T0212725

Lecture Notes in Computer Science   9178

Commenced Publication in 1973
Founding and Former Series Editors:
Gerhard Goos, Juris Hartmanis, and Jan van Leeuwen

Editorial Board

Margherita Antona · Constantine Stephanidis (Eds.)

Universal Access in Human-Computer Interaction

Access to the Human Environment and Culture

9th International Conference, UAHCI 2015
Held as Part of HCI International 2015
Los Angeles, CA, USA, August 2–7, 2015
Proceedings, Part IV

 Springer

Editors
Margherita Antona
Foundation for Research and Technology –
   Hellas (FORTH)
Heraklion, Crete
Greece

Constantine Stephanidis
University of Crete
Heraklion, Crete
Greece

and

Foundation for Research and Technology –
   Hellas (FORTH)
Heraklion, Crete
Greece

ISSN 0302-9743   ISSN 1611-3349   (electronic)
Lecture Notes in Computer Science
ISBN 978-3-319-20686-8   ISBN 978-3-319-20687-5   (eBook)
DOI 10.1007/978-3-319-20687-5

Library of Congress Control Number: 2015942553

LNCS Sublibrary: SL3 – Information Systems and Applications, incl. Internet/Web, and HCI

Printed on acid-free paper

Springer International Publishing AG Switzerland is part of Springer Science+Business Media
(www.springer.com)

Foreword

The 17th International Conference on Human-Computer Interaction, HCI International 2015, was held in Los Angeles, CA, USA, during 2–7 August 2015. The event incorporated the 15 conferences/thematic areas listed on the following page.

A total of 4843 individuals from academia, research institutes, industry, and governmental agencies from 73 countries submitted contributions, and 1462 papers and 246 posters have been included in the proceedings. These papers address the latest research and development efforts and highlight the human aspects of design and use of computing systems. The papers thoroughly cover the entire field of Human-Computer Interaction, addressing major advances in knowledge and effective use of computers in a variety of application areas. The volumes constituting the full 28-volume set of the conference proceedings are listed on pages VII and VIII.

I would like to thank the Program Board Chairs and the members of the Program Boards of all thematic areas and affiliated conferences for their contribution to the highest scientific quality and the overall success of the HCI International 2015 conference.

This conference could not have been possible without the continuous and unwavering support and advice of the founder, Conference General Chair Emeritus and Conference Scientific Advisor, Prof. Gavriel Salvendy. For their outstanding efforts, I would like to express my appreciation to the Communications Chair and Editor of HCI International News, Dr. Abbas Moallem, and the Student Volunteer Chair, Prof. Kim-Phuong L. Vu. Finally, for their dedicated contribution towards the smooth organization of HCI International 2015, I would like to express my gratitude to Maria Pitsoulaki and George Paparoulis, General Chair Assistants.

May 2015

Constantine Stephanidis
General Chair, HCI International 2015

HCI International 2015 Thematic Areas and Affiliated Conferences

Thematic areas:

- Human-Computer Interaction (HCI 2015)
- Human Interface and the Management of Information (HIMI 2015)

Affiliated conferences:

- 12th International Conference on Engineering Psychology and Cognitive Ergonomics (EPCE 2015)
- 9th International Conference on Universal Access in Human-Computer Interaction (UAHCI 2015)
- 7th International Conference on Virtual, Augmented and Mixed Reality (VAMR 2015)
- 7th International Conference on Cross-Cultural Design (CCD 2015)
- 7th International Conference on Social Computing and Social Media (SCSM 2015)
- 9th International Conference on Augmented Cognition (AC 2015)
- 6th International Conference on Digital Human Modeling and Applications in Health, Safety, Ergonomics and Risk Management (DHM 2015)
- 4th International Conference on Design, User Experience and Usability (DUXU 2015)
- 3rd International Conference on Distributed, Ambient and Pervasive Interactions (DAPI 2015)
- 3rd International Conference on Human Aspects of Information Security, Privacy and Trust (HAS 2015)
- 2nd International Conference on HCI in Business (HCIB 2015)
- 2nd International Conference on Learning and Collaboration Technologies (LCT 2015)
- 1st International Conference on Human Aspects of IT for the Aged Population (ITAP 2015)

Conference Proceedings Volumes Full List

Universal Access in Human-Computer Interaction

Program Board Chairs: Margherita Antona, Greece, and Constantine Stephanidis, Greece

- Gisela Susanne Bahr, USA
- João Barroso, Portugal
- Jennifer Romano Bergstrom, USA
- Margrit Betke, USA
- Rodrigo Bonacin, Brazil
- Anthony Brooks, Denmark
- Christian Bühler, Germany
- Stefan Carmien, Spain
- Carlos Duarte, Portugal
- Pier Luigi Emiliani, Italy
- Qin Gao, P.R. China
- Andrina Granić, Croatia
- Josette F. Jones, USA
- Simeon Keates, UK
- Georgios Kouroupetroglou, Greece
- Patrick Langdon, UK
- Barbara Leporini, Italy
- Tania Lima, Brazil
- Troy McDaniel, USA
- Ana Isabel Paraguay, Brazil
- Helen Petrie, UK
- Michael Pieper, Germany
- Enrico Pontelli, USA
- Jaime Sánchez, Chile
- Vagner Santana, Brazil
- Anthony Savidis, Greece
- Hirotada Ueda, Japan
- Gerhard Weber, Germany
- Fong-Gong Wu, Taiwan

The full list with the Program Board Chairs and the members of the Program Boards of all thematic areas and affiliated conferences is available online at:

http://www.hci.international/2015/

HCI International 2016

The 18th International Conference on Human-Computer Interaction, HCI International 2016, will be held jointly with the affiliated conferences in Toronto, Canada, at the Westin Harbour Castle Hotel, 17–22 July 2016. It will cover a broad spectrum of themes related to Human-Computer Interaction, including theoretical issues, methods, tools, processes, and case studies in HCI design, as well as novel interaction techniques, interfaces, and applications. The proceedings will be published by Springer. More information will be available on the conference website: http://2016.hci.international/.

General Chair
Prof. Constantine Stephanidis
University of Crete and ICS-FORTH
Heraklion, Crete, Greece
Email: general_chair@hcii2016.org

http://2016.hci.international/

Contents – Part IV

Orientation, Navigation and Driving

Accessible Security and Voting

Universal Access to Culture

Interactive 3D Digitization, Retrieval, and Analysis of Ancient Sculptures, Using Infrared Depth Sensors for Mobile Devices

Angelos Barmpoutis[1](✉), Eleni Bozia[1], and Daniele Fortuna[2]

[1] University of Florida, Gainesville, FL 32611, USA
angelos@digitalworlds.ufl.edu, bozia@ufl.edu
[2] Museo Nazionale Romano di Palazzo Altemps, 00186 Roma, Italy
daniele.fortuna@beniculturali.it

Abstract. In this paper a novel framework is presented for interactive feature-based retrieval and visualization of human statues, using depth sensors for mobile devices. A skeletal model is fitted to the depth image of a statue or human body in general and is used as a feature vector that captures the pose variations in a given collection of skeleton data. A scale- and twist- invariant distance function is defined in the feature space and is employed in a topology-preserving low-dimensional lattice mapping framework. The user can interact with this self-organizing map by submitting queries in the form of a skeleton from a statue or a human body. The proposed methods are demonstrated in a real dataset of 3D digitized Graeco-Roman statues from Palazzo Altemps.

Keywords: Depth sensors · RGB-D · Kinect · 3d object retrieval · Digital humanities · Statues · Museum studies

1 Introduction

For the past decade, the technological advances in the areas of portable electronic devices have revolutionized the use and range of applications of tablet computers, smart phones, and wearable devices. Furthermore, various multi-modal sensors have been introduced in mobile devices to offer more natural user-machine interactions. Depth sensors (range cameras) have become popular as natural user interfaces for desktop computers and have recently become available for mobile devices, such as the Structure Sensor™ by Occipital.

Depth sensors have been used in various applications related to body tracking such as human detection, model-based 3D tracking of hand articulations [11], human pose recognition and tracking of body parts [12], real-time 3D reconstruction of the articulated human body [3], motion tracking for physical therapy [5],

A. Barmpoutis: This project was in part funded by the Rothman Fellowship from the Center for the Humanities and the Public Sphere and the research incentive award from the College of the Arts at the University of Florida.

M. Antona and C. Stephanidis (Eds.): UAHCI 2015, Part IV, LNCS 9178, pp. 3–11, 2015.
DOI: 10.1007/978-3-319-20687-5_1

and others [7]. The reader is referred to [7] for a more detailed review of RGB-D applications.

In this paper we present a novel application of depth sensors for mobile devices in the topic of digital archaeology. Digital technologies have been adopted in various areas related to museum experience, digital preservation, as well as digitization and study of archaeological artifacts [4].

Digital collections become even more useful educationally and scientifically when they provide tools for searching through the collection and analyzing, comparing, and studying their records. For example an image collection becomes powerful if it can be searched by content, technique, pattern, color, or even similarity with a sample image. The lack of keywords and generalizable annotation for such type of analysis generates the need for keyword-free feature-based analysis.

In this paper a framework is presented for 3D digitization, database retrieval, and analysis of classical statues using depth sensors for mobile devices. In this framework each statue is represented in a feature space based on the skeletal geometry of the human body. A distance function is defined in the feature space and is employed in order to find statues with similarities in their pose. The search query in the presented framework is the body of the user, who can interact with the system and find which statues have poses similar to the user's pose. The proposed methods are demonstrated, using real data from classical statues (shown in Fig. 1) collected in Palazzo Altemps in Rome, Italy.

The contributions in this paper are threefold: (a) A novel application of depth sensors for mobile devices is presented for feature-based retrieval of 3D digitized statues. (b) A scale- and twist-invariant distance function between two given skeletons is proposed. (c) A special type of self-organized maps is presented for interactive visualization of the space of body postures in a low-dimensional lattice.

Fig. 1. Example of an RGB-D frame captured by the camera and depth sensor for a tablet computer (shown on the left). The same depth frame is rendered from two different perspectives —with and without color texture. Images shown with permission from the Italian Ministry of heritage, cultural activities and tourism. Su concessione del Ministero dei beni e delle attività culturali e del turismo - Soprintendenza Speciale per il Colosseo, il Museo Nazionale Romano e l'area archeologica di Roma.

2 Methods

Depth sensors can be used to detect the presence of a particular skeletal geometry, such as human skeletal geometry, by fitting to each acquired depth frame a skeletal model that consists of the following set of parameters:

$$\mathcal{S} = \{\mathbf{t}_j \in \mathbb{R}^3, \mathbf{R}_j \in SO(3) : j \in \mathcal{J}\} \tag{1}$$

where $\mathcal{J}$ is a set of indices of joints connected together in a tree structure of parent/children nodes. Each joint is defined by its location in the 3D space, which is expressed as a translation $\mathbf{t}_j$ from the origin of the coordinate system of the root joint, and its orientation in the 3D space is given as rotation matrix $\mathbf{R}_j$ with respect to the orientation of the root node. There are several algorithms that compute $\mathcal{S}$ from RGB-D, such as those implemented in the Microsoft Kinect SDK [1], in OpenNI library [2], and others [12,14].

2.1 Skeleton Distance Functions

One way to compute distances between unit vectors is the so-called *cosine distance* given by $1 - \cos(\phi)$, where ϕ is the angle between the two vectors. Although the triangle inequality property is not satisfied by this function and therefore is not considered a distance metric, it is computationally very efficient as it can be expressed in a polynomial form. Cosine distance can be extended in order to perform comparisons between elements of $SO(n)$ space by calculating the cosine of the angles between the corresponding rotated orthogonal basis as follows:

$$dist(\mathbf{R}_1, \mathbf{R}_2) = 3 - \cos(\phi_1) - \cos(\phi_2) - \cos(\phi_3) = 3 - trace(\mathbf{R}_1^T \mathbf{R}_2) \tag{2}$$

where ϕ_i denotes the angle between the rotated basis vectors $\mathbf{R}_1 \mathbf{e}_i$ and $\mathbf{R}_2 \mathbf{e}_i$. It can be easily shown that the value of Eq. 2 becomes zero when $\mathbf{R}_1 = \mathbf{R}_2$.

In the case of skeletal geometry, the distance between two poses a and $b \in \mathcal{S}$ can be computed by evaluating Eq. 2 for every joint in $\mathcal{J}$. Such a distance function is scale invariant since it does not take under consideration the locations of the joints, which is a desirable property for our application. Furthermore, the calculated distance can become twist invariant (i.e. invariant under rotations around the line segment that connects two joints) by evaluating Eq. 2 only for the basis vector that corresponds to the axis along the particular line segment as follows:

$$dist(a, b) = |\mathcal{J}| - \mathbf{e}_1^T \sum_{j \in \mathcal{J}} \mathbf{R}_j^{a T} \mathbf{R}_j^b \mathbf{e}_1 \tag{3}$$

where $|\mathcal{J}|$ is the cardinality of the set of tracked joints, and $\mathbf{R}_j^a$, $\mathbf{R}_j^b$ are the corresponding rotation matrices of the skeletons a and b respectively. Without loss of generality, $\mathbf{e}_1$ is a unit vector that denotes the basis of a line segment in the skeletal structure. Equation 3 is scale-invariant and twist-invariant, which are both necessary properties in our application. Scale-invariance guarantees that the distance between skeletons of different subjects will be zero if both are in the same pose. Twist-invariance makes the function robust to possible miscalculations of the rotation of each joint during the skeleton fitting process. In the next section we employ Eq. 3 to achieve 3D object retrieval from a database of human statues using self-organizing maps.

2.2 Interactive Statue Retrieval Using Self-Organizing Skeletal Maps

Given a dataset of skeletons s_1, s_2, $\cdots \in \mathcal{S}$ and a query skeleton $q \in \mathcal{S}$, we need to construct a topographic mapping to a 2-dimensional lattice that satisfies the following 2 conditions: a) q is mapped to a fixed location at the center of the lattice, and b) similar skeletons should be mapped to neighboring lattice locations. The goal of such mapping is to generate an interactive low-dimensional visualization of the multi-dimensional manifold $\mathcal{S}$ for 3D statue retrieval purposes. The user can provide an input query q, which could either belong to the existing dataset s_i (i.e. the posture of a previously digitized statue) or be a new sample in the space $\mathcal{S}$ (i.e. the posture of a human subject or a new statue).

Self-organizing maps have been well-studied in literature and have been employed in various applications related to machine learning and data visualization [6,8,9,13]. A self-organizing map is a type of artificial neural network originally proposed by T. Kohonen [9] that consists of a set of nodes, each of which is located at position x of a low-dimensional lattice (in our application $x \in \mathbb{R}^2$) and is associated with an unknown weight vector in the original feature space (in our application $w_x \in \mathcal{S}$).

The weight vectors produce a dynamic mapping $\mathbb{R}^2 \to \mathcal{S}$ in the form $f(x) = \sum_y w_y K(|x - y|)$, where K is a neighborhood-based kernel function centered at $y \in \mathbb{R}^2$. The mapping is modified by following an iterative energy optimization process using the following update rule:

$$w'_x = w_x - \alpha(t) \frac{\partial dist(s_i, w_x)}{\partial w_x} K(|x - x^*|) \tag{4}$$

where $x^* = \arg\min_x dist(s_i, w_x)$. The derivative of the distance function defined in Eq. 3 can be analytically calculated and results in a $|\mathcal{J}| \times 3$-size gradient vector that contains the coefficients of the vectors $-\mathbf{R}^i_j \mathbf{e}_1 \ \forall j \in \mathcal{J}$, where $\mathbf{R}^i_j$ are the rotation matrices of $s_i \in \mathcal{S}$. Therefore, in our implementation the weight space is $|\mathcal{J}| \times 3$-dimensional and consists of $|\mathcal{J}|$ unit vectors. This mapping of the feature space is due to the scale- and twist-invariance of the distance function, as discussed previously.

Equation 4 is applied iteratively for all s_i in the given dataset and for all lattice locations x except for a predefined central node that corresponds to the query skeleton q (i.e. $w_x = q$). The rest of the weights can be initialized randomly using a Gaussian distribution centered at q. After each iteration the w_x is properly normalized in order to ensure that the components of the weight vector correspond to $|\mathcal{J}|$ unit vectors.

In the next section we demonstrate the presented techniques, using a real dataset of digitized sculptures (Fig. 2).

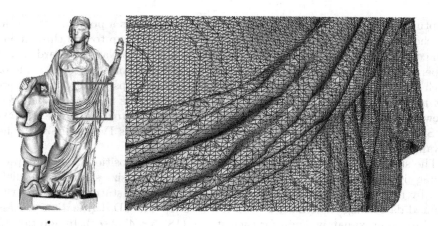

Fig. 2. Left: Example of a statue reconstructed in 3D by fusing a sequence of depth frames. Right: Zoomed view of the reconstructed mesh to show detail.

3   Experimental Results

In this project we used the Structure Sensor™by Occipital, which was attached in front of a tablet computer (iPad Air™by Apple). The resolution of the depth sensor was 640×480 pixels at 30 frames per second and was calibrated so that it records depth in the range from 0.4 m to 3.0 m, which is adequate for capturing life-size statues. Another depth sensor, Kinect™by Microsoft, was also used in our depth fusion experiments, which were performed on a 64-bit computer with Intel Core i7™CPU at 2.80 GHz and 8 GB RAM. Both Kinect and Structure sensors had similar resolution, range of operation, and field of view and were seamlessly used in this project, and therefore we will not differentiate their depth data in our discussion.

In order to create a test dataset for our experiments we digitized in 3D statues from the collection of Palazzo Altemps in Rome, Italy with the permission of the director of the museum, Alessandra Capodiferro. Palazzo Altemps is located in the centre of Renaissance Rome, between Piazza Navona and the Tiber river, in the northern part of Campus Martius. Archaeological excavations have uncovered Roman structures and finds dating from the 1st century AD to the modern age. The current building remained property of the Altemps family for about three centuries, after it was originally acquired by Cardinal Marcus Sitticus Altemps in 1568, who commissioned architects and artists of the time to undertake significant work to extend and decorate the palace. Today the National Roman Museum branch at Palazzo Altemps houses important collections of antiquities, consisting of Greek and Roman sculptures that belonged to various families of the Roman aristocracy in the 16th and 17th centuries [10].

This study focused on statues from three of the collections housed in the museum: Boncompagni Ludovisi collection, Mattei collection, and Altemps collection. Boncompagni Ludovisi is the famous 17th century collection of ancient sculptures housed in Villa Ludovisi in Quirinal, which was a popular attraction for scholars, artists, and travelers from all over the world up to and throughout 19th century. The 16th century Villa Celimontana with its Navicella garden was property of Ciriaco Mattei and was decorated with ancient sculptures, some of which are today in the Mattei collection of Palazzo Altemps. Finally, the important antiquities collection of the Altemps family consists of about a hundred noteworthy pieces of sculptures. These decorated the aristocratic home of Marcus Sitticus Altemps (the grandson cardinal of Pope Pius IV) in line with the prevailing antiquarian taste of the 16th century.

The statues of our interest were in various standing positions and were portraying figures from classical mythology. In total 22 life-size statues were digitized by manually moving the depth sensor around each statue and fusing the acquired data using the Kinect Fusion software [1]. The 3D digitization process lasted for approximately 3 min for each statue ($181.5 \pm 47.2\,sec$). In addition to the 3D reconstructed models, a dataset of the corresponding skeletons was also created by using the skeleton fitting process of the OpenNI library [2] with auto-calibration setting. In the case of fitting errors caused by the presence of adjacent objects or heavy clothing the estimated skeletons were manually corrected. The dataset created from this process is shown in Figs. 3 and 4.

Fig. 3. This figure shows selected samples from our dataset of 3D digitized statues.

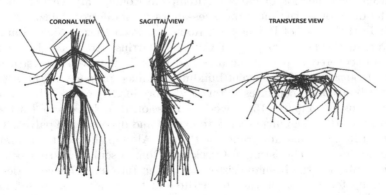

Fig. 4. Visualization of the dataset of skeletons shown from three different perspectives.

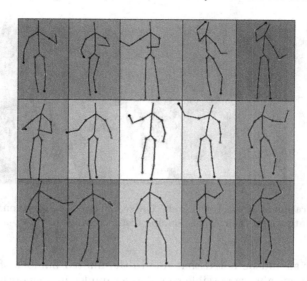

Fig. 5. An example of a self-organized map of skeletons. The map was generated around the query skeleton located at the center of the map. The background intensity shows the distance from the query skeleton.

Figure 4 shows the skeletal samples $s_1, \ldots, s_{22} \in \mathcal{S}$ in the dataset. The skeletons in this plot were normalized in terms of their sizes (full body size and limb size) in order to show the variability of the poses in the dataset. Based on the plots from all three perspectives, it is evident that larger differences are observed in the position of the arms of the statues and smaller yet notable variations are observed in the orientations of the legs and torso as expected.

In the proposed framework, the pose of the statues forms the feature space, which is employed in the comparisons between statues and feature-based database searches for statues with similar poses. The quality of the employed features is determined by their ability to capture the distinct characteristics of each element in the search space; hence the pose variations in Fig. 4 are essential in the proposed framework.

In order to test the interactive statue retrieval framework presented in Sect. 2 we performed skeleton fitting to a human subject who stood in a particular pose in front of the depth sensor. The fitted skeleton was provided as the query input q to a self-organizing 2D map of size 5×3. The central node in the map was assigned to the query vector. The rest of the map was initialized randomly and updated for 1000 iterations, a process that was completed in less than 1 sec in the tablet computer. A representative result is shown in Fig. 5.

By observing Fig. 5 we can see that skeletons with similar poses were mapped in adjacent locations on the map, such as the adjacent skeletons in the center of the map (see also the skeletons in the upper right and the lower right corners). Furthermore, there are smooth transitions between different poses when possible.

Fig. 6. Demonstration of interactive search. The search query is shown on the left. The best matching statues and their corresponding distance from the query are reported.

At this point it should be noted that due to the limited number of samples in our dataset it is not always possible to put the samples in a smooth order.

The gray-scale intensity of the background in Fig. 5 corresponds to value of the distance (given by Eq. 3) between each skeleton and the query skeleton. As expected, the locations around the center of the map correspond to smaller distances (brighter intensities) compared to the areas along the edges of the map.

Finally, Fig. 6 shows the three "closest" statues to the given skeleton query among all statues in the database. The corresponding distance values are also reported. Although the two first statues have similar postures on the upper part of the body, the pose of the first statue's legs better resembles the query skeleton. As a result, the first statue has the smallest distance from the query, which demonstrates the efficacy of the presented framework.

4   Conclusion

The pilot study in this paper shows that the presented framework can be used for keyword-free feature-based retrieval of statues in mobile devices. This has the potential to be used as an interactive guide in museums, but also as a scientific tool that assists scholars in identifying statues with similar characteristics from a large repository of statues. The future use of depth sensors in mobile devices will significantly support the creation of such repositories of 3D digitized artifacts, using limited resources (in terms of scanning time, computational effort, and cost) as well as their computer-assisted study as demonstrated in this paper.

Acknowledgement. The authors would like to acknowledge Alessandra Capodiferro for providing permission to perform this study in Palazzo Altemps and the Italian Ministry of heritage, cultural activities and tourism for providing permission to publish in this paper the collected data. This project would not be possible without the funding support by the Rothman Fellowship in the Humanities to Eleni Bozia from the Center for the Humanities and the Public Sphere at the University of Florida and the research incentive award to Angelos Barmpoutis from the College of the Arts at the University of Florida. The authors would like to thank the sponsors and the anonymous reviewers who provided insightful comments and suggestions.

References

1. Microsoft Kinect SDK. http://www.microsoft.com/en-us/kinectforwindows/
2. OpenNI. http://www.openni.org/
3. Barmpoutis, A.: Tensor body: real-time reconstruction of the human body and avatar synthesis from RGB-D. IEEE Trans. Cybern. **43**(5), 1347–1356 (2013)
4. Barmpoutis, A., Bozia, E., Wagman, R.S.: A novel framework for 3D reconstruction and analysis of ancient inscriptions. J. Mach. Vis. Appl. **21**(6), 989–998 (2010)
5. Barmpoutis, A., Fox, E.J., Elsner, I., Flynn, S.: Augmented-reality environment for locomotor training in children with neurological injuries. In: Linte, C.A. (ed.) AE-CAI 2014. LNCS, vol. 8678, pp. 108–117. Springer, Heidelberg (2014)
6. Bishop, C.M., Svensen, M., Williams, C.K.I.: The generative topographic mapping. Neural Comput. **10**(1), 215–234 (1998)
7. Han, J., et al.: Enhanced computer vision with Microsoft Kinect sensor: a review. IEEE Trans. Cybern. **43**(5), 1318–1334 (2013)
8. Haykin, S.: Neural Networks and Learning Machines (3rd edn). Prentice Hall (2008)
9. Kohonen, T.: Self-organized formation of topologically correct feature maps. Biol. Cybern. **43**(1), 59–69 (1982)
10. La Regina, A.: Museo Nationale Romano. Soprintendenza Archaeologica di Roma. Mondadori Electa S.p.A. Milan (2005)
11. Oikonomidis, I., et al.: Efficient model-based 3D tracking of hand articulations using Kinect. In: Proceedings of the British Machine Vision Association Conference (2011)
12. Shotton, J., et al.: Real-time human pose recognition in parts from single depth images. In: IEEE CVPR Conference, pp. 1297–1304 (2011)
13. Ultsch, A.: Emergence in self-organizing feature maps. In: Ritter, H., Haschke, R. (eds.) Proceedings of the 6th International Workshop on Self-Organizing Maps (2007)
14. Xia, L., et al.: Human detection using depth information by Kinect. In: IEEE Conference on Computer Vision and Pattern Recognition Workshops, pp. 15–22 (2011)

Developing the COOLTURA Resources-Driven Governance Model for Building Scalable Cultural Services in the COOLTURA Platform

María Eugenia Beltrán[1(✉)], Yolanda Ursa[1], Silvia de los Rios[2], Maria Fernanda Cabrera-Umpierrez[2], Maria Teresa Arredondo[2], Maria del Mar Villafranca[3], Lucia María Perez[3], Belén Prados[3], and Carlos Lli Torrabadella[4]

[1] INMARK Estudios y Estrategias, Madrid, Spain
{xenia.beltran,yolanda.ursa}@grupoinmark.com
[2] Life Supporting Technologies, Universidad Politécnica de Madrid, Madrid, Spain
{srios,chiqui,mta}@lst.tfo.upm.es
[3] Patronato de la Alhambra y Generalife, Granada, Spain
{mariamar.villafranca, luciam.perez}@juntadeandalucia.es, belenprados@wonderbrand.es
[4] Universidad Antonio de Nebrija, Madrid, Spain
clli@nebrija.es

Abstract. Cultural institutions and sites currently debate on how to respond to new trends, such as globalisation, exponential growth of digital cultural content and Apps, and reach technological knowledgeable users. In addition, institutions need to look for new ways of engagement, as the engagement of citizens with their cultural heritage environment remains low. This paper presents the preliminary results of a qualitative research performed to evaluate new opportunities for the COOLTURA Platform (output of TAG CLOUD project); as well as the proposal of developing the COOLTURA resource-driven governance model to support the COOLTURA Platform up-take.

Keywords: Engagement · Cultural heritage · Governance in culture · Cultural platform · Cultural apps

1 Introduction: Cultural Heritage Changing Environment

Cultural heritage institutions have invested a lot of money in capturing, digitalizing and digitally storing (as well as preserving) high volume of digital cultural objects in order to cope with the increasing growth of heterogeneous and unstructured data within cultural institutional information ecosystems [1]. Globalisation, massive and pervasive usage of electronic devices, together with the profusion of productivity and semantically web2.0 oriented applications, are being deployed as main support for transactions

© Springer International Publishing Switzerland 2015
M. Antona and C. Stephanidis (Eds.): UAHCI 2015, Part IV, LNCS 9178, pp. 12–20, 2015.
DOI: 10.1007/978-3-319-20687-5_2

and communications in order to find new ways to increase engagement, sharing and consumption of cultural content. We can see for example that the use of smartphones, social media and downloadable applications ("Apps") for mobile devices is growing rapidly in all sectors including the cultural heritage environment and related sectors such as tourism [3]. Altogether, these technologies also shall be able to benefit cultural institutions in managing more efficiently and effectively current, and future, digital cultural objects.

Moreover, cultural heritage institutions are continuously evaluating how to capitalize the investment in digitalization and creation of newly digital content. This process includes changing the way how to produce, present, access, share and consume digital cultural objects [5]. By progressively adopting emerging technologies and putting in place a set of sustainable integrated services to be used before, during and after the visit for lifelong engagement, cultural institutions aim at underpinning and creating cultural experiences, personalisation and customised services [5].

In parallel, many cultural heritage organisations, monuments and cities are also taking a hybrid approach by supporting exhibitions with thousands of digital objects in order to actively encourage cultural learning, debate, action and interaction; furthermore, looking for new and better connections with visitors, and increase engagement of visitors with culture [6].

Under this context, the European Commission co-funded project TAG CLOUD [7] is exploring the use of cloud-based technologies to enable cultural engagement by using cloud-based technologies that leverage adaptability and personalisation of created cultural heritage content, aiming at supporting deeper learning of cultural heritage over time. As a tangible result, the TAG CLOUD project is developing the COOLTURA Platform and COOLTURA App to cope with its objectives.

2 COOLTURA by TAG CLOUD: Managing Cultural Content for Engagement

The COOLTURA Platform and App have been developed following a User-Centered Design (UCD) methodology [8] and using an iterative design cycle that managed a framework of scenarios from three pilot users in Europe: The Monumental Complex of Alhambra and Generalife (Spain), the Barber Institute of Fine Arts (United Kingdom) and the County of Sør Trøndelag (Norway).

The COOLTURA App is the mobile devices oriented application that accesses, uses and re-uses the cultural content processed in the COOLTURA platform. The COOLTURA App aims at exploiting the potential and characteristics of smartphones and mobile devices that allow mobility features, such as geo-location, real time interaction, and thus provide personalised up to date and interactive cultural heritage enriched content. By using embedded tools, the COOLTURA App allows visitors and users to experiment with different types of interactions with cultural objects (e.g. augmented reality), as well as recommend new experiences based on the earlier user behaviour and supporting lifelong experiences. Thus, through the App, visitors are able to experience cultural social interaction, use real-time geographical mapping to increase their user experience, get content that couples with their preferences and interact or consume the cultural content as curiosity arise.

The COOLTURA Platform is a cloud-based and open data oriented platform that enables scalable services for cultural engagement. It is being tested, piloted and firstly exploited with the COOLTURA App. The COOLTURA platform has been conceived as a suite of services that supports harvesting, semantic treatment and curation processes for digital cultural content and objects.

Semantic, intelligent content and analytic tools have been integrated in the platform as an intelligent layer. This layer grants the platform with the ability to abstract complex data and cultural consumption processes, converting them into content and processes that could be more consumable and manageable by the visitors. This layer allows personalisation, adaptability of content and social interactions based on each visitor likes and personal preferences.

Harvesting tools have been integrated, so the platform is able to process curated digital content coming from cultural institutions and other sources, such as Europeana. Through the harvesters, the COOLTURA Platform can map, build and increase the metadata structure moving towards the Open Government Data (OGD) metadata scheme (a standard for the bases for eGovData). This tool shall allow cultural institutions and third parties (software vendors, developers, intermediaries, etc.), to better enrich metadata and benefit from the Open Data eco-systems that will support further use, and re-use, of the curated digital cultural content for cultural engagement in other contexts; such as tourism or smart cities.

In addition, the COOLTURA platform has an analytic layer and a dashboard that allows cultural site curators and managers to get analysed information regarding the usage of the digital content and apps. This layer analyses massive amounts of visitors' data and enable cultural content management decision making in cultural sites, such as support creating/detecting "hot spots" for visitors, as well as creating/improving more demand oriented content and/or new apps.

Thus the COOLTURA platform interoperates with the COOLTURA App, as well as allows the integration of newly and other existing cloud-based tools and/or apps (complying with the platform requirements) developed or managed by cultural institutions registered in the platform. These Apps, also could use innovative tools such as the augmented reality, storytelling or wearable devices. Moreover, the platform enables integration of personalisation, content adaptation and social sharing to the new Apps; allowing cultural institutions to articulate the widest possible reuse of and access to digital content and objects.

3   Current Status of COOLTURA and End User Approach

Both the COOLTURA Platform and COOLTURA App have gone through early-stage evaluations with users, following the scenarios in The Monumental Complex of Alhambra and Generalife, the Barber Institute of Fine Arts and the County of Sør Trøndelag.

Currently, parallel work is being performed: on one hand the TAG CLOUD consortium is working in ways to retrieve information about the user, both passively and actively, in order to explore various parameters that affect the protocols in different context. Information from the users' devices allows us to investigate their interaction with artefacts, and enables the system to form assumptions of their respective interest levels, working towards an optimal approach for personalisation and content adaptability. On the other hand the interoperability and test of the COOLTURA App with the platform's software developments of personalisation, social sharing and content adaptability is being performed. The usability and design of the App interface is being also tested, reviewed and enhanced with real users. In addition developments of the platform have been performed for allowing the STEDR,[1] as an additional App, to be plugged to the COOLTURA platform. This development also tests the scalability of applications in the platform and evaluates requirements needed for adding applications.

In order to evaluate the potential usage, benefits and constrains for up-taking the COOLTURA Platform and App, a qualitative market research that gathers primary information from 50 in-depth interviews with cultural sites, at European level, has been launched. The process aims at capturing how European cultural sites (institutions and cities) shall uptake a platform and an App, based on the experience of the pilot sites of the TAG CLOUD project.

The COOLTURA platform and App are explained from functional and practical point of view to the interviewees at cultural heritage institutions and sites; insights are collected; and later a small evaluation exercise is performed using the "product box" technique.[2]

Insights comprise, comments regarding functionalities, new ways of using digital curated content, current problems that need to be solved, as well as expectations and plans for the future regarding their cultural tangible and intangible heritage and knowledge based services.

4   The Road Ahead: Governance of Apps and Content

Preliminary findings from qualitative market research performed to pilot sites and some cultural institutions in Spain [9], show that cultural institutions and sites debate on how to respond to new trends and changes of society and visitors. Meanwhile these institutions and sites not only suffer of budget constraints, but also look for new ways of engagement with visitors. When approaching what "engagement" means and how should be taken in account for management practices, in general we could infer from interviews that this "engagement need" responds to the fact that cultural institutions and sites have as critical "mission" keeping the perpetuity and the value of the humanity's cultural public and historical heritage; as well as transferring and increasing the knowledge of cultural heritage to current and future generations.

From first insights gathered, we have observed that cultural sites and institutions are clearly influenced by a vast multiplicity of socioeconomically and political processes and trends, which are influencing the structure and dynamics of how these sites interact

---

[1] STEDR: application for story telling. http://stedr.blogspot.com.es/2014/05/about-stedr.html.

[2] Product Box technique allows participants to imagine they are selling a product or service.

with their visitors; and so respond in different manners to the need of increasing engagement. The interviewed institutions have mainly commented on the following trends: the globalisation process; competition for private or public financial resources, new legally enforced protective measures for intellectual assets while at the same time the rights of citizens – individually or collectively – are also enforced; a shift towards a digitalized society with knowledge-based "*services' economy;*" massive and pervasive usage of electronic devices; and the beginning of a new generation of youngsters that have never known a world without the Internet, social media, and mobile technology (technologically-native children born in the digital era - Generation Z [10]), that is foreseen as the future generation of cultural heritage visitors.

In order to cope with these trends, the cultural sites and institutions are shifting from non-digital to digital media; and increasing the development of Apps. The shift towards digital media has escalated both, the digitalization of content and the "born digital" content with heterogeneous formats. This has been driven not only for the need to move toward the provision of content for digital means of visitors, but also by a growing number of sources (individuals, tourism enterprises and content suppliers, as well as curators from cultural institutions and sites) with diverse devices (mobiles, cameras, curators tools, etc.). However, according to the European Commission, still only a fraction of Europe's collections digitised so far (around 12 % in average) [2], on the top to the content that directly is created on digital format. Not only the growth of born digital content is expected to increase, but also the growth of digitalised content. The European Commission has recommended to make the cultural institutions' digitized material accessible through Europeana [4], setting as an objective to provide direct access to 30 million of digitized objects by 2015.

The following points have also been raised during the interviews by the cultural institutions and sites, as key trends that affect their data management processes and costs:

- Exponential growth of digital cultural content also generates new/additional requirements, overheads and needs; for example much more time is needed to the creation and/or selection of high quality of content and/or valuable data to interact and connect with visitors.
- Some digital content is considered as capital and with unique value, as it cannot be recreated or replicated (e.g. in archaeological sites); thus there are new needs that relate with authenticity, preservation, life-cycle and legal rights for reproduction. Also, some of this content is being thought as a new revenue stream in order to create sustainable processes and services; however this thought is not aligned in many cases with the core mission of cultural institutions, which rest on showing, teaching or transferring the humanity's information heritage and providing readily access of the digital patrimony to current citizens and future generations. So new opportunities are being evaluated for this kind of unique cultural heritage content.
- Cultural heritage content now has to be continuously available all day, for the mobile devices and digital means, in order not to cause major problems for digital services offered based in the digital content.
- There is an increasing need of managing context and tracing of information paths, as this allows enrichment of current digital content and adds value when linked with

other digital content (value of content increases when lined and related to other sources, methods, images, data or tools).

Regarding Apps, the insights collected from interviewees reported that Apps are becoming somehow "essential" and very practical tool for the cultural institutions. This comprises the increasing creation of Apps by cultural heritage institutions and sites, as well as its increasing usage by visitors. According to the cultural heritage sites interviewees, Apps reduce costs and provide variety of tools in comparison to large software solutions, improve access to local, geo-located and practical information, reach the visitors easily and increase their interaction with the cultural sites through their mobile devices; also in many cases, integrate or interact with social networks.

According to the Seggitur report this cultural, travel or tourism driven Apps might be in its infancy, but they are expected to grow rapidly, as well as notably evolve in functionalities, user value and market. Apps in the cultural heritage and tourism sector are aggressively increasing and the main differences lie primarily in terms of content and functionality. According to the study in 2011, 23 million of Apps for this sector were downloaded worldwide, while in 2012 it was estimated that Apps would grow by 38 %, reaching 32 million of Apps [3].

To a great extent, our findings show that the lack of understanding and/or budget to confront with all this rapid changes and trends is producing a lack of policies and strategies for efficiently managing digital assets and Apps being produced to exploit the digital content. Notwithstanding, these issues are also creating a phenomenon of change with regards to content production, management and archive/storage, which needs to be approached in cultural institutions or sites.

Thus, when showing the COOLTURA platform interface and structure to the cultural heritage institutions and sites, and asking how they think this platform could respond to their needs, interviewees mainly answered that the COOLTURA platform could be an opportunity and a tool to support the management and governance of digital content and Apps in their institutions.

5 Next Steps: The Vision of the COOLTURA Governance Model

The preliminary insights gathered from our pilot sites and additional institutions, have raised the fact that the COOLTURA platform could be used to support digital content and Apps. So, we started to develop the COOLTURA resources-driven governance model based in the case of The Monumental Complex of Alhambra. This model could be used as best management practices by registered cultural institutions in the platform.

The COOLTURA resources-driven governance model aims at linking the resources allocated in the COOLTURA Platform (Apps, digital cultural content, technological developments such as personalisation processes or new linked technologies such as augmented reality or storytelling.) and the cultural heritage`s institutional framework.

This governance model comprises three main and preliminary steps: planning, implementation and monitoring; and rely on the fact that the COOLTURA platform allows integration of new Apps in a highly scalable way and provides feedback for

Apps and cultural content through the platform's dashboard. These steps are recursive and aim at supporting cultural institutions to manage new scalable cultural services that engage with visitors, the local community and new audiences.

The planning step relates with the fact of linking cultural heritage digital content with institutional policies that address the tangible and intangible value of digital heritage, as well as with making a participatory design of the digital offering, taking in account the feedback and better knowledge of preferences of visitors and locals provided by the COOLTURA platform.

The implementation step will allow identifying new models that provide digital services and cultural content through the different functionalities of the Apps connected to the COOLTURA Platform. The implementation stage should pave the way to connect the digital cultural content and provide:

- New technologies and Apps with "narratives" that link with visitors' enjoyable experiences and to more consumable digital cultural content.
- Exploitation of intangible cultural heritage opportunities through narratives and content that strengthen the identity of local communities and the shared European heritage values; as well as educational values that support sustainable behaviours towards the direct and indirect preservation, re-construction, maintenance and transference of knowledge of cultural heritage.

The monitoring step will identify the valorisation enjoyment, usage and perspectives of visitors (according their profile) regarding the digital services offering (digital cultural content and Apps) through the COOLTURA platform dashboard.

The COOLTURA resources-driven model will also allow to the COOLTURA platform users to build scalable cultural services over the platform in an organized way and support decision-making for selecting, high quality and visitor driven, cultural digital content. Through this governance model, which allows feedback (through monitoring and the COOLTURA Platform) the cultural institutions will be able to manage, in a controllable and visitor driven way, the increasing digital content and applications.

In consequence, through the COOLTURA resources-driven model, the cultural institutions and sites shall be able to manage the potential to improve the management of the user experience and enjoyment of culture, the capacity of building new audiences, increase shared heritage, identity and citizenship, as well as provide new cultural-driven learning environments and narratives.

6   Conclusions

TAG CLOUD project puts users/visitors at the centre of the project, from its inception. All evaluations experiences insights feed not only the TAG CLOUD outputs (COOLTURA Platform and App) but also pilot sites.

From interviews performed with cultural institution pilot sites and additional cultural heritage sites in Spain [9], we perceive the impact of socio-political and technological trends, not only on the way to consume cultural heritage digital content, but the creation and management of this digital content.

Institutions and cultural heritage sites are willing and ready to adopt emerging technologies related with personalisation and customised services, but also there is a need for new processes and technologies that somehow support in an organised way the increasing trend of digital cultural content and Apps. This need is not only driven by above mentioned trends, but also for the need of greater engagement with local communities and visitors; as the visitors experiences need to be untapped by driving differentiated activities and participation, as well as access to new narratives and technologies that allow to digest digital cultural content in an easier way.

In addition cultural heritage institutions and sites also need to link and exploit intangible cultural heritage opportunities to strengthen the identity of local communities, European heritage values, and support sustainable behaviours towards the direct and indirect preservation, re-construction, maintenance and transference of knowledge of cultural heritage.

Thus, the generation of a COOLTURA resources-driven governance model for the COOLTURA platform aims at supporting the growth of planned scalable cultural services and faster take-up of the platform,. This governance model connects and answers to the above needs by linking the resources allocated in the COOLTURA Platform (Apps, digital cultural content, technological developments such as personalisation processes or new linked technologies such as augmented reality or storytelling.) and the institutional framework of the cultural institutions and sites.

Insights and results from evaluations, coupled with above conclusions, are seen as very valuable information for the TAG CLOUD project, the adoption of COOLTURA Platform and App and providing new cultural-driven learning environments that will support the mission of keeping the perpetuity and the value of humanity's public and historical heritage.

Next steps comprise to finish gathering of information of the qualitative approach for the exploitation of the COOLTURA platform and App, as well as complete the COOLTURA resources-driven governance model.

Acknowledgements. This work has been co-funded by the European Commission through the FP7 project TAG CLOUD (Technologies lead to Adaptability & lifelong enGagement with culture throughout the CLOUD); http://www.tagcloudproject.eu/, Grant Agreement No. 600924.

References

1. European Union, & Comité des Sages. The New Renaissance, Report of the 'Comité des Sages' Reflection group on bringing Europe's Cultural Heritage online, Brussels, January 2011. http://www.eurosfaire.prd.fr/7pc/doc/1302102400_kk7911109enc_002.pdf
2. Cultural heritage Digitization, online accessibility and digital preservation. Report on the Implementation of Commission Recommendation 2011/711/EU 2011–2013. Progress report 2011–2013 Working document, September 2014
3. Tourism Apps Market Study. Segittur (2013). http://www.segittur.es/opencms/export/sites/segitur/.content/galerias/descargas/documentos/Segittur_APPS-Turismo.pdf

4. Commission Recommendations of 27 October 2011 on the digitization and online accessibility of cultural material and digital preservation. Official Journal of the European Union 29-10-2011 (2011/711/EU)

5. Beltrán, M.E., Ursa, Y., de los Rios, S., Cabrera-Umpiérrez, M.F., Arredondo, M.T., Páramo, M., Prados, B., Pérez, L.M.: Engaging people with cultural heritage: users' perspective. In: Stephanidis, C., Antona, M. (eds.) UAHCI 2014, Part II. LNCS, vol. 8514, pp. 639–649. Springer, Heidelberg (2014)

6. TAG CLOUD project, CN. 600924, 7th Framework Programme, ICT for access to cultural resources; in-depth interviews for exploitation, February 2013

7. TAG CLOUD project, CN. 600924, 7th Framework Programme, ICT for access to cultural resources, February 2013. http://www.tagcloudproject.eu/

8. Abras, C., Maloney-Krichmar, D., Preece, J.: User-centered design. In: Bainbridge, W. (ed.) Encyclopedia of Human-Computer Interaction. Sage Publications, Thousand Oaks (2004)

9. TAG CLOUD project, CN. 600924, 7th Framework Programme, ICT for access to cultural resources; in-depth interviews for COOLTURA Platform exploitation, February 2013

10. Boost Capital. Say Hello To Generation Z – Digital Natives, Entrepreneurs, The Staff & Customers Of Tomorrow, 17 October 2014. http://www.boostcapital.co.uk/blog/say-hello-generation-z-digital-natives-entrepreneurs-staff-customers-tomorrow/

The Expansion of a Scheme About ACCESSIBILITY in Tourism at the Cultural Sector

Eleni Chalkia[✉], Evangelos Bekiaris, Maria Panou, and Matina Loukea

Center for Research and Technology Hellas, Hellenic Institute of Transport, 57100 Thessaloniki, Greece
{hchalkia,abek,mpanou,mloukea}@certh.gr

Abstract. Accessibility in the tourism domain is already and will be even more in the following years a "must"! Thus, ACCESSIBILITY PASS is an evaluation and certification scheme which has been developed with the scope of evaluating, clustering, analyzing and certifying the accessibility level of a hotel or a conference center taking into account its infrastructure, its offered services and its personnel's certified skills. This paper will explore the possibility of expanding ACCESSIBILITY PASS in the cultural domain buildings like museums, concert centers, etc. where accessibility is very important and it already implemented, but not widely evaluated or certified.

Keywords: Accessibility · Disabilities · Tourism · Infrastructure · Evaluation · Certification · Culture · Museums

1 Introduction

Tourism is a very popular way of leisure, especially in the Western countries, as well as a big industry and a major source of revenue, especially for traditional touristic countries like Greece, Italy and Spain.

Despite the fact that all people, without exception, should have equal opportunities in enjoying tourism, yet nowadays there are still restrictions or even exclusions concerning people with disabilities. For those people, travelling can often be a real challenge, since finding the necessary information on accessible touristic services or even booking a room with special access specifications can be difficult, costly and time consuming.

In order for this problem and inequality to be addressed, an evaluation and certification scheme, entitled **ACCESSIBILITY PASS**, has been developed with the scope of evaluating, clustering, analyzing and finally certifying the accessibility level of a hotel or a conference center taking into account its infrastructure, its offered services and its personnel's skills.

The aim of the **ACCESSIBILITY PASS** scheme is to provide structured and reliable information to people with disabilities globally, regarding the accessibility level of Hotels and Conference Centers, based on actual measurements (not

M. Antona and C. Stephanidis (Eds.): UAHCI 2015, Part IV, LNCS 9178, pp. 21–28, 2015.
DOI: 10.1007/978-3-319-20687-5_3

self-reported) by trained and accredited auditors, with the use of an especially developed application for both Personal Computer (PC) and mobile. The scheme has been designed and developed from a team of experts in accessibility issues and it conforms with the existing international accessibility requirements, while it has been designed for all types of hotel lodgings (regardless of their category).

One of the most important issues regarding **ACCESSIBILITY PASS** scheme is the fact that it focuses on a wide range of disabilities, providing the opportunity to a large rate of disabled people to enjoy equal privileges, during their vacation or business trips, as any other traveler. More specifically, the assets that are being assessed address access for people with motor, visual, hearing and cognitive disabilities, while key issues are also being reviewed for people with other special needs, such as allergic people, people with epilepsy of diabetes.

2 The Need of Accessibility in the Various Domains

2.1 About Disability

Disability is a physical or mental impairment which has a substantial and long-term adverse effect on one's ability to carry out normal day-to-day activities ([2, 3]). A disability may be physical, cognitive, mental, sensory, emotional, developmental or some combination of these. A disability may also be present from birth, or occur during a person's lifetime.

According to the World Health Organization (WHO), over a billion people live with some form of disability. This means that nearly 15 % of the world's population has very significant difficulties in functioning while rates of disability are also increasing due to population ageing and the global increase in chronic health conditions [1].

However, disability is not just a health problem. It is a complex phenomenon that reflects the interaction between the features of a person's body and the ones concerning the society that he/she lives in. Thus, in order for all these difficulties to be overcome, measurements should be received for the environmental and social barriers elimination.

2.2 Disability in the Tourism Domain

Misconceptions and stereotypes for people with disabilities are common. These incorrect assumptions regarding disability is a form of discrimination as it often causes barriers, mainly of social nature, to people with various forms of disability.

As mentioned before, people with disabilities are capable of fully participating in their community life and the same applies as far as the tourism field is concerned. People with disabilities have the same needs and desires for tourism as all others. They have the same motivation to travel as the rest of the population but they need to make a substantially greater amount of pre-planning to undertake travel than the non-disabled.

The general demand for accessibility in Europe exceeds 127 million people. This represents the 27 % of the European population and it has been estimated that 70 % of them have the financial capabilities to travel. If their friends, relatives and careers are included, this figure raises substantially with estimated tourism revenues exceeding €

80 billion [6]. If the members of their families are also included, there are approximately 2 billion persons directly affected by disability, representing almost the 1/3 of the world's population [7].

2.3 Cultural Domain

Closely bonded to the tourism domain is also the cultural domain. The majority of the people, who travel, want to visit some or all the cultural monuments of the place they are travelling too. This mostly refers to museums, galleries, open culture spaces but also other tourist attractions.

An Australia research [8] has revealed that people with a disability are supportive of museums and galleries. They are motivated visitors and see museums and galleries as excellent environments for learning, education and social interaction. People with a disability have strong networks and often visit in groups or with friends and family.

Likewise at the tourism domain, also at the cultural domain, the people, without exception, should have equal opportunities in enjoying the different elements of culture. For example, a visit to a museum, whether of art, local history or technology, is just as worthwhile for the people with disabilities like as it is for visitors without any impairment. Thus all cultural places should be committed to the diversity of all the individuals and communities of different races, countries of origin, first languages, beliefs, cultures, disabilities, genders, sexual orientation, age and income who use, support and work for it; and it recognize that:

- Equality of access for disabled people is integral to that diversity; and that
- Enhancing services for disabled people has a direct and positive impact on the quality of experience for all users.

Not much research has been carried out about the number of people with disabilities that visit museums. Nevertheless, a hint can be given by a Australian survey revealed that 72 % of Australians over the age of 18 with a disability (2.2 million people) had been involved in a community or sporting activity away from home in one year [9]. These rates indicate that people with a disability are an active audience. However, these rates indicate that participation rates decrease as barriers to activities become more pronounced since they are lower than similar statistics for the non-disability population. Thus accessibility barriers hinder people with disabilities in participating in activities outside their houses including cultural events.

3 The Accessibility Pass Scheme

3.1 General Description

Accessibility in tourism sector is of vital importance for people with disabilities. Given this fact, a global evaluation and certification scheme has been developed for the evaluation, clustering, analysis and certification of the accessibility level of a hotel or a conference center taking into account its infrastructure, its offered services and its personnel's skills; the so-called ACCESSIBILITY PASS scheme.

By term "accessible" within ACCESSIBILITY PASS we mean access to any hotel or conference center area or service that the guest with a disability may have unassisted by a third party (hotel staff, escort, carer, etc.); either on his/her own or by using his/her assistive devices, guide dog, etc. Disabilities that are being addressed by this scheme are as follows:

- Motor disabilities
- Visual disabilities
- Hearing disabilities
- Cognitive disabilities

The scheme has been designed and developed by a team of experts in accessibility issues and it conforms with the existing international accessibility requirements, while it has been designed for all types of hotel lodgings (regardless of their category). In the context of ACCESSIBILITY PASS, 4 different certification labels exist, denoting the accessibility level of the hotel/conference center regardless of stars or any other categorization of the facility:

- "CtA" (committed to accessibility)
- "A" (accessible basic services)
- "AA" (full accessibility except leisure and business areas)
- "AAA" (full accessibility)

3.2 Evaluation Procedure

The whole evaluation process of a hotel or a conference center, according to this specific scheme, is based on data and measurements performed by persons specially trained for this purpose, the so-called auditors.

More specifically, the necessary measurements regarding the infrastructure of the hotel or conference center are being taken for further analysis and prioritization, while the services offered in its context are also being taken into consideration (i.e. transport service or health service) for the overall evaluation of the facility's accessibility level.

A very important factor regarding the ACCESSIBILITY PASS scheme is that it assesses the level of service given to a client with a disability in relation to the same level of service offered to all its guests. Thus, only the available hotel/conference center assets, with respect to infrastructure, services and personnel skills, are being assessed (i.e. if a hotel/conference center offers no parking spaces to all of its clients, no accessibility issues for parking will be assessed).

Finally, another aspect of the ACCESSIBILITY PASS evaluation is the evaluation of the skills of its personnel exclusively as far as the service of people with disabilities is concerned. It is worth mentioning that within the overall framework of the ACCESSIBILITY PASS scheme, relevant training may also offered to the perspective staff of the facility, which finally leads to the corresponding certification of each individual.

After the evaluation of the facility's accessibility, for each one of the disability categories mentioned above, and the certification of this specific facility with the assignment of the respective accessibility level, the facility will be entitled to a public registry to a database and a GIS map. This database will interface all the facilities audited and certified under the ACCESSIBILITY PASS scheme and will give the opportunity to all travelers interested in accessible tourism to select the hotel/conference center that best meets their needs.

3.3   Overview of the Assessment Tool

For the realization of the overall evaluation procedure described above, an on-line auditing application has been developed that the auditor has to use in order to insert the data that s/he has measured for every infrastructure element, service and staff category, in order to assess the accessibility level of a hotel. Data are being recorded and locally stored at the device (see Fig. 1).

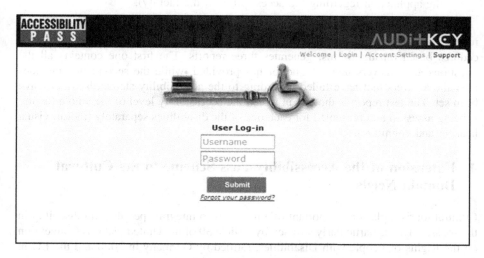

Fig. 1. Home page of the ACCESSIBLITY PASS auditing tool

The electronic auditing applications do not require specific installation and are in general self-explanatory. The system is available as a web application and as an android application. The web application requires only the installation of a web browser. In specific, compatibility has been ensured so far with Internet Explorer, Mozilla Firefox and Google Chrome.

The ACCESSIBLITY PASS electronic auditing system consists of four major components:

- Database: It consists of the questions/items of the auditing process and the auditor responses that are being stored during the audit.
- Evaluation Report Component: It is responsible for the consolidation of the recorded data and the calculation of the hotel's accessibility level (score).

Innovative, unique algorithms are running in the back-end, processing the data provided by the auditor.

- Web application: It is the front-end application which is running in a web browser.
- Android application: It is the front-end application which is running in an android mobile phone.

The different users and/or user groups and the respective authorization rights are as follows:

- Auditor: The auditor can access the web application and/or android application in order to fill in the questionnaires that are required for the audit process.
- Administrator: The administrator has some additional authorization rights, like:
  - Hotel management (the possibility to add/edit/delete information regarding the assessed facility).
  - Reports management (the possibility to add/edit/delete the reports generated by the application regarding the accessibility of the facility).

When the auditor inserts inside the tool all the necessary information (measurements and data obtained by the facility's auditing), the tool, through automated procedures based on algorithms, generates three reports. The first one contains all the questions and answers that the auditor has provided, while the second one includes only the answers that have failed according to the accessibility standards which have been set. The last report is the one in which the accessibility level of the whole facility is being assessed and presented for each one of the disabilities separately (motor, visual hearing and cognitive).

4 Extension of the Accessibility Pass Scheme to the Cultural Domain Needs

Cultural tourism plays an important role in efforts to integrate people with disability in the society. This is particularly stressed by Article 30 of the United Nations Convention on the Rights of People with Disabilities, ratified by Germany in 2008 and the EU in 2010.

People with a disability generally visit museums, and their majority they do this with family or friends, and sometimes this is due to the lack of their accessibility. Thus many visit, and even more would visit, independently when good access is assured. Many more would like to be able to visit independently and wish that more access services were available to make this possible.

The main barriers to access to cultural spaces arise because the needs of people with disabilities were not considered at the original design stage of the construction, or when refurbishments and improvements were planned. Limitations to access can also arise through high admission costs, lack of adequate accessible public transport, inadequate facilities, inhospitable public programs and difficult-to-access visitor information, in particular detailed information about access provisions. Three are main types of access that need to be taken into account in cultural spaces and they are the following:

- physical access
- access to services and staff awareness
- access to information.

The first two types are covered by ACCESSIBILITY PASS scheme. The physical access guidelines in a museum should cover for example, exhibition spaces, labels, lighting levels, hanging heights, audio-visual and interactive experiences, etc. All these are fully covered by ACCESSIBILITY PASS scheme which is actually a hyper-set that covers also the accessibility of spaces which are not meet at a cultural space. Additionally, the access to service is also covered by ACCESSIBILITY PASS, since both the accessibility of the given (electronic) information services and the accessibility of face to face services is covered by the scheme which has a whole part devoted to how people with disabilities should be treated by the staff that is providing the services to them.

The part that is missing from ACCESSIBILITY PASS scheme for the evaluation and the accreditation of cultural places is the access to information. Access to information includes the following issues:

- Provide Auslan interpreting for lectures or have script or synopsis available.
- Provide live captioning for lectures and public talks.
- Provide touch-tours for the blind, deafblind and visually impaired community.
- Provide
  - touch-tours for people with intellectual disabilities, as well as the blind, deafblind and visually impaired community.
  - guided tours specifically for people with intellectual disabilities.
- Provide museum introduction sessions for people with a range of disabilities or access needs.
- Provide privileged costs entrance for people with disabilities and their companions
  - Provide a disability membership price
- Provide options for tours outside of normal visiting hours or at quiet times in the museum.
- Provide captions or signs for the films projected.
- Ensure all lectures/talks/public programs are held in fully accessible venues.
- Promote the museum as space for a social occasion for people with a disability; encourage social groups of people with a disability through the provision and promotion of access services.
- Ensure exhibitions are laid out using a simple, easy to navigate floor plan.
- Provide audio alternatives to all visual material.
  - Provide audio descriptions of spaces, objects, and exhibitions.
- Provide captions or text alternatives for all audio-visual material.
  - Ensure audio-visual material does not dominate the exhibition space, perhaps provide dedicated areas for audio-visual material.
- Ensure all information technology equipment is easy to access, including keyboard settings and design, and is located in a physically accessible environment.
- Provide the option of tours for people who are unable to access written information.

Most of the above are already included in the ACCESSIBILITY PASS scheme as guidelines for hotel open or private spaces. What has to be done is to rearrange the content of the scheme in order to fit the needs of the cultural spaces we would like to include and evaluate.

5 Conclusions

In an ever-developing society, the elimination of marginalization of people with disabilities is an objective to which priority should be given and since the area of tourism and culture is one of the society's key sector, the accessibility of all venues (either for leisure or for business) should be considered as a vital issue.

The ACCESSIBILITY PASS scheme comes to meet this shortcoming, providing the opportunity to people with motor, visual, hearing or cognitive disability to be able to choose and visit accessible facilities, according to their specific needs and preferences (i.e. the scope of their travel). This could and should encompass cultural places also. Ensuring people with disabilities access needs are met offers the potential for cultural places to increase both visitor numbers and the diversity of their audience. In addition, by finding better ways to meet the needs of visitors with disabilities, museums and galleries will be improving the visiting experience for all visitor groups.

The ACCESSIBILITY PASS, being a global evaluation and certification scheme, complies with internationally acknowledged standards of accessibility and aims to help the sector of tourism to be transformed to a more compatible and friendly field for people with disabilities and explore further, at the same time, significant business potentials. This makes this scheme very flexible and extendable to other domains also.

References

1. 10 Facts on Disability. World Health Organization
2. Disability Discrimination Act (1995)
3. Equality Act (2010)
4. http://ec.europa.eu/enterprise/sectors/tourism/accessibility/index_en.htm
5. Improving information on accessible tourism for disabled people. European Commission (2004)
6. OSSATE: Accessibility Market and Stakeholders Analysis (2005)
7. United Nations Convention on the Rights of Persons with Disabilities (2008)
8. Landman, P., Fishburn, K., Kelly, L., Tonkin, S.: Many Voices Making Choices: Museum Audiences with Disabilities. Australian Museum, National Museum of Australia, Sydney (2005)
9. Australian Bureau of Statistics: Community and Sporting Involvement of People with a Disability. Australian Bureau of Statistics, Canberra (2002). http://www.abs.gov.au

EmoActivity - An EEG-Based Gamified Emotion HCI for Augmented Artistic Expression: The i-Treasures Paradigm

Vasileios Charisis[1]([⊠]), Stelios Hadjidimitriou[1],
Leontios Hadjileontiadis[1], Deniz Uğurca[2], and Erdal Yilmaz[2]

[1] Department of Electrical and Computer Engineering, Aristotle University
of Thessaloniki, Thessaloniki, Greece
vcharisis@ee.auh.gr, stelios@psyche.ee.auth.gr,
leontios@auth.gr
[2] Argedor Information Technologies, Ankara, Turkey
{dugurca, erdlylmz}@gmail.com

Abstract. There are important cultural differences in emotions that can be predicted and connected to each other in the light of cultural and artistic expressions. The main differences reflected at the affective space are expressed through initial response tendencies of appraisal and action readiness. Capturing and handling the emotions during artistic activities could be used as a dominant source of information to acquire and augment the cultural expression and maximize the emotional impact to the audience. This paper presents a novel EEG-based game-like application, to learn and handle affective states and transitions towards augmented artistic expression. According to the game scenario, the user has to reach and sustain one or more target affective states based on the level of the game, the difficulty setting and his/her current affective state. The game, although at its first version, has been demonstrated to a small group of potential users and has received positive feedback. Its use by a wider audience is anticipated within the realization of the i-Treasure FP7 EU Programme (2013-2017).

Keywords: Human-computer interaction · Emotion game · Affective state detection · Game-based learning · Contemporary music composition · Valence-arousal space · EEG · Emotiv · Emoactivity · i-Treasures

1 Introduction

1.1 Emotion Recognition (ER) and Human Computer Interaction (HCI)

One of the essential aspects that affect human's daily enterprises that require productive social interaction and communication skills is emotion. Considering the proliferation of machines in our commonness, it is essential that they interact with people the same way people interact with each other. In order to accomplish such a pragmatic HCI, it becomes crucial to imbue machines with the ability to detect, recognize and respond to human emotional states and reactions, that is, to outfit machines with emotional intelligence. The latter is the target of affective computing that deals with the design of

M. Antona and C. Stephanidis (Eds.): UAHCI 2015, Part IV, LNCS 9178, pp. 29–40, 2015.
DOI: 10.1007/978-3-319-20687-5_4

systems and devices that can detect, recognize and process human emotions with the ultimate goal of implementing the aforementioned more reliable HCI.

Emotion recognition is one of the most important issues affective computing brings forward and plays a dominant role in the effort to incorporate computers and generally machines, with the ability to interact with humans by expressing cues that postulate and demonstrate emotional intelligence-related attitude. Successful ER will enable machines to recognize the affective state of the user and collect emotional data for processing in order to proceed toward the terminus of emotion-based Human-Machine-Interaction, the emotional-like response.

1.2   Emotions in Musical Artistic Expression

It is clearly conceivable and apparent that music expresses emotions as personal affective experiences during music listening. However, a lot of research efforts and approaches, from philosophical to biological, have been presented in order to shed light on further insights in this phenomenon [1]. It has been suggested that such music-induced emotions are governed by universality in terms of musical culture, meaning, listeners with different cultural backgrounds can infer emotions in culture-specific music to a certain extent. Such evidence led to the assumption that neurobiological functions underlying such emotional experiences do not differ across members of different cultures, as the neural networks responsible may be fixed. In general, the processing of musical stimuli involves the gradual analysis of music structural elements from basic acoustic features to musical syntax that leads to the perception of emotions and semantic meanings underlying the stimuli [2]. It is becoming evident that the structure of music defines what it expresses. To be more accurate, music does not literally express emotion as it is not a sentient creature, but it is its structural elements and production performance shaping the acoustic outcome that foster the induction of emotional states to the listener, who is indeed a sentient being.

Written music can be performed in different ways, just like a piece of text can be read with various tones. In essence, music exists only when it is performed and performances of the same work can differ significantly. The latter form the concept of performance expression that refers to both; (a) the correlation between the performer's interpretation of a musical excerpt and the small-scale variations in timing, dynamics, vibrato, and articulation that shape the microstructure of the performance and (b) the relationship between such variations and the listener's perception of the performance. It has been proposed that performance expression emerges from five different sources, i.e., Generative rules, Emotion expression, Random fluctuations, Motion principles, and Stylistic unexpectedness, referred to as the GERMS model [3]. Here, the focus is placed on emotional expression that allows the performer to convey emotions to listeners by manipulating features, such as tempo and loudness, in order to render the performance with the emotional characteristics that seem suitable for the particular musical piece. By capturing and handling these emotions, and, even better, their dynamic character during artistic activities, could be used as a dominant source of information to acquire and augment the cultural expression and maximize the emotional impact to the audience.

1.3   The i-Treasures Paradigm

"Intangible Cultural Heritage" (ICH) is defined as a part of the cultural heritage of societies, groups or sometimes individuals and includes practices, presentations, expressions, knowledge, skills and related tools to all of these, such as equipment and cultural sites. This intangible heritage passes from generation to generation and gives people a sense of identity and continuity; it is the result of the continuous interaction of communities and groups with their nature and history and it promotes respect for cultural diversity and human creativity.

The main objective of i-Treasures project [4] is to build a public and expandable platform to enable learning and transmission of rare know-how of intangible cultural heritage. One of the use cases that i-Treasures deals with is Contemporary Music Composition (CMC). According to UNESCO, music is the most universal form of the performing arts since it can be found in every society, usually as an integral part of other performing art forms and other domains of ICH. Music can be found in a large variety of contexts, such as classical, contemporary or popular, sacred etc. Instruments, artefacts and objects in general are closely linked with musical expressions and they are all included in the Convention's definition of the ICH. Music that fits with the western form of notation is better protected. Nevertheless, those that do not fit with the western notation are usually threatened. In order to prevent such ICH expressions from extinction, the aim of CMC use case of i-Treasures project is to provide a tool that will allow people to practice the ICH expressions. Towards this goal, game-like educational applications are developed.

Digital games employed in education can be broadly subdivided in two categories [5]: (1) mainstream games, i.e., games that are created solely for fun, and (2) learning games, i.e., games that are expressly designed with explicit educational purposes. Games in the latter category are also referred to as Serious Games (SGs) [6]. The i-Treasures game-like applications can be reasonably considered SGs, since they have been built having in mind a "serious" educational purpose.

The adoption of SGs in i-Treasures follows a quite well consolidated trend in the Technology Enhanced Learning field. As a matter of fact, at present, digital games are increasingly adopted to sustain learning and training in a variety of educational fields (for example, school education, military training, medical training); this is done for a wide range of target populations, ranging from children to adults [7]. The educational potential of games has been widely explored and highlighted by researchers within the wider research area of Game-Based Learning [8].

1.4   Proposed Application

This paper presents a novel SG emotion Human-Computer-Interaction application, namely EmoActivity, to learn and handle affective states and transitions towards augmented artistic expression of a contemporary music composer/performer/learner. EmoActivity is part of the CMC use case of i-Treasures project. CMC aims to develop a novel intangible musical instrument, which maps natural gestures, performed in a real-world environment, to music by taking into account the performer's emotional status that influences the outputted acoustic result. One of the innovative aspects of EmoActivity is its ER module, based on EEG, as described in the succeeding sections.

2   Electroencephalogram (EEG)-Based ER

Towards effective ER, a large variety of methods and devices have been implemented, mostly concerning ER from face, speech and signals from autonomous nervous system (ANS), i.e. heart rate and galvanic skin response. A relatively new field in the ER area is EEG-based ER, which overcomes some fundamental reliability issues that arise with ER from face, voice or ANS-related signals. For instance, a facial expression recognition approach would be useless for people with inability to express emotions via face or for situations of human social masking. Moreover, voice and ANS signals are vulnerable to "noise" related to activity that does not derive from emotional experience, i.e., GSR signals are highly influenced by inspiration which may not be caused from emotional activity, especially in case of musical performance. The game architecture of the EmoActivity builds upon the EEG-based ER concept via specific time series analysis of the acquired EEG signal to infer for the current emotional state of the user; a detail description of the complete EmoActivity architecture follows.

3   Game Architecture

3.1   Input Data Capture

EEG signals are acquired using the EPOC wireless recording headset (Emotiv Systems, Inc., San Francisco, CA). EPOC (Fig. 2(a)) bears 14 channels (AF3, F7, F3, FC5, T7, P7, O1, O2, P8, T8, FC6, F4, F8), referenced to the common mode sense (CMS –left mastoid) - driven right leg (DRL - right mastoid) ground (Fig. 2(b)), under a 128 Hz sampling frequency. The recorded EEG signals are streamed in real-time to a paired PC. The communication between the headset and the PC is based on a proprietary wireless protocol that requires an EPOC USB receiver plugged in to the computer. The headset is powered by a lithium battery that provides 12 h of autonomy on a full charge.

3.2   Affective States

The most popular model representing the emotional states is the 2D model of valence and arousal [9] (Fig. 1(a)). Valence denotes if an affective state is positive or negative, while arousal constitutes a measure of excitation. Thus, each affective state can be modeled as a point on the plane defined by the orthogonal axes of valence and arousal. In this work, four affective states are discriminated: (a) positive valence – high arousal, (b) positive valence – low arousal, (c) negative valence – high arousal, and (d) negative valence – low arousal.

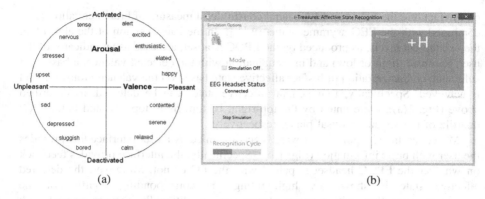

(a)   (b)

Fig. 1. (a) 2D valence-arousal space, (b) Affective state recognition software

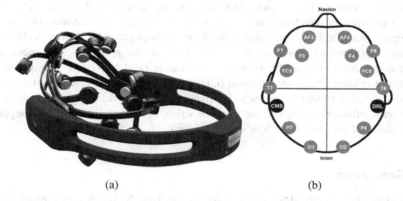

(a)   (b)

Fig. 2. (a) EPOC wireless EEG headset by Emotiv, (b) Electrode positions of the EPOC headset according to the 10/20 International System

3.3 Affective State Recognition Software

The EPOC headset is combined with an in house-developed affective state recognition software. The recognition software gathers the EEG data, in the background, and computes the current affective state of the user. In particular, the software captures the stream of the 14 channel raw EEG data and feeds them to a fractal dimension (FD) threshold-based recognition algorithm, based on the works of [10, 11] that yields the valence (positive or negative) of the users' affective state in real-time. Its recognition cycle requires 4 s; thus, the user's affective valence is outputted every 4 s. In particular, for this time interval, the difference between the sum of the EEG FD values corresponding to channels of the left brain hemisphere and the respective sum corresponding to channels of the right brain hemisphere is computed. If the difference is greater than zero, valence is considered positive; else, it is considered negative, based on the fact that the FD of an EEG signal constitutes a measure of brain activation [12], combined with the EEG asymmetry theory [13]. In the latest version of the algorithm, the excitement levels, as produced by the EPOC headset, are used as an indicator of the user's arousal (high or low) and in combination with the detected valence, a basic, yet sufficient, characterization of his/her affective state based on the valence-arousal model is achieved. Specifically, four general affective states can be detected, as described above (Fig. 1(a)), represented by the top-right, bottom-right, top-left, and bottom-left quartile of the valence-arousal plane, respectively.

Moreover, the recognition software is accompanied by a user interface that provides the user with basic information (Fig. 1(b)). Specifically, the interface provides feedback on whether the EPOC headset is paired with the PC or not. Moreover, the detected affective state is shown by highlighting the corresponding quartile of the valence-arousal plane, with representative colors. Additionally, the progress of each recognition cycle is shown via a progress bar.

The software was developed in C#, while the FD estimation method was realized in Matlab (Math-works, Inc., Natick, MA) and ported as a.NET dynamic link library (DLL). The software interface can be minimised on the task tray (Windows OS) with the recognition algorithm continuing to work on the background. Communication with third-party applications has also been embedded in the software. The recognition module communicates with the visualization module (and Max/MSP if required) via messages over User Datagram Protocol (UDP), i.e., the detected affective state is sent to the visualization module in order to be visualized or used accordingly. In particular, two separate values are sent, i.e., the value of valence (0 for positive or 1 for negative) and the value of arousal (0 for low or 1 for high).

3.4   Game Scenario

EmoActivity is basically designed to prompt the user to reach and sustain certain affective states via a gamified process involving affective images. The game consists of three levels with each level having three difficulty settings (easy, medium, and hard). In Level 1 the user is asked to reach a certain affective state and sustain it, while in Levels 2 and 3 the user is asked to reach two and three consecutive states, respectively. In order to unlock levels 2 and 3, the user should complete successfully Level 1 and Level 2, respectively. In order to facilitate the emotion elicitation, affective images are used. These images are drawn from the International Affective Picture System (IAPS) [14] database based on the valence-arousal rating provided with the database.

The difficulty in each level lies in the difficulty of the affective transition the user should undergo; in other words, the target affective state that the user is asked to reach based on his/her current emotional status. Related studies have shown that conditional dependencies exist between emotional states [15] and the probability of transition from one emotional state to another varies significantly [16]. For example, if difficulty level

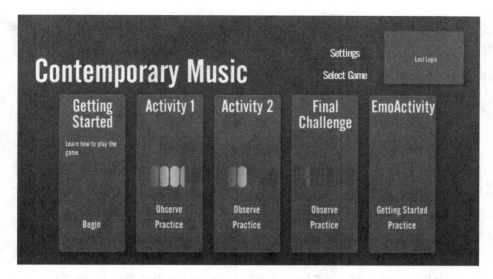

Fig. 3. Main menu of Contemporary Music Composition application

is set to easy and the user is calm (positive valence – low arousal), s/he will be asked to reach a target affective state of excitement (positive valence – high arousal) as this transition is more easy that a state of sadness or anger/fear.

At the completion of each level a performance score is provided according to the performance of the user.

3.5   User Interface

The game interface (visualization module) is implemented by Unity 3D game engine. The reasons to choose this development tool are (a) Unity 3D is an industry proven game development environment, (b) it is easy to deploy the games to various platforms ranging from Desktop PCs to mobile devices, and (c) the development team is highly experienced in Unity.

Main Menu Screen. The main menu screen of the CMC application concerning CMC use case is shown on Fig. 3. The "Getting Started" panel provides a general tutorial about CMC use case whereas the first three activities (Activity 1, Activity 2 and Final Challenge) are focused on the intangible musical instrument. These are not going to be presented because they are beyond the scope of this work. The last activity is Emo-Activity. The "Getting Started" section provides detailed information about the usage, setup and preparation of the Emotiv EPOC EEG headset. A snapshot of the introduction to the headset is shown in Fig. 4. The introduction video provides instructions to the users in order to wear and configure the device on their own. The "Practice"

Fig. 4. Snapshot of the introduction to the EPOC headset video as a "Getting Started" guide

section is the actual game where the user can practice in reaching and sustaining certain affective states.

EmoActivity Screens. By clicking on the "Practice" button the game begins. Each level starts with an introductory screen (Fig. 5(a)) that informs the user about the current level and the target, for example, "Level 1. A series of pictures will be shown. You must reach the target affective state and sustain it". In this screen, each faded color represents a quartile of the valence-arousal plane. After five seconds, the caption disappears and a progress bar is shown for 20 s (Fig. 5(b)). During this period, the current affective state of the user is detected. Then, based on the detected current affective state and the difficulty setting the target emotional state is displayed for five seconds by highlighting the corresponding faded color on the valence arousal space and by displaying a caption "Feel", as illustrated in Fig. 5(c). Thereafter, a series of random affective images are displayed sequentially for five seconds each, as shown in (Fig. 5 (d)) in order to facilitate emotion elicitation. The background of the images has the same color as the corresponding quartile of valence-arousal space that the target affective state belongs. Afterwards, the detected emotional status is displayed by highlighting the corresponding faded color (Fig. 5(e)) and accompanied by a caption "You felt" and a green tick (if the detected affective state is correct) or a red "x" (if the detected affective state is wrong). In case the correct emotional target is achieved, the learner is told that he/she reached the target affective state. However, there are two cases: (1) the learner gets 10 points if the affective target is sustained, otherwise, (2) the learner gets 5 points. On the other hand, if the target affective is not reached the learner gets 0 points and he/she is asked to try again (Fig. 5(f)).

An analogous procedure is applied for levels 2 and 3 but is not described here for space reasons.

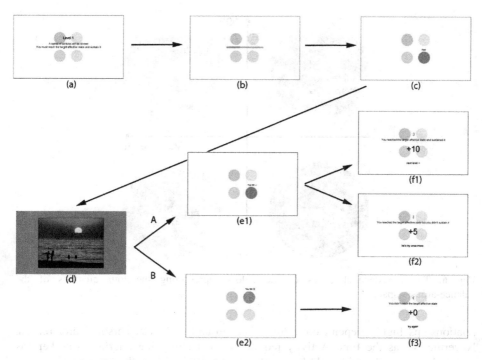

Fig. 5. EmoActivity screens: (a) initial screen, (b) progress bar for current affective state calculation, (c) target affective state, (d) affective pictures display, (e) results screens ((e1) correct affective state reached, (e2) wrong affective state reached), (f) score screens ((f1) correct affective state reached and sustained, (f2) correct affective state reached but not sustained, (f3) wrong affective state reached)

As far as the current affective state detection and the affective state transition/sustenance detection are concerned (see Sect. 3.3 "Affective State Recognition Software"), the user's emotional status is determined by the affective state outputted the most by the recognition algorithm after a number of recognition cycles. For example, during the 20 s of the user's current state detection, five recognition cycles take place; hence, the outcome outputted the most after the five recognition cycles is considered to represent the user's affective state.

Colors. Colors representing the quartiles of the valence-arousal plane are representative of the affective state corresponding to each quartile. In Fig. 6 the colors along with their hexadecimal codes are depicted. In particular, dark red (top-left quartile) usually represents anger or fear, i.e., emotions of negative valence and of high arousal, while dark grey (bottom-left quartile) conveys a feeling of negative valence and of low arousal, such as sadness. On the other hand, the blue color (bottom-right quartile) is linked to the feeling of calmness and serenity (positive valence - low arousal), while orange is representative of excitement and joy (positive valence - high arousal). The latter are based on statistical research [17], mostly in the Western World; however, there is no universal agreement on the association of colors to emotions and such

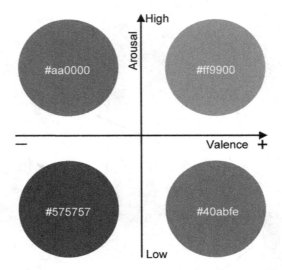

Fig. 6. The hexadecimal codes of the colors representing the four quartiles of the valence-arousal space

relationships highly depend on cultural background and even personal preferences. Nevertheless, as the Emo Activity requires mental effort, the interface was kept as minimal as possible, with only basic information displayed on the screen.

4   Conclusion

This work presents the first version of a novel interactive game-like emotion HCI application that is expected to assist the user to learn and handle affective states and transitions towards augmented artistic expression. Emo Activity is part of the Contemporary Music Composition use case of i-Treasures project that targets the development of an intangible musical instrument that will produce sound through a natural user interface and will be affected by the user's affective state. Acoustic cues manipulated by user's affective states, such as happiness, tenderness, sadness, fear and anger are: pitch, intensity, tempo and timbre [1].

The game entails three levels with three difficulty settings per level. Depending on the current affective state of the user and the difficulty setting, the user is asked to reach one, two or three consecutive affective states at levels 1, 2 and 3, respectively. From a technical point of view, EmoActivity comprises of an affective state recognition software and a visualization module that communicate through UDP. Moreover, the Emotiv EPOC headset is required for capturing and wirelessly transmitting the EEG data.

The first version of EmoActivity has been demonstrated to the Vocational Training Institute of Thermi, Thessaloniki, Greece and Municipal Concervatory of Kalamaria,

Thessaloniki, Greece, and has received positive feedback from both teachers and students. They displayed inspiration and enthusiasm for the concept and scenario of the game while they proactively sought more complex levels.

5 Future Work

Future work includes the use of not only affective images but also sounds and videos in order to achieve improved emotional triggering/elicitation and, consequently, more reliable affective state recognition results. Additionally, more detailed digitization of the valence-arousal space is planned, i.e. four emotional states for each quartile of valence-arousal space leading to 16 states in total; however, such an advance should coincide with an appropriate improvement of the emotional state recognition software to detect 16 emotional states. Last but not least, a new level will be developed where the user will be asked to reach multiple consecutive affective states while listening a contemporary musical piece that will be distorted accordingly in case of failure to reach the targets.

Acknowledgements. This work is funded by the European Commission via the i-Treasures project (Intangible Treasures - Capturing the Intangible Cultural Heritage and Learning the Rare Know-How of Living Human Treasures FP7-ICT-2011-9-600676-i-Treasures). It is an Integrated Project (IP) of the European Union's 7th Framework Programme 'ICT for Access to Cultural Resources.

References

1. Juslin, P.N., Sloboda, J.A.: Handbook of Music and Emotions Theory, Research, Applications. Oxford University Press, New York (2000)
2. Koelsch, S., Siebel, W.A.: Towards a neural basis of music perception. Trends Cogn. Sci. **9**, 578–584 (2005)
3. Juslin, P.N.: Five facets of musical expression: a psychologist's perspective on music performance. Psychol. Music **31**, 273–302 (2003)
4. The i-Treasures project. http://www.i-treasures.eu
5. Kirriemuir, J., McFarlane, A.: Literature Review in Games and Learning. A NESTA Futurelab Research Report – Report 8. NESTA Futurelab Series, Bristol (2004)
6. Michael, D., Chen, S.: Serious Games: Games That Educate, Train, and Inform. Thomson Course Technology, Boston (2006)
7. Charlier, N., Ott, M., Remmele, B., Whitton, N.: Not Just for Children: Game-Based Learning for Older Adults. In: 6th European Conference on Games Based Learning, pp. 102–108 (2012)
8. Van Eck, R.: Digital game-based learning: it's not just the digital natives who are restless. EDUCAUSE Rev. **41**, 17–30 (2006)
9. Russell, J.A.: A circumflex model of affect. J. Pers. Soc. Psychol. **39**, 1161–1178 (1980)
10. Higuchi, T.: Approach to an irregular time series on the basis of the fractal theory. Physica D **31**, 277–283 (1988)

11. Liu, Y., Sourina, O., Nguyen, M.K.: Real-time EEG-based emotion recognition and its applications. In: Gavrilova, M.L., Tan, C.J.K., Sourin, A., Sourina, O. (eds.) Transactions on Computational Science XII. LNCS, vol. 6670, pp. 256–277. Springer, Heidelberg (2011)

12. Accardo, A., Affinito, M., Carrozzi, M., Bouquet, F.: Use of the fractal dimension for the analysis of electroencephalographic time series. Biol. Cybern. **77**, 339–350 (1997)

13. Davidson, R.J.: What does the prefrontal cortex "do" in affect: perspectives on frontal EEG asymmetry research. Biol. Psychol. **67**, 219–233 (2004)

14. Lang, P.J., Bradley, M.M., Cuthbert, B.N.: International affective picture system (IAPS): Affective ratings of pictures and instruction manual. Technical report A-8, University of Florida (2008)

15. Sudhof, M., Emilsson, A.G., Maas, A.L., Potts, C.: Sentiment expression conditioned by affective transitions and social forces. In: 20th ACM SIGKDD International Conference of Knowledge Discovery and Data Mining, pp. 1136–1145 (2014)

16. Baker, D.R.S.J., Mercedes, M., Rodrigo, T., Xolocotzin, U.E.: The dynamics of affective transitions in simulation problem-solving environments. In: 2nd International Conference on Affective Computing and Intelligence Interactions, pp. 666–677 (2007)

17. Cherry, K.: Color psychology: how colors impact moods, feelings, and behaviors. http://psychology.about.com/od/sensationandperception/a/colorpsych.htm

Living Lab Concept Validation Experiment to Experience COOLTURA in the Cité Des Science et de L'Industrie

Silvia de los Rios[1(✉)], Maria Fernanda Cabrera-Umpierrez[1],
Maria Teresa Arredondo[1], Miguel Paramo[1], Charles Tijus[2],
Elhadi Djebbari[3], Federico Mussano[4], and Roberto Santoro[4]

[1] Life Supporting Technologies,
Universidad Politecnica de Madrid, Madrid, Spain
{srios, chiqui, mta, mparamo}@lst.tfo.upm.es
[2] Integrative User Lab – IUL Lutin, Cité Des Sciences et de L'Industrie,
Paris, France
charles.tijus@gmail.com
[3] Universcience, Cité Des Sciences et de L'Industrie, Paris, France
elhadi.djebbari@universcience.fr
[4] ESoCE-Net, Rome, Italy
mussanof@tiscali.it, rsantoro@esoce.net

Abstract. Culture is everywhere; it is part of all citizens, of our past, our roots, our present and key asset for our future. Technology is a good driver to present and allow access to cultural heritage. Within the European FP7 project eCult-Value an open call was launched which allowed the IUL-LUTIN Living Lab to make an experiment using COOLTURA, outcome from the also European FP7 project TAG CLOUD, in the Cité des Sciences et de l'Industrie (CSI) of Paris (France). This paper presents such experiment as well as the interesting results extracted from the participants' feedback.

Keywords: App · Cultural heritage · User experience · Engagement · Augmented reality · Storytelling · Social media · COOLTURA · CSI

1 Introduction

Museums and cultural institutions have invested and are investing a lot to introduce cultural heritage in the digital era. Number of digital objects available in Europeana [1] has increased significantly. Currently, it provides access to over 33 million digitised objects, having already reached 30 million objects in November 2013 [2]. This means that, although around 88 % of Europe's cultural collections (in average) are still not digitised, the trend is to increase these numbers [3]. Digitisation plans are increasing at European level, and a lot of progress has been done in the last years to raise the amount of digitised cultural material as well as with regards to online accessibility of cultural material, including more cross-border collaboration and public-private partnerships [2].

With the aim to re-use the available digitised content and provide it to the user through an adaptive and personalised experience, it has been developed COOLTURA.

© Springer International Publishing Switzerland 2015
M. Antona and C. Stephanidis (Eds.): UAHCI 2015, Part IV, LNCS 9178, pp. 41–52, 2015.
DOI: 10.1007/978-3-319-20687-5_5

It is the outcome of the European funded project TAG CLOUD [4] that aims to explore the use of cloud-based technologies that lead to adaptability and personalisation to increase engagement with cultural heritage. COOLTURA has been developed as a platform and an application following a User-Centered Design methodology [5, 6]. COOLTURA Platform is an open data oriented platform which holds the necessary intelligence, through a set of algorithms, to provide a set of scalable services for cultural engagement. On the other hand, COOLTURA App access the cultural content processed in the COOLTURA Platform and provides the user with a unique personalised cultural experience. This is done through the visualisation of recommended cultural content, itineraries and routes, the exploration of cultural objects through augmented reality, storytelling and games, and the interaction with cultural objects through the usage of QR codes, NFC tags and/or Bluetooth beacons. It also allows the user also to share the cultural experience through social networks.

2   Background

The *Cité des Sciences et de l'Industrie* (CSI), a "universcience" site, is the biggest science museum in Europe, welcoming 3 million visitors per year [7]. In 1981 the architect Adrien Fainsilber decided to open its building to light, a "source of energy of the living world". It is located inside The Park de la Villette, which is the third-largest park in Paris, 35.5 hectares in area, located at the north-eastern edge of the 19th arrondissement.

Through the development of science and technology, the *Cité des Sciences et de l'Industrie* provides the necessary learning tools to better understand the world in constant change around us. Each exhibition space is open to all age groups, from junior to senior, from tourists to professionals/researchers or to the simply curious.

On the other hand, the Integrative Usage Lab (IUL LUTIN) is a Living Lab located at CSI in Paris. IUL-LUTIN has primarily been designed as a Living Lab for usability: a research and development lab that provides facilities for companies who wish to evaluate the usability of new products, services and digital media. Nowadays, it is becoming a place for experiencing scientific mediation and learning within a Living Lab methodology, taking into account ethical issues [8, 9], and with a special focus on digital technologies for museums, mainly because LUTIN is a museum structure for museum validation of technologies dedicated to visitors.

In the past, the *Cité des Sciences et de l'Industrie* (CSI) and IUL-LUTIN carried out several studies and innovative experiments regarding different aspects, such as websites of museums [10], cultural heritage for children [11], Open Science Resources [12], augmented reality [13, 14], learning [15] and tours [16]. The main objective of the most recent experiments was to enrich the visitor experience [17]. Between real and virtual (augmented reality [18], documentary records [19], audio annotation, associated metadata, social media, etc.), the visitor may live a unique experience by combining both, real and virtual environments.

This manuscript describes the Living Lab experiment carried out in the CSI together with IUL-LUTIN to evaluate the TAG CLOUD concept through the experimentation of COOLTURA App. The experiment has been carried out within the framework of the eCultValue project [20], co-funded by the FP7 programme of the European Commission. This project aims to support and encourage the use of new technologies that have the potential to revolutionize new ways to access cultural heritage and experiences offered by cultural resources in real and virtual environments or a mix of both. Concretely, eCultValue is looking at technologies arriving from EU funded projects, promoting these technologies to stakeholders who will apply them and relate technologies to showcase scenarios for easier up-take.

The eCultValue project launched an Open Call for Living Labs to run experiments for the concept validation at European museums of technologies for cultural heritage coming from European projects. COOLTURA, the TAG CLOUD App, was selected to be tested in the validation experiment performed by the Integrative Usage Lab (IUL LUTIN) and CSI in October and November 2014. The COOLTURA application provides a new way to enjoy culture by combining visualisation, exploration and interaction with cultural heritage artefacts. In the context of CSI and IUL-LUTIN Cultural heritage past projects, TAG CLOUD /COOLTURA appears to be the bridge that is conveying an informational richness to visitors: TAG CLOUD /COOLTURA may be a real experience for the Park la Villette visitors. This rich cultural environment in events and entertainment offers fertile ground to test this concept. The experiment focused mostly on the *Cité des Sciences et de l'Industrie* (city of science and industry), the *Géode* (geode), the *Argaunaute* (Argonaut) and the *Bibliothèque des Sciences et de l'Industrie* (BSI – library of sciences and industry). While using mobile devices and COOLTURA, visitors have the opportunity to "augment" their visit with additional information, videos, pictures and social media. They also have the opportunity to be located and discover other activities around them and know, for example, how to book a ticket for an exhibition (Fig. 1).

Fig. 1. Cooltura in the Cité des Sciences et de l'Industrie, Paris, France

The aim for this experiment is based on the analysis of the usage of ICT tools (such as mobiles, PDAs, Augmented Reality Displays, etc.) in cultural institutions. This kind of devices is more and more used for guiding the user through a museum while providing information about the visit and objects in the museum. These devices are often used to integrate or to provide additional information to what is already displayed in the current context. For this reason, when using a mobile device, the user has to choose how to share attention between the intended object (the object of interest), contextual information in the real scene, and the additional information to get from the mobile device. The use of ICT tools for personalising the visit is likely to affect the way visitors explore the museum and the way they learn from the museum contents. How these technologies can influence the visitor's habits and change the museum experience is far from being understood and clearly assessed.

Thus, the main objectives of this experiment consisted in assessing and validating the use of COOLTURA (an App for smartphone or tablet) in real-life settings (museum). For this it was aimed to measure the user acceptance of the proposed technologies, including the effects on the visitors' habits of information searching and attention strategies as well as overall comprehension and learning.

3 Methodology

To prepare and carry on the experiment it was needed, first, to define and design the experiment, second, to prepare the environment for the experiment, and finally to perform it at the *Cité des Sciences et de l'Industrie*.

3.1 Design of Concept Validation Experiment

As mentioned in the previous section, the main objectives of the experiment consisted in assessing and validating the use of COOLTURA App in real-life settings, as in the CSI /IUL-LUTIN. Thus, it was aimed to be performed in real-life conditions with regular visitors of the museum.

In order to measure the effects of using an application, as COOLTURA, in their visit to a museum and how it affects on the visitors' habits of information searching and attention, the LUTIN Mobile Platform was used for observation and evaluation of Users Behaviour, by using eye tracking, camera goggle, audio video recorders and micro cameras. This allowed obtaining quantitative and qualitative data to refine the solutions and services experienced. In addition, questionnaires were used.

The experiment was planned to be carried out in three phases, described below:

- Phase 1: Welcoming

- Welcoming at the *Cité des Sciences et de l'Industrie*;
- Presentation of the COOLTURA application, as an interactive medium to explore several sites (Geode, BSI, Argonaut);
- Exploration of the application by visitors: participants were encouraged to freely explore the application.

- Phase 2: Preparation

- Completing a questionnaire on user's profile (regarding usage of smartphone and museum habits);
- Installation and calibration of equipment (camera, mobile eye tracker).

- Phase 3: Experiment performance

- The visitor must search for the three sites (Geode, BSI, Argonaut);
- Scan the QR code;
- Discover the site information. The test stops when the participant/visitor finds all of the information on the site while visiting the museum.

During phase 3, the experiment performance, supervisors observed visitors using the TAG CLOUD services (i.e. COOLTURA App). In addition, participants were asked to provide their appreciation, ideas about innovation, criticisms and recommendations while performing the experiment, following a Think Aloud Protocol (TAP) [21]. After the experiment, some questions were asked to participants in order to complement the information gathered along the experiment performance.

Participants

Participants were randomly selected from regular visitors of the museum (i.e. *Cité des Sciences et de l'Industrie*) with the following criteria for user's inclusion:

1. To be there for the museum scientific and technical objects, not knowing the places to visit (that were mainly outdoor objects of the museum);
2. To use smartphone or tablet.

By fulfilling these criteria, participants were asked at random to participate in the study that was said to be about a new type of experience while visiting the museum and with the use of a mobile device (i.e. smartphone or tablet).

Materials and tools for test support

A questionnaire was prepared to gather the following information from participants' profile, which was given during the phase 2 of the experiment:

- Age, gender, profession.
- Use of technology.
- Use of Smartphones, specifically.
- Frequency of visits to museums.
- Use of museum guides (printed, human guide, audio, apps).

In addition, to perform the experiment in phase 3, the following materials were planned to be used:

- The "COOLTURA" App.
- The "Barcode Scanner" App.
- Smartphone Samsung Galaxy S5 tablet 5.1 inch (12.7 centimetres) screen diagonal.
- Three QR-codes (for the three sites: Geode, BSI, Argonaut).
- The recording and measurement equipment:

- Eye-Tracking Glasses (recording of fixations and eye movements)
- Camera Scene /GoPro (user behaviour)
- Questionnaire and interview procedure (profile, collection of opinions and of feelings of the user)

With the measurement equipment of the LUTIN Mobile Platform, it was aimed to measure the following variables:

- Interaction:
- a. With menus,
- b. With navigation,
- c. Perception of interactive elements.
- Ergonomics:
- a. Eye fixation on text,
- b. Eye fixation on icons.
- Feelings:
- a. While using COOLTURA,
- b. After using COOLTURA.

Questions driving the research experiment

As mentioned before, the main aim is based on the analysis of the usage of ICT tools in cultural institutions. Thus, during the experiment, participants were asked to provide their impressions of the usage of the App, as well as their ideas and recommendations to improve it. The experiment was driven by the following questions, which were aimed to be answered by using observation and TAP:

1. Are LL participants able to identify the elements of interaction?
2. Are they able to understand their function?
3. Understand how to interact with?
4. Users do they encounter difficulties in the menu navigation?
5. Are the answers offered by the application in line with user expectations? Or are they rather confusing or unpleasant?
6. What do they find to be particularly satisfactory or to be very disappointing? Why are the functions they would use the most? The least?
7. Under what conditions and in what circumstances they would consider using COOLTURA?

3.2   Preparation of the Experiment

Before carry on the experiment, it was needed to prepare the content from the *Cité des Sciences et de l'Industrie* to be included in the COOLTURA App. The first step was to implement the content (videos, images and texts) about outdoor objects (the three included in the experiment: Geode, BSI, Argonaut) of the museum in Android 4.0 for smartphones and tablets.

Once COOLTURA App was ready with the CSI content, training on the usage of the application was given by the TAG CLOUD team to the CSI and IUL-LUTIN team involved in the experiment. Then, an internal testing of the application was carried out by the CSI and IUL-LUTIN team, where all functions were checked as well as the how-it-works.

Next step was to prepare the CSI environment for the experiment, and for this, QR codes were placed in the three spaces included in the experiment in order to interact with the objects (Fig. 2).

Fig. 2. QR code in one of the three sites at CSI (Geode, BSI, Argonaut)

After this, the LUTIN Mobile Platform was prepared to be used, and questionnaires were prepared and placed available online.

Finally, once COOLTURA App, the CSI environment and all materials and tools to be used were ready for the experiment, regular CSI visitors were recruited as participants, according to the criteria mentioned in the previous section.

With these criteria, regular visitors of CSI (n = 12; mean age: 31, 7 y) were recruited as participants, in addition of usability experts (n = 5) [22].

3.3   Experiment Performance

The purpose of the Living Lab study of COOLTURA was the understanding how museum visitors are using the application to visit three sites in the City of Science and Industry (the Geode, Scientific Library and the Argonaut) by evaluating the application in its ability to disseminate content: Do visitors read the texts? What is their perception of QR codes? Is their navigation satisfactory? What's about their user experience?

To do so, the dimensions of the analysis were:

- Their path within the application.
- Their favourite functions and their neglected functions.
- Their understanding of these functions.

The data gathered was related to:

- Project Architecture.
- Navigation /ergonomics.
- Features.
- The proposed interactions with the museum.
- Strengths /weaknesses (advantages & disadvantages).

Finally, participants were using the COOLTURA App with (n = 5) or without eye tracking devices, having then open questions (n = 6) or on line questionnaires (n = 6).

The running of the experiment was done as expected and as described in the above sections.

The use of COOLTURA by the regular visitors was done in real-life settings (CSI), having the task of discovering information about the museum objects while interacting with the App. Regular visitors were regular visitors for the CSI services: Library, Fablab, Living lab (n = 6), but also for exhibitions (n = 6), young adults (n = 8), from both gender: males (n = 9), females (n = 3), as well as with family (n = 2).

Usability experts were CSI (n = 1) and LUTIN members (n = 4) that agree to expertise the App. The use of COOLTURA by usability experts was done as they please according to their rigorous way of evaluating the ergonomy of devices [23, 24].

4   Results

4.1   Results from Visitors

Main results gathered from visitors were that:

1. They all appreciate the graphical design of the interface: simple, enjoyable, readable and nice.
2. 75 % do appreciate navigating with COOLTURA.
3. All of them find easy to use QR code.
4. 25 % find difficult to look for QR code while visiting the museum.
5. Half of them would like to have the App for their next visit.
6. Half of them would pay the App if included in a ticket price.

Participants were wearing eye-tracking glasses while visiting the museum, searching for QR code to flash in order to get the content. The eye-tracking device allowed understanding the process of using COOLTURA:

- (Stage 1) searching for QR code in the environment,
- (Stage 2) flashing
- (Stage 3) getting the content in the content of the museum object.

Fig. 3. Stage 1 of the process of using COOLTURA: searching

Fig. 4. Stage 2 of the process of using COOLTURA: flashing

Fig. 5. Stage 3 of the process of using COOLTURA: getting the content

There were results according to each of the 3 stages of the process.

Stage 1. The participants knew that there were QR codes for some of the museum objects and were searching around it where they could find the corresponding QR code. The sight scan path of the participants show that they were looking at places where the QR code could be located in a goal-directed search, but not paying attention to other things. Although interesting, this was time consuming, attention consuming with sometimes some mental workload.

This was the most problematic phase according to eye movements recording. Participants that were looking at their own eyes movements recording were complaining of this difficult task. They recommended that instead of searching for a QR code, it would be more convenient to discover it: "When you walk and see a QR code then you flash it!" and QR code could have a specific indication for identification in the environment: a large coloured pictogram.

Eye-tracking participants found that installing QR code and pictograms in the environment of the museum was of poor aesthetic. They reminded having this feeling in the real situation while they were viewing their own eye-tracking recording. Some of them (3) were asking why QR code is needed since the museum objects are geo-located: "When you walk, the App (COOLTURA) could inform you that it has some information about closed objects. Thus you at the screen and you decide if you are interested or not". One participant said that "if there are many museum objects, there could have some filters made from your personal interest" (Fig. 3).

Stage 2. When participants found a QR code, participants had to flash it. In fact they always were in the last search-find state. Recording of sight scan path shows that it took some time to go to the flash command and sometimes with errors.

As other participants, they recommend not having to search for the QR code command on the COOLTURA interface (Fig. 4).

Stage 3. Eye-tracking recording indicates two types of strategy. Some content texts were read wholly before exploring and discovering the target objects while with some other contents were partly read before exploring and discovering the target objects (Fig. 5).

While viewing their sight scan path recording, participants said that there could have specific text for specific parts of the museum object. Texts should be more precise: "we don't need general information we could find everywhere but the information we need". They also said that pictures could be displayed according to the viewing point of view and with some augmented reality information for naming parts of the museum objects (Fig. 6).

Fig. 6. Usage of COOLTURA without (left) and with (right) eye tracking

4.2   Results from Experts

Experts found that the structure of the App was a little too complex and could be made simpler. The fact that the QR code function for instance was not attached to the main screen (it was provided in a slide menu) was found uncomfortable. They all recommended having all of the functions always accessible.

Usability experts developed a map of the COOLTURA interaction design showing how one might navigate when using it, according to their expertise.

5 Conclusions

The experiment was of high interest, on one hand, for both the CSI and for LUTIN, to know better about the implementation of mobile applications for the museum. On the other hand, this evaluation was very interesting from the point of view of TAG CLOUD because it provided TAG CLOUD with more information about the evaluation of COOLTURA, from a complementary perspective than the one proposed within the project. This experiment gave information about the User Acceptance and User Experience as well as evaluating the Users' Behaviour measured with different techniques such as eye tracking, camera goggle, audio-video recorders and micro cameras; very useful to enhance the COOLTURA prototype for improving the experience of using it.

After the experiment results, it can be concluded that user experience of using COOLTURA, although generally was positively appreciated, should be improved and made simpler, more intuitive and with more quick access to key elements or functionalities.

Another conclusion is that people generally liked to interact with the environment, but doing it by placing QR codes was found not convenient for outdoor spaces, where GPS location can be used. In addition, quarter of the participants found difficult to find the QR codes. Thus, in case a sensor or code (as a QR code in this case) has to be placed to be searched and scanned to interact with the physical object, it should be easy to identify.

With this experiment, it was also demonstrated that while searching for a code to interact with the environment makes visitors to not pay attention to other objects around. If instead of asking for searching QR codes, the aim is to let the user discover the environment, then the process will be less time consuming, and probably visitors will experience more the whole cultural environment.

Acknowledgements. The work presented in this paper has been partially funded by the EC FP7 projects: eCultValue (Valorisation of EU project results in the area of access to cultural content); https://ecultvalue.wordpress.com/, Gran Agreement No. 601114; and TAG CLOUD (Technologies lead to Adaptability & lifelong enGagement with culture throughout the CLOUD); http://www.tagcloudproject.eu/, Grant Agreement No. 600924.

References

1. Europeana platform. http://www.europeana.eu/
2. Cultural heritage. Digitisation, online accessibility and digital preservation. Report on the Implementation of Commission Recommendation 2011/711/EU. Progress report 2011–2013. Working document, September 2014. ec.europa.eu/information_society/newsroom/cf/dae/document.cfm?action=display&doc_id=7065
3. Stroeker, N., Vogels, R.: Panteia (NL) on behalf of the ENUMERATE Thematic Network. Survey Report on Digitisation. In: European Cultural Heritage Institutions 2014 (January 2014). http://www.enumerate.eu/fileadmin/ENUMERATE/documents/ENUMERATE-Digitisation-Survey-2014.pdf

4. TAG CLOUD project, CN. 600924, 7th Framework Programme, ICT for access to cultural resources, February 2013. http://www.tagcloudproject.eu/
5. Abras, C., Maloney-Krichmar, D., Preece, J.: User-centered design. In: Bainbridge, W. (ed.) Encyclopedia of Human-Computer Interaction. Sage Publications, Thousand Oaks (2004)
6. Nielsen, J.: Iterative user-interface design. Computer **26**(11), 32–41 (1993)
7. Universcience. Web-site. http://www.ecsite.eu/members/directory/universcience
8. Barcenilla, J., Tijus, C.: Ethical issues raised by the new orientations in ergonomics and living labs. Work: A Journal of Prevention. Assess. Rehabil. **41**, 5259–5265 (2012)
9. Tijus, C., Barcenilla, J., Vandi, C.: Challenges and Ethical Issues in Living Labs for Open Innovation. In: Proceeding of the Challenges e-2012 Conference, Lisbon, October 2012
10. WEBCSTI (Websites of museums: Scientific and technical culture on the Web). http://ocim.revues.org/324
11. HANDS ON! (best Culture Heritage for children). http://www.bibliotheque-francophone.org/2009/11/la-biblio-etait-la-cite-des-sciences.html
12. OPEN SCIENCE RESOURCES (OSR: Sharing Resources among Museums). http://www.enssib.fr/chantier-mine/openscienceresources-osr
13. CULTURE CLIC (culture Augmented Reality App on mobile application for France). http://www.cultureclic.fr/
14. MOBILEARN (Augmented Reality for Informal Learning). http://library.ifla.org/903/1/210-djebbari-fr.pdf
15. CULTE (Cultural Urban Learning Transmedia Experience). http://www.agence-nationale-recherche.fr/projet-anr/?tx_lwmsuivibilan_pi2[CODE]=ANR-13-CORD-0018
16. TOUR GROUP GUIDE (tour group guide and communication between the tourist guide and the tour members). http://www.esnc.info/index.php?kat=prototyping.html&anzeige=ll_france.html
17. Vandi, C., Djebbari, E.: How to create new services between Library Resources, Museum Exhibitions and Virtual Collections. World library and information congress: 76th IFLA General Conference Assembly (2010). http://conference.ifla.org/past-wlic/2010/151-vandi-en.pdf
18. Espace "nouveaux modes de lecture", Bibliothèque CSI. http://www.cite-sciences.fr/fr/au-programme/lieux-ressources/bibliotheque/nos-espaces/espace-nouveaux-modes-de-lecture/
19. Dossiers documentaires, Bibliothèque online CSI. http://www.cite-sciences.fr/fr/ressources/bibliotheque-en-ligne/dossiers-documentaires/
20. eCultValue project, CN. 601114, 7th Framework Programme, ICT for access to cultural resources, February, 2013. https://ecultvalue.wordpress.com/
21. Jaaskelainen, R.: Think-aloud protocol. Handb. Transl. Stud. **1**, 371 (2010)
22. Turner, C.W., Lewis, J.R., Nielsen, J.: Determining usability test sample size. Int. Encycl. Ergon. Hum. Factors **3**, 3084–3088 (2006)
23. Scapin, D.L., Bastien, J.C.: Ergonomic criteria for evaluating the ergonomic quality of interactive systems. Behav. Inf. Technol. **16**(4–5), 220–231 (1997)
24. Nielsen, J. Nielsen Norman Group. Internet (2002). http://www.useit.com/papers/heuristic

Evaluating Intimacy and Ludic Engagement with a Musical Interactive Art Installation that Explores Remote Abstract Communication

Steven Gelineck[(✉)]

Aalborg University Copenhagen, A. C. Meyers Vænge 15,
2450 Copenhagen, Denmark
stg@create.aau.dk

Abstract. The main contribution of the paper is a usability evaluation of an interactive art installation where several different factors for ludic and intimate engagement in this specific context of remote face-to-face non-verbal communication are compared. Experiments are carried out with the following different overall goals: (1) to understand the importance of direct eye contact, (2) to understand the influence of using different musical outputs and (3) to understand whether providing participants with more detailed control supports exploration. Results indicate that direct eye contact enhances the intimate connection, that opera sounds are more effective than synthetic sounds in terms of intimacy, control, musical expressivity and exploration, and that participants engaged in more exploration with limited control.

Keywords: Mediated intimacy · Ludic engagement · Evaluation · Usability · Interactive art installations · Musical exploration · Video conferencing · Emotional communication

1 Introduction

Designing interaction for interactive art installations can be challenging. Especially when it comes to evaluation, it is difficult to choose methodological strategies based on objective, reliable and rigorously validated methods in order to produce meaningful, generalizable outcome that can push the research community further. This is in part because the area is under development and there still is a lack of common practices compared to areas that deal with more traditional Human Computer Interaction (HCI). But it also relates to the goal of objectivity that clashes with the art world where experiences are fundamentally subjective [1]. It seems that the majority of art installations presented in the literature are evaluated as they are installed in real world settings – meaning that evaluation is carried out in order to gain insight into how the finished, implemented installation was received. While this is indeed important and meaningful there may be a need for evaluating various parts of the interaction in the stage of development as is common for other areas of HCI. For instance a common practice in HCI usability evaluation is to perform lab experiments exposing users to

© Springer International Publishing Switzerland 2015
M. Antona and C. Stephanidis (Eds.): UAHCI 2015, Part IV, LNCS 9178, pp. 53–64, 2015.
DOI: 10.1007/978-3-319-20687-5_6

different stimuli or different variations of a user interface in order to evaluate the importance of different features. This is often quite challenging when the evaluation takes place in a rich context.

What makes the challenge greater for interactive art installations is that they often deal with evaluation of *softer* concepts such as the ones in question in this paper: intimacy and ludic engagement. Here rigid usability evaluation methods may fall short of measuring the successful or unsuccessful outcome of an interactive activity that is supposed to have an artistic effect on the participant. Höök et al. [1] argues that it is not easy to adapt HCI methods to an artistic context. As they state, *"It would be ludicrous for us to suggest replacing art criticism with HCI evaluation, and we will not answer the question "is this good art?"* Instead they propose using methods inspired by HCI for understanding usability issues that might be part of the experience of interacting with an art piece. Artists should be free to create their art works from their own perspective – but carrying out usability-inspired evaluation during develop-ment can help the artist see the artwork from the perspective the participant [1].

Examples do exist of more experimental comparison studies [2, 3]. The paper presented here can be seen as a contribution to this direction of evaluation within the field. Note that it is not argued that this type of evaluation is more important than more exploratory or ethnographic methods [4]. In fact later in the paper it is argued that evaluation in this field should be multi-faceted using mixed methods approaches in order to evaluate these softer factors often involved in interactive art installations.

This paper deals with issues discussed above while evaluating an installation that is under development and which is meant to provide a *collaborative*, *intimate*, and *ludic* experience to remotely located users. The initial development of this musical interac-tive installation called The OperaBooth has been described earlier in [5] where it was evaluated in an exploratory fashion using qualitative observation and interviews to derive initial feedback uncovering central issues related to user interaction. Here the evaluation is taken a step further by more rigorously evaluating certain aspects found important in the initial exploratory evaluation.

2 Mediated Intimacy and Ludic Engagement

Understanding how technology can be used to mediate emotions between remote users is challenging. Saadatian et al. [6] provide a nice review of technologies for mediated intimate communication. Further on Saadatian et al. [7] describe intimacy as *"the perception of closeness to the extend of sharing the physical, emotional and mental personal space"*, arguing that mediated intimacy can be divided into three overall dimensions (not mutually exclusive): emotional, physical and cognitive. The installa-tion presented in this paper explores all three dimensions, in the sense that *emotionally* we are exploring ludic engagement through a *cognitive/emotional* non-verbal com-munication, while intruding the *physical* space of the participant. Vetere et al. [8] presents a model defining several themes involved with mediated intimacy divided into three stages – prior to the act (Antecedents), the act itself (Constituents), and conse-quences of the experience (Yields). For each stage they outline a set of themes including Self-disclosure, Trust, and Commitment (Antecedents), Emotional, Physical,

Expressive, Reciprocity, and Public & Private (Constituents), Presence in absence and Strong Yet Vulnerable (Yields). This framework has helped steer the development of the installation focusing mainly on the Emotional, Expressive, Reciprocity and Strong Yet Vulnerable attributes. While physicality in a literal sense is often viewed as a strong modality for intimate communication [9, 10] it has not been used directly here. However, the installation explores physicality as the physical space close to the participant in the sense that it became a goal to give the participants the capability of virtually intruding each others intimate space.

Exploring ludic engagement was not a focus from the start of the project but emerged as exploratory evaluations were carried out with test participants. Through these studies [5] it became clear how important the humoristic, playful and exploratory and open-ended properties of the installation were for the intimate connection between the participants. As such this aligns well with the Gaver et al.'s [11] assumptions about designing for ludic activities: *"Promote curiosity, exploration and reflection"*, *"De-emphasise the pursuit of external goals"* and *"Maintain openness and ambiguity"*. Discussions about Ludic Engagement by Gao et al. [12] also fit well here as they state: *"systems that promote ludic engagement should not be concerned with achieving clear goals, or be overly structured with defined tasks"*.

3 The Opera Booth

The installation evaluated in this paper is called the OperaBooth. While still being under development, it is a result of two iterations of development. The initial idea for the interactive art installation was to create a platform where strangers from different parts of the world would be able to experience having a mediated intimate experience together. The goal was to show that humans that come from regions of the world that are politically or otherwise culturally diverse are still just humans and can share human intimate pleasurable experiences. For this, the starting point was to use the *international language of music* as a means for communication. And since most of the potential participants of the installation would not have any musical experience this posed a series of challenges. These challenges did not necessarily deal with the overall artistic intentions of the piece but more with the user experience or usability of the piece. These initial challenges were summarized in the following (note that ludic engagement was not a specific concern at the starting point. Only after carrying out evaluations of the system in use we became aware of the importance of providing users with a ludic experience):

- To provide intimate communication through musical exploration (non-verbal communication)
- Exceed intimate space of the other participant (explore vulnerability)
- Provide simple control mappings catered towards musical novices
- Make the control interface expressive
- Explore different roles for each player for improved musical communication

The following describes in short the development of the installation over two iterations. The evaluation that was part of the second iteration described in the following as Prototype 2 led to the evaluation presented in Sect. 4.

3.1 OperaBooth Prototypes 1 and 2

The premise for developing the OperaBooth was to develop an interface that would provide novice users with a sense of being able to communicate musically with each other. Several different input technologies were considered (including those dealing with more physical and whole body interactions) before settling on exploring facial gestures as the means for making music. This choice was partly based on the idea of participants being able to see each other's faces while performing different gestures. Additionally, it was found that the face-tracking algorithm by Kyle McDonald[1] called faceOSC provided a playful and interesting musical controller. The open-source algorithm detects the face of the user and processes information such as size, position and orientation of the detected face; mouth height and width; eye-size; and eyebrow position. Besides providing an interesting controller for exploration of sound, it was anticipated that face-to-face communication between remote strangers (similar to a Skype video conferencing application) would enhance the intimate connection – especially, since users would have to make many different facial gestures to control the music. Different forms of musical output were also explored including various forms of amplitude and frequency modulation, granular synthesis and sample-based synthesis. While there were many interesting combinations between the controller and different synthesis algorithms it was decided to go for a musical output that connected naturally to the movements of the mouth. Different types of voice were explored including singing, shouting, baby laughter, and bird song. Finally, opera voices were chosen mainly for their theatrical quality.

A simple prototype was built using faceOSC for facial tracking and Ableton Live[2] for handling the audio. A Max[3] patch was used to handle communication between faceOSC and Live. Additionally, Max was used for sending a live video stream of the face of the participants between two laptops – similar to traditional video conferencing. The audio included custom recordings of female and male voices singing "ahh", "ooh" and "bah" notes on a harmonic minor scale (three octaves). From a user point of view, opening one's mouth triggering a random opera singing sample, that was looped using Live's built-in *Sampler*,[4] and thus kept going until the mouth was closed. Both a male and a female voice was implemented. Additionally, a background track was produced as a string section playing harmonic minor chords in the same key as the voices. The two laptops were placed inside a cardboard box and lights were added in order to improve the tracking. Figure 1 (top) gives an impression of the initial prototype (see [5] for more details).

Based on a simple evaluation of the first prototype a high fidelity prototype (Prototype 2, Fig. 1 - bottom) was developed with the following improvements:

---

[1] https://github.com/downloads/kylemcdonald/ofxFaceTracker/FaceOSC.zip- *accessed 03/03/15.*

[2] https://www.ableton.com/.

[3] https://cycling74.com.

[4] https://www.ableton.com/en/packs/sampler.

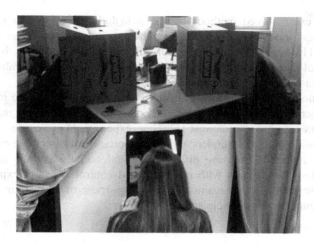

Fig. 1. Prototype 1 (top) and Prototype 2 (bottom) of the OperaBooth

- OperaBooth boxes now communicated with each other over network—dealing with latency issues and synchronization.
- Direct eye-contact between the remote users was enabled.
- Recorded samples were improved.
- Lighting conditions were improved for better tracking.
- Perceived latency was reduced.

This second prototype was also evaluated, outlining factors that were important for the intimate experience between the installation participants. It was suggested that the humoristic and theatrical feel of the opera genre was important for the overall engagement. It was also questioned whether users had too limited control of the musical output suggesting that increased control might lead to increased exploration. Finally, while it was somewhat clear that participants achieved an intimate connection with each other, it was questioned whether that connection was due to the direct eye contact and intrusion of intimate space or to the interactive musical interaction.

4   Evaluation

As described earlier, evaluation of interactive installation art is an on-going challenge as factors like experience, play, exploration and emotion become central, as opposed to function and performance. Morrison et al. [13] suggest approaching such evaluation through a "Lens of Ludic Engagement" by building on works by Gaver [14] arguing how success criteria differ from those of more traditional HCI. Several approaches have been presented for evaluating such criteria both qualitatively and qualitatively. Jaccucci et al. [15] mention several quantitative methods and end up using Positive and Negative Affect Schedule (PANAS) [16] together with interviews and video recordings to evaluate visitor experiences of two interactive art instal-lations. Similarly, Kortbek &

Grønbæk [17] use a mixed methods approach including their own multiple-choice questionnaire and interviews to evaluate interactive installations in an art museum. Gilroy et al. [18] analyse trajectories of affect relating to *Flow* by using the Pleasure-Arousal-Dominance (PAD) model by Mehrabian [19] to evaluate the user experience of an augmented reality art installation.

The evaluation presented here attempts to evaluate and compare the importance of various factors crucial for ludic and intimate communication – factors that have been identified in less rigorous evaluations [5]. Here experiments are carried out with the following overall goals: (1) to understand the importance of direct eye contact, (2) to understand the influence of using different musical outputs and (3) to understand whether providing participants with more detailed control supports exploration. All three goals have been held up against the overall purpose of supporting intimate and ludic engagement between participants.

4.1 Methodological and Technical Setup

The evaluation was a comparative study of how well different versions of the installation performed in terms of whether participants experienced an intimate connection with each other, how ludic engagement emerged and how musical communication was supported. Three different versions of the system were prepared, each with a different mapping between facial expression and musical output (note that only the detected mouth height was used to control the musical output):

- **Regular Opera:** Regular system, where only mouth open/close triggered random opera singing notes.
- **Responsive Opera:** Responsive system, where six different mouth-heights each triggered an opera singing note (pitch increased with height of mouth).
- **Responsive Synthetic:** Responsive system, where six different mouth-heights each triggered a different pitch of an abstract synthetic sound note (pitch increased with height of mouth).

The regular opera version worked as described for Prototype 2. The responsive opera system detected six different thresholds of mouth height each triggering a different pitch of the opera voice. The idea was to give participants a stronger sense of control of the system leading to increased exploration of the system. The responsive synthetic version detected the same thresholds as the responsive opera system but was mapped to abstract synthetic notes – using Ableton Live's built-in *Sampler* (presets *"Lead-Dark Thought"* and *"Lead-Ambient Encounters"*). Reasons for choosing the two specific synthesis timbres included: (1) they accompanied the background musical theme nicely, (2) the two voices were distinct from each other approximating a female and male voice, and (3) the timbres were humoristic when *played* with the mouth.

Finally, the system was setup so participants could either see each in (1) a full screen mode enabling direct eye contact or in (2) a limited screen mode where participants saw each other in a window that filled approximately two thirds of the screen

Fig. 2. Setup used at the evaluation. The two OperaBooths were set up near each other for convenience. Screens between the OperaBooths displaying faces of participants were video recorded.

and was moved slightly to the left on the screen. This setup enabled a simulation of a non-direct eye contact interaction. See Fig. 2 for the setup used for the evaluation.

4.2   Test Procedure

Experiments were carried out over 2 days in February 2015. 24 participants (15 female, 9 male) or 12 pairs took part in the evaluation. Each pair went through three sessions, in each of which they were asked to try a different version of the OperaBooth for 3 min followed by answering a questionnaire with Likert scale questions. Here they were asked to which extent they agreed or disagreed with 12 statements regarding their overall engagement, their experienced connection with the other participant (intimate, playful, humoristic, uncomfortable), their exploration of the system, their perceived control of the system, their ability to express themselves musically, and finally overall pleasure.[5] The test subjects were not told about what the installation was about or how to control it prior to interacting through it. The only instructions they received were to look inside the box and open their mouth. Finally, when all three trials were over, a short interview was carried out asking the participants to explain to each other how they had experienced the installation.

Three different overall versions were tested: (1) Regular Opera, (2) Responsive Opera and (3) Responsive Synthetic. Each pair of participants tried each version in randomized order to avoid learning biases. Finally, since the goal of the evaluation was also to examine the importance of direct eye contact, one of the three versions in each trial was experienced without direct eye contact. Each session was filmed capturing both faces, their tracking data, and the resulting audio in the same.

---

[5] See http://media.aau.dk/~stg/downloads/OperaBoothQuestionnaire.pdf for the specific questions asked.

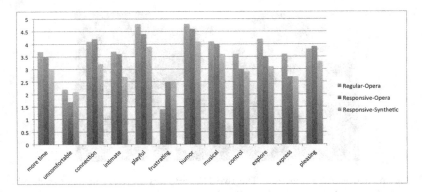

Fig. 3. Shows me an scores for the three versions of the OperaBooth: (1) Regular Opera, (2) Responsive Opera and (3) Responsive Synthetic.

5 Results

5.1 Quantitative Data

Regular Opera scored slightly better than Responsive Opera – see Fig. 3. The only significant differences between the two were found for *expressiveness* where the Regular Opera was rated higher and for *frustrating*, where Regular Opera scored lower. Interestingly, the Regular Opera version, which only responded to opening/closing of the mouth scored higher in both *control* and *exploration* although with p-values of 0.12 and 0.14 respectively.

The Regular Opera version generally scored better than the Responsive Synthetic version. Significant differences were found between all scores except *more time* (p = 0.14), *musical* (p = 0.20) and *pleasing* (p = 0.18). The Responsive Opera version, which provided participants with more control, scored mostly between the other two. Significant differences between Responsive Opera and Responsive Synthetic was however found for *connection* and *intimate connection* scores. This indicates that the participants were not able to connect as well with the synthetic sounds as with the opera sounds. This is also supported by the qualitative data as explained later.

Surprisingly, only marginal differences were found when comparing scores for versions experienced with direct eye contact and non-direct eye contact for connection *(I felt a connection with the other person)*, intimate connection *(I felt an intimate connection with the other person)* as seen in Fig. 4. The only significant difference between the two was found for expressive *(I felt that I was able to express myself musically)* with a p-value of 0.05.

5.2 Observations and Interviews

Video recordings and interviews were analyzed using a critical incidents approach where critical events relevant to the overall purpose of the evaluation were identified. Incidents where participants expressed surprised, bored, confused, in control/non-control,

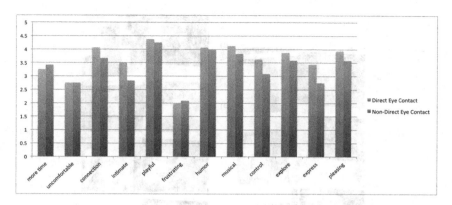

Fig. 4. Shows mean scores for the versions with (1) direct eye contact and (2) non-direct eye contact.

communicative, uneasy (looking away), happy (smiling/grinning), and thea-trical where identified and noted in order to compare between the different versions.

Observations and subsequent interviews generally showed a great appreciation of the installation. For some participants however (approximately 15 percent), the installation was not understood well enough for them to have an engaging experience. Participants never explored the system enough, they were too passive, or the tracking did not work as intended (this was the case for three of the participants).

Generally, subjects seemed confused when first encountering the installation. The participants who tried the Responsive Synthetic version first, found it difficult to understand that they influenced the sound and to understand who was influencing which voice (See Fig. 5a for the passive confusion of the participants). This was most likely to do with the limited naturalness of the connection between mouth and sound. Participants who started with the non-direct eye contact version were also confused about what the other person was able to see. Observation revealed that the commu-nication here was reduced and the exploration of the system became a more personal experience. Participants seem to look more at representations of one another than connecting with one another (see Fig. 5c).

The opposite was observed for the direct eye-contact versions where there was increased non-verbal communication (eye-contact, smiling and grinning as reaction to the movements of the other participant, musical following and turn-taking – see Figs. 5b, d, e, f, g) – confirmed also by interview data. Engaging in direct-eye contact was expressed as feeling intense, as the feeling of sometimes not being able to look directly at each other or as the feeling of being trapped in front another person. One participant even stated: "It felt like he could smell my bad breath". A few participants stated that the musical experience made it easier to maintain eye contact when they were in control of the sounds and were able to "communicate" with each other, in contrast to the silent and doubtful parts that felt very intense and awkward. One participant even felt embarrassment towards the other because she was not able to control the voice. Observations that supported the notion of intense communication included participants looking away or even pulling their head out when laughing too loud.

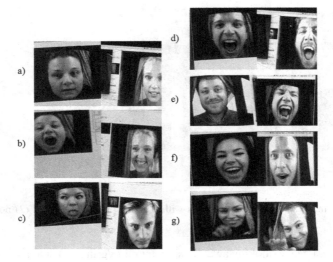

Fig. 5. Shows screenshots of interactions with the OperaBooth representing (a) confusion, (b) engagement, (c) disconnect, (d) competition, (e) exploration, (f) intimacy and (e) added gesturing.

The Responsive Synthetic version seemed more playful for the few who were able to control the interaction (three participants were able to fully control this version and all three tried it as the last version) – see for instance Fig. 5d, where participants are almost battling about who could reach the highest note. Still, the Regular Opera was the most preferred version of the three especially for its musicality, naturalness and appealing sound – even for participants who stated that the synthetic version was more playful. As one participant put it: "The opera voices really the sense that we were really singing together". As also the quantitative data suggests the Responsive Opera version was perhaps too difficult to control and therefor lead to less exploration, probably because participants ended up producing more monotone sounds than the ones experienced where the voices were randomized.

Only few improvements were suggested – these included a more intelligent algorithm that would detect higher level features such as smile, surprise, confused, etc. and express this through sound. A few participants also stated that they felt inhibited because they wanted to use their hands for communicating – even three of the pairs waved to each other during interaction (See Fig. 5g). According to them, including some kind of hand gestures would have enhanced the communication.

6   Discussion and Conclusion

This paper has presented a lab-based usability evaluation comparing different versions of an interactive art installation called the OperaBooth using both quantitative and qualitative data gathering techniques. It is interesting that the observation and interview data does not align with the questionnaire data when it comes to the question of how important direct-eye contact is. A reason could be that when participants provided feedback through the questionnaire they were not conscious about this particular part of the installation, focussing more on their direct interaction and control of the sound. Another explanation could be that even though participants felt a difference, it was overshadowed by the experience of trying to understand how to control the system.

In that respect it can be relevant to ask, whether a quantitative approach like the one presented here is effective for this setting. The answer would probably be: *probably* not if it is to stand alone. However, as part of a multi-faceted mixed method the quantitative approach is effective at bringing forth new insight about certain aspects especially to do with the usability of the system.

Finally, it is the author's strong belief that evaluating *different alternatives*, whether it is using qualitative or quantitative methods brings us a step further at realizing not only whether some forms of interaction work or do not work, but how important certain factors are for the success of those interactions. Understanding the influence of certain factors for enhancing mediated intimacy or ludic engagement is what can help drive the research forward.

Acknowledgments. The author would like to thank Finn Markwardt and Andreas Busk (for co-developing the OperaBooth) and everyone who participated in the evaluation.

References

1. Höök, K., Sengers, P., Andersson, G.: Sense and sensibility: evaluation and interactive art. In: Proceedings of the SIGCHI conference on Human factors in computing systems. ACM (2003)
2. Gonzales, A.L., Finley, T., Duncan, S.P.: (Perceived) interactivity: does interactivity increase enjoyment and creative identity in artistic spaces? In: Proceedings of the SIGCHI Conference on Human Factors in Computing Systems. ACM (2009)
3. Bialoskorski, L.S.S., Westerink, J.H.D.M., Van den Broek, E.L.: Experiencing affective interactive art. Int. J. Arts Technol. 3(4), 341–356 (2010)
4. Sengers, P., Gaver, B.: Staying open to interpretation: engaging multiple meanings in design and evaluation. In: Proceedings of the 6th conference on Designing Interactive systems. ACM (2006)
5. Gelineck, S.: OperaBooth - an Installation for Intimate Remote Communication through Music. In: Proceedings of Audio Mostly. ACM (2014)
6. Saadatian, E., Samani, H., Toudeshki, A., Nakatsu, R.: Technologically Mediated Intimate Communication: An Overview and Future Directions. In: Anacleto, J.C., Clua, E.W., da Silva, F.S., Fels, S., Yang, H.S. (eds.) ICEC 2013. LNCS, vol. 8215, pp. 93–104. Springer, Heidelberg (2013)
7. Saadatian, E., Samani, H., Nakatsu, R.: Anthropologically inspired creative design for intimate telepresence. In: SIGGRAPH Asia 2014 Designing Tools For Crafting Interactive Artifacts. ACM (2014)
8. Vetere, F., Gibbs, M.R., Kjeldskov, J., Howard, S., Mueller, F.F., Pedell, S., Mecoles, K., Bunyan, M.: Mediating intimacy: designing technologies to support strong-tie relationships. In: Proceedings of the SIGCHI conference on Human factors in computing systems. ACM (2005)

9. Mueller, F.F., Vetere, F., Gibbs, M.R., Kjeldskov, J., Pedell, S., Howard, S.: Hug over a distance. In: CHI extended abstracts on Human factors in computing systems. ACM (2005)
10. Wang, R., Quek, F.: Touch & talk: contextualizing remote touch for affective interaction. In: Proceedings of the fourth international conference on Tangible, embedded, and embodied interaction. ACM (2010)
11. Gaver, W. W., Bowers, J., Boucher, A., Gellerson, H., Pennington, S., Schmidt, A., Steed, A., Villars, N., Walker, B.: The drift table: designing for ludic engagement. In CHI extended abstracts on Human factors in computing systems. ACM (2004)
12. Gao, Yi, Petersson Brooks, Eva: Designing Ludic Engagement in an Interactive Virtual Dressing Room System – A Comparative Study. In: Marcus, Aaron (ed.) DUXU 2013, Part III. LNCS, vol. 8014, pp. 504–512. Springer, Heidelberg (2013)
13. Morrison, A., Mitchell J., Brereton, M.: The lens of ludic engagement: evaluating participation in interactive art installations. In: Proceedings of the 15th international conference on Multimedia. ACM (2007)
14. Gaver, W, Boucher, A, Pennington, S, Walker, B .: Evaluating Technologies for Ludic Engagement. In: Proceedings of CHI. ACM (2005)
15. Jacucci, G., Spagnolli, A., Chalambalakis, A., Morrison, A., Liikkanen, L., Roveda, S., Bertoncini, M.: Bodily explorations in space: social experience of a multimodal art installation. In: Gross, T., Gulliksen, J., Kotzé, P., Oestreicher, L., Palanque, P., Prates, R.O., Winckler, M. (eds.) INTERACT 2009. LNCS, vol. 5727, pp. 62–75. Springer, Heidelberg (2009)
16. Watson, D., Clark, L.A., Tellegen, A.: Development and validation of brief measures of positive and negative affect: The PANAS Scales. J. Pers. Soc. Psychol. **47**, 1063–1070 (1988)
17. Kortbek, K.J., Grønbæk, K.: Communicating art through interactive technology: new approaches for interaction design in art museums. In: Proceedings of the 5th Nordic conference on Human-Computer Interaction (2008)
18. Gilroy, S.W., Cavazza, M., Benayoun, M.: Using affective trajectories to describe states of flow in interactive art. In: Proceedings of the International Conference on Advances in Computer Entertainment Technology. ACM (2009)
19. Mehrabian, A.: Pleasure-arousal-dominance: a general framework for describing and measuring individual differences in temperament. Curr. Psychol.: Dev. Learn. Pers. Soc. **14**, 261–292 (1996)

Entangled Sensorium: Subtle Apparatuses for Nonlocal Affectiveness

Clarissa Ribeiro[(⊠)]

Roy Ascott Studio, DeTao Master in Technoetic Arts,
Shanghai Institute of Visual Arts, Shanghai, China
almeida.clarissa@gmail.com

Abstract. This paper aim in waving reflections around the sovereignty of interaction in communicational processes focusing on Human-Computer Interaction subtleties related to informational processes in a quantum level to present and discuss the author series 'Performing Quantum Entanglement: Subtle Apparatuses for Nonlocal Affectiveness'. The approach involves conceptualizing what the author defines as Complex Affective Systems (CAFFS), referring to multidimensional systems of interactions that lead to manifestations and incorporations of the self and the emergence of consciousness. The works selected to conduct the present conversation have been produced for the author's solo show at the Art|Sci Gallery, CNSI/UCLA, in Los Angeles (2014), and recently for the inaugural solo show she designed for the Roy Ascott Studio Gallery in Shanghai (2015).

Keywords: Information · Quantum physics · Interaction · Complex affective systems · Media art · Art and science

1 Introduction: An Entangled Sensorium

Prelude (or) A Manifesto – "Non-Local Affectiveness as an Approach to Media Art"

1. Affectiveness is non-local;
2. In non-local affectiveness there is no in-between;
3. By the nature of non-local information and communication's dynamics, messages emerge simultaneously, and could have the same or similar meaning, in several different places, and the phenomenon is instantaneous.
4. There is no time-lapse between emission and reception (emitter and receiver) considering that instantaneity is the main principia;
5. Information is vibrational;
6. Knowledge and learning are vibrational;
7. Interaction is the sovereign principia that generates realities;

The prelude is an attempt to assemble different but confluent perspectives around transpersonal states of consciousness that emerge from nonlocal informational processes. As a synthesis, it could be seen as a manifesto for a quantum approach to the communicational processes in interactive media art projects. This effort implies in investigating, theoretically and in the practice as an independent artist, ways and

© Springer International Publishing Switzerland 2015
M. Antona and C. Stephanidis (Eds.): UAHCI 2015, Part IV, LNCS 9178, pp. 65–73, 2015.
DOI: 10.1007/978-3-319-20687-5_7

processes through which we affect and are affected by each other and the world around by means of interacting in a quantum level that is vibrational, potential. These could be seemed as knowledge processes attached to the production of entropy externally to the informational systems involved. Bringing this perspective to the discussions around Human-Computer Interaction, implies in considering experience in terms of systems of intercreating processes, coupling with visions like the one of Allan Combs [1], who presents a comprehension of consciousness that incorporates dynamical systems theory and phenomenology, and where the human mind is viewed as a complex dynamic event, constantly engaged in the act of self-creation.

In quantum mechanics, the collapse of the state vector, simultaneous with the process of observation, is so constrained that observers of the process cannot be seen as independent entities – the observers, better to say 'the whole system', are entangled to the point that it involves agreement on the final state of the system itself. This idea of integration, interdependence of observer and observation, from our point of view, could be essential to the contemporary discussions concerning Human-Computer Interaction – a way of thinking in which there has to be considered a continuity between computers and humans – interdependent informational organizations, complementary systems in plurisystemic contexts. Systems that can be described as having a characteristic that couples with its adaptive qualities – affectiveness. From this perspective they can be understood as Complex Affective System (CAFFS) – a term coined by the author to describe and discuss certain Complex Adaptive Systems (CAS) focusing on affectiveness as the main bond between the systems' elements, relating this aspect of system's interconnectedness and the ability its elements have of nonlocal communicating, to the phenomena of quantum entanglement.

In quantum mechanics, in the specific merging of wave theory and of probability theory, by means of 'quantized waves' the information is shared, exchanged and stored. From this perspective [2], it is possible to assert that, decoding a message is a learning transition and, knowledge is extracted from a preexisting negentropy. Considering the cybernetic basilar discovery – the interpretation of negentropy as information, it involves two symmetric procedures – gaining knowledge by decoding a message, and emitting a message, sharing the knowledge acquired. From this point of view, the emergence of consciousness can be related to communicational processes that are going on in the vibrational (quantum) realm, implying no discontinuity between two communicational systemic entities, i.e. humans and computers in their subatomic level. As the researcher explains: "Instead of letting the negentropy of a closed system become uselessly degraded, one can recapture part – or, ideally, the whole – of it, in the form of knowledge. The other facet of the discovery is that existing information can be used to produce macroscopic order, the "negentropy' thus generated being at most equal to the information that has been invested" [3]. Information appears as an organizing power through the dynamics of interacting vibrational entities in a quantum level. From these considerations, a question emerges; how can human-computer interaction systems be conceived to couple with the subtleties of this knowledge processes that take place far beyond materiality and implies continuity, nonlocality, entanglement?

2 Nonlocal Affectiveness: Experimental Incursions and Possible Configurations

What does it mean to be entangled? For her solo show at the ART|SCI, UCLACNSI, in Los Angeles, June 5th to July 5th 2014, the artist presented the series "Performing Quantum Entanglement: Subtle Apparatuses for Extrasensory Affectiveness", an exhibition that was conceived to involve the audience in poetic experiences that explore realms where we are neither waves, nor particles, or may perform both, simultaneously. In this experimental project, the artist invites to think about ourselves and our affective dimension from a semi-material and non-local perspective. Four works integrated the artist exhibition – "The Kiss" (2013-2014), "NLAFF-Non-Local Affectiveness" (2014), "Owner of a Lonely Heart" (2014) and "Microselfies" (2014). Recently, starting from a collaboration with the artist Mick Lorusso for the piece "The Cat's Eyes Nebula' (2015), the artist produced a solo show as the inaugural exhibition for the "Roy Ascott Studio Gallery" in Shanghai, China – "Subtle Apparatuses for Nonlocal Affectiveness", February 20th to March 19th 2015, SIVA – Shanghai Institute of Visual Arts, DeTao Master Academy.

2.1 The Kiss (2014)

In the interactive video installation "The Kiss" (2014), integrated and interacting by what was defined as a semi-material apparatus, couples were invited to perform a 'nonlocal kiss' (Fig. 1) standing face to face, on the top of two different silicon platforms where 12 (twelve) piezo films were placed. The sensors were located in the acupressure reflex points in the planar region of the foot. These points are related to body organs associated to the experience of being in love – the eyes, in the region close to the fingers; heart, liver, stomach, and lung, in the region related to the solar plexus; and the lower pelvic organs. According to reflexology, the emotion of love causes the solar plexus to become active – one of the central energetic points in our informational/vibrational being.

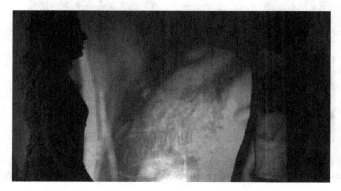

Fig. 1. The Kiss (2014), Clarissa Ribeiro (Source: photo by the author. In the picture, the artists Javiera Tejerina and Diego Ortiz).

In the installation, body subtle vibrations are captured by the piezoelectric gener-
ators' network and emerge as interferences in the transparence of live video – the more
balanced the measurements, the less transparent the image become; the less balanced
the measurement, the more transparent. The images are captured by two webcameras
positioned on the shoulders of the interacting couple. The code developed in the
Processing mixes and interlaces the images.

Despite that the performers are not actually kissing, the kiss is performed in the
projection – a reference to the decay of the wave function in quantum mechanics. 'The
Kiss', is an invitation to think about quantum non-local connectedness – a property of a
quantum mechanical state of a system of two or more objects in which the quantum
states of the constituting objects are linked together even if the individual objects are
spatially apart.

2.2 NLAFF – Nonlocal Affectiveness (2014)

In the installation NLAFF (2014), exploring non-local affectiveness from a poetic
perspective, the audience is invited to join a remote staring experiment. For the artist's
solo show, set up in the center of the gallery, a suspended black cube hides the
performer that is meditating on the top of a wooden base. The interior of the cube was
illuminated by a red light – a reference to the Ganzfeld technique traditionally used in
Parapsychology to test extrasensory perception (ESP). From the outside, the audience
was suggested to focus on staring, looking at the live-feed image of the performer
projected onto one of the faces of the cube. In a second layer of the projection, particles
behave according to the measurements of electrodes connected to the body of the
performer (Fig. 2).

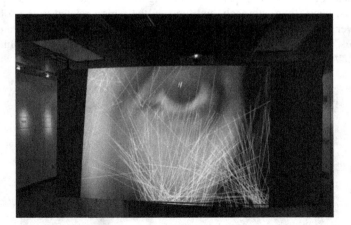

Fig. 2. NLAFF (2014), Clarissa Ribeiro. Particles behave according to the measurements of
electrodes connected to the body of the performer. (Source: photo by Milena Szafir).

The electrode captures live signals of the electrical conductance of the skin measuring galvanic skin response (GSR). The electrical conductance of the skin varies depending on the amount of sweat that is controlled by the sympathetic nervous system — if the sympathetic branch of the autonomic nervous system is highly aroused, then sweat gland activity also increases, which in turn increases skin conductance. In this way, skin conductance can be used as a measure of the way we can non-locally affect each other — entangled interferences in our emotional state.

2.3   Owner of a Lonely Heart (2014)

The 8 (eight) screenshots and the derived (sonified) environmental sound that integrate the piece "Owner of a Lonely Heart" (2014), were traces of an observation — a scientist measuring the heartbeat of a "zebrafish (Danio rerio) embryo's lonely heart" (Fig. 3).

Fig. 3.   Owner of a Lonely Heart (2014), Clarissa Ribeiro (Source: photo by the author)

After recording the data, using a microelectrode precisely prepared for the experiment, the scientist with whom the author was collaborating, Huanqi Zhu, generated a series of graphs using the software OriginPro 8.1 and started zooming in different regions, looking for specific points where the patterns fit his 'expectations' according to the main purposes of the research. The experiment was set up to study the beating patterns of zebrafishes' hearts at different developing stages. The beating patterns serve as markers to identify and differentiate healthy and mutant hearts and were used, in the experiment, to test drugs that can improve specific function of the organ. The work invites the audience to reflect critically about the importance of observation in the creation of 'truth' in science that plays a crucial role in the creation of 'reality', having radical influence in the ways we behave, in our survival strategies, in who we are.

2.4   Microselfies (2014)

The work "Microselfies" (2014) is an exercise of reflection about the creation of reality in the very moment of observation referred, in quantum mechanics, to the collapse of the wave function. Reflected in the surface of a macroscale measuring apparatus – a microelectrode – the author produced, with a superposed apparatus (an Iphone 5S), self-portrait photographs.

In the gallery, the audience was invited to explore the procedures the author went through to produce the images exhibited both in printed and digital formats. Right in front of a LCD monitor where a slide show with the digital series was displayed, inside of a 'petri dish', a microelectrode (Fig. 4) with a reflective surface is the mirror the audience has to face, exploring unusual angles and perceptional subtleness to take their own microselfies.

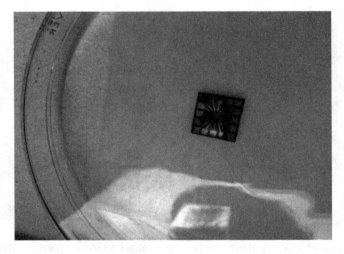

Fig. 4. Microselfies (2014), Clarissa Ribeiro (Source: photo by the author)

2.5   The Cat's Eyes Nebula (2015)

The subtle apparatuses that integrate the work consist simultaneously in a memory and an actualization of possible entanglements between the two artists that were collaborating for its production – Clarissa Ribeiro and Mick Lorusso (Fig. 5). The actual "Cat's Eyes Nebula" (NGC 6543), according to NASA, is a visual 'fossil record' of the dynamics and late evolution of a dying star, and is one of the most complex planetary nebulae ever seen, captured by NASA/ESA Hubble Space Telescope. The structures of the Cat's Eye are so complex that astronomers suspect the bright central object may be a binary star system – a bipolar geometry produced by two stars surrounded by cocoons of gas blown off in the late stages of their stellar evolution. The stars that produced the "Cat's Eyes Nebula" as a memory were in the processes of becoming two giant diamonds silently entangled in faraway skies. Being installed at the same time in

Fig. 5. The Cat Eye's Nebula (2015), opening reception at The Roy Ascott Studio Gallery in Shanghai, February 20th 2015, starting at 8 a.m. (Source: photo by the author).

Shanghai, at the Roy Ascott Studio Gallery, and in Los Angeles, at the Art|Sci Gallery, the work consists of two black boxes where the complex geometric patterns generated by the irregular reflection of a red laser beam, when crossing a diamond-like prism that moves according to visitors' vibrations captured by a piezoelectric sensor, are captured by a hidden webcamera and sent, via live streaming video, to the other entangled exhibition space (Figs. 6 and 7).

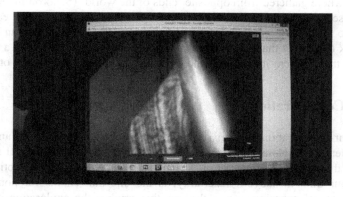

Fig. 6. The Cat Eye's Nebula (2015), screenshot – live video stream: opening reception at The Roy Ascott Studio Gallery in Shanghai, February 20th 2015, starting at 8 a.m. (Source: photo by the author).

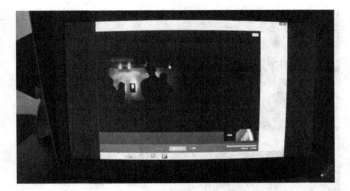

Fig. 7. The Cat Eye's Nebula (2015), screenshot – live video stream: opening reception at The Art|Sci Gallery in Los Angeles, February 19th 2015, starting at 5 p.m. (Source: photo by the author).

The black box is a metaphor to recall the seminal discussion of Erwin Schorönfinger about the phenomenon of Quantum Entanglement (Verschränkung, in Geman) that is in the paper where he presents his imaginary experiment 'The Cat's Paradox' [4]. The dimensions of the box and the proportions are references to multiples of the numbers 5 and 10 (having a hidden 7 as a multiplier); 5 representing the man, 10 representing the whole universe, 7 the magical, supernatural aspect of the phenomenon of entanglement that implies nonlocal connectedness.

In the second part of the above mentioned paper where Schorönfinger discusses a Theory of Measurement, the scientist considers that entanglement cannot be verified if the systems where gathered from opposite 'ends of the world' (Schorönfinger's words) and juxtaposed without interaction because they 'know' nothing about each other. According to him "Any 'entanglement of predictions' that takes place can obviously only go back to the fact that the two bodies at some earlier time formed in a true sense one system, that is, were interacting, and have left behind traces on each other" [4].

3   Final Considerations

If we take our sensory abilities from a quantum perspective, nonlocal communication is to be considered as a natural phenomenon that depends on the vibrational subatomic qualities of the systems in interaction. From this perspective, the perception that is needed in our time to subvert materiality, is the one that claims for nonlocal and entangled states of consciousness – the one that implies the exploration of what is named here as an 'entangled sensorium'.

As emergences from processes through which the author is exploring these ideas, the works presented here embody in the systemic configuration of the apparatuses, reflections around the sovereignty of interaction in communicational processes. These reflections can be seen as incursions on Human-Computer Interaction subtleties related to informational processes in a quantum level.

The 'subtle-apparatuses for Nonlocal Affectiveness' could be understood as semi-material systems conceived as exercises on experimental metaphysics - performing ventures in realms beyond the physical domain, bearing questions about the nature of reality and our bodies, our affective dimension, consciousness and the self. According to Professor Michael Punt, "The fact that technologies rapidly become associated with a class of objects that are fundamentally material should not deflect our attention from the semi-material: another class of objects that emanate in our fullest relationship with the world as necessary mnemonics to our affective dimension" [5].

By means of the author's approach in the above mentioned series, apparatuses are not taken as external forces that operate on bodies from the outside. Following the considerations of Karen Barad, apparatuses could be considered as "[...] material-discursive practices that are inextricable from the bodies that are produced and through which power works its productive effects" [6]. Travelling through the touchable and the untouchable, exploring the power of observation in the creation of the realities we inhabit. In an interconnected world perceived this way, as in the spirituous consideration of Beauregard [3], Schrodinger's cat 'should be able to influence the yes-or-no outcome to which he is subjected.

Acknowledgements. The author would like to thank the Fulbright Program that awarded her a Post-Doctoral grand in Arts (2013–2014) and to the Art|Sci Center and Lab, including the researchers from Professor James Gimzewski's laboratories at the UCLA Department of Chemistry and Biochemistry and the CNSI – California NanoSystems Institute, and from Professor Victoria Vesna's studio at UCLA Department of Design Media Arts, within which she was working during the grant period. A special thanks to the artist's supervisor Professor James Gimzewski, and to Professor Victoria Vesna, for their openness, inspiration, and the opportunity given to conceive, produce and exhibit the experimental project here presented.

References

1. Combs, A., Germine, M., Goertzel, B.: Mind in Time: The Dynamics of Thought, Reality, and Consciousness. Hampton Press, Cresskill (2004)
2. Beauregard, O.C.: Quantum paradoxes and aristotle's twofold information concept. In: Tart, C.T., Puthoff, H.E., Targ, R. (eds.) Mind at Large. Mind at Large, pp. 177–187. Praeger Publishers, New York (1979)
3. Beauregard, O.C.: Time symmetry and interpretation of quantum mechanics. Found. Phys. **6** (5), 539–559 (1976)
4. Schrödinger E.: The present situation in quantum mechanics. In: Proceedings of the American Philosophical Society, vol. 124 (1935)
5. Punt, M.: Synchrony and the semi-material object. In: Ascott, R., Bast, G., Fiel, W., Jahrmann, M., Schnell, R. (eds.) New Realities: Being Syncretic, pp. 224–227. Springer, Vienna (2009)
6. Barad, K.: Meeting the universe halfway: quantum physicsand the entanglement of matter and meaning, p. 230. Duke University Press, Durham (2007)

Immersive Interaction Paradigms for Controlling Virtual Worlds by Customer Devices Exemplified in a Virtual Planetarium

Andreas Schaller[1], Tim Biedenkapp[1], Jens Keil[2],
Dieter W. Fellner[1,2], and Arjan Kuijper[1,2(✉)]

[1] Technische Universität Darmstadt, Darmstadt, Germany
[2] Fraunhofer IGD, Darmstadt, Germany
arjan.kuijper@igd.fraunhofer.de

Abstract. This work provides an insight into the basics of 3D applications in conjunction with various customer devices. In this case, the application is a 3D planetarium of our solar system for a museum. The aim is to create a concept for intuitive and immersive navigation through the virtual planetarium using inexpensive Customer Devices. Visitors should be able to move freely and easily in the solar system. Here, the visitor should be able to focus on the simulation and not quickly lose interest in the complex control application. For this similar approaches and previous research are examined and a new approach is described. As low-cost customer devices, the controller of the Nintendo Wii (Wiimote) and current smartphones are considered in this work. A detailed analysis of these devices is an integral part of this work. Based on the selected devices, there are various possibilities for interaction and resulting interaction concepts. For each device, a concept will be developed to meet the identified needs.

Keywords: Visualization · Immersive environments · Virtual worlds · Interaction devices

1 Introduction and Motivation

VR systems, customer devices and smartphones are enjoying increasing popularity. They offer more opportunities for interaction due to technical development. Customer devices have been designed for a wide range of applications [1,2]. Similarities found in applications can be controlled by different devices. A multi-touch device is suitable, for example, for the direct gesture-controlled manipulation of visible objects. Controller game consoles, however, cover the major interaction paradigms in game genres like EgoShooters and JumpnRun. An EgoShooter is a game form which is controlled from the first-person perspective; usually the player must shoot enemy monster and targets. In JumpnRun the player must move a figure primarily by running and jumping through the course. The smartphone has a small multi-touch display and various sensors. Due to this situation,

© Springer International Publishing Switzerland 2015
M. Antona and C. Stephanidis (Eds.): UAHCI 2015, Part IV, LNCS 9178, pp. 74–86, 2015.
DOI: 10.1007/978-3-319-20687-5_8

the smartphone can to a certain extent be used alternatively as a controller for games and as well as multi-touch device. The smartphone facilitates similar to the multi-touch device applications a virtual keyboard and can be used as a controller for games thanks to the sensors. This raises the question of application areas of customer devices. These can be divided into several classes. The two most interesting are industrial and public areas. They differ primarily in terms of their users. In an industrial environment it can be assumed that trained personnel work frequently with this particular device [3]. In public environments like a museum it must be assumed that the users are one time visitors. In this case, training would be too expensive and the use of customer devices, known to the user from other areas of life, is an option.

In a museum, there are numerous exhibits, of which the function and meaning are not immediately apparent. They can be shown easily by VR systems allowing the viewer a better understanding [4]. Access to these exhibits could be facilitated by a familiar interaction possibility. In the example of the planetarium a replica needs a large space around all planets with orbits and information plastically represent. The VR-based version of the exhibit only requires a sufficiently large 3D-capable presentation medium, such as the HEyeWall. This medium also allows visitors to move freely within the planetarium. The depth of information and updating the content can be accomplished more easily. This type of exhibits needs different DoF for a good navigation. As the visitor does not want to learn how to use a new device for each exhibit, here customer devices are appropriate. They give intuitive operation [5] on the exhibits, if one has familiarized himself at an exhibit with the controller. For the museum operators, this results in the advantage of low acquisition and maintenance costs [6]. Even better is the possibility in which no additional equipment must be purchased and maintained, like a device that all visitors already have. The smartphone features for this scenario by some sensors, a multi-touch display and several communication options (Bluetooth, WLAN, etc.).

In this work, the use of customer devices as remote controller is developed using the example of a virtual planetarium. The system is presented via a room-sized projection. The controller has been guided by a combination of mouse and keyboard in the first version, and a simple touch system. It will now be controlled by smartphone or a Wii Remote. As a result, users are more involved and an immersive interaction through motion detection is designed.

2   Interaction Concepts for the Planetarium

The "Interactive Planetarium" is an interactive presentation and information medium of our solar system. It is used in combination with a HEyeWall 2.0, mouse and keyboard. In this project we use X3D and JavaScript. X3D is an XML-based 3D description language, describing the appearance and behavior of each object in the room. JavaScript is used to calculate the position of the body in space and allows advanced user interaction. The 3D visualization platform in this project is the HEyeWall 2.0 of the Fraunhofer Institute for Computer

Graphics (IGD) in Darmstadt. The HEyeWall has a resolution corresponding to the human eye, so scenes can be represented very realistically and in detail. The high resolution three-dimensional representation of the scene has a cinematically immersive character for the audience. For the user, however, this characteristic is lost due to interaction with mouse and keyboard which need to be avoided. The aim of the application is to impart knowledge about our solar system. The planetarium has a variety of levels of information which can be shown or hidden on demand. There are functions that affect the information content of the entire planetarium or only selected planets. For example, the background of the planetarium can be adjusted in steps, from any background (black) via stars to constellations. In addition, the orbits of the planets can be show. The speed at which the planets move can be adjusted if necessary. To make the planets in the shadow of the sun also clearly visible, the shadow path of the sun can be turned off. In order to estimate the skew of the planets to each other, a north-south axis of each planet provides details. Some planets have additional information; the solar corona can be disabled or Mars and be shown from the perspective of an infrared camera. The Earth as our central element of the solar system provides a wealth of information. Thus, atmosphere and clouds can be hidden to get a better view of the blue planet. It can be showed in a topological, geographical, or black and white view. Information that many visitors are interested in, is the opportunity to view the orbital space debris of the earth. An example of our method showing this is given in Fig. 1.

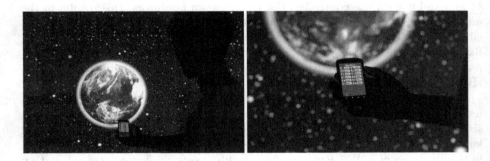

Fig. 1. Earth with space debris.

2.1 Interaction Concept for Control with a Customer Device

The Planetarium is located in a gravity-free space. For navigation in free space, the navigation types "Fly Free" and "Examine" are relevant. There are at least three DoF needed. The considered Devices Wiimote and Google Nexus One can interact in a lot more ways to navigate. These are in addition to the sensors the already mentioned possibilities of the touch screen or buttons.

To navigate to the Planetarium, the rotation around the X and Y-axis and the translational on the Z-axis are used. The rotation about the Z-axis can be ignored to prevent inadvertent misalignment. The interaction in virtual spaces is usually difficult when an intelligent guidance that can prevent an imbalance does not exist [7]. Thus, the user can use all possible degrees of freedom, although he may even change only three. In a planetarium the translations in the X and Y axis, i.e. going to the left or right and up or down, provide no added value. As there is always only one planet in the focus of attention, it can be centered in the image. Therefore, it is assumed that the viewer of a museum application wants to see only the essential information representing the planets and their moons in the planetarium. He does not want to move too long between planets. To facilitate this, an additional control is considered in order to aim at planets directly. The navigation in the planetarium is therefore as follows: It consists in being able to watch a planet from all sides, from near and far. These expectations are a mixture of "Free-Fly", approaching and withdrawal of a planet, and "Examine": turning around the planet in the focus of attention. Intuitive guidance must be done as the user does not want to get lost in the VR world. This should be implemented in a way that does not feel the user as a hindrance. Such guidance may consist, for example, in limiting the distance of the viewer to a planet, so that he always has an orientation point. As a result, the user does not get lost in the vastness of the simulated space and always has a reference point for orientation.

Mapping of the Inputs onto VR. The sensor data provided by the Customer Devices can be implemented in different ways. So one can basically distinguish whether sensor data for a rotational or translational are used. Since in a planetarium, the focus is on the observation of planets, the majority of navigation will consist of rotations. Because of this the exemplary implementation will use sensor data for rotations. The user therefore needs no keys or touch inputs and can largely navigate through intuitive movements. A possible implementation for the two selected Customer Devices are presented as examples. A classification of its input capabilities and its effect in VR are described for each investigated customer device.

Smartphone: The smartphone hybrid device with multi-touch display and sensors allows a combination of sensor and touch interaction. With multi-touch devices the navigation can be implemented by known finger gestures and slides. Thus, the translation of the Z-axis, i.e. the forward and backward movement, can be realized via a touch capture. Such input on the touchscreen allows for fast adjustable interaction. The user can thereby determine himself how fast he wants to move. Accelerometers and the digital compass can allow for the rotations about the X and Y axis. In addition, the neighboring planets can be targeted directly by means of a "single finger vertical slide". It would also be possible to introduce a rotation around the Z-axis by the inclination of the smartphone to the left or right. This was not conceptually planned, since this way the orientation between the rotation over the compass and tilt to the left or right would be more difficult. Using this implementation, all necessary DoF are controllable in speed and unique and intuitive by design. In focus of the intuitive and immersive navigation the smartphone is the most suitable among the analyzed customer devices.

Wiimote: For sensor-based devices such as the Wiimote a concept can be adapted known already in games. The Wiimote combines an accelerometer, a gyroscope and various buttons, permitting a variety of possible interaction concepts. As for the smartphone, the Accelerometer values of the tilt up or down may be used for the rotation around the X-axis. Since the Wiimote does not have a screen, its directional pad can be used here for translation in the Z-axis and alternating between the planets. The rotation around the Y-axis can be realized in analogy with digital compass of the Smartphone using the gyroscope. It should however be noted that the directional pad does not allow control of the speed. A precise, immersive navigation for inexperienced users is therefore hardly possible. In addition, there is no way to select and to target a particular planet as it is possible by the webapp smartphone.

2.2 Overview and Interface Design

For the implementation of a unified interaction paradigm for different customer devices, it is necessary to bring the similarities into a common denominator [8]. Here, the customer devices are combined in a device- and platform-independent interface. Therefore it is necessary to exploit the similarities of the devices. Thus, there is only one adapter that receives the sensor data and unified forwards them to the interface for each device. The goal of a unified interaction interface for VR applications is thus that similar inputs trigger the same actions in VR. So individual devices are connected to the 3D application. The Wiimote is connected directly to an application. The instant reality framework on which the planetarium was developed supports the direct involvement of the Wiimote. In contrast, multi-touch devices and smartphones must be connected via another interface. This interface is a webapp. All devices are connected, regardless of their connection to a central "network script". This accepts all entries and then changes the VR world.

Smartphones and multi-touch devices are passed via the webapp to the Web Interface. Here, the data of the devices are unified and directed to the network script. The data of the Wiimote, which is directly connected to the 3D application, will also be forwarded to the network script. This script then evaluates all the data and manipulates the 3D application. The whole workflow is summarized in Fig. 2.

3   Implementation

With smartphones and Wiimote different interaction concepts can be implemented. This section describes the technical implementation of our concept with the instant reality system. In this case the user is restricted in his movements without knowing. Thus, a control is achieved and disorientation avoided. To realize this, we switch automatically between the perspectives Free-Fly and Examine. In the following, the realization is explained in detail.

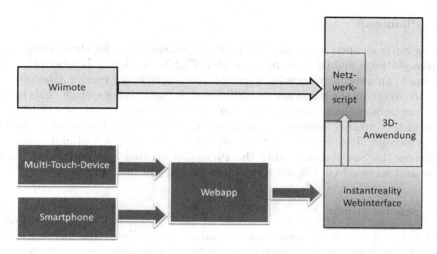

Fig. 2. Workflow.

3.1 Instant Reality

The instant reality Framework is a high-performance mixed-reality system that combines different components of Augmented Reality (AR) and Virtual Reality (VR) for developers [9]. The special feature of this framework is the fact that it works with the standardized data format X3D. 3D content can be described declaratively [10]. A major drawback of many VR systems is generally a lack of standards. instantreality tries to separate by means of X3D between runtime and program logic. The goal behind this is the reusability and exchangeability ("write once, deploy anywhere"). The inputs and outputs are controlled here via the instant reality player, the VR application itself is written in X3D [11].

3.2 X3D

X3D is a further development of the Virtual Reality Modeling Language (VRML). The goal behind this is simple description of 3D objects [12]. "X3D is an official Internet standard allowing to publish three-dimensional images on the Internet. X3D provides the ability to create very complex three-dimensional worlds with which the viewer can interact in a variety of forms. The strength of X3D is the presence of many interactive functions. Moreover, it is in an X3D ISO standard. X3D will therefore also in the future play a certain role. A weakness of the format is the lack of photorealism that we are used to from movies. But the lack of photorealism is a general feature of interactive formats". InstantReality extended X3D with some components. X3D can be expanded and manipulated by JavaScript. Thus, complex calculations, such as the trajectory of a planet described by mathematical formulas can be calculated at runtime.

3.3 Phonegap

"Phonegap is an open source development of open standards for the development of cross-platform mobile applications with HTML5, CSS3, and JavaScript". The developer can use this framework to create web pages, which receive a JavaScript interface to access the hardware capabilities of the underlying system. This hardware functions include camera, GPS and the locally stored contacts database, but also the internal sensors of a smartphone, such as accelerometer, compass and gyroscope. The websites hereby created can be both stored and executed locally on the Smartphone using the Phonegap created app and stored on a server and accessed via the network connection of the smartphone.

3.4 Sencha Touch

Sencha Touch is a web framework to make websites look like native mobile applications. Here, in the context of this work, especially the HTML5 function of gesture recognition on touch screens is important. This functionality allows an application on different devices with the same characteristics to perform. "Sencha Touch has the same basis as the JavaScript framework Ext JS, which is also developed by Sencha and browser-independent functions for DOM traversal (Document Object Model) provides for event handling and asynchronous Server communication (AJAX). Sencha Touch makes use of HTML5 to create, for example, off-line programs and to be able to deliver video or audio files. Furthermore, it uses CSS3 to draw rounded corners, shadows and gradients. The complimentary Framework is available with a commercial license and open source under the GPL (GNU General Public License)" [5].

3.5 Implementation of the Planetarium

The planetarium is built on top of the instant reality Framework X3D scene [13]. The structure language X3D provides for swapping of "objects" with a structure of similar characteristics, called "Proto". With the help of this structure type sub-structure objects can outsourced as planets and thus achieve decoupling. This scene is due to its structure dynamically extensible so newly discovered planets, moons or entire star systems can be integrated easily. This structure can expand individual planets in their functions without affecting the overall system. This dynamism also requires a dynamic navigation option. Specific viewpoints are to be incorporated, with which the user can become a quick and clear view of the entire simulation or can navigate directly to a particular planet or moon.

With a unique combination of numbers for each planet, all planet specific variables are read from a data script. Using these data, the calculation of the orbits and additional information such as different textures are possible. To complement the planetarium with new celestial bodies, thus only one entry with the concrete variables in the data scripts and the creation of a planet proto is necessary.

3.6   Interaction

Especially in the museum context, where every visitor has a different device, a (very) platform-independent control is necessary. To achieve this, it is advisable to use a webapp for control. With the presented framework Phonegap it is possible to make websites as native applications for mobile operating systems and to address the internal sensors of smartphones. Via the Sencha Touch framework, the use of the touch screen is possible. So one can create a webapp using these two frameworks, which has full access to the sensors and input capabilities of a smartphone. For better communication with the VR world this webapp can run on the same server on which the VR world is running and still work from the user perspective as a local native application on the smartphone. Thus, the webapp for the operator is easy to maintain and always up-to-date for the user.

Control of the VR World. To control a VR world, there are several options: Mouse and keyboard are directly linked to the virtual world, as is the case with customer devices, which are normally used as a controller for games consoles. Control devices such as smartphones and multi-touch devices cannot be connected directly to the VR world due to its unlimited possibilities for interaction. For these devices, there are at least two different ways to manipulate the VR world. These include the use of X3D network node or the use of instant reality web interface. In this work the instantreality web interface is used to communicate with the generated webapp and the virtual environment. An interface has been developed that can send all the information from the webapp to the virtual world in its own data format. Through the use of strings as arguments both an unlimited number of possibilities for interaction on the webapp, in the form of buttons or menus, as well as the transfer of sensor data are possible.

3.7   Defined Interfaces

In order to transmit different interactions to the VR world and to receive this transmission in the following the defined interfaces are explained. So touch inputs, sensor values and also directly to the 3D scene connected terminals are through these interfaces linked and their effects on the VR world are combined.

Webapp. All possible inputs implemented on a webapp are transferred in a central JavaScript to VR world. To ensure easy expandability, specially formatted strings are used for communication between the interfaces. The developer can give own unique names for its buttons and to implement them in the VR world. Once the user selects one of these buttons, a unique string is transferred to the virtual environment. Using the example of a planet buttons, the string "switchVP: 'planet name' ' is transmitted. On the opposite side in the VR this string is divided in the command "switchVP" and the parameter" 'planet name. In the VR It then the view point of the desired planet is activated and the user can view it. This type of transmission ensures the action to be executed with

Fig. 3. webapp on a smartphone with planets, features, and info areas.

which parameter. Since the developer must decide how his commands and parameters are established, the diversity of data transfer is not limited. The webapp consists of four main areas: Planet, Features, Navigation Area, and Info.

In Navigation one can, as described, navigate using finger gestures in the VR world. There, apart from the bottom bar, no other elements are displayed. This is by design, because one should not worry about the device in an immersive and intuitive control. The aim is that the user without looking at the page can navigate through the application.

If the webapp is considered within the PhoneGap framework, the webapp has access to the sensor data of smartphones. They are also transferred via the central JavaScript. Due to the uniqueness of the sensors functions are available that can also transfer the parameters as specially formatted strings. In Fig. 3 (left) one can see the planet shortcuts of the webapp. Clicking on one of these buttons, the respective viewpoint of the planet is activated in the simulation. The middle image shows a list of features that one can enable or disable for the planetarium. The picture was taken on the Google Nexus One. In the upper third one can see the features that affect the entire planetarium. Among them come planet-specific features. If a finger is pulled up or down, one scrolls the page down or up, and the remaining features are displayed. The right image shows a screenshot showing the "Info" -Area on the web application on an Android smartphone. Here, the user receives a brief description of what this app can be used for.

Multi-touch Recording. Since the user in the navigation does not want to look at his smartphone to see where he has to push for something to happen, this page is limited to two degrees of freedom. The viewer can go with a swipe of the finger up or down on the screen – in the VR forwards or backwards. Here, the first point of contact on the screen is selected as zero position. The further the current point of contact is removed from the first, the faster the user moves in the virtual environment. Through this realization very small and precise movements are enabled and the user does not type permanently on the screen to enlarge distances in the VC experience. If the finger is pushed back towards the zero point, then the speed is reduced in the VR. When the user drags a finger to the left or right of the respective viewpoint of the neighboring planet is sighted. In this interaction, it is not necessary to look at the screen of the smartphone. The focus is therefore fully on the VR system.

Sensor Detection. The sensor data is summed continuously. Here, the accelerometer has its zero position when the device is held parallel to the floor. The digital compass calculates its rest position from the first recorded data. If the user moves his smartphone now in one direction, the difference between the current value and the zero position is analogously to the multi-touch sensing added to the rotation. The greater the movement of the sensor is, the faster the rotation in the VR. Compared to an absolute mapping of the data in which the virtual environment turns just as the controller is turned, this implementation provides an advantage: the user can bring the viewing direction in the virtual environment in all possible positions and will only have to make a small gesture. If the user wants to rotate once around a planet, he would have to turn around the controller once as well. He would either have to twist his hand, or use the device in his hand. The result in this case would be the loss of immersion and possible inability navigation due to the twisted device.

In Fig. 4 one sees that due to the inclination of the smartphone, the viewpoint around the Earth is rotated. The earth is this fixed in the center and the user can look through a simple hand movement from all sides.

Fig. 4. Tilt to the right

Virtual Environment. The virtual environment is described in X3D and realized by means of instant reality framework. Here, the receiving interface of data is implemented. Therefore, it is necessary to define a script block that expects certain input values and takes over the control of the navigation. The input values include the data from the webapp, which are received via the web interface instant reality and passed to the script and locally integrated customer devices or special equipment. The interaction potential of local devices can be connected at this point in the interaction possibilities of the webapp. This makes it possible to use the sensor data of a smartphone and the Wiimote in the same functions and thus to enable the same navigation. Since the rotation is calculated for simplicity and better constraint to guide the user only for one axis, it is necessary to embed the viewpoint in nested transforms. For this purpose a viewpoint Proto was developed that performs these tasks. This Proto gets passed all the collected data and calculates its own new alignment and positioning in the VR. The developer has thus the advantage of not having to worry about the execution of the navigation. He only needs to place the viewpoint Proto in its virtual environment and adjust the appropriate links to the webapp.

All entries that the user can make are collected in a central location: the webapp. Since it is based on HTML and therefore runs on all major browsers, inputs from various customer devices, such as a multi-touch table or a smartphone can be used. It is also very easy to integrate new devices and interaction, since they must be connected only to the webapp or a new opportunity for interaction must be realized only within the webapp. In addition, the presentation on displays is always the same as the webapp determines the layout and all customer devices with a screen access the webapp. In this way, it is guaranteed that the latest version of the control program is used. The webapp passes all received interactions in the 3D scene, which then changes its current state.

4   Conclusions and Outlook

After creating an interaction concept for Wiimote and smartphone to control the planetarium, more customer devices or interaction concepts remain that could not be investigated in this work. Developments in the field of VR, computer science and consumer electronics in general, generate at relatively short intervals new games consoles with new technical refinements. Each new generation of customer devices brings new interaction concepts and a number of other possible interaction concepts [14,15]. The interaction concepts created here show what possibilities the current controller in the application Planetarium offer. The Kinect is a good example for new generations on the game console market, it combines existing concepts with new technical achievements.The main drawback is the individual user correspondence, though [16]. It remains to be seen what new previously unknown consoles will bring. The possibilities considered in this work are not fully exploited. One could show, for example, the 3D scene also on the screen of the device and put on an immersive and intuitive gesture control. Similarly, the multi-touch aspect that was hardly considered in this work must be regarded as an extension. Since only exemplary functions of the planetarium so far been implemented on the website, this could be extended to all possible functions in the planetarium. An evaluation of the established paradigms of interaction would be to verify the next step is to test the hypothesis. For mixed groups should be formed with and without previous knowledge of a particular controller. Then the VR system is presented with its selected controllers and a first navigation shown by the system. Each of the test persons should fill out a questionnaire at the beginning of each controller. In this questionnaire, expected results of the test subjects should be included on the subject of intuitiveness and degree of immersion. Subsequently, the tester should complete certain tasks with this controller. While performing the tasks, the time required and the number of navigation errors should be measured. A final questionnaire should cover how intuitive the controls was and how immersive the application for the user. Based on the results of the measurements during the implementation and questionnaires, conclusions could be drawn on the quality of the statement.

References

1. Majewski, M., Braun, A., Marinc, A., Kuijper, A.: Providing visual support for selecting reactive elements in intelligent environments. Trans. Comput. Sci. **18**, 248–263 (2013). doi:10.1007/978-3-642-38803-314
2. Braun, A., Wichert, R., Kuijper, A., Fellner, D.W.: A benchmarking model for sensors in smart environments. In: Aarts, E., de Ruyter, B., Markopoulos, P., van Loenen, E., Wichert, R., Schouten, B., Terken, J., Van Kranenburg, R., Ouden, E.D., O'Hare, G. (eds.) AmI 2014. LNCS, vol. 8850, pp. 242–257. Springer, Heidelberg (2014)
3. Engelke, T., Keil, J., Rojtberg, P., Wientapper, F., Webel, S., Bockholt, U.: Content first - A concept for industrial augmented reality maintenance applications using mobile devices. In: IEEE International Symposium on Mixed and Augmented Reality, ISMAR 2013, Adelaide, Australia, 1–4 October 2013, pp. 251–252 (2013)
4. Vayanou, M., Katifori, A., Karvounis, M., Kourtis, V., Kyriakidi, M., Roussou, M., Tsangaris, M., Ioannidis, Y., Balet, O., Prados, T., Keil, J., Engelke, T., Pujol, L.: Authoring personalized interactive museum stories. In: Mitchell, A., Fernández-Vara, C., Thue, D. (eds.) ICIDS 2014. LNCS, vol. 8832, pp. 37–48. Springer, Heidelberg (2014)
5. Grosse-Puppendahl, T., Braun, A., Kamieth, F., Kuijper, A.: Swiss-cheese extended: An object recognition method for ubiquitous interfaces based on capacitive proximity sensing. In: Proceedings of the SIGCHI Conference on Human Factors in Computing Systems. CHI 2013, pp. 1401–1410. ACM (2013)
6. Ardito, C., Buono, P., Costabile, M.F., Lanzilotti, R., Simeone, A.L.: Comparing low cost input devices for interacting with 3d virtual environments. In: Proceedings of the 2nd Conference on Human System Interactions. HSI 2009, pp. 289–294. IEEE Press (2009)
7. Marinc, A., Stocklöw, C., Braun, A., Limberger, C., Hofmann, C., Kuijper, A.: Interactive personalization of ambient assisted living environments. In: Smith, M.J., Salvendy, G. (eds.) HCII 2011, Part I. LNCS, vol. 6771, pp. 567–576. Springer, Heidelberg (2011)

8. Bowman, D.A., Coquillart, S., Fröhlich, B., Hirose, M., Kitamura, Y., Kiyokawa, K., Stürzlinger, W.: 3D user interfaces: new directions and perspectives. IEEE Comput. Graph. Appl. **28**(6), 20–36 (2008)
9. Engelke, T., Becker, M., Wuest, H., Keil, J., Kuijper, A.: MobileAR browser - a generic architecture for rapid AR-multi-level development. Expert Syst. Appl. **40**(7), 2704–2714 (2013). doi:10.1016/j.eswa.2012.11.003
10. Limper, M., Jung, Y., Behr, J., Sturm, T., Franke, T., Schwenk, K., Kuijper, A.: Fast and progressive loading of binary encoded declarative 3D web content. IEEE Comput. Graph. Appl. **33**(5), 26–36 (2013). doi:10.1109/MCG.2013.52
11. Stein, C., Limper, M., Kuijper, A.: Spatial data structures to accelerate the visibility determination for large model visualization on the web. In: the 19th International Conference on Web3D Technology, Web3D 2014, Vancouver, Canada, 8–10 August 2014, pp. 53–61 (2014)
12. Eicke, T.N., Jung, Y., Kuijper, A.: Stable dynamic webshadows in the X3DOM framework. Expert Syst. Appl. **42**(7), 3585–3609 (2015). doi:10.1016/j.eswa.2014.11.059
13. Aderhold, A., Wilkosinska, K., Corsini, M., Jung, Y., Graf, H., Kuijper, A.: The common implementation framework as service – towards novel applications for streamlined presentation of 3D content on the web. In: Marcus, A. (ed.) DUXU 2014, Part II. LNCS, vol. 8518, pp. 3–14. Springer, Heidelberg (2014)
14. Grosse-Puppendahl, T., Herber, S., Wimmer, R., Englert, F., Beck, S., von Wilmsdorff, J., Wichert, R., Kuijper, A.: Capacitive near-field communication for ubiquitous interaction and perception. In: Proceedings of the 2014 ACM International Joint Conference on Pervasive and Ubiquitous Computing. UbiComp 2014 Adjunct, pp. 231–242. ACM (2014) (Best Paper Nomination (best 4%))
15. Grosse-Puppendahl, T., Berghoefer, Y., Braun, A., Wimmer, R., Kuijper, A.: OpenCapSense: a rapid prototyping toolkit for pervasive interaction using capacitive sensing. In: 2013 IEEE International Conference on Pervasive Computing and Communications (PerCom 2013), San Diego, USA, pp. 151–158 (March 2013)
16. Gross, R., Bockholt, U., Biersack, E.W., Kuijper, A.: Multimodal kinect-supported interaction for visually impaired users. In: Stephanidis, C., Antona, M. (eds.) UAHCI 2013, Part I. LNCS, vol. 8009, pp. 500–509. Springer, Heidelberg (2013)

Orientation, Navigation and Driving

Disorientation Factors that Affect the Situation Awareness of the Visually Impaired Individuals in Unfamiliar Indoor Environments

Abdulrhman Alkhanifer[1]($\boxtimes$) and Stephanie Ludi[2]

[1] Computing and Information Science Program, Rochester Institute of Technology (RIT), Rochester, NY 14623, USA
akhnaifer@mail.rit.edu
[2] Software Engineering Department, Rochester Institute of Technology (RIT), Rochester, NY 14623, USA
salvse@rit.edu

Abstract. Developing situational awareness for individuals with visual impairments can be a challenging process, as designers need to understand the environmental aspects as well as the users' needs. In unfamiliar indoor open spaces, individuals with visual impairments need to work around multiple disorientation factors that can affect their orientation and situation awareness levels. In this work, we report our experience and results of longitudinal user studies that were designed to facilitate cues that help raise the situation awareness level of individuals with visual impairments when exploring unfamiliar indoor open spaces. Through our results, we explain in detail users' disorientation factors in such environments.

1 Introduction

Situational awareness (SA) can be explained as the individual's current understanding of the environmental elements and their changes [1]. Picking up environmental cues, such as auditory, can help in maintaining high SA. However, there are some factors that affect this process. In this work, we explain the disorientation factors that we gained through the conduction of three user studies that were designed to formulate our system and SA requirements for an assistive orientation technology to aid individuals with visual impairments in unfamiliar indoors [2]. In our previous paper, we briefly discussed the disorientation factors that affect individuals with visual impairments when obtaining environmental cues in unfamiliar indoor spaces [3]. In this paper, we expand and elaborate upon these factors by providing a detailed user experience.

The aim of this paper is to provide insight for the designers of indoor orientation assistive technologies about the factors that affect users' orientation to be taken into account when designing. The contribution can be summarized as uncovering in detail the disorientation factors that affect the orientation of individuals with visual impairments in unfamiliar indoor open spaces. Using feedback from 95 participants in three different studies, we will shed light on factors and concerns that relate to the visually impaired individual's orientation

© Springer International Publishing Switzerland 2015
M. Antona and C. Stephanidis (Eds.): UAHCI 2015, Part IV, LNCS 9178, pp. 89–100, 2015.
DOI: 10.1007/978-3-319-20687-5_9

in unfamiliar indoor open spaces, such as atriums. Also, we will discuss some implications of designing orientation assistive technologies that were drawn from our results. Understanding the ways that target users orient themselves within environments can provide helpful insight into the design.

2   Related Work

In the past much work has discussed orientation-related issues for individuals with visual impairments. Some work focuses on the orientation process from an orientation point-of-view [4–7], while others focus on providing requirements of indoor assistive technologies [2,8–11]. While the previous work discusses many important issues that relate to the orientation tasks, they do not discuss disorientation factors that can affect users' SA. In this research, we highlight users' experience with the factors that can affect their orientation abilities for the purpose of eliciting requirements for indoor orientation aids. In the rest of this section, we will review examples from each of the previous categories.

Banovic *et al.* [7] describe two user studies where they examined the ways in which individuals who are visually impaired identify surroundings in unfamiliar environments. The first was conducted as a high-level learning study. The researchers initially interviewed nine participants. Participants were then asked to perform exploration tasks in two different outdoor spaces. The second study was directed toward the activities that help individuals who are visually impaired to develop a cognitive map of their environment. Participants were asked to perform two tasks: (1) answer a set of questions that relate to a familiar environment, (2) physically navigate paths that are less familiar to each participant. After completion of the exploration tasks, semi-structured interviews were conducted. Findings from the second study suggested that large indoor spaces were difficult for participants to explore and learn. In our work, we looked into the factors that affect the orientation process in unfamiliar indoor environments and how users employ their skills to overcome them.

Miao, *et al.* [8] elicited requirements to build an indoor navigation system (MOBILITY project) that is intended to provide independence to blind travelers. They interviewed six blind participants and triangulated their interviews with an orientation and mobility (O&M) instructor. They employed structured interviews in their elicitation process. In their paper, they provided proposed functionality to be included in the system such as: contextual information about the surroundings as well as basic building information. In terms of learning the way blind individuals perceive information from the environment, they discussed such issues with the O&M instructor. Also, one of their developers wore a blindfold where he/she experienced non-visual travel.

3   User Studies

In this work, we present a series of three studies: (1) a domain understanding study, (2) Orientation and Mobility (O&M) recommendations, and (3) user survey. The results of each study were used to tailor the design of the next one to enhance the outcomes.

3.1 Methodology

Two of our user studies; domain understanding and O&M recommendations; were presented in the form of semi-structured interviews, while the third study was a validation study in the form of an online survey. To analyze our results, we applied the following qualitative techniques: content analysis [12], and open coding method that is a part of the grounded theory method [13]. Due to the relevance of the three user studies that we conducted the results are collated and can be found in Sect. 5. All studies received ethical approval from the university's IRB.

3.2 Study 1: Domain Understanding

This study was designed to help us understand the domain of indoor orientation and navigation for individuals with visual impairments. We interviewed 24 participants from six different countries to examine the strategies, which are employed to navigate through an unfamiliar indoor environment. This includes identifying the day-to-day challenges faced by individuals with visual impairments when orienting or when locating objects within their vicinity. We also initially investigated users' experience with other indoor orientation and navigation assistive technologies, and their views on accepting new forms of technologies. Participants were recruited from different countries to help us elicit requirements that assist in building an international solution. We designed this user study in the form of semi-structured phone interviews with 66 questions, of which 21 were open-ended and 45 were close-ended. Interview questions were divided into the following categories:

– Mobility issues in indoor environments
– Identification of indoor orientation and navigation tasks
– Identification of frustrations and concerns in different indoor environments
– Exposure and experience with indoor orientation assistive technologies
– User interface and technology preferences for indoor orientation assistive technologies

Participants were recruited through online mailing lists. Table 1 provides a classification of our participants depending on their level of functional vision and the mobility aid they use. G denotes participants who primarily use guide-dogs, while C refers to participants who mainly use canes. The mean age was 49.2 years (14.8 SD). Five of the participants were legally blind, yet could rely on some levels of functional vision, while 19 were fully blind. Legally blind are defined by the US Social Security as persons whose visual acuity is 20/200 or less in the better eye with best sight correction [14]. Twelve among the participants who reported being fully blind were born blind, while the rest lost their vision at a later point. Eleven of our participants primarily use guide-dogs to assist them when traveling, while the remaining 13 used canes. Twenty-three of our participants have received the O&M training.

Table 1. A classification of participants depending on the level of functional vision, mobility aid and geographical locations.

Legally blind	Totally blind	Country	Count
-	G21	Australia	1
-	G3	Canada	1
C17	-	Italy	1
G15	-	New Zealand	1
C11	-	UK	1
C2, G12, G23	C1, C4, C5, C6, C7 C8, G9, G10, G13, C14, G16, G18, C19, C20, C22, G24	USA	19
Total			24

3.3   Study 2: Orientation and Mobility Recommendations

From the previous study, we found that most of the navigation related problems in unfamiliar indoor environments can be categorized into: (1) maintaining orientation, (2) locating a path, and (3) detecting obstacles. Maintaining orientation when entering unfamiliar indoor environments includes but is not limited to understanding the spatial layout of objects within the environment, keeping track of the direction which the user is traveling in, and identifying landmarks that are related to the user's mission. Locating a path was another concern of the participants. The third need was detecting obstacles using their current aid, particularly those which would require time and effort to perceive. The indoor obstacles reported included objects above user's waist and floor signs. One notable aspect regarding participants in our first study was that users with service-animals were less concerned about orientation and obstacles, compared to users with canes. This guided us to reshape our goal and focus mainly on the orientation of cane users as it can greatly impact other challenges. To complement our findings relating to the indoor orientation challenges, we interviewed six certified O&M instructors, as they could provide a unique insight into the behavior of individuals with visual impairments, and the safe practices that enhance their orientation in unfamiliar indoor spaces. We focused our interviews on atrium areas as an example of open spaces and challenging indoor setup. We also discussed the best practices for individuals with visual impairments to navigate indoors from an O&M instructors' point of view.

Participants were recruited through online mailing lists. Participant demographics are shown in Table 2. Three of the participants selected were male, while the other three selected were females. Participants' mean age was 50.5 years (11.9 SD). The oldest participant was 60 years old and the youngest was 27. Participants came from five different states: Pennsylvania, Kentucky, Nebraska, New Mexico, and California. Two of the instructors were sighted, while the other four were visually impaired. Three of the visually impaired were blind since birth, while the remaining instructor lost her sight more than five years

Table 2. Key facts about O&M study participants.

ID	Location	Age	Sex	O&M Experience	Vision
O1	US-CA	53	F	3+ years	Sighted
O2	US-KY	60	F	3+ years	Sighted
O3	US-PA	57	M	3+ years	Blind
O4	US-NE	55	M	3+ years	Blind
O5	US-NM	27	F	Less than a year	Blind
O6	US-KY	51	M	3+ years	Blind

ago. Except one, all instructors had more than three years experience in O&M training. The exception was a new instructor who had less than a year of O&M teaching experience.

3.4   Study 3: Online Survey

As a follow up to our previous user studies, we conducted a third study in the form of an accessible survey. The objective behind our study was to validate and expand our previous findings, as well as to identify initial requirements as the basis for our design. To obtain a wider sample of participants, we recruited via a number of platforms including online mailing lists, social news lists such as reddit.com, emailing previous participants, in addition to word-of-mouth (by those in the aforementioned groups).

Through our previous studies, we have found that the difficulties with orienting one's position occurs more with individuals with visual impairments who rely on their cane to navigate unfamiliar buildings. This, however, guided us to tailor our survey to be more specific to cane users. Additionally, we did not focus on individuals with secondary disability. Our selection criteria can be summarized as any individual with visual impairment who is: an adult, uses a cane only, not hard-of-hearing or deaf, and able to walk unassisted.

Our survey was composed of 27 questions. Different types of question styles were employed including multiple choice, discussion questions and attitudinal questions. We received 65 responses. Participants' mean age was 53.26 years (11.29 SD). The range between participants' ages was 51 years, where the youngest participant was 20 years old and the oldest was 71 years old. The male-female ratio was about half where 32 were female, 31 male, and two preferred not to answer. Table 3 shows a categorization of participants in terms of ages and visual impairment types. We had participants from 27 different geographical locations inside and outside the United States (US). The majority of the participants are from the US (56 participants). Two of our participants preferred not to reveal their location. In terms of the visual impairment types, 41 (63.1 %) of our sample reported that they are totally blind while 24 (36.9 %) of them reported being legally blind. Depending on their age groups, we have categorized our sample under four categories (see Table 3). In terms of sight condition and cane usage, 44 (67.7 %) of our participants reported that they have been

Table 3. Survey participants categorized in age groups and their functional vision.

Age Groups	Gender	Legally blind	Totally blind	Count
18–29	Male	-	-	4 (6.2%)
	Female	S11, S23	S51, S52	
30–49	Male	S27, S29	S13, S19, S26, S34, S62	12 (18.5%)
	Female	S25, S37, S53, S41	S54	
50–64	Male	S10, S36, S38, S43, S60, S65	S5, S9, S14, S15, S20, S31, S33, S39, S44, S49, S61, S63, S64	39 (60.0%)
	Female	S12, S28, S30, S47, S57	S2, S3, S4, S6, S7, S8, S16, S17, S18, S32, S35, S50, S55, S56, S58	
65+	Male	S45, S46, S48, S24	-	7 (10.8%)
	Female	-	S21, S40	
	No answer	S1	-	
No answer	Male	S22	-	3 (4.6%)
	Female	-	S42	
	No answer	S59	-	
Total				65

visually impaired since birth, while 21 (32.3%) of them reported that they were pronounced as individuals with visual impairments more than 5 years ago. Fifty-six participants (86.2%) stated that they received their O&M training more than five years ago, one (1.5%) received the training between 3–5 years ago, seven (10.8%) received their O&M training less than a year ago, and one did not answer the question. Fifty-eight (89.2%) participants had an experience of using their cane for more than five years, two (3.1%) had an experience between 3–5 years, and five participants did not answer our questions.

4   Background

In this section, we provide some relevant results, which are important to under-standing the context of our resulted disorientation factors. The sections provided here resulted from our user studies and aligned with the previous research that was designed to facilitate experience of individuals with visual impairments when exploring unfamiliar indoors.

4.1   Environmental Cues

Paying attention to the environmental cues was reported by O&M instructors as well as the other participants as an important factor that help in gaining a good sense of orientation. Our participants mentioned different cue types that help when exploring unknown indoor environments: auditory, tactile, and olfactory. Auditory cues were often reported as the primary way for users to understand environments. Tactile feedback and olfactory cues were mentioned as well as an important indicator to understand the indoor environment. Participants who primarily use canes appeared to spend more time and effort paying careful attention to environmental cues compared to guide-dog users. In our first study, participants who use guide-dogs reported pausing for moments when entering unfamiliar buildings, while cane users reported pausing for a few *minutes*. For example, participant C1 said "probably the first thing I would do, is get inside and just stand still for a minute and listen. And if there is an elevator I would hear people using it, if it is a busy building that is, or if I'm going to a doctor's office, there would be a receptionist behind the desk you can hear these machines that he/she is using (sic). So, I'd listen for clues [...] to where I might be and then I just start going and see what I come to". This is an important step, as cane users need to have a preliminary understanding of the potential objects and obstacles within an environment before moving forward to walk through it. On the other hand, guide-dog users pause to get a general sense of the environment. Participant G3 said "I usually would stop and listen to get a general sense of my surrounding and then direct my dog accordingly"; however he added, "then I would tell the dog 'go forward' and 'find elevator' or 'stairs'." This is an example that shows that guide-dog users rely on their dogs to orient them in unfamiliar indoor buildings.

Olfactory cues could provide users with information about their surroundings, especially when searching for a landmark that is associated with a unique smell, for example, a coffee shop. However, participants in our first study as well as O&M instructors stated that smells can be used as helpful indicators but should not be treated as a permanent cue. The reason is that olfactory cues may not always be presented due to reasons such as closed doors on the landmark that produce them.

Participants reported the importance of tactile cues when learning and exploring unknown indoor environments. Except for signs, tactile cues can be obtained when individuals with visual impairments finish constructing their initial mental map of layout by listening to the sounds in the environment. Things like floor texture, and feedback from the cane, can help the user to acquire more information about the environment. For example, a floor mat can be an indicator of the building entrance. Another example is the change in the floor texture, which indicates to the individuals with visual impairments that they transitioned to a different part of the building.

4.2   Exploration Strategies

Our participants in the first study reported different techniques and steps that they perform when entering an unknown building. As we decided to focus our design to assist cane users, we investigated the recommended strategies to explore unfamiliar indoor open spaces from the O&M instructors' point of view.

Some of the instructors explain techniques they teach their students when orienting in unfamiliar buildings. Although the O&M instructors we interviewed have different O&M approaches, most of the practices described by them were similar. For example, encouraging the students to learn about the environment while exploring it was a common recommendation. This includes paying attention to the auditory cues such as unique landmark sounds, which can help in indicating the presence of certain landmarks in the environment.

Learning about unfamiliar indoor open spaces can be difficult, as individuals with visual impairments need to construct an initial mental map by listening to the environment and keep updating that initial mental map when they navigate it. Two techniques mentioned by O&M instructors were:

1. Perimeter search: when an individual with visual impairments tries to understand and mentally-map an indoor open space. The individual with visual impairments trails the wall next to his/her side and follows the walls around the space until he/she comes back to the original position. While the individual with visual impairments is trailing walls, he/she tries to collect cues about the landmarks and obstacles near the walls. This strategy gives the individual with visual impairments the ability to understand the environment; however, it might not allow them to understand the area in the middle of the open space.
2. Grid search: when an individual with visual impairments enters an indoor open space, and after paying attention to the environmental cues, he/she starts exploring the space by checking the back side wall (the wall at the beginning of the building), then the user tries to cross the space to the other side and trails the opposite wall. This technique can allow any individual with visual impairments to understand the atrium area and build a better mental map than those who rely only on their perception when standing at the entrance to the building.

Both of the previous reported techniques are aligned with the techniques reported by Jacobson [4]. With the previous techniques, individuals with visual impairments can learn more about the environment if they have the desire to visit that environment in the future.

4.3   User Needs

When visiting unfamiliar indoor environments, individuals with visual impairments expressed their need to understand more than their path information for the purpose of visiting such environments in the future. Among the needs provided: layout understanding, guidance, and obstacle detection. Due to the scope of this paper, we will not provide details about the user needs. More details about user needs as well as user and situation awareness (SA) requirements can be found in our previous paper [2].

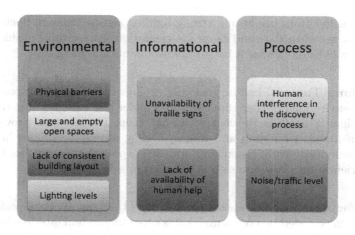

Fig. 1. Disorientation factors in open spaces indoors.

5 Results

In this section, we discuss our findings that relate to the orientation of individuals with visual impairments in unfamiliar indoor open spaces. We have collated our studies' results due to the relevance between the three studies.

5.1 Disorientation Factors

We coded the feedback that was provided by the participants in our validation study (study 3) to formulate the disorientation factors. We used standard coding process [13]. Our coded disorientation factors can be grouped under three categories depending on their context: environmental, informational, and process. Figure 1 shows the disorientation factors under their categories.

Environmental Factors. can cause disorientation to individuals with visual impairments. We coded four types under this category. Physical barriers that separate landmarks from the space where the individuals is located can contribute to a low orientation. Examples of this type are elevators behind walls and reception desks behind closed doors. Such barriers can isolate the auditory cues that are generated from these landmarks, which can lead to a disorientation. The second type under environmental categories is empty space. With fewer landmarks that individuals with visual impairments can relate-to when traveling open spaces makes it harder to travel and rely on a reference point when traveling. Lack of consistent building layout is the fourth type. Stylish and weird building shapes and designs can bring disorientation to the individuals. Such individuals would expect buildings to follow a similar fashion of the ones they experienced. The final type under environmental factors is the lighting levels. Individuals with visual impairments who have little perception to the light might suffer from bright and strong lighting setups indoors. Such lighting effects might generate glare and cause disorientation. An example of this is what participant S28 said, "I wear a hat to manage light and glare..."

Informational Factors. can be generally explained as a lack of information in any indoor environment. There are two types under this category: unavailability of braille signs as well as the lack of human help. Braille signs provide good information about a building and rooms; if they're missing or not in a place where an individual with visual impairments expected them to be, they can cause disorientation. Also, if a sign is installed upside down.

Process Factors. are those encountered factors that can affect the orientation process. We have coded two types under this category: human interference as well as noise and traffic levels. If an individual with visual impairments is listening to the environment and pedestrian traffic is going on around him/her, it is difficult for them to pay close attention. Also, extreme cases of building noise can cause disorientation. In high noise, individuals with visual impairments cannot listen for cues as such cues can be masked. In silent environments, many auditory cues are missing as well.

6   Design Implication on Assistive Orientation Tools

Through the course of our user studies, we elicited much feedback from users where they expressed their needs and preferences in orientation assistive tools as well as how to interact with them. We transformed users' feedback into design implications that can help design for orientation and navigation systems. In this section, we will briefly discuss each guideline.

Adapt to Environmental Changes. As mentioned before, noise and pedestrian activity levels can affect individuals with visual impairments when exploring unfamiliar indoor environments. In such environments, noise and traffic levels can affect the voice feedback provided by any system by interfering or masking its feedback. Also, it becomes much harder to work with voice recognition technologies in such environments. Assistive orientation technologies need to provide different input and output modalities that can help users interact with the system.

Provide Information Beyond User's Context. Systems in such environments need to consider giving users more abstract details about the indoor environment beyond their current context. For example, landmarks that are out of the current user space can be beneficial. In some cases, individuals with visual impairments look for landmarks that do not exist in the atrium area. Also, users would benefit from general information about the atrium such as shape and size.

Support User's Situation Awareness. A goal can be achieved by different tasks. When designing assistive technologies to aid individuals with visual impairments' orientation, it is important to design with user goals in mind not only how to achieve the tasks. Indoor orientation goals can be divided under three goals: obtaining initial mental map, maintaining high orientation, and performing good mobility. Designing to support such goals can help the users to achieve them regardless of their tasks. Our previous paper [2] provided a detailed Goal-Directed Task Analysis (GDTA) [15] for indoor orientation for individuals with visual impairments.

7 Conclusion and Future Work

To maintain their orientation, individuals with visual impairments need to acclimate to many factors that can be present in indoor environments. In this work, we discussed the disorientation factors that can affect individuals with visual impairments' SA indoors. Our results suggest that these factors can be categorized into three groups: environmental, informational, and process factors. Our results can help other researchers who are designing assistive technologies that aid the visually impaired indoors by providing them with insight about some factors that can be taken into account when designing.

Our next step is to incorporate our results in the design process. Soon, we will start our prototyping stage. Later, with help from a number of target users, we will test and validate our prototypes.

Acknowledgments. Authors would like to express their gratitude to all participants. Also, the first author would like to thank King Saud University in Riyadh, Saudi Arabia for the scholarship.

References

1. Dominguez, C.: Can SA be defined? In: Vidulich, M., Dominguez, C., Vogel, E., Mcmillan, G., (eds.) Situation Awareness: Papers and Annotated Bibliography, pp. 5–15. Interim Report No. AL/CF-TR-1994-0085, June 1994
2. Alkhanifer, A., Ludi, S.: Towards a situation awareness design to improve visually impaired orientation in unfamiliar buildings: requirements elicitation study. In: 2014 IEEE 22nd International Requirements Engineering Conference (RE), pp. 23–32, August 2014
3. Alkhanifer, A., Ludi, S.: Visually impaired orientation techniques in unfamiliar indoor environments: a user study. In: Proceedings of the 16th International ACM SIGACCESS Conference on Computers & Accessibility. ASSETS 2014, pp. 283–284. ACM, New York, NY, USA (2014)
4. Jacobson, W.H.: The Art and Science of Teaching Orientation and Mobility to Persons with Visual Impairments. American Foundation for the Blind, New York (1993)
5. Wiener, W., Welsh, R., Blasch, B.: Foundations of Orientation and Mobility, Instructional Strategies and Practical Applications. Foundations of Orientation and Mobility, 3rd edn, vol. 2. AFB Press (2010)

6. Johnson, V., Petrie, H.: Travelling safely: the problems and concerns of blind pedestrians. Br. J. Visual Impairment **16**(1), 27–31 (1998)
7. Banovic, N., Franz, R.L., Truong, K.N., Mankoff, J., Dey, A.K.: Uncovering information needs for independent spatial learning for users who are visually impaired. In: Proceedings of the 15th International ACM SIGACCESS Conference on Computers and Accessibility, ASSETS 2013, pp. 24:1–24:8. ACM, New York, NY, USA (2013)
8. Miao, M., Spindler, M., Weber, G.: Requirements of indoor navigation system from blind users. In: Holzinger, A., Simonic, K.-M. (eds.) USAB 2011. LNCS, vol. 7058, pp. 673–679. Springer, Heidelberg (2011)
9. Engelbrektsson, P., Karlsson, M., Gallagher, B., Hunter, H., Petrie, H., O'Neill, A.M.: Developing a navigation aid for the frail and visually impaired. Univers. Access Inf. Soc. **3**(3), 194–201 (2004)
10. O'Neill, A., Petrie, H., Lacey, G., Katevas, N., Karlson, M.A., Engelbrektsson, P., Gallagher, B., Hunter, H., Zoldan, D.: Establishing initial user requirements for pam-aid: a mobility and support device to assist frail and elderly visually impaired persons, improving the quality of life the european citizen. Improving the Quality of Life for the European Citizen (1998)
11. Rafael, I., Duarte, L., Carriço, L., Guerreiro, T.: Towards ubiquitous awareness tools for blind people. In: Proceedings of the 27th International BCS Human-Computer Interaction Conference, BCS-HCI 2013, pp. 38:1–38:5. British Computer Society, Swinton (2013)
12. Lazar, J., Feng, J.H., Hochheiser, H.: Research Methods in Human-Computer Interaction. Wiley Publishing, New York (2010)
13. Strauss, A.L., Corbin, J.M., et al.: Basics of Qualitative Research, vol. 15. Sage, Newbury Park (1990)
14. Social-Security-Office: Disability evaluation under social security: special senses and speech - adult. http://www.ssa.gov/disability/professionals/bluebook/2.00-SpecialSensesandSpeech-Adult.htm
15. Endsley, M.R., Bolstad, C.A., Jones, D.G., Riley, J.M.: Situation awareness oriented design: from user's cognitive requirements to creating effective supporting technologies. In: Proceedings of the Human Factors and Ergonomics Society Annual Meeting 47, pp. 268–272, October 2003

Informational Geography: Re-writing and Re-reading Maps

Carlos Alberto Barbosa[1,2] and Luisa Paraguai[3(✉)]

[1] School of Arts, Architecture, Design and Fashion, Anhembi Morumbi
University, São Paulo, Brazil
carlosalberto.barbosa@gmail.com
[2] Laureate International Universities, Baltimore, USA
[3] School of Visual Arts, Pontifical Catholic University of Campinas,
Campinas, Brazil
luisaparaguai@gmail.com

Abstract. The text is concerned with how mapping information visualization differs from traditional cartography once the content flows, superposed on physical space, change the way human perceptions deal with space and time. From this point onwards, the text discusses the articulation between spatiality and modes of moving within the city through data representations. Using the Watch_Dogs WeareData Project as an example of how this is done, users can follow distinct syntactic and semantic narratives arranged over individual and public data information made available in Paris, London and Berlin. Each of the three towns is recreated on a 3D map, allowing the users to discover in real time not only the way data organizes and runs cities, but also constructs spatialities.

Keywords: Informational and physical cartography · Data representations and narratives · Hybrid spatialities

1 Introduction

In that Empire, the Art of Cartography attained such Perfection that the map of a single Province occupied the entirety of a City, and the map of the Empire, the entirety of a Province. In time, those Unconscionable Maps no longer satisfied, and the Cartographers Guilds struck a Map of the Empire whose size was that of the Empire, and which coincided point for point with it. The following Generations, who were not so fond of the Study of Cartography as their Forebears had been, saw that that vast map was Useless, and not without some Pitilessness was it, that they delivered it up to the Inclemencies of Sun and Winters. In the Deserts of the West, still today, there are Tattered Ruins of that Map, inhabited by Animals and Beggars; in all the Land there is no other Relic of the Disciplines of Geography. (Jorge Luis Borges)

The text is concerned with different superposed digital data representations and possible maps to configure the everyday activities and to transform the local geography in a poem-palimpsest, as points out O'Rourke (2013) [1] to the ever-changing plots of land. Using the Watch_Dogs WeareData Project as the study object, the text concerns about how the flow of information superposes on physical space changes the way

© Springer International Publishing Switzerland 2015
M. Antona and C. Stephanidis (Eds.): UAHCI 2015, Part IV, LNCS 9178, pp. 101–107, 2015.
DOI: 10.1007/978-3-319-20687-5_10

human being perception deals with space and time nowadays, as much as they can redefine the ideological issues about maps. It makes possible in its own way, different possibilities to think and discover the way data organizes and runs cities, and also reveals a possible sense of spatiality.

2 What Is a Map About? from Territory to Ideology

Basically, territorial maps are (or intend to be) ways of tracing paths or determining territorial positions and limits and constituting a model of spatial representation. In this sense, Harley (apud WOOD and FELS, 2008) [2], calls attention to the fact that maps have been regarded as an epitome of modernity. Nonetheless, once these modes of displacement to a particular piece of land establish the limits of a territory, it is not hard to recognize the ideological element that may be present in these representations, despite the fact that the topographical records and the measurements have been technically and rigorously carried out. Hence, while maps can be man's expression of knowledge about nature, they are also refined manifestations of power and control over a piece of land – a form of supporting the construction and maintenance of the *status quo*, or even, as reported by Passos (2009: 19) [3], "very often anticipating the appropriation of this same space." For such, simply look back to the Treaty of Tordesillas, which, even in 1495, before Europeans occupied portions of land of the so-called New World, already divided and established ownership between the kingdoms of Spain and Portugal.

The point here is not to reflect upon scientific procedures, or about the relations of strength and power (Harley 1988) [4], but to investigate the *WeareData* project and discuss the possible configurations of mapped space as contemporary perceptive modes of operating territories. In this way, we seek to stimulate a reflection about cartography as modes of construction and map reading, seeking to employ Harley's warning (1988: 277) [4]: that "although maps have long been central to the discourse of geography they are seldom read as 'thick' texts or as socially constructed form of knowledge". In this sense, we are interested in researching the social dimension of this process in relation to personal associations and cultural conditionings, within a series of spatial stimuli present in a particular environment, and cognitive and sensory operations. We adopt perception and the relations with the space as learned behavior in different contexts, be them historical, cultural or technological, based on collected and systematically arranged data (Rodaway 2011) [5], by the individuals in their daily activities.

Considering the human experiences of life in cities that grew during the industrial era called for a representation which could provide an understanding of inhabited space in constant change. As noted by Meneses, for this inhabitant

> [...] the daily experience of urban space – once it also starts to get broader and more complex – becomes increasingly insufficient, and he is only able to assimilate disperse fragments. Incidentally, one of the reasons which accounts for the fascination exerted by urban maps as from the 18th century is, precisely, the capacity for synthesis, for instantaneous crystallization of diversity, for an immediate intelligibility of the multiple. (2009: 15) [6]

But to what extent such synthesis and immediate intelligibility of the multiple do not constitute an illusion that tranquilizes the inhabitant of great and complex spaces, as it engenders power structures? The author points out that "spatial perception" and "locational logic", as well as "the understanding of the city as the transformation of nature" are salutary perspectives "[...] for current times, when the said global cities increasingly suffer the loss of their territorial substance or where paradoxically the city's extreme artificiality eventually becomes naturalized" (Meneses 2009: 16) [7]. Such loss of territorial substance that the author refers to implies in a change in the time-space relation, and in the strategies for the maintenance of power. More than the changes in the spaces accelerated by development in great urban centres, the data and information flow that passes over the territory, and the diversity of possible representations of topographical records form rather than a loss of substance, a transformation of the territory's condition and the power instituted over it. Therefore, its transformation does not only unfold due to topographical change, but from what happens on a particular location, orientation, and variation of places, no longer measured only by physical distances, but also by the information operated in digital social networks, financial databases, webcams, synchronous and asynchronous message exchanges.

If for Woods and Fels (2008: 190) [2] "[...] map is nothing more than a vehicle for the creation and conveying of authority about, and ultimately over, territory [...]" the questions that remain concern the way in which power is deployed over a changing territory, and how to counterpoint this established power. As we have seen, for Harley (1988), maps are rarely read as a social construction. They are generally seen as mirrors of nature, but organize themselves as operations of culture. So that they are read critically, "Dialectical relationships between image and power cannot be excavated with the procedures used to recover the 'hard' topographical knowledge in maps and there is no litmus test of their ideological tendencies" (Harley 1988: 280) [8]. In other words, instead of excavating the ideological content and the control mechanisms behind a map, we should observe the dialectical aspects that can be raised from its reading, moving away, as suggests Harley,

> [...] from the canons of traditional cartographical criticism with its string of binary oppositions between maps that are 'true and false', 'accurate and inaccurate', 'objective and subjective', 'literal and symbolic', or that are based on 'scientific integrity' as opposed to 'ideological distortion'. (Harley 1988: 278) [8]

3   The Watch_Dogs WeareData Project: From Physical to Informational Territories

The Watch_Dogs WeareData Project[1] is the first website to gather publicly available data about Paris, London and Berlin, in one location. The interface presents the user with reading modes of three different cities: Paris, Berlin and London, visually organizing data on physical networks of public transport, both of the underground and of

---

[1] http://wearedata.watchdogs.com/

cycling, urban infrastructure such as ATM, traffic lights, public toilets and CCTV cameras. Content that is shared in social networks such as Tweeter, Instagram, Four-square and Flickr contribute to this intricate network of possible narratives [Fig. 1], allowing the user to discover this data.

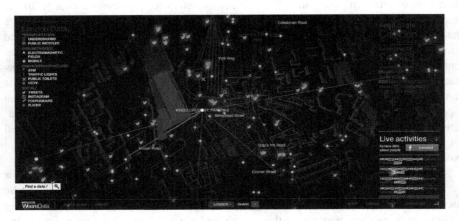

Fig. 1. The watch_dogs wearedata interface with all the icons situated in the city of London, 2014. (http://wearedata.watchdogs.com).

This information is arranged on a 3D map of these cities, where the streets, public buildings and underground stations, for example, are identifiable. As we explore the map as a *flâneur* who roams the city's lanes, alleys and avenues, the user can read the tweets sent from that place, see the images posted on Instagram, as well as official statistics on the region's average salaries, the criminality rate, while monitoring urban displacements and updating the location of urban facilities.

In the first instance the website user is faced with issues related to surveillance, (cf. Foucault 2003) which are based on a system that is constantly fed by data recording; this, according to the author, can be understood by "The practice of placing individuals 'under' observation is a natural extension of a justice imbued with disciplinary methods and examination procedures" (Foucault 2003: 601-602) [9]. However, a closer look at the project reveals to the visitor not only the degree of exposure we are all subject to, but also the synchronous and asynchronous interrelations between physical and informational space. The transmitter, geographically situated by the information he distributed through the network, doesn't always produce content that is directly related to the physical location, but expands the meanings composed contemporaneously with the shared data [Fig. 2]. The time-space articulations become evident in this project – horizontal communication networks that connect the local and the global at chosen times (Castells 2009) [10]. And while the individuals experience these juxtaposed and superposed agency patterns, they seek to organize the dominant logic of each network and ultimately configure other modes of existence.

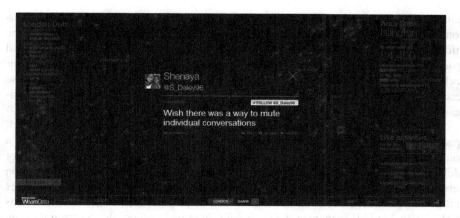

Fig. 2. City of London. Tweet sent from a mobile from Islington area. (http://wearedata. watchdogs.com/start.php?locale=en-EN&city=london).

This information flow emphasizes another outline in the territory, one that is time-based. To strictly carry-out the topographical mapping of a territory, and to try to exert a degree of power over it, seems like a somewhat ineffective activity when the spatial relations are subject to a temporal element. In this way, the transformation of the substance of a territory takes place due to time, an element distinct from space, but more than ever linked to it. The embodiment of the temporal dimension within the same map identifies the relation between the two elements (time and space), but also exposes their separate existence, with distinct forces. Giddens (1991: 27-28) [11] notes that "The separation between time and space should not be seen as a unilinear development, devoid of reversions or which is all-encompassing. On the contrary, as all development trends, it has dialectical aspects which incite opposing characteristics", which allows for separate discussions, even though they occupy the same plane. The place, as defined by the action of the occupant, delimits the space (de Certeau 2013) [12]. But it gives in once again to the powers of space which, in its relation to time reveals the changes which are perceptible to the passer-by who operates new records in the sensory map, establishing a place.

To consider daily life as a field of sensory production is to reference de Certeau (2013: 200) [12] when he proposes narrative structures as spatial syntax, or, in other words, "every story is a travel story – a spatial practice". The author prioritizes the practices that structure space, while the individuals distinctly articulate maps as they pass along given routes. If the place arranges a certain stability of positions, the space presents itself as variable in relation to direction, velocity and time, given by their own operations (de Certeau 2013: 201-203) [12]. In this project, visual interfaces can be understood as transformative powers of space as they give name to structuring orders to narrate spacializing actions, as descriptions of the modes of use, perception and determination of other boundaries.

The Watch_Dogs WeareData Project presents spatial structures defined by the urban experience and conformed by computational language in possible time-space relations, interconnecting databases and distinct physical networks, as in mobile phone calls, online camera video streaming, GPS satellite navigation systems [Global Positioning System] and online social network interactions. In this text we presume that the informational dimension of the digital networks configure themselves with the physical space in non-hierarchical layers, constituting other grids and modes of displacement for each situation – relational systems of spatial notation. The users in this context choose reading paths while organizing the data in narratives, contrary to the discursive processes present in the visualization of the information.

This project explores the relations between modes of perception and construction of space, articulating translation processes of languages where the software acts as a contextualizing element and as a promoter of the project-orientated action. For McWilliams (2012) [13] the computational language acts as "a continuous connection between man and machine", systematizing working methods and techniques, practices and processes of representation and expression, as presentations of the sensible. Reas et al. (2010: 11) [14] recognize the code with three main proposals, "communication, explanation or obfuscation", to the degree that the rules demand previous knowledge from the users and can therefore evoke distinct signification contexts. It is understood that in this project the computational code validates "contemporary techniques of control, communication, representation, writing and interaction" (Manovich 2008: 8) [15], as it assorts data and open profiles derived from databases and social networks, respectively.

The computational language encodes the construction and agency of the visuality, and therefore becomes responsible for the formatting and the expression of the information. Hence, another relevant point raised by the project is the comprehension of these computational objects as cultural practice, as they mediate and elaborate other immaterial dimensions such as the codes of behaviour, habits, rituals, values and significations. These codes are perceived as superposed texts that mediate the human/machine relationship, while they inscribe society. Also, according to Barbero (apud Santaella 2007: 89) [16] "to hybridize the symbolic intensity of numeric abstraction with the perceptive sensoriality" implies accessing and modulating this diverse data and generating complex structures of the networked hypermediatic contexts in the field of the visible.

4 Final Considerations

We understand the emergence of a dynamic cartography, collectively constructed, in which the artists aim to propose forms that articulate the forces of the urban domain, composing complex structures, contingent patterns of society – fragments of time and space translated into actions.

By articulating networks and information flows – physical objects and bodies, times and spaces – the Watch_Dogs WeareData Project considers other perceptions and configurations of the displacement of individuals who perform daily contemporary life, and thus, elaborate an understanding of the world. The audio-visual discourse negotiates spatial orientations, constructs other situations, and as a poetic artefact operates with moments that will be repeated while it composes itself/they are composed, as notes Lefebvre (1960) [17].

References

1. O'Rourke, K.: Walking and mapping – artists as cartographers. The MIT Press, Cambridge (2013)
2. Wood, D., Fels, J.: The nature of maps: cartographic constructions of the natural world. Cartographica **43**(3), 189–202 (2008). University of Toronto Press, Toronto
3. Passos, M.L.P.: O poder dos mapas e os mapas do poder. In: Passos, M.L.P.; Emidio, T. (eds.): Desenhando São Paulo: mapas e literatura 1877-1954, pp.19−21. Imprensa Oficial, Editora Senac São Paulo, São Paulo (2009)
4. Harley, J.B.: Maps, knowledge, and power. In: Cosgrove, D., Daniels, S. (eds.) The iconography of landscape, pp. 277–312. Cambridge University Press, Cambridge (1988)
5. Rodaway, P.: Sensuous Geographies: Body, Sense and Place. Routledge, London and New York (1994)
6. Meneses, U.T.B. Prefácio. In: Passos, M.L.P., Emídio, T., (eds.): Desenhando São Paulo, mapas e literatura 1877-1954, p. 15. Imprensa Oficial; Editora Senac São Paulo, São Paulo (2009)
7. Meneses, U.T.B. Prefácio. In: Passos, M.L.P., Emídio, T., (eds.): Desenhando São Paulo, mapas e literatura 1877-1954, p. 16. Imprensa Oficial; Editora Senac São Paulo, São Paulo (2009)
8. Harley, J.B.: Maps, knowledge, and power. In: Cosgrove, D., Daniels, S. (eds.) The iconography of landscape, pp. 277–312. Cambridge University Press, Cambridge (1988)
9. Foucault, M.: Panopticism. In: Scharf, R.C., Dusek, V. (eds.) Philosophy of Technologie: The Technological Condition, pp. 589–602. Blackwell Publishing, Malden (2003)
10. Castells, M.: Communication Power. Oxford University Press, New York (2009)
11. Giddens, A.: As consequências da modernidade. Unesp, São Paulo (1991)
12. de Certeau, M.: A invenção do cotidiano: 1. Artes de fazer. Editora Vozes, Petropolis (2013)
13. McWilliams, C.B.: Language in the other software. Leonardo Electronic Almanac **17**(2), 102–118 (2012). http://www.leoalmanac.org/vol17-no2-dac09-after-media-embodiment-and-context/. Accessed 9 February 2015
14. Reas, C., McWilliams, C., Barendse, J.: Form + Code in Design, Art, and Architecture. Princeton Architectural Press, New York (2010)
15. Manovich, L.: Media Visualization: Visual Techniques for Exploring Large Media Collections (2012). http://lab.softwarestudies.com/p/publications.html. Accessed 9 February 2015
16. Santaella, L.: As linguagens como antídotos ao midiacentrismo. Matrizes **1**(1), 75–98 (2007). http://www.matrizes.usp.br/index.php/matrizes/article/viewFile/27/39. Accessed 9 February 2015
17. Lefebvre, H.: The theory of moments and the construction of situations Internationale, Situationniste #4 (1960) http://www.cddc.vt.edu/sionline/si/moments.html. Accessed 9 February 2015

Effect of Road Conditions on Gaze-Control Interface in an Automotive Environment

Pradipta Biswas[1(✉)] and Varun Dutt[2]

[1] University of Cambridge, Cambridge, UK
pb400@cam.ac.uk
[2] Indian Institute of Technology, Mandi, India

Abstract. This paper proposes an eye gaze based dashboard control interface for automotive environment so that drivers need not to take their hands off from steering wheel and control the dashboard only by looking at it. With the help of our smoothing and target prediction technology, we found that first time users could operate a dashboard using their eye gaze in approximately 2.5 s for each on-screen item selection in different road conditions. As part of the study we also found that average amplitude of saccadic intrusion is a good indicator of drivers' perceived cognitive load.

1 Introduction

This paper reports a user trial on exploring the possibility of gaze control interface for operating a dashboard in an automotive environment. In particular, we evaluated the effect of two different track conditions on drivers' performance with eye-gaze tracking interface. Previous work [3] has already compared eye-gaze tracking interface with touch-screen control. We took forward that work with a low-cost eye-gaze tracker and intelligent target prediction algorithm [2] that can reduce pointing time.

A second aim of the study was to compute and compare Saccadic Intrusion (SI [1]) in a gaze controlled interface. Saccadic Intrusion is a particular type of eye movement that has been already classified and related to mental workload [4]. SI is more robust than pupilometry based method of cognitive load measurement as SIs are less sensitive to ambient light condition than pupil dilation. Previous work already investigated SI in automotive environment, but investigation of SI parameters in a gaze controlled interface is a new contribution. We investigated whether different SI parameters like amplitude and duration can still be related to mental workload even when users were manipulating their eye-gaze to operate different screen elements.

We have described the user study in the following sections.

2 Participants

We collected data from 12 participants (age ranged from 19 years to 29 years, ; 10 males, 2 females; one student was pursuing a graduate degree; whereas, all others were pursuing undergraduate degrees at the Indian Institute of Technology, Mandi). Out of

M. Antona and C. Stephanidis (Eds.): UAHCI 2015, Part IV, LNCS 9178, pp. 108–116, 2015.
DOI: 10.1007/978-3-319-20687-5_11

these 10 participants, 7 possessed a driving license (one had the license for about 4-years; whereas, others had obtained it in the last 1 to 3 years). Out of these 7 participants, 4 participants drove a 4-wheeler and rest drove 2-wheelers. According to the self-reports, none of the drivers had driven a 2- or 4-wheeler in the mountains before (all drivers reported to have driven vehicles in the plains). Eight participants had driving licenses although the qualities of driving tests were quite different for the participants possessing a driving license. However all participants self-reported to be were expert users of the driving simulator and used to drive cars in the simulator.

3 Design

We designed the test to evaluate the effect of an eye gaze-controlled secondary task on the primary task with participants with varying level of driving skills. The primary task involved driving a car in the left lane without veering off from the lane. We used two different track conditions – a simple track consisting of only two turns and a complex track consisting of 20 turns. There were no other traffic on the road and drivers were instructed to drive safely without veering off the driving lane and simultaneously operating the car dashboard using their eye-gaze. The secondary task was initiated through an auditory cue. It mimicked a car dashboard (Fig. 1) and participants were instructed to press a button on it after hearing the auditory cue. The auditory cue was set to appear between every 5 and 7 s interval. The target button was randomly selected in the car dashboard. The pointing was undertaken through eye gaze of users using an intelligent eye gaze tracking algorithm [2] and selection was done through a hardware button on steering. The secondary task was presented at the centre of a laptop screen (Fig. 2).

a. Experimental Interface   b. Original Car Dashboard

Fig. 1. Secondary task

The study was a 2 × 2 factorial design where the independent variables were

- Track Condition
  - Simple
  - Complex

Fig. 2. Experiment design

- Presence of Secondary Task
  - Driving without Secondary Task
  - Driving with Secondary Task

  The dependent variables were

- Task Completion Time
- Average deviation from centre of road
- Number of correct selections is gaze-controlled interface

We also measured drivers' cognitive load in terms of pulse rate using an Oximeter and NASA TLX scores.

4 Material

We used a Logitech driving simulator hardware and Torque car simulation software. The hardware was set as an automatic transmission car. We used an Tobii EyeX eye gaze tracker and EyeX SDK for the gaze-controlled interface. The primary task was run on a Linux desktop while the secondary task was conduced on a Windows 8 Laptop. The Laptop screen had a dimension of 34.5 cm × 19.5 cm with screen resolution of 1368 × 800.

5   Procedure

Initially participants were briefed about the procedure and trained to use the driving simulator and the gaze controlled interface. Then they undertook the trial in random order of track conditions. After completion of each condition, they filled up the TLX sheet based on their toughest experience during the trial.

We used logging software that recorded the trajectory of the car with timestamp from the driving simulator and cursor and eye-gaze movements from the secondary task. We also recorded participants' pulse rate from the Oximeter with timestamp.

6   Results

We found a statistical significant correlation between number of correct selections in the secondary task and average velocity of the car (Fig. 3, $\rho = -0.46$, $p < 0.05$). Drivers could make significantly higher number [t $(1,21) = -2.2$, $p < 0.05$] of correct selections using eye-gaze control while they were driving in the complex track than the simple track (Fig. 4). In a repeated measure ANOVA, we found

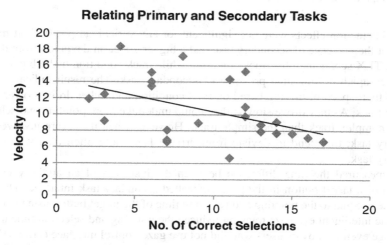

Fig. 3. Average driving velocity is correlated with number of correct selections in secondary task.

- significant main effect of Track Condition on
  - Task completion time F(1, 11) = 88.24, p < 0.01, $\eta^2 = 0.89$
  - Deviation from driving lane F(1, 11) = 6.51, p < 0.05, $\eta^2 = 0.37$
  - TLX score F(1, 11) = 14.58 p < 0.01, $\eta^2 = 0.57$
- significant main effect of Presence of Secondary Task on
  - Task completion time F(1, 11) = 22.07, p < 0.01, $\eta^2 = 0.67$
  - Deviation from driving lane F(1, 11) = 13.69, p < 0.01, $\eta^2 = 0.55$
  - TLX score F(1, 11) = 23.01, p < 0.01, $\eta^2 = 0.68$

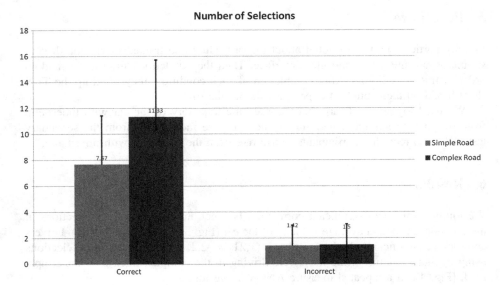

Fig. 4. Number of selections in secondary tasks in different road conditions

The interaction effects were not significant for any variable at $p < 0.05$. It may be noted that the presence of secondary task had a bigger effect on deviation from driving lane and TLX scores than the track condition while track condition had a bigger effect on task completion time than presence of secondary task. The result indicates, users adjusted their speed of driving based on road condition and rather drove slower in the complex track. As they drove slowly, they could undertake more pointing and selection tasks in complex track than the simple track. However when they were involved in a secondary task, they tend to deviate from driving lane more often than without any secondary task.

We measured the time difference between the instances of an auditory cue and selection of a target button in the gaze controlled secondary task interface. This time difference is equal to the pointing and selection time of the target button using eye gaze. Use of the intelligent eye gaze tracking reduced the pointing and selection time to 2.5 s on average even for novice users who did not use gaze-control interface earlier (Fig. 5). The difference in selection times for two different track conditions was not significant at $p < 0.05$.

In summary, we concluded,

- Complexity and presence of dual task significantly increases cognitive load and task completion times.
- Performance with secondary task is significantly related to velocity of car. In complex road, users drove slowly and performed better with secondary task than simple road condition.
- With present state of eye gaze tracker, users needed approximately 2.5 s for pointing and selection

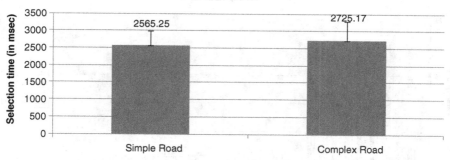

Fig. 5. Average selection times in gaze control interfaces for two different road conditions

7 Saccadic Intrusion (SI) Analysis

We have developed an algorithm to analyze movements of eye gaze and based on the following two criteria:

1. Eye gaze returned to same position between 60 and 870 ms interval
2. Maximum deviation of eye gaze within the interval is more than 0.4° in X-axis

Figure 6 shows an example of eye-gaze movement and corresponding saccadic intrusion. The pink line is the eye gaze movement and the blue line signifies SI.

We calculated the amplitude and duration of all SIs for all participants and Figs. 7 and 8 below show an histogram of SIs for simple and complex track conditions. It may be noted that the highest number of SIs had an amplitude between 0.4° and

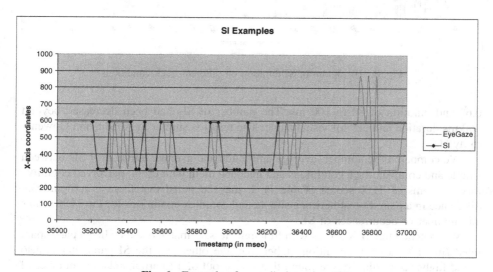

Fig. 6. Example of saccadic intrusion (SI)

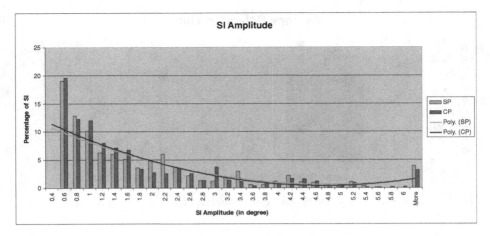

Fig. 7. Histogram of SI amplitude in different track conditions

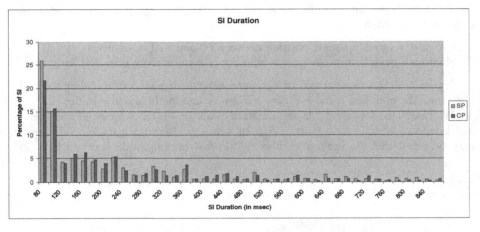

Fig. 8. Histogram of SI duration on different track conditions

0.6° and duration of 80 to 100 ms. The number of SIs had been decreased beyond 360 ms duration and 3.5° of visual angle. The result is similar to Abadia and Gowen's study [1].

We compared the number, average amplitude and average duration of SIs between simple and complex track conditions and matched them with users' perceived cognitive load in terms of TLX scores (Table 1). It may be noted that there is a significant difference in a paired t-test between simple and complex conditions for the TLX scores and number of occurrences of SI.

We matched the TLX scores with SI parameters. A match occurs when a participant rated (in TLX) a track condition higher than the other and the SI parameter is also found higher accordingly. We found that for 10 out of 12 participants, the number of

Table 1. TLX scores and SI parameters in different track conditions

	TLX		SI_Count		AvgSI_Amplitude		AvgSI_Duration	
	Simple	Complex	Simple	Complex	Simple	Complex	Simple	Complex
P1	37	68.51	251	303	2.24	1.70	169.53	181.17
P2	69.16	62	25	224	3.66	1.68	260.09	218.09
P3	52.66	66.32	66	203	1.42	1.63	211.66	194.62
P4	51.17	67.66	67	170	1.25	1.63	238.69	230.09
P5	13.66	42.51	46	172	1.23	1.59	273.02	242.15
P6	65.66	78.17	49	84	1.25	1.87	201.45	246.17
P7	55.5	66.98	61	92	1.85	1.16	250.47	242.74
P8	38.17	54.34	89	143	2.72	2.17	252.31	265.11
P9	54.17	61.34	38	53	0.79	0.81	326.36	255.16
P10	65.49	69.84	84	81	1.58	1.34	230.38	208.84
P11	24.83	67.83	21	52	0.59	1.80	418.63	337.94
P12	39	45.83	77	294	1.10	2.29	226.84	226.37
Ttest		0.002		0.002		0.997		0.113

Table 2. TLX scores and pulse rates in different track conditions

	TLX		MaxPulseRate		AvgPulseRate	
	Simple	Complex	Simple	Complex	Simple	Complex
P1	37	68.51	125	125	61.14	59.5
P2	69.16	62	124	125	64.89	62.33
P3	52.66	66.32	125	124	61.62	60.06
P4	51.17	67.66	125	124	61.97	61.14
P5	13.66	42.51	125	125	60.41	59.32
P6	65.66	78.17	125	127	60.89	64.42
P7	55.5	66.98	121	123	60.87	58.96
P8	38.17	54.34	121	121	61.23	58.82
P9	54.17	61.34	124	124	59.94	60.88
P10	65.49	69.84	118	125	57.79	58.28
P11	24.83	67.83	121	121	60	60.58
P12	39	45.83	127	125	61.78	61.37
Ttest		0.002		0.339		0.278

SIs matched with their TLX scores while for 8 out of 12 participants the average SI amplitude matched with their TLX scores.

However, the maximum and average pulse rate (Table 2) was neither significantly different between simple and complex road conditions nor they matched with TLX scores.

8   Conclusions

Researchers already investigated eye gaze controlled interface in automotive environment for operating dashboard control and even driving the car itself. Our study further demonstrates that

- Eye gaze can be used to operate controls inside the car.
- Saccadic intrusions can be used to detect drivers' mental workload simultaneously with a gaze controlled interface.

Eye gaze is advantageous over existing touch based car interface in terms of the fact that users need not to take their hands of the steering wheel or the gear. In a complex track like a mountainous road, drivers may find it advantageous not to take their hands off the steering. However in the present study, drivers took 2.5 s on average to make a selection in the car dashboard which is slightly higher than the safe time interval that drivers are allowed take their eyes off from road. It may be noted that our present study involved drivers who never used gaze-controlled interface before and our previous studies demonstrated that users can undertake pointing and selection tasks in less than 2 s using gaze-controlled interface after two to three training sessions.

Regarding cognitive load measurement, previous work on saccadic intrusion considered controlled task on free viewing. Our study considered a more realistic task of operating a car dashboard while driving. It has been found that even when drivers needed to manipulate their eye gaze to operate an interface, number of saccadic intrusion and their mean amplitude are indicative o their mental workload in most cases. However, our study did not find any significant difference in pulse rate in different driving conditions.

References

1. Abadia, R.V., Gowen, E.: Characteristics of saccadic intrusions. Vis. Res. **44**(23), 2675–2690 (2004)
2. Biswas P., Langdon P.: Multimodal intelligent eye-gaze tracking system. Int. J. Hum. Comput. Interact. **31**(4), 277–294 (2015). Taylor & Francis, Print ISSN: 1044-7318
3. Poitschke, T., Laquai, F., Stamboliev S., Rigoll, G.: Gaze-based interaction on multiple displays in an automotive environment. In: IEEE International Conference on Systems, Man, and Cybernetics (SMC), pp. 543–548 (2011). ISSN: 1062-922X
4. Tokuda S., Obinata G., Palmer E., Chaparo A.: Estimation of mental workload using saccadic eye movements in a free-viewing task. In: 23rd International Conference of the IEEE EMBS, pp. 4523–4529 (2011)

Usability Evaluation of a Mobile Navigation Application for Blind Users

Márcia de Borba Campos[1]([✉]), Jaime Sánchez[2], Juliana Damasio[1],
and Tasmay Inácio[1]

[1] Faculty of Informatics (FACIN), Pontifical Catholic University of Rio Grande
do Sul (PUCRS), Porto Alegre, Brazil
marcia.campos@pucrs.br, {juliana.damasio,
tasmay.inacio}@acad.pucrs.br

[2] Department of Computer Science, Center for Advanced Research
in Education (CARE), University of Chile,
Blanco Encalada 2120, Santiago, Chile
jsanchez@dcc.uchile.cl

Abstract. This paper presents a usability evaluation of a mobile gaming
application (mAbES) for blind users. mAbES was evaluated with the participation of HCI specialists and experts in video gaming (Group 1) and mAbES
end-users who are blind (Group 2). The instruments used by Group 1 were the
audio feedback questionnaire and the usability evaluation questionnaire. It also
included questions based on video games and game mechanics. For Group 2,
both the audio evaluation and the O&M, tactile feedback and ease of use
questionnaires were applied. Semi-structured interviews were also carried out.
User perceptions and interaction behaviors identified during study and data
analysis allowed to refine the methodology used for evaluating the usability of
mAbES and proposed suggestions for improvements in the use of this application, as well as to make recommendations for developing video games for
blind users for navigation purposes.

Keywords: Users who are blind · Mental map · Orientation and mobility ·
Navigation · Mobile application · Usability evaluation

1 Introduction

This paper discusses the usability evaluation of a mobile navigation application for
people who are blind. The mobile Audio-Based Environments Simulator (mAbES) was
evaluated with the participation of HCI specialists, experts in video gaming and mA-
bES blind end-users. The evaluation included whether or not mAbES would allow the
user to recognize the Science and Technology Museum building at the Pontifical
Catholic University of Rio Grande do Sul (MCT/PUCRS) and, consequently, whether
they could move in this environment from the virtual interaction experience using
mAbES. The main research question was whether mAbES could assist a sightless user
in understanding the real space that it represents without replacing the visitation to the
museum.

© Springer International Publishing Switzerland 2015
M. Antona and C. Stephanidis (Eds.): UAHCI 2015, Part IV, LNCS 9178, pp. 117–128, 2015.
DOI: 10.1007/978-3-319-20687-5_12

Following AbES's functionality [1], mAbES is a mobile audio-haptic environments simulator to assist the refinement of orientation and mobility (O&M) skills in people who are blind. Thus, during navigation the end-user can develop O&M skills that are validated through the construction of mental maps [2]. The navigation capability is related to a person's ability to safely move from one point of origin to a destination.

Vision-based navigation is more of a perceptual process, whereas blind navigation is more cognitively demanding and often requires conscious moment-to-moment problem solving [3]. A person with visual impairment must be competent with orientation and mobility in order to achieve a solid level of navigation, including moving about safely, efficiently and agilely, as well as independently in both familiar and unfamiliar environments [4]. The learning of O&M skills includes a set of predefined techniques that blind or visually impaired children, young people and adults must practice stage by stage. However, learning such skills also involves other aspects such as training and refining perception systems and developing both conceptual and motor skills [2, 4].

Support on a perceptual and conceptual level is important for the development of orientation skills and the construction of cognitive maps [1, 2, 5]. The notion of a map refers to an internalized representation of space, a mixture of objective knowledge and subjective perception.

If real-life surroundings are represented through virtual environments, it is possible to create several training applications that allow a blind user to interact with the elements in the simulated environment during navigation [6, 7].

There are different technological resources that have been developed to aid navigation, and thus allow blind users to better understand the world around them. There are vibrating canes, tactile models, GPS-based applications, indoor environment simulators, RFID (radiofrequency identification) tags, and camera image streaming to a central server via cell phone to process unknown environmental features. There are others navigational technologies available to unseeing users that focus on large scale blind navigation, unfamiliar environments and well-known spaces, besides being potentially useful to users with low vision [3]. The mAbES software was employed including a multimodal interface integrating information feedback via audio and haptic responses. mAbES uses a gaming interaction model proposed by [8, 9] to analyze the barriers that a blind user faces when using a game. The application uses click-based interaction on a Braille matrix, which is represented on a smartphone screen.

There is a research effort towards building interactive systems that can be used autonomously by people who are blind [1–3, 5, 7–11] and that are easy and simple to use. The terms 'usability' and 'accessibility' are related and should be borne in mind along the stages of design, development and evaluation of computer applications [10]. In the mAbES usability evaluation, related accessibility issues were included.

There are different categories of usability and accessibility evaluation methods [12]:

- Automated verification of compliance with guidelines and standards
- Evaluations conducted by experts
- Evaluations using models and simulations
- Evaluations with users or potential users
- Evaluations of data collected during eSystem usage

mAbES's evaluation was conducted with Human-Computer Interaction and video gaming experts in Group 1 and users, or potential users, in Group 2. The goal of the evaluation was to verify mAbES's adequacy to usability criteria (Group 1) and to check that mAbES can help visually impaired people understand a real space that is represented in a virtual environment (Group 2).

The instruments used by Group 1 were the audio feedback questionnaire and the usability evaluation questionnaire. The former identifies the degree of understanding of audio as well as the conformity of the audios to the Brazilian specifications requirements for the description of images in the design of accessible digital material [13]. The latter includes questions that aim to gather information about the suitability of mAbES to the heuristics [14]. It also includes questions based on video games and gaming mechanics [1, 3, 8–11, 15].

For Group 2, the audio evaluation and the O&M questionnaires were applied. The first aimed at verifying if the user could be oriented in space and perceive the objects around them by hearing audio information. The second questionnaire contained questions related to O&M, tactile feedback, ease of use and user satisfaction. In addition to the questionnaires, semi-structured interviews were also carried out.

Tasks were given to the participants of the two groups. Group 1's tasks referred to the use of mAbES without the users been physically in the Museum of Science and Technology of the Pontifical Catholic University of Rio Grande do Sul. Group 2 was organized into two subgroups because some users used mAbES before as well as during the visit to the Museum, whereas others used it only during the visit to the Museum. During the tasks performance, the use of mAbES was videotaped. In the case of Group 2, the videotape served to verify the effect of the use of mAbES on users' perception of the environment, alongside with their behavior when interacting with the technology. After performing the tasks, all participants reproduced the mental map of the museum using concrete material.

Users' perception and interaction behavior identified in the study and the data analysis allowed for refining the methodology used for evaluating mAbES's usability, proposing suggestions for improvements in the use of this application and making recommendations for developing video games for people who are blind for navigation purposes. These issues, together with a description and analysis of the results of the usability evaluation, are presented and discussed in the next sections.

2   AbES

mAbES - mobile Audio-Based Environments Simulator - is a videogame based on AbES [1, 15]. AbES replicates a real, familiar or unfamiliar environment to be navigated by a person who is blind (Fig. 1). The virtual environment is made up of different elements and objects (walls, stairways, escalators, doors, toilets or elevators) through which the user can discover and become familiar with their location. AbES includes three modes of interaction: free navigation, path navigation and game mode.

The user receives audio feedback from the left, center and right side channels, and all actions are carried out through the use of a traditional keyboard, where each set of

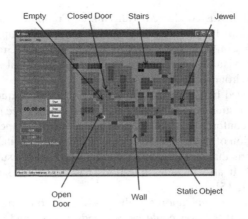

Empty   Closed Door   Stairs   Jewel

Open   Wall   Static Object
Door

Fig. 1. A screenshot of AbES (Source: Sánchez et al., 2009)

keys has different associated actions. All of the actions in the virtual environment have a particular sound associated to them.

3   mAbES

In the development of mAbES, members of the museum team took part in meetings in order to define the scope and to prioritize the functionalities of the software. Then 3 experiments were chosen: Nuclear Power Station (Fig. 2), Energy Train, and Cool House, located on the third floor of the museum.

Fig. 2. (a) Picture of nuclear power station (b) (c) screenshot of nuclear power station

Interface. mAbES is a multisensory (auditory, haptic, graphic) virtual environment simulating real-life space.

The audio interface is responsible for conveying museum information as well as information resulting from user interaction with mAbES. There are four types of audio feedback: (i) when the user collides with an object, the sound is triggered identifying this object, for example "This is an escalator". mAbES also provides an audio-description about its physical appearance, its operation and how the user should use the escalator in the real context of the museum; (ii) during navigation, there is a set of sounds associated with the objects. For example, if the user walks, the step sound cue can be heard; (iii) the instructive component has an audio description of the selected MCT-PUCRS experiments; (iv) while the user interacts with the experiments, they are presented with quizzes/challenges that must be answered.

The haptic interface consists of vibration feedback provided by the smartphone. Every time the user bumps into an object, they feel an intermittent vibration on their hand.

The Graphic Interface represents the characteristics of the museum: size, shape and position of the spaces, the selected experiments (Nuclear Power Station, Energy Train, and Cool House) and objects (escalators, walls, chairs, tables, shelves, etc.). This graphical representation allows mAbES to be used by low-level vision and sighted people alike.

Interaction. The user communicates with the software by interacting with a smartphone screen, which utilizes an array of points of the Braille system (Fig. 3). The movement of the user through the museum is achieved by using the forward button, which represents the user's individual steps. The right and left buttons are used when the user turns either direction (Fig. 4).

Fig. 3. (a) Braille matrix (b) (c) screenshot of the menu

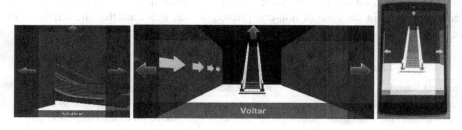

Fig. 4. (a)(b)(c) Screenshot of transitions between floors in MCT-PUCRS

When the user arrives at the third floor, mAbES presents the experiments that are mapped so that the user can choose which one they want to interact with: 1 – Nuclear Power Station, 2 – Energy Train, 3 – Cool House, 4 – Explore the space freely, 5 – More information, 6 – Exit, according to the Braille matrix. When the user comes upon any experiment (Nuclear Power Station, Energy Train, Cool House), mAbES informs the user by naming the object or experiment, and the options or quizzes/challenges that are available to the user. Information on the museum or the experiments is available to the user in audio format. The options for hearing the audio cues are: 1 – Play, 2 – Pause, 3 – Increase speed, 4 – Go back, 5 – Go forward, 6 – Help.

4 METHOD

4.1 Sample

- Group 1: an intentional sample was selected, made up of 3 HCI specialists and 2 experts in video gaming for blind users.
- Group 2: the sample selected for the use with mAbES was made up of 6 learners (3 female; 3 male), of which 2 are between 10 and 14 years old and 2 are between 20 and 36 years old. The 2 remaining users are 44 years old. Across the entire sample, 5 learners were totally blind and 1 person had low vision. All of them were legally blind. This sample was divided into 2 subgroups of 3 users. Subgroup 1 visited MCT without having used mAbES beforehand. Subgroup 2 used mAbES before visiting the museum. The requirement to participate was to not be acquainted with the Museum of Science and Technology, of the Pontifical Catholic University of Rio Grande do Sul.

4.2 Instruments

Sound Evaluation Instrument. Assessment of sound information occurred in two stages: (i) by the authors of this work and (ii) with the participants of Group 1 and Group 2.

The authors of this study evaluated mAbES's sounds from the Technical Note [13]. The authors assessed whether the sounds used in mAbES met the specifications of the Technical Note. In the case of non-compliance, it was indicated that the requirement was not fulfilled and a sound transcription was suggested (Table 1).

Table 1. Example of the comparison between mAbES's sounds

Original Sound	Requirements	Sound suggestion
You are on the second floor. To move up to the third floor, you must use the escalator, which is a few steps ahead.	2	You are on the second floor. To move up to the third floor, you must use the escalator, which is six steps ahead.
This is a counter.	3, 13	This is a white counter 88 cm high.

Of the 156 sounds in mAbES, 30 did not meet what is specified in the Technical Note. Afterwards, a selection was made to discard sounds that referred to the same unmet requirement. Finally, 16 sounds were selected to compose the audio test instrument with the participants in Group 1 and Group 2.

In the second stage, the participants in groups 1 and 2 evaluated the sounds. The instrument contained the identification of the sound cue, the number of times it was run by the user (so as to indicate their preference for the original or the suggested version) and an optional field to include comments on each sound.

Usability Evaluation Tool. Usability evaluation instruments for groups 1 and 2 were based on [1, 11].

- Group 1: 35 questions, of which 28 were based on ten Usability Heuristics for User Interface Design [14], 4 were related to the haptic interface and 3 referred to the sound interface.
- Group 2: 22 closed questions, of which 1 was related to menus, 3 were related to the sound interface, 4 were related to the haptic interface, 2 were related to the graphical interface, 7 were related to ease of use, 1 was related to the Braille matrix and 4 were related to satisfaction. It also had 5 open questions associated with ease of use and user satisfaction.

Evaluation Tool for Orientation and Mobility (O&M). After using mAbES, participants in both groups had to draw the museum's environment. In Group 2, a sheet of paper was used on synthetic foam to enable the drawing to be traced for touch recognition.

4.3 Procedure

Evaluation of Sound Interface. In the evaluation of audio, Group 1 heard the original audio and the audio suggested for each selected sound in mAbES. During execution, they replied to the sound assessment questionnaire.

For respondents in Group 2, the procedure differed in completing the questionnaire, which was conducted with the aid of the authors of this work. The Technical Note [13] was made available in Braille for use as reference.

Usability Evaluation - Orientation and Mobility Evaluation. Participants in Group 1 and Group 2 were explained what mAbES is and the context in which it appears. The application can be used without time restriction.

- Group 1: after using mAbES freely, users drew the museum's environment and gave answers to the usability evaluation tool.
- Group 2: they received the following task: *You are on the ground floor of the museum, near the entrance. You should go to the third floor, and explore the Nuclear Power Station experiment. Afterwards, you should explore the Cool House experiment. In Nuclear Power Station, you should hear the information and respond to challenges. In Cool House, you should come in and see what's in the room.*

– Subgroup 1 used mAbES directly at the museum, without having previously used the software. Then they answered the usability evaluation tool and made the graphic representation of the environment they had visited.
– Subgroup 2 used mAbES and answered the usability evaluation tool and graphically represented the environment of the museum. Only then did they visit the Museum and later they should confirm their answers and, once again, draw their graphic representation. Users in Group 2 (Subgroup 1 and Subgroup 2) were allowed to use headphones during the test, in which case they were to report out loud what happened while moving about with mAbES (Fig. 5).

Fig. 5. A user who is blind interacting with mAbES

5 Results

Evaluation of Sound Interface.

• Group 1: considering the 3 experts in HCI, only one participant chose a set of 5 original sounds instead of their suggestions. The other experts preferred the suggested versions. All experts in video games preferred the suggested sounds. According to their accounts, the option suggested by the sounds was compliant with [13], by which objects are thoroughly detailed.
• Group 2: despite having a strong preference for suggested sound (71 %) in place of the original sound (29 %), according to participants, compliance with the Technical Note [13] made some sounds have excessive information.

Usability Evaluation. For data analysis, the categories 'Strongly agree' and 'Partly agree' were grouped into 'Agree' and the categories 'Strongly disagree' and 'Partly disagree' were grouped into 'Disagree'.

• Group 1: the instrument was organized considering the ten Usability Heuristics for User Interface Design [14], the sound interface and the haptic interface. The result can be seen in Table 2.

Table 2. Usability evaluation – group 1

Category	Questions	Agree	Disagree
Usability heuristics	28	63.5 %	36.5 %
- Visibility of system status	3	53.3 %	46.7 %
- Match between system and the real world	4	85 %	15 %
- User control and freedom	3	26.6 %	73.3 %
- Consistency and standards	2	90 %	10 %
- Error prevention	2	20 %	80 %
- Recognition rather than recall	3	86.7 %	13.3 %
- Flexibility and efficiency of use	3	66.7 %	33.3 %
- Aesthetics and minimalist design	2	80 %	20 %
- Aid in recognizing, diagnosing, and recovering from errors	3	60 %	40 %
- Help and documentation	3	66.7 %	33.3 %
Sound interface	3	86.7 %	13.3 %
Haptic interface	4	100 %	0 %

- Group 2: out of the total of 57 questions, Subgroup 1 agreed with 88.2 % and disagreed with 8.5 %. They were neutral about 3.3 % of the questions. With regard to Subgroup 2, there were differences between pre-test and post-test:
  - Pre-test: 80.3 % agree, 10.8 % disagree and 8.9 % neutral.
  - Post-test: 82.5 % agree, 10.5 % disagree and 7 % neutral.

The answers to the open questions, along with observing mAbES use and the visit to the museum, allowed for a few remarks:

- Rotation: the turns are made based on the hours on a clock. Thus, a 90° rotation requires 3 clicks on the right button. This similarity should be more strongly emphasized.
- Graphical interface: the information should be adjustable and customizable to enable the user to obtain more information on the Museum.
- Haptic feedback: it should be adjustable to the user's preferences. Research has shown that this feature was more useful during the first interactions. After them, users have grasped more from the sound information.
- Help system: it should be contextual to help the user depending on their current virtual location in the museum as well as on the challenges that require responses.
- Routes: when the user leaves an expected route, the application should provide support so that they could recognize the environment and return to the desired point.
- User position: mAbES needs a resource to indicate the user's location in the virtual museum space and should provide information so that they could recognize the space around themselves.

Orientation and Mobility Evaluation.

- Group 1: users were able to understand the Museum space from the use of mAbES and reproduce it in different ways (Fig. 6).

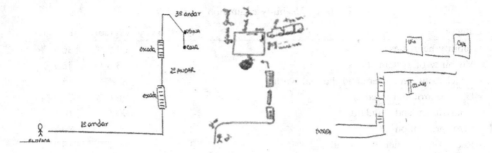

Fig. 6. (a) Representation of museum space by the authors (b)(c) group 1: examples of museum representations.

- Group 2: the majority of participants had no experience in drawing (Fig. 7 Subgroup 1 and Fig. 8 Subgroup 2). Participants of Subgroup 2 could refine their understanding of space when using mAbES before making the visit to the museum (Fig. 8).

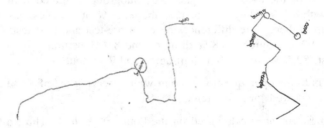

Fig. 7. (a)(b)(c) Group 2 – subgroup 1: examples of museum representations

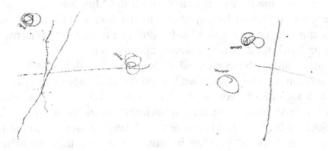

Fig. 8. (a)(b) Group 2 – subgroup 2: drawings made during pre- and post-test stages

Considerations for the Development of Applications to Support Navigation to Users who are Blind. This work allowed making a few suggestions, which may be considered when designing applications for blind users:

- Use of audio cues to describe the images and spaces that are represented in the application.
- Enable control of the user to monitor sound and haptic information.
- Add a contextual help system that can help the user recognize the space in which they are as well as the activities that must be carried out.
- Prevent error that can be triggered when the user performs an action not expected by the software.
- Prioritize sound information over detailing the graphical interface.
- Maintain a standard throughout the actions expected by the user with regard to interacting with the software.

6   Conclusion and Future Work

This paper deals about usability evaluation of a mobile navigation application for users who are blind: mAbES. The evaluation of mAbES was carried out with experts in Human-Computer Interaction and in video gaming (Group 1) and users or potential users (Group 2). Group 1 indicated that mAbES conforms to most usability criteria defined by Nielsen [14].

Group 2 had participants who had never drawn and still been able to establish spatial relationships between the experiments and the space they occupy in the museum. Usage of mAbES before the visit allowed users to explore the museum more autonomously and safely.

Groups 1 and 2 also indicated that most of the original mAbES sounds did not meet that which is specified in the Technical Note [13]. They approved the suggested sounds.

The results obtained regarding O&M skills in blind users who interacted with mAbES demonstrated the positive impact of the software on such skills. Users who are blind understand the space of the museum and interact with the environment based on their use of the software.

This research also collaborates with the design and development of similar applications, and it makes suggestions and precautions that should be considered for users who are blind to better use a system based on sound, haptic and graphic interfaces.

Acknowledgments. This work was supported by the Program STIC-AmSud-CAPES/CONICYT/ MAEE, Project KIGB-Knowing and Interacting while Gaming for the Blind, 2014. It was also supported by the Museum of Science and Technology, of the Pontifical Catholic University of Rio Grande do Sul, Porto Alegre, Brazil (MCT-PUCRS).

References

1. Sánchez, J., Tadres, A., Pascual-Leone, A., Merabet, L. Blind children navigation through gaming and associated brain plasticity. In: Proceedings of the Virtual Rehabilitation 2009 International Conference, pp. 29–36. IEEE, Haifa, Israel (2009)

2. Mioduser, D., Lahav, O.: Blind persons' acquisition of spatial cognitive mapping and orientation skills supported by virtual environment. Int. J. Disabil. Hum. Dev. **4**(3), 231–238 (2005)

3. Giudice, N.A., Legge, G.E.: Blind navigation and the role of technology. In: Helal, A., Mokhtari, M., Abdulrazak, B. (eds.) Engineering Handbook of Smart Technology for Aging, Disability, and Independence, pp. 479–500. John Wiley & Sons, New York (2008)

4. Hill, E., Ponder, P.: Orientación y técnicas de Movilidad, Una guía para el practicante. Comité internacional pro-ciegos, México (1981)

5. Lahav, O., Mioduser, D.: Haptic-feedback support for cognitive mapping of unknown spaces by people who are blind. Int. J. Hum Comput Stud. **66**(1), 23–35 (2008)

6. Sánchez, J., Maureira, E.: Subway mobility assistance tools for blind users. In: Stephanidis, C., Pieper, M. (eds.) ERCIM Ws UI4ALL 2006. LNCS, vol. 4397, pp. 386–404. Springer, Heidelberg (2007)

7. Sánchez, J., Oyarzún, C.: Mobile audio assistance in bus transportation for the blind. Int. J. Disabil. Hum. Dev. (IJDHD) **10**(4), 365–371 (2011)

8. Connors, E.C., Yazzolino, L.A., Sánchez, J., Merabet, L.B.: Development of a audio-based virtual gaming environment to assist with navigation skills in the blind. J. Vis. Exp. **73**, e50272 (2014). http://www.ncbi.nlm.nih.gov/pmc/articles/PMC3641639/pdf/nihms546296. pdf

9. Yuan, B., Folmer, E., Harris Jr., F.C.: Game accessibility: a survey. In: Yuan, B., Folmer, E., Harris Jr., F.C. (eds.) Universal Access in the Information Society, vol. 10(1), pp. 81–100. Springer, Heidelberg (2011)

10. Stephanidis, C.: User interfaces for all: new perspectives into human-computer interaction. In: Stephanidis, C. (ed.) User Interfaces for All - Concepts, Methods, and Tools, pp. 3–17. Lawrence Erlbaum Associates, Mahwah, NJ (2001)

11. Sánchez, J., Campos, M.B., Espinoza, M.: Multimodal gaming for navigation skills in players who are blind. In: XIII Brazilian Symposium on Human Factors in Computer Systems. SBC (2014)

12. Petrie H., Bevan, N.: The evaluation of accessibility, usability and user experience. In: The Universal Access Handbook, Stepanidis, C. (ed.). CRC Press (2009)

13. BRASIL. Ministério Da Educação. Nota Técnica nº 21 / 2012 / MEC / SECADI /DPEE. Orientações para descrição de imagem na geração de material digital acessível – Mecdaisy (2012)

14. Nielsen, J.: Usability Engineering, p. 362. Elsevier, California (1993)

15. Sánchez, J., Sáenz, M., Pascual-Leone, A., Merabet, L.: Enhancing navigation skills through audio gaming. In: Proceedings of CHI EA 2010, pp. 3991–3996. ACM, New York, USA (2010)

Feature Detection Applied to Context-Aware Blind Guidance Support

Hugo Fernandes$^{(\boxtimes)}$, André Sousa, Hugo Paredes, Vitor Filipe,
and João Barroso

INESC TEC and Universidade de Trás-os-Montes e Alto Douro,
Vila Real, Portugal
{hugof,andresousa,hparedes,vfilipe,jbarroso}@utad.pt

Abstract. Human beings have developed a number of evolutionary mechanisms that allows the distinction between different objects and the triggering of events based on their perception of reality. Visual impairment has a significant impact on individuals' quality of life, including their ability to work and to develop personal relationships as they often feel cut off people and things around them, due to their impairment. The need for assistive technologies has long been a constant in the daily lives of people with visual impairments, and will remain a constant in future years. Cognitive mapping is of extreme importance for individuals in terms of creating a conceptual model of the surrounding space and objects around them, thereby supporting their interaction with the physical environment. This work describes the use of computer vision techniques, namely feature detectors and descriptors, to detect objects in the scene and help contextualize the user within the surrounding space, enhancing their mobility, navigation and cognitive mapping of a new environment.

Keywords: Computer vision · Feature detection · Blind · Navigation · Orientation

1 Introduction

From the overall population with visual impairment, about 90 % of the world's visually impaired live in developing countries and 82 % of people living with blindness are aged 50 year old and above. Regrettably, this percentage is expected to increase in the coming decades. Visual impairment has a significant impact on individuals' quality of life, including their ability to work and to develop personal relationships. Almost half (48 %) of the visually impaired feel "moderately" or "completely" cut off from people and things around them [1].

In order to overcome or lessen the difficulties posed by visual impairment, extensive research has been dedicated into building assistive systems. The need for assistive technologies has long been a constant in the daily lives of people with visual impairment, and will remain a constant in future years. Traditional assistive technologies for the blind include white canes, guide dogs, screen readers, and so forth. Modern mobile assistive technologies are becoming more discrete and include (or are delivered via) a wide range of mobile computerized devices, including ubiquitous

© Springer International Publishing Switzerland 2015
M. Antona and C. Stephanidis (Eds.): UAHCI 2015, Part IV, LNCS 9178, pp. 129–138, 2015.
DOI: 10.1007/978-3-319-20687-5_13

technologies like mobile phones. Such discrete technologies can help alleviate the cultural stigma associated with the more traditional (and noticeable) assistive devices [2].

Human beings have the ability of acquiring and using information obtained from the surrounding environment using their natural sensors. They have developed a number of evolutionary mechanisms that allows the distinction between different objects and the triggering of events and complex processes based on their perception of reality. Recently, systems have been developed which use Computer Vision techniques, like pattern matching, to sense the surrounding environment and detect visual landmarks.

Human beings are able to recognize objects without much effort, despite variations in scale, position and light conditions. However, to emulate this detection and recognition with electronic devices is still a major challenge.

In this paper we present the use of computer vision techniques, namely feature detectors and descriptors, to detect objects in the scene and help contextualize the user within the surrounding space, enhancing their mobility, navigation and cognitive mapping of a new environment. Section 2 presents related work and how work enhances previous developments in this field by the research team at the University of Trás-os-Montes and Alto Douro. Section 3 describes the feature detectors used in this work. In Sect. 4 exposes the testing methodology and environment setup. Section 5 shows the results of the study and, finally, Sect. 6 presents some discussion regarding the results found.

2 Related Work

To address the task of finding the user location in indoor environments several techniques and technologies have been used such as sonar, radio signal triangulation, radio signal (beacon) emitters, or signal fingerprinting. All these technologies can be, and have been, used to develop systems that help enhancing the personal space range of blind or visually impaired users [3].

In recent years some research teams [4–6] have developed navigation systems based on this technology. In the case of outdoor environments, some hybrid systems have been proposed that use GPS as the main information source and use RFID for correction and minimization of the location error. In the last few years, the research team at the University of Trás-os-Montes e Alto Douro (UTAD) has given major focus to visual impairment and on how existing technology may help in everyday life applications. From an extensive review of the state of the art and its best practices, three main projects have been developed: the SmartVision [7], Nav4B [8] and Blavigator [9] projects.

The new prototype, developed by the Blavigator project is built with the same modular structure as the SmartVision project. The Blavigator project aimed at creating a small, cheap and portable device that included all the features of the SmartVision prototype, with added performance optimization. In the last optimization of the Computer Vision module of the Blavigator prototype, this module has been developed to work in conjunction with the Location Module [10]. In a known location, the use of object recognition algorithms can provide contextual feedback to the user and even serve as a validator to the positioning and information system modules of a navigation system for the visually impaired.

Based on the previous work described, this paper proposes a method where the use of computer vision algorithms validates the outputs of the positioning system through the use of feature detectors. For this purpose, an analysis of the performance of feature detectors is made as well.

3 Feature Detection

Lately, robust object recognition is a topic of major focus on computer vision. Many researchers have worked for many years to understand how to achieve this goal. Humans can see, detect, recognize and categorize objects in the real world with relative ease. However, this is not an easy task using computer vision.

Many recognition applications are only intended to recognize objects in predefined positions and orientations. However, parts of objects can be of different geometric structure, color, or even hidden. Thus, objects can be viewed from different points of view and even at different scales. The environment or the object itself may cause the occlusion. An object like a book can be hidden in the middle of many others or the facade of a building can have some of its parts hidden by shadow. This additional data should be discarded because it does not help in the recognition of the objects. Recognizing a building or a book cover in different perspectives is a very difficult task using computer vision.

Keypoints are used very often in computer vision, including for object recognition. The term keypoints (characteristic points) generally refers to the set of points that are used to describe certain patterns. The most common approach to detect and recognize objects using keypoints is divided in three steps:

- Detect the keypoints in the image;
- Describe the region surrounding the keypoints;
- Use a method to compare the descriptors (like distance, or similar).

In recent years, various methods have been developed to allow the search of invariant properties that do not differ according to different conditions such as scaling, rotation, and illumination changes. Scale-invariant detectors select regions in places of significance in the image with a corresponding scale parameter, representing the size of the region. Hence, process complexity is reduced because only a limited number of regions remain that are considered as important characteristics.

In order to use the identified characteristic points, the immediate vicinity needs be described in an efficient and compact manner, in order to combine them with similar patterns in other images. A descriptor is used to construct a description of the neighborhood of feature points. The combination of keypoint detectors with feature descriptors enables the robust representation of objects. This article aims to study the performance of detectors and descriptors such as ORB, FREAK, BRISK, BRIEF, STAR, FAST and GTFF for certain classes of objects in order to identify those that behave better, depending on its class.

SURF (Speeded Up Robust Feature) was presented by Herbert Bay in 2006, and can be used in object recognition and 3D reconstruction. It is partly inspired by the SIFT and several times faster, being based on sums of "2D Haar wavelet" making an efficient use of "integral images". SURF cannot be used for commercial purposes without permission of the patent holder [11]. STAR (Solenoidal Tracker at RHIC) derived from CenSurE (Center Surrounded Extreme), uses polygons such as squares, pentagons and hexagons as alternatives computationally less expensive than circles [12]. FAST (Features from Accelerated Segment Test) is a fast detector and an ideal corner detection algorithm for real-time processing. However, it usually detects too many features. For not being selective it is very likely that the selected features are not optimal and are found adjacent to each other [13].

Consequently, after the detection of keypoints, it is necessary to describe them. To this end, descriptors are used. The descriptors analyzed in this work were BRISK, BRIEF, ORB and FREAK, respectively.

BRISK (Binary Robust Invariant Scalable Keypoints) presents an alternative to SIFT and SURF, maintaining the robustness and speed [14]. According to the authors, the key to this speed is the implementation of a detector based on scalable FAST in combination with a "binary string" descriptor, from comparisons obtained from each neighbor sample point of interest. BRIEF (Binary Robust Independent Elementary Features) reduces the size of points of interest, converting them into "binary strings", without having to first obtain the descriptors [15]. For example, when SIFT uses a vector of size 128, all these elements may not be necessary for the "matching" of the descriptors. Thus, these points can be converted to "binary strings" which are very efficient to make the "matching" using the "Hamming" distance which basically uses XOR instructions and processor "bit count". These instructions are extremely fast on processors equipped with SSE instructions. Therefore, BRIEF is an algorithm that uses little memory and is more efficient than descriptors using higher dimensions. ORB (Oriented FAST and Rotated BRIEF) has been proposed as a computationally efficient substitute to SIFT, having a similar performance. ORB is less affected by noise, and can be used for real-time performance [16]. The purpose of this technique is to enable low power devices without GPU acceleration to perform panorama stitching, patch tracking and reduce the detection time of objects. ORB has similar performance to SIFT and better than SURF. ORB is based on the FAST detector and uses BRIEF in regards to recognition. Both technics have good performance and low processing costs. FREAK (Fast Retina Keypoint) consists of a cascade of binary sequences, which are efficiently calculated by comparing pairs of image intensities over a retina-sampling pattern. Interestingly, the selection of pairs to reduce the size of the descriptor produces a highly structured search pattern that mimics the human eye [17].

The techniques in which this study was based for the detection and object recognition were: BRIEF, ORB, BRISK and FREAK. The SURF detector is used together with the BRIEF, BRISK and FREAK descriptors. The ORB detector descriptor is used with ORB as, compared with other descriptors, requires information about the orientation of the keypoints. Moreover, according to the evaluation of Heinly et al. [18], the combined use of the detector and descriptor ORB/ORB exceeded the use of SURF/ORB in most cases. On the other hand, SURF keypoints are invariant to rotation and scaling, being suitable to be used with the BRISK and FREAK descriptors. The authors of the BRIEF [15] confirm the use of SURF as detector.

4   Testing Methodology and Environment Setup

The implementation of any of the methods mentioned in the previous section is similar to each other, according to the aforementioned three essential steps, namely: the detection of feature points, a description of each region around that point as a feature vector using a descriptor, and finally, using a function that allows the comparison of descriptors in order to perform the matching.

Figure 1 illustrates the methodology used to detect and recognize the objects.

The application was developed in Java programming language using the Eclipse IDE and the OpenCV 2.4.9 library for the Android operating system. All methods implemented had the same kind of input images in order to ensure consistency in the comparisons. The only difference was in the feature comparison methods. The methods used were: ORB/ORB, STAR/ORB and ORB/BRIEF. The FAST detector, although recommended for use in real-time applications, in our experiments showed a less acceptable performance due to excessive amount of detected characteristic points, which consequently requires a high processing time.

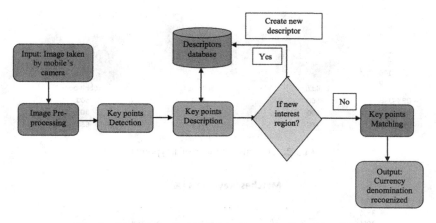

Fig. 1. Flowchart of object detection and recognition [19]

5   Results

The evaluation method used consisted of evaluating three parameters in the processed data: the number of keypoints, the accuracy of matches and processing time (in milliseconds). For this purpose we used a set of 17 images, wherein 13 of them are part of the dataset of Oxford Buildings (Block I and Block C) [20]. The remaining images used are from cover of the book The Hobbit. In these tests, the mobile device used was a Wiko Gateway with camera resolution of 800 × 600 pixels and a Cortex-A7 1.3 GHz quad-core processor.

Figure 2 represents the average number of keypoints for each set of detectors and descriptors used, in particular ORB-ORB, ORB-BRIEF and STAR-ORB. The results show that the ORB detector detects 500 feature points, which is acceptable for processing in smartphones. The STAR detector finds about 700 points, on average, which can be excessive sometimes. Figure 3 represents the ratio (measured in percentage) between the matches and the total number of keypoints detected. The graphic shows that the combination BRIEF-ORB (detector and descriptor) is the one that features better performance, unlike the combination STAR-ORB which cannot match them as efficiently, even after detecting the characteristic points. Finally, Fig. 4 represents the processing time measured in milliseconds. The results show that the STAR-ORB combination has an excessive processing time to be used in mobile applications (about 1050 ms). Since the objective of the implementation is to detect and recognize objects in real time on a mobile device, this is not appropriate to the context. With regard to ORB-ORB and ORB-BRIEF detectors and descriptors it is possible to infer that, in addition to the processing time of the methods ORB-BRIEF being shorter (about 550 ms), they have better accuracy in the matching. Thus, the detector and descriptor chosen for testing in this environment is ORB-BRIEF.

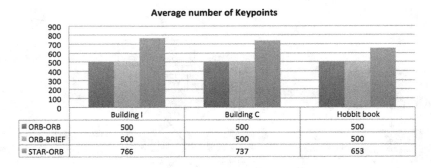

Average number of Keypoints

	Building I	Building C	Hobbit book
ORB-ORB	500	500	500
ORB-BRIEF	500	500	500
STAR-ORB	766	737	653

Fig. 2. Average number of keypoints

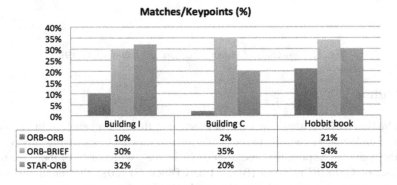

Matches/Keypoints (%)

	Building I	Building C	Hobbit book
ORB-ORB	10%	2%	21%
ORB-BRIEF	30%	35%	34%
STAR-ORB	32%	20%	30%

Fig. 3. Matches/keypoints ratio

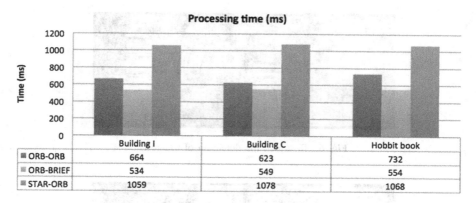

Processing time (ms)

	Building I	Building C	Hobbit book
■ ORB-ORB	664	623	732
▨ ORB-BRIEF	534	549	554
▤ STAR-ORB	1059	1078	1068

Fig. 4. Processing times

After choosing the detector and descriptor, the application was tested to determine if the ORB- BRIEF method is able to detect a set of buildings from the Oxford Buildings DataSet. For this purpose, we used a set of 10 images $(I_1, I_2,..., I_{10})$ of the same building and 15 images $(B_1, B_2,..., B_5, C_1, C_2,..., C_5, D_1, D_2,..., D_5)$ of another three different buildings.

The tests were performed with the mobile device mentioned above. The purpose of the tests was to measure the method performance in recognizing the building in the image. To this purpose, we used a configurable reference value, which allows deciding if the building is the same in both images (true match). This value was determined empirically after a few tests. In our implementation a building is set as found if the number of matches exceeds the value 15.

In Figs. 5, 6 and 7 are shown the overall results of the tests.

It can be seen that there are some critical cases in which, even if the building in the image is not the correct one, there are more matches than normal, particularly in the case of images C_5 (Fig. 7). On the other hand, in the case of image I_3 (Fig. 6) the number of matches is not sufficient to recognize the building, even though the building is the correct one. According to the tests made, the study showed a success rate of 96 %, with only one false negative, in image I_3.

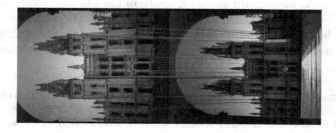

Fig. 5. Result of the detection of image I_8

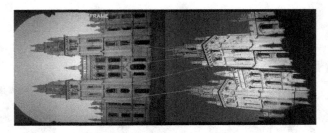

Fig. 6. Result of the detection of image I_3

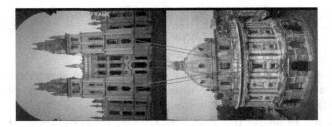

Fig. 7. Result of the detection of image C_5

6   Discussion

From the results obtained it can be seen that the best methods to be used in mobile devices are: ORB, BRISK, BRIEF and FREAK. The work developed was based on the ORB and BRIEF descriptors. The results of these two methods are identical, yet BRIEF shows a slight improvement in the matching of keypoints and processing time which, depending on the situation, may be relevant. Another important factor is the camera resolution. In the case of very small resolutions, the results will not be satisfactory because the image has poor quality. In this case, the response time is relatively small. If the camera resolution is too high, the results are more accurate, but the response time is also increased. Thus, the resolution to use is also a factor to be considered in order to find the best compromise between quality and processing time.

As future work, we intended to use the results of this study in order to enhance the development of the Blavigator system that allows the orientation and navigation of people inside buildings that users are unaware of by identifying natural elements, such as stairs, elevators, ATM, etc. This system is specially developed for people with visual impairments.

Acknowledgements. This work is financed by the FCT – Fundação para a Ciência e a Tecnologia (Portuguese Foundation for Science and Technology) within projects UID/EEA/50014/2013 and UTAP-EXPL/EEI-SII/0043/2014, and research grants SFRH/BD/89759/2012 and SFRH/BD/87259/2012.

References

1. Hakobyan, L., Lumsden, J., O'Sullivan, D., Bartlett, H.: Mobile assistive technologies for the visually impaired. Surv. Ophthalmol. **58**(6), 513–528 (2013)
2. Thomas Pocklington Trust: Research findings no 4: helping people with sight loss in their homes: housing-related assistive technology (2003). http://www.pocklington-trust.org.uk/research/publications/rf4. Accessed 23 November 2014
3. Strumillo, P.: Electronic interfaces aiding the visually impaired in environmental access, mobility and navigation. In: 3rd Conference on Human System Interactions (HSI), pp. 17–24 (2010)
4. Chumkamon, S., Tuvaphanthaphiphat, P., Keeratiwintakorn, P.: A blind navigation system using RFID for indoor environments. In: 5th International Conference on in Electrical Engineering/Electronics, Computer, Telecommunications and Information Technology, Thailand, vol. 2, pp. 765–768 (2008)
5. Willis, S., Helal, S.: RFID information grid for blind navigational and wayfinding. In: Proceedings of the 9th IEEE International Symposium on Wearable Computers, Osaka, pp. 34–37 (2005)
6. D'Atri, E., Medaglia, C., Panizzi, E., D'Atri, A.: A system to aid blind people in the mobility: a usability test and its results. In: Proceedings of the Second International Conference on Systems, Martinique, p. 35 (2007)
7. Fernandes, H., du Buf, J., Rodrigues, J.M.F., Barroso, J., Paredes, H., Farrajota, M., José, J.: The smartvision navigation prototype for blind users. J. Digit. Content Technol. Appl. **5**(5), 351–361 (2011)
8. Fernandes, H., Faria, J., Paredes, H., Barroso, J.: An integrated system for blind day-to-day life autonomy. In: The Proceedings of the 13th International ACM SIGACCESS Conference on Computers and Accessibility, Dundee, Scotland, UK (2011)
9. Fernandes, H., Adão, T., Magalhães, L., Paredes, H., Barroso, J.: Navigation module of blavigator prototype. In: Proceedings of the World Automation Congress, World Automation Congress 2012, Puerto Vallarta (2012)
10. Fernandes, H., Costa, P., Paredes, H., Filipe, V., Barroso, J.: Integrating computer vision object recognition with location based services for the blind. In: Stephanidis, C., Antona, M. (eds.) UAHCI 2014, Part III. LNCS, vol. 8515, pp. 493–500. Springer, Heidelberg (2014)
11. Bay, H., Tuytelaars, T., Van Gool, L.: SURF: speeded up robust features. In: Leonardis, A., Bischof, H., Pinz, A. (eds.) ECCV 2006, Part I. LNCS, vol. 3951, pp. 404–417. Springer, Heidelberg (2006)
12. Agrawal, M., Konolige, K., Blas, M.R.: CenSurE: center surround extremas for realtime feature detection and matching. In: Forsyth, D., Torr, P., Zisserman, A. (eds.) ECCV 2008, Part IV. LNCS, vol. 5305, pp. 102–115. Springer, Heidelberg (2008)
13. Rosten, E., Drummond, T.: Fusing points and lines for high performance tracking. In: Tenth IEEE International Conference on Computer Vision, ICCV 2005, vol. 2, pp. 1508–1515 (2005)
14. Leutenegger, S., Chli, M., Siegwart, R.Y.: Brisk: binary robust invariant scalable keypoints. In: IEEE International Conference on Computer Vision (ICCV), pp. 2548–2555 (2011)
15. Calonder, M., Lepetit, V., Strecha, C., Fua, P.: BRIEF: binary robust independent elementary features. In: Daniilidis, K., Maragos, P., Paragios, N. (eds.) ECCV 2010, Part IV. LNCS, vol. 6314, pp. 778–792. Springer, Heidelberg (2010)
16. Rublee, E., Rabaud, V., Konolige, K., Bradski, G.: Orb: an efficient alternative to sift or surf. In: 2011 IEEE International Conference on Computer Vision (ICCV), pp. 2564–2571

17. Alahi, A., Ortiz, R., Vandergheynst, P.: Freak: fast retina keypoint. In: IEEE Conference on Computer Vision and Pattern Recognition (CVPR), pp: 510–517 (2012)
18. Heinly, J., Dunn, E., Frahm, J.-M.: Comparative evaluation of binary features. In: Fitzgibbon, A., Lazebnik, S., Perona, P., Sato, Y., Schmid, C. (eds.) ECCV 2012, Part II. LNCS, vol. 7573, pp. 759–773. Springer, Heidelberg (2012)
19. Mulmule, D., Dravid, A.: A study of computer vision techniques for currency recognition on mobile phone for the visually impaired. Int. J. Adv. Res. Comput. Sci. Softw. Eng. 4(11), 160–165 (2014)
20. Philbin, J., Arandjelović, R., Zisserman, A.: Oxford Buildings Dataset (2015). http://www.robots.ox.ac.uk/~vgg/data/oxbuildings/. Accessed March 2015

Creating Inclusive HMI Concepts for Future Cars Using Visual Scenario Storyboards Through Design Ethnography

Merih Kunur[1]([✉]), Patrick Langdon[1], Michael Bradley[1],
Jo-Anne Bichard[2], Emilie Glazer[2], Fionnuala Doran[2],
P. John Clarkson[1], and Jean Jacques Loeillet[3]

[1] Engineering Design Centre, Department of Engineering,
University of Cambridge, Trumpington Street, Cambridge CB2 1PZ, UK
{mk831, mdb54}@cam.ac.uk, {pml24, pjcl0}@eng.cam.ac.uk
[2] Helen Hamlyn Centre for Design, Royal College of Art, Kensington Gore,
London SW7 2EU, UK
jo-anne.bichard@rca.ac.uk, emilie.glazer@gmail.com,
fionnuala.doran@network.rca.ac.uk
[3] Jaguar Land Rover, Human Machine Interface, HMI Project, International
Digital Lab, University of Warwick, Coventry CV4 7AL, UK
jloeille@jaguarlandrover.com

Abstract. His paper illustrates the use of scenario writing and storyboard visualisation methods based on ethnographic study of diverse personas, narratives, and user experience to guide automotive engineers and designers for creating innovative ideas and developing inclusive Human Machine Interface (iHMI) concepts for future cars in 2025 and beyond. This paper documents the importance of continuing visual research process based on anthropological case studies that looked into diverse persona, cultural and geographical attributes. These methods are used to visually analyse situational car use, thereby leading to scenario-based HMI tasks that can be applied to generate innovative user oriented future car designs. Storyboard visualisation of narratives is a method that derives from ethnographic interviews with strategically chosen car users from around the world. This is a powerful tool for analyzing situations, describing feelings, and evaluating the usability of functions within the car. With this visual process, future scenarios can be drawn in order to create new and inclusive HMI ideas and design concepts embedded within the storyboards to help engineers and designers' to understand users' different needs, exploring their expectations, emotions and motivations. The realistic details on the character illustrations of each persona are essential for better understanding of the users' including older people, the visually impaired and wheelchair users, child and parent, technophobic or technophile persons. Each HMI concept can be sketched as required in task sequences, with detail and scaled paper model produced for detailed step-by-step design. The required interactions can be observed, photographed and captured on video for in-depth design thinking workshops. A series of HMI working design concepts for future cars will emerge from this pipeline for prototyping and engineering.

© Springer International Publishing Switzerland 2015
M. Antona and C. Stephanidis (Eds.): UAHCI 2015, Part IV, LNCS 9178, pp. 139–149, 2015.
DOI: 10.1007/978-3-319-20687-5_14

Keywords: Human machine interface · Inclusive design · Visual narrative · Scenario storyboards · Concept visualization · Design thinking · User research · User-Centred design · Design ethnography

1   Introduction

The exploration of creative and realistic inclusive Human Machine Interface (iHMI) ideas for future cars requires an understanding of how people around the world drive, travel and use cars of today. Tools of scenario visualization based on ethnographic studies on diverse personas, narratives, and user experience are proven to be beneficial for automotive engineers and designers for creating innovative ideas and developing realistic automotive iHMI concepts. We examine how specific car models could accommodate drivers and passengers who have varying physical, mental and cognitive abilities, as well as varying in their age, gender and culture. Ethnographic research investigates real people with different experiences, lifestyles and needs. Visual representation of such ethnographic findings provides a good understanding of users' behavioural patterns to the designer. Personas set in scenarios (environments and situations) within the context of the persona's response are used in the design process to represent user archetypes.

Rapid growth in population ageing increasingly requires the inclusion of participants from older age groups as well as disabled and less-abled users in the design process. This rise in activity and profile has been catalysed in part by the ten year i~design programme of research (2000–2010) funded by the EPSRC and led by Cambridge University's Engineering Design Centre (EDC) in partnership with the Helen Hamlyn Centre for Design at the Royal College of Art. Scenarios set out for the research are benefiting from the experience of i~design 3 project that has promoted active living through more inclusive design [1].

Inclusive design does not imply that one product fits all nor that there is not a need for specialist products and services for those with particular capability loss or losses. It does however provide an approach to ensure that the accessibility of a designed product or service is maximised, with the attendant reduction in requirements for specialised adaptation and increase in uptake of use.

The need for inclusive design is increasing in an ageing developed world due to the relationship between ageing and capability loss. Currently, half of the adult population in the UK are over the age of 45, a large proportion of these individuals have some form of significant capability loss, whether it is, for example, physical, visual, auditory or cognitive. The iHMI approach assumes that any human user can be impaired (disabled) in their effectiveness by characteristics of their environment, the task, and the design of the user interface they are presented with [2, 3]. Such impairment may take the form of perceptual, cognitive and physical movement functional limitations that then translate into inability. It can arise out of capability limitation or from excessive demands of new technology interfaces.

The purpose of an exclusion audit is to estimate the percentage of the UK adult population excluded from completing a task. It provides a method to estimate the severity of each demand hurdles (e.g. vision, hearing, dexterity) that prevent users with mild capability impairments from achieving, through a metric system using percentage of exclusion to indicate demand magnitude. The audit breaks down a goal into tasks and sub-tasks to enable the demand to be assessed at each step against standard tasks asked from participants.

2 Approach and Methodology

Pruitt and Grudin [4] suggest that the use of personas may be considered 'too arty' for science and engineering based enterprises yet cite the power of fictional characters to engage. This is made even stronger when the narrative is placed alongside visual representations. The place, environment and the situation in which the persona carries out the narrated tasks set the context of the persona. This provides a key set of actions that the persona can undertake. These narratives are known as scenarios and offer a 'sketch of use' in the design process [5]. Present time scenario illustrated frame by frame inspires believable and stimulating new design concepts that are further illustrated in future narrative storyboards to help validate them. It is more effective to show a human face rather than providing abstract data for the user. Scenarios provide the story in which the persona is set, and a sequence of actions that the persona undertakes. They provide the opportunity for wider communication of the user's possible actions. In engineering, the scenario is set as a list of steps and known as a 'usage case'.

3 Design Ethnography and Visualisation

This research is by nature qualitative, as it sets out to grasp the subtleties and details of people's everyday routines. It is concerned with personal experiences, daily rituals, and individuals' understandings of the world set in the broader socio-cultural context [6]. Initial character illustrations provide the viewer with a detailed look of the persona and the clothing. In most cases the photographs provided work to help the visualiser draw as realistic image of the persona as possible, perhaps capturing the important details more effectively than the photographs. It is very important that the personas should not be based just on the designer's own assumptions and experience. Personas require proper details of the users through ethnographic methods that enable to draw out the richness, diversity and nuances of real life experience [7].

The approach taken here developed the persona and usage cases based on interviews with people representing that particular context. Based on these and because of resource limitations a new deliverable format of "Doculets" was proposed. Each persona would generate a small pamphlet/document consisting of professionally printed set of around 5–10 pages. Content consisted of general introductory material on inclusion and future HMI and the Persona description with some illustrations. Key HMI elements of the usage cases were then illustrated with relevant text from user interviews, HMI and the proposed design response. This was accompanied by images in the form of photographs, schematics, interior vehicle sketches illustrating future HMI and the inclusive audit comparisons (Fig. 1).

Fig. 1. Doculet covers depicting each persona within geographical settings using specific car models based on ethnographic research conducted on real people and real places (originals in colour).

In order to gain the most relevant information from the user such as the daily life and routines, needs and desires, experiences and inspirations, questions need to be prestructured by the interviewer to help building a realistic picture of the participant as a persona. Davies [8] tells us that research based mainly on semi-structured interviewing has become a very popular and important form of qualitative research across the social sciences, especially in anthropology (Edgerton 1993; Spradley 1979); sociology (Cockburn 1991; Laws 1990), psychology and other applied social sciences.

During this research, interviews are transcribed and analyzed for keywords and related descriptions; fieldwork generates detailed diary entries on observations of participants [9]. Ethnographic research conducted in strategically targeted different parts of the world within Brazil, USA, Europe, India and China looks for answers for the most likely and diverse personas linked to major car user locations in the world. Each persona appears in a narrative for a typical present day scenario that happens in one geographical place. Every present day scenario is overlapped by the future vision of the same scenario with the innovative HMI concepts likely to change the way cars are being driven or used by the user. Narrative scripts are visualized in storyboard format for the flow of user actions and movements (Fig. 2).

4   Design Thinking /User-Centred Design

One of the key challenges facing designers is to unlock the tacit understanding of how they believe things should be, so that these ideas can be shared, discussed, critiqued and eventually operationalized. Nowhere is this more difficult than in the design of physical interactions, where critical aspects of a design are often neither verbalized nor materialized. And yet, physical movement, behaviors and gestures can be critically important in the design of everyday objects—of cars, of robots, of doors and drawers —where autonomous motion is increasingly being incorporated, and where inexpensive controllers and batteries enable products that can lock and unlock, open and close, move around, wave, hide—act on their own [10].

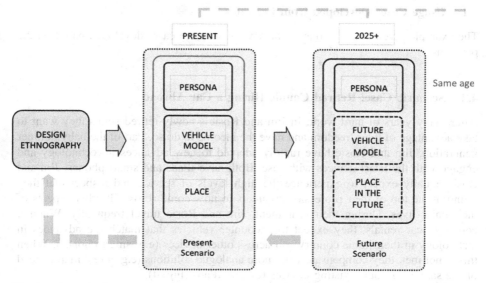

Fig. 2. Diagram of present day user-centred scenario leading to future scenario based on design ethnography.

Each persona, either a driver or a passenger is considered to be associated with an existing car model during the design thinking interaction workshop. Key project engineers, researchers and visualisers discuss and build a realistic storyline around the persona, car, place and environment in a set of tasks and situations (Fig. 3).

Fig. 3. Exploring an executive saloon car from the business user perspective and capturing the sequence of tasks that can be evaluated as potential HMI concepts to be later illustrated in scenario storyboards. Researchers here act as observer-participants.

4.1   Usage Cases Developed from Personas

The example given below is one of the several scenario cases developed based on the personas.

4.2   Scenario Case: Retired Couple Hiring a Car Abroad

After many years of hard work, in Jim and Rosie's newly retired status they want to take advantage of their freedom and have the income to do so. Part of the baby boomer generation, Jim and Rosie have rapidly adapted to new advances in technology and engage with the latest devices with ease. Both have iPads and smart phones. Jim and Rosie equally expect to experience the high levels of service and respect that they found at the top of their professional careers to now come across all other aspects of their daily lives. During their retirement, Jim and Rosie travel frequently. When it comes to car rentals, they expect to encounter vehicles that match the advances in technology in their home country and across other devices (e.g. smart phones). When this is not met, they compensate with more analogue solutions (e.g. a real map instead of the satnav) or their existing devices (e.g. an iPad) (Fig. 4).

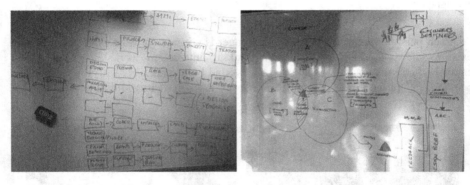

Fig. 4. Inclusive HMI workshops allow the team to analyse narrative scripts, produce visual scenarios and conceptual sketches of iHMI ideas through design thinking and user journey mapping activities. Input from these group sessions feedbacks into ethnographic research and scenario storyboards for the final validation of realistic automotive HMI design opportunities.

4.3   Scenario Storyboarding and Concept Ideation Process

The advantage of using storyboards is the quick changes and additions to the visual flow of the story build-up. In this respect, it is a powerful tool as narrative sequences can be seen altogether; present and future scenarios can be compared almost instantly whether the storyboard frames are laid on the table or stuck on the wall, allowing the project participants to use sticky notes either creating more storyboard frames or moving around or removing them where necessary. One or more visualisers may help capturing ideas by drawing very quick sketches and diagrams that is part of the research phase storyboarding. Thus, during this visual process, each user experience or interaction within the scenario can be broken into its more specific components over time, which allows the group to analyze more closely. Therefore, this visual brain-storming prompts attendees to come up with inspiring and innovative ideas that can be further captured in the future storylines.

A storyboard is a visual narrative of an interaction scenario. With origins in cinema, it is a story-telling device that describes characters, the activities they engage in, the objects that they need and/or use, their motivations, emotions and reactions to interactions, and an environment for those interactions [11].

After completing the initial storyboards through design thinking workshops conceptual ideas emerge. These ideas are drawn in more detailed storyboards to represent the design details as well as the user interactions to reflect the user's action, experience, emotion, feelings and thoughts in many ways leading to storyboard prototypes. Sections of the storyboard that relate to each design idea are discussed within the group. The final working designs that the users would take to overcome the needs or the problems are selected through this decision process. Each project prototype solution becomes a tangible design module used in the overall automobile design. The user remains as the main character to interact with the vehicle [12] (Fig. 5).

Fig. 5. Designers, engineers and researchers going through the storyboard sketches frame by frame in developing the narrative with proposed iHMI design ideas for a specific car model (on the left). Two of the case studies are being presented current and future scenarios in the company technology exhibition 2014.

Final presentation of the storyboard shows each design solution throughout the visual scenario in more detailed and colour drawings focusing on how the user interacts with the car in a specific environment and reveals the experience of certain users due to their age, ability, gender, personality and culture. Thus, engineers and designers have better understanding of creating innovative and inspiring automotive designs that are more inclusive.

4.4 Validity of the Concepts Through Visual Narratives

Visual narratives are quick to draw and sequences of the storyboards can be rearranged and changed where necessary either in the early stages with paper and pencil sketching or scanned digital images on screen in developing stages. Details in drawings, colour, line quality, view angles, pan movements, speech bubbles and other explanatory texts within the storyboards are in continuous progress to capture the most realistic iHMI design ideas that can be well understood and executed by the design engineers. Therefore, the final presentation provides valid design proposals integrated in visual future narratives that are easy to follow. One of the benefits of storyboarding is to understand how technology reshapes human activity and influences the understanding of the reaction to a system [13]. The team analyses the final presentation of visual scenarios and develop further conceptual sketches of iHMI ideas through design thinking and user journey mapping activities. Where necessary paper prototypes and 3D models are produced to provide better feedback from the project team where ethnography and iHMI researchers review the final validation of realistic design proposals.

4.5 The iHMI "Pipeline" to Concepts

The iHMI "pipeline" is a research approach, which allows developing key concepts that take into account the needs of real customers. This approach includes the following steps (Fig. 6):

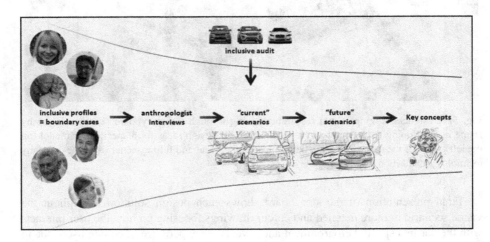

Fig. 6. The inclusive Human Machine Interaction (iHMI) "Pipeline" to concepts

- Persona selection,
- Identification of user needs and usages (anthropology interview),
- Understanding of the current product (inclusive audit),
- Current scenario based on anthropology and inclusive outputs,
- Future scenario,
- Selection of key concepts.

Persona Selection. Marketing departments generally develop one or several persona per products in order to illustrate their typical customers.

Anthropologist Interview. Anthropologists on the team conducted interviews with individuals representative of the persona. Through these conversations, the real lived experience of that individual and as a result their needs in that particular usage case were identified. This enabled us to detail the persona profile based on real feedback, rather than based on the assumptions of designers and engineers.

Inclusive Audit. An inclusive audit is conducted in order to identify the most difficult functions to operate/use.

"Current Scenario". The current scenario illustrates the usage and the needs of each persona and details the outputs of the inclusive audit. The persona is represented using a current vehicle.

"Future Scenario". The future scenario illustrates the same persona using a 2030 vehicle. This methodology allows presenting future concepts and visualising their value for the customer. At this stage, concepts are created without technical limitations.

Concept Selection. As a group, engineers and designers select the key concepts taking into account value for the customer and business priority.

5 Conclusion

At the present time scenario presented with its future version next to it helps us to have a good comparison of the two timelines. The importance of the storyboarding tool lies on the visual execution techniques to explore and understand drivers and passengers, automotive technologies and the interactions in between especially from the inclusive design perspective. Scenario boards provide the necessary visual language that the researchers, visualisers, automotive designers and engineers communicate in a more effective way [11].

Therefore, in this ongoing project, the aim is to create visual material such as a series of booklets that are self-explanatory brief documents each focusing on one persona case, design sketches and drawings of the future design ideas and interfaces. It also includes CAD drawings of future vehicle detailing the interiors, door apertures, seating, driver and passenger areas, and set of storyboards for each scenario. The storyboards show how each user interacts with the vehicle and its environment. These may differ inclusively from each other due to different needs and expectations. A consistent visualization for a number of inclusive design based personas using cars with future HMI interfaces are being generated.

Storyboards executed to date are twofold: present day scenarios where the persona is interacting with a current vehicle and environment, and future scenarios where the same persona is visually tested against an imaginary future car. Storyboards mainly focus on two elements: (1) user perspective that portrays the characteristics of the user including age, gender, profession, cultural background and disability, and (2) the vehicle perspective that combines components and devices within the vehicle where the user interacts with the interface of controls and displays. This arrangement of the storyboards allow the team some potentially useful design thinking in order to resolve the issues; whether through redesign of the interface, or perhaps through changing the order of tasks. It is expected that more investigation will be required for better understanding of the user's expectations of the right layout and right location of controls and displays as well as other components, such as: seats, storage, arm, head and foot rests, cup holder, sound, light, air units and work stations. The usage cases will be matched to design using inclusive design metrics [14].

At the end of the initial phase of the project 2 scenario cases were introduced during the company technology exhibition 2014. Each case study illustrated the users' relationship with the vehicle and the surrounding environment. The success of the approach has been measured through the feedback from the company automotive engineers and during the company technology exhibition. This has demonstrated the effectiveness of this type of technique in relating user needs to engineered technology and design.

References

1. Waller, S.D., Langdon, P.M., Clarkson, P.J.: Using disability data to estimate design exclusion. Univ. Access Inf. Soc. 9(3), 195–207 (2010)
2. Bichard, J.-A., Coleman, R., Langdon, P.: Does my stigma look big in this? considering acceptability and desirability in the inclusive design of technology products. In: Stephanidis, C. (ed.) HCI 2007. LNCS, vol. 4554, pp. 622–631. Springer, Heidelberg (2007)
3. Sears, A., Lin, M., Jacko, J., Xiao, Y.: When computers fade... Pervasive computing and situationally induced impairments and disabilities. In: Proceedings of HCI International, pp. 1298–1302 (2003)
4. Pruitt, J., Grudin, J.: Personas: practice and theory. In: Proceedings of the 2003 Conference on Designing for User Experiences, pp. 1–15 (2003)
5. Rosson, M. B., Carroll, J.M.: Scenario-based design. In: Jacko, J., Sears, A. (eds.): The Human-Computer Interaction Handbook: Fundamentals, Evolving Technologies and Emerging Applications. Lawrence Erlbaum Associates, pp. 1032–1050 (2002)
6. Geertz, C.: Available Light: Anthropological Reflections on Philosophical Topics, pp. 11–17. Princeton University, New Jersey (2001)
7. Cooper, A., Reimann, R., Cronin, D.: About Face 3: The Essentials of Interaction Design, pp. 77–86. Wiley, Indianapolis (2007)
8. Davies, C.A.: Reflective Ethnography: A Guide to researching Selves and Others, pp. 169–170. Routledge, London (1999)

9. Bichard, J-A., Gheerawo, R.: The designer as ethnographer: practical projects in industry. In: Design Anthropology Object Culture in the 21st Century. Springer, Wien, New York, USA, pp. 45-55 (2010)

10. Sirkin, D., Ju, W.: Embodied design improvisation: a method to make tacit design knowledge explicit and usable. In: Plattner, H., Meinel, C., Leifer, L.J. (eds.) Design Thinking Research. Building Innovators, pp. 195–210. Springer, Heidelberg (2015)

11. Van der Lelie, C.: The value of storyboards in the product design process. Pers. Ubiquit. Comput. **10**(2), 159–162 (2006)

12. Sirkin, D., Ju, W.: Using embodied design improvisation as a design tool. In: International Conference on Human Behaviour in Design. Center for Design Research, Stanford University, Stanford, Ascona, Switzerland (2014)

13. Truong, K.N., Hayes, G.R., Abowd, G.D.: Storyboarding: an empirical determination of best practices and effective guidelines (2006)

14. Langdon, P.M., Johnson, D., Huppert, F., Clarkson, P.J.: A framework for collecting inclusive design data for the UK population in applied ergonomics. Appl. Ergon. (2013). pii: S0003–6870(13)00050-1. doi:10.1016/j.apergo.2013.03.011

Wide-Range Auditory Orientation Training System for Blind O&M

Yoshikazu Seki[✉]

National Institute of Advanced Industrial Science and Technology (AIST),
1-1-1 Higashi, Tsukuba, Ibaraki 305-8566, Japan
yoshikazu-seki@aist.go.jp

Abstract. Authors started to develop a training method that combined "sound localization" and "obstacle perception" by using acoustic virtual reality technologies for the orientation and mobility training for the blind people in 2003, and we finally developed an auditory orientation training system (AOTS) in 2005. As a modified version of AOTS, the first WR-AOTS was released April 2013 for the blind rehabilitation and/or education facilities. By January 2015, about 70 requests for use of it were received from the blind rehabilitation and/or education facilities. We will keep providing update on the facilities' demands in future.

Keywords: Orientation and mobility (O&M) · Visual impairment · Virtual reality · 3-D sound · Head-related transfer function (HRTF)

1 Introduction

People with blindness must be able to cognize their environment using acoustic information through their auditory sense when they are walking or conducting daily activities. This skill, known as "auditory orientation", includes sound localization and obstacle perception. Sound localization is the ability to identify a sound source location, such as a vehicle or pedestrian. Obstacle perception is the ability to detect a silent object, such as a wall or pole, using sound reflection and insulation. It is sometimes called "human echolocation" [1].

Training of auditory orientation is usually conducted for people with blindness as an one lesson in orientation and mobility (O&M) instruction. Such O&M instruction is usually conducted in a real environment; the trainee is expected to acquire auditory orientation capability by listening to ambient sounds experientially [2]. However, training in a real environment where actual vehicles are running is sometimes danger and stressful for novice trainees. Furthermore, the trainee must spend a long time to acquire auditory orientation using this training method because it is very difficult for the novice trainee to discern and listen to important sounds selectively from many other environmental noises. To reduce the risk and stress, and to shorten the period of training, a new training method in an ideal sound field reproduced by acoustical simulation is considered very effective.

Some studies of acoustic training technology have been conducted in Japan and overseas to solve these problems [3]. However, these studies have covered only a very

© Springer International Publishing Switzerland 2015
M. Antona and C. Stephanidis (Eds.): UAHCI 2015, Part IV, LNCS 9178, pp. 150–159, 2015.
DOI: 10.1007/978-3-319-20687-5_15

small part of auditory orientation, called "sound localization". The acoustic training systems developed from these studies are too expensive to introduce into actual training sessions and are not suitable for practical use. Therefore, there is a need for a practical auditory orientation training system for safe and efficient rehabilitation to encourage the visually impaired to participate in social activities.

2 Auditory Orientation Training System (AOTS)

In 2003, National Institute of Advanced Industrial Science and Technology (AIST) and National Rehabilitation Center for persons with Disabilities (NRCD) started to develop a training method that combined "sound localization" and "obstacle perception", and in 2005, we developed an auditory orientation training system (AOTS).

2.1 Composition

AOTS comprises ten 3-D sound processors (RSS-10; Roland Corp.), ten sound recorders/players (AR-3000; Roland Corp.), two sound mixers (RFM-186; Roland Corp.), a magnetic 6DOF position and direction sensor (3SPACE Fastrak; Polhemus), headphones and an amplifier (SRS-4040; Stax Ltd.), and a computer (iBook G4; Apple Computer Inc.). Software was developed (REALbasic; REAL Software Inc.) to function on Apple Mac OS X. The 3-D sound processors and sound recorders/players are controlled through MIDI; the magnetic sensor is controlled through RS-232C (Figs. 1 and 2).

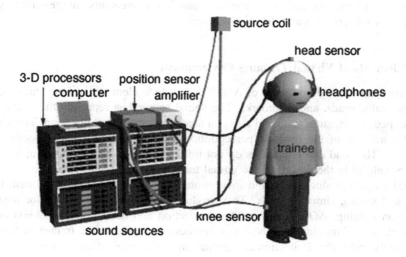

Fig. 1. Outlook of auditory orientation training system (AOTS). AOTS was developed in 2005 by AIST and NRCD.

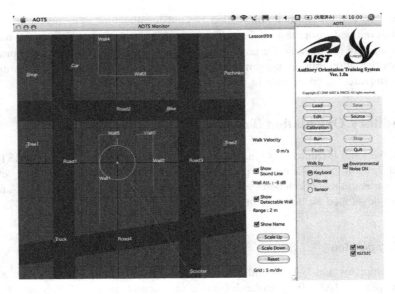

Fig. 2. Application window of auditory orientation training system (AOTS)

2.2 User Interfaces for Trainee

A trainee can listen to sounds in the virtual training environment through headphones while changing the head direction. A trainee can also walk though the virtual training environment by moving their feet. The head and foot movements are measured by the magnetic 6DOF position and direction sensors.

2.3 Elements of Virtual Training Environment

The virtual training environment of AOTS can include elements of four kinds: sound sources, walls, roads, and landmarks. The sound source can represent the sound of a vehicle, pedestrian, store, etc., and move in a constant speed and direction. The wall is used for training of the obstacle perception, and gives rise to sound reflection and insulation. The road and landmarks do not influence the sound propagation, but they are very helpful in the design of the virtual training environments (Fig. 3).

AOTS can reproduce six sound sources and four ambient noises (from east, west, north, and south), simultaneously. To reproduce the presence of a wall for obstacle perception training, AOTS can reproduce reflection and insulation of ambient noise, and insulation of moving sounds. These reproductions enable the trainee to learn to detect walls and paths. Reflection and insulation of the ambient noises are reproduced when the listener approaches to within 2 m of a wall; sound insulation is reproduced by attenuating the sound by 6 dB. The O&M instructor can design and "construct" the virtual training environments easily by describing them in extensible markup language (XML), which was originally proposed for this system.

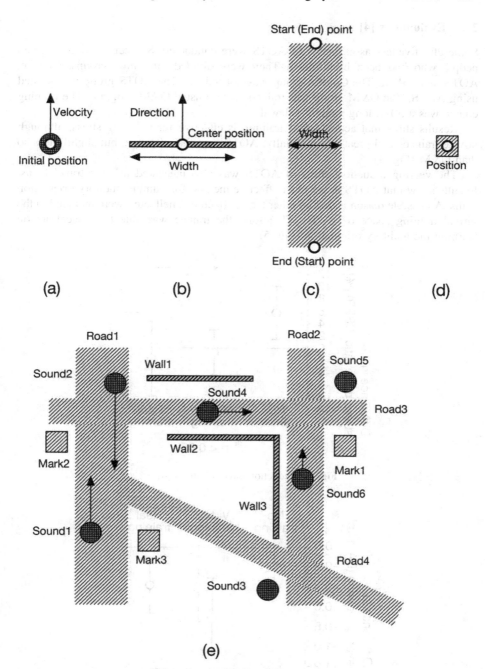

Fig. 3. Elements of virtual training environment. (a) Sound, (b) Wall, (c) Road and (d) Mark. (e) Example of the virtual training environment.

2.4   Evaluations [4]

Some effectiveness assessments of AOTS were conducted. Subjects were 30 sighted people who had been blindfolded. They were divided into three groups: Control, AOTS, and O&M. The Control group was not trained. The AOTS group was trained using AOTS. The O&M group was trained using a usual O&M program. The training course was a 50-m-long straight sidewalk.

Results show that actual O&M training is effective for reducing stress, although novice trainees feel great stress initially. AOTS was also effective, but slightly less so than O&M (Fig. 4).

The veering reduction effect of AOTS was also measured using a travel locus. Results show that AOTS is the most effective method for training auditory orientation skills. A possible reason is that no other factors (tactile, smell, etc.) were included in the virtual training space of AOTS. Therefore, the trainee was able to concentrate on learning the auditory orientation (Fig. 5).

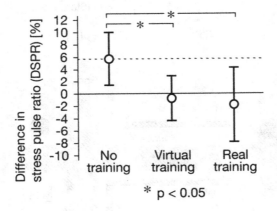

Fig. 4. Reduction effect of stress [4].

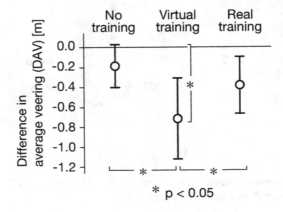

Fig. 5. Reduction effect of veering [4]

2.5   Ploblems

However, at about 5 million yen (about 50 thousand dollars) the system was expensive. Also, it was too large to carry and enabled the position and orientation of the head to be measured over a distance of no more than 1 m at a time. Thus trainees cannot walk while using it.

3   Wide-Range Auditory Orientation Training System (WR-AOTS)

Since 2008, Author has been jointly attempting to reduce the size of the auditory orientation training system with Tohoku University, et al., to expand its coverage, and to reduce its cost, and finally developed an improved system.

3.1   Composition

The developed training system consists of special-purpose software, "WR-AOTS™ (Wide-Range Auditory Orientation Training System)", a personal computer (PC), a stereo headphone set, and a commercially available game controller (for wide-range positioning) (Figs. 6 and 7).

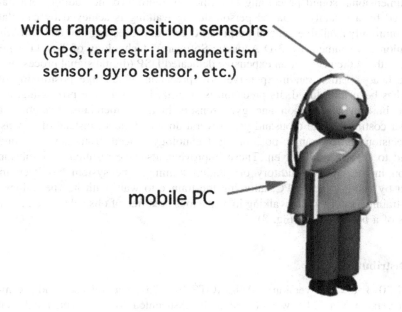

Fig. 6. Outlook of wide-range auditory orientation training system (WR-AOTS). WR-AOTS was developed in 2013 by AIST, Tohoku University, et al.

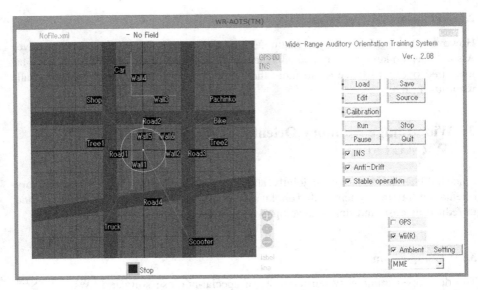

Fig. 7. Application window of wide-range auditory orientation training system (WR-AOTS).

3.2 Improvement

Three-dimensional sound processing to artificially reproduce the auditory orientation clues used by a visually impaired person during walking is achieved by calculation with a commonly available general-purpose PC central processing unit and "SifASo™ (Simulation environment for 3-D Acoustic Software)" technology of Tohoku University [5], without the need for an expensive dedicated DSP (digital signal processor). To measure head position, an inexpensive, low-precision wide-range positioning technology has been introduced. Its precision is stabilized by software processing, and it uses the built-in acceleration and gyro sensors in a commercially available game controller costing several thousand yen (several dozens dollars), instead of expensive, high-precision narrow-range positioning technology priced from several hundred thousand to several million yen. These improvements have resulted in a substantial reduction in the cost of auditory orientation training. The system has been made compact by using a laptop PC, allowing the trainee to walk with it. The trainee can receive training safely while walking in a spacious area free of obstacles, such as in the grounds of a blind school (Fig. 8).

3.3 Distribution

In April 2013, the first version of WR-AOTS Ver. 2.04 was released and the minor updated version Ver. 2.06 was started to be distributed for the blind rehabilitation and/or education facilities.

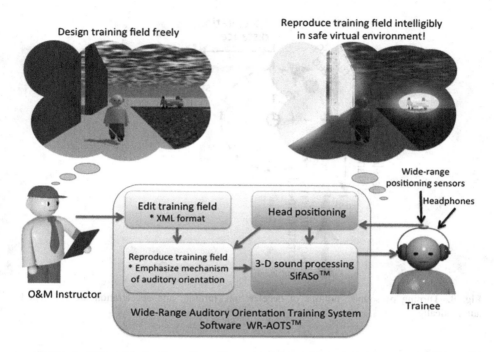

Fig. 8. Principle of wide-range auditory orientation training system (WR-AOTS)

4   Updates of WR-AOTS

After the first version was released, we have been keeping providing update on the facilities' demands.

4.1   Ver 2.07

Turning of Sound. The most remarkable request from the O&M instructors was to enable the sound source to turn a curve. The sound image motion when the car runs straight, turns a curve, and runs away is very important cue to detect a crossroad for the Blind people. In Ver. 2.06 and before, the Sound could move only straight in constant velocity. In the updated version Ver. 2.07 and after, the Sound can turn. The situation where a car turns a curve can be reproduced by this improvement. The training to detect a crossroad by using car running sound can be performed. The blind people can learn how to detect a crossroad by sound motion in our system (Fig. 9).

Volume Control of Sound. In Ver. 2.06 and before, volume of the Sound could not be controlled. In Ver. 2.07 and after, the volume can be controlled. It is possible that specific Sound is loud and other Sounds are small. The difficulty of the listening training can be adjusted by controlling volumes.

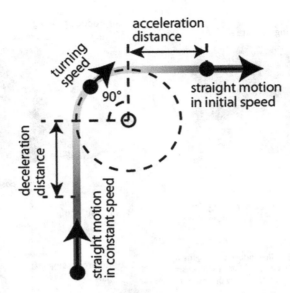

Fig. 9. Turning of sound. motions of deceleration, turning, and acceleration are calculated automatically.

Kind, Direction, and Volume Control of Ambient Sounds. In Ver. 2.06 and before, kind, direction, and volume of the ambient sounds could not be changed. In Ver. 2.07 and after, these can be controlled.

- For the kind of the Ambient sound, constant white noise (that includes all frequency component) and pink noise (lower frequency is stronger) can be selected as well as conventional town noise. They are suitable for the novice trainee, who feels difficulty to use complex town noise, to learn how to listen to the specific sound in the ambient noises, or acquire the obstacle perception by using reflection and/or insulation of the ambient sounds.
- For the direction of the Ambient sound, as well as the four points of the compass, two directions or one direction can also be selected. Generally, wall can be detected easier as less direction. Thus, they are suitable for the novice trainee.
- The volume of the Ambient sound can be controlled. The difficulty of the training for listening to specific sound in ambient sounds can be adjusted.

4.2   Ver. 2.08

Screen Reader. In Ver. 2.07 and before, screen readers could not be used. In Ver. 2.08 and after, principal buttons etc. can be read by screen readers, and can be selected by TAB key. Operation is available by screen reader and keyboard in some degree.

Training Field Data Based on Japanese Rules of Public Sounds. In Ver. 2.08 and after, the sounds of the accessible pedestrian signals (APS) and the silent vehicle approach notification equipment are added. Japanese rules of public sounds that must be learned in O&M can be learned by this system.

5   Conclusions

Authors started to develop a training method that combined "sound localization" and "obstacle perception" by using acoustic virtual reality technologies for the orientation and mobility training for the blind people in 2003, and we finally developed an auditory orientation training system (AOTS) in 2005. As a modified version of AOTS, the first WR-AOTS was released April 2013 for the blind rehabilitation and/or education facilities. By January 2015, about 70 requests for use of it were received from the blind rehabilitation and/or education facilities. We will keep providing update on the facilities' demands in future.

References

1. Seki, Y., Ito, K.: Obstacle perception training system and CD for the blind. In: Proceedings of CVHI 2004, CD-ROM (2004)
2. Blasch, B.B., Wiener, W.R., Welsh, R.L.: Foundations of Orientation and Mobility, 2nd edn. AFB Press, New York (1977)
3. Inman, D.P., Ken Loge, M.S.: Teaching orientation and mobility skills to blind children using simulated acoustical environments. In: Proceedings of HCI International, vol. 2, pp. 1090–1094 (1999)
4. Seki, Y., Sato, T.: A training system of orientation and mobility for blind people using acoustic virtual reality. IEEE Trans. Neural Syst. Rehabil. Eng. **19**, 95–104 (2011)
5. Iwaya, Y., Otani, M., Suzuki, Y.: Development of virtual auditory display software responsive to head movement and a consideration on deration of spatialized ambient sound to improve realism of perceived sound space. In: Principles and applications of spatial hearing, pp. 121–135 (2011)

A Spot Navigation System for the Visually Impaired by Use of SIFT-Based Image Matching

Hotaka Takizawa[1]([⊠]), Kazunori Orita[1], Mayumi Aoyagi[2],
Nobuo Ezaki[3], and Shinji Mizuno[4]

[1] University of Tsukuba,1-1-1 Tennodai, Tsukuba 305-8573, Japan
takizawa@cs.tsukuba.ac.jp
[2] Aichi University of Education,Kariya, Japan
[3] Toba National College of Maritime Technology,Toba, Japan
[4] Aichi Institute of Technology,Toyota, Japan

Abstract. In this report, we propose a spot navigation system to assist
visually impaired individuals in recalling memories related to spots that
they often visit. This system registers scene images and voice memos
that are recorded in advance by a visually impaired individual or his/her
sighted supporter at various spots. When the individual visits one of the
spots, the system determines the current spot from the results of image
matching between the registered images and a query image taken by the
individual at the spot, then plays a voice memo which corresponds to
the spot. The system is applied to actual indoor and outdoor scenes, and
experimental results are shown.

1 Introduction

In 2014, the World Health Organization reported that the number of visually impaired individuals was estimated to be approximately 285 million worldwide [1]. Many of them are trained by sighted supporters to move along paths,
for example, from their houses to offices. During such training, they are often
taught information related to important locations (called *spots*) on the paths.
For example, a visually impaired individual is taught that there is a restroom
just outside a ticket gate at a station. If the individual remembers the information about the restroom, he or she can use it later. However, otherwise, he or she
cannot at all. The individual is strongly affected by whether he or she remembers
such information. It is necessary to build an assistive system that helps visually
impaired individuals remember information related to spots to visit.

There are several systems that help visually impaired individuals remember the information on everyday environments. The Digital Sign system [3] and
the NAVI system [4] determine the current positions of visually impaired individuals by use of passive and AR markers, respectively. These systems need to
deploy markers in large scale infrastructure for everyday use. A navigation system [2] determines the current position of a visually impaired individual by use
of GPS, and then guides the individual along the predefined route. This GPS-
based system cannot be used in, for example, reinforced concrete buildings. Sekai

© Springer International Publishing Switzerland 2015
M. Antona and C. Stephanidis (Eds.): UAHCI 2015, Part IV, LNCS 9178, pp. 160–167, 2015.
DOI: 10.1007/978-3-319-20687-5_16

Camera [5] is an AR application on mobile phones. Digital information, called Air Tag, can be virtually attached to the real world, and a user can know the local information from the Air Tag. The main targets of this system are sighted people, and thus it is difficult for visually impaired individuals to use this system. e.Typist Mobile [6] converts characters in environments to voices. Tap Tap See [7] and LookTel Recognizer [8] help visually impaired individuals to identify objects.

In this paper, we propose the concept of spot navigation to help visually impaired individuals remember information related to spots to visit. This concept is implemented as an application software on a mobile system, which is applied to actual indoor and outdoor scenes.

2   Concept of Spot Navigation

Spot navigation is a framework to assist visually impaired individuals in recalling the memories related to spots that they often visit. In this framework, first, a visually impaired individual visits several spots with a sighted supporter, and then records the position data and voice memos of the spots onto a mobile system. Later, when the visually impaired individual visits one of the recorded spots, the mobile system determines the spot position and then plays the voice memo that corresponds to the spot. The visually impaired individual can obtain the spot information by hearing the voice memo.

3   Implementation of a Spot Navigation System

3.1   Spot Navigation System

The spot navigation concept is implemented as an application software on an Android smartphone system (Google Nexus 4 [9]) and our Kinect cane system [10–12]. The application software has the following two modes:

1. **Registration mode:** A visually impaired individual visits each spot with his or her sighted supporter. The individual takes scene images with several perspectives by use of a camera on a mobile system, and records a voice memo about supplemental information related to the spot. The system registers the images and the voice memo to a dictionary in the system. The images are used as keys in the dictionary to determine the spot positions.
2. **Spot navigation mode:** When the visually impaired individual visits one of the recorded spots, he or she takes a scene image, and then inputs the image as a query into the system. The system determines the current spot from the results of image matching between the query image and the dictionary images. The system plays the voice memo corresponding to the matched dictionary image.

3.2   Image Matching Based on the SIFT

The Scale Invariant Feature Transform (SIFT) [13] can extract pixels that have distinct features, which are described by 128-dimensional vectors. The feature vectors are invariant against the changes of scale, rotation and illumination. Such pixels are called *key points*.

Let k^q and k^d denote key points in a query image q and a dictionary image d, respectively, and v_i^q and v_i^d denote the i-th feature value of k^q and k^d, respectively. The system searches for the key point pair which minimizes the following distance:

$$\delta(v^d, v^q) = \sqrt{\sum_{i=1}^{128}(v_i^d - v_i^q)^2}. \tag{1}$$

Fig. 1 shows a matching result where lines represent the key point pairs.

Fig. 1. Example of key point pairs in a query image and a dictionary image at an indoor spot.

The system evaluates the following six criteria based on geometrical relations between key point pairs:

1. too few pairs,
2. size consistency,
3. direction consistency,
4. 2D affine constraint,
5. area size and,
6. axis inversion,

which are proposed by Kameda et al. [14,15]. If all the criteria are satisfied, the query image is determined to correspond to the dictionary image.

4   Experimental Results

4.1   Image Matching Test 1

Conditions: 22 indoor spots and 22 outdoor spots were selected for the experiment, and eight images were taken at each spot. The resolutions of the images were 144×192 pixels. A two-fold cross-validation test were employed with the following parameters: $K_0 = 10$, $t_{size} = 0.35$, $t_{dir} = 45$, $t_{affine} = 12$, $t_{area} = 15$, which are used in the image matching.

Results: Table 1 lists the accuracy of the image matching. *Correct detection* represents a situation where the system can find a dictionary image that corresponds to a query image. *False detection* represents a situation where the system mistakenly selects a dictionary image that does not correspond to a query image. *No correspondence* represents a situation where the system determines that the dictionary does not include any images that correspond to a query image. In this test, no correspondence is the failure of the image matching, because the image dictionary includes at least one image corresponding to a query image.

In this result, the 317 query images were matched successfully, but the 35 query images cannot be matched. Figure 2 (a), (b) and (c) show the matching results where the right and left images are dictionary and query images, respectively. Figure 2 (a) shows the images which are taken at the same indoor spot. 25 key point pairs are obtained correctly from the same objects. All the criteria are satisfied (i.e. $K = 25$, $E_{size} = 0.05$, $E_{dir} = 2.4$, $E_{affine} = 5.5$ and $E_{area} = 38.8$), and thus the system successfully determines the spot. Figure 2 (b) shows the images which are taken at different spots, and no key point pairs are obtained from the images. The number of the key point pairs is smaller than the threshold K_0, and thus the system successfully determines that they are the different spots. Figure 2 (c) shows the images which are taken at different spots. 19 key point pairs are obtained, but the size consistency, the direction consistency and the axis inversion are out of permissible ranges. Therefore, they are successfully determined to be different spots.

4.2   Image Matching Test 2

Conditions: We verified whether the system correctly returns no correspondence in cases where the dictionary does not include any images corresponding

Table 1. Matching accuracy in Test 1.

	# of images	Ratio
Correct detection	317	90%
False detection	0	0%
No correspondence	35	10%

(a) The same scenes.   (b) A pair of different scenes.

(c) Another pair of different scenes.

Fig. 2. Matching results in Test 1.

Table 2. Matching accuracy in Test 2

	# of images	Ratio
False detection	0	0%
No correspondence	28	100%

to a query image. 28 images were taken at other spots (14 indoor spots and 14 outdoor spots), and the image matching were performed by use of the 28 images and the dictionary images.

Results: Table 2 lists the matching results. In this test, no correspondence represents that the system successfully indicates that there is no dictionary images corresponding to a query image. All the query images are correctly determined to be no correspondence.

Figure 3 (a) and (b) show matching results. Figure 3 (a) shows the images which are taken at different outdoor spots. The system successfully determines that they are different spots, because the size consistency and the direction consistency are out of permissible ranges. Figure 3 (b) shows the images which are taken at indoor and outdoor spots. These images provide only two key point

(a) A pair of different scenes.   (b) Another pair of different scenes.

Fig. 3. Matching results in Test 2.

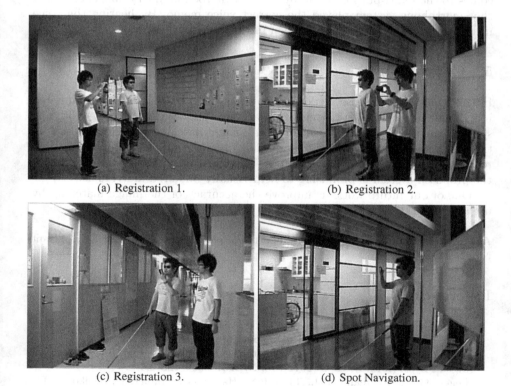

(a) Registration 1.   (b) Registration 2.

(c) Registration 3.   (d) Spot Navigation.

Fig. 4. Registration and spot navigation modes in user study.

pairs. The number of the pairs are smaller than the threshold K_0. Therefore these spots are successfully determined to be different spots.

4.3   User Study

We conducted a user study where a blindfolded subject used an Android smartphone system in which the spot navigation method was implemented. In Fig. 4(a), a person having a white cane played a role of a visually impaired individual, and a person in a white T-shirt played a role of a supporter. They were in an entrance of a building. The supporter set a smartphone, took an image of the scene, and input a voice memo, *"Here is an entrance. There is a direction board."* In Fig. 4(b), they were in front of a multi-purpose room. The supporter input a voice memo, *"Here is a multi-purpose room. There is a kitchen inside."* In Fig. 4(c), they were in front of our laboratory. In this case, the visually impaired individual input a voice memo, *"Here is our laboratory"*, under the advice of the supporter. Figure 4(d) shows a situation where the visually impaired individual comes to the multi-purpose room by himself. He took an query image, and then the smartphone system played the correct voice memo. By hearing the voice memo, he could remember the kitchen in the multi-purpose room.

5   Conclusion

In this report, we propose a spot navigation system to assist visually impaired individuals in recalling the memories related to spots that they often visit. The system can identify spots by use of the image matching technique based on the SIFT, and give a visually impaired individual the supplemental information related to spots by use of voice memos. The experimental results indicate that the proposed system is promising to help visually impaired individuals.

One of our future works is improve the accuracy of the image matching by use of, PCA-SIFT [16], BSIFT [17], and CSIFT [18].

Acknowledgment. This work was supported in part by the JSPS KAKENHI Grant Number 25560278.

References

1. World Health Organization, Media Centre, Visual impairment and blindness, Fact Sheet No 282. http://www.who.int/mediacentre/factsheets/fs282/en/
2. Gaude, M., Candolkar, V.: GPS Navigator for Visually Impaired. Int. J. Electron. Signals Syst. (IJESS), vol-2 (2012), ISSN: 2231–5969, ISS-2,3,4
3. Legge, G.E., Beckmann, P.J., Tjan, B.S., Havey, G., Kramer, K., Rolkosky, D., Gage, R., Chen, M., Puchakayala, S., Rangarajan, A.: Indoor navigation by people with visual impairment using a digital sign system. PLoS One 8(10), e76783 (2013)

4. Zöllner, M., Huber, S., Jetter, H.-C., Reiterer, H.: NAVI – a proof-of-concept of a mobile navigational aid for visually impaired based on the microsoft kinect. In: Campos, P., Graham, N., Jorge, J., Nunes, N., Palanque, P., Winckler, M. (eds.) INTERACT 2011, Part IV. LNCS, vol. 6949, pp. 584–587. Springer, Heidelberg (2011)

5. Sekai Camera Support Center BEYOND REALITY. http://support.sekaicamera. com/ja/service

6. e.Typist Mobile. MEDIA DRIVE CORPORATION. http://mediadrive.jp/ products/etmi

7. TapTapSee - Blind and Visually Impaired Camera. TapTapSee. http://www. taptapseeapp.com

8. LookTel Recognizer Documentation. LookTel. http://www.looktel.com/recognizer-documentation

9. Nexus 4 - Google. http://www.google.co.jp/nexus/4/

10. Takizawa, H., Yamaguchi, S., Aoyagi, M., Ezaki, N., Mizuno, S.: Kinect cane : an assistive system for the visually impaired based on three-dimensional object recognition. In: The Proceedings of the 2012 IEEE/SICE International Symposium on System Integration, vol. 1, No. 1, pp. 740–745 (2012)

11. Takizawa, H., Yamaguchi, S., Aoyagi, M., Ezaki, N., Mizuno, S.: Kinect cane : object recognition aids for the visually impaired. In: The proceedings of the 6th IEEE International Conference on Human System Interaction (HSI 2013), 6 p. (CDROM proceedings) (2013)

12. Orita, K., Takizawa, H., Aoyagi, M., Ezaki, N., Mizuno, S.: Obstacle detection by the kinect cane system for the visually impaired. In: 2013 IEEE/SICE International Symposium on System Integration (SII 2013), pp. 115–118 (CDROM proceedings) (2013)

13. Hironobu, F.: Gradient-based feature extraction : SIFT and HOG. In: PRMU, CVIM 160, pp. 211–224 (2007)

14. Kameda, Y., ohta, Y.: Image retrieval of first-person vision for pedestrian navigation in urban area. In: ICPR, pp. 364–367 (2010)

15. Kurata, T., Kourogi, M., Ishikawa, T., Kameda, Y., Aoki, K., Ishikawa, J.: Indoor-outdoor navigation system for visually-impaired pedestrians: preliminary evaluation of position measurement and obstacle display. In: Proceedings of ISWC 2011, pp. 123–124 (2011)

16. Ke, Y., Sukthankar, R.: PCA-SIFT: a more distinctive representation for local image descriptors. In: Proceedings of IEEE Conference on Computer Vision and Pattern Recognition (CVPR), pp. 511–517 (2004)

17. Stein, A., Herbert, M.: Incorporating background invariance into feature-based object recognition. In: Proceedings of IEEE Workshop on Applications of Computer Vision (WACV), pp. 37–44, January 2005

18. Abdel-Hakim, A.E., Farag, A.A.: CSIFT: a SIFT descriptor with color invariant characteristics. In: Proceedings of IEEE Conference on ComputerVision and Pattern Recognition (CVPR), pp. 1978–1983 (2006)

Accessible Security and Voting

Toward Private and Independent Accessible Write-In Voting: A Multimodal Prediction Approach

Shanee Dawkins[1,4], Wanda Eugene[2(✉)], Tamirat Abegaz[3],
and Juan E. Gilbert[2]

[1] Department of Computer Science and Software Engineering,
Auburn University, Auburn, AL 36830, USA
dawkins@nist.gov, swright0206@gmail.com
[2] Computer and Information Science and Engineering Department,
University of Florida, P.O. Box 116120, Gainesville, FL 32611, USA
{weugene, juan}@ufl.edu
[3] School of Computing, Clemson University, 100 McAdams Hall, Clemson, SC
29634-0974, USA
tabegaz@g.clemson.edu
[4] National Institute of Standards and Technology, 100 Bureau Drive, MS 8940,
Gaithersburg, MD 20899, USA

Abstract. The overall objective of this research is to design a multimodal system to write-in a candidate's name that addresses the issues of time, privacy, and accessibility. In order to determine if these issues were met, the design is analyzed and compared against alternate methods of writing-in a candidate's name. An experiment was performed to assess two aspects of the multimodal system: speech interaction and switch interaction. The research intends to capture and analyze the efficiency and effectiveness of writing-in a candidate's name anonymously through multimodal interactions. Though the essence of this research embodies universal of design for everyone everywhere, the design and experiments put forth in this paper will focus on the U.S. voting population.

Keywords: Accessibility · Universally usable interfaces · Electronic voting systems · Multimodal interaction · Text prediction

1 Introduction

The design of ballots is the foundation of successful election operations. Today, a properly designed ballot interface is one of the key aspects to running a successful election; an interface that enables all voters to have independent access to the ballot. As technology for electronic voting systems continues to develop, there is an increased need for universal design in these systems [1, 2]. A universal design ensures that systems are as usable as possible by as many people as possible regardless of age, ability or situation [3]. By focusing on the needs of the voter, the design of electronic voting systems can satisfy the aforementioned usable criteria. With ballot privacy

© Springer International Publishing Switzerland 2015
M. Antona and C. Stephanidis (Eds.): UAHCI 2015, Part IV, LNCS 9178, pp. 171–181, 2015.
DOI: 10.1007/978-3-319-20687-5_17

constantly being a major concern in the design of voting systems, it is often difficult to implement voting technology that incorporates a private, yet universal, design. Some developers today address this issue through the design of their electronic voting systems [4]; however, these electronic voting systems have yet to integrate universal design into the writing-in of a candidate's name.

The objective of this research is to develop a system in which a person, regardless of ability or disability, can efficiently, anonymously, independently, and effectively spell a candidate's name through multimodal interaction. The research conducted captures and analyzes the efficiency and effectiveness of writing-in a candidate's name anonymously through multimodal interactions. Broadly speaking, the purpose of this research is to design a method to write-in a candidate's name that addresses the issues of time, privacy, and accessibility.

2 Background

The Help America Vote Act (HAVA) of 2002 was created [9] as a result of the major issues faced in the 2000 United States Presidential Election. HAVA aimed to prevent these problems, such as interpreting voter intent, from happening in future elections. The Voluntary Voting System Guidelines (VVSG), which expand access for individuals with disabilities to vote privately and independently [5], is a byproduct of HAVA. The VVSG addresses the advancement of technology and provides requirements for voting systems to be tested to ensure functionality, security, and accessibility [4]. The VVSG states that all voters must have access to the voting process without discrimination, and that the voting process must be accessible to individuals with disabilities, including non-visual accessibility. It also states that voting systems should be independently accessible to as many voters as possible, which further emphasizes the need for a universal design. A universally designed system requires no special adaptation or additional cost to be usable by as many people as possible thus is accessible to people with disabilities [6–9].

In United States' elections, voters have the option to vote for a person who is not listed on the ballot by writing that person's name in a dedicated space on the ballot. Because election law is not mandated federally, laws pertaining to writing-in a candidate vary across all states [5]. Most, but not all states allow write-in candidates for general elections. Similarly, some states require people to pre-register as a write-in candidate for an election, while others do not. Some states do not allow candidates to be written-in at all [5]. Election write-ins can introduce a host of challenges that often result in turmoil. The 2010 general election in Alaska was the basis of one such controversy [10]. Joe Miller and Lisa Murkowski were candidates for U.S. Senate in the election on November second. Murkowski was registered as a write-in candidate, and upon completion of the vote tallies, was declared the winner of the race. Murkowski obtained more than 97 percent of the write-in votes; 11 percent more votes than Joe Miller [10]. Miller, however, filed a lawsuit, claiming that write-in votes were not counted properly according to Alaska state law. Miller's argument was that elections officials accounted for voter *intent*, from which certain ballots, like those shown in Fig. 1, were counted as votes for Murkowski. By designing a usable ballot interface, voters can feel certain about their votes being casted as intended, and election officials are able to feel confident about interpreting voters' intent.

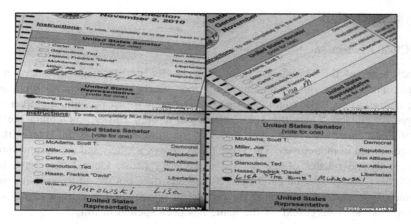

Fig. 1. Ballot variations for write-in candidate, lisa murkowski

2.1   Accessible Write-In Voting

Due Electronic voting systems that employ the use of a touchscreen often feature a virtual keyboard for voters to input the write-in candidate's name. When the VVSG was released, many voting system manufacturers opted to utilize the audio ballot – reading the on-screen content aloud via headphones – to meet the accessibility standard for writing-in candidate's names. For the write-in option, traditional audio ballots present the alphabet to the voter in a linear fashion from A to Z, one letter at a time, wrapping around to start over from "A" when the end is reached. The voter then spells the candidate's name, letter by letter, by making a selection when the desired letter is heard through the headphones. The presentation style of the alphabet and manner in which voters make selections vary between voting system designs.

The presentation style of voting system designs is to traverse the alphabet via automatic scanning or voter input. With automatic scanning, the system's audio will prompt the voter with a letter and pause to give the voter time to select the letter. If the voter does not make a selection, the system continues automatically to the next sequential letter. When automatic scanning is not used, the voting system will only continue to the next letter when the voter chooses to do so. In this case, the voter has options to select the letter, or to skip the letter.

Traditional voting systems implement a wide range of techniques for voters to make letter selections when writing-in a candidate in conjunction with audio ballots. The systems can provide the voter with a button to select a letter, e.g., buttons for selecting and skipping letters; buttons for selecting, skipping, and returning to the previous letter; a button to select and a rotary dial to scroll through the letters; or touchscreen guides for selecting and skipping letters.

The research discussed here builds on the Prime III voting system prototype [11], which features multimodal inputs (physical and speech) with automatic scanning. Using these methods, enhanced with a clustering and prediction model, it is hypothesized that voters will have a more efficient, effective, and satisfactory accessible write-in experience.

3 System Design

3.1 Cluster Selection

For each letter of the candidate's name, the clusters are presented to the voter for selection. The voter begins by making the proper selections, through a microphone or switch button, to spell the candidate's name. The system first prompts the voter with the alphabet clusters. Once the voter selects the desired cluster, containing the first letter of the intended candidate's last name, the system then prompts the voter with the letters contained in that cluster. The voter then chooses a letter, and the system moves on to get the next letter of the desired candidate's name. Once letters have been selected, the name prediction can begin. If the voter does not intend to write-in one of the names suggested, s/he continues the process of selecting clusters, then letters, until the correct name is suggested, or the name has been spelled in full.

As can be seen from Table 1, the alphabet is broken down into five standard clusters; four clusters of five letters, and one cluster of six letters. When selecting the first letter of each of the candidate's names, the voter is first prompted to choose from one of the five standard clusters. The first cluster presented to the voter is chosen at random, with the prompts for the remaining clusters following in alphabetical order, in a round robin fashion. This method for presenting a randomly selected initial cluster increases voter privacy by preventing selection detection via eavesdropping bystanders.

Table 1. Standard letter clusters

Cluster Letters
A, B, C, D, E
F, G, H, I, J
K, L, M, N, O
P, Q, R, S, T
U, V, W, X, Y, Z

The purpose of this randomization is to secure ballot anonymity by ensuring that bystanders would not be able to decipher for whom the voter voted. The initial cluster is chosen using a weighted random; each cluster may not have an equal chance of being chosen first. The weights for the clusters depend on the letter position of the name being spelled and the names in the database. Once the first letter has been selected, the system is able to present a common letter cluster prior to the presentation of the five standard letter cluster prompts. This common letter cluster consists of the three most common next letters, given the letters previously selected by the voter. The most common letter cluster is a special cluster that is dependent on the presence of database name matches to the letters already selected. For example, suppose the voter is spelling the intended candidate's last name, and has selected 'C' as the first letter. Based on the records in the database, the three most frequent letters that follow 'C' as the first letter are presented in this "most common letter" cluster.

The most common letter cluster expedites the selection process since the voter is able to make selections at this point, rather than potentially traversing each of the standard letter clusters. If the next letter of the name is not in the most common letter cluster, the voter is then prompted to select one of the standard clusters.

Figure 2 demonstrates the process of presenting cluster prompts to the voter. Once the voter selects the correct cluster containing the next letter of the desired candidate's name, s/he is prompted to choose from those letters: if the voter selects the cluster of letters {A, B, C, D, E}, s/he is prompted to choose from those letters within that cluster; if the voter selects the cluster of the most common letters, for example, {R, A, E}, s/he is prompted to choose a letter from that common letter cluster. Once the desired letter is chosen, the system moves on to the set of prompts for the voter to select the next letter of the write-in candidate's name.

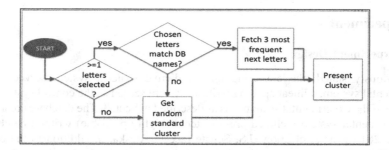

Fig. 2. Auditory write-in cluster prompt algorithm

3.2 Name Prediction

The prediction system for writing in a candidate's name is made possible through the use of a local database of names. The database contains two types of names; common names and names that have the highest probability of being written-in. The high probability names stored are based on pre-registered write-in candidates and other highly popular write-in names (e.g. Mickey Mouse). The database also contains a table of the top 1000 ranked surnames, a table containing the top 1000 ranked male names and the top 1000 ranked female names from the 1990 United States Census [12, 13]. Because there is a single database table for given names, the Census rankings of each name needed to be altered to form a single ranking scheme for both male and female names. This new ranking scheme, combining male and female names into a single list, was based on the percent frequency of name popularity rather than the sole rank.

In order to effectively reduce the amount of time a voter spends to write-in a candidate's name, this system utilizes a name prediction method built on the name database. The names suggested are fetched from the name database depending on the letters already chosen by the voter. If one of the predicted names is correct, the voter does not need to go through the entire spelling process. There are various aspects in the timing of the name predictions. A visual summary of the name prediction operation is shown in Fig. 3.

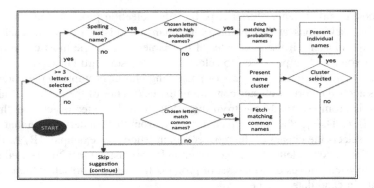

Fig. 3. Auditory write-in prediction algorithms

4 Experiment

4.1 Experiment Design

As previously stated, the clustering and predictive write-in system served as the experimental system; a linear spelling write-in system served as the control system. The interface of the experimental system was as described in Sect. 3. The database created for the experimental system included pre-registered (highly probable) write-in candidates from the 2010 general election U.S. Senate race in Alaska, in addition to the census names. The linear system was modeled after the write-in methods used in the DRE systems described in Sect. 2, and uses neither clustering nor prediction during the write-in process. To write-in a name using the linear system, participants were presented each letter of the alphabet sequentially, beginning with the letter 'A', selecting one at a time until the spelling is complete. This linear system was used for the comparison of results of the experiment.

The experiment was designed to randomly divide the participants into two groups. The participants in the first group interacted with the systems via speech input (herein referred to as the "speech group"); the participants in the second group interacted with the systems via switch input (herein referred to as the "switch group"). Participants in both groups were prompted to make selections via speakers (for observation). Speech group participants made selections via microphone; switch group participants interacted with the system via a 2-button switch – pressing the right button moved to the next prompt, while pressing the left button made selections. Within each group, two tasks were completed on both the experimental and linear systems.

4.2 Tasks

System prompts can only be interrupted when using the switch input method, and not using the speech input method. Therefore, completing the evaluation tasks via the speech input method on the linear control system would overburden the study participants. Instead, the corresponding tasks were simulated under a best-case scenario for the speech input group in order to evaluate the efficiency of the control system vs. the experimental system.

4.3   Participants

There were 40 participants in this study; all were recruited from Auburn University. The demographic results indicated that the age range for the participants was 19 to 27, with an average 20.2 years of age. There were 34 males to participate in this study, making up 85% of the participants. Three of the participants listed that they had disabilities; one indicated dyslexia, another indicated loss of hearing in one ear, and another indicated poor vision.

5   Results and Discussion

The performance metrics evaluated during the experiment in this study were effectiveness and efficiency. The effectiveness is determined by analyzing the accuracy of task completion. Efficiency is determined by measuring the task completion time. User satisfaction was measured based on the participants' response from the post-experiment questionnaire. The following sections report on the findings for each of the usability metrics individually.

5.1   Effectiveness

In this study, the effectiveness was measured discretely as success and failure. A task was deemed successful if the participant completed the spelling of a name correctly. If a participant was unable to complete the spelling, or if upon completion the name spelled was incorrect, the task was declared a failure. As previously stated, one of the expected outcomes of the experiment was that the participants would be able to accurately complete the given tasks using both input methods. 93.75 percent of the tasks were completed successfully on the experimental system, including participants in both the speech and switch groups. Zero participants failed multiple tasks. Of the five failed tasks, one task ended before the spelling of the name was complete; four were incorrectly spelled name submissions.

5.2   Efficiency

An expected outcome of the experiment was that the experimental system would be more efficient than the linear system. The results of this investigation are reported in this section. The experimental procedure for participants in the speech group differed from that of the switch group. Therefore, efficiency data for each of the two groups was analyzed separately. Tables 2 and 3 are discussed in the reporting of both groups.

Speech Interaction. The average time-to-task for Task A (user-chosen names) on the experimental system was 5.19 m; the average time-to-task for the same names on the linear system was 8.12 m (see Table 2). A total of 21 user chosen names were spelled during the study. 81 percent of the names' chosen had a record in the database; 88 percent of those names were suggested to the participants. Of the names suggested, the participants selected 87 percent (see Table 3).

Table 2. Analysis summary for user chosen names for speech and switch interactions

Interaction Type	Measure	Experimental System	Linear System
Speech	Average Time-to-Task	5.19 mins (std. dev. 1.99)	8.12 mins (std. dev. 2.07)
Switch	Average Time-to-Task	3.51 mins (std. dev. 0.97)	4.90 mins (std. dev. 1.58)

Table 3. Common name records, speech and switch interaction selection percentage

Measure	Speech	Switch
Number of User Chosen Names Spelled	21	19
Names with Database Records	80.95%	73.68%
Intended Names Suggested to Participant	88.24%	92.86%
Suggested Names Selected by Participant	86.67%	100%

Figure 3 provides a more in-depth comparison of both systems used in the speech group. The shortest surname chosen was "Doe" (three letters); the longest surnames spelled were "Johnson" and "Patrick" (seven letters). The surname length with the fastest time-to-task was the three-letter group on the experimental system, at 2.83 m. The surname length with the slowest time-to-task was the seven-letter group on the linear system, at 11.00 m. The smallest difference in time-to-task between the two systems was the three-letter group, with a time difference of 0.85 m. The largest difference was the six-letter group, with a time difference of 4.02 m. The time-to-task

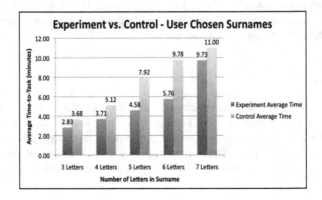

Fig. 4. Time-to-task by name length for user chosen names for speech interaction

data was evaluated statistically via the Wilcoxon Rank Sum test, showing that the experimental system is faster than the linear system ($p < 0.0001$) (Fig. 4).

Switch Interaction. The average time-to-task for Task A (user-chosen names) on the experimental system was 3.51 m; the average time-to task for the same names on the linear system was 4.9 m (see Table 2). Of the 19 surnames chosen in the switch input group, there were records in the database for 74 percent of these names; 93 percent of the names with database records were suggested to the participants. When names were suggested, 100 percent of the participants selected the name (see Table 3). Figure 5 provides a more in-depth comparison of both systems used in the switch group. The shortest surname chosen was "Doe" (three letters); the longest surnames spelled were "Newton" and "Dawkin" (six letters). There were four, four-letter surnames spelled, averaging 2.94 on the experimental system and 3.61 on the linear system. Averaging 3.34 and 5.18 on the experimental and linear systems, respectively, were 12 five-letter surnames. The time-to-task data was evaluated statistically via the paired t-test, showing that the experimental system is between 1.4 and 2.5 m faster than the linear system (95% confidence). The results of the t-test ($p < 0.0001$) suggest that the experimental system is faster than the linear system. Figure 4 depicts a summary of the statistical analysis of the time-to-task for the speech interaction method.

5.3 User Satisfaction

The post-questionnaire was used to gain knowledge of the participants' opinion of the system designs used in this experiment. Since only the participants in the switch group performed tasks on the linear system, user satisfaction data on the linear system was not collected from the participants in the speech group (Table 4). The Signed Rank Wilcoxon test shows that, for statements one through five, there was not enough evidence to show a difference between the two systems ($p > 0.05$). However, in response to the usability statement, results suggest that the linear system was more usable than the experimental system ($p = 0.03$). In addition, Table 4 shows the results of a combined analysis of the questionnaire responses. Overall, there was insufficient evidence to show a significant difference in the user satisfaction between the two systems ($p = 0.17$) (Fig. 5).

Table 4. Switch interaction method – experiment vs. control user satisfaction analysis

User Satisfaction Statement	Wilcoxon p-value
1. This method is easy to use.	0.5547
2. It was easy to understand the instructions.	0.0781
3. It was easy to correct my spelling mistakes.	0.9375
4. I feel that I made selections privately.	1.000
5. This method should be used for voting during elections.	0.3828
6. Usable	0.0313
Overall User Perception	0.1698

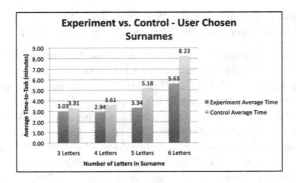

Fig. 5. Switch interaction- user chosen summary by name

6   Conclusion

The ultimate goal of electronic voting systems today should be to allow anyone to vote privately and independently. The VVSG provides useful and necessary guidelines to ensure that all eligible citizens have the same access when voting, regardless of a person's disability. The primary objective of this research was to embrace these guidelines by developing a universal design in which a person can efficiently, anonymously, and independently write-in a candidate's name during an election. The method designed allows voters to spell a candidate's name discretely through multimodal interaction. This method uses a clustering and predictive approach in order for the voter to get through the voting process of writing-in a candidate's name quickly and accurately.

The objective of this research was evaluated by analyzing different methods of writing-in a candidate's name. The evaluation measures were the time taken to complete write-in tasks, accuracy of the task completion, and user perception of the write-in method used. Analysis of these three measures led to the determination of the predictive system's efficiency, effectiveness, and user satisfaction. The evaluation results suggest that the system is effective, given that 94 percent of all tasks were completed, efficient, with statistically significant evidence showing that voters can write-in names faster with the predictive system than with the linear systems in use today, and provides user satisfaction, with statistical significance that the overall user perception of the system is significantly above a mid-range neutral ranking. Overall, the results of the experiment show that the designed system is an effective and efficient solution to writing-in a candidate's name.

References

1. Keele, L., Titiunik, R., Zubizarreta, J.: Enhancing a geographic regression discontinuity design through matching to estimate the effect of ballot initiatives on voter turnout. J. R. Stat. Soc: Ser. A **178**(1), 223–239 (2012)
2. Mauer, R.: Miller Files Suit in State Court Over Senate Vote Count. Anchorage Daily News (2010). http://www.adn.com/2010/11/22/1567823/miller-files-vote-suit-instate.html#ixzz 169P30wmY

3. Mace, R., Hardie, G., Plaice, J.: Accessible environments: toward universal design. In: Preiser, W.E., Vischer, J.C., White, E.T. (eds.) Design Interventions: Toward A More Humane Architecture, p. 156. Van Nostrand Reinhold, New York (1991)
4. Voluntary Voting System Guidelines Recommendations to the Election Assistance Commission (2007). http://www.eac.gov/files/vvsg/Final-TGDC-VVSG-08312007.pdf
5. Helm, B.: Ins and Outs of Write-Ins.(2004). http://www.businessweek.com/bwdaily/dnflash/nov2004/nf2004112_5680_db038.htm
6. North Carolina State University Center for Universal Design (2008). http://www.design.ncsu.edu/cud/about_ud/about_ud.htm
7. Institute for Human Centered Design (2008). http://www.adaptiveenvironments.org/index.php?option=Content&Itemid=3
8. Independent, Secret and Verifiable: A Guide to Making Voting an Independent and Accessible Process for People Who Are Blind and Visually Impaired . American Council of the Blind, September 2002. http://www.acb.org/resources/votingbook1.html
9. Dix, A., Finlay, J., Abowd, G., Beale, R.: Human Computer Interaction, 3rd edn. Prentice Hall, London (2004). ISBN 0-13-046109-1
10. State of Alaska Division of Elections. General Election Results (2010). http://www.elections.alaska.gov/results/10GENR/indexWI.shtml
11. Prime III: One Machine, One Vote for Everyone. http://primevotingsystem.org/
12. United States Census Bureau (2011). http://factfinder.census.gov/
13. Butler, R. (2005). http://names.mongabay.com/

Virtual Fingerprint - Image-Based Authentication Increases Privacy for Users of Mouse-Replacement Interfaces

Viktoria Grindle[1], Syed Kamran Haider[2],
John Magee[1(✉)], and Marten van Dijk[2]

[1] Math and Computer Science Department, Clark University,
950 Main St,Worcester, MA 01610, USA
{vgrindle,jmagee}@clarku.edu
[2] Department of Electrical Engineering and Computer Science,
University of Connecticut, Storrs, CT 06269, USA
syed.haider@uconn.edu, vandijk@engr.uconn.edu

Abstract. Current secondary user authentication methods are imperfect. They either rely heavily on a user's ability to remember key preferences and phrases or they involve providing authentication on multiple devices. However, malicious attacks that compromise a user's device or discover personal information about the user are becoming more sophisticated and increasing in number. Users who rely on mouse-replacement interfaces face additional privacy concerns when monitored or assisted by caregivers. Our authentication method proposes a way of quantifying a user's personality traits by observing his selection of images. This method would not be as vulnerable to malicious attacks as current methods are because the method is based on psychological observations that can not be replicated by anyone other than the correct user. As a preliminary evaluation, we created a survey consisting of slides of images and asked participants to click through them. The results indicated our proposed authentication method has clear potential to address these issues.

Keywords: Human-Computer Interaction · Mouse-replacement interfaces · Security · Privacy · Behavioral biometric · Authentication · Camera Mouse · Virtual Fingerprint

1 Introduction

We investigate privacy implications of users with severe motion impairments that use mouse replacement interfaces. Users of such interfaces interact with a computer via an on-screen pointer that is always visible to anybody who is also able to see the screen. This creates privacy concerns, for example, when such an interface is used with an on-screen keyboard to enter a password. We propose to use a "virtual fingerprint" to authenticate such users in a way that maintains privacy despite observation yet can be accomplished entirely on-screen with mouse-replacement interfaces.

© Springer International Publishing Switzerland 2015
M. Antona and C. Stephanidis (Eds.): UAHCI 2015, Part IV, LNCS 9178, pp. 182–191, 2015.
DOI: 10.1007/978-3-319-20687-5_18

We work with people who use the Camera Mouse [4] – a mouse replacement interface that tracks head motion to move a mouse pointer on the screen. Users of other pointer-manipulation interfaces such as trackballs, accessible joysticks, or head and mouth actuated controllers face similar issues. Previous investigations of this interface modality revealed that users were concerned about their privacy while using a variety of software programs [10].

Online social networks can be used to address loneliness and isolation issues that people with disabilities sometimes face. However, some challenges include lack of privacy (the caregiver is always present), lack of autonomy, and inadequate computer literacy of caregivers [2,5,9].

Users of the Camera Mouse typically use the software with a caregiver. It can be difficult to maintain privacy and security while authenticating (i.e., "logging in") to various services. Beyond social networks, users may need to authenticate to email, file or photo sharing, online banking, or health care-related services. Users are faced with a choice of letting a caregiver observe the password as it is entered in an on-screen keyboard, allowing the caregiver to know the password and enter it themselves, or trust them to look away as it is entered.

A "virtual fingerprint" is a behavioural biometric way to authenticate users of mouse-replacement interfaces that is tolerant to observation. It involves authentication through the selection of images. An initial investigation of this approach for secondary user authentication (e.g., replacement of security questions) was conducted.

2   Related Work

2.1   Graphical Passwords

Using images to authenticate a user has been studied in the past. One such common area of study is on the use of graphical passwords. Graphical passwords are intended to replace regular passwords [7]. These passwords are easier for the user to remember and are also more difficult to brute force since there are no weak passwords. A couple early studies tested how well graphical passwords could be used to authenticate users.

One early pioneering study, called "Deja Vu" [7], had participants select images they liked and then had them find the images later on among a large assembly of other random images. A second early study, "Hash Visualization" [11], also had users select previously seen images. However, these images used "random art" [11] (a randomly generated image) to generate an image for the user to memorize rather than having the user pick their own images. Both studies as well as others concluded using images for authentication is easier for users as well as just as secure as regular textual and numeric based passwords against brute force [8]. Numerous other studies have also been conducted in the area of graphical passwords. The glaring problem with these authentication techniques is that they are intended to provide the user with an easier time with passwords rather than to specifically prevent certain kinds of attacks. If the user's device is compromised or if a malicious attacker is observing the communication between a user and the service provider they could still easily observe what images the user is clicking on (similar to observing what textual password a user is typing in) and use those images to log into the user's account in the future.

2.2 Biometrics

Recent research in the category of behavioral and physiological biometrics as authentication techniques [1] also has shown a lot of promise. Physiological biometrics are traits that can be used to distinguish one person from another such as a physical fingerprint, DNA sample, retina scan, and many others. Behavioral biometrics on the other hand focus more on behavioral traits and tendencies that define an individual. For example, observing how a user types or how they phrase sentences is a behavioral biometric. Other commonly studied behavioral biometrics to use for authentication purposes include observing "keystroke dynamics" and "mouse dynamics" [1].

One particular study tested out the effectiveness of using keystroke and mouse dynamics to detect "computer intrusions" [1]. The implementation they proposed and experiments conducted were shown to be extremely effective in detecting intrusion and identifying users. However, these biometrics still present issues. First of all, a lot of individual key and mouse habit data is needed to form a profile for the user. This tends to take time to gather and is not entirely feasible or convenient for a company to do for each of their users. Secondly, in order to record this data, special software usually needs to be installed on the client's machine. Lastly, although it would be significantly more difficult than with graphical passwords, if a malicious attacker is observing the user's mouse and/or key strokes they could potentially gather enough data to replicate the user's style in the future. This study intended for the implementation to be used to detect general computer intrusions rather than for a service provider to authenticate a user.

3   Methodology

A virtual fingerprint of a user is a measure of their personality and behavior. The fingerprint is created by a user upon account creation and stored in the system. Each subsequent time the user logs in they would go through a short series of slides which generates a fingerprint and compares it to the one currently stored for him to determine if its a close enough match. The slides contain images that correspond to previously determined personality categories. The categories and images are randomly selected with each generated slide. The categories are also unknown to the user or any other observer, making it difficult for a malicious attacker to replicate a user's personality pattern. A user is instructed to click on images he likes which are then used to form his personal image selection pattern, what we call his virtual fingerprint. The slides are generated based on an algorithm to test for particular features used to categorize users and derive correlation (Fig. 1).

Fig. 1. Sample slide displaying 4 randomly selected images.

3.1 Design

In order to test out the potential effectiveness of using personality based images to authenticate a user we conducted a study that enrolled approximately 160 participants. This study was conducted using two online surveys. The first survey recorded responses from approximately 100 participants and the second from approximately 60 participants. Our participants were mostly volunteers from Amazon Mechanical Turk, which is an online service that allows users to take surveys and perform small tasks in exchange for compensation. The participants were required to be 18 years of age or older and be living in the USA. We created an online survey that consisted of 60 slides. Each slide contained 4 randomly selected images and each image corresponded to a particular personality category. No category was repeated on the same page and we developed an algorithm to make sure each category was seen an equal number of times. This prevented any unnecessary polluting of the results from a participant seeing some categories more than others. The image database consisted of a total of 224 images and 28 personality categories. Each category consisted of 8 images. Before deploying the second survey the image database was doubled. Each category then contained 16 images instead of 8 in order to see if having a larger number of images and less image repeats would affect the results. We also implemented a 5 s timer on each slide which refreshed the page if an image was not clicked. The timer was included in the survey design to promote an initial reaction from participants and prevent long periods of decision making from adding bias to the results. Each participant was instructed to simply select images they liked. Additionally, a 'can't decide' button was added to each slide in case the participant had no immediate preference for any of the images.

Users of mouse-replacement interfaces would be able to complete this survey simply by moving the mouse pointer over the image they wish to choose. We hypothesized that the two features we tested for would be significantly different if a participant was looking at their own slides versus if they were looking at another participant's slides (Fig. 2).

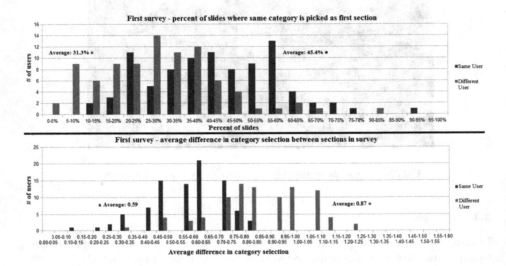

Fig. 2. Results of category selection from preliminary authentication experiment.

3.2 Feature Testing

After a user went through the first 20 slides, these 20 slides were selected again at random and shown to the same user. Each slide of this set of 20 contained the same 4 categories as a slide from the first set of 20. However, a different image was randomly selected from each category so neither an attacker nor a participant would be aware what slide or category he was being shown. This second set of 20 slides tested for one of two features. Firstly, it tested to see what percent of the time a participant would select the same category from a set of 4 categories as they did previously. This, we believed would be a much higher percentage than if the participant selected categories from another participant's set of first 20 slides. The second feature we tested for was overall variance in category selection. Each of the 28 categories was selected a certain number of times in a participant's first 20 slides. We compared that number to the number of times each category was selected in the next 20 slides and computed an average difference in same category selection. This, we believed would be a much smaller difference between category selection if a participant was looking at their own slides than if he was looking at another participant's slides. The third and final set of 20 slides randomly selected slides from a different randomly selected participant's first 20 slides. The purpose of this third set of 20 slides was to compare the features we tested for in the participant's first 20 slides with a different participant's first 20 slides. We hypothesized that the two features (mentioned above) we tested for would be significantly different if a participant was looking at their own slides versus if they were looking at another participant's slides. To determine how correct this assumption is, we performed linear regression analysis on the first half of the data set from the second survey (30 participants) and tested that model on the second half of the data set from the same survey as well as all of the data from the first survey (100 participants). The linear regression model quantified the correlation between the two features. It output a predicted value which was then compared to the actual value for each user. If the actual value was higher than the predicted, the authentication would be approved. If it was lower, the authentication would be rejected. This model had a correct positive and correct negative prediction rate which will be discussed in the next section.

4   Results

4.1   Distribution of Data

The second feature we tested for showed more weight in authenticating a user than the first feature. This can be seen in the normal distribution graphs for both features (Fig. 2). Participants on average selected the same categories on the same slides as they had previously 45.4 % (first survey) and 41 % (second survey) of the time. On the other hand participants only selected the same categories of another participant's slides as that participant had selected an average of 31.3 % (first survey) and 29.5 % (second survey) of the time. As for the second feature, participants on average had an average difference between overall category selection on their own slides of 0.59 (first survey) and 0.62 (second survey). They also on average had an average difference between overall category selection on another participant's slides of 0.87 (first survey) and 0.89 (second survey). It is obvious from the normal distribution that neither feature can solely be used to predict if a user is who they say they are or not. This is apparent from the overlap between a true user and a 'hacker' present in both normal distribution curves.

4.2   Regression Analysis

As mentioned previously both features were plotted against one another and ana-lyzed using a linear regression model. After performing linear regression analysis on the first half of the data from the second survey, we came up with the follow-ing regression model: $Y = 45.596X-2.238$ where Y represents the percent of same categories picked and X represents the average difference in category selection. After running the rest of the data from the second survey through the regression equation, our model correctly predicted that a user was truly who he claimed to be (correct positive rate) 75 % of the time and correctly predicted that a user

Regression Model: Y = 45.596*X − 2.238	First Survey
Y = percent of same categories picked as on previous slides	Correct positive rate: 78%
	Correct negative rate: 68%
X = average difference in category selection for each category	Second Survey
If actual user's Y > predicted Y approve authentication else, reject authentication.	Correct positive rate: 75%
	Correct negative rate: 75%

Fig. 3. Summary of linear regression statistics

was not who he claimed to be (correct negative rate) 75 % of the time as well. This created an overall accuracy rate of 75 %. In the first survey the correct positive rate was 78 % and the correct negative rate was 68 % which makes for an overall accuracy of 73 % (Fig. 3).

On a quick side note, as mentioned previously the second survey was designed the same as the first but with twice as many images to determine if authentication was affected by a participant seeing repeated images. From our results we concluded that doubled image database size had little effect on the accuracy (73 % is close to 75 %). The second survey also added a third set of 20 slides which tested for the same two features on the same random participant picked from the second set of 20 slides. This was designed to determine if a participant would have consistent results for both of their features if given another participants 20 slides twice. Our accuracy statistics above point to yes since there was about the same level of accuracy for each survey, one with the additional 20 slides and one without. Overall, it is clear that there is promising probability that our theory of using personality based images to authenticate a user could be a viable option (Fig. 4).

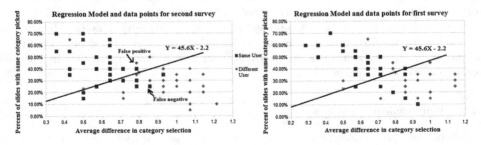

Fig. 4. Linear regression model.

5   Conclusion and Future Work

Although our regression model shows high potential for further implementation, there are a few weaknesses and concerns we noticed in the overall system. Firstly, motivating users to be active participants that pay attention to their image selection can be difficult. Any amount of randomness to their selection technique will quickly lead to a false negative. Some users may find it inconvenient to go through 20 slides of images after providing their user name and passwords. For implementation in the real world, this technique might serve better as an optional authentication method, unless a service provider is able to turn the authentication into a type of game or reward system that will provide incentive for the user. The second issue is a vulnerability in dealing with a particular type of malicious attack. The proposed virtual fingerprint method is theoretically secure from a brute force attack. There are many possible answers to a set of N slides which grows exponentially in N. Finding the exact desired answer is therefore hard to find. Of course, the authentication procedure is threshold based and large subsets of possible answers will lead to authentication: in the study a malicious attacker has 25 % probability (for N=20) to be successful in correctly guessing a member of such a larger subset. This probability corresponds to being able to guess a set of answers whose "distance" to the exact desired answer is within some threshold. As N grows larger, a malicious attacker will have a much lower probability of achieving a successful guess. From the user perspective, a large N is user unfriendly. For this reason we will investigate techniques that allow to capture more authentication content per slide. The Virtual Fingerprint is also theoretically secure from device compromising, and observation of communication between a client and server, since the images are random and unpredictable and also only have significance to the user. However, the one point of vulnerability is if the attacker personally knows the user very well and could potentially predict what images the user will select. We consider it to be a low risk for an attacker to personally know the user that well. However, it is still worth testing out.

The accuracy of our regression model is high enough to be promising but low enough to indicate that much more research is needed to bring up the accuracy before this authentication method can be implemented in a real world setting. We plan on adding dimensions to our survey and re deploying it to test for further correlations and reduce overlap between 'true users' and 'hackers'. In this study we only tested for two features. However, adding an additional one or two features would create for a more accurate regression model and overall prediction. Additionally, we also plan to test to see if increasing the number of initial slides (which for this experiment was 20) will increase accuracy of the regression model. Also, more research is needed to better determine potential personality categories as well as what images are proper representatives of each personality trait. Lastly, after raising the accuracy for this study we plan on doing a time based analysis where we have participants do the survey twice with a certain amount of time (at least one month) in between. This will determine how well our method can authenticate a user repeatedly and over time.

Using the "virtual fingerprint" with mouse-replacement interfaces is a promising approach to providing privacy and security for users with disabilities. Improvements to the accuracy of the system via additional research is ongoing, and user studies with people with disabilities are planned. We believe that this approach could be implemented as part of a password manager (software that stores user's passwords and fills them in automatically) or a strategy in an accessible authentication framework [3]. Such a password manager with virtual fingerprint authentication would provide a good level of usability and some level of privacy for our users.

Acknowledgments. The authors would like to thank their participants. We would also like to thank John Chandy for his extensive guidance and the University of Connecticut for hosting the Research Experience for Undergraduates where much of the study discussed in this paper was conducted. Lastly we would like to thank the NSF for providing funding through the CNS-1359329 grant.

References

1. Ahmed, A.A.E., Traore, I.: Detecting computer intrusions using behavioral biometrics. In: PST (2005)
2. Ballin, L., Baladin, S.: An exploration of loneliness: communication and the social networks of older people with cerebral palsy. J. Intellect. Dev. Disabil. **32**(4), 315–327 (2007)
3. Barbosa, N.: Strategies: an inclusive authentication framework. In: Proceedings of the 16th International ACM SIGACCESS Conference on Computers & Accessibility (ASSETS 2014), pp. 335–336. ACM (2014)
4. Betke, M., Gips, J., Fleming, P.: The camera mouse: visual tracking of body features to provide computer access for people with severe disabilities. IEEE Trans. Neural Syst. Rehabil. Eng. **10**(1), 1–10 (2002). IEEE
5. Cooper, L., Baladin, S., Trembath, D.: The loneliness experiences of young adults with cerebral palsy who use alternative and augmentative communication. Augment. Altern. Commun. **25**(3), 154–164 (2009)
6. Denning, T., Bowers, K., van Dijk, M., Juels, A.: Exploring implicit memory for painless password recovery. In: Proceedings of the SIGCHI Conference on Human Factors in Computing Systems (CHI 2011), pp. 2615–2618. ACM (2011)
7. Dhamija, R. Perrig, A.: Deja vu: a user study using images for authentication. In: Proceedings of the 9th Conference on USENIX Security Symposium, SSYM 2000, vol. 9. USENIX Association (2000)
8. Jermyn, I., Mayer, A.J., Monrose, F., Reiter, M.K., Rubin, A.D.: The design and analysis of graphical passwords. In: Usenix Security (1999)
9. Lewis, M.: Cerebral palsy and online social networks. In: The 12th International ACM SIGACCESS Conference on Computers and Accessibility (ASSETS 2010). ACM, October 2010
10. Magee, J.J., Betke, M.: Automatically generating online social network messages to combat social isolation of people with disabilities. In: Stephanidis, C., Antona, M. (eds.) UAHCI 2013, Part II. LNCS, vol. 8010, pp. 684–693. Springer, Heidelberg (2013)
11. Perrig, A., Song, D.: Hash visualization: a new technique to improve real-world security. In: International Workshop on Cryptographic Techniques and E-Commerce, pp. 131–138 (1999)

12. Schmidt, A-D., Bye, R, Schmidt, H-G., Clausenm J., Kiraz, O., Yuksel, K.A., Camtepe, S.A., Albayrak, S.: Static analysis of executables for collaborative malware detection on android. In: IEEE International Conference on Communications, ICC 2009, pp. 1–5. IEEE (2009)

Joystick Interaction Strategies of Individuals with Dexterity Impairments: Observations from the Smart Voting Joystick Usability Evaluation

James E. Jackson[1(✉)], Jennifer Ismirle[1], Sarah J. Swierenga[1], Stephen R. Blosser[2], and Graham L. Pierce[1]

[1] Usability/Accessibility Research and Consulting, Michigan State University, East Lansing, MI, USA
{jamesedj,ismirlej,sswieren,glpierce}@msu.edu
[2] Resource Center for Persons with Disabilities, Michigan State University, East Lansing, MI, USA
blossers@msu.edu

Abstract. In order to develop a joystick as a universal access device for accessible voting machines, it is necessary to observe and understand the strategies of users with disabilities when operating joysticks in this context. For this study, researchers analyzed video and audio recordings as well as written notes and user feedback from the usability evaluation of the Smart Voting Joystick to identify, document, and understand the interaction strategies individuals with motor or dexterity related disabilities employ when using a joystick to interact with a mock voting system.

Keywords: Assistive technology · Accessible voting · Joystick · Interaction strategies · Usability

1 Introduction

The Help America Vote Act of 2002 (or HAVA) was passed in order to reform the U.S. voting process, requiring polling places in all states to be physically accessible and to provide at least one accessible voting system for voters with disabilities, thereby allowing for independent and private voting [1]. However, although progress has been made, current electronic voting system equipment that is deemed "accessible" for persons with disabilities is inadequate and requires time and effort that can be prohibitive for these individuals to independently vote with confidence [2].

The U.S. Government Accountability Office found in 2013 that 46 % of polling locations still utilize voting systems that are not completely accessible, such as stations that do not accommodate wheelchairs [3]. In addition, the turnout rate in the November 2012 elections for voters with disabilities was 5.7 % less than the voter turnout rate for those without disabilities (if these voting rates had been the same, approximately 3 million more persons with disabilities would have voted), and 30.1 % of persons with disabilities reported encountering difficulties when voting in-person at a polling place

© Springer International Publishing Switzerland 2015
M. Antona and C. Stephanidis (Eds.): UAHCI 2015, Part IV, LNCS 9178, pp. 192–203, 2015.
DOI: 10.1007/978-3-319-20687-5_19

(versus 8.4 % of voters with no disabilities) [4]. As a result, the right to independent and private voting is often not guaranteed for individuals with disabilities, as they are likely to need assistance at a polling place with current systems.

According to the Voluntary Voting System Guidelines (VVSG) 1.0 of the U.S. Election Assistance Commission, voters with disabilities should be provided with support that is built into voting equipment and should not be required to provide their own personal assistive technology to vote successfully [5]. Allowing voters with disabilities to connect personal assistive technology to voting equipment has been under consideration recently, but security concerns need to be addressed. Therefore, there is a need for universal access devices to allow persons with disabilities to easily and successfully vote at polling places.

Because the usefulness of joysticks as assistive technology for computers has been studied and discussed in previous research involving users with motor or dexterity impairments [6–10], we developed the Smart Voting Joystick [11] as a universal input device for accessible voting systems. A force feedback feature was also included in the design, as studies have shown that this force can enhance user performance and accelerate learning when using a joystick to control a computer [12] and a powered wheelchair [13].

1.1 Understanding Interaction Strategies for Joysticks and Other Input Devices

Usability evaluations of the Smart Voting Joystick made it apparent that individuals with motor and dexterity impairments use a variety of interaction strategies to manipulate a joystick and buttons to vote. These interaction strategies are not well documented in the existing literature, particularly in the context of voting and universal devices. For instance, hand poses and how various input devices are handled are briefly described in some studies [14–16], and some research has documented the interaction styles of individuals with motor and dexterity impairments when using touchscreen devices [17]. However, research on joysticks and other alternative input devices has primarily focused on the accuracy and success encountered when using these devices [8, 18, 19] and when using specific gestures in the case of touchscreens [20–22], and on developing adaptive interface systems that adjust based on the capability of the user [14, 23, 24].

Therefore, to address the need for a universal input device for voting systems that is accessible to the widest range of users and requires the least individual customization, it is essential to observe and better document the interaction strategies of users with motor and dexterity impairments when using joysticks in order to understand and appropriately accommodate voting for these users.

2 Methodology

Researchers analyzed video and audio recordings as well as written notes and user feedback from one-on-one usability evaluations of the Smart Voting Joystick [11].

2.1   Materials

The Smart Voting Joystick setup (see Fig. 1) included a dual-axis joystick (which allowed users to navigate in four directions) with haptic feedback and three external buttons (Enter, Review, and Help). For this study, the Smart Voting Joystick was connected to a desktop computer, via USB port.

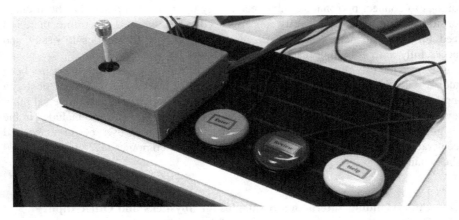

Fig. 1. The Smart Voting Joystick with Enter, Review, and Help buttons

The Smart Voting Joystick has adjustable features which were kept consistent during evaluation to allow for comparison across users. The force feedback (felt as a "pulse" when the joystick is moved) was set to a 30 ms pulse of 2.5 N, and the return-to-center force (how much effort is required to move the joystick) was set at 0.6 N. The button repeat delay (minimum time between inputs that are accepted by the system; actions taken within this interval are ignored) was set at 100 ms to filter tremors and other unintentional actions.

For the purposes of the usability evaluation, a simple user interface was developed which allowed users to vote the NIST Test Ballot [5]. This interface was optimized for the joystick and allowed users to navigate between contests using the joystick in conjunction with the buttons (e.g., to move to the next contest, users could move the joystick to the right to select an arrow icon, then press the Enter button to move to the next contest) or to move between contests with the joystick alone (e.g., after moving the joystick to the arrow icon, users could move it to the right again to move to the next contest). To ensure consistency during the evaluation, participants were instructed to vote for specific candidates.

2.2   Participants

The usability evaluation included six participants (five male and one female) with a wide range of dexterity impairments. These participants clearly split into two groups:

four participants with moderate dexterity impairments, primarily muscular weakness (Group 1); and two participants with much more significant dexterity impairments, including functional limitations of spasticity and control (Group 2).

All participants had previously voted in a federal or state election. Three participants voted by absentee ballot/mail-in, two participants had another person assist them in filling out a paper ballot at a polling place, and one participant filled out a paper ballot at the polling place without assistance.

3   Results

3.1   Group 1: Participants with Moderate Dexterity Impairments

Three of the four participants in Group 1 were able to complete the ballot accurately using the Smart Voting Joystick, and one participant voted incorrectly on only a single contest. All of the participants indicated that they would recommend the joystick to those with similar needs as themselves. Participants were only given minimal guidance by the moderator to complete the task. For example, when one user accidentally went past a contest before voting and then became confused, the moderator directed the user to go back to the previously missed contest and continue voting.

Joystick Interaction Strategies. The majority of users in Group 1 pushed or pulled the joystick with one or more fingers (see Figs. 2 and 3). Two participants grasped the joystick at times while pushing or pulling, and one participant grasped the joystick for nearly the entire session (see Fig. 4). Three of the participants rested the side of their hand or their wrist on the joystick box while using the joystick.

Fig. 2. Nudging with side of index finger (left) and thumb (right)

Pushing or Pulling. Pushing or pulling ranged from participants softly nudging the joystick (Fig. 2) to somewhat more forceful pushing or pulling (Fig. 3). Pushing or pulling of the joystick also varied from participants using one or two fingers (from the side or on top of the knob), a thumb, or all of their fingers or palm from the side. While pushing or pulling, participants rested their hand on the joystick box or hovered just above it.

Fig. 3. Pulling with all fingers (left) and pushing with two fingers (right)

Grasping. At times, participants grasped the joystick knob or stem with one or two fingers and their thumb, or used a hand resting on top of the joystick with one finger making most of the joystick movements (Fig. 4, left and center). One participant grasped the joystick for nearly the entire session, varying between grasping the joystick with the whole hand to move it (Fig. 4, right), or switching to a looser grip to nudge the joystick with only a thumb or fingers. This participant also switched to slightly wrapping their fingers around the stem of the joystick near the end of the session to scroll down, possibly due to fatigue. At times, when this participant was using a looser grip to move the joystick, they would pass a desired candidate or go on to the next contest before voting, accidentally moving the joystick more than intended while using this type of grip.

Fig. 4. Grasping knob and stem with two fingers and thumb (left), resting hand on top of joystick (center), and grasping with entire hand (right).

Button Interaction Strategies. Three of four participants in Group 1 used one hand for the joystick and the other hand for the buttons, and one participant used the same hand for both the joystick and the buttons. The three participants who used both hands rested their button hand on the table at times and occasionally hovered over the buttons. Two of the participants in Group 1 used one finger to press buttons, and two participants used their whole hand to press buttons.

Additional Observations. While participants in this group recommend improvements to the joystick design, they still indicated that they would recommend the joystick to those with similar needs. Participants in this group also expressed a preference for the dual-axis (four direction) joystick, as opposed to a single-axis (two direction) joystick.

The majority of participants in this group indicated that they would prefer less force feedback. Two participants were very surprised when they first moved the joystick and encountered the feedback, and one participant also thought that the feedback was a warning that they had pushed the joystick too far. One participant felt fatigue in their arm at the end of the session, and mentioned that they would prefer a joystick with less return-to-center force.

None of the four users in Group 1 held the joystick down to scroll through long candidate lists as expected, instead moving the joystick up or down one selection at a time. One participant specifically mentioned a preference for moving the joystick up or down one selection at a time, and noted that including page-up and page-down functions would be useful for long lists.

Two participants felt that a shorter and thicker joystick, more like those found on typical powered wheelchairs, would be easier to use and would allow more control. One participant indicated it was easier to move up and down with the joystick than left or right.

3.2   Group 2: Participants with Severe Dexterity Impairments

Both participants from Group 2 employed a wider variety of usage types and strategies than participants in Group 1, including operating the joystick with the forehead or chin. Because their impairments limited their ability to make fine movements, these users encountered a significant number of unintended actions and mistaken inputs that increased the time and effort required to vote.

One participant from Group 2 completed the ballot successfully with only minimal help (similar to participants in Group 1), and the second voted a portion of the ballot independently, then encountered difficulties and was unable to complete the voting tasks successfully. These difficulties primarily related to a lack of arm support, and problems with the size and shape of the joystick played a contributing role. This participant was given significant help with navigating the ballot throughout the session and, as a result, this session functioned more as an in-depth interview where researchers were able to collect important qualitative data.

Despite the fact that only one participant in Group 2 was able to vote successfully and that the testing demonstrated that the Smart Voting Joystick as it is currently configured does not cater to the needs of this user group specifically, both participants strongly endorsed a joystick in principle, and noted that adjusting specific features of the joystick, buttons, and user interface would improve its usability.

Joystick Interaction Strategies.   The two participants in Group 2 used a variety of strategies (usually in conjunction with each other) to operate the joystick, including pushing, pulling, striking, and flicking, as well as grasping the joystick at times while making these movements. Neither of these participants rested their hands on the table, though one used the joystick box at times to stabilize or rest their hand when bringing it toward the joystick to make a movement.

Pushing or Pulling.   Like Group 1, this group used pushing and pulling movements to interact with the system, ranging from nudges to more forceful movements. Movements were generally more forceful and were far more varied than in Group 1, including the use of a forehead (Fig. 5, left) or chin, closed fist, palm of hand (Fig. 5, right), knuckle of a finger or thumb (Fig. 6, left), a thumb, all fingers, fingertips over the top of the joystick, or a gap between fingers (Fig. 6, right).

Fig. 5. Pushing with forehead (left) and nudging with palm (right)

Fig. 6. Nudging with knuckle of index finger and thumb (left) and pushing with gap between index and middle finger (right).

Striking or Flicking.   Unlike Group 1, this group also used striking and flicking, which are more forceful movements than pushing or pulling, to navigate and make selections. Participants used their hands to strike the joystick at times in order to move it or to grasp it (Fig. 7, left and center), and they also flicked the joystick with their palm, fingers, or fingertips to move it (Fig. 7, right).

Grasping.   At times throughout the voting process, both participants in Group 2 grasped the joystick stem or knob with one or two fingers and a thumb to move the joystick (Fig. 8, left and center). Participants also grasped the joystick with their entire hand (Fig. 8, right), alternating between grasping from the left and right side of the joystick and with a hand or palm on top of the joystick. For these participants, grasping resulted in the most unintended actions (e.g., accidentally switching to a new contest) of any usage type. However, most of these errors were related to aspects of the test ballot's interface design and could be resolved with minor changes, such as requiring the use of multiple input devices to switch between contests (e.g., requiring the users to navigate to an arrow icon via the joystick and then pressing the Enter button to move between contests).

Fig. 7. Striking with back of hand (left), striking down with closed fist (center), and flicking with fingertips (right).

Fig. 8. Grasping stem of joystick with thumb and finger (left), grasping knob (center), grasping and holding with whole hand (right).

Button Interaction Strategies. When pressing the buttons, both of the participants in Group 2 used an entire hand, a fist, side of the hand, or fingertips. Neither of these participants rested their hands on the table (as Group 1 often did), but instead hovered over the joystick and buttons between movements.

Like the participants in Group 1, the participant who completed the ballot successfully used both hands to operate the joystick (one to press the buttons and one to operate the joystick). The second participant used one hand for both the joystick and the buttons (as well as their forehead and chin at times). This participant also used the foot pedal on their wheelchair as the Enter button, along with the other two tabletop buttons (Help and Review) to the left of the joystick.

Additional Observations. Both users in Group 2 were more successful when striking, flicking, or occasionally nudging the joystick, whereas grasping the joystick caused the most unintended actions, including unintentionally switching between contests and scrolling farther than intended. As a result, both users relied primarily on striking and flicking to vote the ballot, but also indicated they would have preferred a joystick they could hold without causing unintended inputs.

Although motions like striking and flicking were more successful, there were still a significant number of unintended inputs when participants employed this usage type. For instance, when one participant would move a hand toward the joystick to strike or flick it with an open palm, and when this participant would move a hand away after such an action, they would often accidentally hit the joystick with a thumb or finger. One participant indicated that moving the joystick away from their body was easier than moving it towards their body (presumably because moving the joystick to scroll down required either flicking or pulling, while moving it to scroll up allowed the use of nudging or striking motions). When asked, this participant said that the voting process would have been easier if the cursor had started at the bottom of the list of candidates instead of the top (so that they would need to scroll down less often).

For the participant who did not complete the voting process, many of the obstacles they experienced operating the joystick related to a lack of arm support. For instance, to operate their wheelchair joystick, this participant relied on the strong support provided by the wheelchair armrest to stabilize a forearm and then operate the joystick largely with wrist and fingers. However, because of the joystick position during the study, similar arm support was not possible, and the participant therefore needed to utilize their whole arm, unsupported, to operate the joystick. Furthermore, this participant was fully able to independently operate their wheelchair using a joystick (which was shorter, thicker, spherical joystick, and had substantial arm support via the armrest), indicating that their difficulties may be related to features of this specific joystick design.

While one participant experimented with scrolling quickly through the list of candidates while grasping and holding the joystick up or down, both participants preferred to scroll through candidates one by one like the participants in Group 1. Also similar to the other group, both participants in this group indicated that they would have preferred a joystick that was shorter and thicker, which would have been more consistent with joysticks these participants used previously for successfully interacting with information technology, and operating powered wheelchairs.

Unlike the participants in Group 1, one of the participants in this group expected the joystick to operate as a single-axis joystick, and felt that this would have been easier to use than a dual-axis joystick, and both participants in this group stated that they wanted a joystick that was "stiffer" (offering more return-to-center force) and provided stronger force feedback.

4   Discussion

From observing and analyzing the interaction strategies of individuals with dexterity and motor impairments while using the Smart Voting Joystick, we determined considerations which are critical for a universal access voting joystick and buttons. A variety of interaction strategies were used between and within the moderate and severe groups, and the majority of participants used more than one strategy throughout the voting task. Thus, it is necessary to accommodate a variety of joystick strategies, including both gentle and forceful movements (from pushing and pulling to striking and flicking). In addition, grasping is a potentially effective usage type that users will likely employ during the voting process, but joystick and interface designers need to ensure that grasping does not result in a high number of unintended inputs.

To meet the needs of a variety of users and support their preferred interaction strategies, the force feedback and return-to-center force levels of a voting joystick should be easily adjustable (by users and/or poll workers before voting begins). Both single-axis and dual-axis modes should also be offered.

As indicated by nearly all participants, a shorter and thicker (similar to the joysticks on powered wheelchairs) would facilitate a variety of interaction strategies, such as grasping or pulling the joystick. For example, a shorter, rounder joystick could prevent users with low motor control from "snagging" the joystick when moving their hand toward or away from the joystick.

Sufficient arm support needs to be provided to facilitate control and aid in reducing fatigue. For example, participants in Group 1 often rested their hands on the joystick or the table for support, and participants in Group 2 had difficulties using the Smart Voting Joystick because they could not stabilize their hand or arm as they could with their armrest while operating a wheelchair joystick.

The size and spacing of buttons used in conjunction with the joystick needs to accommodate the various interaction strategies of users, allowing the use of fingers and an entire hand without unintended inputs. Button sensitivity and careful timing of when buttons are active and inactive are crucial to preventing unintended inputs.

5 Conclusion

In order to further the development of a universal access voting joystick and buttons for the individuals, interaction strategies of individuals with motor and dexterity related disabilities were identified and documented during the usability evaluation of the Smart Voting Joystick. Further research and testing needs to be conducted in order to determine the range of feedback and default settings that need to be available to users, as well as to determine optimal joystick dimensions and button repeat delay. Arm support options for joysticks and buttons, such as universal access mounts, also need to be considered and researched to determine the best option to accommodate voters using wheelchairs.

Acknowledgements. This research was funded through a grant from the Information Technology & Innovation Foundation (ITIF), Accessible Voting Technology Initiative to Michigan State University (ITIF Subgrant No. 2013004; Prime Grant No. EAC110149B – U.S. Election Assistance Commission). PI: Dr. Sarah J. Swierenga, Michigan State University, Usability/Accessibility Research and Consulting (UARC). The Smart Voting Joystick was developed in partnership between UARC, rehabilitation engineers from the MSU Resource Center for Persons with Disabilities (RCPD), and MSU Engineering students.

References

1. Help America Vote Act of 2002, Pub. L. No. 107-252, 116 Stat. 1666-1730, codified at 42 U.S.C. §§15301-15545 (2002)
2. Swierenga, S.J., Pierce, G.L.: Accessible voting system usability measures. J. Technol. Persons Disabil. **1**, 146–154 (2013)
3. Bovbjerg, B.: Voters with Disabilities: Challenges to Voting Accessibility. U.S. Government Accountability Office, Washington, D.C. (2013)
4. Schur, L., Adya, M., Kruse, D.: Disability, Voter Turnout, and Voting Difficulties in the 2012 Elections. Report to U.S. EAC and RAAV (2013)
5. U.S. Election Assistance Commission: Voluntary Voting System Guidelines 1.0. U.S. EAC, Washington, D.C. (2005)
6. Blosser, S., Eulenberg, J.B.: A customized joystick for computer control. In: 38th Annual Conference on Engineering in Medicine and Biology, p. 47.4. AEMB, Chicago (1985)
7. Brodwin, M.G., Star, T., Cardoso, E.: Computer assistive technology for people who have disabilities: computer adaptations and modifications. J. Rehab. **70**(3), 28–33 (2004)
8. LoPresti, E.F., Romich, B.A., Hill, K.J., Spaeth, D.M.: Evaluation of mouse emulation using the wheelchair joystick. In: RESNA 27th International Annual Conference, Orlando (2004)
9. Nischelwitzer, A.K., Sproger, B., Mahr, M., Holzinger, A.: MediaWheelie – a best practice example for research in multimodal user interfaces (MUIs). In: Miesenberger, K., Klaus, J., Zagler, W.L., Karshmer, A.I. (eds.) ICCHP 2006. LNCS, vol. 4061, pp. 999–1005. Springer, Heidelberg (2006)
10. Begnum, M.E.N., Begnum, K.M.: On the usefulness of off-the-shelf computer peripherals for people with Parkinson's disease. Univ. Access Inf. Soc. **11**, 347–357 (2012)
11. Swierenga, S.J., Pierce, G.L., Blosser, S.R., Mathew, A., Jackson, J.E.: Smart Voting Joystick for accessible voting machines. J. Technol. Persons Disabil. **2**, 144–154 (2014)
12. Rosenberg, L., Brave, S.: Using force feedback to enhance human performance in graphical user interfaces. In: Conference Companion on Human Factors in Computing Systems, pp. 291–292. ACM, New York (1996)
13. Chen, X., Agrawal, S.K.: Assisting versus repelling force-feedback for learning of a line following task in a wheelchair. IEEE Trans. Neural Syst. Rehabil. Eng. **21**(6), 959–968 (2013)
14. Gajos, K.Z., Wobbrock, J.O., Weld, D.S.: Improving the performance of motor-impaired users with automatically-generated, ability-based interfaces. In: SIGCHI Conference on Human Factors in Computing Systems, pp. 1257–1266. ACM, New York (2008)
15. Trewin, S., Swart, C., Pettick, D.: Physical accessibility of touchscreen smartphones. In: 15th International ACM SIGACCESS Conference on Computers and Accessibility, Article No. 19. ACM, New York (2013)
16. Carrington, P., Hurst, A., Kane, S.K.: The gest-rest: a pressure-sensitive chairable input pad for power wheelchair armrests. In: 16th International ACM SIGACCESS Conference on Computers and Accessibility, pp. 201–208. ACM, New York (2014)
17. Anthony, L., Kim, Y., Findlater, L.: Analyzing user-generated youtube videos to understand touchscreen use by people with motor impairments. In: SIGCHI Conference on Human Factors in Computing Systems, pp. 1223–1232. ACM, New York (2013)
18. Hwang, F., Keates, S., Langdon, P., Clarkson, P.J., Robinson, P.: Perception and haptics: towards more accessible computers for motion-impaired users. In: Workshop on Perceptive User Interfaces, pp. 1–9. ACM, New York (2001)

19. Wobbrock, J.O., Gajos, K.Z.: Goal crossing with mice and trackballs for people with motor impairments: performance, submovements, and design directions. ACM Trans. Accessible Comput. 1(1), Article 4, 1–37 (2008)
20. Froehlich, J., Wobbrock, J.O., Kane, S.K.: Barrier pointing: using physical edges to assist target acquisition on mobile device touch screens. In: Proceedings of the 9th International ACM SIGACCESS Conference on Computers and Accessibility, pp. 19–26. ACM, New York (2007)
21. Guerreiro, T., Nicolau, H., Jorge, J., Gonçalves, D.: Towards accessible touch interfaces. In: 12th International ACM AIGACCESS Conference on Computers and Accessibility, pp. 19–26. ACM, New York (2010)
22. Irwin, C.B., Sesto, M.E.: Performance and touch characteristics of disabled and non-disabled participants during a reciprocal tapping task using touch screen technology. Appl. Ergon. **43**, 1038–1043 (2012)
23. Keates, S., Clarkson, J., Robinson, P.: Investigating the applicability of user models for motion-impaired users. In: 4th International ACM Conference on Assistive Technologies, pp. 129–136. ACM, New York (2000)
24. Kurschl, W., Augstein, M., Stitz, H., Heumader, P., Pointner, C.: A user modelling wizard for people with motor impairments. In: Proceedings of International Conference on Advances in Mobile Computing and Multimedia, p. 541. ACM, New York (2013)

A Universal Ballot to Enable Voting for All

Seunghyun "Tina" Lee$^{(\boxtimes)}$, Yilin Elaine Liu, Ljilja Ruzic Kascak,
and Jon A. Sanford

Center for Assistive Technology and Environmental Access,
Georgia Institute of Technology, Atlanta, GA, USA
{tinalee,Y.ElaineLiu,ljilja}@gatech.edu,
jon.sanford@coa.gatech.edu

Abstract. Voting is a glocalized event across countries, states and municipalities in which individuals of all abilities want to participate. To enable people with disabilities to participate accessible voting is typically implemented by adding assistive technologies to electronic voting machines to accommodate people with physical and visual disabilities. To overcome the complexities and inequities in this practice, two interfaces, EZ Ballot, which uses a linear yes/no input system for all selections, and QUICK Ballot, which provides random access voting through direct selection, were designed with multi-modal inputs and outputs to provide one system for all voters. This paper reports on the results of Phase I usability testing of EZ Ballot with 21 adults with visual, dexterity and cognitive limitations, which indicated the need for the second interface and describes the Phase II efficacy testing of both interfaces that is currently ongoing. Participants performed a standard set of voting tasks including: voting for one and two candidates, using the write-in function, voting on a referendum and changing their vote. Task performance was recorded by video. Post-trial interviews solicited feedback about ease of use and preferences. Overall, the study demonstrated that people with different limitations could perform voting tasks on a single system, although their preferred input and output methods varied, suggesting that providing flexibility through multi-modal inputs is important to ensure participation of all individuals in the voting process.

Keywords: Accessible voting · Ballot design · User interface · Multi-modal · Interactions

1 Introduction

Voting is a glocalized event across countries, states and municipalities in which individuals of all abilities want to participate. Compared to older voting system technologies such as paper ballots, levers, or punch cards, newer electronic voting machines that provide random access selection of candidates have the potential to enable individuals with a broad range of disabilities to vote independently through the use of a variety of multi-modal inputs and outputs [1, 2]. To date in the U.S. and many countries, providing voting accessibility has focused primarily on accommodating voters with vision and dexterity impairments, which are the types of limitations that are most likely to impact use of electronic voting machines. Not surprisingly, accessibility

© Springer International Publishing Switzerland 2015
M. Antona and C. Stephanidis (Eds.): UAHCI 2015, Part IV, LNCS 9178, pp. 204–214, 2015.
DOI: 10.1007/978-3-319-20687-5_20

for these users has primarily been accomplished through the addition of alternative inputs (e.g., track ball) and outputs (e.g., speech recognition) to existing hardware and/or software architecture. However, while the added-on features may be technically accessible, they often more complex and difficult for poll workers to set up and require more time for the targeted voters with disabilities to use (e.g., listening to each candidate selection in a contest one at a time) compared to the direct selection interfaces (e.g., point and click) that enable voters without disabilities to select any candidate in a particular contest at any time. Moreover these interfaces generally do not address the needs, and can exacerbate difficulties experienced by voters with cognitive limitations.

To address the complexities and inequities with the accessible alternatives, a universal design approach was used to seamlessly integrate a range of integrated input and output (I/O) interfaces with two new ballot interfaces, EZ Ballot and QUICK Ballot, to provide one voting system on a Windows Surface tablet for all voters. In addition, EZ Ballot was designed with a linear, binary yes/no input system for all selections that fundamentally re-conceptualizes ballot design to provide the same simple and intuitive voting experience for all voters, regardless of ability or I/O interface used. In contrast, QUICK Ballot, uses touchscreen input system to provide random access selection that minimizes voting effort. Nonetheless, whereas the provision of universal design voting systems is important to ensure participation of all individuals in the voting process, the proliferation of electronic and mobile devices suggests that glocalized development of universal design systems has implications for participation of all individuals in all aspects of the society.

2 Background

Voters with vision, cognition and dexterity limitations experience different types of problems using accessible voting machines. For blind and visually-impaired voters, voting takes significantly longer (31 vs. 5 min) compared to sighted voters [2] and navigating a ballot often leads to confusion [3–5]. These difficulties can often be attributed to the accessible features that are added to standard ballots, which are designed to be used visually. For voters with cognitive limitations who can be confused and overwhelmed by the amount of information and visual complexity of a full-face or the lack of overall orientation in page-by-page ballots, there is a need to incorporate more cognitive supports [6].

To provide access to voters with dexterity limitations, a variety of assistive technology inputs (e.g., sip-and-puff, jelly switch devices) have been added to voting machines. In addition to creating set up problems for poll workers who are unfamiliar with these input devices [5], they can negatively affect the voting experience. In contrast, simple touch screen and gestural input could ease physical effort.

A number of efforts have been undertaken to develop alternative ballots, such as the zoomable voting interface which provides an overview of the entire ballot as well as a detailed zoomed view of each race [1], and Prime III, which offers multimodal touch and/or voice and/or A/B switch inputs [7]. However, each of these systems only accommodate voters with specific limitations. To date, there are no voting systems that accommodate all voters across the range of ability.

3 Ballot Design

EZ Ballot breaks down the voting process (e.g., contests, candidates, review of the ballot and casting the ballot) into simple questions that are easy to understand and answer using either a "yes" or "no" response, which provides consistency and simplicity. Each screen contains only one question that is presented both visually and verbally (see Fig. 1). For example, "Do you want to vote for democratic Barack Obama & Joe Biden for president and vice president?" will be displayed visually and through audio. The question itself serves as a prompt that can remind and orient voters. Responses on the existing prototype are limited to pressing a physical buttons on the left and right sides of the device or by using touch buttons on the screen.

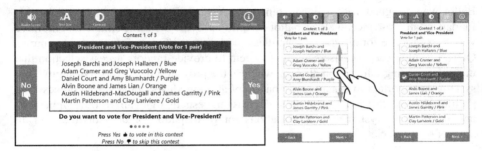

Fig. 1. EZ Ballot (left) and QUICK Ballot (right) interfaces

Design decisions for the two interfaces were based on the UD Principles [8] described below.

Principle 1. Equitable Use. The design goal is one voting system for all rather than accessible design for people with disabilities. As a universally designed system, the ballot design avoids segregating or stigmatizing users by providing the same means of use for all users.

Principle 2. Flexibility in Use. The use of two ballot interfaces, in itself, provides flexibility in use. In addition ballot I/O features were specifically designed to accommodate a range of abilities including the cognitive, visual, and manipulative abilities that are most likely to be adversely affected by ballot design. Multimodal inputs include physical tactile input, touch screen input, and gestural inputs. The prototype of the physical tactile buttons (see Fig. 2) are two conductive rubber buttons covered with aluminum metal. For both ballot interfaces, physical tactile buttons and touch screen buttons are placed on each side of the screen where the tablet is typically held. Speech inputs for EZ Ballot allow voters to answer either "Yes" or "No" verbally. This also ensures privacy as others do not know the specific candidate that is being selected (i.e., any audio output is provided through headphones). Gestural interfaces can be 2D touch gestures that use of fingers on touchscreens or 3D air gestures that involve free movement in space [9]. Although not yet developed for the working prototype, the goal is to embed 2D multi-finger gestures (e.g., pinching and scrolling) for magnification and navigation which recognizes defined gestures, such as swipe, circle, or zoom, or a gestural development kit, which permits user-defined gestures such as a check. For 3D gestures Kinect technology or Apple iSight, which recognizes air gestures using the iPad camera, will be used to record head gestures, such as shaking up and down, or hand gestures, such as thumbs up or down. The ballots were also designed with multimodal outputs that use visual, speech, and tactile feedback to provide orientation to the structure of the ballot (i.e., a progress bar to identify where the voter is in the voting process) and non-speech cues (i.e., sounds) to provide feedback about indicate that the voter actions (e.g., candidate selection) have been recorded. To ensure that all users have access to all inputs and outputs, the default mode is to have all modalities turned on rather than forcing users to select those that they need and then limiting the types of modalities.

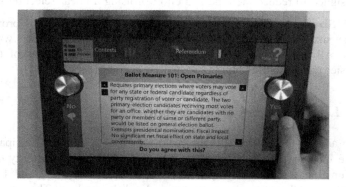

Fig. 2. Multimodal inputs of EZ Ballot prototype

UD Principle 3. Simple and Intuitive Use. While many users are familiar with random access direct selection on touchscreen interfaces, QUICK Ballot is a familiar, intuitive interface. However, for those who are not familiar with these types of interfaces or are unable to see the touchscreen, EZ Ballot has a simple and linear structure that provides two main advantages: directed guide and matched audio interface. Directed guide allows users to follow a particular sequence of steps so that users can easily manage to stay focused. Studies [10, 11] have suggested a linear structure rather than a hierarchical information structure for low-literacy or novice users because they lose focus during navigation. In addition, the nature of the linear structure resembles that of the linear audio interface, which can benefit users who are visually impaired or reading disabled.

UD Principle 4. Perceptible Information. EZ Ballot integrates simultaneous visual and audio output interfaces desired by visually-impaired voters [3, 5], rather than using separate outputs that are found on most current systems. In addition, all touch screen buttons provide redundant visual cues through color, icons, and text. Internationally recognizable green and red represent "Yes" and "No" buttons are also differentiated by text and common icons. The tactile cover that sits above a touchscreen helps users with limited or no visual abilities who have difficulties to locate the virtual buttons on the screen. The initial tactile cover indicated the location of virtual control buttons by adding indentations to the inner edge of the frame.

Principle 5. Tolerance for Error. The ballots provide verification to confirm a selection or identify mistakes during voting process. EZ Ballot has two levels of confirmation, a prompt after each yes or no response (e.g., "Are you sure you want to vote for Daniel Court?") with reversion back to the previous selection question when users press "No". In both ballots a sub-review message (e.g., "You voted for Daniel Court") reverts back to the first candidate page when users press "No".

Principle 6. Low Physical Effort. To reduce effort in pressing buttons while holding the device, "Yes"/"No" buttons are located along the sides of the device where they can be activated by a user's thumbs or fist. In contrast the random access system of QUICK Ballot is designed to reduce the time and effort of using a linear selection system.

Principle 7. Size and Space for Approach & Use. All soft buttons provide large enough target size (i.e. minimum width measure of 20 mm) [12] for users with a range of dexterity. All the buttons are placed in the corners or the edges of the screen allowing easier navigation for blind or visually-impaired users [13, 14].

4 Phase I. User Studies of EZ Ballot

Twenty one adults (11 female; 10 male) who are eligible to vote participated in the study. These include visual disabilities (6 blind, 6 low vision), dexterity disabilities (2 no arm function, 2 hand dexterity limitations, 1 wheelchair user), and 4 mild cognitive disabilities. All participants were native English speakers. The age range was 21-64 years, with a mean age of 45.4 ± 11.74 years. Participants' mean level of self-reported touch screen devices was 6.00 ± 3.2, where 1 = novice and 10 = expert. Twelve out of twenty one participants were smartphone owners.

4.1 Procedures

After signing an informed consent form approved by Georgia Tech IRB, pre-trial interviews consisting of demographic information including age, types of disabilities, previous touch screen experiences, and smartphone ownership were conducted. Participants then simulated voting tasks as directed (e.g., voting for one candidate, voting for two candidates, reviewing the vote, and changing the vote) using EZ Ballot. During the trials, researchers observed the participants' interaction and recorded usability issues. Following each test trial, participants completed a post-trial interview to elicit qualitative feedback about the usability of each design feature (e.g., ease of use, preferred input). Each session lasted 90 min.

4.2   Results

Participants self-reported their perceived ease of use on voting using just "Yes" and "No" as a range from 2–5 with a mean of 4.2 ± 1.0 (where 1 was very difficult and 5 was very easy). Participants who responded that Yes and No voting was very easy commented that the Yes and No voting is simple and intuitive enough to vote independently: "I think it simplifies it. It makes it easier and you don't have to think about it." Participants who responded that "Yes" and "No" voting was difficult commented they had some difficulty with touch screen itself. Significantly, smartphone users' reported statistically greater (p = .042) perceived ease of use of EZ Ballot than non-smartphone users.

Participants' preferences for input methods were varied. Ten participants (50.0 %) preferred to use touch screen input. Four (three blind, one dexterity) (20.0 %) preferred to use physical push buttons. Three participants (15.0 %) preferred to use the stylus: one low vision participant used stylus to help reading the text, one cognitive participant commented that stylus is comfortable because of the habit of using the pen, and one dexterity participant used mouth stick since he had no arm functions. Three (two low vision, one dexterity) (15.0 %) preferred to use speech input: "I can just say 'Yes' and it will repeat back who I voted for. That would be the best I think". One dexterity participant commented that he would choose the speech input over his mouth stick if it responds well.

4.3   Discussion

Overall, the Phase I study demonstrated that individuals with various types of disabilities could perform voting tasks on a single voting interface, EZ Ballot, using their preferred inputs. Despite the high self-reported rating and positive feedback such as the simple linear process, redundant confirmation messages, and helpful audio guidance, the user study recommended the refinement of the user interface (i.e., instruction pages and tactile cover design) and providing enhanced features (i.e., custom adjustment settings and direct selection of candidates). The issues included locating the "Yes" and "No" buttons (58.3 % coming from visually-impaired users), changing a vote (28.6 %), going back (23.8 %), and selecting a candidate (19.0 %). Overall, the issues came from confusion in understanding the instructions for EZ Ballot and the linear interface, which may not be as familiar to most touch screen interfaces, which use direct selection. In addition, negative feedback includes a lack of control of visual and audio characteristics, dissatisfaction with the linear design, and vagueness about the use of the tactile cover design. Based on the user study, a number of design changes were made, including the addition of the direct touch QUICK Ballot interface and refinements to the tactile cover and instruction pages.

5 Design of the QUICK Ballot Interface

Participants who have enough visual abilities and touch screen experience preferred direct selection among the list of candidates rather than going through each of the candidate's pages as well as the capability of going back to the previous pages. Thus, a random access ballot structure that uses a touchscreen to provide direct selection of candidates as an alternative means of input was designed. The visual appearance of QUICK Ballot (see Fig. 1) is similar to a standard ballot, although, other than the linear structure, it incorporates the same universal design features used in EZ Ballot. When the user touches the box of the candidate's name, the box changes to the highlighted dark background and white text with a check mark icon that visually emphasizes the selection of the candidate. If the user wants to change the selection, the user can touch the box again to deselect the candidate. For navigating through the page of contests, the user can touch the "Next" and "Back" buttons located at the bottom corner of the screen.

The audio interface of QUICK Ballot provides unique touch speech interactions, particularly for visually-impaired users. Using a "touch to hear" feature [15] the user can hear what is being touched on the screen including a dragging motion of a finger along the screen. For example, when a voter is touching the candidate name "Joseph Barchi and Joseph Hallaren/Blue" the voter can hear the text "Joseph Barchi and Joseph Hallaren Blue party". The voter can drag the finger on the screen to scan all the names of the candidates. When the voter finds the desired candidate's name "Daniel Court and Amy Blumhardt/Purple", the voter can simply lift his/her finger to select the name and hear the sound "Selected Daniel Court and Amy Blumhardt Purple party" (Table 1).

Table 1. Differences between EZ Ballot and QUICK Ballot

	EZ Ballot	QUICK Ballot
Across Contests	Linear selection • Yes or No • Swipe gesture	Linear selection • Back or Next
Within Contests	Linear selection • Yes or No • Swipe gesture	Random selection • Direct touch for sighted • One-finger scan and lift for non-sighted

5.1 Tactile Cover

The tactile cover that sits on top of the touchscreen (see Fig. 3) enables users with limited or no vision to locate the 3 control buttons on the screen (i.e., contrast, text size and audio speed). The initial tactile cover indicated the location of virtual control buttons by adding indentations to the inner edge of the frame. The refined tactile cover design is simplified with raised tactile indicators that allow users to find the edges of the screen as orienting cues without inadvertently activating the touchscreen control buttons adjacent to the tactile indicators.

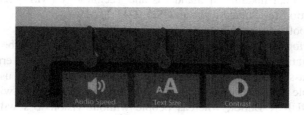

Fig. 3. Tactile cover

5.2   Instruction Pages

The instructions were redesigned as a four-page section at the beginning of the voting process. To maintain the "Yes" and "No" binary structure of EZ Ballot, each instruction page provides a "Yes" touch button to go to next page and a "No" touch button to skip the instructions. The first page explains how to select and navigate using "Yes" and "No" buttons. The second page describes the locations of the 3 control buttons that can be found using the raised tactile indicators. It also describes how to adjust the volume using the tactile rocker switch on the side of the tablet. The third page explains swiping gesture used to navigate between contests and candidates (Fig. 4). Swiping is visualized using horizontal and vertical navigation dots. Finally the fourth instruction page describes the use of the scroll buttons. Each instruction page has constant audio instructions that can be turned on and off depending on the user's need and preference.

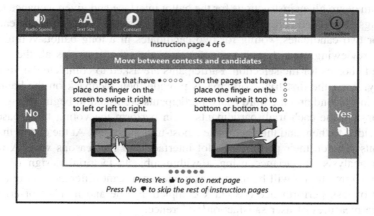

Fig. 4. Instruction page for swiping gestures

6   Phase II. Efficacy Study

Efficacy studies are currently being conducted to determine the effectiveness, efficiency and user satisfaction for both EZ Ballot and QUICK Ballot using metrics recommended by the U.S. National Institute of Standards and Technology (NIST) and the International Organization for Standardization (ISO 9241-11, 1998).

Specific hypotheses include:

H1. The performance on the voting tasks using QUICK Ballot will be faster than EZ Ballot for navigating and selecting candidates, but will result in more erroneous selections and more assists compared to the performance on the voting tasks using EZ Ballot.

H2.2. People with vision loss will have higher satisfaction with EZ Ballot compared to QUICK Ballot; whereas people without vision loss will have higher satisfaction with QUICK Ballot compared to EZ Ballot.

H2.3. People with vision loss will prefer to use EZ Ballot, whereas people without vision loss will prefer to use QUICK Ballot.

A total of 30 participants, including people who are blind or have low vision, and people without vision loss are being recruited. Participants perform three trials of voting tasks using the two ballot interfaces. The order of the ballot interface is counterbalanced across participants. The first trial includes adjusting custom setting process for those who need, instructions how to use the particular ballot interface, and voting tasks. The voting tasks include voting for one candidate, voting for two candidates, and voting for one candidate in a long ballot that requires page navigation. In each trial, participants are given a slate with names of candidates and choices of propositions that they are supposed to vote. To reduce the memory loads, participants vote for candidates with the same names on each contest. For example, using a slate I, participants vote John Smith and Daniel Lee for all three contests. The reason for doing second and third trials is for the purpose of measuring the learnability. Thus, the second and the third trials require participants begin voting without going through instructions and custom setting process.

Each participant is randomly assigned to use one of the ballots first and the other second. Participants perform a total of three trials with same ballot contents. For the first trial, they are given instructions for the ballot interface and given a chance to adjust any settings. They then perform a series of voting tasks (e.g., voting for one candidate, voting for two candidates, voting for two candidates in a long ballot, voting for referendum, reviewing, and changing a vote) on a slate that provides all the candidate names and choices for the selection. Participants are asked to complete the voting task accurately. After the first trial, participants provide their feedback on the ballot interface. For the second and the third trials, participants are asked to begin voting without instructions. In the each trial, participants again perform the voting tasks based on a Slate provided to them and then complete a post-trial interview. At the end of third trial, participants provide their preferred ballot interface and the reasons why. A repeated measures analysis of variance using a within-subjects factorial design (two ballot interfaces x three trials) will be used to examine significant differences in quantitative measures of task performance (i.e., task completion time and number of errors) and qualitative measures of user satisfaction/preference.

7 Discussion

In addition to the ballots themselves, this paper makes two important contributions to the field of universal design. First, it makes a strong case study for extending the Universal Design Principles beyond the physical world to the design of digital interfaces. Whereas there has been past criticism that the Principles only apply to physical artefacts, this project used the Principles to seamlessly integrate physical hardware and a digital ballot to develop a product that would be usable by all individuals. Second, the project suggests that two ballots, both designed according to Universal Design Principles, can be differentially usable by individuals with disabilities. This approach clearly distinguishes this project from previous efforts, which have focused on developing one universal design solution for everyone. Whereas, this "one-size-fits-all" approach is useful to prove the efficacy of UD, it assumes that if equitability (Principle 1) and usability (Principles 2−7) are achieved, that the UD artefact will be desirable and effective for all users. This approach fails to consider that the 7 UD principles are not black and white, but shades of grey that may require trade-offs in design that favor one principle over another. In contrast, using different "doses" of various principles, this project designed two different UD ballots. It is expected that both ballots will achieve equitability and usability, although it is hypothesized that the degree of usability (as measured by speed and errors) will vary according to a user's abilities.

These assumptions appear to be born out based on preliminary data from the Phase II study. Early findings indicate that participants with and without vision are able to use both ballots independently. However, users with vision loss make fewer errors and prefer EZ Ballot; while users without vision loss make fewer errors and prefer QUICK Ballot. Clearly, these findings begin to suggest that while UD, by definition, is design to be usable by all people by the greatest extent possible, this does not mean that design is equally usable by all people. Rather, by applying the Principles of Universal Design, designs, whether physical, digital or a combination of both, may not only be differentially usable based on ability, but they may also be differentially desirable based on preference. Most importantly, this suggests that universal design does not dictate a one-size-fits-all approach, but rather celebrates flexibility in use.

Acknowledgments. This study was funded, in part, by the Information Technology & Innovation Foundation as part of a grant from the U.S. Election Assistance Commission.

References

1. Herrnson, P.S., Niemi, R.G., Hanmer, M.J., Francia, P.L., Bederson, B.B., Conrad, F.G., Traugott, M.W.: Voters' evaluations of electronic voting systems: results from a usability field study. Am. Polit. Res. **36**(4), 580–611 (2008). doi:10.1177/1532673x08316667
2. Piner, G.E., Byrne, M.D.: The experience of accessible voting: results of a survey among legally-blind users. Proc. Hum. Factors Ergon. Soc. Annu. Meet. **55**(1), 1686–1690 (2011). doi:10.1177/1071181311551351
3. Burton, U.: The ballot ballet: the usability of accessible voting machines. In: AFB AccessWorld, vol. 5,4. American Foundation for the Blind (2004)

4. Gilbert, J., McMillian, Y., Rouse, K., Williams, P., Rogers, G., McClendon, J., Mitchell, W., Gupta, P., Mkpong-Ruffin, I., Cross, E.: Universal access in e-voting for the blind. Univ. Access Inf. Soc. **9**(4), 357–365 (2010). doi:10.1007/s10209-009-0181-0
5. Runyan, N., Tobias, J.: Accessibility review report for california top-to-bottom voting systems review. In: Report to the Secretary of State of California (2007)
6. Ott, B.R., Heindel, W.C., Papandonatos, G.D.: A survey of voter participation by cognitively impaired elderly patients. Neurology **60**(9), 1546–1548 (2003). doi:10.1212/01. wnl.0000061481.46191.75
7. Gilbert, J.: PRIME III: One Machine, One Vote for Everyone. http://www.juangilbert.com/ (2005)
8. Connell, B.R., Jones, M., Mace, R., Mueller, J., Mullick, A., Ostroff, E., Sanford, J., Steinfeld, E., Story, M., Vanderheiden, G.: The principles of universal design. In: NC State University, The Center for Universal Design (1997)
9. Saffer, D.: Designing Gestural Interfaces: Touchscreens and Interactive Devices. O'Reilly Media, Sebastopol (2008)
10. Chaudry, B.M., Connelly, K.H., Siek, K.A., Welch, J.L.: Mobile interface design for low-literacy populations. In: Paper presented at the Proceedings of the 2nd ACM SIGHIT International Health Informatics Symposium, Miami (2012)
11. Parikh, T., Ghosh, K., Chavan, A.: Design studies for a financial management system for micro-credit groups in rural india. In: Paper Presented at the Proceedings of the 2003 Conference on Universal Usability, Vancouver (2003)
12. Jin, Z.X., Plocher, T., Kiff, L.: Touch screen user interfaces for older adults: button size and spacing. In: Stephanidis, C. (ed.) HCI 2007. LNCS, vol. 4554, pp. 933–941. Springer, Heidelberg (2007)
13. Oliveira, J., Guerreiro, T., Nicolau, H., Jorge, J., Gonçalves, D.: Blind people and mobile touch-based text-entry: acknowledging the need for different flavors. In: Paper Presented at the Proceedings of the 13th International ACM SIGACCESS Conference on Computers and Accessibility, Dundee (2011)
14. Leporini, B., Buzzi, M.C., Buzzi, M.: Interacting with mobile devices via VoiceOver: usability and accessibility issues. In: Proceedings of the 24th Australian Computer-Human Interaction Conference OzCHI 2012, pp. 339–348 (2012)
15. Vanderheiden, G.C.: Using extended and enhanced usability (EEU) to provide access to mainstream electronic voting machines. Information Technology and Disabilities, **10**(2) (2004)

Universal Design (UD) Guidelines
for Interactive Mobile Voting Interfaces
for Older Adults

Ljilja Ruzic Kascak[(⊠)], Seunghyun "Tina" Lee, Elaine Yilin Liu,
and Jon A. Sanford

The Center for Assistive Technology and Environmental Access CATEA,
Georgia Institute of Technology Atlanta, Atlanta, USA
{ljilja,tinalee,y.elaineliu}@gatech.edu,
jon.sanford@coa.gatech.edu

Abstract. Current mobile interfaces have numerous usability problems, especially when used by older adults, population of users diverse in ranges and combinations of dis(abilities). However, user interfaces need to be usable by all users, including older adults and disabled people. Universal design (UD), Design for Aging (DfA), and Universal Usability (UU) consider designing systems and interfaces usable by all people, to the greatest extent possible. Set of more inclusive UD guidelines emerged from this integration of the three approaches with mobile design guidelines in order to address usability of user interfaces by diverse population of older adults. An example of an application of the inclusive UD guidelines was universally designed interactive voting interface, EZ Ballot, designed to improve usability of voting systems for older adults. This paper presents the results of the usability testing of the voting system with young and older adults, and reports equal usability of the ballot for both age groups.

Keywords: Design for ageing · User interface adaptation for universal access · Design guidelines · Older adults · Universal design · Usability

1 Introduction

Older adults encounter numerous barriers associated with aging while interacting with user interfaces (UIs) [1]. Small touch and physical buttons, menus that require precise movements, small fonts, content placement, color contrast, and large contents that require memory recall are some of the many barriers that older adults encounter while using interfaces [2, 3]. These barriers lead to longer and less successful task completion times [2].

Universal design (UD) is "design of products and environments to be usable by all people, to the greatest extent possible, without the need for adaptation or specialized design" [4]. The purpose of UD is to overcome the barriers that come with aging and disabilities [5] within a framework of typical everyday design [6]. It advocates for usable design by the greatest number of people, addressing wider range of limitations and combinations of limitations one might have [7]. In addition, Design for Aging (DfA) [8] explores the factors that limit the use of user interfaces (UIs) by older adults,

© Springer International Publishing Switzerland 2015
M. Antona and C. Stephanidis (Eds.): UAHCI 2015, Part IV, LNCS 9178, pp. 215–225, 2015.
DOI: 10.1007/978-3-319-20687-5_21

as well as aspects of UI design which assist older users with age-associated disabilities and limitations (i.e. memory, cognitive, hearing, visual, dexterity, and physical impairments) [9]. All of these limitations vary within a day, from day to day, and over times within an individual [6]. DfA addresses these problems by meeting the needs and abilities of older adults throughout their lifetime. There is a need to design usable UIs for older adults and thus integrate UD approach with DfA in order to have the complete set of design guidelines that would address all the usability problems older adults encounter while interacting with user interfaces. Based on UD approach universal usability (UU) was developed to make information and communication technology usable and accessible by all people, with and without disabilities [10]. Based on Eight Golden Rules, UU was defined as "having more than 90 % of all households as successful users of information and communications services at least once a week" [11]. Moreover, mobile design guidelines and recommendations were proposed to a general population to assist future development of mobile technologies. Integrating mobile design guidelines [12], Universal Usability guidelines [11], DfA approach, with UD we have developed more robust and inclusive set of UD guidelines for interactive mobile interfaces for older adults.

One interface with which older adults have usability problems is the UI of current voting systems. Specifically, research suggests that older adults have problems due to unfamiliarity with interfaces, poor task performance, long completion time, large number of errors made, difficulty in viewing a computer screen, and problems understanding the relationship between touchscreen button manipulation and response of the system [3, 13]. As a case study, more complete UD guidelines were used to design the interactive ballot interface prototype, EZ Ballot [14]. This paper describes the implementation of the more complete set of UD guidelines for mobile interactive interfaces to design EZ Ballot and the usability study to determine the effects of the interface on voting performance.

2   Inclusive UD Guidelines

Mobile interfaces for older adults need to be usable, engaging, easy to use, meaningful, and motivate the adoption of technology [15]. However, current mobile technologies do not meet the needs, experiences, and limitations of older adults, and have many usability problems [16, 17]. A number of web design guidelines [18–21], design principles [22, 23], heuristics [23], and mobile and touch screen design guidelines and recommendations [12, 24] were developed to address the usability problems with interfaces for general population. However, current design guidelines and principles address focus on specific limitations and disabilities, mostly vision impairments, as well as cognitive and motor limitations. This approach fails to account for the entire range of limitations and combinations of limitations that characterize the diversity of the population of older adults.

Due to the gap between the current mobile design guidelines for user interface design and the needs of the diverse population of older adults, this paper describes a project to provide an overarching set of inclusive and complete UD guidelines for mobile interactive interfaces for older adults. The set of inclusive UD guidelines was developed integrating mobile design guidelines [12], UU principles [11], results of the usability studies with older adults [16], and DfA approach with UD principles and guidelines [14]. It was also expected that the design of usable user interfaces for older adults would also enhances the usability for all other user groups and improves the users' overall experience [25].

Voting interface EZ Ballot was designed using design criteria which were based on the set of integrated inclusive UD guidelines for UIs [14] with the addition of the UD guidelines applicable to the voting systems (6a, 7a, and 7b). Design criteria for the voting interface are measurable and performance-based criteria. Guidelines and criteria are listed below based on each UD principle (guidelines are numbered, and corresponding design criteria, DC, are listed below each guideline):

Principle 1: Equitable Use: The design is useful and marketable to people with diverse abilities.

1a. Provide the same means of use for all older adults: identical whenever possible, equivalent when not.

DC: Provide one type of voting system to all voters regardless of their abilities.

1b. Avoid segregating or stigmatizing any older adults.

DC: Avoid specialized voting systems for voters with disabilities.

1c. Provisions for privacy, security, and safety should be equally available to all older adults.

DC: Reduce the chance of older adults being vulnerable by providing several error-proof and privacy-proof mechanisms. Provide a touchscreen not visible to people standing next to the voting poll but the voter himself.

1d. Make the design appealing to all older adults.

DC: Seemingly integrate simultaneous visual and audio ballot interfaces. Use familiar design features. Avoid institutional appearance. Use a human voice as an audio sound.

Principle 2: Flexibility in Use: The design accommodates a wide range of individual preferences and abilities.

2a. Provide choice in methods of use to allow older adults to feel they are in control [26].

DC: Provide choices of input (e.g., touch, stylus) and navigation methods (e.g., Yes/No (Next/Back) touch buttons, scroll, and swipe gestures). Provide multiple choices of visual (text size, color contrast) and audio (speed, volume) characteristics. Candidate selection could be linear or random access. Provide consistency in system navigation in order to make older adults feel they are in control. Allow for easy reversal of actions (as described in 5c.) and easy access to all the content (main control pane with Review, Instructions, Audio speed, Text size, and Contrast touch buttons).

2b. Accommodate right- or left-handed access and use.

DC: Make any inputs usable for right- or left-handed older adults by making the navigation accessible and touch buttons easy to reach with either left of right fingers.

2c. Facilitate the older adult' accuracy and precision.

DC: Use large touch-buttons and provide enough space between the buttons. The big size facilitates accuracy by reducing fine finger movements. The whitespace between buttons allows older adults to have a clear idea of the location of the target buttons.

2d. Provide adaptability to the older adults' pace.

DC: Locate Review and Instruction touch buttons on the main control panel, easily accessible at any point of the voting. Ballot UI should support any voter's pace (e.g. provide multiple audio speed options, have linear and random access interfaces). Provide a choice for skipping instructions, any races or propositions.

Principle 3: Simple and Intuitive Use: Use of the design is easy to understand, regardless of the user's experience, knowledge, language skills, or current concentration level.

3a. Eliminate unnecessary complexity.

DC: Provide guided linear or random access structure that matches the audio interface. Locate Review and Instruction touch buttons as described in 2d. The piece-by-piece process breaks down a complex task into several easy-to-complete subtasks to reduce complexity. Remove visual clusters. Avoid multiple contest pages in one screen.

3b. Be consistent with older adults' expectations and intuition.

DC: Answer with Yes/No (Next/Back) to the question on each page. Design touchscreen buttons to look touchable.

3c. Accommodate a wide range of literacy and language skills.

DC: Use universal/recognizable icons for text size, audio speed, and contrast. Use simple Y for Yes, N for No, and I for instructions. Provide step-by-step instructions how to use the ballot (e.g., how to navigate pages, how to select a candidate).

3d. Arrange information consistent with its importance.

DC: Arrange page information consistent with its importance (e.g., title of the page: president and vice president, voting information: vote for one pair of candidates and name of the candidate). Design instruction pages so that these can be skipped at any point. Arrange these pages based on the importance of the information (page 1: use of the instruction touch button and navigation using Yes/No (Next/Back) touch buttons; page 2: adjusting the audio volume; page 3: adjusting audio speed, text size, and contrast; page 4: navigation between instruction or contest pages; page 5: navigation between candidate or review pages; page 6: use of scroll buttons; page 7: review of the selections; page 8: use of write-in page). Location and background color of ballot progress indicator need to be less distractive but noticeable. Make Yes and No (Next and Back) buttons accessible. These need to stand out visually. Choose a different font sizes to differentiate levels of importance of the context.

3e. Provide effective prompting and feedback during and after task completion.

DC: Provide two ways for verification, a prompt and a sub-review message. A prompt message (e.g., "Are you sure you want to vote for Daniel Court and Amy Blumhardt from the Purple party?") reverts to the previous question if older adults press No. A sub-review message (e.g., "You voted for Daniel Court and Amy Blumhardt from the Purple party.") reverts to that specific candidate page if older adults press No. Indicate the progress by color-coding the current candidate. Provide visual and audio prompting and feedback during and after the voting process.

3f. Design dialogs to yield closure [26].

DC: Interface should provide older adults with the satisfaction of accomplishment and completion, a sense of relief, and an indicator to prepare for the next group of actions.

Principle 4: Perceptible Information: The design communicates necessary information effectively to the user, regardless of ambient conditions or the user's sensory abilities.

4a. Use different modes (pictorial, verbal, tactile) for redundant presentation of essential information.

DC: Provide simultaneous visual and audio ballot interfaces. Provide tactile indicators for locating the touch buttons. Use universal icons along with redundant cues (e.g., color, text, and symbols).

4b. Provide adequate contrast between essential information and its surroundings.

DC: Use internationally recognizable color-coding (e.g., Yes (Next) touch button is green, and No (Back) touch button is red). Place all other touch buttons on the main control panel (text size, color contrast, audio speed, review, instruction). Provide high contrast (black text on a white background) as a default mode.

4c. Maximize "legibility" of essential information.

DC: Display information in sans serif and in at least two font sizes: 3.0–4.0 mm (the height of an upper case letter in the smaller text size) and 6.3–9.0 mm (the height of an upper case letter in the larger text size); based on the VVSG (Sect. 3.2.2.1.b.) recommendation. Make page title bold.

4d. Differentiate elements in ways that can be described (i.e., make it easy to give instructions or directions).

DC: Provide color-coded visual representation (e.g., match a color of instruction button with instruction pages).

4e. Provide compatibility with a variety of techniques or devices used by people with sensory limitations.

DC: Allow use of three text sizes, where increased text size would be compatible with the use of a magnifier for visually impaired older adults. Accommodate other input devices (e.g., Sip and puff, mouth stick, pedal switch, speech input).

4f. Design for multiple and dynamic contexts [26].

DC: Implement context-awareness, self-adapting functionalities, and/or universal control feature, which would work regardless of the context and environment. Derive input indirectly from the user.

Principle 5: Tolerance for Error: The design minimizes hazards and the adverse consequences of accidental or unintended actions.

5a. Arrange elements to minimize hazards and errors: most used elements, most accessible; hazardous elements eliminated, isolated, or shielded.

DC: Begin the UI with instructions. Locate Yes (Next) and No (Back) touch buttons as described in 4c. Locate other touch buttons on the main control panel. Locate Review and Instruction touch buttons on the main control panel (easy to find) while isolated from the most used Yes/No (Next/Back) touch buttons.

5b. Provide warnings of hazards and errors.

DC: Provide any warnings (under voting, over voting) to prevent mistakes during a voting process.

5c. Provide fail safe features.

DC: Provide two ways for verification, a prompt and a sub-review message. A prompt message (e.g., "Are you sure you want to vote for Daniel Court and Amy

Blumhardt from the Purple party?") reverts to the previous question if older adults press No. A sub-review message (e.g., "You voted for Daniel Court and Amy Blumhardt from the Purple party.") reverts to that specific candidate page if older adults press No. Provide a way for changing the vote (Review touch button).

5d. Discourage unconscious action in tasks that require vigilance.

DC: Locate different function of control buttons far apart (e.g., Yes/No (Next/Back) touch buttons).

Principle 6: Low Physical Effort: The design can be used efficiently and comfortably and with a minimum of fatigue.

6a. *Allow older adult to maintain neutral body position.*

DC: Provide main input buttons at the locations where older adults' hands are in neutral body position.

6b. Use reasonable operating forces.

DC: Take out the physical buttons and instead use large touch buttons. Provide capacitive touchscreen rather than resistive touchscreen that requires more physical force.

6c. Minimize repetitive actions.

DC: Avoid multiple actions (e.g., double tap, split-tap) and use a single tap.

6d. Minimize sustained physical effort.

DC: Take out the physical buttons and instead use touch-buttons. Use tactile icons to navigate the older adults' fingers to the location of the touch buttons. Use touch buttons that require only single tap.

Principle 7: Size and Space for Approach and Use: Appropriate size and space are provided for approach, reach, manipulation, and use regardless of user's body size, posture, or mobility.

7a. *Provide a clear line of sight to important elements for any seated or standing older adult.*

DC: Place the important information (questions, referendum content, etc.) at the center of the screen. Provide adjustable height of the tablet stand for any seated or standing older adults.

7b. *Make reach to all components comfortable for any seated or standing older adult.*

DC: Make a tablet detachable from the stand. Provide tilted tablet stand for any seated or standing user.

7c. Accommodate variations in hand and grip size.

DC: Use large touch buttons and large tactile icons on the cover of the screen. Provide sufficient space between buttons for different size of fingers and grip.

7d. Provide adequate space for use of assistive devices or personal assistance.

DC: Use large touch buttons that can be activated using the assistive devices.

3 A Case Study: EZ Ballot Voting Interface

3.1 Interface Design

EZ Ballot was designed as a one voting system to all voters regardless of their abilities (1a). It is a linear structure voting interface (2a, 2d, 3a) which integrated visual and

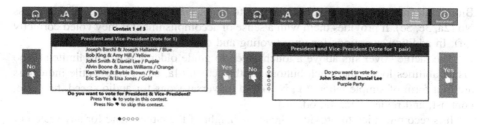

Fig. 1. Linear structure of the EZ Ballot: a single question per page (Color figure online)

audio output (1d, 4a) without any special adaptation (1b) [27]. A candidate can be selected by answering a single question per page (3a, 3b), and by selecting Yes or No touch-buttons (6d) on the sides of the touchscreen (2b, 3b, 4c, 5a, 5d, 6a). A binary structure of navigation and selection requires Yes and No responses following a particular sequence of steps (2a) (See Fig. 1). In order to accommodate for ranges of abilities in older adults, settings for audio speed, text size, and contrast features were designed (2a, 2d). Audio speed, text size (3d, 4c, 4e), and contrast have three levels, where large text size is compatible with the use of a magnifier for visually impaired older adults (4e). These touch-buttons (6d) were located on the main panel (2a, 4b, 5a), with universal icons (3c) and color-coded in blue to match the settings pages (4d). High contrast (black text on a white background) is set as a default mode (4b). Page title is bold (3d, 4c).

The ballot allows for the use of natural gestures (e.g. swipe and scroll) for faster navigation between candidates (2a, 2d). Single tap was used throughout the whole interface (6c, 6d). EZ ballot has a horizontal layout with Yes (green) and No (red) touch-buttons on the side of the screen (3d, 4b, 5a, 5d). The important information (questions, referendum content, etc.) is located at the center of the screen (7a). All touch buttons are at least 20 mm wide (2c, 6b, 7c, 7d).

When they start the voting process users are on the first page of instructions (3c, 4d, 5a). They can skip the instructions and begin voting (2d, 3d), or navigate further (2a, 2d). Instruction touch button (6d) is easy accessible located on the main control panel (2a, 2d, 3a, 4b, 5a) with simple icon I (3c) and color-coded with light blue to match the Instruction pages (4d). Instructions were designed as an eight-page introduction section that informs the users about all the features, navigation, and selection (3c, 3d, 4d). Pages are arranged based on the information importance (page 1: use of the instruction touch button and navigation using Yes/No (Next/Back) touch buttons; page 2: adjusting the audio volume; page 3: adjusting audio speed, text size, and contrast; page 4: navigation between instruction or contest pages; page 5: navigation between candidate or review pages; page 6: use of scroll buttons; page 7: review of the selections; page 8: use of write-in page) (3d). Audio instructions are consistent with visual instructions and slightly more detailed (1d, 3a, 4a). These can be turned on and off, as the rest of the audio output (2a, 2d).

A prompt message (e.g., "Are you sure you want to vote for Daniel Court and Amy Blumhardt from the Purple party?") reverts to the previous question if older adults press No. A sub-review message (e.g., "You voted for Daniel Court and Amy

Blumhardt from the Purple party.") reverts to that specific candidate page if they press No (2a, 3e, 5c). It provides them with a sense of accomplishment if they voted correctly (3f). In addition, warnings for under voting and over voting are provided (5b).

The tactile cover sits above a touchscreen to guide older adults with limited or no visual abilities locate the touch buttons on the screen (4a, 6d). Large tactile indicators are in a form of simple letters (Y, N, I) and universal icons for audio speed, text size, contrast, and review (3c, 4a, 6d, 7c).

It is recommended to provide adjustable height of the tablet stand for any seated or standing older adults (7a), make a tablet detachable from the stand, and provide tilted tablet stand for any seated or standing user (7b) at the voting pole.

3.2   Usability Testing

Methods. A study was conducted at the Georgia Tech Research Institute (GTRI) with two groups of participants, 9 young adults (age 44 to 65) and 15 older adults (age 65 and older). Young adults group had 5 female and 4 male participants, 44 to 64 years old, mean age 57.78 years (SD = 6.14). A group of older adults consisted of 11 female and 4 male participants, 65 to 77 years old, mean age 70 years (SD = 4.19). 14 participants had vision impairments including macular degeneration, cataracts, glaucoma, blindness, or other conditions that affected reading ability. Some of them had signs of mild cognitive impairment (4 participants) and/or upper mobility impairments (9 participants) including arthritis, peripheral neuropathy, and carpal tunnel. 1 participant had chronic obstructive pulmonary disease (COPD) and 1 had slight hearing loss.

Participants were asked to perform a voting process as they would have done it at the actual voting poll. Use of instructions was not mandatory. Participants were given a slate with names of candidates and choices of propositions that they are supposed to vote (See Table 3). Participants were asked to vote for candidates with the same names for each contest (e.g. participants were asked to vote for John Smith and Daniel Lee for all three contests), in order to reduce their memory load.

Results. Effectiveness and efficiency were measured assessing the error rates and task completion times, respectively. Errors were coded as mistakes, assists, did not recover from the error, overvote, undervote, wrong vote, and touchscreen error. We counted the total number of errors in order to report the average number of errors per participant (See Fig. 2).

Differences across the age groups in the average number of errors per participant were not found statistically significant (p = 0.291, df = 22, t = 1.082). Thus, EZ Ballot voting system is equally accurate for both young and older adults.

Completion rates of the voting tasks were 100 %. Task completion time was measured as time it took participants to vote not including the instruction time (See Fig. 3).

Young adults voted faster on EZ Ballot compared to older adults (p = 0.173, df = 22, t = −1.408). However, differences in task completion times across the age groups were not statistically significant. We can say that it took both young and old adults the same time to vote on EZ Ballot.

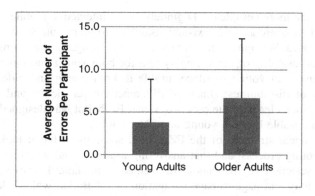

Fig. 2. Young and older adults' average number of errors per participant for EZ Ballot

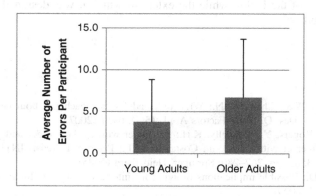

Fig. 3. Young and older adults' average task completion time in minutes

4   Conclusion

EZ Ballot was designed as a linear ballot interface, with integrated visual and audio output [28]. Navigation and selection had a binary structure with Yes and No responses following a single question per page. A usability study with young and older adults tested the effect of design of the voting interface on usability. We found that there were no significant differences in task completion times and number of errors between the two age groups. Therefore, results show equal efficiency and effectiveness of the ballot for both age groups, and thus equal usability of the voting interface for young and older adults. This leads to a conclusion that EZ Ballot was a successful example of the universal voting interface, usable to older population of users as well as to the rest of the population.

In the research described here, we expanded existing UD guidelines in order to make those more robust and inclusive for design of mobile interactive interfaces for older adults and address the need for usable interfaces for the ageing population of users. Integrating UD principles and guidelines with DfA, UU, and mobile design guidelines into the more complete UD guidelines for interactive mobile interfaces, we have attempted to overcome the existent usability problems older adults have with mobile technologies. We applied the guidelines to the design of the voting interface of EZ Ballot to test usability of the voting system for both young and older adults. This resulted in a universal voting interface, usable to both young and older adults with various ranges of dis(abilities). Lack of differences in efficiency and effectiveness across the age groups leads to the conclusion that EZ ballot was designed as universal voting interface, usable by both young and older adults.

Due to the linear structure of the EZ Ballot, some users felt it took too long to complete the voting process, and that answering a prompt and a sub-review message following the selection of the candidate seemed redundant. However, other users preferred simplicity and page-to-page navigation of EZ Ballot, which allows for slow pace and sufficient time for information processing. Results showed that EZ Ballot was found equally usable by older adults and the rest of the population. This confirms universal design of the ballot, while the extent to which it was designed as universal can be improved.

References

1. Jastrzembski, T.S., Charness, N.: What older adults can teach us about designing better ballots. Ergon. Des. Q. Hum. Factors Appl. **15**(4), 6–11 (2007)
2. Siek, K.A., Rogers, Y., Connelly, K.H.: Fat finger worries: how older and younger users physically interact with PDAs. In: Costabile, M.F., Paternó, F. (eds.) INTERACT 2005. LNCS, vol. 3585, pp. 267–280. Springer, Heidelberg (2005)
3. Hawthorn, D.: Possible implications of aging for interface designers. Interact. Comput. **12** (5), 507–528 (2000)
4. Mace, R.: Universal Design: Housing for the Lifespan of all People. US Department of Housing and Urban Affairs, Washington DC (1988)
5. Law, C.M., et al.: A systematic examination of universal design resources: part 1, heuristic evaluation. Univ. Access Inf. Soc. **7**(1–2), 31–54 (2008)
6. Sanford, J.A.: Universal Design as a Rehabilitation Strategy: Design for the Ages. Springer Publishing Company, New York (2012)
7. Falls Among Older Adults: An Overview. Centers for Disease Control and Prevention 2013 (cited 2014 April 21). http://www.cdc.gov/homeandrecreationalsafety/falls/adultfalls.html
8. Nichols, T.A., Rogers, W.A., Fisk, A.D.: Design for aging. In: Salvendy, G. (ed.) Handbook of Human Factors and Ergonomics, 3rd edn, pp. 1418–1445. Wiley, Hoboken (2006)
9. Zajicek, M.: Interface design for older adults. In: Proceedings of the 2001 EC/NSF Workshop on Universal Accessibility of Ubiquitous Computing: Providing for the Elderly. ACM (2001)
10. Meiselwitz, G., Wentz, B., Lazar, J.: Universal Usability: Past, Present, and Future. Now Publishers Inc (2010)
11. Shneiderman, B.: Designing for fun: how can we design user interfaces to be more fun? Interactions **11**(5), 48–50 (2004)
12. Gong, J., Tarasewich, P.: Guidelines for handheld mobile device interface design. In: Proceedings of DSI 2004 Annual Meeting. Citeseer (2004)

13. Bederson, B.B., et al.: Electronic voting system usability issues. In: Proceedings of the SIGCHI Conference on Human Factors in Computing Systems. ACM (2003)
14. Kascak, L., Rébola, C.B., Sanford, J.: Integrating Universal Design (UD) principles and mobile design guidelines to improve design of mobile health applications for older adults. In: 2014 IEEE International Conference on Healthcare Informatics (ICHI). IEEE (2014)
15. Gaver, W., et al.: The photostroller: supporting diverse care home residents in engaging with the world. In: Proceedings of the SIGCHI Conference on Human Factors in Computing Systems. ACM (2011)
16. Kascak, L., et al.: Icon design for user interface of remote patient monitoring mobile devices. In: Proceedings of the 31st ACM International Conference on Design of Communication. ACM (2013)
17. Kascak, L., et al.: Icon design to improve communication of health information to older adults. Commun. Des. Q. Rev. 2(1), 6–32 (2013)
18. Pruitt, J., Adlin, T.: The Persona Lifecycle: Keeping People in Mind Throughout Product Design. Morgan Kaufmann, San Francisco (2010)
19. Kurniawan, S., Zaphiris, P.: Research-derived web design guidelines for older people. In: Proceedings of the 7th International ACM SIGACCESS Conference on Computers and Accessibility. ACM (2005)
20. Zaphiris, P., Kurniawan, S., Ghiawadwala, M.: A systematic approach to the development of research-based web design guidelines for older people. Univ. Access Inf. Soc. 6(1), 59–75 (2007)
21. Hart, T., Chaparro, B.S., Halcomb, C.G.: Evaluating websites for older adults: adherence to 'senior-friendly'guidelines and end-user performance. Behav. Inf. Technol. 27(3), 191–199 (2008)
22. Redish, J., Chisnell, D.: Designing web sites for older adults: A review of recent research. vol. 9, p. 2008. Accessed June 2004
23. Fisk, A.D., et al.: Designing for Older Adults: Principles and Creative Human Factors Approaches. CRC Press, Boca Raton (2012)
24. Parhi, P., Karlson, A.K., Bederson, B.B.: Target size study for one-handed thumb use on small touchscreen devices. In: Proceedings of the 8th Conference on Human-Computer Interaction with Mobile Devices and Services. ACM (2006)
25. Chisnell, D., Redish, J.: Designing web sites for older adults: Expert review of usability for older adults at 50 web sites. In: AARP, vol. 1, pp. 1–60 (2005)
26. Shneiderman, B.: Universal usability. Commun. ACM 43(5), 84–91 (2000)
27. Lee, S., et al.: EZ ballot with multimodal inputs and outputs. In: Proceedings of the 14th International ACM SIGACCESS Conference on Computers and Accessibility, pp. 215–216. ACM, Boulder (2012)
28. Lee, S., et al.: EZ ballot with multimodal inputs and outputs. In: Proceedings of the 14th International ACM SIGACCESS Conference on Computers and Accessibility. ACM (2012)

"Biometric Dental Rosette" - Introduction into New Method of Dental Identification

Michał Rychlik[1(✉)], Agnieszka Przystańska[2,3],
Dorota Lorkiewicz-Muszyńska[3], and Mariusz Glapiński[4]

[1] Division of Virtual Engineering, Poznań University of Technology,
ul. Piotrowo 3, 60-965 Poznań, Poland
rychlik.michal@poczta.fm
[2] Department of Anatomy, Poznan University of Medical Sciences,
ul. Świecickiego 6, 60-781 Poznań, Poland
[3] Department of Forensic Medicine, Poznan University of Medical Sciences,
ul. Świecickiego 6, 60-781 Poznań, Poland
{aprzyst,dlorkiew}@ump.edu.pl
[4] Oral Rehabilitation Clinic, Poznan University of Medical Sciences,
ul. Bukowska 70, 60-812 Poznań, Poland
mariusz.glapinski@gmail.com

Abstract. The hypothesis of the study was that human dentition is unique. This study was performed to analyze whether biometric methods using measurements and proportions are suitable for dental identification. The use of 3D models with specialized systems for computer aided engineering (CAE) and Reverse Engineering (RE) allowed for a number of point surface and volume comparative analyses. "Mapping" was carried out next on the dentition models. This procedure results in a set of curves and points depicting the characteristic features of the teeth and their edges respectively. Based on the "mapping" the so-called "biometric dental rosette" was created for the dentition models. The "biometric dental rosette" was created for maxillary and mandibular dentition models. Every rosette was individual thus unique. The method allowed for positive identification of all the volunteers. The presented studies are of preliminary character, and the continuation is necessary.

Keywords: Bitemarks · Biometrics · Forensic odontology · 3D modeling · Reverse Engineering · CAME – Computer Aided Medical Engineering

1 Introduction

The bitemarks are not rare in practice of forensic odontologists [8]. Aside from bite mark analysis being the most challenging it is also the most controversial of all the tasks assigned to forensic odontologists. The literature concerning bitemark methodology is

---

"Biometric Dental Rosette" – a term invented by the authors and used in print for the first time.

© Springer International Publishing Switzerland 2015
M. Antona and C. Stephanidis (Eds.): UAHCI 2015, Part IV, LNCS 9178, pp. 226–236, 2015.
DOI: 10.1007/978-3-319-20687-5_22

sorely lacking in rigorous scientific testing [5]. It is recognized that an urgent need for high quality studies on bitemarks analysis is required [11, 13, 14]. Although an ideal method probably does not exist, the classical pattern analysis has been continuously developing, as have new computer-aided methods [2–4, 10, 12, 15, 20, 22]. In spite of extensive work in the field of forensic odontology, bitemark analysis has come under increasing scrutiny because of wrongful convictions [11]. The introduction of new, scientifically proven methods could facilitate bite mark analysis, help forensic experts avoid erroneous opinions and thus take away the arguments of opponents.

Many characteristics of human anatomy and physiology (fingerprints, iris, hand geometry and facial appearance) are considered to be unique. Thus, they are suitable for biometric recognition [16]. Biometrics (Greek: *bios = life, metron = to measure*) deals with the use of measurable anatomical, physiological and behavioral features. It includes automated methods of measuring and comparing of anthropometric and behavioral characteristics. The aim of biometrics is personal identification or verification based on the analysis of unique and constant features.

The most commonly known is identification based on the facial appearance. Literally this is what a child does when it recognizes the face of its mother. A mother and father can recognize their child perfectly from a distance, even if they are one of a pair of identical twins. The reason is not just the facial appearance. Although single distances between the characteristic points may be similar in many people, four or five distances as well as the proportions between them are unlikely to be identical.

Pretty [13] is of the opinion, that the studies are not required to determine the uniqness of the human dentition, but how it is represented within the bitemark. However, the basis of this study was the assumption that human dentition is unique. There is no proof that it is, but also no proof, that it is not. The uniqueness in term of human dentition means characteristic shape, size, and pattern, and any individual features within the particular arch (i.e. broken crown, a developmental malformation, anomaly in eruption) [6]. The single distances between the teeth and their dimensions can be similar in many people, however the series of measurements and the proportions between them seem to be appropriate for biometrical methods. Nonetheless, every method has its limitations, thus to apply biometrics to bitemark analysis, it must guarantee certainty.

The Computer Aided Engineering (CAE) systems are very well known by designers in their every day practice and numerical analysis. Many of engineering technologies, especially CAD/CAM techniques, have an application in biomechanics, bioengineering, biometrics [17–19] presently known also as Computer Aided Medical Engineering (CAME).

The study was performed to analyze whether biometric methods using measurements and proportions are suitable for bitemark analysis.

The scope of work includes the following elements:

- maneuvering of the 3D models of the tooth geometry to compare with the bitemarks left in the cheese,
- three-dimensional "mapping" of the position of the characteristic points of the teeth "biometric dental rosette",
- comparison of the "bite-in" profile with the bite mark line of mandibular teeth.

2   Materials and Methods

Registration of Volunteers' Dentition. Twelve adult volunteers of different gender and age were involved in the study. A standard dental examination was performed and dental records were created for every person. According to standard dental procedures the impressions of maxillary and mandibular teeth were made in order to prepare the gypsum models of the volunteers' dentitions.

Experimental Bitemarks. Experimental bitemarks were collected from every person involved in the study. The bitemarks were left on the previously prepared rectangular piece of medium-hard cheese (approx. 2 cm thick). The volunteers were asked to bite-in and bite-off a piece of cheese.

3D Scanning of Dental Casts and Bitemarks. Both, the gypsum models of the dentition and the bitemarks registered on the cheese were immediately scanned. The 3D scanning was performed using an optical scanner GOM Atos II Rev.01 with a measuring volume of 120 × 96 × 80 mm. The resolution of the camera was 1.4 megapixels. Distance between points during scanning was 0.18 mm.

The reference data for computational analyses were 3D models of the dentition and fragments of cheese with bitemarks (Fig. 1).

The 3D Analysis of Dentition Models and Bitemarks. The 3D analysis was performed with the use of specialized CAE programs (Computer Aided Engineering) as well as Rhinoceros 4.0 and Reverse Engineering software, as Geomagic Studio (a specialized program for processing and analysis of the models obtained from 3D scanners).

Creation of "Biometric Dental Rosette". The method comprises the following steps:

(1) development of a computer model of the dental arch - based either on data from a three-dimensional scanner (dental cast scanning) or on direct scanning within the patient's oral cavity;
(2) identification of the characteristic features (points) on the crowns of the teeth;

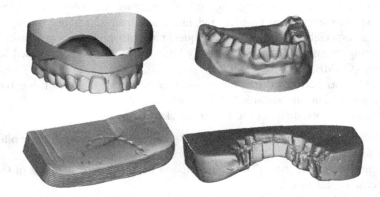

Fig. 1. 3D models of the dentition and fragments of cheese with bitemarks

(3) determination of a system of axes and reference planes - based on the characteristic points;

(4) determination of quantities characterizing the dental arch features.

As the result of the above steps is three-dimensional "Biometric Dental Rosette".

3   Results

The use of 3D models, and specialized programs for computer aided engineering (CAE), allowed for a number of point surface and volume comparative analyses. Models obtained from 3D scanning are fully parametric, retaining all essential geometric parameters of their originals.

Implementation of individual analysis of 3D models is presented in the following sections.

3.1   Geometric Matching of 3D Models of Dentition with Bitemarks Left in the Cheese

Matching the 3D models of dentition with bitemarks left in the cheese was performed first. Matching was done separately for "bite-in" (Fig. 2) and "bite-off" marks (Fig. 3).

The ability to manoevre the dentition models and bitemarks in 3D space aided analysis of the indentations of the teeth into the cheese.

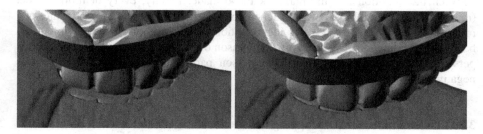

Fig. 2. Three dimensional matching of dentition with bitemarks for "bite-in" marks

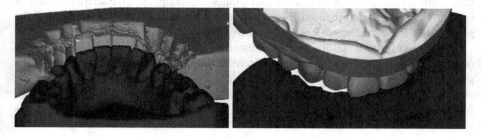

Fig. 3. Three dimensional matching of dentition with bitemarks for "bite-off marks"

Using 3D methods, 864 blind trials of matching the dentition models to the bitemarks were made. Every model of maxillary dentition was matched sequentially to every "bite-in" mark (to its superior and inferior surface-144 matches each) and to the superior surface of "bite-off" mark (144 matches). The models of inferior dentition were matched in the same way: every model was matched sequentially to every "bite-in" mark (to its superior and inferior surface-144 matches each) and to the inferior surface of "bite-off" mark (144 matches). Adjusting was conditioned by the type of the bitemark. The "bite-in" mark represents the edges of the maxillary (on the superior surface of the bitemark) and mandibular teeth (on the inferior surface of the bitemark). Because it is not always clear which surface of the bitemark is superior or inferior, both dentition models, the maxillary and mandibular, were matched to both surfaces of the "bite-in" mark. The superior surface of the "bite-off" mark represents the edges of maxillary teeth (an anchor), while on its inferior surface the profiles of mandibular teeth are visible. The inferior teeth penetrate deep into the material when the jaws are closed leaving behind marks on the material's vertical surfaces along its entire thickness.

The edges of the maxilla and the mandible were transformed into the corresponding positions of the bitemark and the edges of the maxillary and mandibular incisors and canines as well as cusps of premolars were adjusted to the bitemarks in 1:1 scale.

In this 3D pattern comparison, the structure of several teeth, as well as the relationship to the surrounding teeth was compared. The width and shape of the maxillary and mandibular arches, width and shape of the projection of the incisive edges and cusps of the teeth, and other characteristics of the teeth (position, rotations and restorations) were analysed. This allowed conclusive results regarding the correspondence between the dentition and the bitemark to be made. Finally, every dentition model (maxillary and mandibular) was matched to corresponding "bite-in" and "bite-off" marks. This allowed for a positive identification to be made of all the 12 volunteers based on the bitemarks they left. Any comparison of the dentition characteristics of one person to the bitemark left by another person participating in the experiment was negative.

3.2   Three Dimensional "Mapping" of the Position of the Characteristic Features (Points) of the Teeth

"Mapping" was carried out next on both the dentition models and the bitemarks. This procedure results in a set of curves and points depicting the characteristic features (points) of the teeth and their edges respectively (Fig. 4). Based on the "mapping" the so-called "Biometric Dental Rosette" was created for the dentition models.

The "Biometric Dental Rosette" is initiated by the determination of the closing line (a straight line connecting the first characteristic point to the last one). Afterwards, the straight lines between points are plotted and extra lines between the centre of the closing line and the various characteristic points are spanned. An established "rosette" functions similarly to the so-called "Golden Triangle", known for biometric systems used in face recognition. Similarly, the "rosette", was created for bitemarks (Fig. 5).

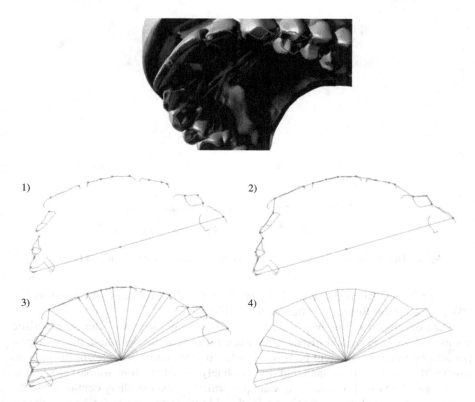

Fig. 4. "Mapping" the position of characteristic features (points and curves) of the teeth and stages of creating the three-dimensional "Biometric Dental Rosette": (1) characteristic features (points and curves) of tooth, (2) curve connecting characteristic points and closing straight line, (3) setting of rosette arms, (4) final "Biometric Dental Rosette".

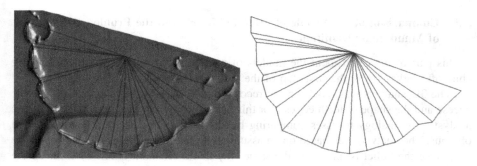

Fig. 5. "Mapping" the position of characteristic features (points and curves) of the bitemark and three-dimensional "Biometric Dental Rosette".

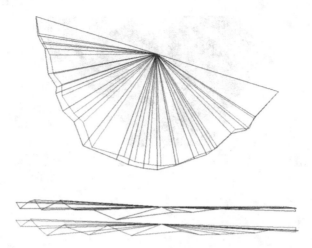

Fig. 6. The "Biometric Dental Rosette's" comparison of the dentition and bitemarks

Finally, the "Biometric Dental Rosette" of the dentition was compared to the "Biometric Dental Rosette" of the bitemark (Fig. 6).

Data developed in this way include not only the coordinates of the characteristic points, but also the mutual distances between them as well as a whole range of proportions between the different parts of triangles. It is the entire complex of 3D data, as rosettes do not lie in one plane, but are absolutely 3D (three-dimensional) structures.

A total of 144 trials of matching were performed for the maxillary dentition and the superior surface of "bite-in" marks and another 144 trials were made for the mandibular dentition and the inferior surface of "bite-in" marks. All the individuals were positively identified as the biters. Any comparison of the dentition of one person to the bitemark left by another person was negative.

3.3   Comparison of the Profile of "Bite-in" Mark and the Profile of Mandibular Dentition

In this part of the experiment the models of mandibular dentition and corresponding "bite-off marks" (from the first step of the study) were used.

The 3D analysis was based on the reconstruction of both the bitemarks left in the cheese and the shape of teeth edges. For this part of study we were inspired by ballistic analysis. An analogy to cases comparing bullets fired from rifles and pistols seemed obvious. The analysis was based on an assumption that the trait left of the barrel on the surface of the bullet is unique in the same way that a bitemark is left by teeth on the surface of the cheese.

Transversely to the course of the bite line the plane was appointed and the curve of bitemark was plotted. Then, based on the curve, the projection (prolongation) of the bitten surface was made and its representation in 3D space was created (Fig. 7). The analogical procedure was made of the mandibular dentition (Fig. 8). The image

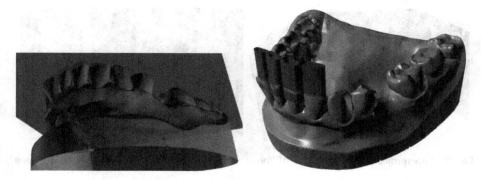

Fig. 7. Projection of the profile of mandibular dentition and their 3D representation

Fig. 8. Projection of the surface profile of "bite-in" mark on cheese

obtained in the space corresponds to the surface, theoretically left by the teeth if they had moved vertically from top to bottom.

Finally, both surfaces were superprojected and their concordance was analyzed (Fig. 9). In all investigated cases the correlation was observed, the more accurate the marks left by mandibular teeth, the higher the correlation.

4   Discussion

Any biological or behavioral characteristics could be used to identify individuals if it meets the following requirements:

(1) Collectability = accessibility (the element can be measured or easily acquired);
(2) Universality = availability (the element exists in entire population);
(3) Unicity = distinctiveness (the element must be distinctive to each person, the biometric characteristic should show great variation over the population);
(4) Permanence = robustness (the property of the element should be stable and remain constant over time) [7].

Fig. 9. Superprojection of the profile of "bite-in" mark and the profile of mandibular dentition

Contextually, the human dentition meets all the above requirements with a little controversion on its permanence. Considering the fact, that behavioral characteristics can change over time and it is not a precluding factor for biometric analysis, it can be concluded, that biometric methods applied for bitemark analysis have to accept some degree of variability.

What we consider advantageous is that all the presented analyses may proceed the standard bitemark analysis.

The "biometric dental rosette" may be created for maxillary and mandibular dentition models as well as for the bitemarks and appropriate number of matches can be performed.

The pairs of rosettes showing the highest concordance will show the dentition model and corresponding bitemark, making the identification of the biter possible. Likewise, the reconstruction of the bitten surface and the creation of the hypothetical surface left by the mandibular teeth, followed by the appropriate number of matches, will enable the mandibular dentition model to be matched to the corresponding bitemark. The maintenance of size and proportions of the original, both dentition model and the bitemark is an absolute condition for comparative analysis [21]. The first step in computer analysis of biological/medical objects is to obtain the correct and high accurate 3D model [17–19]. Models obtained from 3D scanning are fully parametric, retaining all essential geometric parameters of their originals.

The 3D models of scanned cheese reproduce the bitemarks with high resolution and are highly accurate. The bitemarks preserved by scanning were clear and legible.

The ability to maneuver the models in 3D space significantly facilitates bitemark analysis by allowing the assessment of bitemarks and the maxillary and mandibular arches from different angles. It also allows the depressions of the teeth in the material to be observed.

However, biometrics is not a perfect method [1, 9] and some limitations of our analysis should be discussed. Some inaccuracies in the implementation of computer models, as well as relations arising from the nature of food as well as the chewing process have to be emphasized. We also found the following elements affected the results:

- inaccuracy of mapping the geometry of the teeth caused by food elasticity;
- shortages of food elements caused by rupture of food by the action of shear forces between the teeth and food;

– inaccuracies in the reconstruction of the 3D model due to its recreation based on bitemarks and scanning of the gypsum model. The intermediate elements can be eliminated when the teeth directly, not their model are scanned.

It has to be emphasized that the presented studies are of preliminary character, and the continuation is necessary. The increase of the sample number and the trial to eliminante the imperfections of the methods are the most required.

Nevertheless, we believe that the introduction of "biometric dental rosette" is both legitimate and can of great benefit in the analysis of bitemarks.

5   Conclusions

All the above methods can be successfully used in the identification of the biter. The introduction of "biometric dental rosette" into bitemark analysis seems to be a scientifically reasonable idea. Further development of methods and their adoption in practice can be advantageous.

Acknowledgements. The authors thank Mrs. Ruth Hounam for her language support.

References

1. Aas, F.K.: The Body does not lie: identity, risk and trust in technoculture. Crime Media Cult. **2**, 143–158 (2006)
2. Al-Talabani, N., Al-Moussawy, N.D., Baker, F.A., Mohammed, H.A.: Digital analysis of experimental human bitemarks: application of two new methods. J. Forensic Sci. **51**(6), 1372–1375 (2006)
3. Bernitz, H., Owen, J.H., Heerden, W.F.P., Solheim, T.: An integrated technique for the analysis of skin bite marks. J. Forensic Sci. **53**, 194–198 (2008)
4. Blackwell, S.A., Taylor, R.V., Gordon, I., Ogleby, C.L., Tanijiri, T., Yoshino, M., Donald, M.R., Clement, J.G.: 3-D imaging and quantitative comparison of human dentitions and simulated bite marks. Int. J. Legal Med. **121**, 9–17 (2007)
5. Bowers, C.: Problem-based analysis of bitemark identification. The role of DNA Forensic Sci. Int. **159S**, 104–109 (2006)
6. Dorion, R.B.J. (ed.): Bitemark Evidence, 2nd edn. CRC Press, Boca Raton (2011)
7. Emilio, M., Massari, S.: Body, biometrics and identity. Bioethics **22**(9), 448–498 (2008)
8. Freeman, A.J., Senn, D.R., Arendt, D.M.: Seven hundred seventy eight bite marks: analysis by anatomic location, victim and biter demographics, type of crime, and legal disposition. J. Forensic Sci. **50**(6), 1436–1443 (2005)
9. Jain, K.A.: An introduction to biometric recognition. IEEE Trans. Circuits Syst. Video Technol. **14**(1), 1–10 (2004)
10. Martin-de-las-Heras, S., Tafura, D.: Comparison of simulated human dermal bitemarks possessing three-dimensional attributes to suspected biters using a proprietary three-dimensional comparison. Forensic Sci. Int. **190**, 33–37 (2009)
11. Metcalf, R.D., Lee, G., Gould, L.A., Stickels, J.: Bite this! The role of bite marks analyses in wrongful convictions. Southw. J. Crim. Just. **7**, 47–64 (2010)

12. Naether, S., Buck, U., Campana, L., Breitbeck, R., Thali, M.: The examination and identification of bite marks in foods using 3D scanning and 3D comparison methods. Int. J. Legal Med. **126**(1), 89–95 (2012)
13. Pretty, I.A.: The barriers to achieving an evidence base for bitemark analysis. Forensic Sci. Int. **159S**, 110–120 (2006)
14. Pretty, I.A., Sweet, D.: The scientific basis for human bitemark analyses—a critical review. Sci. Justice **41**, 85–92 (2001)
15. Przystańska, A., Lorkiewicz-Muszyńska, D., Rychlik, M., Glapiński, M., Łabęcka, M., Sobol, J., Żaba, C.: The effectiveness of 2D and 3D methods in analysis of experimental bitemarks Dent. Med. Probl. **52** (2015) (in press)
16. Rosenzweig, P., Kochems, A., Schwartz, A.: Biometric Technologies: Security, legal and policy implications. Legal Memorandum **12**, 1–10 (2004)
17. Rychlik, M., Stankiewicz, W.: Extraction of 3D geometrical features of biological objects with 3D PCA analysis and applications of results. In: G.R. Naik (ed.) Applied Biological Engineering – Principles and Practice, Chapter 4, pp. 85–112. InTech (2012)
18. Rychlik, M., Stankiewicz, W., Morzynski, M.: 3D facial biometric database – search and reconstruction of objects based on PCA modes. In: Stephanidis, C., Antona, M. (eds.) UAHCI 2014, Part I. LNCS, vol. 8513, pp. 125–136. Springer, Heidelberg (2014)
19. Rychlik, M., Stankiewicz, W., Morzynski, M.: Numerical analysis of geometrical features of 3D biological objects, for three-dimensional biometric and anthropometric database. In: Stephanidis, C. (ed.) Universal Access in HCI, Part II, HCII 2011. LNCS, vol. 6766, pp. 108–117. Springer, Heidelberg (2011)
20. Santoro, V., Lozito, P., De Donno, A., Introna, F.: Experimental study of bite mark injuries by digital analysis. J. Forensic Sci. **56**, 224–228 (2011)
21. Sheets, H.D., Bush, M.A.: Mathematical matching of a dentition to bitemarks: use and evaluation of affine methods. Forensic Sci. Int. **207**, 111–118 (2011)
22. Thali, M.J., Braun, M., Markwalder, T., Brueschweiler, W., Zollinger, U., Malik, N.J., Yen, K., Dirnhofer, R.: Bite mark documentation and analysis: 3D/CAD supported photogrammetry approach. Forensic Sci. Int. **135**, 115–121 (2003)

Polling Place Support Tool; User Interface to Plan and Run Polling Places

Ted Selker[1(✉)] and Shama Hoque[2]

[1] CITRIS University of California, Berkeley, USA
Ted.Selker@gmail.com
[2] Research Alliance for Accessible Voting, Dhaka, Bangladesh
shama.hoque@gmail.com

Abstract. We describe a scenario and enabling system to provide assistance to election officers in several ways. The new user interface approach supports polling place design, training, operations, problem solving, and auditing. It presents a spatial/graphical user interface for interacting with representations of voting space, furniture, and equipment layout, to assist election officers in better fulfilling polling place administrative activities before, during, and after the election. The application, Polling Place Support Tool, is designed to improve on the current paper-based checklists an election officer uses to remember the different activities he or she has to perform. The RAV Polling Place Support Tool is a simulation that allows poll workers and officials to explore the possibilities for optimizing the design of an accessible and compliant polling place, auditing its use and intervening in to solve problems as they arise.

Keywords: Voting · Process · User interface · Web service

1 Introduction

Polling places are notoriously difficult for individuals with disabilities to navigate and accessible voting devices might even be improperly setup. In the aftermath of the 2000 presidential election, research and statistics showed that polling place operations were responsible for losing over a million votes [1].

M. Antona and C. Stephanidis (Eds.): UAHCI 2015, Part IV, LNCS 9178, pp. 237–247, 2015.
DOI: 10.1007/978-3-319-20687-5_23

Polling place problems-rank as one of the top three aspects of the voting process that hinder and disenfranchise voters. Setting up the polling place during an election is a process that requires following strict guidelines and rules, as well as understanding how to efficiently control voter flow. Indeed, in 2013 President Obama convened a task force to look at the problems, such as long lines in polling places [2].

Fig. 1. New Orleans 2006. 50 precincts voted in this accessible warehouse. Polling place workers with poll books used registration lists to direct people efficiently. There were no lines.

Several mechanisms have been employed to teach people how to design and plan polling places. One is the lecture hall approach, where those learning how to operate a polling place face an instructor at the front, who discusses various parts of the undertaking. At another extreme, some poll workers might only get a color-coded leaflet that helps people to understand some parts of it.

Live presentations and leaflets might not have been the most effective approaches to teaching or motivating election workers to create seamless, functioning spaces to hold elections, especially as polling place design relates to accessibility to all voters. Significant problems often arise during the actual operation of polling places on election days.

1.1 Polling Place - Examples

A couple examples might illustrate the value of planning polling place operations. In Boston in 2006, Dr. Selker watched a dark polling place with many people having trouble reading their ballots. Additional lights were installed so people could vote without flashlights in a dimly-lit auditorium polling place at 9:30 AM, 1.5 h after the polling place opened (Fig. 1). At a polling place in Nevada in 2004, Dr. Selker watched as all twenty voting machines at the site were plugged into a single power outlet. A breaker tripped, losing power. When all of the batteries died 2 h later, the polling place ceased operation. An ad hoc decision was then made: all of the machines were plugged into a different (single) outlet. That outlet, it turned out, had a microwave oven plugged into it. When a pollworker was asked, "Shouldn't the microwave be unplugged?" another pollworker replied, "No, it's okay" [3]. In a separate problem at that polling place, people discovered that they were only allowed to vote for federal elections (Fig. 2) which was caused by a pollworker setting up the voters activation cards for "provisional" in-stead of registered voters.

Fig. 2. People not able to vote on local elections due to polling place problem

In the above two examples and hundreds of other ones we have witnessed, the pollworker is navigating complex issues of planning execution and need for external support. Bad training can cause problems and good training and care and attention of poll workers can sometimes overcome inherent problems with polling place design and planning. Post-Katrina in New Orleans, Dr. Selker watched an election day in which dedicated helpers from the Secretary of State's office came from Baton Rouge to help people identify their voting place, reach it, and even get their cars parked. The largest polling place that day had 50,000 people assigned … and had no lines! This was the famous Ward 9 that had flooded during Katrina. For that reason only 5,000 – several times the number of people that typically vote in a polling place – not 50,000 showed up to vote. But, 5,000 people going to one polling place would be a debacle in most polling places. It was accessible and easy to navigate, because it was spacious, organized, and there were people telling voters which of the 50 different precinct polling places inside that warehouse they should go to, or if they had to go to another site (Fig. 2).

1.2 Polling Place - Training

Poll worker training varies from election to election and jurisdiction to jurisdiction. We have visited some polling places staffed with poll workers that were enlisted the morning of the election. It is also not uncommon for poll workers to have spent hours or days in classroom settings learning about voting. It is less common for them to role-play or simulate accessible processes. We see the training practices in polling

Fig. 3. Voting not private, pencil given voter makes selection much harder than finger

places lean on support of more experienced poll workers, a telephone helpline, or a poll worker pamphlet on the day of election when the process is happening.[1]

When a problem arises in the polling place, poll workers have to make decisions in the moment without supervision, and possibly without proper analysis of the problems. Figure 3 shows a poll booth that was setup incorrectly, putting ballots in plain view of onlookers. As well, by giving the voter a pencil to poke the touch screen, the pollworker inadvertently made the touch screen very difficult to use. Many of the problems that polling places face might be avoided just by conceptually walking through the experience ahead of time and role playing the experience for the voter and poll worker.

1.3 Poll Worker Training User Interface Alternative[2]

"Polling places should be organized so that all voters can be processed efficiently and voters with disabilities can navigate the voting area and participate in the electoral

---

[1] We pollwatched in CA, IL, LA, MA, NV, NY, and talked to pollworkers from many other states.

[2] http://researchinaccessiblevoting.bitbucket.org

process without assistance" [4]. As easy as the task might sound, it can take 178 pages to explain which guidelines and rules to follow and which activities to do before, during, and after the election to create a well-organized polling place layout.

From a "ostraca" shard of pottery to indicate a vote in Greece to paper and voting machines over the last century technology has been used in assisting voters to make their voting experience easier. Technology to assist pollworkers have normally included pamphlets, registration books, and their replacements in electronic versions in electronic poll books and telephones. There are several reasons that more technology hasn't been available to ease the work of pollworkers. First, each jurisdiction potentially has its own guidelines and procedures to set up a polling place. Another reason is that in some states the elections office will do a "site survey" [Rick Urps, personal communication] to identify the features of the facility where the polling place will be set up, and create the layout for the polling place.

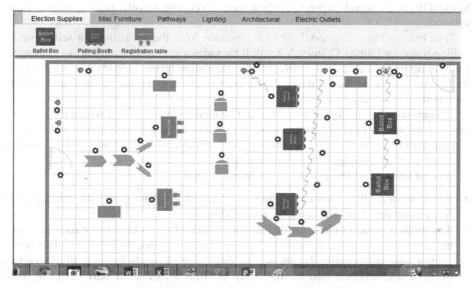

Fig. 4. Example of paths, outlets, cords, equipment and existing furniture in final polling place support tool

The layout should not be changed once it is set by the office; poll workers are compelled to faithfully reproduce the diagram. Third, so far people have not used tablets to assist in polling place setup. As an attempt to make some tasks easier for the elections officer, we have designed and created a prototype for a web application that will help officers and workers in setting up the polling place more quickly, and also in completing a long list of "to-dos" to comply with the laws regarding elections and regarding Americans with Disabilities Act (ADA) [5].

The RAV Polling Place Support Tool provides an alternative to teaching with a slide-based presentation or paper-based instruction. Its goal is to encourage election officials to plan the polling location beforehand, test it, and document how to do it.

The novel user experience started as a project in a CMU accessible voting technology class. It includes two main functions: creating a diagram on how to set up the polling place, and interaction for checking the tasks that need to be done before, during, and after the election. Documentation and communication to potentially reduce difficulties for poll workers to get help during an election was added. The application provides a reflection tool for the poll worker to be able to easily figure out the proper layout to make the voting area accessible with good traffic control. It should also provide enough information for the poll worker to quickly perform the tasks associated with the voting process.

2 Polling Place Support Tool Overview

The tool was built to be scalable. It is written in JavaScript using the MEAN Stack, MongoDB, Node.js and Express.js for the web server, and Angular.js for the client-side software.

The Polling Place Support Tool took guidance from the guidelines for setting up a polling place for Fairfax County, VA [6]. It provides visual representations of entrance, exit, voting booths, accessible voting booths, tabulation boxes, help station, registration station, waiting areas, and walking directions which allow the user to plan and reflect on a polling place layout.

It contains a list of "to-do" tasks that can be marked as completed within the tool. In this way the officer might be more aware of the tasks he or she needs to do, and also be certain about which tasks have already been completed. This live system can be accessed at http://pollingplace.nettempo.com.

List of features of the Polling Place Support Tool:

- Room layout: allows a user to block out parts of a square grid with architectural features or furniture that can't be moved (Fig. 4)
- The toolbox presents elements that should be part of the polling place such as: exit, entrance, help station, registration station, ballot station, ballot box, observers' station, accessible voting booth, and so forth. The elements in the toolbox can be dragged and dropped into the room layout from a toolbar to start designing the voting area layout (Fig. 4)
- Furniture manipulation: The elements in the toolbox could be dragged and dropped into the room layout. Once an item is added to the layout, Handles allow sizing and rotation.
- The user can click on the image to show the different activities the poll worker needs to do to set up that particular furniture. Clicking on an item's gear Icon produces a popup menu note, checkbox duplicate, and delete (Fig. 7). The important items associated with each station can be checked (Fig. 8) by selecting.
- The application allows a user to login and use a database of polling places to create various polling place layout and equipment configurations.
- Beside the activities that the poll worker needs to do for the polling place station, the tool provides information on the activities that he or she needs to do before the

election, when opening the polls, during the Election Day, and when closing the polls. These lists are in a database that can be edited.

Polling place activities are organized to aid poll workers understand the sequence of the tasks they need to do.

Rick Urps, Deputy Director of Maryland State Board of Elections, provided feedback on the prototype. He wasn't sure that the Board would use the layouts previous to the election during a 'site survey', but he saw a lot of potential for associating checklists positions within the polling place. He said "Combining the site survey map with checklists is where we see potential for an app such as this. In Maryland, we envision that the app would be used to initially map out the polling place during the site survey, or the existing polling place map is entered into the app. On Election Day, the map and checklists are there for the chief judges to reference."

Poll workers are often undertrained or new to the activity. We held a workshop for ten persons with little or no experience in the polling place to try using the first iteration of the application. They worked in pairs using the application and reading the guidelines. They found it easy to start creating a layout but found the manipulation impoverished. The final iteration below includes simple handles for sizing and rotating items.

Some users of the first iteration used the app first; some of them used the paper guidelines first. It took them several minutes to read the documentation to start using the application. The final version below simplified learning and using though a simpler user interface. They wanted better information on the use of the checklist and other elements of the system; the final version below makes it easier to add modify and delete items. People wanted more status feedback; the second version below treats the poll designer and pollworker differently.

For physical accessibility, the Polling Place Support Tool focuses on making physical obstructions and paths through the polling place a priority. It allows a user to put blocks on a grid to define it. The user experience focuses most of the screen real

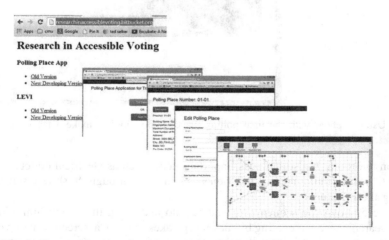

Fig. 5. Screens showing the steps to using the final polling place support tool

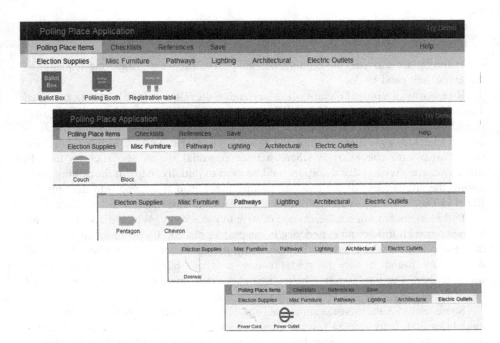

Fig. 6. Toolbars available for adding elements in the final polling place support tool

Fig. 7. Using a photo with the final polling place support tool to make a tag record for an incident.

estate on the room. It also includes important items such as electrical outlets, existing furniture, wires, illumination, and notes. Figures 4 through 8 shows screenshots showing these features.

Figure 5 shows the sequence of getting into and using the application. Going to http://researchinaccessiblevoting.bitbucket.org takes you to a screen where you can choose the new polling place application. From there, a screen allows you to try a demo

Fig. 8. Student sample checklist

or log in. If you try the system by default, you are shown polling place number 01-01, which you select to edit layout. This takes you to the architectural layout that you can experiment with. The application's polling place screen presents a polling place floor plan grid and tabs for things to place in it, as in Fig. 4. A grid of 1-foot by 1-foot flooring tiles indicates specifically where various elements of the polling place can be placed. The elements, such as an entrance in an architectural diagram, can be dragged from the "toolbox" at the top to where they should be on the grid.

Polling place designers can place a polling place element in a spot on the grid, then click on it to see relevant information. The toolkits in the new application are in tool bars shown in Fig. 6. The objects include election supplies, furniture, pathways, lighting, architectural elements, and electrical outlets. Selecting one of these tabs shows a set of items that can be dragged onto the polling place grid, such as the ballot box, polling booth, and registration table icons, in the election supplies tab in Fig. 6. Each placeable item has 'handles' to position, rotate, or stretch it. Selecting the gear icon next to the item brings up a popup menu including note, checklist, duplicate, and delete, as shown in Fig. 7. Building and exploring with the system is meant to have a spatial game-like experience to inspire new poll workers to learn about and succeed in setting up a polling place. The simulator becomes an interactive experience that is likely to be memorable to them.

For each of the elements on the grid, there is the option to create a Note which can be used to leave a note and record the position and time as shown in Fig. 7. If someone is using this application on an election day, as an aid for setting up a polling place, or as an educational tool, the note tag option allows this person to rate a problem, or add text and/or a photo that will appear with the element on the polling place grid. A photo of a help station in an actual polling place can be added and might be useful to whomever looks at the note tag. The photo could show how the setup election device should look on Election Day. The photographs could also be used by an online help desk to diagnose problems remotely, such as a poorly positioned sign hanging below the desk. An employee at a town or city's election office could view various polling places prior to the election with the application and, upon noticing an ineffective aspect, attach text to the help desk to indicate the need to post important material in a more accessible spot.

3   Polling Place Support Tool - Conclusion and Future Work

Two iterations of a Polling Place Support Tool were made. The final one is created as a web services app that should be deployable for testing in jurisdictions.

This platform demonstrates a range of support that can make polling places more functional, reliable, and accessible. The web-based interactive polling place design and management system can be used on most any web-enabled desktop or mobile device. Poll workers access to the app, their checklist activity, and note tags can play a role in auditing. The system can be used for polling place site analysis and preparation of layouts prior to an election. It can be used for procedural support for opening polls, for closing the polls, for facilitating communication about problems and solutions during Election Day. Such visual and text records of polling places created with the software can be used as a reference to analyze things that happened and to consider and improve operations for the future. The next step in exploring this approach would be to deliver it for a pilot trial in a jurisdiction.

Figure 9 shows a rendition of a future use. It includes a control panel that could allow an election headquarters to keep track of and communicate with polling places through this application. Without phones, the central support people could then be made aware of and address problems throughout the jurisdiction. "Pins" on a map could indicate pending requests for communication. The official could view the polling place, its checklists, and its notes to be oriented as they work with a pollworker who is grappling with a problem. As well, the MIT Voting Technology Project have shown interest in working with the system to add a simulation mode. Integrated simulation code could allow users to see how various changes to the polling place affect throughput and other aspects of efficiency.

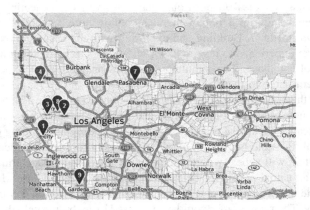

Fig. 9. Artist's conception of an election control room user experience to access polling places especially when they have red, important tagged problems.

The Polling place support tool described in this paper demonstrates how a user experience can help aspects surrounding an activity: training planning: logistics and problem resolution. Polling places are set up episodically with little margin for error and tremendous pressure for perfection; all recipes for difficulty. As small problems in the polling place can disenfranchise disabilities, it is especially useful for them. As many solutions that attempt to help people with special needs do, the tool demonstrates universal design, helping everyone. Integrating education, planning, process compliance, and problem resolution can be daunting. This web app shows how such hurdles can be mitigated with an integrated solution.

Acknowledgements. This work was supported by the RAAV Federal Election Assistance Commission grant to the Research Alliance for Accessible Voting. Early prototypes were made by Linda Angélica Avendano Franco Dan Gillette assisted with all aspects of this research as well.

References

1. Alvarez, R.M., Ansolabehere, S., Antonsson, E., Bruck, S., Graves, S., Palfrey, T., Rivest, R., Selker, T., Slocum, A., Stewart, C.: Voting – What Was, What Could Be. Caltech/MIT Voting Technology Project, July 2001. http://www.votingtechnologyproject.org/reports/2001report. htm
2. Presidential Commission on Election Administration, The American Voting Experience: Report and Recommendations of the Presidential Commission on Election Administration (2014)
3. Selker, T.: A Day of Poll Watching, Reno and Sparks Nevada User Experience Magazine, vol. 4, no. 1 (Spring 2005)
4. United States. Election Assistance Commission: Voluntary Voting System Guidelines. vol. 1, Version 1.0 (2005)
5. United States Department of Justice Civil Rights Division: ADA Best Practices Tool Kit for State and Local Governments 2003. Retrieved from Americans with Disabilities Act: Retrieved, June 2014. http://www.ada.gov/pcatoolkit/chap5toolkit.htm
6. Virginia Polling Place: checklists and procedures. Fairfax. VA, 06 November 2012

The Impact of Literacy on Usable and Accessible Electronic Voting

Kathryn Summers[1]([⊠]) and Jonathan Langford[2]

[1] University of Baltimore, Baltimore, USA
ksummers@ubalt.edu
[2] Interactive Educational Systems Design,
River Falls, USA
Jlang2@pressenter.com

Abstract. Electronic voting interfaces present particular challenges for voters with low literacy. Research has found that individuals with low literacy typically encounter problems in electronic interfaces related to their tendencies to read every word, act on every word, interpret words literally, skip text, become distracted, and stop reading too soon. Based on a growing body of research about the experiences of low-literacy voters in electronic interfaces, this paper presents eleven principles to address these challenges. It also translates those principles into specific best practice recommendations related to language, navigation, visual design, and interaction in electronic voting interfaces.

Keywords: Low literacy · Electronic interfaces · Interaction design · Voting · Ballot design · Plain language · Plain interaction · Usability

1 Introduction

Key goals for any electronic ballot interface include the following:

- Allow voters to cast their votes as intended, and to verify that their votes were cast as intended
- Provide an easy, non-frustrating voting experience
- Enable voters to vote with minimal assistance, while preserving privacy and confidentiality

These goals are more difficult to achieve for voters with low literacy. This is particularly true of voters who also lack computer expertise, which is the case with many low-literacy voters.

This paper describes current best practices for designing electronic ballot interfaces that will achieve these goals for low-literacy voters, in light of what is known about the behavior of low-literacy readers in general with electronic interfaces and more specifically when using electronic ballots.

M. Antona and C. Stephanidis (Eds.): UAHCI 2015, Part IV, LNCS 9178, pp. 248–257, 2015.
DOI: 10.1007/978-3-319-20687-5_24

1.1 Understanding Low Literacy

What is Low Literacy? Low literacy among adults is difficulty at reading and processing written information at the level that is expected of adults in modern society.

Literacy has multiple dimensions. The National Assessment of Adult Literacy measures three types of literacy: prose, document, and quantitative literacy. Of these, *document literacy*—the previous knowledge and skills required to perform tasks like filling out applications and understanding maps, tables, or drug labels—relates most directly to the voting experience [1].

Low literacy doesn't necessarily mean an inability to read. Rather, it means being weak in skills such as word recognition, understanding sentence structure, being able to locate a piece of information in text, drawing inferences, applying the information that has been read to the reader's own situation, and being able to connect one piece of information to another. Voters with low literacy may read slowly, with great effort, and may come away with an incomplete or incorrect understanding of what they've read.

Who has Low Literacy? In some cases, low literacy is related to lower education levels. More often in the United States, it is related to other circumstances that prevent people from reading well. These may include:

- Learning disabilities
- Mild cognitive impairment
- Decrease in reading capability due to aging
- Limited proficiency in English
- Other conditions that can interfere with reading

Literacy issues affect 43 % of the adult population in the United States, based on the 2003 National Assessment of Adult Literacy. Low literacy skills tend to correlate with lower income, higher rates of chronic health challenges, and lower rates of participation in voting activities. Only 53 % of adult citizens with below basic prose literacy reported voting in the 2000 presidential election; only 62 % of voters with basic prose literacy skills voted in 2000. In contrast, 84 % of voters with proficient literacy skills reported voting in 2000 [1].

1.2 Low-Literacy Behaviors

Researchers have observed several characteristic reading strategies and behaviors that are likely to affect voters when interacting with electronic ballot interfaces:

Read every word—Competent readers typically focus on the key information that is relevant to them. In contrast, low-literacy readers often read every word in an effort to make sure they don't miss the information they are looking for [2].

Act on every word—When low-literacy readers see language that implies an action, they often will act immediately on it without reading further or considering what they are reading in context. For example, if the instruction say to touch the screen, they are likely to immediately touch the screen, even if they are on a help screen [3].

Interpret words literally—Low-literacy readers have difficulty making inferences, and interpret words and sentences literally.

Skip—Because reading can require a lot of cognitive effort for people with low literacy skills, they may try to do as little reading as possible by skipping instructions, hard words, or even whole sections of dense text [2, 4, 5].

Get distracted—Readers with low literacy skills can easily be distracted from reading. In the case of voting, extraneous information or visual design elements can divert cognitive resources away from reading, reducing voters' success in casting their votes as intended [2, 6].

Stop reading too soon—Both competent readers and low-literacy readers typically read only as much as they think they need to know before taking action. However, low-literacy readers often stop reading too soon. In a voting context, this can lead either to undervotes or to random or semi-random choices [4].

2   Principles of Electronic Ballot Design for Low-Literacy Voters

Effective ballot design for low-literacy users requires that ballots and supporting messages and instructions must be written in plain language [7, 8]. Additionally, electronic interfaces for low-literacy users must employ plain interaction: i.e., interaction that is designed to help the user clearly understand the information presented to them, the actions expected of them, and the results of their actions [9].

In general, research confirms that electronic design that supports low-literacy readers also improves the experience of voters in general. Similarly, electronic ballot design for low-literacy voters can help improve the experience of voters with other disabilities and voting challenges by decreasing the mental and physical processing that is needed in order to complete the ballot.

Principle #1: Make language simple and easy to understand. Use of plain language improves the experience of all voters [10, 11], but is crucially important for low-literacy voters. Plain language in electronic ballots is also important for voters who may be less comfortable or less familiar with electronic interfaces—which includes many low-literacy voters.

Principle #2: Make it look easy to read. Effective use of visual layout and cues can help readers process text more easily by indicating main points, signalling transitions, and making the text look less intimidating [12]. These cues are useful for all voters, but particularly important for voters with low literacy.

Principle #3: Create a linear flow. It's important not to split the attention of low-literacy readers. A logical, linear flow of information helps voters to focus their attention on one thing at a time, reduces possible anxiety and the need for decisions about what to do next, and helps to guarantee that voters have the information they need before they are asked to make a decision [5].

Principle #4: Support a narrow field of view. Readers who have difficulty processing text—including low-literacy readers—are less likely to notice content above, below, or to the sides of their focus of attention. This means they are less able to pay attention to cues about what might be coming up and may not remember where they have previously been. They also are less likely to notice page interaction that is "in the margins" [9].

Principle #5: Prompt voter actions and choices. People process information better when they know what they are expected to do. This is particularly true of low-literacy readers. Low-literacy readers also have difficulty making inferences. They are likely to be confused by directions that indirectly suggest actions they can take without making those actions explicit.

Principle #6: Support immediate action. Because low-literacy readers voters tend to act on every word, it is important to integrate instructions with the interface so that voters can take action at the same time and in the same space where the information is provided [9].

Principle #7: Support users' preferred actions. Voters expect to be able to carry out certain actions in an electronic interface, based on prior experiences, assumptions from print documents, and the needs of the moment. As much as possible, the interface should behave how voters expect [9].

Principle #8: Communicate the results of voters' actions through immediate feedback. Voters need opportunities to make sure that what they did was what they intended to do. This kind of feedback is much easier to process right after voters have taken the action, and provides opportunities for them to take immediate additional action (e.g., adding a vote for another candidate). Immediate feedback is also reassuring—something that is particularly important for low-literacy voters. Immediate feedback includes not only written feedback, but also visual changes to the interface (e.g., immediately showing that a choice has been selected) [3].

Principle #9: Make it easy to fix errors. Low-literacy voters tend to have much more difficulty in seeing and understanding the errors they make, and then in figuring out how to fix them [5]. Messages need to explain clearly and specifically what they need to change and how to change it, without causing anxiety or embarrassment.

Principle #10: Provide a simple and intuitive experience for all voters. Best practices for improving the experience of low-literacy voters incorporate and expand on language and design recommendations for making the voting experience simple and intuitive for voters in general. In general, research confirms that electronic design that supports low-literacy readers also improves the experience of voters in general [2, 3, 5, 9, 10, 11, 14].

Principle #11: Test to ensure usability. Low-literacy voters do not always react to design elements in ways that designers and researchers expect. This is particularly true of low-literacy voters who also lack computer expertise. The only way to be sure electronic ballots work for low-literacy voters is to test the design with low-literacy voters.

3 Language

The general principle related to language in electronic ballots for low-literacy voters is to make language simple and easy to understand. This applies not only to the language of the ballot itself (ballot questions, explanations, etc.), but also to instructions, feedback, and any other text voters may see.

Text Content and Structure.

Guideline: Don't require voters to remember information.

Explanation: Requiring voters to remember something they read elsewhere—even in a previous paragraph—makes it harder for them to process what they are reading. In many cases, low-literacy voters simply won't remember such information. Each paragraph, piece of instructions, and feedback messages should include the information voters need in order to understand what they are being told.

Guideline: Don't provide information voters don't need.

Explanation: Unnecessary information isn't just distracting; it also takes up mental processing resources that low-literacy voters need in order to focus on the essentials. There's an important balance between providing information that voters will find useful (such as a candidate's party affiliation) and information that is likely to prove distracting (such as non-essential instructions or a link to a candidate's position statement).

Guideline: Use headings to provide context.

Explanation: Headings can help orient readers within text. Such cues are particularly important for low-literacy readers. Headings should make sense independently: i.e., without needing to take into account the context of the existing page or information that was read earlier. Example: Instead of "What to Do Next," use "How to Vote."

Guideline: Use short paragraphs that make sense independently.

Explanation: Even remembering information from one paragraph to the next can cause difficulties for low-literacy voters.

Vocabulary and Tone.

Guideline: Use simple and familiar words. Use the same words throughout the ballot for the same actions or concepts.

Explanation: Voters perform better with instructions that use plain language instead of technical voting terminology [13].

Guideline: Avoid possible misunderstandings.

Explanation: This includes not only avoiding words and phrases with ambiguous meanings, but also avoiding words and phrases that may be clear to most voters but that low-literacy readers have been shown to misinterpret. For example, low-literacy voters often have a hard time with the word *choices*, misinterpreting it as either *choose* or *chose*. This can be solved by rewording: e.g., changing "You have 2 choices left" to "You can choose 2 more" [9].

Guideline: Avoid language that could be read as disapproving or scary. Keep the tone positive with a focus on reducing anxiety [9, 13].

Explanation: Low-literacy voters who lack confidence may read unintended meanings into messages. For example, "Are you sure you have finished voting?" could be interpreted as a hint that they have not yet done everything that was expected of them.

Writing Effective Instructions.

Guideline: Place instructions where they are needed and where voters can act on them—not all at the beginning.

Explanation: Instructions generally make more sense in the context where they are needed. Low-literacy voters in particular are unlikely to remember instructions provided ahead of time.

Guideline: Make instructions clear but short.

Explanation: Voters need to know their options, but thorough, complete instructions can cause problems for low-literacy voters. Whenever possible, make interfaces simple enough that they need little explanation [9]. Then provide the minimal amount of help right where the voter can act on the instruction.

Guideline: Write instructions directly to the voter as positive statements.

Explanation: For example, instead of "If you want to vote straight party, you can touch the party name," write "To vote straight party, touch the party name."

Guideline: Put the purpose before the action.

Explanation: For example, instead of "Touch here to vote for someone," write "To vote for someone, touch here."

For additional guidelines related to writing clear voter instructions, see the *Guidelines for Writing Clear Instructions and Messages for Poll Workers* [13].

4   Navigation

Guideline: Provide a separate page for each race, ballot measure, or other voting interaction. Do not split a race, ballot measure, or other voting interaction over multiple pages.

Explanation: This signals voters when each separate race begins and when they are being offered an opportunity to vote on an issue or set of candidates.

Guideline: Provide persistent navigation on each page that shows current location and allows voters to move to any of the main pages in the ballot. Include a Next and Back button, or equivalent, on every page.

Explanation: Persistent navigation allows voting in whatever order voters prefer. It also communicates the overall structure of the ballot and tells voters how far they have to go. This is particularly important for lengthy or complex ballots.

5   Visual Design

5.1   General Guidelines

Guideline: Create a consistent visual design.

Explanation: Low-literacy voters are particularly reliant on consistent visual cues, and are likely to become confused by inconsistency.

Guideline: Use a visual design that shows a clear visual hierarchy.

Explanation: This includes elements such as the following:

- Consistent and clearly distinguishable heading levels
- Closer spacing between related elements
- Strategic use of indentation

5.2   Page Layout

Guideline: Present the ballot in a single active column [2].
  Explanation: Multiple active columns can confuse voters.

- Instructions, active area, and feedback should all be in a single column.
- Candidates should be listed in a single column.
- Navigation can be included to the left of the active column.

  Guideline: Use visual cues (headings, boldface, color, etc.) sparingly to highlight key content and guide voters toward actions they will take.
  Explanation: Visual cues can provide important clues to help low-literacy voters process information and move through the ballot easily. However, too much use of visual cues can prove distracting and confusing.
  Guideline: Maintain a clean, uncluttered layout.
  Explanation: This helps prevent voters from becoming confused or distracted. This can be crucial for voters with low literacy skills, who are already struggling to process all the information on the ballot.

5.3   Buttons

Guideline: Make buttons easy to see and easy to recognize as buttons. Use labels or icons that clearly communicate the purpose of each button to voters.
  Explanation: Buttons should have a consistent format, with rounded corners. Shadow, bevel, gradient, and other effects that make them look more like physical buttons can also help. Make sure labels on buttons are easy to read (e.g., by putting the text in bold and using high contrast). User testing can help determine whether low-literacy voters recognize and use the buttons as intended.
  Guideline: When voters select a button, change the visual appearance to signify that it has been selected.
  Explanation: This provides valuable feedback for voters.

5.4   Text Format and Font

Guideline: Use a text format and font that is clear and easy to read.
  Explanation: For example:

- Text should be flush left, in mixed case (not all capitals), using a simple and easy-to-read font [14].

- Text should be big enough to read easily. While most guidelines call for 12 point text, low-literacy voters often find it easier to complete ballots that are in a larger text size.
- Do not use long blocks of italicized text.
- Voters should be able to change the text size at any point in the voting process.

Guideline: Make sure text does not run wider than 3-4 inches.

Explanation: Longer lines make text harder for low-literacy voters to process. This is particularly important to keep in mind when designing interfaces for small screens that might also be used with larger screens.

Guideline: Visually emphasize key information.

Explanation: This is often done through using bold text or color. However, overuse of boldface and other visual cues can reduce the impact and lead to confusion.

6   Interaction

6.1   General Guidelines

Guideline: Provide an option for voters to hear text spoken.

Explanation: Voters with difficulty reading may benefit from hearing text read. This is particularly true for items such as instructions and feedback messages.

Guideline: Give voters control over their voting experience (text size, contrast, audio, etc.).

Explanation: Both initially and at any point in the voting experience, users should be able to change any of the following:

- Text size
- Contrast levels
- Audio (on/off) and volume

Guideline: When text extends past the visible screen, provide both a scrollbar and a clearly labeled button to view additional text.

Explanation: Voters with computer experience expect scrollbar functionality and are likely to be frustrated if it is not available. However, some voters have difficulty using scrollbars. Additionally, scrollbars do not provide a strong signal of the presence of additional text, particularly for voters with low computer experience. For such voters, a clearly labeled button provides essential additional support.

6.2   Support for Vote Selection

Guideline: When a list of candidates extends past the visible screen, strongly signal the availability of more candidates.

Explanation: It is important to draw the attention of voters to additional candidates. However, users should not be forced to view the entire list. One possible solution is a large button reading "Touch to see more names," presented in a different color at the bottom of the visible list of candidates—plus an active scrollbar at the side of the list.

Guideline: Provide signals to help voters know whether they have selected a candidate or made a choice before moving on.

Explanation: For example, before voters select a candidate or make a choice, the button to move on could read "Skip." Afterwards, it could change to "Next."

Guideline: If using a touchscreen interface, let voters select candidates by touching anywhere on the candidate's name.

Explanation: Voters expect this functionality and are frustrated when it is not available. It also makes the interface easier to use for voters with motor impairment.

6.3 Feedback

Guideline: Whenever voters take an action, immediately communicate the results of the action through visual cues and through text messages when appropriate.

Explanation: Immediate feedback is a principle of universal good electronic interface design, but is particularly important for low-literacy readers.

Guideline: Communicate results of a voting choice by using multiple signals.

Explanation: For example, results could be communicated through color change plus a check mark, or through color change plus contrast change.

Guideline: Show text feedback messages in an overlay box on top of the active area, with multiple ways to close the message box.

Explanation: More specifically:

- In light of low-literacy voters' narrow field of view, it is particularly important that feedback messages be presented where they will be sure to see them.
- The message feedback box should not obscure the entire screen, but instead should let voters see enough of the original screen that they do not lose context. The original screen should be darkened, compared to the message box.
- Low-literacy voters are more likely to have difficulty closing the message box. Message boxes should include a button that says "Close"; it is also helpful if voters can make the message box disappear by clicking outside the box.

6.4 Help

Guideline: If help is provided, make it context-sensitive and focused on the problems voters are most likely to have.

Explanation: If voters ask for help when they are in the write-in interaction, it should help them figure out how to write in a candidate; if they are on the review screen, it should explain what they can do on the review screen and how to do it.

Guideline: Any help text that is provided should be in plain language and should be tested with low-literacy voters.

Explanation: Explanations on help screens should be more simple than the language that is used in the body of the ballot, if possible.

Acknowledgements. This work was funded by grant 70NANB13H180 from the National Institute of Standards and Technology.

References

1. Kutner, M., Greenberg, E., Jin, Y., Boyle, B., Hsu, Y., Dunleavy, E.: Literacy in Everyday Life: Results From the 2003 National Assessment of Adult Literacy (NCES 2007–480). U.S. Department of Education. Washington, DC: National Center for Education Statistics (2007)
2. Summers, K., Summers, M.: Reading and navigational strategies of web users with lower literacy skills. Proc. Am. Soc. Inf. Sci. Technol. **42**(1), 1–10 (2005). doi:10.1002/meet. 1450420179
3. Chisnell, D., Davies, D., Summers, K.: (2013, July 24). Any Device, Anywhere, Any Time: A Responsive, Accessible Ballot Design. The Information Technology and Innovation Foundation, Working Paper #007. Retrieved November 20, 2014 from. http://www. elections.itif.org/reports/AVTI-007-Chisnell-Davies-Summers-2013.pdf
4. Summers, K., Summers, M.: Making the web friendlier for lower-literacy users. Intercom **51** (6), 19–21 (2004)
5. Summers, K., Langford, J., Wu, J., Abela, A., Souza, R.: Designing web-based forms for users with lower literacy skills. Proc. Am. Soc. Inf. Sci. Technol. **43**(1), 1–12 (2006). doi:10. 1002/meet.14504301174
6. Gribbons, W.M.: Universal accessibility and low-literacy populations: Implications for human-computer interaction design and research methods. In: Jacko, J.A. (ed.) The Human-Computer Interaction Handbook: Fundamentals, Evolving Technologies, and Emerging Applications, 3rd edn., pp. 913–931. CRC Press, Boca Raton (2012)
7. Federal Plain Language Guidelines, Revision 1. (2011, May). Retrieved November 30, 2014 from. www.plainlanguage.gov/howto/guidelines/FederalPLGuidelines/FederalPLGuidelines. pdf
8. PLAIN [Plain Language Action and Information Network]. (n.d.). What Is Plain Language? Retrieved November 30, 2014 from. www.plainlanguage.gov
9. Summers, K., Chisnell, D., Davies, D., Alton, N., McKeever, M.: Making voting accessible: designing digital ballot marking for people with low literacy and mild cognitive disabilities. USENIX J. Election Technol. Syst. **2**(2), 11–33 (2014)
10. Redish, J., Chisnell, D., Newby, E., Laskowski, S.J., Lowry. S.: Report of Findings: Use of Language in Ballot Instructions. NISTIR 7556. National Institute of Standards and Technology (NIST) (2008)
11. Kline, K., Bell, C., Jahant, H., Price, C., Jones, A., Mosley, S., Farmer, S., Harley, L., Fain, B.: A Study of Plain Language Writing Style for Ballots in English, Spanish, and Chinese (Working Paper #014). The Information Technology & Innovation Foundation (2013). http://elections.itif.org/wp-content/uploads/AVTI-014-GTRI-PlainLanguage-2013a.pdf
12. Doak, C., Doak, L., Root, J.: Teaching patients with low literacy skills, 2nd edn., J.B. Lippincott Company, Philadelphia (1996)
13. Redish, J., Laskowski, S.: Guidelines for Writing Clear Instructions and Messages for Voters and Poll Workers. NISTIR 7596. National Institute of Standards and Technology (NIST) (2009)
14. Norden, L., Quesenbery, W., Kimball, D.: Better Design, Better Elections. University School of Law Brennan Center for Justice, New York (2012)

Universal Access
to the Built Environment

Flexibility as an Instrument of Social Stabilization of Residential Environment

Wojciech Bonenberg[(⊠)]

Faculty of Architecture, Poznan University of Technology, Poznan, Poland
wojciech.bonenberg@put.poznan.pl

Abstract. This paper presents the results of research conducted at the Faculty of Architecture PUT, regarding flexibility and human factors in the design of housing environment. It points to the need of flexible approach at the initial design stage of decision-making; public opinion has to be considered and emphatic analysis needs to be undertaken to establish the required scope of flexibility. The paper presents the main features of flexibility in the design of flats/houses as opposed to the design of other facilities, such as offices, industrial and commercial areas. The results of research reveal significant differences in the demands regarding the interior of flats/houses and those regarding the residential area. Flexibility turns out to be a crucial factor in the creation of residential areas that stabilize social relationships and include human factors.

Keywords: Flexibility · Housing environment · Social stabilization

1 The Description of the Problem

The issues of flexibility accompany the design-related decisions that an architect faces when designing new facilities and refurbishing or adapting the existing buildings.

In architecture, flexibility involves forecasting the course of future events and choosing between various scenarios of future developments. Uncertainty related with the foregoing is a basic risk factor occurring in architecture. Redevelopments, adaptations, reconstructions of architectural facilities, and city planning may bring about positive spatial consequences, but they may also cause a functional degradation of the facility and result in serious financial losses. Risk control in this respect includes taking decisions regarding the functional layout, the structural parameters, the method of laying pipes and other systems in the building, the selection of building materials, the performance standards of the equipment. In terms of urban planning, it includes taking decisions regarding the size and the location of land reserves for future development, the system of pedestrian and motor routes, the arrangement of underground infrastructure and overhead lines.

Forecasting the course of future events and choosing between various scenarios of future developments are inextricably linked with the flexibility of architectural structures [1]. In this understanding, flexibility involves openness to change, ensuring an

© Springer International Publishing Switzerland 2015
M. Antona and C. Stephanidis (Eds.): UAHCI 2015, Part IV, LNCS 9178, pp. 261–269, 2015.
DOI: 10.1007/978-3-319-20687-5_25

easy adaptation of a facility to potential, difficult to anticipate, functional needs. Uncertainty regarding the future is the major reason behind thinking about flexibility in architecture [2].

Due to this uncertainty, there arises a question relating to the usefulness of designing flexible facilities. Perhaps it would be more sensible to demolish the old buildings, which do not meet new needs and build new, fully adapted buildings, in the place of the demolished ones? If our tastes, preferences, and needs change so quickly, what is the point of designing buildings that would be easy to adapt to the uncertain wishes and requirements of their future users?

This problem is particularly noticeable in the residential environment. The staff mobility dictated by global trends involves frequent changes of the place of residence and, what follows, quick turnover on the real estate market. Each new resident or new buyer wants to adapt the flat to his or her individual needs, which are usually different to the preferences of the former inhabitants.

The following questions arise:

- Should new buildings be designed only according to the current needs, or should the possible future changes in their function, appearance and equipment be considered as well?
- How long can a building fulfil its tasks in view of the dynamic and difficult to predict economic changes, the changes of clients' preferences and tastes arising from new, currently unknown needs?

Over the recent decades, these issues have emerged as a significant architectural problem. Their rank varied, depending on the types of facilities. In some kinds of buildings flexible solutions have been applied more or less effectively for over a hundred years - for instance in industry, commerce, trade exhibition and office construction. In other areas such as housing, the problem of flexibility is currently gaining importance.

2 Flexibility in Residential Environment

In housing developments flexibility is characterized by specific features. A good flat should be adjusted to human needs; it should "fit" a person like a tailor-made outfit. A residential estate should be adjusted to the requirements of the local community. It should follow demographic changes, cultural preferences, and the changes in spatial behavior resulting from fashion, lifestyle, affluence, and the age of its inhabitants. A house/flat should be characterized by:

- adabtability – being adaptable to the residents' changing tastes;
- transformability – being adaptable to the technological progress;
- convertibility – easy exchange of components;
- multifunctionality – being applicable to multiple purposes, e.g. organizing parties, holding meetings, working, etc.
- partitionability – easy partition of space to create extra rooms;
- extensibility – potential to enlarge.

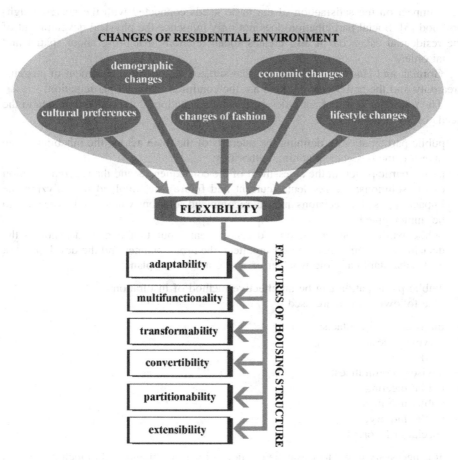

Fig. 1. Flexibility in residential environment: reasons and implications

Is it possible to achieve such flexibility? The achievement of an ideal is definitely very difficult, which does not mean that an architect should not make efforts towards this goal (Fig. 1).

Residential estates can be analyzed in functional, aesthetic, social and environmental terms. In this sense, many contemporary residential areas are, to a large extent, ugly, and infected with social and environmental problems. In connection with this situation, one may ask about the reasons for it. Maybe the cause lies in the lack of flexibility of the residential estate.

It seems that one of the most frequent mistakes includes the lack of flexible approach as early as at the stage of preliminary design decisions. Namely, the question of ensuring social participation of the members of the local community in the process of taking decisions connected with the development of their neighborhood. Flexible participation approach assumes that space is common good and each person should have impact on the satisfaction of the basic needs connected with the nearest neighborhood [3]. Social participation does not only influence the physical development of the residential estate but it also creates social relations that bring about spatial and social order.

Górniak and Hausner [4] point out that subjective and equal treatment of citizens, creativity and the activity of partners are the condition of social participation.

The following types of activities ensure the adaptation of the residential area to the needs of its inhabitants [5]:

− public participation in defining the interests of the main actors: the inhabitants, the investor, the designer, planning authorities;
− public participation in the assessment of the consequences and the recommendation of the solutions: the residents (current and future) are involved in analyzing the impact of possible decisions and can recommend solutions which can be accepted to be implemented;
− public participation in the final decision: real input to the final decision − the decision is not only made by the architect, the urban planner and the developer, but each inhabitant can vote whether or not to accept the plan.

Public participation can be an effective method of inspiration.
The following tools are used:

− informal local contacts;
− surveys, questionnaires;
− workshops;
− advisory committees;
− public meetings;
− public hearings;
− public inquiry;
− special task forces.

It is necessary to get to know the opinions of the inhabitants and to include them in the process of taking decisions related to the design of the neighborhood while determining the form of spatial development [6].

Flexibility is required at this stage, because even at the highest level of social participation in the process of architectural design and urban planning most people will have to live in a neighborhood designed by someone else (an architect). Even if this neighborhood fully met the clearly identified and formulated needs of the inhabitants, one should be aware of the fact that social preferences change over time.

In order for most inhabitants to live in satisfactory environment, the designer must put considerable effort. The design of the neighborhood must be adjusted to the requirements of particular inhabitants to the highest possible extent. The empathic analysis is a reliable base for decision-making in order to define the required scope of flexibility. Urban empathy is especially useful in grasping the context in a comprehensive manner. The idea behind this method is that the designer is part of the situations/conditions of the local inhabitants, and observes their immediate surroundings through their own eyes, as if travelling together with them through the events which happen to them on the street, in a square, or in their house [7].

In this sense, flexibility manifests itself in the practical-functional and symbolic aspect.

2.1 The Practical-Functional Aspect

The idea is to provide the possibility of adjusting the residential environment to the current needs and functional requirements of the inhabitants. This relates to amenities which facilitate running a household, easy installation of the equipment offered by the dynamically developing market of kitchenware, sanitary systems, energy-saving ventilation and heating systems, TV and multimedia devices [8]. The major problem is related to the anticipation of space for future systems and piping enabling the installation of new sanitary fittings, easy connection to new energy-saving devices, ventilation and air-conditioning.

It is also important to have the possibility to partition the housing area in adjustment to the changing family life cycle (growing up children, ageing parents, the death of a spouse, etc.). Ideally, the total area of a flat should be possible to increase or decrease, depending on the family's needs, for instance, the separation of an independent flat at the moment when parents are left alone in the flat after their adult children moved out should be possible. Based on his own design experience, the author defined the following characteristics of a flexible residential environment [9]:

- changeable, universal, multifunctional plan and movable partition walls;
- appropriately selected span of the load-bearing walls, the construction module cannot limit space arrangement;
- appropriate construction system, optimally a skeleton construction;
- centralized system of utilities delivery, integration of the building management systems;
- modularization of installation elements which enables quick assembly of additional equipment and fittings without additional costs of connection;
- leaving space under the floor for additional systems (e.g. air-conditioning, heating, structural network, installation of home entertainment systems including the sound system);
- in the case of flush mounted wiring, the determination of the installation zones on the walls and "free" zones for safe hanging of decorative elements (paintings, shelves);
- easy to adapt house/flat interior: moveable partition walls equipped with ducts for the "plug in" system installation;
- the possibility of connecting the house/flat to alternative energy sources;
- segment systems of network infrastructure enabling an easy separation of the systems, extension, branching and independent measurement devices for the separated zones;
- the possibility of installing internal control systems for micro-climate quality;
- integrated design approach, cooperation between the architect, the developer, the local council, the energy and water suppliers, the sewage collection companies, and the construction material and technical equipment manufacturers;

– the possibility of the application of closed-loop water circulation systems, and waste recycling inside the residential unit.

2.2   The Symbolic Aspect

The idea is to be able to change the image of a flat easily to mark one's own personality. In order to achieve this, it is necessary to ensure adaptation flexibility and innovation flexibility.

- Adaptation flexibility. Each new resident attempts to adapt the space to his or her own tastes and systems of values, confirming one's individuality and personality. This is a relatively new phenomenon, which has been indicated by Bonenberg [10]. The author notices that the willingness to distinguish oneself in the environment is a growing phenomenon in the post-industrial society.
- Innovative flexibility. This kind of changes results from the fact that, after some time, the residents cease to approve of the environment that they formed themselves in the past. They consider it outdated, unfashionable, in need of innovation and adjustment. The reasons for change in this respect may be explained by the general principles of human nature, and in particular, the impact of fashion on the behavior of the residents [11].

The analysis of the residential environment flexibility requires significant differentiation between two basic types of space: public space (a street, a square) and private space (a flat, a house). While the tendencies presented above refer mainly to private space (where the variability of needs is significantly high), the rules governing public space are different.

The author of this paper has conducted studies in fifteen residential areas. They reveal that, in general, the residents are reluctant about changing their local space. Changes implemented there are the cause of many local conflicts because the existing status quo is the result of a difficult compromise. Changing the location of a bus stop or a playground, even if it is substantiated with functional reasons, always gives rise to many controversies and conflicts. The inhabitants are not fond of the changes in the profiles of the local shops or service outlets, often mentioning the former bakers, shoemakers or florists with nostalgia. Being accustomed to the looks of the street, the existing façades, and the old greenery is part of the local identity that develops for years.

The sentiment to the appearance of public space, which people were attached to for years, brings on severe social protests in the case of an attempt to change its form or function, even if it seems that it will be more functional and attractive.

Thus, the art of flexible designing of residential environments consists in a skillful combination of two requirements: keeping the historic continuity of the public space (keeping the homeliness of public spaces) and implementing the necessary adaptations and innovations in private space.

3 The Characteristics of a Flexible Residential Environment

3.1 The Residential Area

- The residential area ensures a harmonious social development and neighborhood integration; it gives the effect of social synergy owing to common space that favors the cooperation of the residents and uses their potential and activity.
- The residential area ensures access to basic services within a walking distance from one's house, in a safe public space, giving the possibility of meeting neighbors whom we can talk to, share our worries with or tell about our success.
- The residential area ensures open, functional-spatial structure that allows for the location of workplaces for as many inhabitants as possible within the area, in accordance with the principle that work should be brought to the place of residence rather than putting the residents in a difficult situation of commuting to remote places. This is possible as the result of the creation of new workplaces in the sector of specialized creative services (software and computer games, design, advertising, antique art market, art restoration, second hand book shops, multimedia, fashion, etc.), in the sector of recreational and health services and modern office services of the Small Office Home Office type. These are the workplaces for young creative specialists who are able to find employment in their neighborhood. This is also an ideal solution for parents with small children and people searching for flexible forms of part-time employment.

3.2 The House/Flat

- A flexible house/flat is characterized by a spatial layout that is adjusted to the family's lifestyle, rather than making the family adapt to the spatial layout.
- A flexible house/flat is characterized by the constant following of the needs of its successive residents/tenants. This means the ease of adaptation over time and quick and cheap implementation of changes that improve life quality.
- A flexible house/flat is characterized by the ability to adjust to the changing needs in the partition of space and equipment in connection to the family life cycle.
- A flexible house/flat means that the resident can be "growing with the house", without the need to move. This is a step forward towards the members of the local community, who wish to lead a stable life among neighbors, live with children and elderly parents and grow into the local community. This is a house/flat for people who do not want to be anonymous and who intend to be active members of the local community (Fig. 2).

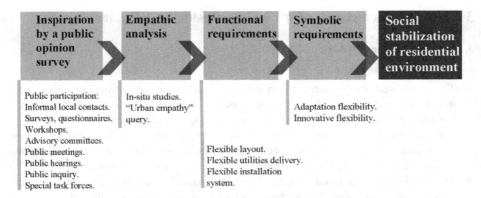

Fig. 2. Social stabilization and flexible approach to the housing design

4 Summary

To sum up, it may be stated that a high level of flexibility has a beneficial effect on the sustainable development of a residential estate. It stabilizes social composition and, simultaneously, strengthens the social bond. The residential environment that is characterized by the lack of flexibility imposes high inhabitant turnover, which destabilizes the social composition of the area following the changing family life cycle. A flexible residential environment requires greater effort on the part of the architect. However, in the long-term perspective, this effort gives positive consequences resulting from social stabilization: place attachment, place identity, sense of place and stronger neighborhood relations.

References

1. Bonenberg, A.: Design for the information society. In: Stephanidis, C. (ed.) Universal Access in HCI, Part I, HCII 2011. LNCS, vol. 6765, pp. 12–19. Springer, Heidelberg (2011)
2. Rabeneck, A., Sheppard, D., Town, P.: Housing flexibility? Architectural Des. **43**, 698–727 (1973)
3. Pawłowska, K.: Idea i metody partycypacji społecznej w ochronie krajobrazu i kształtowaniu przestrzeni. Fundacja Partnerstwo dla Środowiska, Kraków (2010)
4. Górniak, J., Hausner, J., Kołdras, S., Mazur, S., Paszowska, R.: Komunikacja i partycypacja społeczna. MSAP, Kraków (1999)
5. Schill, C., Koch, B., Bogdahn, J., Knapp, S., Coors, V.: Public participation comment mark-up language and WFS 1.1. In: Coors, V., Rumor, M., Fendel, E.M., Zlatanova, S. (eds.) Urban and Regional Data Management - UDMS Annual 2007, pp. 93–104. Taylor & Francis, London (2008)
6. Charytonowicz, J.: Social Effects of Integrating Design. Global Ergonomics, pp. 203–207. Elsevier, Oxford (1998)
7. Bonenberg, A.: Beauty of the City - Urban Empathy. Case Study Catania in Sicily. FA, Poznan University of Technology, Poznan (2011)

8. Forty, A.: Words and Buildings. A Vocabulary of Modern Architecture. Thames & Hudson, London (2000)
9. Bonenberg, W.: The architecture of the future exemplified by an experimental residential complex in pobiedziska. Środowisko Mieszkaniowe – Hous. Environ. **10**, 44–48 (2012)
10. Bonenberg, W.: Przestrzeń publiczna w osiedlach mieszkaniowych, pp. 17–21. Urbanista, Oxford (2008)
11. Altas, N.E., Özsoy, A.: Spatial adaptability and flexibility as parameters of user satisfaction for quality housing. Build. Environ. **5**, 315–323 (1998)

Risk Analysis in the Process a New Workplace

Hanna Gołaś[(⊠)]

Faculty of Engineering Management, Chair of Ergonomics and Quality
Management, Poznan University of Technology, Poznan, Poland
hanna.golas@put.poznan.pl

Abstract. In this paper the author presents the use of selected risk analysis
tools in the process of authorising a new workstation. The company selected for
the study belongs to the automotive industry, where customer requirements are
high in terms of quality and performance as well as in terms of safety of work,
employees and the process.

Keywords: Workstation · Employee safety · Labour standards · Risk

1 Introduction

Problems associated with the preparation of and launching a new workstation in a
production process occur most often in situations of implementation of a new product or
modernisation of an existing workstation. The focus of the managing staff responsible
for production on the quality of the products, their parameters and properties, means that
they often forget about the various aspects of ergonomics. Ergonomics is inextricably
linked to the provision of employee safety, proper work system and the relevant technical solutions as well as personal protective equipment. Ergonomics also ensures the
comfort of work in terms of access to relevant information, tools, documentation and
explanation of the entire spectrum of requirements posed to the employee.

A good solution in this situation is to develop a standard for the workstation and for
the process of the approval of the workstation.

The Subject Matter. A workstation is a work space along with all the means and
objects for work in which an employee or group of employees do the work [10]. In
other words, workstation is a combination and spatial arrangement of work equipment,
surrounded by the work environment under the conditions imposed by the work tasks
[7, 9]. He tasks to be carried out at a workstation and the tools necessary determine
what and in what order or distance from the employee should be placed at the workstation. The range of issues to be taken into consideration is very broad. Among others,
the following are worth specifying:

- what will be supplied to the workstation (e.g. raw materials, packaging),
- what will be collected from the workstation (e.g. finished products, waste),
- what is the necessary equipment (e.g. machinery, devices, measuring instruments),
- what information the employee must be provided with (e.g. qualitative and quantitative requirements),

© Springer International Publishing Switzerland 2015
M. Antona and C. Stephanidis (Eds.): UAHCI 2015, Part IV, LNCS 9178, pp. 270–279, 2015.
DOI: 10.1007/978-3-319-20687-5_26

- where at the production hall the workstation will be located (e.g. its surroundings, lighting),
- what qualifications the operator and the staff of the workstation must have (e.g. experience, skills),
- how the workstation will be maintained in continuous technical efficiency and productivity (e.g. inspections, information about and elimination of malfunctions)
- what information from the employee will be required to measure their work (e.g. the results of the qualitative examination of the product, performance).

The scope of the above mentioned issues is shown in Fig. 1.

Preparing and launching a new workstation, especially in a production process, requires the involvement of employees with different levels of competence and performing different functions in the work system. This process requires the participation of a workstation operator, who will not always act as a "workstation designer", as well as the participation of the employees of service departments (planned repairs, breakdowns, improvement, modernization), inspection departments (quality, process) and departments providing materials for production. The human role in the manufacturing system is shown in Fig. 2, while the description of the requirements for each role are included in Table 1.

A new workstation is a new element affecting the quality of a production process, and therefore there are many factors to be considered in order to ensure adequate and stable flow in the process. Nevertheless, the systems-based approach provides opportunities to consider the multi-dimensionality of the workplace in a comprehensive manner at a given time. The systems-based approach may consist of the following steps (among others):

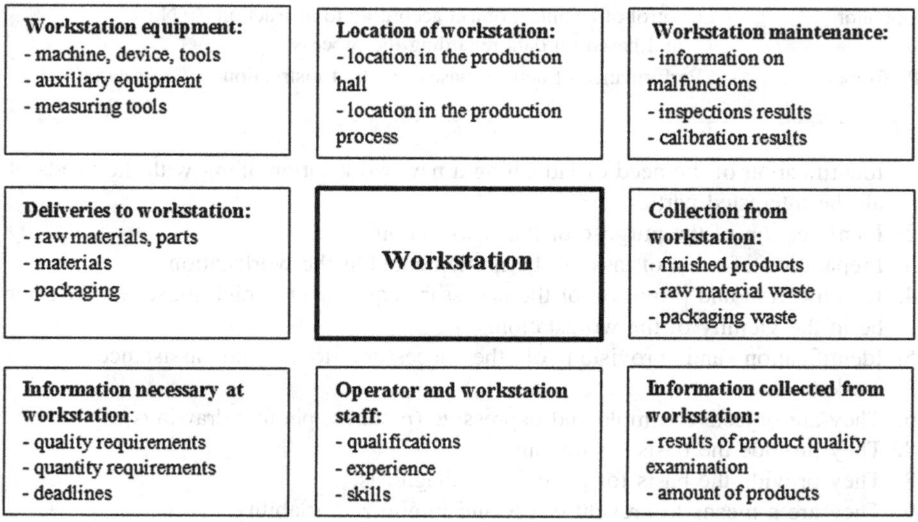

Workstation equipment: - machine, device, tools - auxiliary equipment - measuring tools	Location of workstation: - location in the production hall - location in the production process	Workstation maintenance: - information on malfunctions - inspections results - calibration results
Deliveries to workstation: - raw materials, parts - materials - packaging	**Workstation**	Collection from workstation: - finished products - raw material waste - packaging waste
Information necessary at workstation: - quality requirements - quantity requirements - deadlines	Operator and workstation staff: - qualifications - experience - skills	Information collected from workstation: - results of product quality examination - amount of products

Fig. 1. The scope of information and organizational jobs for a workstation (Source: author's own work)

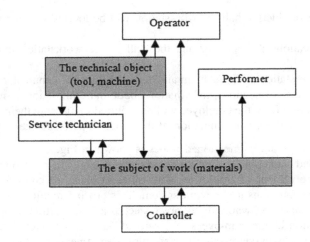

Fig. 2. The human role in the manufacturing system (Source 6)

Table 1. Levels of human function in a production system (Source 6)

Function in the production process	Required level of intelligence	Ability to replace the function
Controller	Conformity assessment of process and product, decision making during disruptions	Partly
Service technician	Servicing of technical objects according to instruction, state of the object and engineering knowledge	No
Operator	Control of technical object according to instruction and based on data regarding the process	No
Performer	Performance of actions based on strict instruction	To a large degree

1. Identification of the need of launching a new workstation along with the needs of all the interested parties.
2. Identification of the purpose of the workstation.
3. Preparation of a list of tasks to be implemented at the workstation.
4. Identification and provision of the necessary equipment, which must be part of or be in the vicinity of the workstation.
5. Identification and provision of the necessary tools and assistance at the workstation.
6. They are objective, simple and expressive (pictures, photos, drawings).
7. They provide the basis for training.
8. They provide the basis for control and diagnosis.
9. They are a means to prevent errors and minimize variability.
10. Identification, documentation and provision of the criteria for the evaluation of the performance of the workstation.

2 Safety at the Workstation

According to the International Labour Organization every day, 6,300 people die due to occupational accidents or work-related diseases, which constitutes more than 2.3 million deaths per year. In addition, 313 million accidents happen on the job yearly what often leads to extended absences from work. The human cost of accidents is estimated at 4 per cent of global Gross Domestic Product each year (Safety at work 2013). Thus, there is a need to increase the awareness of the scope and consequences of work-related accidents, injuries and diseases, and make an attempt to find an explanation for them and their causes [8].

The above cited figures focus on the typical approach to the issue of safety, that is they are focused on accidents at work. For an employee who does their job at a workstation located in a production hall it is not only health and safety conditions that are important. Interviews and observations show that access to information and clear requirements are an important element in shaping safe work conditions. Only an employee who knows what is expected of them and how they will be evaluated is able to ascertain the management of the organization that the work is properly done. In the longer term, it provides the effect of quality in the production process. Building a safe and healthy work environment is one of the most important elements of the quality of life at work [1].

In leading a team of people, especially when dealing with employees who perform work for a customer, one can notice that their comfort of work is dependent on giving them clear and understandable criteria for the evaluation of their work. Therefore, when shaping work safety one must take into account not only the legal requirements in the field of health and safety, the requirements of the Labour Code and the general principles applicable in the industry, but also the issues which stem from the specific nature of the production process. The production process, often subjected to evaluation by customers, also generates work requirements for the workstation. Speaking about safe work then means looking at the workstation from two perspectives: the employer's and the employee's. Figure 3 shows the extent of the requirements faced by the employee but also by the employer.

The employer is responsible for the safety at a workstation. They equip the employee with everything that they are obliged by law and by the requirements of customers. However, those requirements will not be respected if the employee will not perform their work in accordance with the applicable rules, procedures and instructions.

Works Standard. A standard is a set of parameters which ensures that an appropriate level, characteristic for the purposes of a given object, is reached. In the case of a workstation the standard is a card describing the tasks, tools, acceptance criteria, the resources required for the implementation of the standard work at a workstation or for a given activity. A standard is not a permanent document, it is subject to continuous updates and changes resulting from changing requirements, resources and employee qualifications.

The basic properties of standards [4]:

1. They present the best, easiest and safest method of performing a job. They take into account employees' long-term experience and knowledge of the scope of their duties.
2. They are the best way to preserve knowledge and expertise.

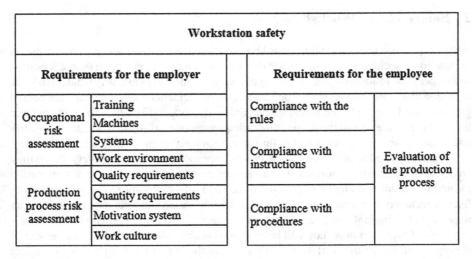

Fig. 3. Safety of a workstation from the points of view of the employee and the employer (Source: author's own work).

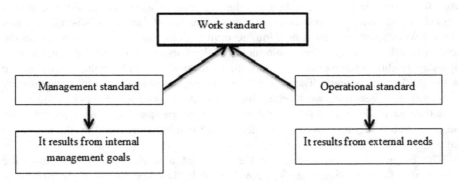

Fig. 4. The construction of a work standard (Source: author's own work)

3. They are the criterion for measuring work - an objective way to evaluate work.
4. They show the cause and effect relationship.
5. They provide the basis for maintaining the right level of work and its improvement (When there is a variability due to the lack of a standard one should be introduced. If there is a variation in spite of compliance with a standard, it must be validated and refined or the operators must be trained to carry out their work in accordance with the standard) (Fig. 4).
6. They are objective, simple and expressive (pictures, photos, drawings).
7. They provide the basis for training.
8. They provide the basis for control and diagnosis.
9. They are a means to prevent errors and minimize variability.

To develop a standard for a workstation in a production process one must (among others):

- specify the target to be achieved,
- make a list of tasks performed at the workstation,
- determine the movements of the employee working at the workstation,
- determine the arms' reach of the employee,
- determine the order of movements,
- determine the working area of the workstation,
- establish the time of work,
- identify the planned performance,
- identify the types of information that an employee must have at the workstation,
- define access to the above mentioned information,
- determine the health and safety requirements for the workstation,
- define fire prevention requirements for the workstation,
- determine the environmental requirements for the workstation,
- define the principles for assessing the employee's work.

Organization of a new workstation requires employers to take all kinds of measures to ensure the proper functioning of this workstation. The requirements that must be met by an employer result from the legal requirements, the specific features of the technology, the conditions of production organization, the available resources, customer requirements and the organizational culture.

Risk Analysis. Risk is a product of the probability of risks and the severity of their effects. The key aspect then is to skilfully identify the potential hazards and to define their effects. However, the first step is to determine the purpose of risk analysis, since it determines the types of risks [3].

Risk analysis is a tool to ensure that the risks associated with launching a new workstation will be identified and recognized, and that the preventive measures will be properly implemented. Methods worth applying for risk analysis are: an audit of standard work at the workstation, brainstorming, FMEA, FTA, ETA, a checklist. In this article, the author will present excerpts from an application of a checklist and an FMEA.

The Basics of Risk Analysis. When launching a new workstation, in order to ensure the safety of the employee, both in terms of health and safety measures and their psychophysical comfort, a systems-based approach to risk management [2] must be applied, and on this basis the following information should be considered:

- analysis of reported complaints (recognized and not recognized, 8D reports, analysis of the causes of the complaint),
- analysis of the internal audit reports of the production process,
- analysis of the internal audit reports of the condition of health and safety,
- evaluation of the minimum health and safety requirements for the production machinery and equipment,
- legal requirements for machinery, equipment, industry,
- customer requirements for control and regulations operations, access to information, labour standards,

- internal requirements resulting from the existing principles of work,
- health and safety requirements for production workstations,
- environmental requirements for the physical work environment as well as for the handling of waste and energy factors.

The Use of Selected Risk Analysis Tools When Launching a New Workstation. A company in the automotive industry was selected for the research, whose main production process is the casting of lead products. The essential parameters of this process are the temperature of the cast lead, the temperature of the mould and the temperature of the brass insert flooded with liquid lead. The brass insert, while waiting to be flooded with lead, is stored on trays heated to the temperature of 60 degrees Celsius. Also, due to the employees being exposed to lead, it is important to uphold hygiene at work and conform to the principles of work at a foundry.

In the analysed company, as a result of customer audits and the requirements of the top management, a checklist has been developed to ensure the proper functioning of workstations, especially during the process of launching a new workstation.

It contains a list of requirements that must be met so the production management, the health and safety inspector, and the quality control inspector can authorise the workstation for the production process. The forms are presented in Figs. 5 and 6.

ALCOMOT°	Integrated System of Quality and Environment Management ISO 9001:2008 i ISO 14001:2004			KLI-P1/F1		
	Principles for the authorization of a new workplace			Issue 1		
				Date of issue: 25.06.2014r		
Name of workplace		Room	Date	OK	N/A	Date,signature
1 Check the condition of the electrical system (including connections)				□	□	
2 Check if the power cord and plug are not damaged.				□	□	
3 Check the operation of warning signals.				□	□	
4 Check if the main switch is operational.				□	□	
5 Check the lighting of the workplace.				□	□	
6 Perform a health and safety and fire protection survey.				□	□	
7 Work out workplace hazards.				□	□	
8 Perform a health and safety and fire protection training.				□	□	
9 Has the employee been trained for the workplace?				□	□	
10 Inspect the equipment.				□	□	
11 Check whether the cutting tool is in good condition.				□	□	
12 Check whether the cutting tool is correctly and firmly fixed in the holder.				□	□	
13 Check whether the tool is running smoothly, without vibration or noise.				□	□	
14 Check if there is any visible damage to the body of the tool.				□	□	
15 Have the tools necessary for work been provided?				□	□	
16 Is the main switch visible and within easy reach of the operator?				□	□	
17 Is the operating manual available at the workplace?				□	□	
18 Is the OK/NOK product standard available?				□	□	
19 Are process parameters displays, e.g. temperature, visible?				□	□	
20 Is there a light signal showing that temperature is below the assumed value?				□	□	
21 Is the above mentioned light signal visible for the operator during work?				□	□	
22 Has the workplace got quality control forms?				□	□	

Fig. 5. A checklist for launching a new workstation (Source: author's own work)

ALCOMOT°	Integrated System of Quality and Environment Management ISO 9001:2008 i ISO 14001:2004		KLI-P1/F3
	Completeness of technical and production documentation for new production		Issue: 1
			Date of issue: 25.06.2014r

Product:			Type	
Customer			Date	

				OK	N/A
1	Customer inquiry			✔	⌐
2	Material specification of the customer				
3	Material specification - ZAK-P2/F2				
4	Construction drawing of insert				
5	Construction drawing of cast before processing				
6	Construction drawing of cast after processing				
7	Quality requirements of customer - arranged with customer KLI-P1/F2				
8	Authroisation of new workplace				
9	Customer acceptance of "The first items examination report"				
10	Product control before authorising the mold for production				
11	Documentation of the mold				
12	Production manuals				
13	Packaging manual				
14	Forms for recording dimensions controls				
15	OK/NOK manuals				
16	Measuring tools and calibration certificate				

Fig. 6. A checklist for quality a new workstation (Source: author's own work)

In the analysed company the checklist has been divided into four areas: electrical, health and safety, operation maintenance and quality. Before switching the workstation on the employee responsible for the given area will perform a control check and reply to the questions. In the form there is only room for two types of replies: "OK" or "not applicable". The workstation will only be allowed to be operated only in a situation where each of the areas will contain an OK reply (unless "not applicable" is marked). If the workstation is not ready then the fact must be reported to the production manager, who implements corrective action for the workstation to meet the requirements. The corrective actions are carried out until they are accepted by the employee responsible for the evaluated area.

Another tool is the FMEA analysis carried out for the entire production process in terms of meeting customer requirements, including the preparation of the workstation to work in the process. The FMEA is a recognized and widely used method which allows for identification of errors and which helps to eliminate them. The FMEA analysis is used to identify and assess the risk of potential errors which can occur in various elements of the product or in the process of its production as well as the consequences of their occurrence [5].

Among the most common hazards in the process of launching a new workstation in the analysed company there are:

- lack of the required temperature of the mould used at the workstation,
- failure by the employee to follow the production manual,
- lack of the required temperature of the crucible,
- lack of the required temperature of the tray,
- lack of appropriate tools,
- lack of the proper mould,
- insufficient lighting,
- mess at the workplace,
- lack of the required pressure in the system,
- malfunction of the workstation.

This approach ensures that every time the FMEA is updated, for example as a result of a change of the location of the workstation in the production hall, the hazards affecting the safety at the workstation will also be subjected to analysis (Fig. 7).

Application of the described tools is beneficial to the employee and the employer, provides a systematic approach to risk analysis and provides the basis for the implementation of corrective actions.

Summary. The application of selected risk analysis tools in the process of launching a new workstation presented in this paper is just an attempt to signal a wide range of issues related to the safety of employees and to the analysis of the risks that occur when launching a new workstation. The company selected for the research undergoes annual audits by its clients and it must meet the quality requirements and any other to which it has committed itself or is obligated to. Increasingly, customers evaluate certain aspects of work safety and environmental issues. As the automotive industry has high quality

ALCOMOT°			ANALYSIS OF POTENTIAL CAUSES AND CONSEQUENCES OF DEFECTS (FMEA OF THE PROCESS)											FMEA number: 1 Page:				
															Effects of actions			
Number	Name of operation	Potential defect	Potential consequence	consequence	Potential cause of defect	Occurrence	Prevention	Method of detection (control)	Detectibility	Risk	Correction action LPR>100	Responsibility and deadline	Action taken	Result	Occur	Defect	Risk
160. Mass production																	
160.3/1	Preparation of workplace for casting	inappropriate mold temperature	production downtime	3	heating system malfunction	4	visual inspection before use	temperature gauge	6	72							
160.3/2	Preparation of workplace for casting	workman does not follow production instructions	non-compliant product	9	warning system malfunction	2	foreman inspects and records temperature	forman's inspection	5	90							
160.3/3	Preparation of workplace for casting	insufficient pot temperature	production downtime	3	heating system malfunction	4	visual inspection before use	temperature gauge	5	60							
160.3/5	Preparation of workplace for casting	lack of appropriate tools	production downtime	3	wear of tools	3	visual inspection before use by employee	employee reports	7	63							
160.3/8	Preparation of workplace for casting	insufficient light	production downtime	2	lighting malfunction	2	replacement before work	visual	7	28							
160.3/9	Preparation of workplace for casting	messy workplace	production downtime	3	lack of 5S standards for workplace	3	cleaning workplace after work	visual, change of shifts	7	63							
160.3/10	Preparation of workplace for casting	insufficient pressure in the system	production downtime	3	compressor malfunction	4	compressor inspection	documents control	5	60							

Fig. 7. An excerpt of an FMEA to launch a new workstation (Source: author's own work)

requirements and it requires a guarantee of on-time deliveries, it becomes critical to ensure continuity of the production process. These requirements will be met provided that each of the workstations will be efficiently and safely operated. The identification of risks in a systematic and formal manner (which is often criticized by employees forced take care of the formal side of the process) gives a chance for the elimination of barriers and obstacles in order to ensure continuity of production.

References

1. Drożyner, P., Mikołajczak, P., Szuszkiewicz, J., Jasiulewicz-Kaczmarek, M.: Management standardization versus quality of working life. In: Robertson, M.M. (ed.) EHAWC 2011 and HCII 2011. LNCS, vol. 6779, pp. 30–39. Springer, Heidelberg (2011)
2. Gołaś H.: Podejście systemowe do zarządzania ryzykiem. Logistyka 5 (2014)
3. Gołaś, H.: Risk management as part of the quality management system according to ISO 9001. In: Stephanidis, C. (ed.) HCI 2014, Part II. CCIS, vol. 435, pp. 519–524. Springer, Heidelberg (2014)
4. Imai, M., Kaizen, G.: Zdroworozsądkowe, niskokosztowe podejście do zarządzania, Wydawnictwo MT Biznes sp. Z o.o., Warszawa (2006)
5. Mazur, A., Gołaś, H.: Zasady, metody i techniki wykorzystywane w zarządzanie jakością, Wydawnictwo Politechniki Poznańskiej, Poznań, s. 113 (2010)
6. Misztal, A., Butlewski, M., Jasiak, A., Janik, S.: The human role in a progressive trend of foundry automation. Metalurgija 54(2), 429–432 (2015). ISSN 1334-2576
7. Misztal, A., Butlewski, M.: Life improvement at work, Wyd. PP, Poznań (2012). ISBN: 978-83-7775-177-0
8. Mrugalska, B., Nazir, S., Tytyk, E., Øvergård, K.I.: Process safety control for occupational accident prevention. In: Arezes, P.M., Baptista, J.S., Barroso, M.P., et al., (eds.) Occupational Safety and Hygiene III. International Symposium on Occupational Safety and Hygiene (SHO), Guimaraes, 12–13 February 2015, pp. 365–369. Taylor and Francis Group, London (2015)
9. Norma ISO PN-EN ISO 6385:2005 - Zasady ergonomiczne w projektowaniu systemów pracy
10. Rączkowski, B.: BHP w praktyce, Ośrodek Doradztwa i Doskonalenia Kadr Sp. z o.o. Gdańsk (2012)

Ergonomics of the Urban Villa's Form as an Element of Sustainable Architectural and Urban Design

Paweł Horn[(✉)]

Wrocław University of Technology, Wrocław, Poland
pawel.horn@pwr.edu.pl

Abstract. Article is a presentation and discussion of the complex of multi-family buildings which were built in Wroclaw in an interesting and challenging historical urban context. Discussion of the complex serves to define characteristic parameters that allow to consider the buildings as example of urban villa and to illustrate the process of reaching the optimum of these parameters in the context of urban environment. Ergonomics of the object's dependency from its surroundings will be analysed and considered as an aspect of sustainable design in a conscious decision-making process in an integrated interdisciplinary and computer-aided design environment. Discussed design process due to its flexibility and value is to show the urban villa's advantages as an answer to the needs of contemporary inhabitants of a big city. At the same time the author intends to highlight the influence of sustainable design on ergonomics of an architectural object nowadays, taking into account the degree to which it is possible to use and create computer tools for ergonomic and sustainable design.

Keywords: Ergonomics in sustainable design of residential architecture · Ergonomics of urban villa · Computer-aided design environment for housing designers

1 Introduction: Ergonomics Versus or in Line with Sustainable Design?

Architectural design is a multidisciplinary field. It is as vast and profound ascertainment as it may sound obvious. Each building is a unique result of combination of all relevant disciplines, where aspects and requirements of some have to be fulfilled in 100 % (safety and reliability of structure, fire safety, accordance with technical regulations and building standards, etc.), and some are more or less negotiable. This negotiation happens on various levels, where those various disciplines involved meet: investor's needs and financial ability, site or localization parameters, functional and aesthetic aspects versus indications at the local and national level of spatial policy, short and long term environmental impact, third parties interests (if applicable), and so on. These negotiations' main battlefield is architect's competences in connection with his or her main task of coordinating all disciplines in design process. However, today

© Springer International Publishing Switzerland 2015
M. Antona and C. Stephanidis (Eds.): UAHCI 2015, Part IV, LNCS 9178, pp. 280–290, 2015.
DOI: 10.1007/978-3-319-20687-5_27

the more measurable factors the design involves (resulting from precisely specified regulations and initial requirements), the more tools can be elaborated to support the optimization of design process. It takes the form of either computer aided design applications for everyday use in architects' and other disciplines designers' practice or elaborated systems aimed at special tasks, which are the external to designer's office environmental rating systems (international or nation specific). Both result from increasing role of sustainability in design at all levels: planning, urban and architectural design, interior and product design. In this article the author wants to discuss the levels of urban to interior design, but this important multidisciplinary approach applies equally to planning, simply involving other ones than at subsequent stages, leading from decisions at regional level to a particular complexes of buildings and single objects, and then their fitting, equipping, furnishing and final performance. It is very important to understand the continuity of this process and to see a building with its internal environment is a final result of the complicated and multilevel process. Thus to discuss ergonomic or sustainability aspects in reference to buildings one has to consider its dependencies on multiple mutual connections between those aspects influencing its coming into existence. This comes from the simple reason that building an architectural object requires usually a significant amount of money, time, energy and materials, also engages a fairly big group of professionals. The resulting structure has final shape and parameters which cannot be easily modified. Both ergonomics and sustainable design increasingly play an important role. But in the author's opinion these two disciplines often are seen as competing or almost conflicting; one can get the impression that they act at the opposite ends in design process. Sustainable design imposes set of rules from a very starting point, not even of a particular building but already at the stage of creating technical regulations in accordance with country's policy,[1] with the focus on limits for energy consumption and diminishing negative environmental impact of the whole building process, including dismantling and recycling the materials. The main task of sustainable development in general is to allow realization of our goals and needs without diminishing possibilities of doing so for future generations. This is however often connected with such harsh requirements that it puts realizations on or beyond threshold of feasibility, due to economic factors. On the other side stands the end user of a building, who often is the actual investor, expecting the project and the building to comply with its destination and cost limits. Ergonomics developed for decades to protect the end users of work station and then of all working and living built environments from negative or harmful effects. It refers not only to sufficient level of safety. What becomes important, meeting the requirements of sustainable development, especially in reference to energy efficiency is beginning to have increasingly higher costs and it can lead to savings on quality of other aspects of design within the project's budget – functionality and aesthetics. In this light tension between sustainability and ergonomics may be easier to understand. In author's opinion and from the point of view of practicing architect, these two disciplines should be integrated into design as

---

[1] In European Union it refers to general directives to be implemented in all member states. Currently the author in his practice of an architect observes difficulties in compliance with these regulations as they are being applied to buildings as requirements at final stage of building process – design and realization, without preparation of the whole building process and participants.

mutually influential. At the moment it is very difficult, because higher demands for energy efficiency increase the cost of a building while payback time of a construction of a building is still as long as the time after which expensive devices like heat pumps etc. need to be replaced.

On one hand, it can be observed in research that sustainability and ergonomics tend to be seen in some way parallel [1], dealing with incompatible aspects of design and use of buildings; on the other hand, it is satisfying that ergonomics is becoming to find its crucial place as an integral criterion and inclusive part in sustainable design. Discussion of these aspects of ergonomics' contribution to sustainability is based on analysis of complex of two urban villas in Wroclaw, Poland. Firstly, urban villa is a reasonable way of shaping the downtown and suburban housing space in the context of single-family housing complexes and multifamily estates of a small scale, providing the basic elements of social bonds, a sense of security, belonging and identity of the inhabitants. Secondly, buildings of this type provide spatial comfort on a scale of an urban development/housing estate and a dwelling unit, and ensure a variety of residential structures and architectural forms [2]. The important feature is economic optimization of this form of inhabiting a city with the chance to achieve desired advantages. Economy conditions crucial sustainability aspect in the architectural design – participation of future users. The way of integrating ergonomics into sustainable design is mainly by one of its five principles, which is respect for user in terms of realization of needs of each human, broad education and social participation in design and use process. This also means healthy residential environment achieved by allowing contact with nature, selection of safe and healthy materials [3]. In such an approach ergonomics will no longer have to be applied at final stage of design as a response only to general rules of proper shaping of work station and selection of aids or tools for home use by generic users, what in effect draws the necessity for future surveys of satisfaction and health of these specific end users and then the potential need for extra costs of corrections or major changes [1]. In this discussion it is also important to remember, that user friendly living spaces influence the rest of human activities e.g. productivity at work [16]. Their initial targeting of strengthening positive social behaviors is very important as well.

2 Complex of Two Multifamily Buildings as an Example of Ergonomic Sustainable Design

The buildings are located in the corner of the streets converging at an acute angle, at the same time such a location can be read as the spatial boundary between green area around and the highly ordered and dense residential development inside the wedge. The confluence of streets is also the place of confluence of architectural periods:

Olszewski Street was formed as an avenue of pre-war[2] German single-family houses [4] with strictly reproducible scale and dimensions (Fig. 1); Bacciarelli Street contrary became a communication route during post-war development based on groups of multi-family buildings, in their own independent spatial system and different orientation to north-south axis (Fig. 2). This post-war buildings in the vicinity of discussed complex of two villas happily had been shaped in the form of three apartment blocks, giving the newly build complex of urban villas "A" and "B" the chance to be transition from not very high, intense forms of blocks of flats to a smaller scale residential single-family homes in close proximity (Fig. 3). Forms of both buildings are functionally interrelated and refer to surrounding houses as a spatial continuation. Complex forms a closure and complement through the transition from cubic forms of blocks of flats from eighties of the XX c. organized around central staircase and a row of ascetic forms of pre-war villas with a steep gable roof without eaves.

Fig. 1. Context of villa "A"

While the urban context and historical features were somewhat external, objectively existing and impossible to adapt to one's needs, standard of living and cost optimization were the criteria arising from individual assumptions on which this investment - newly designed unit was based as a starting point for design. Cost optimization in this case started with looking for the most effective way of using the plot due to a location within the city limits and high costs of land. Additionally placement in the prestigious green district of Wroclaw further increased the value of the property together with the character of the historic neighborhood [4, 5] causing the area to be under the supervision of the Municipal Conservator. But this was associated with interesting aspect of this location - awareness of local population, which determines the choice of it as a place for continuing residence in subsequent generations, e.g. for the price of smaller

---

[2] Wroclaw is one of the biggest and oldest Polish cities, located in Lower Silesia, with a more than a thousand years of history. It was under the rule of the Czech kings since XIV c., in 1741 during the Silesian Wars, the city, along with most of Silesia, was conquered by King Frederick II and became part of Prussia, and therefore since 1741 the official name of the city was, Royal Capital and residential city Breslau (Ger. Königliche Haupt- und Residenzstadt Breslau). During the Napoleonic wars the year remained under the dominion of France. Returned under the rule of Prussia and remained German until the end of World War II. On August 2, 1945 r. at the Potsdam conference it was decided to include Silesia with Wroclaw in new area of Poland, and the German population, which had not left the city before the siege of 'Festung Breslau' (fortress Breslau), was deported to the Soviet occupation zone in Germany. Polish people began coming to Wroclaw mainly from the central Poland (Kielce region, Lodz) and Wielkopolska region and displaced residents of prewar Polish eastern borderlands, mostly from Lviv and the surrounding area and from Vilnius. [15].

Fig. 2. Context of villa "B"

size of a dwelling. This had been emphasized in talks with investor (Housing Cooperative Biskupin), to consider the will of current inhabitants and their descendants to remain within the district. It meant that future inhabitants preferred to live there in medium sized flat than move somewhere else and for the same price buy a house or bigger apartment. While the world's class monuments proximity does not always affect the decisions of individual residents, one can understand the sentiment, taking into account the other advantages of this district: close proximity to the city center, very good communication with the rest of the city through the center, recreational areas and the Odra river area's enormity of greenery, parks at your fingertips, the proximity of some of the largest universities in Wroclaw, as well as presence of basic services in place. It is a legacy of the post-war rational building of the past century, when urban standards of proper proportion of residential buildings to others like schools, shops etc. conditioned their existence as a prerequisite for the construction of residential complexes, contrary to other present commercial developments, where shops are in a great distance and schools or medical practices remain only in master plan's guidelines.

When the site is accepted and recognized and the size of dwellings approximated, optimization of building costs is the next aspect of ergonomic design, what in terms of respect for future user and response to their needs for decent dwelling at the reasonable cost is decisive both for sustainable design and feasibility of investment. Of course, the building could had been designed to higher standard and built for profitable sales, however the Cooperative activity is not directed for making commercial profits but only uses its incomes for statutory objectives. This is also the situation where consultations of future users' needs preceding design where possible. 26 flats were designed, 6 in building "A", 20 in building "B". They are provided 32 car parking places according to 'building indications' for this investment (local authorities' document issued in case master plan is not yet prepared). 13 of car parking places are located in underground garage, joining the building and offering a common terrace at the roof. Site area equals 6892 m^2 what gives apartment to area ratio 38 (precisely

Fig. 3. Localization of complex of two urban villas "A" and "B" as a "keystone" of neighboring surroundings from subsequent historic periods of two nations in one city. Aerial view 2011.01.04 Google Earth, access 2015.02.04. Olszewski Street is a continuation of main road where famous Centennial Hall by Max Berg of 1913 and WUWA - modern movement experimental "living and workspace exhibition" of 1929 [5] are located, the site characteristic is close proximity to the river Odra, also the adjacent district value apart from famous historic monuments and Wroclaw ZOO are vast park areas and a mixture of single family housing and blocks of flats with a lot of greenery. Complex built in 2009, design Horn Architects.

37,72) flats per ha. It is typical ratio indicator for urban villa typology[3] [2]. Buildings' area at ground level: 181 m² of "A" villa, 667 m² of "B" villa and 848 m² of the whole complex with garage. Villa "A" is three storey high (third under the gable roof with an extra entresol), two flats at each storey, flats at ground floor with an extra entrance to green backyard. Villa ends and closes the row of pre-war villas of similar scale and shaping, thus its design solution was shaped to corresponding but contemporary stylistics and form. Villa "B" is four storey high, five flats per each storey. Both buildings share underground garage with green terrace accessible for all dwellers, and in terms of aesthetics – the same set of stylistic solutions (character, details, windows, doors, railings, etc.) and what concerns colours – each building is a reverse of the other (black-white, colourful-grayscale, white staircase's walls + orange railings – orange staircase's walls + white railings, and so on). Buildings are designed in compliance with building standards. In terms of ergonomics it is an important note – technical

---

[3] On the basis of analysis of a group of various examples made by the author, where for the site ranging from 0,1 ha to a few ha this ratio was 27 to 50 flats per ha depending on the size of residential buildings or complexes.

regulations and standards have been set to ensure the minimum requirements intended to keep proper and sufficient conditions for safe use and health protection of occupants. In terms of sustainable development the design reflects standards for energy efficiency, (preservation of resources at level of particular object), the complex is designed to fit into its unique surroundings in the best possible way (respect for terrain, integration with urban landscape), the site development project complies with initial requirement for preserving of 30 % biologically active part of it and green terrace is designed (because it is allowed to be counted as 50 % of its green floor area) adding this way to "4 r" rule of sustainable development: reduce, reuse, recycle, renewable – this solution helps to economically use building site area while at the same time contributes to rainwater management [3]. Both buildings with underground garage constitute a composite whole and are relatively simple in terms of technical equipment. However as indicated earlier, their design is representative at urban level in spatial and social meaning. Challenge in case of this project comprised fitting it into strong historic context with conservation protection and respond to future users' needs and expectations. The form of urban villa had been deliberately chosen and main features of this type of building incorporated. (Figure 4) Characteristic parameters of this form: free-standing with one staircase, with high standard of finishing and architectural details, limited number of storeys and size of the site. For comparison – the minimum site area in this district in case of master plan regulations is defined as 600 m^2 while the maximum for an urban villa - 1200 m^2. The site of the complex of two villas is bigger but at the time of design no master plan had been in force, and as described, it allowed building of two villas with a garage with preserving required distances between buildings and other elements of site project. At the site of two multi-family villas of 6892 m^2 11 single family houses could be placed instead (600 m^2 allowed per each), so, taking into consideration Polish building regulations (single family house definition allows it to include two separate flats) the number of apartments would be 22. Due to particular situation parameters only two villas could have been placed in discussed complex but at site of comparable size one could have 5 urban villas 10–12 apartments each (in case of master plan the number of storeys is usually restricted to three).

The following comparison shows the process of optimization:

- "A" + "B" villas: 26 apartments, 265 m^2 of site per apartment
- Comparative 11 single family houses: 22 apartments, 313 m^2 of site per apartment
- Comparative 5 urban villas: 50–60 apartments, 115–138 m^2 of site per apartment

The comparison is intended to show the importance of cost of grounds in Polish cities, especially in dense urban fabric, especially in this particular case where free building plots are practically unavailable or extremely expensive. The complex was built at ground which already had been the property of Cooperative 'Biskupin' (Investor) and was formed of two villas because apart from the external municipal requirement of leaving 30 % of the site for biologically active area, other factors and regulations restricted the part of site where it was possible to build buildings (distance from site borders, necessity to allow space for children's playground, car parking places, waste container – all of these also with regulated distances to residential building). The Cooperative sells the flats together with a ground, and if it had not been building on its own plot the cost for this investment would have been enormous.

Fig. 4. Summary of urban villa features represented in "A" and "B" buildings: 1. freestanding building – open all elevations allow for best use of location parameters and contact with surroundings. 2. Maximum three to four floors – optimization of costs and profitability of the investment 3. High quality of architectural details – crucial for wellbeing and identification with place of residence 4. Apartments in relation with green space – recreation and ecology (water retention, living space for animals). Drawing and description by the author.

Crucial factor is often the required amount of car parking places – which is regulated according to a particular localization and building type, not all of them and sometimes none can be designed in underground garage – in Wroclaw the level of underground waters is very high so it is connected with high costs of heavy watertight insulations. Contrary to building of a single family house, in Cooperative's multi-family building each family or occupant needs to spend less for purchase of building plot, and from the point of view of sustainable development the municipal grounds are used more efficiently (more inhabitants at comparable site than in case of single family housing, while urban villas not only provide conditions close to the quality of life in single family housing but offer much more in terms of social cooperation and common spaces). Technical equipment designed to serve 26 apartments in one integrated system instead of 22 houses requiring 22 separate systems is in result cheaper and easier to regulate, joint initiative allows shared costs for better energy efficiency of buildings, and also lower costs are connected with fitting and furnishing of apartments ranging from 25–75 m^2 than of single family houses of at least 120 m^2.

Unfortunately in Poland typical master plans' requirement for minimum building plot for single family house is 600 m^2, and it is simply uneconomical to build a tiny house of 80–100 m^2 at such a small site. Smaller plots are allowed for semi-detached or terraced houses which in fact also turn uneconomical – from functional point of view it is even harder to organize the living spaces at multiply levels while only three or two sides are available for windows, and keep the floor area small. So the choice is either big, expensive plot and small house or smaller plot and big house. In every case of single family house investor must individually bear the costs of heating and all other installations. This shows in short the economic and spatial efficiency of small multi-family houses, which can take the form of an urban villa in case of particularly demanding contexts or investor's needs or requirements. This is an ergonomics at urban level. Due to higher functional and aesthetic standard (common recreation spaces, contact with greenery, extensive scale) occupants can reach the quality of living similar to the one in single family housing at lower costs and extra social and environmental advantages. They can simply afford to live in environmentally and socially sustainable building. The level of satisfaction and comfort in this case together with efficiency at urban and economic level is a result of bottom-up approach – respect for future users guarantees ergonomics of a living environment by sustainable design. However, success of such a way of designing is conditioned by high level of architect's competences, imagination, ability to foresee potential problems and sensibility. If more data of post occupancy surveys taking into account not only the sole aspects of energy efficiency were available, architects' plane of reference would be more independent from their personal skills. In Poland post-occupancy surveys are not yet popular, what reflects the lack of knowledge in general in regard to sustainable design and ergonomics. But residential architecture design is a vast and complicated domain, and simple applying typical tools used somewhere else (e.g. for office or industrial buildings design, maintenance and monitoring) does not necessarily work. In Great Britain for example, very advanced in environmental sustainability of building market, domestic building performance evaluation is still an emerging research area for which survey methods and principles need to be elaborated [9], and researchers observe barriers in sampling a representative data for benchmarking purposes in residential buildings [10]. Thus to draw conclusions, the author of this article refers to own practice as the architect and available surveys or research performed in Denmark [6–8], Great Britain [10] and Sweden [11] in multifamily houses in recent years. These countries are member countries of European Union, as well as Poland, and are similar to Poland in terms of climate, culture and share sense of community of values and of nationalities. To understand these contemporary problems regarding sustainable design it is important to remember, that architectural design accompanied human creation since we started to build cities. The process of learning and experimenting took centuries, according to the development of human built environment. The situation changed rapidly and dramatically in last two decades [14]: severe technical regulations are being put to force most of newly built homes to be low-energy, and it often acts against human sense of comfort and needs, which become subject to research only when systems do not work properly or health problems are reported.

3   Conclusions

All of these aspects show that ergonomics and sustainability meet in architectural design simultaneously and inseparably, reflecting general characteristics of it – multidisciplinary. The architect needs to be a man of a great knowledge and experience, familiar with building regulations and able to integrate all aspects into design:

technical, functional, ecological, economic, social, and many others. This is why the bigger project the more specialists of various disciplines are involved. Today the design team is supported by helpful computer aided design tools. They give useful calculations, simulations and visualizations in almost any discipline: architectural (how the building will look like, how it will use sun light) structural (its static or dynamic behaviour) and mechanical or electrical (thermal performance, artificial lighting, ventilation, etc.) But the tools alone, the same as sole fulfilment of raw technical requirements will not create good and user friendly living environment. Firstly – each realization is unique, and different set of aspects, requirements and expectation is to be joined together in the design. In human-computer interaction the tools used by designers can help in dealing with particular aspect of design, but the final interpretation of all information and data put together, and decisions are made by human. In author's opinion it is rather impossible to produce such a universal application to take the place of human designer. The reason for this is not only the extreme level of complication of so many parameters. Also available Danish [6–8] and Swedish [11] post-occupancy surveys of residential buildings show that the occupants' sense of comfort often refers not only to measurable factors like the possibility to control or regulate indoor environment but also important were aspects which in fact result from artistic sense and creative talent of a designer and the ability to make pleasurable spaces of high aesthetics and functionality – for example a peaceful atmosphere, contact with nature and the view through a window. The important factor was also indicated: the proper functioning of systems, in terms of thermal effect and costs of adjustments.

This factor is even more important in single family houses - frequent problems of occupants to make use of sophisticated systems regulating their homes show to what extent sustainable design requires ergonomic approach. Incorrect use of devices is sometimes caused by the lack of clear information and communication between user and the system, what can reduce efficiency or disorganise the work of installation system of a so-called "intelligent house". The inevitable troubles connected with use of the system by subsequent tenants or residents are to be avoided only when the systems are the simplest possible, even at the price of efficiency [12] And contrary to commercial buildings, possibility to have control over one's living space is very important due to vast number of living styles, personal preferences, family models and health and climate parameters. Also the range of activities performed at home varies from sleeping and relaxing to working at home, with all intermediate necessities including preparation of food, children's playing, elderly caring etc. Interface between system and user [13] in this case may become a barrier in functioning of the system or satisfaction and well-being of user.

It is very important not only from the point of view of human needs, but also holistically bearing in mind human place in the world. Today, nature is no longer perceived as resources undergoing the irresponsible exploitation, but the place of coexistence with other creatures deserving our respect. Today we have to create our cities and architecture in the spirit of thinking about the future of the next generations and the planet. From the point of view of natural science, we find that often it is not the nature who comes to the cities – it is us who expand habitats into other species' ecosystems which either adapt to changed circumstances, have to migrate or perish. This is not without significance for urban villa, which is the form of the specific characteristics. Urban and architectural solutions are of economic and environmental importance in the process of optimization of costs and use of available space: the modern urban villa must be the result of finding the best combination of all these material and ideological aspects, to achieve its best ergonomics in contemporary sustainable design.

References

1. Hedge, A., Dorsey, J.A.: Green buildings need good ergonomics. Ergonomics **56**(3), 492–506 (2013). Taylor & Francis
2. Horn, P.: Urban Villa as a modern interpretation of extensive residential building development. Ph.D. Thesis. Department of Architecture, Wrocław University of Technology. Wrocław (2003)
3. Schneider-Skalska, G.: Design – between nature and culture ABC Architekta Budownictwo Zrównoważone 1/2014, pp. 5–6. Publikator, Białystok (2014)
4. Thum, G.: Uprooted: How Breslau Became Wroclaw during the Century of Expulsions. trans. Tom Lampert, Allison Brown, W. Martin, Jasper Tilbury; Princeton and Oxford, Princeton University Press (2011)
5. Urbanik, J.: 1929 WUWA 2009 Wroclaw exhibition of Werkbund. Muzeum Architektury we Wrocławiu, Wrocław (2009)
6. Frontczak, M.: Human comfort and self-estimated performance in relation to indoor environmental parameters and building features, Ph.D. Thesis Department of Civil Engineering Technical University of Denmark, p. 40 (2011)
7. Frontczak, M., Wargocki, P.: Literature survey on how different factors influence human comfort in indoor environments. Build. Environ. **46**, 922–937 (2011). ELSEVIER
8. Frontczak, M., Andersen, R.V., Wargocki, P.: Questionnaire survey examining factors influencing comfort with indoor environmental quality in Danish housing. Build. Environ. **50**, 56–64 (2012). ELSEVIER
9. Leaman, A., Stevenson, F., Bordass, B.: Building evaluation: practice and principles. Build. Res. Inf. **38**(5), 564–577 (2010). Routledge
10. Baborska-Narozny, M., Stevenson, F.: Performance evaluation of residential architecture – scope and methods applied in two case studies based in north england. In: the 5th International Conference on Applied Human Factors and Ergonomics AHFE 2014, Kraków, Poland 19–23 July 2014, pp. 109–115. Advances in Human Factors and Sustainable Infrastructure. Edited by Jerzy Charytonowicz. AHFE Conference (2014)
11. Zalejska-Johnson, A.: Evaluation of low-energy and conventional residential buildings from occupants' perspective. Building and Environment **58**, 135–144 (2012). ELSEVIER
12. Baborska-Narozny, M.: POE and BPE evaluations – the postulated standard in British design practice in time of transformation to zero emission architecture. Reports of Institute of Architecture, Wrocław University of Technology, Ser. SPR, No. 1, p. 27 (2013)
13. Stevenson, F., Leaman, A.: Evaluating housing performance in relation to human behaviour: new challenges. Build. Res. Inf. **38**(5), 437–441 (2010). Routledge
14. Radjiyev, A., Qiu, H., Xiong, S., Nam, K.: Ergonomics and sustainable development in the past two decades (1992–2011): research trends and how ergonomics can contribute to sustainable development. Appl. Ergon. **46**, 67–75 (2015). ELSEVIER
15. http://pl.wikipedia.org/wiki/Wroc%C5%82aw
16. Interview of Ewa Szumowska with prof. Jerzy Charytonowicz "let's talk about ergonomics". http://strefaergonomii.pl/porozmawiajmy-o-ergonomii/

The Effect of Technological Progress on the Quality and Aesthetics of Modern Sanitary Facilities

Anna Jaglarz and Jerzy Charytonowicz[✉]

Department of Architecture, Wroclaw University of Technology, St. Prusa 53/55,
50-317 Wroclaw, Poland
{anna.jaglarz,jerzy.charytonowicz}@pwr.edu.pl

Abstract. Taking into account the possibilities of modern technology and its application in the area of hygiene and sanitation, we can observe a significant change in the quality of the bathroom resulting from the transformation of individual bathroom systems and devices that do not avoid rapid technological development, adapting them to the requirements of modern times.

Although the latest technology achievements in the field of bathroom facilities often surprise with their complexity, the amount of features and capabilities of the technique, by which apparently may seem complicated, however, degree of comfort which they offer is convincing about the proper actions of designers and manufacturers. Actions which primary purpose is the convenience, safety and functionality of the use of technologically and aesthetically advanced devices. Also, their hygiene, mobility and ease of use and the ability to easily keep clean are necessary. The solutions used in modern bathrooms are designed to simplify and reduce the cost of their construction. Saving of water and energy is also an important issue.

The possibility to use any innovations provides much greater freedom in shaping and arranging, the opportunity to implement the original design ideas, and thereby the ability to create individual, unique hygienic-sanitary objects. All these actions result from the requirements of the present times and emerging needs of the modern user and are based on numerous studies and analyzes concerning the possibility of shaping the bathroom.

Keywords: Sanitary facilities · Technological progress · Modern bathroom design trends · Modern technology in the bathroom · Sustainable bathroom · Ergonomics

1 Introduction

Realizing the potential of modern technologies in the field of hygiene and sanitary area, now understood not only as a place of hygiene, but also a place of recreation, significantly helped to change the appearance and functionality. An important change of

© Springer International Publishing Switzerland 2015
M. Antona and C. Stephanidis (Eds.): UAHCI 2015, Part IV, LNCS 9178, pp. 291–302, 2015.
DOI: 10.1007/978-3-319-20687-5_28

bathroom quality is the result of transformation of individual bathroom systems, equipment and appliances. Many of them were subjected to continuous development and numerous modifications and completely changed their appearance, becoming independent of the prior models, and even eliminating them. Their shape, structure, production technology, and even the principles of operation, have been changed. In other with coexisting bathroom fittings and devices occurred only slight changes, often imperceptible at first glance. Referring to the solutions of many years ago, while retaining their basic characteristics, they have become a kind of continuation of the older generation devices. However, they did not avoid rapid technical and techno-logical development, adapting them to the requirements of modern times and the changing needs of the contemporary user.

2 The Technical Quality of Tap Fittings

Elements which not only permanently changed the appearance, but primarily affected the functionality of the bathrooms are elements of tap fittings. For a long time the classic models with handles and two separate valves were the only choice. They consumed relatively large amount of water while achieving the desired temperature. Also the control process was uncomfortable, and the position of the handles did not give even an approximate idea of the temperature of the water flowing from the faucet. It was completely out of the control of the user eyesight. Therefore, the structural simplicity and low price of these solutions have been relegated to the background. Need of eliminate defects caused that designers and manufacturers of fittings have started working on the idea of the device that does not require too much force for handling, and using free hand movements could be a quick and easy way to control both stream flow and water temperature. The solution that emerged at the turn of sixties and seventies, the so-called "ceramic cartridge", in its basic form has survived to this day, and affects the shape of modern single lever mixer taps. Single lever faucets were not the only solution that has affected the quality of use of sanitary fittings. Already known thermostatic faucets have become more and more popular in the early seventies significantly increasing safety and comfort of use of tub and shower. Systems used in thermostatic faucets have allowed precise and stable maintenance of the water tem-perature setting, regardless of changes in the installation. The main idea of the ther-mostat has remained unchanged to this day [4, 11, 15] (Fig. 1).

Fig. 1. Sample forms of modern tap fittings as a fusion of the latest technology and design (Source: own work).

The real breakthrough in creating a modern tap fittings came with the use of electronics. In the second half of the eighties a small group of the largest tap fittings manufacturers began to widely introduce its first touchless electronic taps. In addition to water-saving features, electronic taps also enabled unprecedented hygiene of use through free-touch operation. These solutions have largely contributed to improving the quality and comfort of use of bathroom fittings by persons with disabilities. These devices are constantly innovated, which is reflected in the latest top achievements in the field of digital and electronic batteries. They represent a new quality in terms of water flow control. For maximum hygiene, they provide possibility to program regular automatic flushing one to few days after the last usage to avoid water stagnation – an important feature for facilities that are not used on a daily basis [5, 17].

3   The Impact of Technological Progress on the Quality of Use and Aesthetics of Bathing Facilities

Among the complex bathroom equipment, shower is an element that despite the common associations related to standard shower head, handle and wall bar focuses the attention of designers and manufacturers of fittings. Since the time of the introduction of the shower bar by Hansgrohe in the fifties, can be seen two ways to find the perfect shower. First is a continuous process of improving the classic version of the shower, or modifications of shower head and handle and their fasteners and connections. The second is the search for a new form of shower set [8, 11].

3.1   Modifications of Shower Head and Handle

The first way has led to various forms of shower heads that provide several types of flow, in addition to the standard and diffuse stream, also special streams - massage jet, aerated, economic, etc. The shower heads are protected against limescale and other impurities, which are probably the greatest threat to their efficient functioning. Other improvements, which strongly affect the quality of shower set are a silicone nozzles at the outlet openings, filters hidden in the handle that can be rinsed and special pins hidden in the head that push the sludge from the nozzle [11].

Numerous innovations also include the entire hand shower. In the latest hand showers traditional handles are equipped with the Rota Head - pressing the button allows you to rotate and set the head in any position. The direction of the stream is determined by the rotation of the head, without moving the handle. This feature also allows the massage side stream even when the shower is mounted on a immovable wall bar. Shapes and sizes of mobile hand shower have been adapted to the different sizes of the hand and provide selected direction of the stream offering three types of this - gentle, uniform and normal. Modification the type of stream can be done in a simple way, by moving the slider on the side of the hand shower [3, 8, 11] (Fig. 2).

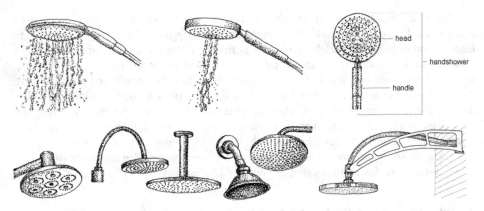

Fig. 2. The classic version of the shower head and the handle is still improved (Source: own work).

3.2 Modification of Shower Sets

Complex modifications influencing the form of shower and shower sets are the result of the continuous analysis of designers and manufacturers. In solutions combining the idea of panel and shower set, classic handle is replaced with rotating arm (angle of rotation 180 degrees) to which two shower heads are fixed. Movable heads with handle allow for easy set the shower at the top or side position. Two types of stream, plain and pulse, make the user, in addition to the classic shower, can take advantage of the massage panel [11] (Fig. 3).

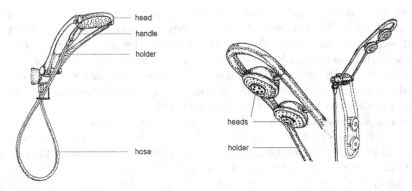

Fig. 3. Movable heads with handle allow for easy set the shower at the top or side position (Source: own work).

Shower panels and columns are other interesting solutions. With a combination of recessed and surface-mounted components all elements of the installation can be hidden in the wall. Column resembling classic shower bar, topped with shower head usually with the function of rain shower, is the outer, visible part. Shower handle and retractable shower hose is pulled out in the bottom of the column. The heads are usually equipped with numerous nozzles and in addition to conventional shower, allow for hydromassage, or imitate a waterfall [1, 6, 8, 11] (Figs. 4 and 5).

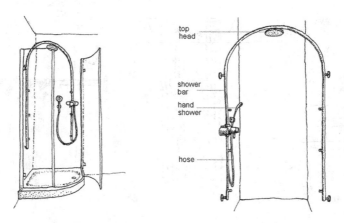

Fig. 4. The arc-shaped shower set, upper and hand, can be mounted both in the cabin and between two walls (Source: own work).

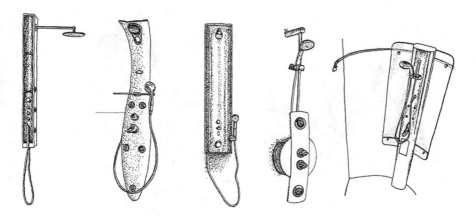

Fig. 5. Additional side shower nozzles are used for hydromassage. (Source: own work)

Modern shower features were supplemented not only the possibility of a massage, but also an increasingly popular "rain". Rainfall shower heads are mostly in the form of flat plate or bowl. However, you can find more unconventional solutions different from traditional forms. Evolution includes not only the form of rainfall showerhead, but also the ways of their installation. Rainfall showerheads can be installed directly on the

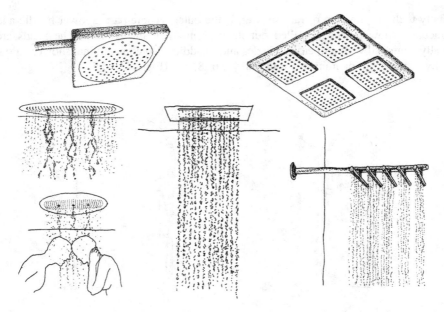

Fig. 6. Innovative ideas for rainfall showerheads helped create functionally and stylistically interesting solution of shower for two people (Source: own work).

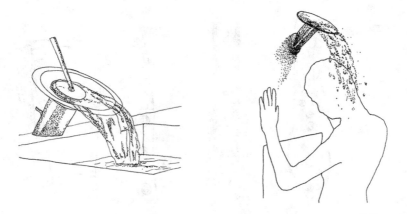

Fig. 7. In the cascade systems flow of water is regulated by a recessed mounted thermostat. (Source: own work).

ceiling or on the wall. This allows for independent of the other elements of the shower construction [8, 11, 16].

Cascade or waterfall shower is one of the modern trends in bathing facilities. This system is used for shower sets and basin mixer fittings [3] (Figs. 6 and 7).

Recessed-mounted shower-massage system is a solution that is becoming increasingly popular. Flush-mounted on one, two or three walls it gives you more opportunities to arrange in comparison with shower panel. It's not just about the number of side nozzles, but also about their setting that allows you to direct the stream to any part of the body, and thus adjusts the massage to individual preferences [7, 11] (Fig. 8).

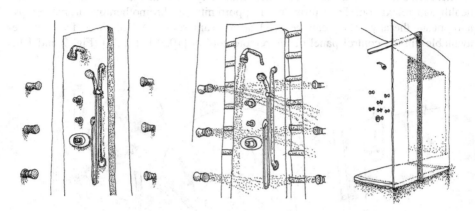

Fig. 8. The use of flush-mounted massage - shower systems, has introduced a new quality in the field of shower equipment (Source: own work).

3.3 Modifications of Shower Cabins

Modern shower cabins are equipped with functions for both hygiene and relaxation. Among them you can find models suitable for standard bathroom and for bathing room. Cabins are made of high quality materials, with a tendency to a maximum of lightness and transparency. They allow the user to have the easiest access to the shower and the comfortable use of it, without causing complete closure and a sense of isolation from the rest of the bathroom during this action. Contemporary trends in the design of the cabins tend strongly towards minimizing the number of structural profiles for the maximal surface of fillings which diversity of materials and patterns is practically unlimited. The user can choose between the smooth, transparent surface, or decorated, structural. The surface of the cabin is usually made of polystyrene and "safety" tempered glass. In order to increase the comfort of use of cabins, for the sake of maximum hygiene, on their surfaces are used special coatings that protect against dirt, sludge and bacteria [14, 22].

An important issue in terms of convenience and safety of cabin use is easy access to the inside. Such structures and attachments are used that allow for effortlessly maneuver to open the cabin door. They also enable fast, easy, possible without additional tools, moving them from the guides for precise cleaning of places that are often inaccessible. An important feature of modern cabins is diversity in terms of size, which allows for easy adaptation to the needs of users. Cabin seal is a separate issue which is appreciated by the users especially in the case of any problems. More perfect sealing systems are used for this reason. Also, other elements of shower cabins, such as hinges, handles, or various types of connectors are gradually modified. Easy access to the interior of the cabin is also possible thanks to modern shower bases that are very low and shallow. Increasingly, they are completely eliminated, and such solutions are the best complement to the modern concept of removal of divisions in the bathroom space [14, 22].

Modern shower cabins are multifunctional. They combine the functions of hygiene, health and relaxation. They provide an opportunity of chromotherapy, aromatherapy and music therapy. They can be used as a steam room. All of these features are available via the control panel or the remote control [10, 13, 19, 21] (Fig. 9 and 10).

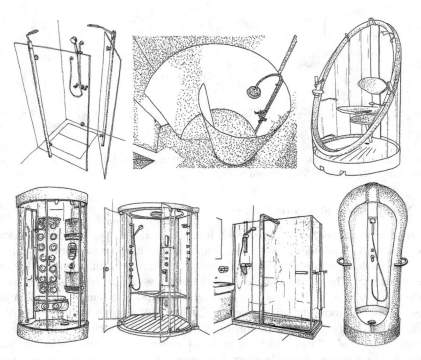

Fig. 9. Examples of forms of shower cabins (Source: own work)

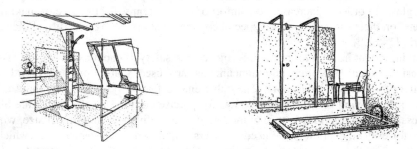

Fig. 10. The glass elements in the bathrooms (Source: own work)

3.4   Characteristics of Contemporary Bathtubs

The trend in the pursuit of transparency also includes another part of bathroom equipment such as bathtubs. We can talk about a unification of the bathroom because transparent tubs are referring in its design to modern shower cabins. Sometimes the glass is the predominant part of the tub, reminiscent of "aquarium", sometimes its use is limited to glass fragments or entire walls. The use of glass does not interfere with the placement of hydromassage nozzles in the tub, on the contrary, their launch and the introduction of water into a dynamic movement can affect the visual and aesthetic quality of use of the bath. Illuminated bathtubs are an additional attraction [2, 12, 20] (Figs. 11 and 12).

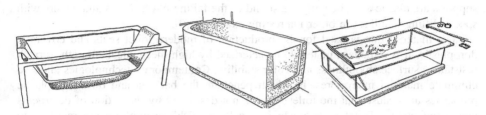

Fig. 11. Examples of the use of glass in bathtubs (Source: own work)

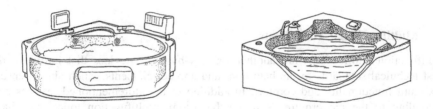

Fig. 12. Bathtubs with hydromassage and with glass „window" (Source: own work)

4   Contemporary Trends in Shaping of the Toilet Seats

The toilet seat is an integral part of the toilet bowl, while perhaps the most decisive for the convenience of using it. The first toilet seats, as the name suggests, were made of wood. A variety of shapes and colors appeared, when the plastic, easily and well formed, began to be used in their manufacture. The shape of the toilet seat can be unrestricted. Usually, however, it is a subordinate to sanitary ceramics form. Nowadays, it is not always conventional, so among the toilet seats can also be found other than the traditional - round, oval, square, octagonal, etc. Also, the cover of toilet seat may not be typical. It can be smooth, textured, decorated with various patterns. Wooden toilet seats are still manufactured. They are usually simple and smooth, very often treated with special preservatives [9].

Proper mounting toilet seat on the toilet bowl is an important matter, on which depends the convenient use of the toilet. Various methods are known, however usually attachment made of plastic, chrome-plated or gold-plated metal is used for this purpose. Systems for rapid assembly and disassembly of the toilet seat, which play an important role when it comes to maintaining the hygiene of both toilet seat and bowl are becoming increasingly popular. Special hinges or so-called "quick couplers" are used in these systems. Automatic, "soft close system" of closing toilet seat and cover is already quite standard solution. Soft close system features hinges that gently lower the toilet seat and cover to a close when pushed down. The quantity and quality of the support elements also determines the functionality of the toilet seat. Number of supports depends on the hardness of the seat. Toilet seats made of soft plastic with inflexible supports are more susceptible to deformation or fracture. Preferably, the supports are elastic and silencing the sound of the falling cover. Seats and covers with special lifting handles are other interesting examples [9].

The material that is used for the production of modern toilet seats and covers is duroplastic. It is a modern material characterized by high mechanical strength, scratch resistance, surface smoothness and color stability. Contemporary technologies allow to eliminate material micropores, in which penetrate the bacteria and dirt. Duroplastic properties also cause that the toilet seat are not destroyed by the action of detergents and disinfectants. Toilet seats made in the "sandwich" technology are resistant to cracking and breaking. This is a technology based on high-performance composite structure of polypropylene with elastic filling of the toilet cover [9].

4.1 Multifunctional Toilet Seats

Multifunctional toilet seats are another sanitary-hygienic devices that introduce the latest technical standards to the bathroom and another elements which aim to ensure maximum functionality and comfort. In addition to the aforementioned features corresponding to the modern trends in the bathroom, multifunction toilet seats have additional properties affecting the quality of their use [18].

Automaticity and reducing to a minimum manual operation, make use of them is easy and comfortable. Water washing toilet seats indicate not only hygiene and comfort, but their use has a positive impact on the alleviation or elimination of many inconvenient health problems. They are also indispensable in the care of the elderly, the disabled, people after surgery, women in the postpartum period. Properly selected streams of water allow dispense with the need for toilet paper for a more delicate form of hygiene. Nozzles placed on the moving arms are essential elements of multifunctional toilet seats. The first models were equipped with nozzles responsible for the traditional function of a bidet. Systems with duplicate nozzles and shoulders for individual functions have been developed recently [18].

Washing function, or the use of a oscillating water stream having carefully programmed temperature and pressure of the flow is an essential function of the multifunctional toilet seats. Retractable nozzles placed on mobile spray arms are extended only to the working position at the moment of use, otherwise they allow the unfettered traditional use of the toilet seat. The electronic control system is responsible for maintaining the purity of the individual elements. Automatic cleansing the arms and nozzles takes place before and after use of toilet seat with special disinfectants dispensed by the electronic system. Washing system of multifunctional toilet seats is complemented by drying systems. Electronically controlled dryers significantly increase comfort and hygiene of using the toilet seats and also improve their health benefits. Numerous solutions, including thermostats and thermal safety-valves, ensure safe use (Fig. 13).

Fig. 13. Examples of the multifunctional "intelligent' toilet seat (Source: own work)

The Japanese toilet company Toto, excels in the production of "intelligent" toilets, in which the most advanced technology is used. Electronic toilet seats with washing and drying systems offer many functions. They feature a heated seats, warm water massage system, warm air drying system, built-in automatic deodorizer and digital thermostat. Automatic opening and closing toilet seat and cover are additional features. Stimulator of toilet flushing sound can mask any unwanted sounds made by the user. Latest toilet devices have additional medical functions, enabling the analysis of urine and blood pressure measurement and data transfer via modem to doctor. The electric raised-seat toilets that provide a lift mechanism to assist the user in getting on and off of the toilet serve as an aid to the elderly or disabled [18].

5   Conclusion

Selected from coexisting in the hygienic and sanitary area and discussed in the article systems and devices, belong to a group of bathroom solutions and equipment, which characteristically and permanently have changed the image of the place - appearance, but in particular its functionality, and significantly have influenced the change in its quality.

The main directions of contemporary designers and manufacturers activities and features of innovative components of bathrooms are:

- multifunctionality - which is a response to the diverse needs of users,
- safety - primarily safety in use, meaning not only comfortable use of the facilities, but also their efficiency, reliability and ease of maintenance,

- ease of use - the possibility of a simple, rapid control method that does not require too much manual dexterity and understanding of complex principles of operation,
- hygiene - ability to keeping cleanliness and easy maintenance and cleaning,
- saving water and energy - allowing for minimal use of the necessary natural resources without the effect of reducing the comfort of using the bathroom,
- aesthetics - application forms and materials that ensure aesthetic appearance of equipment and finishing regardless of the period of use, the so-called technological durability
- freedom in the design and arrangement of bathrooms - mobility of devices, the ability to choose any place of their location and moving them after installation.

These examples are intended to illustrate phenomena and achievements related to the evolution of the bathroom equipment, which until recently were only an idea. It has been implemented as a result of experience, research and creative work on the possibilities of shaping the sanitary-hygienic area. Therefore contemporary user can use the bathroom as it did before, except that it is more readily available, much more comfortable, safer, more pleasant and often more economical.

References

1. Baran, P., Markowska, M.: Goscinny egoista, Dobre wnetrze, Murator, Warszawa (7/2005)
2. Baran, P., Markowska, M.: Wodne przezrocza, Dobre wnetrze, Murator, Warszawa (7/2005)
3. Baran, P., Markowska, M.: Z rynny pod deszcz, Dobre wnetrze, Murator, Warszawa (7/2005)
4. Bathroom Products. http://www.us.kohler.com
5. Digital & Electronic Taps. http://www.grohe.com
6. Freehander. http://www.grohe.com
7. Galicka, J.: Hydromasaz spod tynku, Lazienka, Publikator, Bialystok (12/2004)
8. Hansgrohe products. http://www.hansgrohe.com
9. Inteligentna deska sedesowa, Lazienka, Publikator, Bialystok (12/2000)
10. Kubasik, A.: Lazienka jako maszyna? Lazienka, pp. 52–55. Publikator, Bialystok (2000)
11. Lazienkowa kronika polwiecza, Lazienka, Publikator, Bialystok (6/2004)
12. Matracka, M.: Przejrzec wanne. Publikator, Bialystok Lazienka (2005)
13. Nowe oblicze łazienki. Brodziki i kabiny natryskowe, Instalacje, pp. 70–73. Bud-Media, Bydgoszcz (3/2000)
14. Poliszczuk, P.: Anatomia kabiny, Lazienka, Publikator, Bialystok (2/2002)
15. Pusz, A.: Ewolucja baterii termostatycznej, Lazienka, pp. 28–29. Publikator, Bialystok (3/2002)
16. Rain Sky. http://www.dornbracht.com
17. Strzalowski, P.: Bezdotykowe baterie elektroniczne, Lazienka, Publikator, Bialystok (2/2004)
18. Topczewski, A.: Wiecej niz bidet, Lazienka, Publikator, Bialystok (4/2004)
19. Zacharewicz, K.: Niekonwencjonalny natrysk, Lazienka, Publikator, Bialystok (4/2005)
20. Zacharewicz, K.: Wanny przyszlosci?, Lazienka, Publikator, Bialystok (2, 3/2005)
21. Zukowski, J.: Dwa pomysly pod prysznic, Lazienka, Publikator, Bialystok (2/2003)
22. Zukowski, J.: Gdzie wziac prysznic, Lazienka, Publikator, Bialystok (6/2000)

Development of the Ecological Bathroom Ideas

Anna Jaglarz[✉]

Department of Architecture, Wroclaw University of Technology, St. Prusa 53/55,
50-317 Wroclaw, Poland
anna.jaglarz@pwr.edu.pl

Abstract. Shaping the ecological bathroom includes various activities allowing optimal usable, health and aesthetic conditions to reside and perform specific actions by users with minimum interference in the environment and low use of natural resources. The main objective of these activities is to create a harmonious compounds in the system: user - bathroom - the environment. The basic features of ecological bathrooms and its ecological equipment include efficiency and savings of water, energy and materials. Equally important is the friendly treatment of the environment and the maintenance of healthy and hygienic conditions of use of the bathroom.

Bathroom industry, taking care of the environment, is offering more and more products that prevent waste of natural resources and control their consumption. As a result of work on ever new, sometimes surprising, possibilities of their optimal use, numerous projects appear in response to needs for solutions that are economical in operation and at the same time comfortable to use.

Keywords: Ecological bathroom · Eco friendly bathroom · Sustainable bathroom · Modern bathroom design trends · Hygienic and sanitary facilities · Technological development · Modern technology · Ergonomics

1 Introduction

Nowadays, having to deal with health and hygiene conscious society, and when the innovations in the bathroom relate primarily to its aesthetic and technological side, the problem of natural resources turns out to be extremely important. Despite this ecological imperative, the quest for total comfort of use of hygienic and sanitary zone and experience in this area greatest pleasure still continues. Hedonistic lifestyle of many people is associated with the desire to achieve well-being, from enjoying the aromatherapy baths, and ending with the luxury brands of bathroom facilities, signed with the names of well-known designers. Paradoxically, the user, on the one hand, being aware of the opportunities of bathroom facilities and encouraged by manufacturers offers, at the same time realizes that his worldly pleasures take place at the expense of diminishing natural resources. Water as a natural resource and an essential element of the bath becomes a luxury. We can look for the good balance, for example, by saving water at home activities during the day, for the evening bath in a bathtub full of water, but such behavior is not entirely consistent with contemporary trends directed towards the comfort of using the bathroom and the whole apartment [12].

© Springer International Publishing Switzerland 2015
M. Antona and C. Stephanidis (Eds.): UAHCI 2015, Part IV, LNCS 9178, pp. 303–310, 2015.
DOI: 10.1007/978-3-319-20687-5_29

The basic principle is verification of the current water consumption and awareness of the need of water-saving. It turns out that the installed water meters are the most effective elements causing rational use of water. Measurements affect the need to search for solutions directed towards the reduction of water bills. The second step is identification of areas for the application of improvements and obtainment savings. The implementation of appropriate solutions for water management should be proceeding.

Saving water is just one of the activities associated with the formation of the ecological bathroom and its ecological equipment. Saving energy and materials is also an important issue. This ecological attitude is intended to provide a healthy and hygienic conditions of use of the bathroom with due respect for the natural environment, minimum interference in the ecosystem and low utilization of natural resources. Friendly treatment of the natural environment and creation of harmonious relationships in the system: user - bathroom - the environment are key activities associated with the formation of the ecological, environmentally sustainable bathroom.

2 Daily Habits

Reasonable use of the water is one of the main rules. Precise observation of water usage can show that even simple changes in daily habits are sufficient to significantly reduce the consumption of water in every home. Brushing teeth, washing hands, or shaving, are examples of activities that, despite appearances, require use of the large amounts of water. Therefore, should not be done as continuous use of flowing stream of water - close the tap while brushing teeth or shaving foam overlap. For example, rinsing teeth after brushing using a cup instead of under running water is a consumption of 0.5 liters of water instead of 16. You can also replace a full bath, with a content of about 100–150 liters of water, on a more economical shower and save at least one third of the amount of water [11].

3 The Quality and Condition of the Bathroom Installations and Equipment

You should also pay attention to the quality and condition of installation and fittings of the bathrooms, especially the faucets and taps. Leaky valve and tap, from which drips one drop per second causes a waste of 16.8 liters of water a day - that's more than half a liter per hour, and each year about 4.7 cubic meters, or 4 700 liters. The tap, from which leaking 2 mm water stream leads to loss of water in an amount of 277 ml per minute and 146 cubic meters per year (146 000 liters). Therefore, both the competent installation and proper maintenance of fittings can be very important. Quality control, verification of the guarantee and certificates required by building regulations and authorizing the sale of faucets are also recommended. They are evidence of the use in the production of faucets materials that guarantee safety of the use. Also, the quality of toilet flushing devices is an important issue. Leaky toilet cistern wastes up to 32 liters of water per day. Water saving flush systems with dual flushing and start/stop flushing can help save about 1.5–2 liters of water with every flushing [9, 11].

4 Water Recycling and Reuse

Possibility of recycling and reuse wastewater, is an effective way to reduce water consumption in the household. Increasingly effective systems allow, for example, through proper filtration, use the waste water from the bathtubs and shower cabins for flushing the toilet bowls. In a domestic installation, users have opportunity of recycling and reuse consumed water, the so-called "grey water" or process water. Properly designed and installed system is needed for this purpose. Waste water is collected from bathtubs, shower trays and washbasins. Waste water is collected from bathtubs, shower trays and basins, and then is passed through a natural filter system (sand and gravel) and biological and mechanical filter systems. Purified water is stored in underground tanks and used for flushing the toilet, cleaning or watering the garden. In the single-family house also rainwater can be used. It is suitable for irrigating the garden, flushing the toilets, washing the car, and even doing the laundry [11, 13].

5 Modern Devices Limiting the Consumption of Water and Energy

Modern equipment limiting water and energy consumption can also help in saving and at the same time in environmental protection. Bathroom industry, taking care of the environment and implementing ecological programs, is offering more and more products that prevent waste of natural resources and control their consumption. Solutions as a result of work on their optimal use are becoming increasingly frequent. They do not reduce the comfort of using the bathroom, on the contrary, they contribute to improving quality and standard of this place. Among them you can find economical energy-efficient washing machines, which have special functions of washing and consume less water with less clothes, environmentally friendly faucets with special solutions allowing to avoid water waste while providing the comfort of their use and a modern, efficient flushing device and ecological bathing facilities. Other ecological solutions include waterless urinals and dry toilets. Energy efficient hand dryers and energy-efficient lighting, such as LED type are further examples of environmentally friendly solutions.

5.1 Ecological Bathroom Fittings and Fixtures

Faucets are elements of bathroom facilities that can help you save water. Ecological solutions that are used in them do not allow for the water losses and provide comfort of use. Single-lever mixer taps and thermostatic faucets provide control and regulation of the stream intensity and the temperature of the flowing water. Therefore setting of the optimal parameters is fast and prevents wasting even a drop of water. One handle is easier to open the outflow of water for children and the elderly. In this way, you can easily adjust the intensity and temperature of the water, while holding in your other hand another thing such as a toothbrush. This solution helps to save water that would be consumed during long lasting regulation of the pressure or temperature with double handle faucets. Electronically controlled touchless faucets running only when your hand or other object comes within range of the sensors are another way to control the amount of water consumed. The water flow stops automatically after removal of the hands - so there is no risk that a child or elderly person forgets to close the tap, pouring in an uncontrolled manner many liters of precious water. Also, bathroom faucets operated electronically - via the remote control are effective in saving water. With their help, you can set both the required water temperature and a suitable size of water flow: 2, 5 or 13 liters/min, and by pressing the corresponding button save setpoints. Touchless faucets and taps with the remote control may limit water consumption by even more than 50 %. Faucets fitted with a stop the flow of water so-called eco-button are also effective solution. It is usually located on the back or on the side of the tap. In order to obtain the maximum flow of water out of the spout (13–14 liters per minute), button must be pressed. After closing tap the button automatically returns to its previous position, and after re-opening tap, water flows already in the amount of 5–7 liters per minute. In this way, the water flow is reduced by approximately 50 %. Also the faucet with a special water-saving head, which is equipped with the lock - brake is offered by manufacturers of sanitary fittings. Strong resistance is felt at the time of lifting up the faucet holder - from the tap flows 5–7 liters of water. Maximum outflow in an amount of about 13 liters/min is achieved only after overcoming this resistance. Water consumption using the water-saving head can be reduced by up to half. Another proposal is to use the aerator - an element in the form of special fine-mesh sprinkler, which is fastened at the end of the spout in order to aerate the water flowing stream. Despite this reduction in the intensity of the stream, it seems that the same amount of water flows from the tap, because it is enriched with thousands of air bubbles. Such a change does not reduce the effectiveness of cleaning, and reduces water consumption by about 15 % in the case of using the traditional aerator. The eco-aerator, designed specifically for effective water saving, can reduce the outflow from the spout even by 40–60 %. Also, shower head and hand shower may have a special construction to minimize water consumption. As a result, the strength of the water stream and enjoyment of the shower does not change, and water consumption is reduced by 50 % [7, 9].

5.2 Ecological Flushing Devices

The toilet bowls designed for efficient flushing are now the new standard. The amount of water needed to flush the toilet bowl depends on its shape. Older models of toilet bowls with the so-called ledge (obsolescent) require a larger amount of flushing water - usually around 9 liters. For flushing new model of toilet bowl 6 liters of water is usually sufficient. In modern flush tanks, the amount of water, that flushes the toilet bowl, can be adjusted. In most containers, it is in the range of 6 to 9 liters. The flush mechanism is equipped with a dual button. Pressing the first button releases 6–9 liters of water (and causes complete emptying of the reservoir), pressing the second button releases only 3 liters (limited but efficient flushing). The buttons are usually marked (for example, the first - a large drop, the second - a small drop), or one which empties the entire tank is larger. The use of the toilet bowl with a flush tank equipped with a dual flush button

(3 or 6 liters of water) compared with the bowl with a conventional system allows to save 22 m3 of water per year for a family of 4 people. The single button with "stop" function that allows - by pressing again - to stop the flow of water at any time, is a slightly different, but also environmentally friendly alternative. Modern non-contact flush devices respond to the presence of at least 6 s the user in the impact zone of photocell. Automatic water flow occurs within 3 s after leaving the zone by the user. In case of necessity of additional flushing, this is possible with the help of manually operated button. The flushing installation with the use of waste water from the bathtub and the shower cabin is now becoming more and more frequently used solution [3, 8, 10, 13].

5.3 Ecological Bathing Facilities

The bath in the tub, although pleasant, is not a pro-ecological. Filling the bathtub requires about 180 liters of water, while each minute of the shower is the consumption of about 10 liters of water. For persons, who in addition to water, save time, the choice seems obvious. However, if you wish to take a long baths, both tub and shower are a problem from an ecological point of view. High-tech shower cabins, such as hygienic capsule designed by Fabio Lenci, are programmed in such a way that the water consumption during washing is low as possible. It can be a water saving system, similar to that used on the spaceships, in the form of three separate functions. The first function, used to wet the entire body with a consumption of only three liters of water, the second function, atomizing water, that helps to soap and rinse the body with two liters of water, and the third function using a further three liters for the final rinse. Additional water filtration methods allow the water reuse. The toilet set integrated with the cabin is equipped with special system that separates excrement and urine, and which allows to use of less contaminated wastewater [4, 5].

5.4 Ecological Toilets and Urinals

The present ecological sanitation methods help to save water, energy and reuse of human waste. The waterless toilet systems do not require any water to function. They utilize a natural biological processes to break down human waste into dehydrated odorless compost - as material. They not only save water, but they are also entirely isolated from the surrounding environment and cannot contaminate underground water resources.

Given that 40 % of the water consumed in the household is used for flushing the toilet bowl, the solutions in the form of toilets without flushing seem to be a very ecological proposals. The so-called composting toilets, separating toilets or a so-called dry toilets are suitable for use, among others, in the residential buildings, especially toilets which have a central composting module, which can collect waste from many toilet in the building [2].

In addition to waterless toilets we have waterless urinals. Waterless urinal known today does not use a single drop of water. This is due to the use of a replaceable cartridge filled with a special biodegradable substance which transmits urine into the drain, but on the other hand blocks the release of odors outside without the need of flushing. Operation consists of replacing the cartridge - on average every 4–6 months, depending on frequency of use. However, the price of the cartridge is considerably less than the amount saved on the water consumption. Waterless urinals allow for a significant reduction in operating costs. They do not require flushing, and consequently reduce the amount of wastewater compared to traditional urinals. This ecological device, saving water and environment, is willingly used in public buildings. No water consumption saves on water and wastewater, so provides economic advantages, but it also gives the environment protection, so provides ecological benefits. Some waterless urinals have the potential to get extra points for LEED and BREEAM - certification for "green buildings" [1].

6   Peculiar Ideas of Ecological Bathroom and Its Equipment

There are also some strange ideas and concepts in the form of various solutions related to the unlimited possibilities of use bathtubs and shower cabins, born under the inspiration of the modern, multi-function devices, which, although based on advanced technologies, however, are not always equipped with water saving systems and their use requires large amounts of this precious natural resource. They were processed under the influence of certain philosophies of life, desire for contact with nature and its contemplation, and at the same time the need to protect natural resources, especially water. Many interesting projects were created as a result of this. It is to be hoped that they will get the chance for realization.

Several designers, drawing on the experience of countries facing water scarcity, have presented a number of unusual and unconventional proposals. The bathtub *"Ben Hur"* and the shower *"True Trunk"* are French examples. *"Ben Hur"* is a large bathtub on wheels equipped with a set of accessories that can be used not only for bathing and washing. Person taking a bath does not need to break away from their daily activities, such as laundry, cleaning, cooking, or working at a desk etc. The wheels allow for easy movement around the house. Thanks to them, the person can also go to the garden. Sunshade which is part of the bathtub equipment effectively protects against the sun. The user can take a bath in the presence of other people, treating this action as an element of social life [12].

Unknown eclectic group of designers, writers and artists from Marseille, Les Pas Perdus, with roots in Mauritius, has approached to the subject of bath with wealth of experience from the Third World, combining them with the "visual euphoria." The use of recycled materials returning to favor in the form of secondary raw materials, and artistic installations and structures realized with them, are the result of the search of unlimited possibilities. Plastic cover creates a shower cabin, and a barrel full of water mounted on a tree trunk, allows you to see the level of the water for use. This simple, realized according to the principle of "do-it-yourself", shower is designed to provide the unusual sensations in contact with nature treated as a valuable natural goodness. Projects *"X-les Bain"* designed by Olivier Peyricot, are another bathing inventions, which give water equal status with human. *"Roombath"* is an example of the bath architecture, which is closed within a large plastic bathtub warm and nice to touch giving shelter from the surrounding world. The users, sitting on small chairs in its interior, can use a small, water-filled bowls to wash up. Transparent plastic hose enables precise control of water stream. Portable mattress designed for relaxation and accessories for massage and personal care are additional bathtub equipment. This form of bath refers to the rituals that are part of Muslim or Japanese bathing culture. The bathtub is a health and rest center, with a small amount of precious water. *"Wombath"*, flexible, latex bathtub in the shade of human skin, is referring to the womb of a pregnant woman. It has been shaped in such a way that allows the user bathing in a fetal position, so that even a small amount of water reaches up to his shoulder. This position relating to the first moments in the womb, promotes relaxation, meditation and even allows napping during the bath. Flexible but durable material "softens" the light and dampens the sounds reaching into the interior, providing total peace of mind and undisturbed relaxation for user. *"Washchair"* like a tub of our ancestors, can be used for bathing and washing clothes. It is made of soft polyurethane. Its shape, high back and rounded edges resembles nineteenth-century tub, designed for hygiene in a sitting position, and as it allows for a comfortable bath in the "cosy chair". Textured back provides a shoulder massage, and, if necessary, can become functional tare for washing. By maintaining the central parts of the body in a small amount of warm water, *"Washchair"* is another example of its ecological use [6, 12].

"Four Seasons" is a project of a luxurious spa bath. Its bottom is covered with a synthetic grass and flooded only a small amount of water. The grass is intended to stimulate blood circulation of user. The bathtub cover has openings which can be filled with vegetation corresponding to the current season. It may resemble a pond or a small lake. In order to enhance the sensations associated with the passing seasons, you can use the cherry blossom-scented bathing salt in the spring and in the summer seaweed and algae that may turn bathtub into the sea beach. Herbs in the autumn and eucalyptus oil or extract from spruce and juniper in winter, can be very helpful in the treatment of colds, and in addition the bath becomes a soothing, regenerating and uniting with nature experience [6, 12].

Aside from a number of changes "in the bathtub", seen as a sign of luxury in areas of water scarcity, shower as a more economical solution when it comes to about the bath, were also not left out. But although its use was always associated with time saving and water saving, today the term "quick shower" is already outdated. Currently in the cabin, you can spend even more time than in the bathtub. Therefore just as relaxing bath in the tub showering should become an experience similarly pleasant, with the participation of music therapy and aromatherapy, that also does not waste precious water resource. In this case, the water can be, for example, an element of fun recalling childhood memories. *"Popshower"*, a form of shower that offers the benefits of thalassotherapy while having fun is exactly such a solution. Various shower heads arranged in the wall and floor of the suitably shaped cabin provide a different types of water stream. It can take the form of a rushing waterfall, a gentle sprinkler grass or a light sea breeze. Each of the water outlets is closed with a rubber stopper with a suitable handle for easy release of the plug and trouble-free start of each shower forms [6, 12].

7 Summary

User of contemporary bathroom is motivated both by ecological and economic considerations, so he would like to use water and energy wisely, reasonably and sparingly, but at the same time without sacrifice and without giving up the pleasures that provide modern bathroom facilities. Therefore, the society, which on the one hand wants to care about health, hygiene, appearance and well-being, on the other hand, is aware of the problem of natural resources, is looking for functional, comfortable to use, and at the same time economical in operation, solutions. Developing bathroom industry, taking care of the needs both of users as well as the environment, is offering more and more products that provide a high quality of use, while preventing the waste of valuable resources and control their consumption. Many interesting ideas, concepts and finished products resulting from the development of new, sometimes unexpected, possibilities of optimal use of natural resources are a response to the needs of users. The solutions discussed in this article are only examples of far-reaching and multifaceted environmentally friendly actions of designers and manufacturers that significantly contribute to development of the ecological bathrooms.

References

1. Bezwodny pisuar – co to wlasciwie jest? http://blog.ekoforte.com
2. Ekotoaleta kompostujaca. http://www.ekogazeta.com.pl
3. Filipkowski, K.: Podtynkowe systemy splukujace, Lazienka, Publikator, Bialystok (8/2000)
4. Kubasik, A.: Kapsula kosmicznej higieny, Lazienka, Publikator, Bialystok (5/2001)
5. Kubasik, A.: Mobilne konfiguracje, Lazienka, Publikator, Bialystok (9/2002)
6. Morozzi, C.: Linee d'acqua. Cultura del bagno e del corpo, Miller Freeman I Mostra Convegno Expocomfort, Mediolan (2000)
7. Oras – nowe standardy, Lazienka, Publikator, Bialystok (9/2000)
8. Oszczedne splukiwanie. http://www.kolo.com.pl
9. Oszczedzanie wody w kuchni i lazience. http://www.muratordom.pl
10. Oszczedzanie wody w toalecie. http://www.muratordom.pl
11. Szkoła oszczedzania. http://www.archipelag.pl
12. White, L.: Kapielowe paradoksy, Lazienka, Publikator, Bialystok (8/2000)
13. Woda i scieki. http://www.life.epce.org.pl

Does a Computer Have Control Over an Architect? Reflections on the Example of Sports Arenas

Nina Juzwa[1], Adam Gil[2], and Katarzyna Ujma-Wasowicz[2(✉)]

[1] Faculty of Civil Engineering, Architecture and Environmental Engineering,
Technical University of Lodz, Łódź, Poland
nina.juzwa@polsl.pl
[2] Faculty of Architecture, Silesian University of Technology, Gliwice, Poland
{adam.gil,katarzyna.ujma-wasowicz}@polsl.pl

Abstract. Considerations on the subject were carried out by a comparative analysis of modern architecture of large volume sport objects that originated i.a. in Poland at the turn of the 20th and 21st centuries with references to earlier objects and trends in worldwide architecture. Case studies are an effective tool that allows to observe changes and on this basis to draw conclusions for the directions of development. It is a chance to comment on the relationship between computer tools and the form and method of solving selected problems of architectural designing. Analysis of selected examples leads to the conclusion that modern architecture of sports arenas probably not have been built without participation of computer programs.

Keywords: Large-scale objects for sports and entertainment · Architecture of sports arenas and stadiums · Computer programs in architectural design

1 Introduction

The design of large scale objects has been the subject of our research led within a university team for a long time[1] [1]. In recent years, Poland has hosted sports competitions of international reach – in 2012 the EUFA European Football Championship and in 2014, the World Men's Volleyball Championship. These occasions provided an opportunity to enlarge and modernize Polish sports infrastructure which allowed to decrease the difference between architectural technology and engineering in Poland and other parts of the world. The newly built objects had to fulfill very high standards. This new reality was the initial impulse for our research and thoughts.

---

[1] Part of the research is presented in the paper Juzwa N., Ujma-Wasowicz K.: "Large scale architecture. Design human factors and ergonomics aspects based on state-of-the-art structures. Does new architectural geometry require a reinspection of comfortable usage and the user's emotions?" during AHFE International Conference 2012.

© Springer International Publishing Switzerland 2015
M. Antona and C. Stephanidis (Eds.): UAHCI 2015, Part IV, LNCS 9178, pp. 311–321, 2015.
DOI: 10.1007/978-3-319-20687-5_30

The merit of the current contribution are large-scale sports and show (entertainment) objects.[2] This paper consists of three parts:

- introduction;
- discussion of the tradition of large-scale objects for sports and entertainment;
- presentation of selected examples of sports arenas and stadiums in information driven era;
- summary and conclusions.

Probably the most important feature of modern architecture is a constant search for a diversity of solutions. We witness the disintegration of the regular, Cartesian net of spatial arrangements and in many modern examples we see the aesthetic and engineering capabilities in the transition from geometric to organic forms. The variability of form is accompanied by a variability and diversity of the material creating the new architectural space.

Architecture, in particular from the end of last century is a continuous search for novelty. Dariusz Kozłowski talks about searching novelty and weariness: "… the recipient can be weary, but it is rather the impatience of the bored artist, which drives the innovative character of solutions in ever new facilities" [2]. At this point doubts arise; on the one hand, architecture as Umberto Eco said, should contribute to the destruction of its own codes [3], on the other, according to Kozłowski, it should operate with elements understood by the recipients, elements which they are accustomed to. This characteristics gains particular gravitas when utility is the most important characteristics for the investor – when the object is to serve a particular function. Architecture of large forms is usually created for the needs of a person or an institution. In many cases, to the investor aesthetic matters are of secondary importance, more stress is placed on utility and the cost of the planned construction. In such cases, the architectural form and aesthetics of the solutions become important mainly for the anonymous recipient, the future user.

Architectural decisions concerning a large-scale – public – object, become important for the city in which the object is being created. Such an object, especially when it is architecturally characteristic and noticeable becomes an important element – an icon – of the urban landscape.

Objects serving shows and sports events have always been present in human cultures and new eras introduced contributions from previous generations, also in architecture. Each historical era, starting in antiquity, introduced into architecture a characteristic specific to its time. From the oldest times the balance between utility, durability and beauty have been a measure of the quality of architecture; logics of construction was added in the gothic and transfer of emotions, in baroque. From the last years of the 19th century until mid-20th century rationalism dressed in the philosophy of modernism was the most important feature which concerned the object and its context.

The medial modern times adapt to the increasing variability of social needs – the variability itself has various dimensions and stems from the need to individualize everything; as if in opposition to the increasing unification of the world, societies feel the need for individualization and the importance of non-standard solutions increases. This concerns

---

[2] The difference between the solutions of the hall and stadium was not explored as it did not seem important to the thoughts expressed here.

also architecture. This cognitive fluidity, the ability to freely amalgamate contents having their source in various spheres of interaction – functional, aesthetic, in "familiarity", identity, prestige – is encountered in current architecture. Such free combination of functional and aesthetics contents with the simultaneous availability of new design techniques and new technologies available in the realization of the work result in an extremely individual image of the architectural space. Innovation of the manner in which search for architectural solutions is performed is also a characteristic feature of sports architecture.

Apart from features common for a whole range of architectural solutions, large-scale sports arenas have features that distinguish them from others buildings. In authors' opinion the most important are:

– geometric nonlinearity – elliptical projection which is the result of a natural formal and functional shaping – it appears as a sine qua non element, equally in historic, as in modern arenas;
– spatial size – the need for a accumulation in one space – under one roof – of thousands of spectators and ensuring that they have a good view and sound;
– shaping of the form as a spatial reflection of the "architecture of emotions" – making a reference to places of events – creating objects whose core of functionality is enabling a joint experiencing of emotions;
– adaptability of solution as a results of a design process using advanced computer tools as well as their affordability as an answer to the changing market needs;
– accessibility of the space to various groups of users, which stems from pro-social legal requirements, architects' attitudes and economy of usage.

These features in confrontation with newly designed objects leads to the inference that nowadays sports architecture draws conclusions or provides solutions that are the effects of tradition and coexistence of sports and society spanning many centuries, as well as an effect of excellent contribution of computer aided design.

2 Sources of Tradition of Modern Sports Arenas

The title of the presentation contains a question of the uniqueness of the investigated objects. For the clarity of the message it is important to draw attention to some objects that seemingly contributed to the modern examples solutions and those mentioned special features that are important also today. The point of focus are: the Roman Colosseum, Wroclaw Centennial Hall, Katowice Spodek (pol. "saucer") Arena and the Munich Olympiastadion.

Colosseum, Rome, Italy 80 (Fig. 1). Known as the Flavian Amphitheatre, was erected in the 70 s of the first century of our era. This elliptical building measuring 156x188 m and having a height of 48.5 m was used for gladiators' fights, hunting for wild animal and similar spectacles funded by the emperor and Roman aristocrats. The auditorium could contain 50 000 sitting spectators located around the arena according to a strictly defined hierarchy: senators, the rich and less rich Romans from the lowest to higher rows. Women and commoners at the very top. On very hot or rainy days there was a possibility of partial coverage of the auditorium and arena. For this purpose velarium was used, a large, waterproof canvas stretched on ropes. The arena that measures 54x86 m was once covered with a wooden floor and a thick layer of sand. Two stores of cellars were located under the floor; they were used for keeping animals and humans participating in the spectacles. The cellar interiors had corridors, external exits and lifts which allowed to elevate large animals to the level of the arena. Also the auditorium had a well-conceived system, 80 entrances and exits allowing to distribute the spectators and for a relatively rapid exit from the object. The building survived hardly changed over many years and, even in the years of the fall of Rome AD 458 and 508, renovated. It was destroyed during an earthquake in 1349. From the mid-18th century it was under a constant care as a place commemorating the suffering of first Christians. It was also then when the tradition of the Stations of the Cross started, a procession within the ruins of the large amphitheatre on Good Friday. In 2007 the object has been included in the list of the "New7Wonders of the World" – the motto has become "joy and suffering". When today on TV screens around the world the Good Friday stations of the Cross can be viewed, we are still impressed by the magnificence and beauty of this place, as well as the vision of the architects and constructors of those times.

Centennial Hall, Wrocław, Poland 1913 (Fig. 1). This arena was designed by Max Berg and built to commemorate the 100th anniversary of the victory over Napoleon in the Battle of Leipzig. The hall served the international fairs. It was used for sports events, concerts, opera performances. In 2006, the object was included in the list of UNESCO World Heritage Site together with the four-dome pavilion authored by Hans Poelzig. The huge, expressionistic building inspires admiration thanks to the magnificent reinforced concrete construction. The construction of the large reinforced concrete dome (span of 62 m and height of 42 m) was at the time of construction the largest cupola in the world and a model for modernist solutions of similar constructions. The modernization of the elevation and the interior conducted in 2007 adapted the building to the use according to the current needs. The total reconstruction of the auditorium and lowering of the floor by 2.7 m allowed to increase the capacity to 10 000 spectators. The size of the arena is 25x45 m.

Spodek Arena, Katowice, Poland 1971 (Fig. 2). In the 1960s in Katowice, on the terrain of the old steelworks Franz and Fanny, next to the coal mine Ferdinand (Katowice), began the construction of a large object, sports and entertainment hall. It was created by the architects Maciej Gintowt, Jerzy Hryniewiecki and Maciej Krasiński and constructors Wacław Zalewski i Andrzej Żurawski[3]. The architecture of the this building is one of the most recognisable Polish sport and spectacle arenas. It is the prototype of the roof structure known in the world and in classic engineering designs as Geiger's Dome[4]. The geometry of the object can be imagined as an inverted cone with the base intersected by a slanted plane. The tilting of the roof is caused by the solution

---

[3] The creator of the spatial- construction concept was Wacław Zalewski, and after he left Poland Andrzej Żurawski.

[4] The dome of a span of 126 m has the shape of a tilted plate – hence the name "spodek" – in Polish: saucer. The construction system known as "tensegrity" ensures a perfect arrangement of tensions in the integrating structure According to M. Pelczarski "O kształtowaniu dachu katowickiej hali spodka. Rozważania z wywiadów z Profesorem Zalewskim" [w:] Architectus 2013 (34), WAPWr, Wrocław. DOI:105277/arc.130205 (On shaping the roof of the Katowice Spodek Arena. Discussions from interviews with Prof. Zalewski.).

of the interior, ensuring the alignment of the main seats on the tribune and ensuring the organization of the stage and auditorium. The worldwide unique formal, spatial and construction solutions are probably a result of cooperation and talent of the creators who had to face extremely difficult local foundation conditions - the object was built in the area of active mining damage. The hall of the "Spodek" Arena provides flexibility of spectacles, events, concerts and a wide offer of the mode of use of the rooms accompanying the main hall. The object was modernized in 2014, the audience was enlarged to ca. 8 000 people (some sources quote 10 000). In 2014, the hall was a witness of the happiness and emotions connected with the Polish men's team winning the World Championship in Volleyball.

The Olympiastadion, Munich, Germany 1972 (Fig. 2). The Olympic Stadium in Munich, designed by architect Gunter Boenish and constructor Otto Frei, was built on the occasion of The Olympic Games in 1972.[5] The authors accepted a task thinking of the motto of the Olympics: "The Happy Games". A concept of the stadium was to reflect the Alps, their rhythm, variability and the drama of the image. This idea was expressed by a curve of a hanging decking: acrylic panels supported by a cable structure suspended on vertical steel posts. The most notable feature is the great meaning of structure and, simultaneously, the feeling of emotional reception of the architecture of a place. The stadium, designed for 80 000 spectators, is a part of a sports complex located in the park area. The complex consists of a sports hall, stadium, swimming pools and other sport facilities, as well as an Olympic Village and a conference and press center. The mentioned fantastic acrylic roof was the most controversial issue for the inhabitants. Its size is approx. 80 000 square meters and it spreads over the stadium and a part of the Olympic Park. Extensive use of sports and entertainment function, along with the scale of the facility and clearly noticeable integration of land and architecture, made the structure the biggest tourist attraction of the city.

3 Large–Scale Sports Architecture in the Era of Information

On the one hand contemporary state-of-the-art architecture for sport and entertainment for sure fits to thoughts of architects deconstructivists "Coop Himmelb(l)au": "We want architecture that has more to offer. Architecture that bleeds, exhausts, that turns and even breaks... Architecture that glows, that stabs, that tears and rips when stretched. Architecture must be precipitous, fiery, smooth, hard, angular, brutal, round, tender, colorful, obscene, randy, dreamy, en-nearing, distancing, wet, dry and heart-stopping. Dead or alive. If it is cold, then cold as a block of ice. If it is hot, then as hot as a tongue of flame. Architecture must burn!".[6] In such reference (going parallel to thinking about the structure) it seems that today the most simple and most obvious way is to "sell"

---

[5] According to: www.archdaily.com/109136/ad-classics-munich-olympic-stadium-frei-otto-gunter-benisch.

[6] http://en.wikipedia.org/wiki/Coop_Himmelb(l)au; Their Sports' Arenas projects: "Rhein Main Arena" in Germany 2006 (Frankfurt/M), "Soccer Stadium Zaragoza" in Spain 2008 (Zaragoza) or "Silk Leaf Stadium" in Japan 2012 (Tokyo).

emotions outside the object, outside place where the event is held, through not only architectural form, but also illumination and changing pictures around. On the other hand such large scale architecture posses characteristic feature - adaptability of solution that can be reached depending on the needs of the specific event or the time of using. Certainly those are possible thanks to modern, controlled by a computer, progressive technology. To illustrate such thesis several examples of the objects are discussed below: National Stadium in Beijing, Allianz Arena in Munich, Municipal Stadium in Wroclaw (Breslau), Arena Kraków in Cracow, Wembley Stadium in London, Aquatics Centre in London, AAMI Park Stadium in Melbourne.

"Bird's Nest", Beijing, China 2008 (Fig. 3)**.** Named "Bird's nest" Beijing National Stadium was designed by the duo Jacques Herzog and Pierre de Meuron for The Olympic Games in Beijing in 2008. China, with its philosophy of metaphoric way of seeing the reality, was a difficult market for the team of architects known for treating architecture very literally: "A building is a building. It cannot be read like a book; it doesn't have any credits, subtitles or labels like picture in a gallery. In that sense, we are absolutely anti-representational. The strength of our buildings is the immediate, visceral impact they have on a visitor". Jacques Herzog.[7] Prior to the competition architects, conscious of the need to refer to the local culture and the Chinese passion for metaphors as well as the risk of encountering cultural differences, asked the Chinese artist Ai Weiwei to cooperate. From the beginning of work representatives of Arup Company, later responsible for detail designs including the structure, were participating in the project. Already at the stage of the competition Arup designers created a CAD model of the building proposing a system of pillars and beams hidden in the thicket of elements. "Bird's Nest" is one of the largest stadiums in the world (220 m x 320 m, 70 m high) – it accommodated 91 000 spectators during the Olympic Games. Due to the risk of earthquakes the stadium structure was designed as two independent structures – reinforced concrete stadium bowl and a steel "shell" forming the walls and the roof over the stands. Both the stadium bowl and its cover were designed using parametric methods (CATIA software v.5 by Dassault Systeme) enabling changes and testing alternatives. Later stages of parametric design defined shapes of membrane fillings (ETFE) between structural elements. Digital models, used in the initial phase of the project, did not decide on the shape and the nature of the building. They were rather used for optimizing assumptions, testing them, reducing costs and for preparing documentation. Ultimately, the work of an international team "has nested" in its place not thanks to models, but thanks to conscious and derivative references to the local identity.

Allianz Arena, Munich, Germany 2005 (Fig. 3)**.** The history of Allianz Arena Stadium in Munich is a history of emotions. The history originates from the decision of FC Bayern to resign from the use of the existing Olympic stadium designed by Gunter Benisch and Frei Otto. After a heated discussion the idea to renovate the stadium was rejected and two Munich clubs (FC Bayern and TSV 1860) decided on a joint realization of a brand new stadium. A competition was announced and later won by

---

[7] Words of Jacques Herzog [in] "The Pritzker Architectural Prize Jacques Herzog and Pierre de Meuron 2001 Laureates Biography" Martha Thorne, Executive Director. The Pritzker Architecture Prize 2001 The Hyatt Foundation.

Herzog & de Meuron architecture firm. The stadium size is 200 x 250 m and it is 50 m high. The stadium capacity is over 70 000 spectators. The structure of the stadium and technical solutions of the exterior are designed by Ove Arup & Partners. An innovative concept is the solution which enables color changes of the entire structure depending on what team is playing. For example: when Bayern plays – the color is red, when TSV plays – the color is blue. Such an idea needs a façade which enables easy color change. The architects proposed covering the facade with large ETFE foil (ethylene-tetrafluoroethylene) "pillows" lit from the inside by white fluorescent tubes. There is approx. 2,8 thousand of such "pillows" in the façade, each of a different shape and size. Detail solutions (precise shape, mounting points, seals shapes, apertures) were developed by Covertex Company with advanced parametric CAD/CAM solutions and a form-finding technology. Colors can be changed in the real time, independently for each "pillow". Thanks to that the stadium can reflect ongoing events and react to the emotions of spectators. All that, combined with the fact that the stadium can be seen from the distance of many kilometers, shows architecture as a real emotion transmitter.

Municipal Stadium in Wrocław, Wroclaw, Poland 2011 (Fig. 4). The stadium was built as a part of an investment associated with "UEFA European Football Championship" organized in Poland and in Ukraine in 2012. It was designed by a polish consortium JSK Architects (also known for designing "The National Stadium" in Warsaw). The stadium looks like a lantern which symbolizes the dynamic development of the city of Wroclaw. The project distinguisher is a fiberglass mesh covered with Teflon and mounted on steel rings around the stadium. This semitransparent façade gave the lightness to the stadium. Specially designed lighting allows the change of colors around the circuit, depending on the event taking place. The capacity of tribunes oscillates around 43 000. Different events were planned at the stadium (sports, concerts and mass events).

Arena Kraków, Cracow, Poland 2014 (Fig. 4). Tauron Arena Kraków is a sports and entertainment hall completed in Poland in Cracow in 2014. It was designed by a consortium of companies: Perbo-Projekt Sp. z o.o. from Cracow and Modern Construction Systems Sp. z o.o. from Poznan. The hall was created to host "Volleyball Men's World Cup" in the same year. It is currently the largest in Poland and one of the most modern facilities of this kind in Europe. It accommodates, depending on the event (sports, concerts, congresses, exhibitions, etc.), from 11 000 up to 18 000 spectators. Its façade is a distinctive architectural element (its special feature). It is the largest LED screen in Poland (with a height of 14 m) encircling the hall all along its perimeter. The screen enables projection of the events taking place inside the hall or it is used for advertising.

Wembey Stadium, London, Great Britain 2007 (Fig. 5). Reconstruction and expansion of the old Wembley Stadium (built in 1923) is an unprecedented example of a new quality and spectacularity of a national sports facility. The authors of architectural changes were Foster & Partners and HOK Sport (Populous after 2009). The stadium can seat up to 90 000 people and it is the second largest (right after Spanish "Camp Nou") stadium in Europe. Like other discussed objects, it is multifunctional. For example in case of athletic competitions the level of the floor is raised 3 meters up (reducing the number of seats to 68 000). According to the designers, the stadium façade (besides the glass entrance area) was supposed to be neutral to emhasize the line of thr construction arch. This arch is the strongest architectural element: it is 133 m high, 315 m long, and its diameter is 7 m at the widest point. During the night the arch is illuminated and it can be seen from distant parts of London. Lightning conditions as well as ventilation conditions were modeled digitally for the best evaluation of the grass growth level.

Aquatics Centre, London, Great Britain 2012 (Fig. 5). A competition to design "London Aquatics Centre" was won by Zaha Hadid. The building was completed in 2012. Swimming competitions took place in The Centre during The Olympic Games. Organic architecture of "Aquatics Centre" is characteristic for its designer. The object is formed by a decking inspired, according to the author, by changeability of waving water. To complete the designed spatial effect, the collaborating Arup firm used complex and integrated digital models enabling constant interbranch coordination. These tools enabled implementing possibilities of adapting the building for further needs. Under the decking are swimming pools and an auditorium for 2 500 people. Originally the project assumed a greater auditorium (for approx. 15 000 people) decked with a three times bigger roof. During the initial analysis it was calculated that the total cost, including construction and maintenance, significantly exceeds the budget. This caused a change in the approach to the project. Reduction of the size of the Center and construction of temporary auditoriums on both sides of the structure were proposed. Thanks to that the Centre accommodated 17 000 spectators during the Olympics. Temporary tribunes included not only auditoriums but also some of the service rooms (e.g. toilets). It was not until the end of the Olympics when the Centre received its proper shape. Tribunes were removed and sold and side walls of the building were closed with glazing.

AAMI Park Stadium, Melbourne, Australia 2010 (Fig. 6). The newest stadium in Melbourne is an initiative of Victoria State authorities. It was built in 2010 and its capacity is about 30 000 spectators. The city, despite having a number of large-scale sports facilities, did not have a stadium for football and rugby matches. The AAMI Park Stadium was designed by Cox Architects and Planners and detail projects were completed by Arup firm. Arup was engaged to develop tribune structure, the stadium shell, fittings, and the mass motion analysis. 80 % of seats are decked with a characteristic shell roofing (180 x130 m). The roof is the biggest architectural attraction of the structure and it consists of 20 intersecting geodesic shells. Each shell forms a slice of a geometrized flattened sphere consisting of a net of triangular planes. These planes are filled with metal panels or with a transparent material. Roof generatrices were covered with a mesh of LED lamps from the inside. Thanks to a digital control, lamps can generate changing images on the surface. Therefore the stadium, like other mentioned previously, can transmit emotions experienced at the stadium. To create the geometry of the stadium many parametric digital tools were used. During the concept stage a combination of Catia models and 3-D CAD was used (with Cox Architects and RMIT University's Spatial Information Architecture Laboratory). During later stages of the project Arup company used Bentley's Generative Components software enabling dynamic analysis of structure tensions, its parametric modifications, and verifying calculations in the real time. Further optimizations were conducted on analytic software dedicated specifically to Arup needs. After completing optimization the parametric model was imported to the Bentley Systems software and it was used to generate documentation. An independent and interesting matter was a digital optimization of a functional structure of the building. As the complex consists not only of the stadium, but of many accompanying functions, an attempt to analyze the model of visitor traffic, inflow and outflow of fans and their evacuation was undertaken. To do that software for analyzing the movement of masses was used (Oasys MassMotion). The software enables tracking and analyzing in 3-dimentional model environment of human motions represented by single avatars (in this case 31 000 "agents" were used). Vertical and horizontal circulation, waiting areas in front of entrances and ticket offices were analyzed considering various sports events. On the basis of these analyses several changes were made in the functional structure of the building (i.e. staircases were widened and redesigned). The whole project required close cooperation between architects, other designers, and consultants to develop an optimal solution.

Fig. 1. [L.] Colosseum, Rome, Italy, 80 ("New7Wonders of the World" list 2007). Capacity: 50 000; [R.] Centennial Hall, Wrocław, Poland, 1913 (UNESCO list 2006). Capacity: 8 000 (Author: Adam Gil).

Fig. 2. [L.] Spodek Arena, Katowice, Poland, 1971. Capacity: 11 500; [R.] The Olympiastadion, Munich, Germany, 1972. Capacity: 69 2500 (Author: Adam Gil).

Fig. 3. [L.] "Bird's Nest", Beijing, China, 2008. Capacity: 80 000 (Olimpic Games 2008: 91 000); [R.] Allianz Arena, Munich, Germany, 2005. Capacity: 70 000 (Author: Adam Gil).

Fig. 4. [L.] Municipal Stadium in Wrocław, Wroclaw, Poland, 2011. Capacity: 45 105; [R.] Arena Kraków, Cracow, Poland, 2014. Capacity: 22 800 (Author: Adam Gil).

Fig. 5. [L.] Wembey Stadium, London, Great Britain 2007. Capacity: 90 000; [R.] Aquatics Centre, London, Great Britain, 2012. Capacity: 2 500 (Olimpic Games 2012: 17 500) (Author: Adam Gil).

Fig. 6. [L.] AAMI Park Stadium, Melbourne, Austalia, 2010. Capacity: 30 050; [R.] Stonhenge, Wiltshire, Great Britain, prehistoric (UNESCO list 1986) (Author: Adam Gil).

4 Summary and Conclusions

At the beginning of our deliberations on forming architecture of large – scale structures for sports and entertainment two periods were distinguished for the purpose of the paper. Summarizing the period of seventies to the twentieth century one notices a particular influence of structural solutions on an architectural concept. The innovation of the structure is the most important feature for the meaning of architecture. It influences significantly the importance of architecture when considering the history and the theory. In contemporary architectural discourse appears a notion of "an event" which takes place in urban space. Bernard Tschumi increases the meaning of an event which takes place in space and combines architecture with the idea, experiencing and using. He writes: "The value of architecture no longer results from creating shapes in space, but rather from fostering relationships within it. Combined relationships and actions – reactions in (and for) a definitively "open" and non-predetermined reality; the more qualitative, the more potentially interactive in positive synergy with environment. This point to a latent change in the figure of architect, no longer formable only in terms of a designer of objects, but rather in that of "strategist of processes" [4].

A characteristic feature of contemporary large-scale sports and entertainment facilities is attention to the functionality of solutions, expressed by accessibility to all potential participants of the show, while preserving the diversity of esthetic and formal solutions. Modern development of techniques and technologies of constructing allows expressing users' emotions also trough the architectural form of a building. This occurs at the fullest in the night when a building is illuminated with colors of joy, emotions and optimism. Both in the past and today, a cooperation of architectural solutions and structural concepts is the greatest value of these large structures. However one element always remains constant: as in the mythical Stonehenge we like to experience emotions in a circle (Fig. 6).

Returning to the question, included in the title of the paper, one can conclude, after analyzing the examples, that contemporary sports architecture probably would not emerge without computer software. The ongoing studies [1, 5] allow noticing a tendency for humanizing, as well as dehumanizing the form of a building. Whilst many examples lead to a conclusion that the increasing flexibility of tools enhances the designer's work possibilities (leading to humanization of architectural space), other examples may suggest occurrence of "Uncanny Valley"[8] effect. Creating architecture, which is dedicated to people, can actually lead to dehumanization of architectural space. If we agree on the fact that architecture is in close relation with art, we will also approve a fact that the development of modern information technologies changes communication conventions in art. The development of the artistic activity stored as a digital layer, understandable for the calculating machine, leads to further integration of cultural and digital meanings. Information sharing can be performed thanks to the transfer into the bit language. Looking at the process of creating architectural space itself, one can notice further opportunities as well as new "traps". An architect – a designer who is overwhelmed by new system solutions must find the balance in the variety of choices. In the pursuit of endless originality and shortening the design process, solutions may occur as products repeated in fragments or in greater parts …
Architecture in the past and in the present is developed in the struggle between a creative thought of the designer and the social context, expectations of the investor and the client.

References

1. Juzwa, N., Ujma-Wasowicz, K.: Large scale architecture. Design human factors and ergonomics aspects based on state-of-the-art structures. Does new architectural geometry require a reinspection of comfortable usage and the user's emotions? In: Conference Proceedings 4th International Conference on Applied Human Factors and Ergonomics AHFE International 2012, pp. 3580–3589 (2012)
2. Kozłowski, D.: Defining the architectural space. Durability and Fleeternes of Architecture. In: Czasopismo Techniczne, pp. 208–209. Krakow (2011)
3. Eco, U.: Pejzaż semiotyczny. PWN, p. 324. Warszawa (1982)
4. Tschumi, B.: Event Cities, p. 69. MIT Press, London (2001)
5. Juzwa, N., Gil, A., Sulimowska-Ociepka, A., Witeczek, A.: Architektura i Urbanistyka współczesnego przemysłu. Wydział Architektury Politechnika Śląska, Gliwice (2010)

---

[8] The term was drawn from the terminology which functions in robotics. Moris's influence on the world of robotics is immeasurable. His classic hypothesis the "UncannyValley" published in 1970, is still key work defining robotic design.

The Impact of Solar Radiation on the Quality of Buildings: Research Methods

Dariusz Masły, Michał Sitek[✉], and Klaudiusz Fross

Faculty of Architecture, The Silesian University of Technology,
ul. Akademicka 7, 44-100 Gliwice, Poland
{dariusz.masly,michal.sitek,klaudiusz.fross}@polsl.pl

Abstract. Daylight analyses presented in this paper are fragments of a wider research project. The daylight simulation study focused on the influence of various facade solutions on lighting environment in office buildings located in the south of Poland. The development of scientific principles lying behind correctly daylit workspaces in offices was the main project's aim. The another, equally crucial purpose was the development of design guidelines for office buildings in the southern Poland. Selected architectural solutions were compared in this study. They included facade solutions (window placements and shapes, glazing-to-wall (GWR) ratios), solar radiation reflectors (light shelves) and deflectors (venetian blinds). Moreover two types of daylight performance metrics were explored, static and dynamic. The objective of this document is to promote the use of the most advanced and sophisticated computer simulation methods, techniques and tools for sustainable building design regarding quality of daylit indoor environment.

Keywords: Daylight analysis · Indoor environment quality · Natural lighting design strategies · Sustainable office buildings

1 Introduction

A recent study showed that most architects don't understand energy use, even though they acknowledge its importance. Architects in all types and sizes of practice can and should be leaders in energy modeling, taking responsibility as designers for assuring that buildings perform to high standards. To do so, we must learn new terms, strategies, and methods of calculation, as well as how to integrate this knowledge into the early decision making of a project. Design of modern buildings should be carried out using the knowledge about conditions at a particular location, taking into account the environmental and urban space conditions. Using knowledge about conditions at a particular location and Climate Base analysis, we can plan and test different variants of solar geometry and architectural solutions for building models in order to select the optimal strategy of passive. The purpose of the passive design is the search for solutions that will reduce pEUI = predicted Energy Use Intensity the facility demand for energy.

The passive design is based upon climate considerations, attempts to control comfort (heating and cooling) without consuming fuels. Easiest way to control heat gain and heat loss and air flow is to use proper orientation and shape of the building. This actions helps

© Springer International Publishing Switzerland 2015
M. Antona and C. Stephanidis (Eds.): UAHCI 2015, Part IV, LNCS 9178, pp. 322–331, 2015.
DOI: 10.1007/978-3-319-20687-5_31

also to maximize the use of free solar energy for heating and lighting and apply a free natural ventilation for building cooling. This can be achieved by finding such a building solid geometry to reduce its overheating. Therefore, in the study of the location of the object is needed to simulate the effect of body shaping to reduce energy gains. Reducing susceptibility to overheating of the object, we must bear in mind the special role in the preservation of natural light comfort. Architects must relearn how to use shade (natural or architectural) to control heat gain. Modern building facades are like balloons, very thin, and very important to the overall energy efficiency of the structure. They are also an expression of architect skills and create the building image-quality [17]. Office buildings and other objects studied in Poland as a university [18] or laboratory facilities [19] are particularly sensitive to the formation of the facade. This is due to the particular climatic conditions. Proper technical solution of the building envelope with planned routes depths less than 5 m, create a user-friendly environment. The authors decided to investigate the effect of solar radiation on the conditions in office buildings with a detailed analysis of the quality of daylight available for selected weather conditions, geolocation, and other technical - forming elements of the facade.

2 Researches - Introduction

Daylight analyses presented in this paper are fragments of a wider research project [11]. The daylight simulation study focused on the influence of various facade solutions on lighting environment in office buildings located in the south of Poland. The development of scientific principles lying behind correctly daylit workspaces in offices was the main project's aim. The another, equally crucial purpose was the development of design guidelines for office buildings in the southern Poland. Selected architectural solutions were compared in this study. They included facade solutions (window placements and shapes, glazing-to-wall (GWR) ratios), solar radiation reflectors (light shelves) and deflectors (venetian blinds). Moreover two types of daylight performance metrics were explored, static and dynamic. The objective of this document is to promote the use of the most advanced and sophisticated computer simulation methods, techniques and tools for sustainable building design regarding quality of daylit indoor environment.

3 Researches - Theoretical Background

The thesis that daylight and a view of the outside are appreciated by buildings' users have been proved by numerous researches in recent years. The effects of properly daylit indoor spaces are linked to advantages for occupants' productivity, learning, health and wellbeing [3, 5, 7–9]. A relatively new area of study is non-visual, physiological effects of daylight on human biological processes [1]. Daylight controls many biochemical processes in the human body, for example it synchronises the circadian clock and regulates discretion of hormones. More and more researches are showing that indoor lighting standards are inadequate for biological stimulation. Numerous studies have recently been devoted to an estimation of physical, quantitative measures: light distribution, daylight factors, illuminance and luminance [2, 4, 6, 8, 10, 11, 14, 15].

This study was based on three main conclusions. They were:

1. daylight is desirable by office's occupants and has an enormous influence on users' comfort, health and well-being,
2. the most promising strategy for energy efficiency and visual comfort in Polish offices appears to be the use of exterior automated retractable venetian blinds [10, 11],
3. 100 % glazed offices do not provide significantly more daylight at the height of office desk than offices glazed from table height up to a suspended ceiling [2, 10, 11].

4   Researches - Methods

This paper presents results of daylight computer simulations done for 4 different facades of an office building, various window placements, shapes, and glazing-to-wall (GWR) ratios were analysed. Various ways to distribute and redirect daylight (light shelves) and shading devices (venetian blinds) were also compared. The simulations were made with the assistance of the Autodesk Ecotect, Radiance, Daysim and Evalglare software. The reference office represented a south-facing sidelit open-plan office located in Cracow in the southern part of Poland (latitude: 50°N, longitude: 20°E). The footprint of the analysed building was designed along the east-west axis. The building was not obstructed by any objects in the neighbourhood. The analysed floor area was intended to give daylighting conditions typical of an open-plan space in a naturally ventilated and daylit office building with a narrow floor plate. The office room was situated on the second floor of a four-story office building. Its dimensions were: 10.8 m in width, 9.0 m in depth (office area of 97.2 m^2), a suspended ceiling was placed at a level of 3.0 m. The four facades' glass area-to-wall area ratios were as follows, see Fig. 1: O1 – 25 % (8 m^2/32.4 m^2); O2 – 60 % (19.5 m^2/32.4 m^2); O4 – 27 % (8.6 m^2/32. 4 m^2); O5C – 33 %

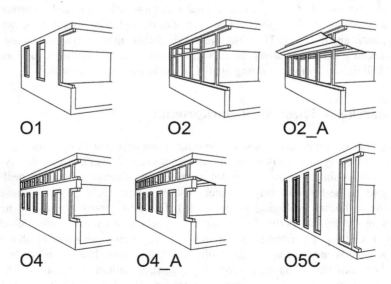

O1   O2   O2_A

O4   O4_A   O5C

Fig. 1. Analysed facades

(10.6 m²/32.4 m²). The visual transmittance of the double glazing was 64 %. The reflectances of room surfaces were: ceiling – 85 %, floor – 35 %, walls – 65 %, light-shelf – 70 %, blinds – 63 % and furniture – 50 %. An analysis grid of "virtual sensors" was located on a plane 80 cm above the floor. That was approximately at a height of a standard office desk. During the computer simulations conventional, static daylight performance metrics as well as dynamic performance metrics were applied.

4.1   Static Daylight Performance Metrics

Static daylight performance metrics include daylight factor, view to the outside, and avoidance of direct sunlight. The static daylight studies consisted of three parts. Daylight Factor levels analyses, illuminance levels analyses and visual comfort analyses were done successively. Daylight factor is the superior static quantitative performance metric, it is the most widely used one, and it remains the only widely accepted one [13]. It is defined as the ratio of the internal illuminance at a point in a building to the external horizontal illuminance. DF is calculated under a CIE overcast sky. DF of 2 % on the work plane is at the present time recommended as an adequate daylighting level for office work. The first part of the static studies was devoted to the influence of various facade solutions on daylight availability (DF levels). The differences in lighting conditions are displayed in Fig. 2. The main limitations of the DF metric results from the fact that it does not consider season, time of day, direct solar ingress, variable sky conditions, building orientation, and building location [13]. The consequences are that DF analyses cannot help to develop shading strategies and glare prevention strategies. The aim of the two successive parts of the static studies (illuminance levels analyses and visual comfort analyses) was to balance

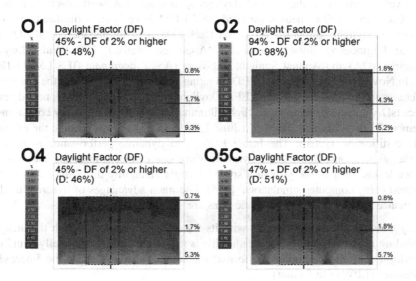

Fig. 2. Calculated daylight factor

DF metric limitations. Authors used a method of static daylight analyses, combining three types of analyses.

1. Daylight Factor levels analyses: they enabled preliminary assessment of architectural solutions. The worst cases were rejected. Selected solutions that had been best performing were analysed comprehensively.
2. Comprehensive analysis of lighting conditions throughout the year: illuminance levels (lx) analyses were done for two days of the year: 21st of June (summer extreme regarding solar heights) and 21st of March (the midpoint of the year). Sunny conditions were studied. The crucial aim of this part of the study was to evaluate the influence of various shading systems (external retractable venetian blinds 30° and redirecting blinds 5° + 30°) and lightshelves. Significant limitation of the analyses was that only the performance of fixed shading devices could be simulated. In practice Authors considered firstly various blinds' slat angles (0°, 15°, 30°, 45°) to find a glare free environment (see next point), secondly illuminance levels analyses were done for optimal lighting environment. The other goal was to ensure that direct sunlight was avoided.
3. Visual comfort analyses - luminance levels analyses (cd/m^2). It was assumed that if a value of luminance had not exceed the recommended maximum value of $2000 \ cd/m^2$, a glare free environment would have been achieved.

4.2 Dynamic Performance Metrics

An alternative to the static daylight performance metrics are dynamic ones. They are founded on a precise computational method called 'climate-based daylight modelling' (CBDM). The concept of dynamic performance metrics is relatively new, an incomparable level of activity in the field of daylighting research has been observed in recent years. Until now a few metrics founded on CBDM have been formulated, the most popular are Daylight Autonomy (DA) and Useful Daylight Illuminance (UDI). US Illuminating Engineering Society published 'Approved Method: IES Spatial Daylight Autonomy (sDA) and Annual Sunlight Exposure (ASE)' document (IES LM-83-12) in 2013. In November 2013 the new LEED v4 rating system was launched at the Greenbuild Conference in Philadelphia and the LEED Daylight credit changed entirely, new dynamic metrics (sDA and ASE) replaced daylight illuminance levels in a clear sky conditions on September 21 at 9 a.m. and 3 p.m.. At June 1, 2015 LEED v4 will become the exclusive LEED certification system. The future belongs to dynamic performance metrics and computer simulations. Reinhart has written: 'since one cannot realistically measure illuminance levels for a whole year in a space, daylight autonomy distributions have to be calculated using computer simulations' [x15]. The main advantages of dynamic daylight performance metrics compared to static ones are:

• they consider the actual climate with its weather variations in which the analysed building is placed (An annual weather file is imported while dynamically simulating daylight. The most popular file format for annual weather data is the EnergyPlus Weather (EPW) file format);

- some daylighting computer programmes enable simulating of the performance of dynamic shading devices;
- the new approach considers too occupant requirements of the building.

The daylighting tool that was used to carry out dynamic daylight simulation was Daysim. This is Radiance-based simulation program. A grid of upward facing illuminance sensors that extended throughout an area of 10.8 m (width) x 6.0 m (depth) was defined. The grid resolution was 0.325 m x 0.25 m. Sensors were placed at 0.8 m above the floor (work plane height). Some of these sensors were selected as sensors close to where the occupant who operated shadings was located (core work plane sensors). Four cases of user behaviour were analysed (Daysim uses the Lightswitch algorithm (user behaviour model) created by Christoph Reinhart):

- no shading: space without shading;
- active A: dynamic shading device, active user sitting near the window;
- active B: dynamic shading device, active user sitting at depth of 5.0 m;
- passive: passive user.

Different user behaviours and locations of an occupant that controls shading devices were simulated to evaluate extreme daylighting conditions in an open-plan office. Dynamic shading device (venetian blinds) were controlled manually. Annual illuminance profiles were calculated for two shading device settings (blinds up, blinds down - slat angle of 45°). The analysed office was occupied from 8.00 to 17.00, Monday to Friday, and the minimum illuminance level was 500 lx.

5 Researches - Results

The first part of the static daylight studies (DF analyses) showed that although the glass area of facade O5C was larger than of facades O1 and O4, the DF values were almost the same, see Fig. 2. The conclusion is that the best solution is a glazing from table height up to a suspended ceiling. The highest light levels are for the case O2 that represents the best facade for an office building. The most interesting are the results of sunny conditions analyses after sidelighting systems and shading devices were proposed. Proper design choices (example of facade O4_A) can improve lighting conditions significantly, what is seen in Fig. 3.

Dynamic daylighting studies identified also the facade O4_A as the best case (the optimal reference case O2 is not considered), see Fig. 4. Moreover, they showed the percentage of the year when required illuminance levels were achieved by daylight alone. Authors calculated all the most popular dynamic daylight performance metrics: Daylight Autonomy, Useful Daylight Illuminances, Continuous Daylight Autonomy. Useful daylight levels (UDI 100-2000 lx) and exceeded UDI (> 2000 lx) for the cases O1 and O4 are displayed in Figs. 5 and 6. Results for various cases of user behaviour are also interesting. The best design solution should guarantee a comfortable daylight environment regardless of user behaviour. Seen from this point of view, the case O4_A performs incomparably better than O1.

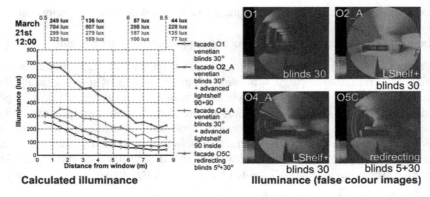

Calculated illuminance   **Illuminance (false colour images)**

Fig. 3. Illuminance levels analyses - 21st of March (the midpoint of the year)

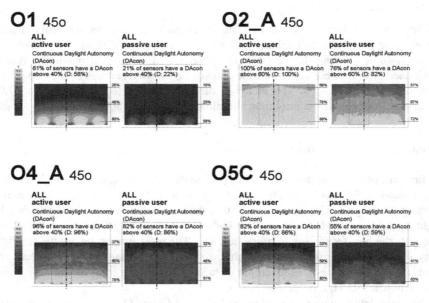

Fig. 4. Selected dynamic daylight performance metrics: Continuous Daylight Autonomy, Useful Daylight Illuminances 100–2000.

The O5C case represents one of the most fashionable facade solutions in recent years. The daylight analyses results confirm that fashionable facade solutions very often decrease the daylight levels and do not provide a balanced daylight distribution throughout the room.

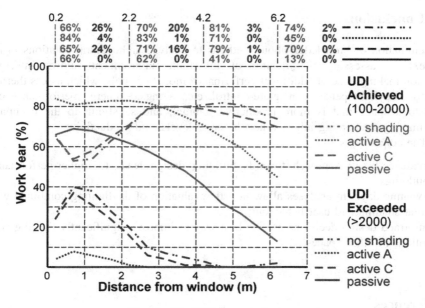

Fig. 5. O1: UDI – user behaviour

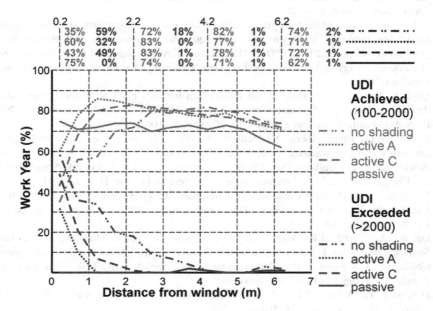

Fig. 6. O4: UDI – user behaviour

6 Conclusions

Dissemination of knowledge about methods to analyze architectural solutions in the context of assessing the quality of the built environment allows informed decision-making. Use of additional performance modeling tools, which assess thermal comfort, daylight penetration, glare-control, etc., alongside energy performance can lead to a space that is more productive, vibrant, and satisfying to the occupant. Maximizing daylighting improve health, stress levels, and productivity.

The conclusions are:

- evidence-based approach towards building design leads to higher-performance buildings;
- dynamic daylight analyses allow holistic evaluation of daylighting combined with solar shading and user behaviour;
- informed design decisions are the best way to improve significantly lighting conditions in office spaces.

References

1. Altomonte, S.: Daylight and the Occupant. Visual and physio-psychological well-being in built environments, PLEA 2009 - The 26th Conference on Passive and Low Energy Architecture, Quebec City (2009)
2. Bulow-Hube, H.: Daylight in glazed office buildings. A comparative study of daylight availability, luminance and illuminance distribution for an office room with three different glass areas. (Report EBD-R–08/17). Department of Architecture and Built Environment, Division of Energy and Building Design, Lund University, Faculty of Engineering, Lund, Sweden (2008)
3. Choi, J., Beltran, L.O.: Study of the relationship between patients' recovery and indoor daylight environment of patient rooms in healthcare facilities. In: Proceedings of the 2004 ISES Asia-Pacific Conference, Korea, 17–20 October (2004)
4. Dubois, M.C., Blomsterberg, A., Flodberg, K.: Towards zero energy office buildings in northern europe: preliminary results of daylighting simulations. In: SB11 Helsinki - 6th World Sustainable Building (SB) Conference, proceedings, vol. 1, Finnish Association of Civil Engineers RIL, VTT Technical Research Centre of Finland, Helsinki (2011)
5. Fontoynont, M.: Daylight Performance of Buildings. James & James (Science Publishers) Ltd. for the European Commission Directorate General XII for Science, Research and Development, London (1999)
6. Galasiu, A.D., Atif, M.R.: Applicability of Daylighting Computer Modelling in Real Case Studies: Comparison between Measured and Simulated Daylight Availability and Lighting Consumption. A report of IEA (International Energy Agency) SHC Task 21/ IEA ECBCS Annex 29: Daylight in Buildings, November 1998
7. Heschong, L., Wright, R.L., Okura, S.: Daylighting impacts on human performance in school. J. Illum. Eng. Soc. **31**, 101–114 (2002)

8. International Energy Agency: Daylighting in Buildings. A Source Book on DaylightingSystems and Components. A Report of IEA Solar Heating & Cooling Task 21/Energy Conservation in Buildings and Community Systems Annex 29. Lawrence Berkeley National Laboratory, USA, July 2000. http://gaia.lbl.gov/iea21/
9. Keeler, M., Burke, B.: Fundamentals of Integrated Design for Sustainable Building. Wiley, Hoboken (2009)
10. Masły, D., Sitek, M.: Zastosowanie symulacji komputerowych do analizy wpływu rozwiązań elewacyjnych na jakość oświetlenia naturalnego w biurowcach (The Use of Daylight Simulation Studies to Analyse the Influence of Facade Solutions on Quality of Daylight in Offices). In: Bać, A., Kasperski, J. (eds.) Kierunki rozwoju budownictwa energooszczędnego i wykorzystania odnawialnych źródeł energii na terenie Dolnego Śląska. Praca zbiorowa, Oficyna Wydawnicza Politechniki Wrocławskiej, Wrocław, Poland (2013)
11. Masły, D., Sitek, M.: Analysis of natural lighting with regard to design of sustainable office buildings in poland. In: Stephanidis, C., Antona, M. (eds.) UAHCI 2014, Part IV. LNCS, vol. 8516, pp. 227–236. Springer, Heidelberg (2014)
12. Niezabitowska, E., Masły, D.: Research Projects in the field of architecture – experiences of the faculty of architecture at the silesian university of technology in gliwice, poland. In: ICERI 2010 - International Conference of Education, Research and Innovation, Proceedings of International Conference, IATED, Madryt, Hiszpania, November 2010
13. Reinhart, C.F., Mardaljevic, J., Rogers, Z.: Dynamic daylight performance metrics for sustainable building design. Leukos 2006 3(1), 1–25 (2006)
14. Reinhart, C.F., Petinelli, G.: Advanced Daylight Simulations Using Ecotect, Radiance, Daysim – Getting Started. National Research Council Canada, Institute for Research in Construction (2006)
15. Reinhart, C.F., Wienold, J.: The daylighting dashboard – a simulation-based design analysis for daylit spaces. Build. Environ. 46, 386–396 (2011)
16. Reinhart, C.: Daylighting Handbook I. Fundamentals Designing with the Sun (2014)
17. Tymkiewicz, J.: The Advanced Construction of Facades. The Relations Between the Quality of Facades and the Quality of Buildings. Book Group Author(s): Kaunas Univ Technology Press, Conference: 2nd International Conference on Advanced Construction; Location: Kaunas Univ Technol, Kaunas, Lithuania; Date: November 11–12, 2010; Book Series: Advanced Construction, pp. 274–281 Published: 2010
18. Winnicka-Jasłowska, D.: Internet Based - Study on Users's needs. Students' functional and Spatial needs in facilities of Architecture Faculties at technical Universities in Poland. A. Ajdukiewicz (eds.): ACEE Architecture, Civil Engineering, Environment, vol 1 1/2008, The Silesian University of Technology, Gaudeo (2008)
19. Winnicka-Jasłowska, D.: Ergonomic solutions of facilities and laboratory work-stands at universities. In: Stephanidis, C., Antona, M. (eds.) UAHCI 2014, Part IV. LNCS, vol. 8516, pp. 314–321. Springer, Heidelberg (2014)

The Human Factor in the Revitalization of the Historic Polish Cities

Robert Masztalski[✉]

Faculty of Architecture, Wroclaw University of Technology, Wroclaw, Poland
robert.masztalski@pwr.edu.pl

Abstract. There are cities in Poland, which suffered as a result of World War 2, and after 66 years is still not rebuilt. This is particularly true of historic towns with historical pedigree. The monument conservators trying to keep full control over the reconstruction of these city centers and are blocking investment processes. Revitalization of these areas needs to be redefined in terms of procedures of conservation of cultural heritage in the context of modern ergonomic requirements. Case study is the city of Strzelin in the south-west Poland.

Keywords: Modern ergonomic requirements · Revitalization · Historic cities in Poland

1 Introduction

2nd half of the twentieth century was not lucky for the small towns of Lower Silesia. Most of them survived the war with more or less damage. The scale of devastation in the case of the Strzelin town center reached even 90 %. The destruction of small towns of Lower Silesia as a result of World War 2 of up to 50 % or more, occurred in such units as: Międzyborz, Wasocz, Nowogrodziec, Bierutow, Scinawa, Piensk, Sobotka, Sycow, Trzebnica, Wołow, Strzelin, Brzeg Dolny, Chojnow and Strzegom. The damagea of less than 50 % occurred in towns such as Lubomierz, Prochowice, Katy Wroclawskie, Zmigrod, Przemkow, Sroda Slaska, Lwowek Slaski, Milicz, Gora. This means that this problem affects one third of the small towns of Lower Silesia. This problem is one of the most important determinants of the development of these towns. Many of them still cannot cope with this "heritage". This issue is discussed in detail in the publication entitled "The transformation of the spatial structure of small towns in Lower Silesia after 1945" (Masztalski 2005, pp. 80–88) These towns and villages of Lower Silesia generally are of medieval origin. Locations of most of them were taking place between 1242 and 1399 (respectively Strzegom and Sobotka). The towns of Lower Silesia developing over the centuries, in 1939 reached a certain state of urbanised spaces, which over the next 6 years was at different times and to different degrees destroyed. Some of these towns lost most of it's historic downtown buildings. Such towns are: Trzebnica, Strzelin, Pieńsk, Ścinawa, Brzeg Dolny, Wołów, Nowogrodziec, Syców. In the subsequent post-war decades, this group was joined by the new small towns in which the lack of political will and money for the renovation of existing residential and commercial downtown area building has led to a similar state of

M. Antona and C. Stephanidis (Eds.): UAHCI 2015, Part IV, LNCS 9178, pp. 332–339, 2015.
DOI: 10.1007/978-3-319-20687-5_32

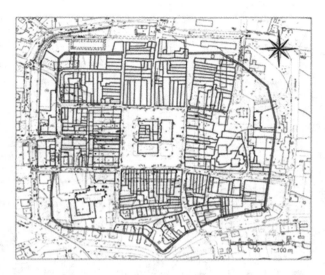

Fig. 1. Historic breaking up quarters on the basis of historical materials. (its own)

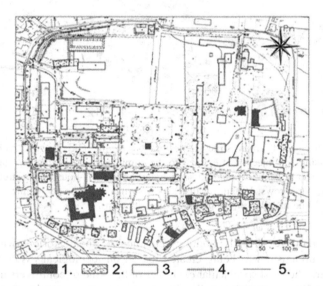

■■■ 1. ▨▨ 2. ☐ 3. ------ 4. —— 5.

Fig. 2. Inventory of the Old Town buildings detailing the conservation of protected objects. Symbols: 1-objects included in the register of monuments; 2-objects that appear in the list of monuments of architecture and construction PSOZ; 3 other objects that exist; 4-historic walls, fences, 5-border development. (its own).

destruction. These towns are, primarily, small urban organisms, such as: Prusice, Lubomierz, Radków, Wlen, Wiazow.

The work of destruction was completed by a post-war policy of implementing the new, modernist building on the outskirts of towns. In some of the towns, where as a

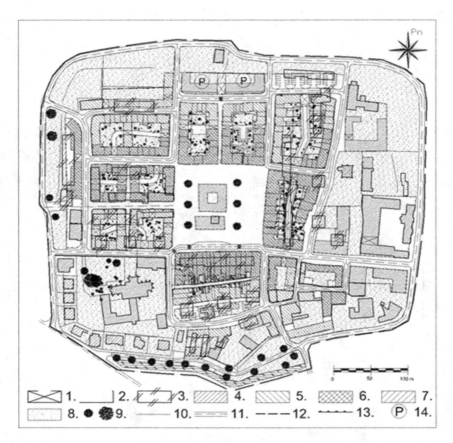

Fig. 3. The concept of urban structure restoration of the Old Town Strzelin. Symbols: 1-crossing, crossings; 2-objects that exist; 3 to the elimination of existing facilities; 4-building service; 5-apartment housing; 6-building service and housing; 7-housing construction; 8-green park, recreation; 9-tree rows; 10-fence walls; 11-key strings of public communication; 12-border development; 13-line installation; 14-parking zone. (its own).

result of war damage virtually nothing remained of the historic town center, the so-called new urbanism was being created, based on ideological assumptions of the Athens Charter. The most spectacular examples of this kind of controversial actions can be observed in Trzebnica and Strzelin. Other towns were, in varying degrees and for different reasons, "beautified" with only single buildings. In this way the urban systems of Klodzko, Wolow, Sobotka, Sroda Slaska, and many other towns were destroyed. Only a few towns have managed to maintain in an almost intact state its historical urban layouts together with the original building that fills them. Among those few are Ziebice and Zabkowice Slaskie. An additional element of a destabilizing effect on the urban areas of Lower Silesia was the state of uncertainty as to further political fate of this part of Poland. The present population of these towns has been resettled from the former eastern territories of the Republic, and for many decades, they weren't feeling at home here. Throughout this period there prevailed a sense of temporariness here. This was not helping in restoring the identity of these towns in any form, whether it was based on the existing historic material culture or the heritage contained in the cultural identity of the resettled population. This state of affairs was additionally encouraging the authorities and decision-makers to experiment with various forms of urban planning and architecture activities, and the then heritage doctrine was often focused on discovering and exposing of so-called "signs of the Slavic heritage" - especially in small towns The bottom line is, the period of the 2nd half of the twentieth century was not a lucky time for the small towns of Lower Silesia.

2 Spatial Development of Strzelin in the 2nd Half of the Twentieth Century

The population of Strzelin in 1939 was 12,337 [2] residents, and in 1946, according to the General Summary Census, there was only 7334 [2] inhabitants remained in the town. Population policy of the relocation of the local German population, carried out by the then administrative authorities of the country, led to the further reduction of the number of Strzelin inhabitants. Only in the late fifties, after the political changes of the year 1956 the increased population growth took place. From this point the town population was growing at a steady rate of several percent per year. In the eighties of the twentieth century, the town has reached pre-war population, but since the end of the nineties of the twentieth century a slow decreasing of the population could be seen. In the 2000 the town was inhabited by 13,228 people, and at the end of 2010, the number of inhabitants was 12,113 people.

   Parallel to the increase in the number of inhabitants the urbanized areas of the town were developing. The largest increase in the urban area occurred in the seventies and eighties. At the same time it is characteristic that in the eighties, they invested mainly in the outskirts of the town, with no interest in the town center undeveloped since the war. The historical shape of the town market has been changed as a result of war damage and the post-war buildings and the currently existing town market space has dimensions of 140 by 230 m (Figs. 1 and 2). The empty spaces left after the buildings demolished during the fighting in 1945 and after the World War II, in the sixties was complemented by modernist residential buildings, what substantially changed the proportions of the square.

   The shape of the historic town market in Strzelin is readable only by the granite pavement of the square. The town market frontage virtually ceased to exist as a result of the warfare. Until today there are only some of the western facade buildings preserved as well as the House of the Princes of Brzeg closing the market in the corner, which was rebuilt after the war. The design work on the concept of rebuilding the destroyed old town of Strzelin was started in the mid-60 s. The concept assumed the demolition of all buildings completed before 1945, leaving only the religious buildings, school buildings, a small complex of residential buildings at the Kosciuszki Street and two buildings At the Wodna Street. Fortunately, they failed to realize that vision to its completion. Significant areas still remained not developed. Based on this project only two frontages of the market were developed. Only eastern and southern frontage was built with prefabricated blocks of flats, simultaneously changing its proportions. The development line was moved well over 10 m, completely changing the spatial shape and climate of this most important place in the town. In addition, failure to restore the block of mid-market building together with the Town Hall and Town Hall tower, changed the human friendly centre into a void, anonymous space. The hostile space, without the characteristic points, restrictions and view closures in which a man feels alienated.

Today, the market square centre is occupied by a green square with the remains of the currently reconstructed town hall tower (Fig. 3). In the area of the pre-existing quarters of the market square developments an open town market operates. The seat of the Municipal Council and District Office are located away from the town center. The market is neglected and not well maintained. The residential and commercial buildings located in the vicinity of the main transport hub of the town took over the role of the town centre. Towards the railway station there is a district from the late nineteenth and early twentieth century. It was less destroyed during the war and part of the pre-war buildings have been used here for offices. The outskirts of the town are dominated by the post-war blocks of multi-family housing and one family housing.

For many years after the war, the construction investments in the town were limited to the reconstruction and modernization of existing, partially damaged and neglected buildings. A significant increase in new development occurred only in the late sixties and early seventies. The eighties initiated the realization of the large number of detached houses. Multi-family residential development virtually ceased to be realized. In 1994, a local spatial development plan of the town was enacted. It sanctioned the heritage protection zones and banned the developing of the Old Town in a manner inconsistent with the objectives of the heritage protection. For the next 15 years nothing new was built in this area. The town centre of Strzelin has become a kind of ghetto, which deterred with emptiness in the urban as well as the social space. The town authorities have unsuccessfully tried for many years to revitalize the area but without the determined change in the attitude of the Heritage Office the area will be deterring with the emptiness for the next few decades. The problem of creation of the modern Strzelin town centre on the ruins of the urban system from the 1939 requires redefining and setting new modern principles and priorities of the reconstruction of this part of the town.

3   Ways Revitalization of Historic Cities

For many years in the Polish town planning reality we come across what might be called "radical conservatory doctrine". A manifestation of this approach is an attempt to have heritage preservation board control over as many buildings as possible. The Heritage Protection and Preservation Act in the first article says that: "The act specifies the subject, scope and forms of heritage protection and preservation, the creation of a national program for Heritage Protection and Preservation and the financing of restoration works, renovation and construction works on historical monuments as well as organization of heritage protection services" [3]. In subsequent articles the act explains in detail how to evaluate and protect historic buildings. In this part of the statutory regulations are clear and undisputed. But in 2010 this just task of protecting cultural heritage was - without a reason - extended in the following manner. Following sentence: "The projects and changes in the space development plan of the region and in the local spatial development plan are subject to consultation with the regional inspector of monuments" was expanded to include the words: "in forming the housing development and land management." [3]. This means that not only objects under the heritage protection but even the contemporary planned buildings will be subject to agreement by the heritage conservation services regarding the form and method of land management. Why someone wanted the heritage conservation services to control the way of shaping the development and management of the areas that are not the subject to heritage protection? Could it be that the only correct architectural and urban ideas was the domain of the officials of the Regional Conservators of Historic Monuments only? Or perhaps some over-zealous officials want to enrich the concrete housing estates from the 70 s with the steep roofs covered with tiles in natural color of ceramics?

Such activities could be associated with attempts to halt the progress of civilization and with strive to create a kind of open air museum of architecture and urbanism from the days before World War 2. Another surprising thing is the lack of constant reminders from the Boards of professional architects and planners about this curiosity and the lack of desire to fix it. The search for the contemporary urban doctrine must begin with a complete denial of the current provisions of law on spatial planning and development, starting with the Act on The Profession of Town Planner and the Spatial Planning and Development Act, through all the separate laws related to urban planning and space management and ending with the implementing regulations referring to them. The current Acts are a patchwork of random and inconsistent legal provisions, resulting from the actions of the subsequent parliamentary lobbys. These regulations are so "infected" with the subsequent conjectural and lobbystic updates and amendments, that they do not give a chance to repair the current space management law. The space management law must be rewritten anew and in isolation from the momentary political coalitions and local lobbying needs.

It has been publicly said about such principles as sustainable development and spatial order that are permanently engraved into current legal regulations. And that's it because those who established them were only interested in them until the end of the legislative process. What counts afterwards is a pragmatism, a business logic, political correctness and measurable economic benefits. The effects of the current heritage conservation policy are the projects - unfinished for decades, that rebuild the war-damaged downtown areas of such towns as Elblag, Głogow, Strzelin and many others. In addition, we have many buildings maintained in a state of so-called "permanent ruin", what comes from rather megalomanic martyrdom than from their desire to maintain the cultural heritage (Figs. 4 and 5).

The Regional Inspector of Monuments Services were transformed from the power protecting the most valuable achievements of the material culture of our country into a fundamental slowing down factor of reasonable civilization changes in our urbanized area. The register and documentation of historical monuments evolved from a tool of protection into a tool of blind repression. In most cases, the heritage conservation management is limited to the search for the forms that reproduce or rather imitate the historical past. This leads to the formation of the most bizarre architectural forms.

The documenting of the history and cultural heritage evolved into the creation of artificial sets, based on motives that try to be historical. Any progress towards modern

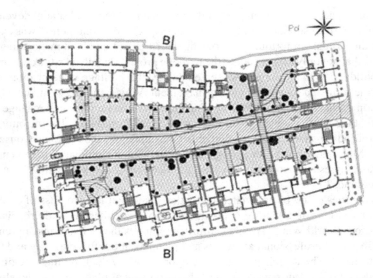

Fig. 4. Project of reconstruction of historic buildings in the center - a first floor view's (its own)

Fig. 5. Project of reconstruction of historic buildings in the center - vertical section. (its own)

technology and the needs of the information civilization is blocked. Not all towns have to look like design models from different periods of the past centuries. It's just about time to start creating the bustling modern towns in place of the ruins and archaeological remains, instead of increasingly degrading areas that count on tourist and sponsors with an open and unrestricted bank account. Today it is easier to build businesses on the outskirts of the town than to invest money in archaeological research, that nobody can predict how and when they will end.

4 Summary

After 70 years since the end of World War 2 in the downtowns of many small towns of Poland, we can still see the empty tracts of land which are remnants of wartime and postwar devastation. These spaces are often not built-up because the existing heritage protection policy with its fundamentalism turns the existing architectural relics of the past into ruin or causes their rapid physical elimination from our surroundings. The reason for this is the thoughtless recognition of each architectural object realized before 1945 as a monument worthy of protection. Why it's not possible to plan the demolition of the object, which - apart from the date of creation - has no other rational reason for continued existence. The lack of reflection and realistic assessment of what is worth protecting and what is likely to survive without government financial assistance is a fundamental shortcoming of current conservation policy. The space finally must be created for the investment modernization and renovation activities without any inter-ference and any heritage conservation requirements. And finally we should demand more faith in logic and reason of local authorities, architects and investors. One of those abnormal situations is no downtown site planning for most of damaged by war old town areas. Such city, which has got that problem is Strzelin, where for 70 post-war years no one was able to face the problem of downtown building reconstruction. It had its consequences, because it changed centre of gravity for administration and service from old town to other parts of the city.

References

1. Masztalski, R.: The transformation of the spatial structure of small towns in Lower Silesia after 1945, Wroclaw (2005)
2. Statistics towns and settlements 1945–1965, Central Statistical Office, Warsaw (1967)
3. The Act of 23 July 2003 on the conservation and care of monuments, Polish Journal of Laws, Warsaw (2003)

Designing Kitchens for Small Domestic Spaces

Przemyslaw Nowakowski[✉]

Faculty of Architecture, Wroclaw University of Technology, Prusa st. 53/55,
50-317 Wroclaw, Poland
przemyslaw.nowakowski@pwr.edu.pl

Abstract. The role of kitchen area in the house environment has been changing over the course of history. The changes concerned the share of kitchen space in apartment functional structure, as well as the course of everyday chores. Currently, as well as in the past, kitchen areas remain placed either in separate rooms, or they constitute a part of a bigger space (usually the living room). At present, two characteristic domestic kitchen models are preferred: "laboratory" and multi-functional (with a dining room). The space limitations, especially in multi-family housing, favored the "laboratory" kitchen model, or so-called partial kitchens in living rooms. Technical progress enabled creating various types of small kitchen areas, which are adjusted to diverse needs of users, according to their lifestyle.

Kitchen areas are crucial places for completing various household chores. Among everyday duties performed in the kitchen there are: preparing meals, doing the washing up and cleaning up. Those chores frequently are technologically complicated activities. In order to perform them more efficiently, household members use various devices and home appliances. Conducting of chores, storing the appliances and food products etc., requires a vast share of the apartment structure. Providing sufficiently big maneuver and storage spaces is particularly difficult in small kitchens. Shortages in available space may have a negative influence on, among others, the correct layout of working space or ease of movement in small kitchens.

The following paper concentrates on the evolution and examples of types of small kitchens, as well as selected rules concerning the improvement of conditions of their arrangements.

1 Introduction

Throughout the centuries, preparing of meals has constituted one of the main house-related activities. However, the role of household chores, preparing of meals, and kitchens themselves have significantly changed with time. Initially "the kitchen space" was limited only to the space near the fire. With time it took up the space of a dedicated room, where other, even profit-making, household chores were performed. Another factor which constitutes kitchen's quality and looks is the way of heat treating of dishes. Furnaces with open of closed fire, and gas and electric "cold stoves" determined forms of kitchen space. Formerly, the process of storing and processing of food produce rarely took place in one room. Storing of food supplies and firewood, water access and waste disposal required using of other rooms of the house, even areas outside the housing building.

M. Antona and C. Stephanidis (Eds.): UAHCI 2015, Part IV, LNCS 9178, pp. 340–351, 2015.
DOI: 10.1007/978-3-319-20687-5_33

With time people aimed at clear distinction between areas concerning household chores and leisure. However, it was not until 20th century when a fully monofunctional kitchen model was devised, which combined all the functions connected with preparation of meals. The complexity of kitchen-related chores also led to a spatial distinction of zones used for performance of particular activities using properly chosen and placed equipment.

Preparation and consumption of meals at home formerly took place in "the kitchen area" in the broad sense of the term, or, in wealthy households, also in the adjoining room – dining room. Such a term is justified, as assigning a monofunctional "kitchen" with a full usage program is a solution which has been commonly used only for a couple dozens of years. In such a space, despite typical activities connected with preparation of meals, various household chores (mainly cleaning activities) are also performed. Contemporary kitchens usually are not only the center of household chores, but also the place of family bonding, studying and spending free time with family and friends. However, it is difficult to carry out those activities in small, monofunctional kitchens.

2 Separation of the Kitchen Area in Former Houses

The central place which formerly designated the living and, in particular, kitchen area was the hearth with an open fire. Fire was necessary to maintain comfortable conditions in households (rooms heating function), as well as to process food produce (heat treating) into easily assimilated and warming meals. Together with gasification and electrification the form of the heating medium has changed. Traditional flame was replaced by invisible thermal radiation transferred directly into the dishes. Using of stoves with closed hearth and central heating enabled separation of rooms used exclusively to prepare meals – monofunctional kitchens. Division of flats into separate spaces – chambers and rooms (also with an assigned kitchen) was an effect of successive improvement of life standards and living conditions.

3 Beginnings of the "Laboratory" Kitchen Model

Various economic and social changes took place after the World War I. Among common phenomena of that time one can distinguish: a proceeding decline of big families, emancipation and employment of women, ceasing of using services of domestic workers, etc. Those tendencies influenced social relations, as well as forms of residence. The contemporary need for housing initiated new trends in design. The demands concerning the improvement of housing conditions were formulated mainly by lower social classes, for whom cheap housing with a higher standard than previously was planned to be built. In Europe the idea of tenement housing was abandoned for the sake of social housing.

Withdrawing from the model of household with servants required a different perception of the functional and spatial program of apartments. Maintaining spacious houses with separate utility rooms (kitchens, pantries, laundry rooms), as well as rooms for servants was no longer possible. The household chores were started to be performed single-handedly and an interest in smaller houses and apartments without chore rooms increased. Simultaneously, mechanization and automatization of chores adapted to the housing environment gained importance. Those developments were introduced thanks to the advancements of industrial productions. However, the aforementioned processes were undertaken mainly in industrialized regions and countries.

Functional construction layouts of buildings created in 1920s were transformed into considerably small apartments, however with both kitchens and bathrooms in standard. Moreover, the aesthetic experiences connected with decorative details were replaced by the superiority of practical needs. That is why the expression "housing machines" gained popularity, as it described the living space as a place of fulfilling only specific utilitarian needs. This expression also resulted from introduction of unification and prefabricated elements in the housing industry.

Designing of modern housing ("housing machines") was based on, among others, the analysis of everyday needs of residents and graphic diagrams determining the traffic patterns between the zones in a test kitchen during performing of the most important chores. Separation of kitchen from other parts of the house was justified by hygienic and health considerations [1]. The reduction of traffic patterns led to certain limitations, especially in the kitchen, where a complex course of activities requires multiple changing of places. Those theoretical considerations were merely a formal justification of needed savings, resulting from the unfavorable economic situation, together with a big shortage of housing and poor sanitary conditions in cities.

It is at that time when the new program of building new housing estates in Frankfurt called "*Das neue Frankfurt*" (The New Frankfurt) was commenced. In the project the model of "laboratory", also known as "Frankfurt", kitchen was proposed. The author of this project was an architect from Vienna, Margarete Schütte-Lihotzky, who, in 1926, designed a kitchen on the area of 6.5 m^2. Her idea was inspired, among others, by the works of Ch. Frederick, an American home economist and household reformer [2].

The size and proportions of the "Frankfurt" kitchen, as well as the galley shape layout, enabled to considerably reduce the distance between the appliances. The measurements of the kitchen amounted to 187 × 344 cm [3]. It had a functional connection with the hall and it was directly adjoined to the living room. Prefabricated elements and standard kitchen furniture was fitted to it. The furniture was manufactured and then assembled inside the room. Due to a careful workmanship, the countertop was smooth and with invisible technological connections. This created a possibility of uninterrupted performing of chores in any place of the countertop and an ease of maintaining it clean. Another new features in the "Frankfurt kitchen" was lack of movable furniture (including the traditional kitchen cabinets) and a dining table. The furniture was fixed permanently to walls. An addition to the furniture, there was a gas stove and a sink with running water. The maneuver space was limited to the minimum. Using of a particular kitchen required just a turn, or taking a few steps to the side. The technology of work was an overriding criterion deciding on the way of particular arrangement of furniture, however the functional and aesthetical variants were not planned.

It was assumed that the kitchen chores would be performed by one person. Therefore the kitchen was an effect of implementation of rules of technical improvement and functionality of the equipment. Specialization of housewives concerning the kitchen chores aimed at reflecting the organization of work in the gastronomic industry, as it was a popular belief that those activities are a waste of time and an excessive overload, which need to be performed as quickly as possible [3]. In a prototype "Frankfurt kitchen" both the traversed distance, and the time spent on performing the activities was measured. It was estimated that the distance traversed while performing the chores in kitchens of the old type amounted to 19 meters, while in the kitchen designed according to the Frankfurt model it was only 6 meters [4]. It was also noticed that some distances require to be traversed several times, for instance, from the cabinet with kitchenware to the stove, or from the sink to the cabinet with dinnerware. That is why the aforementioned functional segments became adjacent, in order to minimalize the walking distance and the number of unnecessary manual activities.

The comparison of the distance covered while working in a traditional and new kitchen was only seemingly a decisive factor in the introduction of the features of small "Frankfurt kitchen", since the role of the dining area adjacent to the working zone was not included. Appreciating the close placement of dining table, stove and sink in old, traditional rural and bourgeois kitchens, M. Schütte–Lihotzky postulated placement of the table in the living room, in the distance not longer than 3 meters from the kitchen working area [2]. The arrangement of furniture and appliances in "Frankfurt kitchen", in accordance with technological manner of preparing meals can be considered as influential in relation to older, often randomly designed multifunctional kitchens with traditional tables used for consumption of meals.

The placement of wall cabinets and standing cabinets, as well as characteristic aluminum storage scoops was also carefully thought through. The technological requirements of the work space and reach dimensions of users in various working positions were also considered. The project envisioned performing of activities along the walls in a standing position and next to the window, in a sitting position (Fig. 1).

A narrow room with a simple traffic pattern and parallel functional working zones enabled only one person to work. Therefore the working areas were placed in accordance with the technological course and order of performing chores. Such an arrangement enabled to shorten the distance covered during performing the activities. However, strictly systematized arrangement of chores resulted in boredom. The routine

Fig. 1. "Frankfurt kitchen" with furniture fixed to walls and a countertop under the window.

and alienation in the kitchen were deepened by a lack of a multifunctional table, where all the members of family could gather.

The "laboratory" character of the "Frankfurt kitchen" and latter mini-kitchens lead to ceasing of the traditional role of this room – integration of household members. Kitchens became only places of "service" in relation to other parts of the house (the living room in particular). Despite achieved improvements, and both investment-related (financial) and functional limitations in apartments built at that time, the majority of society preferred bigger multifunctional kitchens. Users demanded for kitchens and rooms to be big enough, so that they could individually furnish them and, above all, assign an area for meals consumption [5]. Nevertheless, the "Frankfurt kitchen", and, in a broader understanding, the "laboratory kitchen" with an ordered layout, became a model kitchen design for the following decades, especially in multi-family housing.

4   Popularization of Small Kitchens in Housing Development

Resignation from the services of domestic workers enforced having just one person managing the household. Those changes were particularly dynamic in the USA. Therefore, typical kitchens from 1920s and 1930s were small, and had a "laboratory" character. Frequently they had built-in closets with many doors and drawers, coal and gas stoves, or coal and electric stoves. Among other appliances which became gradually more popular there were: refrigerators, sinks with a dish drainer shelf, waste burning heaters, and smaller household appliances [6], [7]. The models of "laboratory" kitchens equipped with the newest appliances were mainly popularized. While multifunctional and open kitchens were built in bigger detached houses.

The technical and furniture equipment had a better ergonomic quality and characteristic visual features, such as streamlined shapes. It is then, when the term "Streamline Kitchen" gained popularity. Using of streamlined shapes in household appliances was inspired by the contemporary aviation and motorization. Such forms were considered as a visual synonym of speed, efficiency, as well as mechanization of household [8]. The term *streamline* did not refer only to the shapes, but also to ensuring of the continuity and fluency of performed activities [9]. Although kitchens were assembled from the prefabricated elements, various layouts were available, as wall to wall fitted furniture enabled creating an in-line and galley shape layouts in "L" and "U" shapes, etc. [10].

5   Domestic Kitchens After the World War II

The economic and social changes after the World War II contributed to equalization of the status of households. This, in turn, led to a considerable unification of forms and qualities of housing. As a result, average standard of newly built housing was improved. A higher technological standard, mainly of kitchens and bathrooms, became more accessible, despite the wealth of their users.

The economic considerations and significance of class-less societies decided on an averaged standard space of apartments. The savings and cutbacks usually affected the space of kitchens and bathrooms. That is why they were usually the smallest of all rooms. Providing the installations (mainly waterworks and sewage system) resulted in a higher technical standard of housing. Apartments built in 1950s and 1960s were not very spacious. That is why, the functional program was limited to the basic needs. Placement of functional zones was strictly prearranged, and the space and proportions of rooms excluded a possibility of any flexibility in the interior design. The measurements of kitchens at that time amounted to 4–6 m^2. They were joined together with bathrooms creating a "wet functional block". A serious disadvantage of this solution was, among others, a small surface, resulting in both functional and social consequences. The size of traffic and maneuver space, as well as work space enabled only one person (usually a woman) to work in the kitchen. The participation of other household members, and resulting from it integration of the family, was strongly hindered [11]. Also the consumption of meals could only take place in the living room.

Because of financial reasons, the concepts of multifunctional kitchens were rejected in favor of the "laboratory model", which was sometimes joined with the living room (which usually served also as a bedroom). Another consequence of this solution was a spatial separation of kitchen and dining zone, and moving the dining area to the living room [12]. The reverse of this trend took place only in 1970s, when the model of multifunctional kitchen gained popularity at the expense of the "laboratory model" [13]. This change did not result from returning to the old family structure and the role of the "housewife" who did not have gainful employment. The reason for it was perceived in the possibility of activation of other members of family, by delegating to them certain chores, such as laying the table. In the sample arrangements one of the crucial features was a comfortable work flow, by, among others, installing countertops in between the main work hubs. The rule of the "work triangle" (refrigerator – sink – stove) was gaining popularity at that time, which coincided with popularization of various technological and kitchen appliances, in particular: washing machines, refrigerators, dishwashers, etc.

The size of an average kitchen in post-war multi-family housing was similar to the "Frankfurt kitchen". The "laboratory model" of kitchen, which was strongly popularized and realized until the end of 1960s, still did not gain a considerable recognition. The need of having a dining area was important, even at the expense of correct arrangement of the working area and comfort of work. The division into separate rooms resulted in doubling of the dining area, which was placed both in the kitchen and in the living room (Fig. 2).

1970s was the time of an increase in welfare of societies. Focusing the manufacturing on production of consumption goods favored the improvement of technical standards and

Fig. 2. Sample layouts of small kitchens (often with faulty arrangements of the working area equipment).

sizes of apartments. It applied mainly to the kitchen areas, where most of the household chores were performed. Popularization of mechanical devices led to a change in approach to household and kitchen chores. A common use of food processors, dishwashers, microwaves, washing machines, electric irons, etc. resulted in reduction of the most laborious and unpleasant activities. A return to a traditional role of the kitchen, and considering joint preparing and consuming of meals as a means to integrate the members of the family, commenced a withdrawal from the "laboratory" model, in which the kitchen was an area isolated from the rest of the household. Big multifunctional kitchens, became open, and connected with the living room, which was an expression of practical quality of the apartment [11]. This trend was more visible in wealthier, capitalist countries. At this time, in the socialist countries, there were still struggles concerning the insufficiency of housing and various socio-economical limitations. The preferred model of housing was still large-panel buildings with rigid functional layouts. Small apartments, out of necessity, still contained kitchens designed according to the "laboratory" model. Short layouts usually contained not enough work space and storage room.

The layout of work zones with cabinets along the walls creates a necessity of working facing the wall, with the back to the room. Separation of kitchen from the rest of apartment with walls additionally strengthens the isolation of a person preforming the kitchen chores from other activities and members of the household. This issue was first discussed at the beginning of 1980s by a German designer Otl Aicher, who in his book "A kitchen for cooking" (Die Küche zum Kochen) postulated that kitchen chores be should also considered as "social and communicative activities" [14]. His books commenced a process of changes in functional and social approach towards kitchen chores. The author criticized the previous model of performing chores at the module work space, which relied on routine preparation of meals (mainly from ready-made frozen products and canned food) and the fact that the person who was cooking was facing the wall [14].

A new functionality was the location of main countertop in the middle of the room, in a form of an island with an openwork shelf for the most necessary accessories. Therefore the person who was working was "in the center of events" and could maintain visual contact with other members of the household [14]. Otl Aicher perceived preparing of meals as an important part of home life, also in the social context, particularly concerning the development of interpersonal ties. This new idea also aimed at including guests in the process of meal preparation.

The island layouts may be used on relatively big spaces. They can be also recommended in small kitchens opened into a living room. Such a layout may lead to considerable savings of space (Fig. 3).

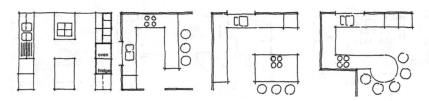

Fig. 3. Outline of a multifunctional island kitchen according to O. Aicher and a small laboratory kitchen with an island opening into a living room.

"Laboratory kitchens" are mainly dedicated to young and single people and those who spend the majority of day outside home (at work), who also often use food services. The traditional kitchen model with a dining area is recommended to families with children, as well as people having a particular lifestyle (for instance those who entertain their guests with a joint preparation of meals). As a result, kitchens again started to serve various functions of daily activities of household members.

The diversity of offered furniture systems and household appliances influenced the popularity of the open kitchen model, as the kitchen area is often a part of living room. This solution led to creation of impression of a spacious room, together with reducing the traffic zones. Those concepts are particularly popular in smaller flats. Stylistic merging of the zones became possible, nevertheless opening of kitchens required a disconnection of gas system installation in the apartments.

6 Measures of Small Kitchen Design

The functional and spatial program of kitchen includes all the functions connected with feeding of householders and their guests, furniture equipment, as well as appliances used for preparation and consumption of meals. The equipment aims at enabling an effective and well-balanced work, together with reduction of needed time and effort, in accordance with users' needs. The functional and spatial program of kitchen depends on the following factors:

- location of kitchen in the house structure;
- proportions of the room and the kitchen area;
- possible layout and length of the work zone;
- number of household members;
- lifestyle, diet and personal preferences.

Other factors which influence the kitchen layout are features connected with traits of the members of household (relatedness, age, relations between members of different generations, education, social and work status, lifestyle, preferences, diets etc.). That is why, especially in the monofunctional kitchens (covering small spaces), it is necessary to fulfill accompanying functions in other parts of the apartment, such as: spending time together, taking care of children, learning and playing and performing household chores not related with preparation of meals (e.g. cleaning, ironing).

Efficient preparation of meals, cleaning works, making stocks, etc. requires appropriate arrangement of space. It is especially vital in small kitchens, whose space is mainly taken by the furniture and mechanical devices. There are various organizational and architectural factors which can contribute to making the kitchen chores more efficient. Among the organizational factors one can distinguish:

- doing shopping more often (possibility of reduction of space needed for making stocks);
- purchasing of partially processed products (ground coffee, juice, frozen foods, etc.) and reducing the number of additional kitchen appliances;
- purchasing of ready-made products (sauces, stewed fruit, jams, etc.) and meals (pizza, soups, risotto, and ready-to-cook foods, etc.) sold in bulk, in jars, cans or frozen;

- using of multifunctional kitchen appliances (e.g. food processors, pressure cookers, microwave ovens).
- The architectural factors are as follows:
- appropriate layout of the working area;
- right choice and arrangement of particular elements of furnishings (furniture, equipment and kitchen appliances);
- minimalization of the length and avoiding of crossing of traffic patterns;
- ensuring of optimum microclimate conditions (temperature and humidity of air, natural and artificial lighting, proper ventilation, etc.);
- elimination of possibilities of accidents (tripping, spilling, falling, burns, cuts, etc.).

A well-balanced placement of the most often used equipment enables to limit the necessity of working in uncomfortable positions, such as: kneeling or squatting. While a proper placement of furniture and appliances may lead to a reduction of time of work and covered distance.

Modern kitchen furniture systems enable to match the equipment precisely to the size of the kitchen area, as well as to the size and movement abilities of its user. It is accomplished by the choice of cabinets and work surfaces with specific height, depth and width. It is also possible to arrange the equipment according to individual needs of users (placing of refrigerator, stove etc. in any part of the working zone and on individually chosen height) despite the location of installation connections.

The situation of the doorway in the kitchen has a big influence on a well-balanced arrangement of this room. Its edge should be placed minimally 60-65 cm from the corner of the room. In case of a smaller distance, the placement of the countertop or kitchen cabinets with a depth of 60 cm is impossible, and a narrow unused space covered up with a door and with limited traffic pattern possibilities is created. Increasing the space to 70 cm enables placement of tall cabinets, as well as installation of a light switch (Fig. 4).

The minimal assumed width of the kitchen doorway, amounting to 80 cm (in case of people with disabilities who use wheelchairs – 90 cm) can be considered as sufficient in order to provide a free traffic pattern, even while carrying big trays and bags. However, for preventive reasons (the possibility of health deterioration of the household members), and in order to increase the comfort and meaning of the kitchen in the housing structure, it is

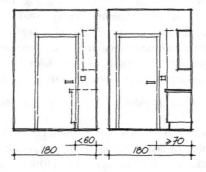

Fig. 4. Narrow and recommended space between the door and the corner of the room.

recommended to use unified, extended width of the doorway, amounting to 90 cm. Nevertheless, the number of doors in the kitchen area should be limited to the minimum. The door to the hallway (the entry and traffic zone of apartment) and a potential door to the living room (the dining area) may be considered as sufficient. Meeting the demand concerning the extension of doorway might therefore result in the necessity of increasing the traffic area in the apartment, especially in the hallway.

The window should provide a sufficient amount of day light for both working zone, and the whole room. Windows may have one or multiple panes, however, big glass surfaces are more difficult to open and clean, and, after opening, they take up a lot of space. The most convenient are double casement windows, with a possibility of full or ajar opening. However, an ajar window does not allow to quickly and effectively air the room. A wide opened window should not block often used cabinets or force to move tableware from the countertops.

The height of window sill should create a possibility of installing cabinets and countertop underneath it, and it should be 85-110 cm (e.g. "L" or "U" shaped). In this case it is recommended to connect the sill and countertop into one element on the same level. The window sills built in multi-family housing, with the height of 85 cm practically hinder the possibility of installing higher worktops adjusted to the standing work of taller people. If the sink is placed under the window, it is advised for the opening window to be installed approximately 30 cm higher, because of, i.a., sink standing taps. Therefore, the opening of windows should not be constricted by furniture or placed on it equipment, appliances and tableware.

Both standing and wall cabinets are usually installed up to the corner of the external wall. They should not block the window opening (Fig. 5). Therefore the window should be in a distance of at least 40–45 cm from the corner of the room (assuming that, at the same time, the window sill is above, or on the same level as the countertop). In many apartments window openings take up the whole wall of the room. Then, wall cabinets are moved away from the window, creating an unused corner; the space gained in that way still prevents from a full opening of the window. Resulting in difficulties in cleaning of the window from the outside.

As a result of putting the countertop in front of the window (which is the case in all kitchen layouts except one wall kitchen and galley layout), it is difficult to reach the

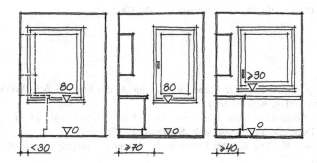

Fig. 5. The influence of the size of the window proportion on the possibility of moving the work zone to the external wall.

window handle. That is why it is advised to install it lower, so that it is easier to grip from behind the countertop under the sill.

7 Summary

Kitchen plays a special role in every household. It is a place for preparing meals, but also of creating culinary art and feasting. That is why designing a kitchen is not only a technical process considering potential changes and technological improvements. The design should encompass the philosophy of life of its users, as well as a possibility of changes of their lifestyle and social relations.

Throughout the centuries, the role of kitchen in social and spatial structure of house has been reflecting the attitude towards work. Although kitchen has been the center of home activity for a long time, it did not use to have a representative role. It was often spatially and functionally isolated from the rest of the house. Thanks to the scientific rationalization of housework and considerable savings of space in the first half of 20th century, kitchens were considered as "service" areas in comparison with the leisure areas of the house. What is more, the social recognition of housework declined together with the emancipation of women and their work activation.

Introduction of a small kitchen in a "laboratory" model, requires a detailed planning of the kitchen activities. The equipment should be well chosen and installed in appropriate places. However, in most cases the work zones are placed intuitively, without the analysis of courses of activities. This leads to functional errors, and, in a result, to extension of the way traversed during everyday chores.

Small kitchens usually enable only one person to work inside. Because of their separation from the rest of apartment, the kitchen chores are isolated from other household activities. Moreover, kitchen is viewed only as a monofunctional secondary room, which cannot be used to integrate the household members. Therefore, other common needs of house-dwellers are to be met in different rooms.

The current view of preparation of meals as a pastime, opportunity to relax and means to entertain guests changed the rank of kitchen in the house structure. Nowadays, in many houses kitchens became prestigious areas, alongside with the living rooms. As a result, they are even considered to be "kitchen rooms". Prospective achievement of such a value by small kitchens requires both functional and spatial connection of them with adjacent rooms (living rooms).

References

1. Petsch, J.: Eigenheim und gute Stube Zur Geschichte des bürgerlichen Wohnens, vol. 154. DuMont Buchverlag, Köln (1989)
2. Kähler, G.: Geschichte des Wohnens 1918–1945 Reform, Reaktion, pp. 219–277. Zerstörung. Deutsche Verlags-Anstalt, Stuttgart (1996)
3. Spechtenhauser, K.: Die Küche: Lebenswelt, Nutzung, Perspektiven. Birkhäuser Verlag, Basel (2006)
4. Andritzky, M.: Oikos Von der Feuerstelle zur Mikrowelle Haushalt und Wohnen im Wandel, pp. 104–105. Anabas Verlag, Giessen (2000)

5. Beer, I.: Architektur für den Alltag Von sozialen und frauenorientierten Anspruch der Siedlungsarchitektur der zwanziger Jahre, vol. 125. Schelzky & Jeep, Berlin (1994)
6. Carlisle, N.: America's Kitchen, vol. 123. Historic New England, Boston (2008)
7. Plante, E.: The American Kitchen: 1700 to the PresentFrom Hearth to Highrise, pp. 225–229. Facts on File Inc., New York (1995)
8. Giedion, S.: Die Herrschaft der Mechanisierung, pp. 655–659. Ein Beitrag zur anonymen Geschichte. Europäische Verlagsanstalt, Hamburg (1994)
9. Lupton, E.: The Bathroom, the Kitchen and the Aesthetics of Waste, p. 65. Princeton Architectural Press, New York (1996)
10. Malnar, J.M.: The Interior Dimension: A Theoretical Approach to Enclosed Space, p. 215. Van Nostrand Reinhold, New York (1992)
11. Flagge, I.: Geschichte des Wohnens. Von 1945 bis heute. Aufbau – Neubau – Umbau, pp. 755–761. Deutsche Verlags-Anstalt, Stuttgart (1999)
12. Weresch, K.: Wohnungsbau im Wandel der Wohnzivilisierung und Genderverhältnisse, p. 131. Dölling und Galitz Verlag, Hamburg (2005)
13. Wenz-Gahler, I.: Die Küche, p. 282. Rohwolt Taschenbuch Verlag, Reinbeck, Lernbereich Wohnen (1979)
14. Aicher, O.: Küche zum Kochen. Das Ende einer Architekturdoktrin, pp. 40, 45, 57. Callwey Verlag, München (1982)

Human-Computer Interactions
in Contemporary Office Environment

Elżbieta Dagny Ryńska and Ferdynand Górski[✉]

Warsaw University of Technology, Warsaw, Poland
dagny.rynska@arch.pw.edu.pl, home@fgda.pl

Abstract. The article is a voice in the discussion on ergonomics and efficiency in the operation of ITC devices in the context of the office environment and its ongoing changes. Increased mobility which followed technological advances is redefining office work. With the restraint of having to create designated workstations lifted, the possibilities of work-related interaction became more diverse, creating new chances but at the same time also design challenges.

Which aspects of the workspace have proven to be effective in creating a good work environment? Proper temperature and humidity, daylighting, aesthetics, greenery and an interesting view outside are the top of the list; but is there really a single answer to that question? Even within one industry, requirements regarding the optimal workspace may differ, depending on the task at hand. This should be a hint that maybe flexibility and diversity of spaces made available to the employee is the best solution to that problem.

In the first part of the article we explain how the office environment has evolved into what it is today, showing the most important factors influencing that change.

The second stage of the analysis centers around the tools employed in working mobile, focusing on displaying their current limitation and usability in the work-related context.

Keywords: Office environment · Productivity

1 Introduction

Office buildings and, on a smaller scale, office spaces are a particular type of facilities that have emerged as a result of work specialization, driven by the goals of lowering costs and increasing productivity—being a fine example of economy of scale—starting from alloted divisions within a company to handle specialized task like managing archives, or accounting, and ending with a whole new industry called BPO (business process outsourcing).

The conceptual approach to designing office spaces is closely tied to advancements in technology and management theory. The shift from traditional cellular offices was clearly related to mass production, because the creation of large quantities of identical goods has lead to attempts to standardize and optimize.

© Springer International Publishing Switzerland 2015
M. Antona and C. Stephanidis (Eds.): UAHCI 2015, Part IV, LNCS 9178, pp. 352–359, 2015.
DOI: 10.1007/978-3-319-20687-5_34

The research performed by Frederic Winslow Taylor at Bethlehem Steel has inspired the management consultants that followed to try to apply the same ideas that comprised the so-called scientific management to office work. The experiments were successful—open space was indeed more effective in terms of utilization of floor space, as no space was wasted on partitions and doors, and its openness allowed the managers to get a snapshot view of the whole floor at any given moment, giving them a sense of having control.

After World War II, product lifetimes have gotten shorter due to fashion-driven product design and there was much more data to be processed in the office. Around 1960 Robert Propst at the Herman Miller Research Corporation had conducted a lengthy study, came to the conclusion that in this new data-intensive reality an office worker would benefit from individual private space to process that data, and designed a special type of furniture system, called the Action Office. It was quite elaborate but unfortunately also too expensive, and therefore not that design but a much cheaper version of it has taken the world by storm in the form of the much-despised cubicles.

Then, in the eighties, another paradigm shift took place in management. U.S. companies were outperformed by Japanese and eventually started importing foreign management concepts such as JIT (just in time), and *kaizen*. Production, accounting, management—everything had to be *lean*. Big hierarchical management structures had to be dismantled and small *agile* teams were formed instead. As a result, workplace design had to include an ever increasing amount of collaboration spaces, where those small task groups could work. And that brings us to the office environment we have today, where collaboration not only is still a key aspect, but has reached a new level.

2   The Office Environment of Today

Office work is not what it used to be just a few decades ago. Thanks to better network connectivity, distributed systems, miniaturization of computer devices, and a largely electronic flow of documents, there barely is a need for a dedicated office space for an employee anymore. As long as the computing tools were stationary or hard to move around, the concept of the workstation was thriving and ergonomists were tasked with trying to figure out the best relation between the user and the equipment: the monitor, keyboard, desk, and seating instrument. Although this research is still valid, work-related interaction with computers has become more diverse.

Now, a designated workstation is just one of the places where work can be performed on a computer. Other places include: the company's canteen, a café around the corner, open teaming areas, focus areas, a library, or different rooms, some of which look more like they belonged in a fancy club and not in an office business. Portability of computing devices makes that possible but doesn't explain the cause. Why such a great variety of spaces is being provided? Flexibility and creativity are the keywords that can help to shed some light on this phenomenon.

In the survey of emerging real estate trends in 2013 conducted by PwC and the Urban Land Institute [2, p. 45] respondents, when asked about office property types in perspective, have pointed out that "long-term investors are looking for mixed-use angles [...] business space intertwined with lifestyle uses", and that the occupiers are interested in campuses, returning to cities, and not just "being stuck in an office in the middle of nowhere". The surrounding facilities grow in importance—employees want to be able to get to work on bikes or "hang out in quirky cafés at lunchtime".

The report [2] showcases the TMT sector (technology, media & telecommunications) as being quite a special case with regard to tenant requirements and expectations, when compared to more traditional sectors such as banking and finance, since much more emphasis is put on creativity, and creative spaces, i.e. spaces that support and help to express the creativity of the employees.

The surge of creativity came with the DotComs at the end of the XX century, when a big idea and a vision of exaggerated and unsubstantiated network effects at an unknown moment in the future was all it would take to attract money from VCs. We know how that ended, but the culture of creativity did not burst along with the bubble.

An article [1, Table 1] mentions several papers from years 1999–2006 that discuss the influence of office environment characteristics on creativity, listing such factors as:

- plants in the office inspiring employees,
- variation in colors,
- multi-discipline groups,
- informal meetings (80 % of the creative ideas are said to come from them),
- coffee lounges to stimulate those informal meetings,
- spaces for meetings and interaction,
- creating breaks with toys,
- sharing desks to stimulate new ideas.

Increased mobility and connectivity has made it possible to work from basically anywhere, and in order to collaborate with others directly one could meet for example at a café. So, is there still a need for a company office? Yes, for many firms an office building is a sign of prestige and a strong branding message. Furthermore, management may be concerned that a café is not the best place to discuss some sensitive projects, because it is less secure than the office. A solution to that problem would be to open a café in the office building itself, so that employees won't have to use outside services. But in result this leads to the company basically competing with all the fancy places equipped with Wi-Fi where workers could have met instead of meeting at the company. As it was phrased in the CBRE report [4, p. 3], "smart organizations recognize the need to provide a great workplace experience for their employees by creating an environment where they *want to be* rather than where they *have to be*".

Peter Greenspun [6] wrote, that (paraphrased): "your success in the IT business depends on the extent to which programmers will practically live in your office". But to make that happen, the facilities must make the employee feel very comfortable and relaxed, include home cinema, pinball, a piano—everything that an individual might not afford to install at his house and that would increase social bonding at work, giving a stronger sense of community. All spaces should also allow for ad hoc sharing of knowledge, because genius might strike unexpectedly. Hence, IT company premises start to resemble university campuses, one reason for it being that in case of younger employees they may in fact be competing against real university campuses.

ITC businesses are fighting for top talent and if one of them provides extraordinary workspace attractions, making its offices a great place to work, others start feeling the pressure to match or beat that offer. As it turns out, the most important factor when deciding upon a job is flexibility. According to CISCO Global Trends Report 2010, "3 of 5 workers would choose jobs that were lower-paying but had leniency in working outside of the office over higher salaried jobs that lacked flexibility". On the other hand, if the provided facilities were great, employees would be more likely to stay and work inside the office.

IT and media companies are at the forefront of this undergoing change in office environment, due to their strict reliance on creativity resulting in undertaking attempts to boost it, but offices in other, more conservative sectors also start to follow suit. One cause for that are real estate consulting companies that monitor closely what concepts are being successfully implemented in offices and then try to suggest or implement them in other businesses. A good example of that is CBRE Workplace Strategy, who develop solutions that link business strategy to workplace initiatives.

The other cause for change in workspace is the omnipresence of sustainable building assessment systems. Employee comfort and well-being is becoming a very important factor in those systems. Those systems are all quite similar, LEED and BREEAM being most popular. Let us look at the DGNB System, which was created in Germany and starts getting traction worldwide. The DGNB System [8, p. 15] presents a catalog of evaluation criteria for new office and administrative buildings. A table divides them into sections: Environmental quality (ENV), Economic quality (ECO), Sociocultural and functional quality (SOC), Technical quality (TEC), Process quality (PRO), and Site quality (SITE). It may come as a surprise to some that the most populated section is the one regarding sociocultural and functional quality (SOC), and not the environment (ENV), despite the evaluation systems being commonly described as "green certificates". Thus, the well-being of users is of great relevance in the assessment. The following criteria are included in the SOC section:

- Thermal Comfort,
- Indoor Air Quality,
- Acoustic Comfort,
- Visual Comfort,
- Occupant Control [1],
- Quality of Outdoor Spaces,

---

[1] Occupant Control—meaning of course the ability of occupants to control thermal and other conditions in the rooms, and *not* monitoring employees by the management.

- Safety and Security,
- Access for All (i.e. universal access),
- Public Access,
- Cyclist Facilities,
- Design and Urban Quality,
- Integration of Public Art,
- Layout Quality.

As we can see, points are being awarded not only for assuring psycho-physical comfort, but also for the quality of outdoor spaces, layout, design, and even integration of art. With building assessment being so ubiquitous, new office development will have to take those aspects into account in order to get a high score and proof of high quality at the same time.

3 Usability and Portability of Devices

As much as has been said about flexibility and mobility being the driving force behind current changes in the office environment, the mobility of the tools being used is still quite limited, or more accurately: the portability of the right tools required for a non-trivial tasks is. The barriers in the evolution of work concepts are not architectural but technological.

There is a productivity gap between desktops/laptops and smaller computing devices. Smart phones and small tablets are undoubtedly mobile, because they can fit into the pocket and therefore be easily carried around practically anywhere, but on the other hand they are almost useless for doing most "serious work", and by serious work we mean performing tasks such as:

1. editing a complicated spreadsheet,
2. developing and compiling a computer program,
3. doing a side-by-side comparison of two documents,
4. writing a chapter of a book or a report.

The first two tasks show how limited the capabilities of those highly portable devices are. As long as they only run simplified versions of desktop applications under the control of special-purpose operating systems (and because of that), they cannot be considered a viable general replacement for desktop and laptop computers, even after the other issues are addressed, and the device has sufficient processing power (many of them already have). It is the choice of architecture that has the most impact on what software tools will be available on a given platform, limiting user's selection.

It is impossible to perform the third task on smaller devices simply due to the small form factor of their displays (all other tasks are affected by this as well), and it is probably the hardest problem to overcome. For a device to be truly portable and accessible anytime, anywhere, it would have to fit into a pocket—the device would have to be less than 3.5" (for a shirt pocket) or 5" wide (for a jacket pocket), that being the shorter dimension, while the longer edge could be roughly about 1.4 times that. Therefore, only the bigger version of the device would make comparing two texts side-by-side doable, barely, and only under the assumption that line lengths would not exceed 80 characters, give or take. In the old days it was considered good practice to keep code line lengths under 80 characters, because the standard terminal was 80×25, but nowadays many software projects do not honor that rule, taking advantage of usually quite large desktop displays used for development.

What would be a good solution to this problem, other than having to use for example a full-size laptop? In the case of the device fitting into a jacket, having a screen that folds in half and was originally 10" wide would be a good start. Unfortunately the shirt pocket display wouldn't be wide enough even when built from two pocket-sized parts. A possible answer could be a display made of thin elastic film with shape memory that can be folded multiple times and that returns to the original shape when taken out of the pocket.

In the case of screen size, the more is generally the better, especially for software developers. For this group of users even a 15" laptop screen would be considered small, but still acceptable on the go if no other choice is available. Jeff Atwood [9] once wrote, that one can never have too much screen space, and suggested using a setup with not even one but multiple large monitors. If one was to follow that advice, it would basically mean a come back to stationary desktop workstations. So the user would still be free to roam company premises, enjoying the creativity-boosting facilities, but actual coding would have to be performed at a designated place.

The last task is related to text input. We can disregard speech interface (it is distracting others, too ambiguous, and not expressive when it comes to input symbols: it is unclear whether something is a word, a symbol, or a control sequence) and handwriting (it is expressive but has too much variation in general, requiring the input handling software to be extremely context-aware). That leaves us with the keyboard as the most reliable method for text input, with a one-to-one relationship between input and output symbols.

The on-screen virtual keyboard available on mobile devices is a poor substitute for the traditional keyboard for a few reasons. First of all, it lacks tactile feedback—by comparison, when operating a physical keyboard, during key presses and while hovering fingers over it the brain receives sensory feedback from the fingers and the shape of the keys instantly tells if the finger "registered" correctly on the center of the key, or if it was moved a bit to the side, and which side that was. While it is possible to provide audible feedback from a virtual keyboard, passing on all that extra information, like offset, would come at the price of the sound becoming too complicated to decipher. Therefore, such finger position information is usually not presented and, as a consequence, the user can be less confident when using such an input method.

The problem is more widespread. Over the recent years we could observe a rapid reduction of tactile feedback in the design of devices—from the flattening of keyboards to replacing buttons with a "touch" interface. Touch, but not feel, one could add, because the primary and often only feedback received is visual.

Physical buttons, sliders, or dials available in the older generation of equipment
provided greater control and, what is very important, could be easily operated
by a person with impaired vision. They were also of benefit to anyone who did
not want to avert their eyes from whatever they were doing in order to look at
the interface. It is deeply concerning to encounter examples of flat, attention-
grabbing interfaces being used on automobile dashboards. But let us return to
the office setting.

In addition to the lack of tactile feedback, the on-screen keyboard is simply
too small, when compared to a physical keyboard in which the main block of keys
alone is almost 12" wide. And finally, a virtual keyboard obscures the premium
space of the already small display. To solve this dilemma, external bluetooth
keyboards are sometimes used. To have the best of both worlds, foldable keyboards have been manufactured, such as the 4-part foldable Stowaway keyboard
from the good old days of Palm and PocketPC.

The use of a full-size physical keyboard brings big productivity gains. Fast
typists, like pianists, don't look at the keyboard while typing. After months
of practice with a keyboard its general layout is memorized along with many
common short series of key presses (recalling what finger combination handles
them best, what are the displacements between key coordinates, etc.), and they
can be combined into longer, fast passages almost unconsciously.

Foldable keyboards are the portable counterpart of the traditional keyboard,
but even a small deviation from the traditional layout may generate usability
problems. For example one customer that bought a Verbatim Wireless Bluetooth
Folding Keyboard on Amazon wrote in a review [10] that he had to return it
because he just could not get used to it. The actual experience is interesting:

> The fatal flaw [...] is the keyboard layout. It is sort of laid out like a
> standard keyboard, and they tried to make up for its size by making
> the letter keys larger and the number and function keys smaller. Even
> so, the relative positions are off slightly from a standard keyboard, and
> not all the letter keys are the same size. The V key for instance is twice
> as wide and the adjacent B key. The 1 key is centered of the W, not
> slightly to the left of the Q, that's where the escape key is on this one.
> Also the tiny backspace and tab buttons throw me off and I find I often
> am hitting keys I don't intend.

The examples discussed show that efficiency-preserving portability is still an
open issue of HCI, with no clear solution, because productivity and portability
are often opposite goals. This makes desktops and laptops still the best choice for
involving, non-trivial tasks, even when it comes at the price of reduced mobility.

4   Conclusion

As we have seen so far, the office environment has evolved over the course of the
XX century, with the last generation of workplaces putting strong emphasis on
flexibility, various types of collaboration, comfort, and promoting creativity.

When the new kinds of office spaces offered are related to the creative thought process and social interaction, the use of computers can be an orthogonal issue, because it does not have to influence the layout. There are however companies experimenting with an organizational culture imposing special types of HCI, such as firms in which the employee, or even the director, does not have his own desk but can instead use whatever "hot-desk" terminal or conference room he desires that is available at the moment, or can alternatively connect to the corporate network from the outside. Most of the space in such offices is open space, with a few added team work and conference rooms, leaving HR and accounting as the only closed areas with limited and controlled access.

Whether such experiments prove successful in different office sectors, remains to be seen. Nevertheless, both architectural surroundings and the design of interfaces have a great impact on the type, quality and efficiency of work that can be done, and therefore are an integral part of studying the changing contemporary office environment.

References

1. Vink, P., de Korte, E., Blok, M., Groenesteijn, L.: Effects of the office environment on health and productivity 1: effects of coffee corner position. In: Dainoff, M.J. (ed.) HCII 2007 and EHAWC 2007. LNCS, vol. 4566, pp. 157–162. Springer, Heidelberg (2007)
2. PwC and the Urban Land Institute: Emerging Trends in Real Estate Europe 2013. PwC and the Urban Land Institute, London (2013)
3. CBRE: Poland Office Occupiers Survey–What's Next? 2013. CBRE, Warsaw (2013)
4. CBRE: The evolving Workplace. How U.S. Office Space is Changing. CBRE Research and Consulting, July 2014
5. Davis, M.C., Leach, D.J., Clegg, C.W.: The physical environment of the office: contemporary and emerging issues. In: Hodgkinson, G.P., Ford, J.K. (eds.) International Review of Industrial and Organizational Psychology, vol. 26, pp. 193–235. Wiley, Chichester (2011)
6. Greenspun, P.: Managing Software Engineers (2002). http://philip.greenspun.com/ancient-history/managing-software-engineers
7. CABE: The impact of office design on business performance, CABE (2005)
8. DGNB: Excellence defined. Sustainable building with a systems approach. DGNB–German Sustainable Building Council (2012)
9. Atwood, J.: Three Monitors For Every User, 4 April 2010. http://blog.codinghorror.com/three-monitors-for-every-user/
10. Horne, A.: Review of the Verbatim Wireless Bluetooth Folding Keyboard, 7 July 2011. http://www.amazon.com/review/R2WAM0KB2EOERJ/

Shaping of the Architectural Detail in View of Energy Saving

Andrzej Skowronski[✉] and Maciej Skowronski

Faculty of Architecture, Wroclaw University of Technology,
Ul. B. Prusa 53/55, 50-317 Wroclaw, Poland
andrzej.skowronski@pwr.edu.pl

Abstract. Global warming observed has provoked the tendencies to reduce the emission of CO2. In January 2014 Poland also introduced much stricter building-law regulations referring to how buildings should be designed in respect of heat insulation and a permissible value of EP coefficient (defining a yearly demand for primary energy). The changes introduced result from the general strategy included in the European EPBD (Energy Performance of Buildings Directive) which imposes (up to 2020) the reduction of greenhouse gases at least by 20 %. In December 2014 the European Union took up another obligation- to reduce greenhouse gases by 30 % by the end of 2030.

The consumption of energy in the building industry is vastly influenced by the thermal insulation of buildings, as well as by such things as: thermal Bridges, air tightness of a building.

When an architectural detail is not designed carefully enough or some other errors occur in the process of construction, one can observe a large energy loss which escapes through thermal bridges or other leaky places in the building. Energy loss may then reach even dozen or more per cent.

The European Union has changed legal regulations for the building industry, concerning mostly energy effectiveness. Those refer not only to the insulation capacity (passive protection from the heat loss) but also impose the obligation for new buildings to use renewable energy, which is understood as an active share of alternative energy. While doing their designer's job, architects must now dedicate their time to the calculations how much heat is lost and to computer simulations of the energy balance, including the energy coming from solar panels, heat pumps, wind energy, etc.

The changes and limits to energy consumption introduced gradually influence the character of architect's profession. The buildings designed as extensively segmented or glazed will become less economical than simple but carefully insulated blocks. Also, the role of an architect is about to be changed giving way to a new profession which could be dubbed as: a specialist in energy saving and the building physics.

Keywords: Architecture · Saving energy · Detail

© Springer International Publishing Switzerland 2015
M. Antona and C. Stephanidis (Eds.): UAHCI 2015, Part IV, LNCS 9178, pp. 360–369, 2015.
DOI: 10.1007/978-3-319-20687-5_35

1   Introduction

In local Polish publications one may come across faulty solutions referring to the process of shaping the so-called modern architectural detail. These can result in thermal bridges created, and consequently a large energy loss. Such a situation often occurs when foreign solutions designed for a different climatic zone have been applied directly, which should not be done in Poland where a former adaptation to the local climate conditions is fairly needed. In other cases, this may be an error in the designing or building process that matters. The growing costs of energy, as well as more and more strict legal regulations concerning energy saving make it necessary to design the architectural detail even more carefully.

The latest amendments to the Polish building regulations including the ordinance by the Minister of Infrastructure concerning technical conditions…., in force from 1 January, 2014, defines much stricter requirements to be applied to the building design in respect of thermal insulation [6]. This amendment refers to the original building, as well as its later alterations, including any changes in the way of using those buildings, both over and under the ground, which perform a usable function. In clauses: 148, 151 and 154, in individual passages, the Legislator has defined new requirements concerning the ventilation of buildings. In the ordinance of Chapter 10 on Energy saving and thermal insulation, in clauses: 328 and 329 the requirements defining the EP coefficient (yearly demand for non-renewable, primary energy) and the rules for its calculation were imposed. From now on the buildings must meet both requirements which concern:

- minimum thermal insulation of outer partitions in the building (walls, floors, roofs, ceilings, windows and doors)
- permissible value of EP coefficient influenced mostly by the central heating, hot water storage and electricity systems.

Up till now, it was enough to meet one of the requirements mentioned. Meeting both of them may be a real challenge for designers as the value of EP is defined by a combination of many different factors, such as: thermal insulation, method of ventilation, specific kind of fuel used for heating the building, etc. In the ordinance mentioned, clause 328, passage 1a, the requirements for alterated or reconstructed buildings were defined.

The changes introduced in the Polish building-law regulations result from the common strategy of the European Union (Energy Performance of Buildings Directive) aimed at the reduction of energy used by buildings, as well as the obligatory certificates defining the energy-effectiveness of buildings, which is specified in the directives issued by the European Parliament and Council [1]. The new EPBD directive no 2010/31/UE of 19 May 2010, point (3) says: *Buildings account for 40 % of total energy consumption in the Union. The sector is expanding, which is bound to increase its energy consumption. Therefore, reduction of energy consumption and the use of energy from renewable sources in the buildings sector constitute important measures needed to reduce the Union's energy dependency and greenhouse gas emissions. Together with an increased use of energy from renewable sources, measures taken to reduce energy consumption in the Union would allow the Union to comply with the Kyoto Protocol to the United Nations Framework Convention on Climate Change (UNFCCC), and to honor both its long term commitment to maintain the global temperature rise below 2°C, and its commitment to reduce, by 2020, overall greenhouse gas emissions by at least 20 % below 1990 levels, and by 30 % in the event of an international agreement being reached. Reduced energy consumption and an increased use of energy from renewable sources also have an important part to play in promoting security of energy supply, technological developments and in creating opportunities for employment and regional development, in particular in rural areas.* In December 2014 the European Union made another resolution - to increase the renewable energy sector up to 30 % by 2030.

All those legislative decisions in EU countries will result in the situation that only energy-saving buildings are built and in the future these will be mainly passive or even zero-energy objects. Unfortunately, no definition of such objects has been defined yet. An energy-saving home is also a home in which energy is obtained from renewable sources (sun, air, wind, biomass, earth and water) and where energy-saving equipment has been installed. The transitional period from 2014 up to 2020 (until energy saving standards have been precisely defined) in EU countries will be used for a gradual adaptation of the building sector to the very strict requirements awaiting, as well as for education and propagation of the idea for energy-saving buildings. In Poland since the mid - 2013 the National Fund for Environmental Protection and Water Economy has activated the program of supplementing credits for the building and purchase of energy-saving homes. Individual investors who within the years 2013–2018 start the investment or purchase an energy-saving building may apply for extra money as high as 30 to 50 thousand PLN. The sum of supplementary money depends on a very strict energy-saving parameter - respectively: NF40 or NF15 (energy consumption lower than 40 or 15 $kWh/m^2/year$).

The money invested in the construction of a new building or modernization of the existing object tends to grow steadily and can be easily lost due to a wrongly designed architectural detail. It may occur that the building which at a quick glance looks correct (in respect of insulation) is faulty in respect of solutions for the details applied that diminish energy effectiveness.

2 Thermal Bridges

The thermal bridge, also called the cold bridge is a commonly known phenomenon. Thermal bridges are created in places which are not sealed properly or remain not efficiently insulated, i.e. where the U-coefficient of heat transfer is significantly higher (worse) than the one for the adjacent building elements. Due to this along with a big difference in temperatures outside and inside the building in the winter time, one can observe the point or linear cooling of the partition. Through a thermal bridge the heat is lost beyond any control. The heat loss is proportional to the area of the bridge. In the place where the thermal bridge has been created the temperature of the building partition in the winter time lowers so much that the dew point is exceeded and steam is resolved into water. This phenomenon provokes a risk that the walls and ceilings in rooms become wet, as well as many other negative consequences, such as formation of fungi and molds. In extreme cases, in the places which are not properly thermally insulated, the process of freezing may occur, which consequently leads to biological corrosion of the building elements.

The standard definition of the thermal bridge is the following [5]: *The cold bridge is a part of the building housing in which a usually equal heat resistance has been changed through:*

- *full or partial piercing of the building housing by a material of a different heat conductivity,*
- *changed layer thickness of the materials,*
- *difference between outer and inner surfaces of partitions, as in the connections: wall-floor-ceiling.*
  Thermal bridges may have a point or line form.

In individual European countries fairly different standard regulations as to how to calculate thermal bridges are in a mandatory use. So far in Poland a simplified method to measure the heat loss due to thermal bridges has been applied [12]. It involves the correction of the U-coefficient depending on the question if:

- the outer wall has windows and doors - $\Delta U = 0{,}05$ [W/(m^2 × K)],
- the outer wall has windows and doors with balcony brackets - $\Delta U = 0{,}15$[W/(m^2 × K)] (see Fig. 1).

There are no particular data which would define the energy loss provoked by thermal bridges. The correction coefficients ΔU, as well as some other sources of information make us think of the heat loss as big has even 20 % [8]. This happens mainly due to long linear bridges as a result of inefficient insulating of the cover wall in the place of connection with:

- the floor on the ground,
- the ceiling above unheated basement rooms,
- uncovered passages or drive-ins downward under the building,

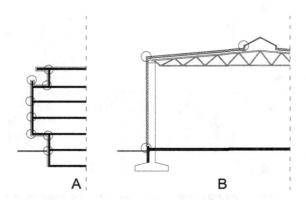

Fig. 1. Typical locations of linear thermal bridges: A – in a building of services and apartments, B – in industrial building (Source: Author's drawing of December 2014)

- ring beams on subsequent stories,
- projections,
- cornices and attics,
- roof surfaces.

Thermal bridges may occur in any building objects, and the lack of tightness may result from a wrongly developed design or a careless execution of the investment.

An extensive energy loss in buildings may also result from windows, doors or balcony brackets that have been wrongly positioned in the cover wall. Then thermal bridges are created in specific locations (points) around those places. The more windows, doors or balconies are designed and then wrongly or carelessly installed and insulated, the bigger energy loss may occur–even as high as a dozen or more per cent. Presently, however, new technologies are available that make it possible to assemble balcony brackets tightly enough to prevent any thermal bridges. In this case, the warming layer is located between the cover wall and the balcony bracket through a specially shaped reinforcement of the balcony panel (see Fig. 2).

The heat loss in buildings, generated by windows and doors, results from their worse insulation from outer walls as well. The standard heat conductivity coefficient required for the outer wall, e.g. for a detached one-family home has now a minimum value of $U = 0, 3$ [W/(m^2 × K)], while its value for a window is $U = 2 \div 2, 6$ [W/(m^2 × K)]– depending on the climatic zone. In the market, there are three-pane windows available which are characterized by a much better coefficient reaching $U = 0, 7$ [W/(m^2 × K)]. The heat conductivity coefficient for a triple-pane joint window, with a low-emission coat and an inter-pane void filled with argon may be as low as approx. $U = 0, 55 \div 0, 6$ [W/ (m^2 × K)]. Yet, the heat loss may occur on the window profile whose insulation capacity does not usually exceed the coefficient value $U = 1, 0$ [W/(m^2 × K)]. As the share of window profiles in the whole middle-sized window area is about 15–20 %, the value of the heat conductivity coefficient for the whole window (profile + glass pane) does not usually exceed the coefficient value $U = 0, 7$ [W/(m^2 × K)].

The window insulation capacity and its proper assembling should be treated as two different problems. The largest heat loss occurs in the place of connection between the

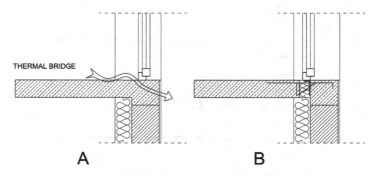

Fig. 2. Two ways in which a ferro-concrete balcony panel can be fastened: A – traditional way with a thermal bridge, B – energy-saving way within the "Isocorb" system (Source: Author's drawing of December 2014)

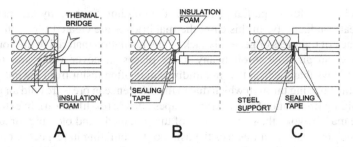

Fig. 3. Methods of window assembly: A–traditional with a thermal bridge, B and C – energy-saving methods (Source: Author's drawing of December 2014)

window and the cover wall, especially in the place where the window sill is fastened. A careless and not tight enough fitting-up may significantly lower the heat comfort of the room even if the best window is installed. Nowadays, a new method of window assembling has been developed in which windows are installed on the outside of the wall, even in the outer warming layer of the multi-layer cover wall. In this case, windows are fastened on special steel anchors (brackets) in the outer warming layer, not directly inside an opening in the brick wall. Recently, the sellers of window and door joinery have been offering various solutions for assembling windows at different prices, such as:

- commonly used the so-called traditional assemble method, i.e. inside the window opening, where a thermal bridge usually occurs (A - sealing made of polyurethane foam),
- energy-saving assembling inside the wall, in its outer part before the warming layer (B - sealing made of polyurethane foam + additional foil belts from the inside and outside of the polyurethane foam),
- energy-saving assembling on the outside of the window opening (C – within the thickness of the warming layer on the outside of the wall, on steel brackets + foil belts from the inside and outside of the window) (see Fig. 3).

Typically, thermal bridges that occur in industrial halls result from a wrongly designed warming layer applied to pad stones in the place where they contact the so-called foundation beam. Prefabricated foundation beams can now be manufactured in the warmed-up version, which means that they possess an inner Styrofoam (polystyrene foam) core. Nevertheless, designers often forget that the pad stones must also be warmed as this is where the foundation beam and the main bearing construction of the industrial hall are supported. In this case, thermal bridges occur locally, i.e. on the floor around the foundation.

3   Air Tightness of the Building

The standard definition of thermal bridge given above [5] is not precise as it does not clearly emphasize the lack of tightness of cover walls and roofs, which significantly influences the energy characteristics of the building. The building standard explains thermal bridges as: full or partial piercing of the building housing by the material of a different heat conductivity. In this case, thermal bridges are created for another reason, which is a lack of tightness or generally lack of any insulation material in the housing and, consequently, an air flow through any leaky places in cover walls and roofs. Not everybody knows that the heat loss in buildings may often result from the untight, leaky housing of the building through which due to the difference in pressure cold air penetrates into the building (infiltration) or warm air escapes outside (ex-filtration). In extreme cases the leakage may provoke the phenomenon of the so-called wind blowing (draught in the rooms), which extensively influences the using of the building in respect of comfort and ergonomics. Recently in Poland, there have appeared a lot of companies that deal with the measurement of the building tightness. The method of such air-tightness measurements is based on the Polish standard [4] and allows to measure the size of the air stream which flows through the gauge called the Blower Door. This device consists of a ventilating fan which is to pump the air into or out of the room in order to create a specific pressure, as well as measuring apparatus connected with a computer which measures the air flow at the specified difference of outside and inside pressures [7]. The measurement is done both for overpressure and under-pressure in the room, and the average value of the air stream flowing at the pressure difference equal to 50 Pa, is taken as a basis for defining the value of n50 coefficient. All the leaky places, located due to the pressure created by the Blower Door, can also be spotted by thermo-vision (a thermo-vision test by means of a camera makes it possible to observe the air flowing), as well as the using of an anemometer and smoke generator (See Fig. 4).

In the attachment to the ordinance issued by the Minister of Infrastructure on the technical conditions… [6], in point 2.3.1. the Legislator writes: *In residential buildings, blocks of flats, buildings of common use and industrial objects the outer non-transparent partitions, connections between the partitions themselves and between their parts (such as connections of flat roofs and roofs with the outer walls) all passages for the elements of installations (such as ventilation and fume ducts through outer partitions), as well as connections of windows with jambs, should be designed and*

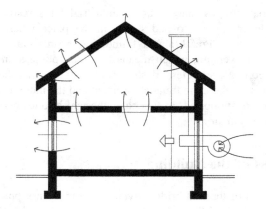

Fig. 4. Pattern for testing the air tightness of the building (Source: Author's drawing of December 2014)

performed so carefully that a full air tightness is achieved. Further on, in point 2.3.3., a recommended value of the building air tightness is given, depending on the kind of ventilation system designed (mechanical or gravitational). At the moment the testing of buildings in respect of their air tightness is not mandatory but fairly recommended, according to the attachment to the ordinance mentioned above, in point 2.3.4. which says: *It is recommended that the executed residential buildings, blocks of flats, buildings of common use and industrial objects are tested in respect of tightness and that the test is done according to the Polish Standard on air penetration so that the required tightness is achieved as it was defined in point 2.3.3.*

Testing buildings in respect of air tightness is not yet obligatory in EU countries, except for United Kingdom, while in Germany and Denmark it is required only for buildings equipped with mechanical ventilation [2].

The studies done in Poland in which a few passive or energy-saving buildings (those were designed and performed very carefully when it comes to air tightness) were tested in respect of tightness show that the improvement in tightness made it possible to save up to 40 % of energy [2]. In industrial buildings a typical place where air leaking occurs is the connection of multi-layer panels used for the so-called light building structures:

- with the foundation beam,
- with the roof,
- internally between the panels in the place of connection by means of special locks,
- where the roof ridge is covered with tinware,
- where skylights and smoke vent flaps are situated.

Any leakage may result not only from a careless execution of the project but also from some inner faults of building elements designed for the so-called light structures (e.g. untight locks between the panels, which should tightly connect them one to another). The leading manufacturers of multi-layer panels have introduced a new generation of protective panels which make it possible to save up to 20 % of energy needed for heating homes [11].

4 Conclusion

The beginning of 2014 brought in a lot of changes as to the requirements concerning the energy effectiveness of buildings. Among those, there is an obligation for the building to meet simultaneously both conditions of heat conductivity through partitions U and the permissible value of the coefficient defining the demand for non-renewable original energy EP. As for the required values of the U coefficient, compared with those of the late 2013, one may say that they are still kept on a safe level and will not make the architects change their attitude to partition designing dramatically. More controversy among architects is raised by the newly introduced values of EP coefficient (original energy). Those are much more difficult to respect, especially in some categories of buildings, as they refer to the energy balance of the whole building, including the method of heat delivery (heating, cooling, electricity) to the building, as well as the source of energy used. Therefore, to meet the EP demands the designers may need to apply solutions that so far have not been popular with those categories of buildings, which will consequently increase the cost of investment.

To achieve the standard EP coefficient (of primary energy), first both the EU coefficient (of usable energy) and the EF (final energy) must be calculated according to the rule defined by the following formula: EU > EF > EP [3]. The architect may influence only the EU coefficient through a proper designing of the function and body of the building, as well as the kind of outer partitions (of adequate U coefficients). An excessive segmentation of the building body leads to a higher energy loss. This is defined in Clause 329: *on technical conditions...* [6] giving permissible factors of the building segmentation A/V (coefficient of the building shape), where:

- A - is the sum of surfaces of all building partitions separating the heated part of the building from the outside air, ground and the adjacent unheated rooms, calculated on the outline,
- V - is the cubature of the heated part of the building minus arcades, balconies, loggias, galleries, etc. calculated on the outline.

What also provokes energy loss is an excessive glazing and therefore the current legal regulations define the permissible glazing quotient A0max, for specified types of buildings.

The theories, commonly used only few years ago, which stated that windows should be a little leaky as the inflow of fresh air prevents the dampness in rooms, as well as molds and fungi, now belong to the past. So do the gravitational ventilation systems in favor of mechanical ventilation with recuperation. Within a few years from now on, recuperative ventilation will probably become the only legally admitted solution, even for detached one-family homes.

One of significant factors of a modern building, along with energy effectiveness, is its air tightness. The designer should pay a special attention to it by choosing an adequate sealing for windows and doors. What also matters is how the steam-proof foil is connected and any piercing in installations insulated.

While designing architectural details, one should aim at the maximum air tightness.

The new architectural detail has been introduced for common use. As an example one can mention the assembling of:

- balcony brackets to prevent thermal bridges,
- windows and doors installed within the warming layer of the outer wall and sealed with belts.

In the near future, due to much stricter regulations concerning energy saving, new building technologies focusing on saving energy are going to be developed. Among others, a more and more common system of building certificates, based on energy effectiveness (energy-effectiveness certificate) as merely one of many factors, will play its role. The most prestigious buildings have to meet many other (more than a dozen) demands to be granted a prestigious certificate LEED [9] or BREEM [10].

All in all, the circle of Polish architects is deeply concerned about the changes introduced. They ask a question if the coefficients: A/V and A0max., included in the building law regulations, will put an end to segmented, sculptured and glazed buildings? Will the European Union after 2030 allow only simple blocks with eye-sockets (small windows) and those more spectacular objects can be done only at a great cost? The question arises if the changes implemented may diminish the role of an architect giving way to a new profession called for instance: the building physicist. The newly introduced building-law regulations may also make it necessary to modify the methods of educating future architects.

References

1. Directive of the European Parliament and Council 2002/91/UE of 16 December 2002 on the energy characteristics of buildings changed by the Directive of the European Parliament and Council 2010/31/UE of 19 May 2010
2. Firląg, Sz.: Szczelnosc powietrzna budynkow pasywnych i energooszczednych - wyniki badan [Air tightness of passive and energy-saving buildings - study results]. In: Czasopismo Techniczne [Technical Magazine], 2B/2012 file 3, pp. 105–113. Krakow University of Technology, Krakow (2012)
3. Osowski, S., Zarembowski, J.: WuTe architekcie Part 2. In: Zawod: architekt [Occupation: Architect], Ogolnopolskie Czasopismo Izby Architektow RP [Nationwide Magazine of Architect's Chamber], no. 38/, pp. 97–102. Izba Architektow RP, Warsaw (2014)
4. PN-EN 13829:2001: Wlasciwosci cieplne budynkow. Metoda pomiaru cisnieniowego z uzyciem wentylatora.[Polish standard: Heat qualities of buildings. Method for pressure measurement by means of a ventilator]
5. PN-EN ISO 10211–1:1998: Mostki cieplne w budynkach. Strumień cieplny i temperatura powierzchni. Ogolne metody obliczania. [Polish standard: Thermal bridges in buildings. Heat flow and surface temperature. Guidelines of measurement]
6. Rozporzadzenie Ministra Infrastruktury [Ordinance by the Minister of Infrastructure] of 12 April 2002 w sprawie warunkow technicznych, jakim powinny odpowiadac budynki i ich usytuowanie [on technical conditions applied to buildings and their location] (Dz. U. no 75, item 690) – legal status after the change introduced by Minister of, Building Industry and Sea Economy, valid from 1 January 2014 (Dz. U. no 0, item 926)
7. Blower - door – test. http://www.blowerdoortest.pl
8. Czy wiesz ile tracisz przez mostki termiczne [Do you know how much you lose through thermal bridges]. http://www.cte.fea.pl
9. Amerykanski system wielokryterialnej certyfikacji budynkow LEED [American system of multi-criterion building certification LEED]. http://www.ecosquad.pl
10. Angielski system wielokryterialnej certyfikacji budynkow BREEAM [English system of multi-criterion building certification]. http://www.ecosquad.pl
11. Systemy fasadowe Ruukki [Facade systems Ruukki]. http://www.ruukki.pl
12. Mostki termiczne [Thermal bridges]. http://www.zarzadcy.com.pl

Changes in Shaping the Banking Environment

Krystyna Strumiłło[✉]

Institute of Architecture and Urban Planning, Lodz University of Technology,
90-924 Łódź, Al. Politechniki 6, Łódź, Poland
kstrumillo@interia.pl

Abstract. The goal of this article is to show the changes in shaping the banking environment. The analysis of these changes caused by the technological development aims at illustrating which banking functions have lost their original meaning or vanished, and which functions developed from scratch. The research method is based primarily on the selected examples from existing banks in cities, as well as on the analysis of source materials, i.e. scientific literature. The process of computerization and automation of banking operations becomes an important issue. The rapid development of technologies is mirrored in the bank and client relationship. This development affects not only the way of shaping the interior, but also the operations performed and appearance of banks. New technologies have fundamentally transformed both buildings design and the whole financial services sector. Electronic banking, which definitely has many advantages, is the most popular type of banking. It leads to wider savings and also helps to reduce the need to open traditional branches of banks. Now, the percentage of the financial and banking operations conducted via electronic means is increasing and clients are also supported by ATM machines and retail offices.

Keywords: Banking environment · Banking space · Bank building

1 Introduction

Ever since the creation of the first bank buildings, the interiors with a certain spatial organization were shaped. This was due to the specificity of banks and their specific needs. It resulted also from the specific need within the relation between the banker and the client. Originally, simple banking operations did not require sophisticated interior. Over the centuries, the gradual broadening of the bank functions, and then the change triggered by technological development, influenced the changes in the objects' functionalities. Since the beginning of banking history, the most important area of the bank was the banking hall. However, banks combined also many different functions. In the recent years, we can observe the gradual vanishing of banking halls. Daniel M. Abramson [1] argues that this is the most unexpected feature of the contemporary banking architecture. The traditional functions of banks are preserved only in some modern buildings of medium-sized banks, mostly in regional offices. Another crucial issue is the appearance of automation and computerization of banking transactions. It is necessary to add that banks excel in the use of most modern achievements of technology. Currently, a growing percentage of banking and financial transactions are conducted virtually, by electronic means, but the client is also supported by ATMs and

© Springer International Publishing Switzerland 2015
M. Antona and C. Stephanidis (Eds.): UAHCI 2015, Part IV, LNCS 9178, pp. 370–377, 2015.
DOI: 10.1007/978-3-319-20687-5_36

retail branches. Computer and information technology have radically changed the functional needs of bank architecture to the extent that transactions can now take place through terminals in the wall. The introduction of self-service and work automation was the source of revolution in banking as well as in shaping bank architecture.

In the middle of the 20th century, banks began to change their appearance from closed fortresses symbolizing wealth to open institutions attracting clients. They are meant to represent hospitality and safety. Their clients must be sure that their money is and will be well kept safely. It is commonly considered that the architecture of banks should send a visual message confirming that a bank is a trustworthy institution.

2 Historical Context

Buildings of banks are objects with rich and long history. The oldest historical trace of the existence of banks dates from Babylonia, where a bank house existed in the 6th century B.C. The House of Egibi were a mercantile Babylonian family whose financial activities are known. It is necessary to mention that the lively commercial exchange in the Near East, in the Mediterranean area, resulted in the need of crediting of mercantile transactions and the invention of money. The bank house mentioned above accepted deposits for safekeeping, for which it paid interest. It also mediated in purchase and laid out part of the money from its own funds [2].

The first bank offices designed and built concerning the needs of merchants and bankers appeared at the beginning of the 15th century. They were stock exchanges. Their buildings were simple structures, something between a market hall and a guildhall, a single space hall with or without aisles. The demand for buildings of this kind did not change remarkably from their beginnings. Private houses and residences of great bank dynasties were the most characteristic buildings. Big palaces of bank families in Florence are considered to be the initiation of the growth of the power of money and the status of bankers.

Palaces in Florence performed various functions, they were presentable housing residences and workplaces at the same time, from which bankers and merchants managed their businesses. Among the most important ones is the Medici-Ricardi Palace, the construction of which was started in 1444 by Michelozzo. The Palace was built for Cosimo I de' Medici. Thanks to its owner and his influences, the structure became a pattern for other palazzos not only in Florence, but also in Italy and, later on, throughout the world. The Rucellai Palace and the Strozzi Palace are among other impressive residences in Florence worth mentioning.

With time, the activity of Italian bankers broadened and banks started to appear in England, France and Spain. The first bank building as a separate institution was erected in Barcelona in 1401. It was the Tabula di Cambi.

The second half of the 17th century and the 18th century involved the invention of paper money and the creation of central banks. The Bank of England, the first bank to have its own headquarters, was an exemplar for others. Sir John Soane became its architect in 1788. It was extended in later years, finally occupying almost a whole quarter of 1, 3 hectare. In the following decades, in the 19th century to be more specific, banks (and other types of public architecture buildings) often reached for ancient patterns. In the second half of the 19th century, the Bank of England created a network of regional branches. The buildings were to symbolize reliability and confidence. How vast was the influence of the Bank of England can be proved by the creation of the first bank building in the United States [3], i.e. that of the First Bank of the United States (1791) in Philadelphia. The bank was designed by Samuel Blodget in the classical order. The interiors were quite simple and functional, the banking hall was decorated with a Corinthian colonnade and a conference room was designed upstairs.

In Poland, the first bank houses were created in Cracow at the end of Middle Ages.

The first key-realizations mentioned above, the milestones of the bank domain, as they can be called, developed and evolved. They became the foundations of modern banking. At the end of the 20th century, the high-tech style, a technological variety of international modernism, became the favorite fashion of contemporary institutions, including banks of course, wishing to emphasize their modernity and progressive attitude to reality. The bank began to transform from a traditional, sound public building into a universal, corporate one.

3   The Evolution of Bank Spaces

Historic buildings of banks were reflections of societies which created them. Contemporary bank structures are projections of economic as well as social processes. Bank architecture has nowadays become a commercial tool, the building has become a machine that makes functioning of the institution easier and more efficient.

The traditional bank building of the 19th and the 20th century had a few distinctive features: it had a public space for the realization of its basic function, i.e. financial transactions, the so called banking hall, and a safe space for storing money – the vault.

Furthermore, as Majewski [4] describes, the bank building usually combines many various functions. Traditionally, it is:

- a public building
- a financial operations center
- a place to meet and exchange information
- an office building
- a place to store money and valuables
- a centre of modern technologies

Banks usually bring all of the above functions together in a single building or in a complex of buildings. Today, we can observe a tendency to split the functions of banks and to transfer them into separate objects: bank headquarters take the form of an office building, often inaccessible for customers. Retail points take over the function of customer service. Electronic centers of data processing and storage, the so called data centers (most often doubled for the sake of data safety) are situated (also for the sake of safety) as separate and most diligently guarded buildings. Similarly, banks more and more often build separate structures for storing and distribution of money: central vaults and distribution centers.

The factor that determines the current stage of banking architecture and banking space development is automation of the banking industry. The interaction between human and computer has a special meaning here. The introduction of automation and computerization of banking processes has become a trigger for the revolution in banking industry, as well as in modern banking architecture. Today, as a result of automation, credit cards usage and accessibility of the electronic operations, the amount of cash in the banking transactions is steadily decreasing. Cash has been replaced by electronic money. There are fewer customers physically coming to banks, the traditional division for cashiers, administrators and counselors is steadily disappearing. The most characteristic area in banks, i.e. banking hall, is disappearing as well, together with the traditional cash desk-treasury relation. The number of cash transactions is decreasing and will continue to decline.

Machines facilitate paying cash in and out. ATMs and other automated facilities have significantly influenced the shape of bank branches, which had to create the so called night zones – self-service, twenty-four-hour spaces enabling safe cash banking. The first ATM (Automatic Teller Machine) in the world was activated in a branch of Barclays Bank in Enfield Town, northern London, on June 27, 1967. It is estimated that over 2 million ATMs operate currently throughout the world, yet the number will rise up to 3 million towards the end of 2015. The rate of ATM network development is different depending on the region of the world but the highest number of these machines is to be found in Asia, Pacific islands and the USA [5]. The invention of the ATM initiated a further development of automated banking devices: automatic cashier machines, safes and multi-safes, electronic depositories, payment and withdrawal terminals, counting machines, assorting machines, etc. Yet is was the development and popularization of electronic devices that brought a true revolution in banking itself and changed (and is still changing) the outlook and planning of bank offices. The need to rebuild already existing structures also appeared. Unfortunately, there are many difficulties to overcome when trying to adapt historic interiors to the demands of contemporary banking technology. It is in Poland, however, that the oldest historic banks, i.e. the former Commercial Bank (*Bank Handlowy*) (Fig. 1) and the former Russian State Bank, both dating back to the beginnings of the 20th century, now Bank PKO BP and the National Bank of Poland and operate in renovated historic interiors. They are examples of beautiful, impressive spaces which, on the other hand, are expensive to maintain. Their banking halls with well-preserved, attractive and rich decorations have a typical bank character. They are among the most beautiful banking halls in Poland, which makes efforts to preserve the originals so reasonable. In the banks, there are also other fine and well equipped rooms, such as the president's offices, boardrooms, etc.

Nowadays banks have ceased to be strongholds, financial bastions. Bars and massive counters no longer separate clients from bank employees. More and more often, the arrangement of banking halls has the character of unconstrained, informal space full of light and color. Clients are attended in a sitting position. Friends can be met here, you can talk to your financial consultant.

Technology had freed bank architecture from traditional role: huge, imposing halls have been replaced by banking suites and tellers behind computer screens, rather than behind counters; back-rooms full of clerks have been replaced by telephone banking centres in anonymous out-of-town locations; bustling, high maintenance dealing floors at heart of the city by trades at terminals in lower rent offices on the outskirts.

Fig. 1. The banking hall in the historic building of the former Commercial Bank (*Bank Handlowy*) in Lodz, preserved until today. Currently Bank PKO BP. (photo by author)

Fig. 2. A banking service point of Cooperative Bank (*Bank Spółdzielczy*), situated in the building of the Revenue Office in Lodz. (photo by author)

New technologies have also been the reason of growing competitiveness. Companies and key clients are attended electronically and are able to conduct their financial operations online, practically from every corner of the world. A growing number of banking and financial operations is realized virtually, without participation of money. The individual client is served by a network of ATMs and retail branches (Fig. 2). The automation of collecting, processing and transforming data has contributed to a substantial reduction of costs and personnel.

It can be observed in Poland that many bank buildings have been put up for sale while networks of retail branches expand significantly. The most dynamic development of such networks fell on the nineties of the previous century. At present, a tendency to verify networks and to optimize branch locations can be observed. Their number in Poland is not growing any more, the number of personnel is decreasing.

4 Forms of Banking

Electronic banking is currently the most popular form of banking. Banks are developing its telephonic forms, i.e. access through ordinary or mobile phones, call centers, Short Message Service or WAP technology. Electronic banking is being intensively developed by most banks all over the world. Separate divisions are created to meet the needs of this kind of customer service.

Internet banking (access through a computer, a web browser and the Internet) and home banking (access through a computer, a dedicated communication link and specialized software on the client's side) are becoming increasingly popular. It is worth mentioning that in 1998, in Germany, the world's first virtual bank came into being. NetBank had neither any branches nor a call center. Internet banks are also being established by non-banking institutions. For example, Prudential, a British insurance company, has founded an Internet banking service called Egg.

Individual banking, traditionally playing a subordinate role in comparison with corporate banking, has completely changed its face through last decades and has become a spontaneous, attractive field of banking activity. Even banks which traditionally served corporate clients, such as Goldman Sachs, Morgan Stanley in the USA or CitiBank in Poland, are now investing in the development of retail networks. It is worth mentioning that Goldman Sachs and Morgan Stanley opened their offices in Warsaw a few years ago.

Currently, only buildings of bank branches have preserved characteristics typical for banks. The other types are no longer banks. Headquarters buildings are standard, contemporary corporate office structures. Bank retail branches are usual commercial places. Interestingly, the following functional conditions were included into the architectural competition for the European Central Bank: according to the plans, the building should have enabled the realization of various users' demands, support and strengthen contacts between users in order to eliminate organizational barriers and favor group work. It should have maximized the probability of meetings and personal interactions above the organizational network of internal hierarchy.

5 The Influence of Changes on Perceiving Bank Architecture in the City

Bank buildings have always occupied an important place in the hierarchy of architectural structures. They have often been exposed within the tissue of the city, being a significant element of the tissue at the same time.

It is necessary to notice that changes in banking are very fast, which sometimes compels selling historic banks or gaining new function. It can even apply to new banks which have not been able to operate for a longer time. Of course, it is not a rule, the examples (mentioned above) of which can be the former Commercial Bank (*Bank Handlowy*) and the Russian Bank of State (*rosyjski Bank Państwa*) in Lodz, which operate in well-kept, historic interiors. Occupying presentable locations along one of the main city streets, they are situated on street corners, which makes them exposed from both sides. There is no doubt they still remind of the splendor of banks as financial institutions.

New bank buildings, on the other hand, are becoming increasingly universal, cosmopolitan and anonymous. There is a symbol of new times in it, a new approach to architecture that should serve the human being, not just to be presentable. Such architecture is a result of a complete change of understanding the form of financial institutions. Contemporary banks, without large vaults, without classic cash desks (replaced with cash automats), are office-like structures. With time, we can observe changes in the hierarchical arrangement of city objects, changes concerning the size and scale of the object. Banks are often engaged into office activities, their buildings being strongly marked within the city profile. So, the significance of office buildings has risen much recently.

The fact that big cities have banking districts, also called financial districts, cannot be omitted. Frankfurt, Germany, with the most important institutions of Commerzbank and the European Central Bank, is one of such cities. The buildings prevail the city skyline, they are easily recognizable, they even became symbols [6].

Commerzbank headquarters (architect Foster Associates) is still one of the most modern facilities of its kind. The building is undoubtedly the pride of the city and a dominant part of the landscape, which is why it is easily remembered by the observer. By 2003, the bank was the highest building in Europe (it is 298 m high).

It can be noticed that the biggest banks are taking part in a race to build the highest, the most expensive and the most technologically advanced premises to emphasize their significance. Heathcode notices [7] that the German financial capital has fought hard to assert itself as the new financial capital of a united Europe. London has traditionally been the banking centre of Europe and Frankfurt has struggled to usurp London's dominance of international money markets. A major component of the effort a credible new financial capital in competition with London has been the construction of Commerzbank building, DG Bank and recently the European Central Bank on a huge scale. To define Frankfurt's new character, one cannot omit bank architecture. Yet, it is not the banks that have to dominate with the height of their buildings to become characteristic objects in the city. The original premises of the former BreBank (nowadays mBank) are a perfect example of a bank that became the flagship of the city of Bydgoszcz, Poland. The building creates characteristic landscape of the Brda River waterside recalling the commercial identity of the city.

K. Lynch, an American urban planner, pointed out the image-creating role of a city forum. He distinguished two features of urban landscape: clarity and imaginability [8]. According to Lynch, clarity is the ease with which different parts of the city are recognized and organized into a coherent whole. Clear city is a place where individual areas, neighborhoods and distinctive buildings are easily identified and merged into an overall arrangement. The physiognomy of a city and the form of development affect the identification of a place. The space of a city, which contains informative and aesthetic values, is very important in creating the indicative and cultural basis. Such distinctive buildings can be contrasted with small retail branches, which have originated so numerously in recent years, on ground floors of accidental buildings, with advertising so aggressive that one can talk about littering of the space.

It must be stated that the process of architecture unification and standardization, the disposal of its identity, either local or typological, is characteristic not only for bank architecture, but also for other cotemporary buildings. Yet banks that have become characteristic elements of the city outline can still influence the city's image.

6   Conclusion

Taking into account the process of globalization, it should be noticed that it is the development of technology that determines the direction of bank spaces development. Furthermore, new forms of banking, which make the relations between the client and the bank easier, lead to further evolution of the building.

Banks undergo constant changes as a result of reactions to innovation in the world of technology. This is accompanied by erecting new objects since adaptations do not always rise the occasion.

The perspectives of bank space development in the present world are difficult to foresee. It can be stated for sure that banks need a flexible architectural model for the growth of banking services. The psychological aspect, indispensable for ensuring the feeling of safety of the client, must be taken into account as well.

Despite the technical revolution, bank headquarters still exist. Banks are continuously adapting to the changing requirements of modern world, still being a crucial element of the city space. The power of banks is immeasurable and modern technocratic societies would collapse instantaneously without them.

References

1. Abramson, M.D.: Building the Bank Of England. Money, Architecture, Society 1694–1942. Yale University Press, New Haven, London (2005)
2. Biasiotti A., Galeazzi L.: Progetto banca, Milano (1986)
3. Belfoure, C.: Monuments to Money. The Architecture of American Banks. McFarland & Company, Jefferson (2005)
4. Majewski, S. J.: Według klasycznego wzorca. Architektura-Murator, vol. 2, pp. 39–40 (1999)
5. Automatyka bankowa. Najnowsze trendy i rozwiązania z zakresu technologii bankowych. http://www.automatykabankowa.pl/bankomaty-pokonaly-kryzys-i-ich-liczba-na-swiecie-bedzie-rosla/
6. Strumiłło K.: Special form in the landscape of a city. Bank building as a symbol-vs. an identity of a place. In: A Special Element in its Surroundings. The Identity of Place, pp. 436–445. Oficyna Wydawnicza Wyższej Szkoły Ekologii i Zarządzania w Warszawie, Warszawa (2013)
7. Heathcote, E.: Bank Builders. Wiley-Academy, Chichester (2000)
8. Lynch, K.: The Image of the City. The MIT Press, London (1994)

Some Paradoxical Aspects of the Use of Computers for Architectural and Structural Design

Romuald Tarczewski[✉]

Faculty of Architecture, Wroclaw University of Technology, Wrocław, Poland
romuald.tarczewski@pwr.wroc.pl

Abstract. The architectural form determines visual perception of the building and its social acceptance. From it depends also fulfillment of functional and utilitarian assumptions, adopted at the project beginning. The aim of architectural modeling is primarily to create a geometric model of the future facility. It has also influence on the ability of modeling of the structural system which is a carrier of architectural form. All limitations of the structural system translate into limitations of architectural form. As long as only straight lines and planes were readily available, and any curves and non-planar surfaces were extremely difficult to model – architectural form was characterized by preference of orthogonality. If one looks at the restrictions in both architectural and structural modeling, resulted from the shortcomings of the underlying theory, and the impact that introduction of modeling with use of numerical tools had on change of that situation – it can lead to surprising conclusions.

Keywords: Building modeling · Numerical models · Shaping of form

1 The Complexity of the Form and the Complexity of Means of Expression

While admiring the beauty of classical forms of ancient buildings, we not always remember through how simple means of expression it has been achieved. We do not always remember that it was largely the result of the consistency of the architectural form and construction system.

In terms of static we are dealing with only a few very simple elements: single- and multi-span beams, cantilever bar. Joined together in various combinations they allowed developing well known elements: column, architrave, cornice, frieze, triglyph, metopes, pediments, which became the main components of the style, later supplemented by numerous details, Fig. 1. Thanks to them, we can admire the distinction between Doric, Ionic and Corinthian styles, each of which has been materialized in many, often greatly differing, objects [1]. The same was true in ancient Egypt and other great civilizations, in which their own original architectural forms emerged on the basis of available material and technological solutions. Indirectly, the objects thus manifested their reliability and durability, allowing their users to break away from a purely

M. Antona and C. Stephanidis (Eds.): UAHCI 2015, Part IV, LNCS 9178, pp. 378–389, 2015.
DOI: 10.1007/978-3-319-20687-5_37

utilitarian function – protection against environmental conditions, and focus on the symbolic function – temple, palace etc.

Fig. 1. Basic components of form and structure in the ancient Roman temple in Ebora (Portugal): 1 – stereobate, 2 – stylobate, 3 – column base, 4 – column shaft, 5 – column capital, 6 – architrave, 7 – frieze, 8 – cornice

The complexity of the architectural form was therefore not directly related to the complexity of the structural system. Homogeneous understanding of technology enabled precise communication between the participants of the investment process with use of relatively simple tools.

1.1 Communication in the Investment Process

Every building object emerges first as an abstract idea related to the needs of investor. This idea is translated onto architectural language and converted to the architectural concept. The initial concept is developed up to the stage of detailed design, which must be then communicated to the contactor, craftsmen etc. Information is produced and exchanged at every stage of the investment process. The amount of information and number of connections between the participants in the process, for its exchange increases rapidly with the transition to the successive phases of investment. Since the exchanged information covers a variety of specialized fields and are produced and stored in various forms, their exchange requires the use of appropriate tools, such as classification, coding, graphic conventions, textual descriptions, etc. The ability to exchange information is a precondition for design and construction of a building. Information is exchanged through the model of building, specific to a particular task, which can be used with different agents.

Model of the building, created in the investment process, exhausts contemporary definition of the interface: it denotes a *"point of interaction between a number of participants in the process [...], coordination and interaction between several work groups, is used to communicate plans and control production activity. This interaction can be a human interaction, computer systems, or any other medium of communication"* – as stated by the popular definition in Wikipedia. Building models are created to allow the exchange of information between all those involved in their realization – from the investor, through designers up to the craftsmen working on the construction site.

Any limitations on the possibilities of creating models of buildings, as well as the exchange of the information contained therein, in a direct way limits the range of solutions available for the designer. If the architect cannot build a geometric model that describes the required spatial form, he is not able to transmit information about this form to the other participants of the investment process, and thus such a form cannot be constructed. If the structural engineer is not able to build a calculation model of a complex system, he will use the simpler systems, which he is able to consciously use.

1.2   Impact of Building Modeling on Architectural Form – Observations from Antiquity to the Beginnings of the 20th Century

Models of buildings reflect both the needs for which they are created, and the technical determinants of the period in which it originates. All available media were used as an information carrier. In ancient Mesopotamia these were the clay tablets with drawings and cuneiform descriptions. A little later, in ancient Greece, textual description was sufficient as a complete building mode, however physical models were also created. This was due to a common understanding of the general patterns and samples used in construction, called *paradeigmata* [2–4]. Have been also preserved Egyptian drawings used in contract documents, and there are information (e.g. Vitruvius) about drawings used by designers in ancient Rome. It's amazing how much these ancient drawings are close to the modern graphic conventions [5].

This situation remained broadly to the beginning of the twentieth century. Progress in the building modeling was related mainly to media and way to write on these media. In the field of media, it was a shift from a very expensive (and therefore spared) papyrus, parchment and vellum, to the cotton- and linen-based paper and ultimately to the wood-based paper. New recording technologies included printing press with movable type, graphite pencils, color pencils, modern drawing instruments, typewriter, blueprints etc. [3].

In a relatively small extent this development affected theoretical concepts underlying the modeling of buildings. As important steps can only be mentioned: the introduction of "Arabic" numerals, perspective drawing and standardized measurement system. All of these improvements, however, relate only to the technology of presentation in the building modeling and do not have a significant impact on its form. They do not change the scope of shaping forms available for designers. Penchant for orthogonality, strongly disclosed in this period results both from the limitations in the transfer of information about more complex geometry, as well as the inability of its structural analysis.

2   Contemporary Revolution in the Methods of Building Modeling

Visionary work "As We May Think" by Vannevar Bush in 1945, and Memex system described in it, created the ideological basis for development of computer graphics. Another important step in its development was made in PhD thesis of Ivan Sutherland, defended in 1963 at MIT, in which he presented his revolutionary program Sketchpad. This pioneering program changed the way of human-computer interaction, among others things by introducing a light pen as a universal interface. This idea was taken up and creatively developed by Douglas Engelbart, who, in his presentation at the Fall Joint Computer Conference in San Francisco in 1968, later called "The Mother of All Demos", presented fully mature, comprehensive way of working with a computer – the one we know today. The doors to the use of computers in modeling of buildings have been opened.

Currently, the primary carrier of information is a digital recording in computer memory. However, more important than the type of media, aspect of the model is the way in which it represents a modeled object. It is always dependent on the degree of advancement of knowledge in the specific field.

Hitherto, building modeling technology was only a consumer of general scientific knowledge, especially in the field of geometry and applied mechanics, developed independently of the needs of the investment process, so to speak. This situation changed when the graphic computer programs have ceased to be merely intelligent drawing board, but allowed easy handling of complex geometric objects that have emerged along with new theoretical solutions, such as B-splines, biquadratic flexible surfaces, sponges (labyrinths) and many others, e.g. Fig. 2. It is obvious that the emergence of such forms influenced also the forming of the modern aesthetic paradigm.

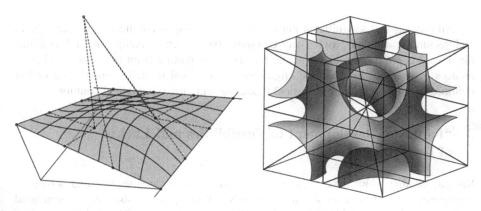

Fig. 2. Two examples of new geometric structures that have been discovered thanks to the possibilities offered by computer graphics: on the left – NURBS surface with visible control vertices (CV) [6]; on the right – single repeatable frame of sponge i.e. a system of saddle surfaces connected with a single polyhedron (the edges of the frames pass through the tunnels of labyrinth) [7]

In structural modeling, the geometric model is just a starting point for the formulation of a model describing the static, dynamic and strength properties of the system. Historically, for a very long time this modeling was based mainly on the accumulated experience and intuition of designers. Since the emergence of the science of structural mechanics and strength of materials, structural models were based on analytical solutions, describing the relationship between the load, internal forces and deformations in different types of construction. The catalog of these types of structures is, however, limited, and any attempt to go beyond it can cause a loss of mathematical support for modeling. Numerical methods, particularly finite elements method, enabled the digitization of structural systems, and thereby description of very complex structures, for which previously did not exist analytical solutions, Fig. 3.

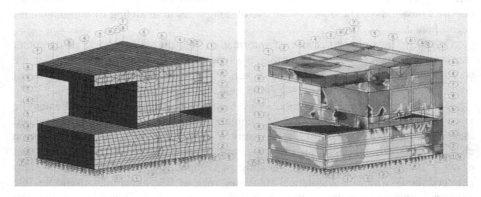

Fig. 3. An example of the analysis of the Opera House in Wroclaw (Poland) using the Finite Element Method (FEM): on the left – division of the building structure into finite elements; on the right – distribution of extreme stresses in the form of maps on the walls of the building

All this has had a significant impact on the modeling in architecture and design. In architecture, it enabled provide any complex spatial forms, manipulate and visualize them, evaluate the impact of climatic factors – a departure from the orthogonal preferences in shaping. In structural engineering, numerical modeling supplanted earlier methods of analyze, such as physical modeling and closed analytical solutions).

3   "Fantastic Development of Possibilities and Lack of Guidelines"

Radical change – increase of modeling capabilities in architecture and structural engineering, occurred almost simultaneously, allowing that modeling of structural systems can keep up with the modeling of architectural form. This led to the widespread belief that "anything is possible". The mere fact that the form is feasible is often sufficient reason for designing it.

Usually unnoticed limitation of structural modeling by means of the finite element method is the need for accurate geometric data, as input to build the model. It is possible to analyze any number of variants of the object model, but they all must be pre-defined. So, can be analyzed only objects whose form has already been geometrically defined earlier, in the stage of architectural modeling, which – as mentioned above – gained almost total freedom to create forms.

In such a process, disappeared – developed over the centuries – common search for forms by architect and structural engineer. And the latter one lost the tools to creatively support architect.

Thus appeared a belief that everything that is possible is reasonable and should be constructed. Sometimes this view is supported by a quote from G.W. Leibniz – *"Omne possibile exigit existere"* – Everything that is possible demands existence (De veritatibus primis, 1686).

In architecture, this became the conviction that there are no ugly or inappropriate forms. More important is originality, understood as otherness and astonishment – sometimes even shocking – of recipient by the visual effect.

In structural design, became possible modeling of "everything". Designers began to create complex computational models, fleeing from the intellectual effort related to the deep understanding of the essence of the problem. This phenomenon constantly increases with entering into working life successive generations of engineers. Mathematics becomes a kind of alibi to justify the lack of their own creative invention.

This situation has led to the emergence of a whole series of forms that can be boldly called pathological. On the one hand, their visual attractiveness attracts the attention of the public opinion, they are widely reported and commented, on the other hand, it is difficult to find for them any (except perhaps for prestige) functional or economic justification. One of the most famous such examples in recent years is undoubtedly the Olympic Stadium in Beijing, constructed in 2008, Fig. 4.

Fig. 4. Olympic Stadium in Beijing (arch. J. Herzog and P. de Meuron)

A huge amount of steel consumed for the construction this object, the structural elements of a very complex geometry and large dimensions, as well as the determination of the investor in the pursuit of the project (during construction were a number of fatal accidents) – were repeatedly subjected to criticism and even condemnation.

Another example of an object whose form is based on a fairly random inspiration (pappardelle pasta) is a new building at the Fair in Milan, Fig. 5. Witty, in the early stages of design, inspiration, has led to the need to design a structural system that is difficult to define other than "forced by the architectural form". The author of this project, a prominent structural engineer, M. Majowiecki, pointed out on this occasion that indiscriminate "adding" of the structural system, to the arbitrary given architectural form, carries a lot of risks that did not exist before, in the traditional design process [8]. This includes such issues as: a lot more complex configuration of loadings (particularly wind load), unclear scheme for verification of the spatial stability, complicated diagram of exhaustion of cross-section capacity, dynamic problems, etc. Thus, thoughtless pursuit of originality may, in extreme cases, even lead to failure threatening the safety of users of the object.

Fig. 5. "Cometa" Milano Portello Fair in Milan (arch. M. Bellini, struct. eng. M. Majowiecki)

The title of this paragraph, which is a quotation of A. Einstein's statement, is a brilliant punchline of that situation: we can design and analyze (almost) everything – but do we know what we should design and analyze?

4   Intuition Rediscovered

The reaction to this situation is an attempt to restore, in numerical version, formerly used tools which allow designer not only to control the calculations of the given form, but also allow to actively shaping it. These are e.g. advanced development of long known graphical static methods, reverse catenary modelling, flow of forces method and the use of prototypes of structural forms found in Nature.

On this occasion one can observe a paradox. New possibilities for shaping the geometry led designers to focus on the visual effect of their work, leading up to a "showiness". Today, however, just methods associated with visual perception give hope for healing situation.

An example would be the latest trend in the development of methods for the calculation of structural systems. In the above-mentioned Finite Element Method (FEM) first and very important step is to divide the analyzed area (surface, space) onto sufficiently small parts. Current methods of division are based on algorithms originally developed for other purposes, e.g. rendering in movie animation (e.g. Coons patches). What's more, they referred to the division of the "traditional" surfaces rather than today's popular free-form surfaces. Thus, very often they are based on triangularisation. The isolation of these algorithms from geometric description with use of e.g. NURBS, is obvious.

Intensively developed for last ten years, area called the "Isogeometric Analysis" is focused on working out such algorithms of division, and then calculation procedures in FEM, to obtain homogeneous, using the same geometric tools, description of both the geometry and mechanical properties [9]. The aim of this approach is to bring unity in the geometrical and mechanical description of the modeled object.

Another very interesting and promising trend is to restore to use methods that were once widely used, and then almost forgotten. By combining them with numerical modeling, appeared entirely new capabilities of creating the form.

An example of such a "revitalization" of design methods is intensively renewed interest in graphical statics methods. These methods, which peak development was in the second half of the nineteenth century, have subsequently been almost completely supplanted – initially by iterative calculation method, e.g. the H. Cross's method, and then by the above mentioned finite elements method. Now, in last few years, appear publications in which authors not only highlight the reasonableness of the use of these methods in design practice, but also propose new, very interesting extensions and generalizations of these methods [10].

Physical modeling for a long time was the only available method to analyze complex structural systems. Spectacular examples of this approach for the formation of the whole object can be found in the works of Antoni Gaudí, especially the famous Sagrada Familia in Barcelona. Appearance of numerical methods caused that the scope of the physical modeling is currently limited to testing the individual components, while this approach is not applied as a comprehensive tool to shape the form.

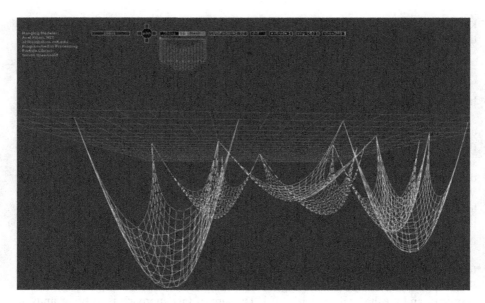

Fig. 6. Interface screen in the Hanging Modeler program, developed by Axel Kilian

A. Gaudí used a special form of physical modeling by building catenary models in which flexible strings likely to transmit only tensile forces, represented arches and vaults of designed structure. After reversing the model upside down, the designer receives a structure which, for the dominant loading schemes, is only in compression. This allowed, for example, constructing impressive structures of stone blocks. Currently, has been developed software based on particle-spring systems, which allows construction of virtual catenary models [11]. This software allows easy creation, through an intuitive graphical interface, Fig. 6, of complex catenary models, which can then be further processed in other programs until the full value structural model is achieved, Fig. 7.

Fig. 7. An exemplary structure shaped in the Hanging Modeler program

Another very interesting example of the numerical implementation of the physical modeling is a software that allows a virtual representation of the process of creating origami structures. This traditional Japanese art of paper folding has been used for the design of deplayable structures of different applications – from construction industry to the space antennas [12]. Freeform Origami software [13] allows to perform and test virtual models based on this concept.

An example of the modeling of the structure of the roof covering of the building shaped as folded shear beam structure is presented below [7]. A simple initial pattern, Fig. 8 left, has been deformed by origami method, Fig. 8 center and right, until the desired geometry was achieved. The resultant model of roof covering, Fig. 9 left, was then transferred to the finite element method the program, in order to determine the values of internal forces caused by snow load, Fig. 9 right. Easy and clearly legible, visual binding of the obtained geometrical form and static structural behavior is a great advantage for the designer in the initial stage of shaping the form.

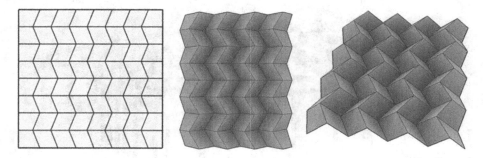

Fig. 8. Successive stages of shaping form of roof covering by means of origami method

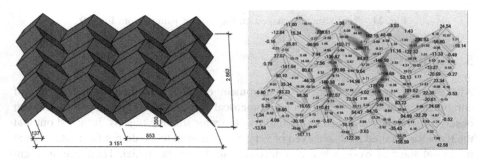

Fig. 9. Analysis of the structure of Fig. 8, by using the FEM program

Still other possibilities results from the use of natural prototypes of structural forms. Using patterns found in the Nature, one can reconstruct them in a scale of the building, while maintaining their interesting structural properties. Interestingly, sources of inspiration are not necessarily obvious and may be based on purely visual associations. Below is an example of using the pattern formed on cracked ice cap, Fig. 10, to design a roof structure of the building, Fig. 11 [7, 14].

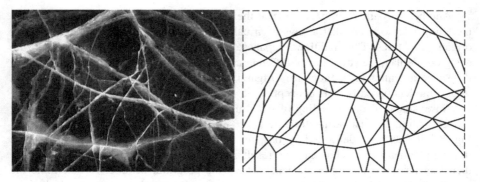

Fig. 10. A pattern formed on cracked ice cap

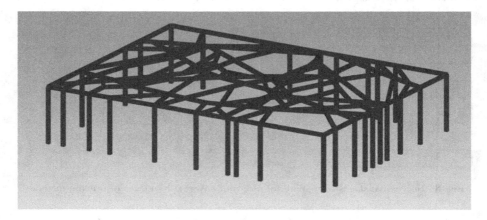

Fig. 11. Roof structure shaped on the base of pattern from Fig. 10

5 Conclusions

After several years of intensive development of design methods with the use of computers, both for modelingin the geometrical form and structural system, one can observe a tendency to return to the intuitive tools for shaping objects. It turned out that the tools for detailed analysis, even of very complex structures, do not facilitate work at the initial stage of work, when it is necessary to define the model. Therefore in recent years emerged the methods and tools to fill in this gap. They allow using computers in the traditional pre-design process.

Traditional, experience based methods of structural design must be replaced by designing based on mathematics, which combines static and aesthetic problems. Lightness (freedom) of architectural form does not automatically translate into a lightness and freedom of structural form.

Artur Loeb's remark, that *"Space is not a passive vacuum; it has properties which constrain as well as enhance the structure which inhabit it"* [15] is confirmed once again.

References

1. Koch, W.: European Architectural Styles. W. Foulsham & Co Ltd, London (1978)
2. Jeppesen, K.: Paradeigmata – Three Mid-fourth Century Main Works of Hellenic Architecture Reconsidered. Aarhus University Press, Aarhus (1958). Jutland Archaeological Society Publications Vol. IV
3. Gelder, J.: Specifying architecture: a guide to professional practice. Construction Information Systems Australia, Sydney (2001)
4. Ziolko, J.: Byggesaksdokumenter. Norske standarder og bruk av EDB-methoder. Universitetsforlaget, Oslo (1991)
5. Heisel, J.: Antike Bauzeichnungen. Wissenschaftliche Buchgesellschaft, Darmstadt (1993)
6. Tarczewski, R.: Evolution of building modeling methods in the investment process. In: Obrebski, J.B. (ed.) XX LSCE International Seminar on Lightweight structures in Civil Engineering – Contemporary problems. Micro-Publisher, New York (2014)
7. Tarczewski, R.: Topology of structural forms. Natural and man-made prototypes of structural forms. Oficyna Wydawnicza Politechniki Wrocławskiej (2011) (in Polish)
8. Majowiecki, M.: Personal experiences in structural architecture: from form finding to free form design. Architectus 4(40), 79–92 (2014)
9. Cottrell, J.A., Hughes, T.J.R., Bazilevs, Y.: Isogeometric Analysis: Toward Integration of CAD and FEA. Wiley, New York (2009)
10. Akbarzadeh, M., Van Mele, T., Block, Ph: Spatial equilibrium networks using 3D reciprocal diagrams. In: Obrębski, J.B., Tarczewski, R. (eds.) IASS 2013 – Beyond the Limits of Man. Oficyna Wydawnicza Politechniki Wrocławskiej, Wrocław (2013)
11. Kilian, A.: Linking digital hanging chain models to fabrication. In: Fabrication: Examining the Digital Practice of Architecture. ACADIA 2004 Proceedings of the 23rd Annual Conference of the Association for Computer Aided Design in Architecture, Cambridge and University of Toronto, pp. 110–125 (2004)
12. Miura, K.: Method of packaging and deployment of large membranes in space, In: Proceedings of 31st Congress of International Astronautics Federation (IAF-80-A31), Tokyo, pp. 1–10 (1980)
13. Tachi, T.: Design of infinitesimally and finitely flexible origami based on reciprocal figures. J. Geom. Graph. 16(2), 223–234 (2012)
14. Tarczewski, R.: Natural and geometrical prototypes of organic forms in architecture. In: Obrębski, J.B., Tarczewski, R. (eds.) IASS 2013 – Beyond the Limits of Man. Oficyna Wydawnicza Politechniki Wrocławskiej, Wrocław (2013)
15. Loeb, A.L.: Space Structures: Their Harmony and Counterpoint, p. 1. Wiley, New York (1991)

Interior Architecture and Humane Design

Elzbieta Trocka-Leszczynska and Joanna Jablonska[✉]

Faculty of Architecture, Wroclaw University of Technology, Wrocław, Poland
{elzbieta.trocka-leszczynska,
joanna.jablonska}@pwr.wroc.pl

Abstract. There is a distinct correlation between the interior design architecture and ergonomic quality of space in hotel rooms. However, is an increase in standard paired with human comfort and safety? Does a higher standard of a hotel unit type, i.e.: Superior, Comfort or Suite, provide optimal spatial solutions? The article presents a continuation of a study on the following elements: design solutions, internal finishing, furnishing and appliances; investigating their influence on the well-being and safety of people with or without any type of disability. Research based on literature and numerous case studies was focused mainly on the needs of independent travelers, who wish to live in a hotel space without a need to rely on help from a third party. The scope of study includes hotel bedrooms, sitting rooms and bathrooms.

Keywords: Room standard · Appliances · Ergonomics of a hotel residential unit · Ergonomics of a hotel room

1 Introduction

A hotel room is undoubtedly the most significant part of a hotel, as its standard and furnishing determines the guests' level of comfort and safety. Beside objective factors, i.e. fulfillment of one's most important daily and nightly needs, optimal size, adjusted furniture and appliances, quality of finishing materials; a person's quality of stay is ensured by other individual subjective or psychophysical factors, e.g. "coziness", sense of spaciousness, "hominess", "modern style", beautiful interior design solutions or acoustics. Moreover, some of the previously mentioned parameters may be mutually exclusive, while hotels undergo a constant innovative process, understood as development in the area of "productivity, quality, competitive positioning, market shares, etc." [1, p. 702]. The presented variety of factors necessitates a continuous study of hotel rooms in order to determine ever new ergonomic guidelines for the safety and comfort of use.

Another premise for the undertaken study is related to the equally significant commercial aspect of the hotel industry. Room décor and design are crucial factors determining a customer's choice. Cited by various sources, Dube's study from 2000 indicates that the "physical property" and "guest-room design" are, respectively, the third and fourth factors on a 10-point list of attributes used in hotel selection [1, p. 703]. Therefore, the discussed aspects should be designed properly and from good materials,

© Springer International Publishing Switzerland 2015
M. Antona and C. Stephanidis (Eds.): UAHCI 2015, Part IV, LNCS 9178, pp. 390–400, 2015.
DOI: 10.1007/978-3-319-20687-5_38

because, as indicated by Robson and Pullman, [2] even the most insignificant corrections of appliances may prove very expensive for large hotels.

It is worth noting that the above described room features are strictly connected with room type and standard. The same hotel may offer residential units of various levels of comfort, decor and furnishing. A common practice includes also a frequent renovation of interiors of the Suite type in correspondence with the Standard or Economy type.

Thus, considering all of the above, the paper is focused on the correlation between the standard and furnishing of hotel rooms, while taking into account the guests' level of comfort and safety. Additionally, a range of other means facilitating a comfortable usage of space by people with various psychophysical disabilities, such as allergies, arthritis, minor hearing or visual impairments, was examined.

1.1 Methodology and Research Aim

The basis of the conducted research was to establish categories according to which hotel rooms, bedrooms and bathrooms are evaluated. Jaremen D.E. in his work from 2006 suggested the following relatively clear criteria in this aspect: size (subjectively-objective factor), cleanliness (culturally determined objective factor), functionality (culturally determined objective factor), aesthetics (subjective factor), completeness (objective factor), comfortableness (subjectively-objective factor), contemporary style (subjectively-objective factor), basic furnishing (objective factor), additional furnishing (subjectively-objective factor), decorative elements (subjectively-objective factor), lighting and room temperature (objective factor regulated by law, yet dependent on subjective impressions) [3]. Other significant factors are: acoustics (objective factor regulated by law, yet dependent on subjective impressions), fire safety (objective factor), and safety of use (objective factor). At the same time, it should be discussed weather to include the previously mentioned criteria of contemporary style and decorative elements, as, overall, they seem irrelevant to ergonomics. While in the paper, the authors refer to Jaremen's list of criteria, the classification of factors given in brackets is original [3]. Due to the need to limit the scope of the research, the categories of decorative elements (as less significant) together with lighting and temperature (as factors regulated by law) are not discussed in the paper. They have, however, been discussed in detail in literature.

In regard to methodology, the study was based on the following methods: analysis, graphic and critical analysis, synthesis, comparative synthesis; and sources: literature, Internet and case studies. In terms of furnishing, size and other comfort providing factors, 19 hotel facilities located in Poland and other European countries were comprehensively studied. All researched facilities, including those reconstructed according to national heritage regulations, were adapted to the needs of modern-day guests. Moreover, the research scope included facilities rated from 3 to 5 stars.

The goal of the undertaken study was to establish ergonomic solutions aiming at ensuring comfort and safety of users according to the hotel's type and standard. Taken into account were the needs of a healthy, yet possibly suffering from various temporary or permanent ailments, person. This was due to the fact that deteriorations in one's psychophysical state, i.e. arthritis, hearing and visual difficulties, heart diseases [4], are not classified as disabilities, however they may hinder normal functioning.

2 Discussion

For hotel guests, a hotel room provides possibly the only private zone during the course of their trip. Therefore, its separateness and integrity should be preserved, as it fulfills a basic human need [5]. Moreover, for the room to serve the guests adequately, it needs to provide several activity zones. Among those, Robson and Pullman list: sleep area, workstation, room for clothes changing, and a fully equipped bathroom [2]. This is confirmed by other sources [4, 6], indicating a need to provide room for man's daily and nightly (sleep) activities, as well as entertainment and rest. Additionally, Rutes, Penner and Adams [4] point to the crucial interconnection between the distribution of functions and supplied daylight through the creation of adequate zones, namely: daily rest by the windows (seats), workstation (desk, table), bed and TV in the center of the room, and, finally, changing area by the door, i.e. a wardrobe and clothes rack [6]. The cited authors state further that each of the discussed activities takes up a certain area of floor surface. Hall [5] also draws attention to the need to provide space for additional activities, e.g. stepping away from the desk and stretching ones back. However, in hotels, due to technical and economic factors, all activities are reduced to fulfill the minimal space requirement [6].

2.1 Floor Surface and Comfort

Next to legal documents, in Poland it is the Minister of Economy and Labor Regulation of August 19 2004 regarding hotels and other facilities providing hotel services (uniformed text, Journal of Law 2006, No. 22, Item 169) with subsequent amendments, legislation in force as of January 26 2015 (later in the text referred to as Regulation) [7], the minimal size of a room is adjusted according to the projected furniture and free space necessary for the utilization of each appliance. Hall, in regard to the function of providing a workstation zone, defines 3, so called, "invisible" usage zones:

"1. Immediate workstation area, including a chair and desk;

2. Area located within an easy reach from the desk;3. Area in which one can move away from the desk and work without getting up from the chair" [5, p. 73].

The same zones can be established for the bed, i.e. an area enabling the arrangement of bed linen, an area providing sitting space and possibility to maneuver bedside tables and night lamps. Similarly, armchair and closet should be preceded by free floor space, enabling the user to stand before them, change, etc. Failure to provide all necessary zones will result in the impression of a tight area and will obstruct the usage of appliances. This is connected with the so called "kinesthetic space", i.e. range of human hands. Hall claims that in most American hotels, there is not enough of it, and any try to circle the room would result in collision with furniture [5, p.74].

Therefore, it is not surprising that the accepted floor surface norm (dependent on the construction and floor plan structure) is diverse and adjusted according to the type of a room. This is clearly visible in the case of suites – the higher the standard, the bigger the residential unit. Moreover, a raise in standard results in the enlargement of a bathroom in order to provide room for deluxe sanitary equipment and inducing a feeling of luxury [2]. In the aspect of room décor it is recommended to provide mirrors in the room and strong lighting in the bathroom so as to optically enlarge space [4].

The interconnection between standard and space management is presented on the following illustration and based on simplified floor plans of the 5* Aquila Atlantis Hotel in the center of Heraklion in Crete (Greece). With the subsequent standard/size dimensions ratio: Comfort/Business – 24 m², Superior/Executive – 26 m², Junior Suite – 35 m², Family Superior – 36 m² (See Fig. 1).

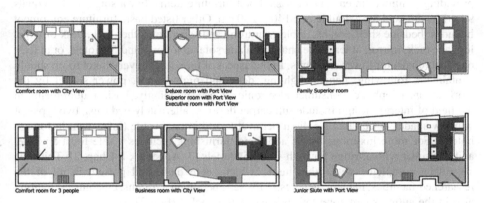

Fig. 1. Diverse room configurations in the Aquila Atlantis Hotel in Heraklion, Crete (Greece) – elevated standard visible in the space management method (compiled by J. Jablonska, 2014 based on [8]).

While discussing the interconnection between floor surface and comfort, it is crucial to mention methods of furniture arrangement. Hall talks about 2 basic tendencies in this aspect, indicating cultural differences between Japanese and European culture [5]. While the Japanese place furniture in the center of a room leaving empty peripheries, the Europeans arrange it along the walls. As a result, while in the first instance a feeling of spaciousness is evoked, in the second one may feel overwhelmed. [5].

Moreover, it needs to be noted that space management is only one of the factors creating the sense of comfort, as the latter is further dependent on guests' individual characteristics. For example, some may feel uncomfortable in large interiors, as in such environments there is a risk of disorientation (vision deterioration) or of an excessive reverberation time (hearing deterioration). At the same time, relatively small, but optimally furnished rooms with an interesting interior design may seem "cozier" or more appealing than multi-room presidential suites. This is further confirmed by sources stating that a guest's well-being is determined not exclusively by the size of a residential unit, but also through furnishing, décor, and color [6]. The given set could also be supplemented by the type of surface and its texture (soft, warm, smooth, cold, etc.).

2.2   Furnishing and Standard

In literature one may find a suggestion to limit the number of furniture items through a skillful process of joining their functions together [4]. For example, a chest of drawers may serve as a TV cabinet and have an additional function of a folding table for working purposes. Seat height adjusted to enable comfortable typing or laptop usage would help to eliminate extra chairs. Finally, installation of night lamps above the bed allows for the use of smaller bedside tables or shelves only, while at the same time installing a wide countertops below the mirror in the bathroom reduces the need to provide additional furniture [4] (Fig. 2).

In Poland the law [7, Appendix I, Chap. 2] specifies the standards of equipment, providing minimal dimensions of basic hotel furniture items. For a single bed it equals 90×200 cm, and for a double bed 140×200 cm. Other listed basic furniture equipment includes: bedside shelf or table, table, wardrobe and separate clothes rack, desk or table, luggage rack, mirror, at least one chair, sofa and sofa table for 4 and 5* hotels, or at least one seat (chair) for lower standards. In the aspect of furnishing, every hotel room should contain the following: general lighting, desk and night lamps, power socket by the workstation, telephone, consumer electronics. Correspondingly, basic requirements in the field of interior design include full carpet flooring, alternately bed rugs, two types of window shades or curtains, i.e. light permeable and impermeable (infrequent in foreign hotels). For more luxurious hotels additional furnishing includes a safe for a 5* hotel and a minibar with a fridge for both 4 and 5* hotels [7, Appendix I, Chap. 2]. This data should be completed with other items, which seem basic and present in all of the researched facilities, namely: headrests, TV sets, bed linen, curtains, customized lighting also in the sitting room zone, mirrors and paintings [4] (Fig. 2).

Furthermore, according to Polish regulations a telephone set is a mandatory device in all hotel rooms [7, Appendix I]. An interesting discussion regarding the best placement of this appliance took place in the US, suggesting either a place on the desk or by the bed. At first, high class hotels provided telephone sets in both places, but later resorted to a telephone headset with a docking station [4]. In the mobile phone era this problem may be perceived as outdated and the presence of a phone set in the room as questionable. Nevertheless, for a person with any type of psychophysical disability a possibility to quickly connect with the reception desk in order to obtain information, request service or medical help, proves absolutely crucial. In this case, a telephone set should be located by the bed as well as in the bathroom, always in a clearly visible and easily accessible place. In life threatening situations one should not rely strictly on wireless appliances, which may run out of battery or have no signal.

It is worth noting that sanitary facilities should be present in all hotel rooms. Polish building law [7] regulates basic bathroom equipment, listing an all in one bathtub with shower or shower cabin, bathroom sink with a cabinet or shelf with adequate lighting, and a toilet. Other elements include a bathtub shield, bath mat by the bathtub and shower cabin, handles by the bathtub and shower cabin (for all interiors, not only the adapted ones), clothes racks, toilet roll holder, and a soap dish. Mandatory furnishing items include electrical sockets with safety covers, hair dryers (not for 3* hotels), wastebasket and a telephone (the latter only for 5* hotels) [7].

Conducted case studies illustrated that an upgrade in a hotel room standard (especially for Economy, Standard and Comfort), even with the same floor surface, is clearly influenced by additional or more luxurious furnishing. In the aspect of furniture this included: customized furniture, beds with an increased width or length or fitted with spring mattresses, ergonomic chairs, armchairs and beds. Among the appliances were: flat-screen TVs of various size, designer coffee makers, high end sound systems, tablets, docking stations for iPods, and, finally, lighting adapted to individual activities. In sanitary facilities the standard upgrading furnishing comprised of separate bathtub and shower cabin with a shower rain head. The equipment facilitating a more comfortable use of a hotel room for all guests included: floor level shower trays, extended horizontal door and balcony window handles, handheld shower heads (in place of permanently mounted and rain shower heads), supporting handles in slippery and exposed to moisture areas, a supporting handle by the toilet, large and visible device buttons and light switches [4]. Moreover, sound insulation and allergy friendliness are seen as additional factors creating a more attractive environment for prospective visitors [2, 8]. Other solutions increasing the comfort of utilizing a room include the possibility to control lighting and bed curtains, fast Wi-Fi and touch panels enabling the control of various parameters, i.e. lights, temperature [4].

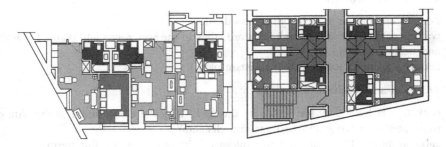

Fig. 2. Furnishing and standard – on left: InterContinental Hotel in Warsaw – the scheme of layout part with double rooms of a higher standard, typical for levels VIII-XXII; on right: Kraków Park Inn – double rooms with twin option (compiled by J. Jablonska, 2014, based on: [6, p. 321, Fig. 2 and p. 316, Fig. 2]).

As it was previously mentioned in the "Floor surface and comfort" paragraph, next to furnishing, furniture arrangement is equally crucial. Robson and Pullman [2] point to the need of providing a possibility to watch TV from the bed, a comfortable usage of one's own laptop in the workstation, or collision free deposition and storing of clothes in the wardrobe. Research conducted by Robson and Pullman confirms that guests expect an ergonomic but also an interesting interior [2]. In one of the studied hotels the guests were asked to choose the best and most interesting room furnishing and listed the following: adequately located soap dispensers in the shower cabins, paintings hanging over the bed and view outside the window. It is noteworthy that in the same study customers also identified inconveniences, i.e. bathroom headphones easily falling to the floor, lack of a shelf for cosmetics over the bathroom sink, tangled electrical wires under the desk, faulty wardrobe doors [2]. The latter issue is connected with another crucial element ensuring the users comfort, i.e. the need of efficacy of all devices located in a residential unit [6, 7].

2.3 Atmosphere and Star Rating

Citing Countryman and Jang (2006) [1, p. 703] sources indicate three elements creating atmosphere: light, color and style (Figs. 3, 4). Texture, often neglected by designers or chaotically applied, could also be added to the list [5]. All these factors are elements of interior design and are distinguishable based on the standard of a given hotel room:

For rooms:

- floors – carpets, carpet flooring, tiles (warm climate), wooden flooring with rugs (suites),
- walls – painted plaster, wallpaper, stucco, wall paneling and baseboards (high standard),
- ceiling – painted plaster, acoustic materials (rarely),
- doors – acoustic panels or wooden (high standard),

for sanitary facilitites:

- floors – ceramic or stone (high standard) tiles,
- walls – ceramic or stone (high standard) tiles in the wet zones and painted plaster and wallpaper in the dry ones,
- ceiling – painted plaster (water resistant paint),

electrical and mechanical appliances:

- sockets – at least 2 by the bed, 1 by the desk, 1 by the closet and 1 in the sitting room zone (for computers and vacuum cleaners),
- cable system – TV, 2 phone lines, Internet (wireless or cable), fire alarm,
- air-conditioning (for 4 and 5* standards) and air supply exhaust system in bathrooms,
- fire detectors and sprinklers (according to local regulations) [4, 8].

Ambience may be influenced also by other factors. For example, Robson, Pullman [2] indicate two tendencies in creating interiors of modern-day hotel rooms. The first one is directed at enlarging space, mainly by broadening rooms in order to create interesting furnishing arrangements, while the second is creating small, but very cozy areas in the existing buildings, characteristic especially for boutique hotels. In Poland, facilities of this type are located usually in the existing building stock and may fall under certain exemptions according to Sect. 3. 1. of the Regulation [7]. The referenced paragraph indicates that in the aspect of facilities on the national monument list certain exceptions from the building regulations are acceptable. For example, rooms 32 m2 large "with a garden view" in The Granary La Suite Hotel (located in the ruins of an old granary), situated in the historical part of the building allow guests to admire the 17th century ceilings, parts of original walls and especially customized furniture. Undoubtedly, original building features are very attractive for customers.

Fig. 3. Atmosphere of the Aquila Atlantis Hotel in Heraklion, Crete (Greece) is created by simple but high-quality materials (photograph by J. Jablonska, 2014) (Color figure online).

Fig. 4. Atmosphere of the Hotel Yasmin in Prague (The Czech Republic) is created with the use of color, textures of materials and mirror effects (photograph by J. Jablonska, 2013) (Color figure online).

On the other hand, it is proved that innovative solutions may also draw clients. This was exemplified by findings from research conducted in the 5* Granada Hotel in Alanya in Turkey, particularly popular among guests from Germany and Russia [1]. The cited researched involved a questionnaire distributed among 200 guests and 97 hotel employees. Undoubtedly, the findings indicate a significant role of architectural innovations in fighting competition on the market [1].

Based on the cited source materials as well as case studies, it becomes clear that creating hotel ambience is not just about referencing tradition, maintaining a classical style, or blindly following trends. On the contrary, it is considerably more important to create an original offer which would "stand out from the crowd". In conclusion, interior design should always provide an ergonomic décor and not overwhelm the user (Figs. 3, 4).

2.4 Other Comfort Ensuring Factors

Internet sources indicate that the basis for a well-designed hotel is comfort: comfort of use, sanitary and acoustic [6]. Factors determining a comfortable use of a residential unit were listed above.

In the sanitary facility it is important to provide hotel guests with a sense of cleanliness and freshness [6]. Next to providing proper service, finishing materials resistant to cleaning processes and able to maintain immaculate appearance in the course of use are absolutely crucial. Their aesthetics and durability are therefore essential. Yet, it is worth noting that certain materials popular in contemporary interior design, i.e. raw concrete, scratch coat plaster, stone vein ceramic tiles, old-styled wood, may reduce the feeling of cleanliness and freshness.

Another aspect of sanitary hygiene is smell. "Olfactory space" in architecture, a term coined by Hall, influences the feeling of comfort as well as memories from a given environment [5, pp. 64-65]. "Smell invokes far deeper memories than image or sound" [5, p. 64]. Designing space in the aspect of smell may seem difficult, however, in choosing finishing materials it is crucial to pay attention to the scent they emit. Rather dangerous in this aspect are all types of textiles and carpet flooring, as artificial glues and water-proofing substances are often used in their production. Hence, it is also crucial to evaluate the risk of emitting unpleasant odors by this type of materials.

Acoustics is a crucial element of a hotel's space. Properly soundproofed interiors eliminating noise from the outside as well as other rooms and halls, provide the guests with necessary privacy and rest. Hall, in his book "Ukryty wymiar" (English: "The Hidden Dimension"), cites examples of complaints regarding a certain manager's qualifications, which came to a halt when the acoustic environment of the conference room, where the meetings with employees were held, was corrected [5, pp. 62-63]. The sound proofed walls eliminated traffic noise and the manager's assessment among employees was greatly improved. Except from isolating outside noise, it is necessary to provide acoustic comfort related to interior design.

Large areas of the suite type are especially at risk of the echo effect. Sound reproduction (e.g. of impact noise) may lead to a feeling of confusion and general anxiety. In contrast, small rooms (Single, Double type) are in danger of excessive absorption of acoustic waves, which may results in a guest feeling overwhelmed, entrapped or generally claustrophobic. The simplest method of sound adjustment in both rooms is an adequate distribution of soft (upholsteries, textiles, curtains, carpet flooring, carpets, etc.) and hard (plastered and painted walls, wooden, ceramic or stone cladding tiles, etc.) materials and surfaces. A more sophisticated method includes an additional optimization of acoustic structures, for example on the ceilings (Fig. 5).

Fig. 5. Interior sound adjustment with a proper layout of materials in Sofitel Chicago Water Tower, Chicago Il. (USA) (photograph by J. Jablonska, 2013).

3   Conclusion

Comfort in a hotel room is provided by the following: floor surface, functionality (including completeness), standard of furniture and appliances, atmosphere, cleanliness and hygiene, equipment efficiency, interior design aesthetics, acoustics, lighting and room temperature, etc. Certain solutions favorable for hotel guests, i.e. handles by sanitary appliances, wide handles and door knobs, lowered shower trays, are characteristic for all hotel rooms. However, based on case as well as literature studies, it is very clear that the level of functionality in a residential unit is strictly intertwined with its standard. For example, comfortable matrasses, ergonomic seats and office chairs, as well as healthier finishing materials (natural, noble) were present in rooms with higher standard such as: Comfort, Executive, Superior, Exclusive, and Suite.

Therefore, we would like to conclude by stating that optimal design requires the use of safe ergonomic solutions in all types of hotel interiors. The standard should be raised by providing more luxurious appliances, furniture, and finishing materials, however not at the expense of hotel guests' health.

References

1. Doğana, H., Nebioğlub, O., Aydına, O., Doğana, İ.: Architectural innovations are competitive advantage for hotels in tourism industry? What customers, managers and employees think about it? Procedia - Social and Behavioral Sciences **99**, 701–710 (2013). http://www.sciencedirect.com/science/article/pii/S1877042813039864. Accessed on 21 January 2015

2. Robson, S., Pullman, M.: Hotels: Differentiating with Design. In: Implications, vol. 03, no. 06. The Regents of the University of Minnesota, (2002–2005). www.informedesign.umn.edu. Accessed: 24 January 2015

3. Jaremen D.E.: Ofensywa jakości dla hoteli i pensjonatów. Kierunki doskonalenia jakości. Metodologia badań, Partnerstwo na Rzecz Rozwoju Nowe szanse dla transgranicznego rynku pracy i gospodarki Euroregionu Nysa, Jelenia Góra (2006). www.vip.karr.pl/pliki/METODOLOGIA.pdf. Accessed: 21 January 2015

4. Rutes, W.A., Penner, R.H., Adams, L.: Hotel Design, Planning and Development. Norton and Company Inc., New York (2001)

5. Hall E. T.: Ukryty wymiar, trans. In: Hołówka E. (ed.) Warszawskie Wydawnictwo Literackie "MUZA". SA, Warsaw (2003)

6. Nowoczesne hotelarstwo: od projektowania do wyposażenia. In: Błądek Z. (ed.) Palladium Architekci – Błądek. Manikowski, Poznan (2010)

7. Minister of Economy and Labor Regulation of August 19 2004 regarding hotels and other facilities providing hotel services (uniformed text, Journal of Law 2006, No. 22, Item 169) with subsequent amendments, legislation in force as of January 26 2015

8. www.booking.com. Multiple access between: September 2014 - February 2015

Ergonomics and Universal Access

Aiding Self-reliance of the Elderly and the Disabled - Modular Cupboard with Mobile Internal Units

Agata Bonenberg[✉]

Faculty of Architecture, Poznan University of Technology, Nieszawska 13 C,
60-021 Poznan, Poland
agata.bonenberg@put.poznan.pl

Abstract. Changes in the age structure of societies, development of medical care and, even more importantly, the drive of the elderly and the disabled towards self-reliant and satisfactory lives make the creation of space devoid of any barriers a fundamental goal of the architectural design. The subject of the study presented in this paper is the design of the modular cupboard with mobile internal units. The purpose of such a unique construction of this piece of furniture is to make the users able to optimally use the space available in the upper parts of the room. The paper consists of the three main elements: description of the inventive design, analysis of the customization options for the modular cupboard frame, and the research including the assessment of the modular cupboard frame according to the *kansei* method.

Keywords: Designing for the disabled and the elderly · *Kansei* method · Customization

1 Introduction

In the face of the demographic and social phenomena of the 21st century, related to the changes in the age structure of societies, the development of medical care and, even more importantly, the drive of the elderly and the disabled towards self-reliant and satisfactory lives, the creation of space devoid of any barriers has become an imperative of the modern architectural design. Adaptation of the surroundings to the needs of the users, who have diversified mobility impairments and high expectations related to their old age, is an important element of the therapy of accident victims and the disabled as well as the prolongation of self-reliance of the elderly.

The above-mentioned assumptions are viable thanks to the new inventive design of a modular cupboard with mobile internal units. The purpose of such a unique construction of this piece of furniture is to make the users able to optimally use the space available in the upper parts of the room. The aim of the project is to facilitate the kitchen work for the disabled, performing everyday tasks, and developing interest in cooking. The project meets the European principles of universal and inclusive design (Branowski and Zabłocki 2006).

M. Antona and C. Stephanidis (Eds.): UAHCI 2015, Part IV, LNCS 9178, pp. 403–412, 2015.
DOI: 10.1007/978-3-319-20687-5_39

2   Structure of the Study and Research Methods

The design of the modular cupboard allows for the most important achievements and stylistic trends in the modern architectural design and the public utility design, which include:

- popularization of electric drives that support the mobility of the pieces of furniture,
- employment of the remotely-controlled mechanisms,
- discrete interior design that employs the unobtrusive spatial solutions related to the physical impairment of the user,
- following the modern stylistic patterns and the universally accepted trends of the furniture design.

The above-mentioned achievements and stylistic trends have been defined through the literature research and the analysis of model solutions offered by the leading manufacturers of the kitchen furniture.

The paper consists of the three main elements:

- description of the inventive design, prepared on the ground of the literature research and the analysis of model solutions,
- analysis of the customization options of the modular cupboard frame,
- research including the assessment of the modular cupboard frame according to the *kansei* method.

3   Core of the Modular Cupboard Concept

Solutions employed in kitchens that are designed solely for the purpose of serving people without any disabilities significantly differ from those dedicated to the users with limited mobility, chiefly in the aspect of ergonomics related to the vertical accessibility zones. In case of the kitchens used by the elderly and the disabled, the vertical dimensions of the basic kitchen planes, that is the height of worktops and the height of wall cabinets, are designed individually.

The modular cupboard is aimed at enabling persons using a wheelchair or persons with a limited scope of manipulation movements convenient access and use of storage space located at higher levels of rooms which are usually inaccessible to them (Bonenberg A. 2013).

The invention solves the problems of storage space availability and it relates to persons with near-ground reach and manipulation zone resulting from anthropometric characteristics (e.g. low height of a person), the musculoskeletal system mobility (e.g. at older age) or motor disability (e.g. persons using a wheelchair). At the same time the piece of furniture enables traditional manner of use by persons with full motor skills.

The comfort of use both by disabled persons and able-bodied persons makes the piece of furniture meet the European standards of universal design (Figs. 1 and 2).

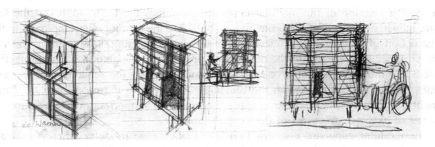

Fig. 1. Drawings presenting the preliminary concept of the modular cupboard [A. Bonenberg]

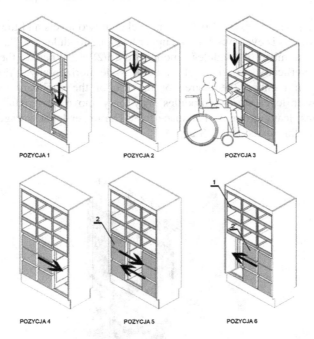

POZYCJA 1   POZYCJA 2   POZYCJA 3

POZYCJA 4   POZYCJA 5   POZYCJA 6

Fig. 2. Principles of operation for the modular cupboard. Six possible positions of the internal baskets. Positions 1, 2, 3 – upper baskets have been pulled down. [by A. Bonenberg]

4   Structure of the Modular Cupboard

In terms of its structure, the cupboard is comprised of two systems: the support-and-drive system and the protective system. The protective system is designed in accordance with the stylistic concept of the remaining furniture in the room and as a self-supporting element that remains independent from the support-and-drive system.

The design solution of the modular cupboard combines the technologies of the furniture industry (in terms of the protective system) and the technologies employed in the construction of machines with mechatronic drives (in the support-and-drive system). This provides comfort within the design and production. Separation of the protective system and the support-and-drive system is simultaneously the separation of the aesthetics, which is consistent with the remaining furniture in the room, and the functionality. This way it is possible to apply the universal support-and-drive system in a number of external structures of the kitchen furniture.

The modular cupboard contains two levels of storage modules where the availability of upper modules is ensured owing to the possibility of sliding them to the lower level. The movement is supported with the electric drive and mechatronic control. Modules may be equipped with shelves, drawers, cabinets or pull-out cargo type elements.

Modules are placed in skew drive system socket at two levels and the total number of skew drive sockets is even n > 2. In the upper level n/2 modules are placed and in the lower level the number of modules amounts to (n/2)−1. Whereas the upper level modules slide vertically, lower level modules slide horizontally. Along with the increase in the n number, the degree of the use of the cupboard usable area is increasing. Lower level storage modules may only move horizontally, to strictly defined positions, leaving one socket space free. The upper level storage module can easily move into this space (Figs. 3 and 4).

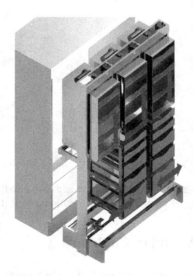

Fig. 3. Support-and-drive system of the modular cupboard. [by A. Bonenberg]

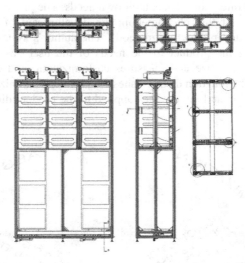

Fig. 4. Support-and-drive system of the modular cupboard. [by S. Głowala]

The construction of the modular cupboard has been awarded with prestigious prizes: the gold medal at the INPEX exposition in the USA (Pittsburgh) and the gold medal at the European EUROINVENT exposition. The question of further development of the product has been brought into the spotlight. The patented system of mobile units constitutes the ground for further development while the next step should be the decision concerning the frame of the cupboard that would exhibit its values and render it attractive for its future users. The decisions taken in terms of the industrial design were based on two research methods:

- analysis of the mass customization options of the modular cupboard frame,
- assessment of the proposed visualizations of the modular cupboard frame according to the *kansei* method.

5 Analysis of the Mass Customization Options of the Modular Cupboard Frame

The separation of the support-and-drive system and the protective system enables the designers to match the frame of the cupboard to any existing set of furniture. The popular strategy of adapting the product to the individual user's needs is customization, which has become a standard feature of the industrial production (Bonenberg W. 2013). According to the studies[1], as many as 30 % of consumers would like to receive the

---

[1] The study has been conducted on a sample of 1000 customers who make their purchases online. Source: Forbes, access on 06.11.2013. (http://www.forbes.com/sites/baininsights/2013/11/05).

individually prepared offers that reflect their own needs. The process of co-designing is the attractive element of this phenomenon: the development of modular solutions, flexible technologies and production methods. The author's systematics showing the stages of customizing the product to the needs of the user has been based on the functional customization, size and measures customization, and the aesthetical customization (Fig. 5). The diagram distinguishes the product customization at the stage of the industrial production and the changes applied to the product directly by the user.

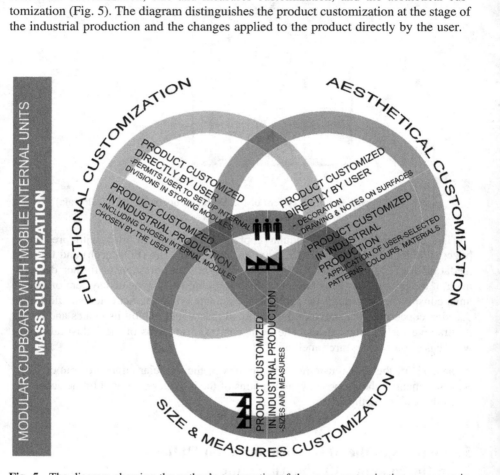

Fig. 5. The diagram showing the author's systematics of the mass customization processes in designing the modular cupboard. [by A. Bonenberg].

In case of the modular cupboard, the customization is carried out at the functional level which can be personalized on the user's request both at the stage of the industrial production and personally by the user (secondary partition of the space available in drawers and cabinets, which determines the position of tools and products stored inside the cupboard). The customization of the size and measures can be undertaken only at the stage of the industrial production whereas the aesthetical customization of the modular cupboard is possible both during the industrial production and directly by the user. Two solutions in terms of the modular cupboard frame has been suggested: a high-tech solution with the front made of the polycarbonate resin and aluminum and a traditional one that employs a bended and lacquered MDF (Fig. 6).

6 *Kansei* Method in the Selection of the Modular Cupboard Frame

In case of the mass customization in the furniture industry, the manufacturer is required to offer a large number of available finishes, functional solutions, and sizes while the customer often faces a difficult decision in terms of choosing the optimal solution.

Thanks to the kansei method (Nagamachi 2011; Mori 2002), it is possible to examine the feelings of potential users towards the studied object. This method allows for a human factor in the assessment of a given project, that is the emotions and feelings which usually slip out from the fully measurable assessments, e.g. functioning of the device. The basic purpose of employing the kansei method is to limit the number of design variants of the furniture without the risk of reducing the attractiveness of the offer. It is possible to predict the decision of the customer. Therefore, it is crucial to maintain proper balance between the diversification of the offer and the number of options available to the customer. Kansei is the method of creating the product value and consists in the statistical examination of the interrelation between the customer's feelings and the product's measurable features. The reduction of the number of available variants of the product constitutes the reason for which the manufacturers attempt to understand the stimulus responsible for the customer's satisfaction.

The applied research method is based on seven consecutive stages:

1. Defining the scope and aim of the research.
2. Appointing 20 competent judges (the expert method).
3. Determining the criteria to describe the product (in form of a semantic differential).
4. Determining the criteria weight by comparison in pairs and standardizing the extreme values (the expert method).
5. Conducting surveys.
6. Averaging out the expert assessments of the furniture and hierarchizing the results.
7. Conclusions.

The purpose of the research is the selection of a final solution from among a high-tech solution with the front made of the polycarbonate resin and aluminum and a traditional one that employs a bended and lacquered MDF. Thus, the scope of the research embraces two suggested design proposals.

20 competent judges, aged 41–68, were appointed and then the criteria describing the product were formulated in the form of a semantic differential. The concepts included in the table are related to the reception and associations evoked in the judges by the presented modular cupboard frames. The assessment was based on a five-point grading scale (Table 1).

Then, the criteria weight was determined by comparison in pairs and the extreme values were standardized (Tables 2 and 3).

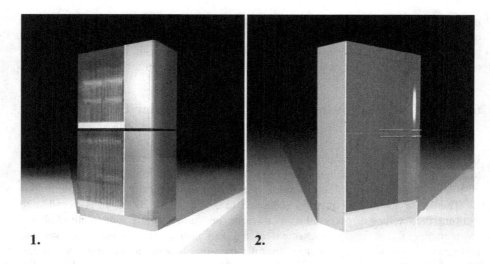

Fig. 6. Comparison of a high-tech solution with the front made of the polycarbonate resin and aluminum and a traditional one that employs a bended and lacquered MDF. [by A. Bonenberg].

Table 1. Semantic differential [by A. Bonenberg]

CRITERIA	CONCEPTS
K1 COMPLEXITY	(complex ↔ simple)
K2 MODERNITY	(modern ↔ traditional)
K3 UNIQUENESS	(original ↔ common)
K4 INNOVATIVENESS	(innovative ↔ imitative)
K5 INTEREST	(interesting ↔ boring)
K6 DANGER	(safe ↔ dangerous)
K7 USABILITY	(multi-functional ↔ mono-functional)
K8 INDUCTION OF EMOTIONS	(emotion-inducing ↔ neutral)

Table 2. Summary table of the averaged-out assessments of the furniture provided by 20 competent judges. [by A. Bonenberg].

CRITERIA and CONCEPTS	FRAME 1	FRAME 2
K1 COMPLEXITY (complex ↔ simple)	5.5	1.8
K2 MODERNITY (modern ↔ traditional)	6.7	4.5
K3 UNIQUENESS (original ↔ common)	3.4	3.3
K4 INNOVATIVENESS (innovative ↔ imitative)	5.6	3.8
K5 INTEREST (interesting ↔ boring)	7.5	6.9
K6 DANGER (safe ↔ dangerous)	3.9	6.8
K7 USABILITY (multi-functional ↔ mono-functional)	4.5	4.8
K8 INDUCTION OF EMOTIONS (emotion-inducing ↔ neutral)	8.2	6.7

Table 3. Summary table of the averaged-out and hierarchized assessments of the furniture provided by 20 competent judges. [by A. Bonenberg].

CRITERIA	FRAME 1		FRAME 2	
K1 COMPLEXITY	5.5 × 0	0.1	1.8 × 0.1	0.18
K2 MODERNITY	6.7 × 1	6.7	4.5 × 1	4.5
K3 UNIQUENESS	3.4 × 1	3.4	3.3 × 1	3.3
K4 INNOVATIVENESS	5.6 × 0.78	4.4	3.8 × 0.78	3.0
K5 INTEREST	7.5 × 0.71	5.3	6.9 × 0.71	4.9
K6 DANGER	3.9 × 0.14	0.5	6.8 × 0.14	1.0
K7 USABILITY	4.5 × 0.5	2.3	4.8 × 0.5	2.4
K8 INDUCTION OF EMOTIONS	8.2 × 0.07	0.6	6.7 × 0.07	0.5
		$\sum$ **23.2**		$\sum$**19.28**

After summing up the score, it becomes noticeable that the first variant (FRAME 1) with a high-tech stylistic design is preferred among the group of 20 judges.

7 Summary

The design and aesthetics of the product constitute crucial elements of the adaptation of the surroundings to the needs of the elderly and the disabled. The furniture dedicated to this target group may be modeled in a futuristic pattern since this way it does not evoke associations with the restrictions caused by the disability and the old age. On the contrary, it remains attractive and draws attention. The frame of the modular cupboard that was chosen by the group of judges only confirms this thesis. Despite their advanced age, the group of 20 competent judges found the modern high-tech design more attractive. Such a result was unexpected since this age group is commonly considered to be strongly attached to the traditional design of the furniture.

Adaptation of the surroundings to the needs of the users with mobility impairments constitutes a crucial element of improving life quality for the accident victims and the disabled as well as of prolonging self-reliance of the elderly. In the face of the demographic and social phenomena of the 21st century, related to the changes in the age structure of societies and the development of medical care, seeking solutions that employ the principles of universal and inclusive design becomes the necessity. The proposed construction of the modular cupboard provides a step towards the available space.

References

Bonenberg, A.: Shaping an integrating kitchen space with gesture-based control system. In: Stephanidis, C., Antona, M. (eds.) UAHCI 2013, Part III. LNCS, vol. 8011, pp. 12–21. Springer, Heidelberg (2013)

Bonenberg, W.: The impact of visual impressions on human work environment–based on the example of industrial design. In: Stephanidis, C., Antona, M. (eds.) UAHCI 2013, Part I. LNCS, vol. 8009, pp. 255–263. Springer, Heidelberg (2013)

Branowski, B., Zabłocki, M.: Kreacja i kontaminacja zasad projektowania i zasad konstrukcji w projektowaniu dla osób niepełnosprawnych. In: Jabłoński, J. (ed.) Ergonomia produktu. Ergonomiczne zasady projektowania produktów. Wydawnictwo Politechniki Poznańskiej, Poznań (2006)

Hall, R., Mace, R.: Design for physical and mental disabilities. In: Wilkes and Packard (ed.) Encyclopedia of Architecture: Design Engineering and Construction, p. 755, New York (1998)

Nagamachi, M.: Kansei/Affective Engineering. CRC Press, Boca Raton (2011)

Mori, N.: Rough set approach to product design solution for the purposed "Kansei". The Science of Design Bulletin of the Japanese Society of Kansei Engineering (2002)

Ergonomic Implications of Technological Innovations in the Development of Computer Workstations

Marcin Butlewski[✉], Aleksandra Dewicka, and Edwin Tytyk

Chair of Ergonomics and Quality Management, Poznan University of
Technology, 11 Strzelecka Street, Poznan, Poland
{marcin.butlewski,aleksandra.dewicka,
edwin.tytyk}@put.poznan.pl

Abstract. Relentless technological progress creates change in the work environment, including that of commonly used computer workstations. Determinants of change in this respect are both the changes in information and communication technologies as well as the more often exhibited concern for the welfare of employees. Technological innovations derive from a multifaceted improvement of a specified element of the technical environment (e.g., contrast, energy consumption for the next generation of computer screens), with the assumption that they will bring a benefit in terms of ergonomic quality of working conditions. Technological innovations can, however, cause a deterioration of identified in advance or often unknown parameters of the working environment, in particular, they can have negative consequences for ergonomic working conditions. The analysis found that technological changes satisfactory from the point of view of ergonomics.

Keywords: Ergonomic design · Heuristic methods · Design · Ergonomics · Devices for the elderly

1 Introduction

Innovations related to the human working environment clearly affect the ergonomic dimension of work systems. In many cases, however, an ergonomic evaluation of the resulting situation is a consequence of irregularities in the functioning of the anthropotechnical system. Innovations include both events of a technical, organizational nature as well as financial – economic. There is therefore a need to consider the ergonomic potential of introduced innovations, particularly in the area of computer workstations as the fundamental work unit of any modern organization. For this purpose, the term innovation must be defined. The broadest and currently classic definition of innovation was presented by J.A. Schumpeter, who interpreted innovation as a discrete undertaking of new combinations of production factors relating to five instances [20]:

- the introduction of a new product,
- the introduction of a new method of production,
- the opening of a new market,

© Springer International Publishing Switzerland 2015
M. Antona and C. Stephanidis (Eds.): UAHCI 2015, Part IV, LNCS 9178, pp. 413–421, 2015.
DOI: 10.1007/978-3-319-20687-5_40

- the acquisition of new sources of raw materials or half-manufactured products,
- and the conduction of a new method of organization of business processes in production as well as in the sphere of the circulation of goods.

The innovation process is inextricably linked with progressive phenomena of change, reforms and ideas that seek to better exploit existing knowledge, capital, and infrastructure of the information society. Currently, innovation is interpreted in two ways, narrow and broad, i.e. sensu *stricte* and sensu *largo*. In the narrow sense, innovation is defined as a change in manufacturing methods based on new, not previously used, knowledge. One of the proponents of such a narrow interpretation of the concept of innovation was, among others, E. Mansfield, who believes that "innovation is the first application of the invention" [14]. A similar view is expressed by Ch. Freeman, who defined innovation as "the first commercial introduction of a new product, process or machine" [7].

In the broad sense, according to J. A. Allen "innovation is the introduction of new products, processes or procedures to wide application" [1]. P. R. Whitfield stated that innovation is a sequence of complex acts of solving problems, the result of which is some comprehensively developed novelty [23]. In Kotler's broad definition "the concept of innovation refers to any good, which is seen by someone as new" [13], and Rogers' innovation "is an idea, practice or object that is perceived as new by an individual or other receiving entity" [18].

According to the Oslo Manual, used in Europe for research on innovation and which accumulates all created definitions to date, innovation occurs when a new or improved product is introduced to the market, or a new or improved process is used in production, wherein the given product or process is new at least from the point of view of the introducing organization.

Innovation includes all sorts of phenomena and processes related to technological, organizational, economic, social, and psychological progress. Innovations can be created by one person or a group of people or institutions, which is why there are many divisions depending on the type and complexity.

The most frequently proposed breakdown occurring in literature is the division into technological innovations, which include product and process innovations, and non-technological innovations, including marketing and organizational innovations. In addition to the subject criterion in the typology of innovation there can be found a number of divisions based on the criteria:

- originality of changes; pioneering or replicating innovations;
- novelty; new innovations on a global scale, for the market or business;
- magnitude; radical or incremental innovations;
- scope and duration of exposure; revolutionary, evolutionary, strategic or tactical innovations;
- source; foreign, domestic, internal, external, demand or supply innovations;
- complexity; conjugated or not conjugated innovations;
- psychosocial factors; reflective, intentional or unintentional innovations;
- scope of impact; innovation outside the organization or within the organization;
- technological and capital intensity; innovations of advanced or simple technology;
- types of knowledge; tangible or intangible innovations;
- motive for innovative action; autonomous or induced innovation.

In studies devoted to technical progress it is assumed that innovation has an original character, and the main criterion for its distinction is its size, its so-called radicality or groundbreaking nature.

A groundbreaking innovation is defined as the application of a previously unused technical solution that brings about revolutionary change in the way of solving the previously unsolved problem of a particular group of potential recipients – users [21].

One type of "creative destructions" aimed at the recipient – user are ergonomic innovations generated as a result of human creativity, courage and ingenuity. Ergonomic innovation can be defined as the process of introducing a "new solution" to production and use by applying anthropocentric, social, biotic and technical combinations which alter the existing parameters of objects and products in terms of size, quality, novelty and effectiveness. Ergonomic innovation can thus be an approach to design which will allow for obtaining results in the form of solutions that are much more resistant to human error [3] or also resistant to any interference in the process [17] which can lead to a dangerous situation or crisis [2].

One form of innovation can be those that are ergonomic, which collate achievements of many sciences attempting to humanize the living and working environments so that they are friendly to the psycho-physical needs of users, but bring tangible benefits when they completely fulfil the needs of the changing recipient – operator – user. However, they are only a part of the introduced changes, the ergonomic consequences of any innovative changes taking place at computer workstations should also be assessed.

2 Innovations in Operator Workstations

In the era of entrepreneurial culture manifested as a strong attachment of an individual to work, employees devote most of the day to work, which is why it is important to carry out a series of tangible and intangible actions of a scientific, research, technical and organizational character to improve the quality of working life [16]. Ergonomic innovations handle the adaptation of technical tools, positions and methods of work and the material work environment to the biological and psychological needs of the human – operator. The main objective of ergonomic innovations is to ensure healthy and safe working conditions to the human – operator. These activities, which improve the quality of life, are inherent in the pilot concept of the so-called "innovative workplace," which thanks to the commitment of the European Economic and Social Committee will be in the centre of the strategy "Europe 2020."

Rational innovations in the workplace are conducive to social and organizational change which incorporate integrated and sustainable approaches, improve companies' performance and in the long-term reduce operating costs [11]. Striving for improvement can occur in many areas, but the most common are: work processes, work organization, working methods, work tools, physical working environment, professional qualifications, as well as management operating procedures [6].

In the twenty-first century, most work processes are executed by operators – users of different types of machinery, devices and computer equipment. Operators for many hours are performing hard visual and mental work while seated or standing, causing

Fig. 1. Innovative workplace with a computer

eye strain, feeling of fatigue – monotony, as well as pain within the shoulders, back and arms. The complexity of equipment operators' work involves the simultaneous introduction and processing of data – messages, use of preferential equipment, while maintaining a continuity of communication with other employees or superiors. The needs of the stressed, carrying a huge responsibility sector of the market have been noticed by many producers of work equipment, who offer many pioneering and precursory solutions. The most common and most gladly used of them in the Polish economy is presented below.

One of the first innovative solutions from which operators of mobile and computer equipment can benefit is the optimization of seating. The concept of an ergonomic chair for work with a computer was proposed by the company mPosition, which came to the conclusion that the best and safest way is to work in a sitting-lying position, where the line of the vertebral column makes a 135 degree angle with the line of the femur (Fig. 1).

Source: www.officomeble.pl

However, even though all applied ergonomic innovative solutions for improving the quality of working life are subject to criteria and an analysis of the consequences of changes, many of the implemented solutions have not been analyzed in terms of ergonomics, both directly and indirectly.

In view of the large number of various modifications and their variable strength, only an identification of groups of innovations in computer workstations was performed, without indicating the relationship between them. Therefore highlighted were innovations related to:

- logical schema of cooperation between human – computer – e.g. human enters information in machine-readable form – digital encoding,
- software at the workstation – achieving a range of functions at the workstation,
- physical performance of control functions – e.g. speech control,
- hardware components – e.g. different families of processors,
- working environment – e.g. ergonomic seat.

Changes in even one element can belong to multiple groups, additionally the direct motivation for undertaking them (ergonomics of the position) does not eliminate the need for ergonomic assessment of the consequences of the innovation, both because of the uncertainty that assumptions are met as well as due to the possibility of accompanying changes.

3 Ergonomic Assessment Criteria of Consequences of Innovative Changes

The ergonomic evaluation of changes is associated with estimation of the level of quality of use and ergonomic quality before and after the completion of the change. In practice, this assessment is carried out as a form of estimating the future situation and after its occurrence the degree of reaching the initially expected level of performance is assessed. For consequence assessment, different sets of criteria which may be subject to evaluation should be characterized, The following factors can be evaluated [4, 5, 8, 9, 16]:

- (PL) physical load – deviation from the optimal level of load (energy expenditure);
- (MO) motion overload – overload of musculoskeletal system resulting from repetitive and unilateral movements;
- (MS) mental strain – deviation from optimum for a given employee's level of mental strain resulting from factors such as load monotony – described separately, (the term used in this regard corresponds to the effects of stress on the employee as defined in ISO 10075, where strain is – the immediate effect of mental stress within the mentally strained individual (not the long term effect) depending on his or her individual habitual and actual preconditions including individual coping styles, while stress is the total of all assessable influences impinging upon a human from external sources and affecting it mentally);
- (PC) physical conditions – including lighting (luminance, contrast, glare); climatic conditions (temperature, humidity, air movement, atmospheric pressure); noise (sound level, frequency); vibrations (low level vibrations, resonance); weather (rain, storm); odours (disgusting or strongly influencing) – these categories will also have an effect on mental strain;
- (BA) balance – balance between individual factors and a sustainable course of their variability over time limiting overload which would cause a decline in the employee's efficiency;
- (US) usability, which consists of (ISO 9241):

  - *Functionality (Functional completeness, Complexity, Adequacy, Integrity, Traceability, Testability)*
  - *Performance (Execution efficiency, Interaction performance, Stability, Scalability)*
  - *Dependability (Reliability, Error-tolerance, Safety, Security, Testability)*
  - *Satisfaction (Ease of use, Understandability, Learnability, Productivity, Acceptance)*
  - *Flexibility (Portability, Modifiability, Configurability, Ease of testing)*

Some of the elements are considered jointly under the term mental fatigue, which does not allow for analysis because this factor aggregates many others, resulting from:

- (MS-TR) Task requirements;

  - Sustained attention (watching a screen for prolonged periods);
  - Information processing (number and quality of signals to be detected, drawing inferences from incomplete information, deciding among alternative ways of action);
  - Responsibility (for health and safety of co-workers, loss of 1 production);
  - Duration and temporal pattern of action (hours of work, rest pauses, shift work);
  - Task content (controlling, planning, executing, evaluating);
  - Danger (underground working, traffic, handling dangers or valuable objects);
- (MS-SO) Social and organizational factors (which can also may be a consequence of operators' workstation):

  - Conflicts (among groups or individuals);
  - Group factors (group structure, cohesion);
  - Social contacts (work in isolation, customer relations);

It should be added that in the case of factors such as physical load and mental strain, in accordance with ISO 6585 appropriate load is also assessed for an insufficient level – and thus underload.

Therefore, a record of an ergonomic assessment of consequences of innovation in the field of computer workstations can be made as a function of changes in meeting the requirements of specific groups of criteria (PL, MO, MS, PC, BA, US) - (Fig. 2).

The above mentioned groups of criteria can also be evaluated by the directness and indirectness of the change's impact. The reasoning in this regard is made much more difficult due to the complexity of the situation and a repeated inability to isolate it from the others. Thus indicated here are possibilities of using more fuzzy ergonomic assessments – fuzzy index to qualitative and quantitative evaluation [15].

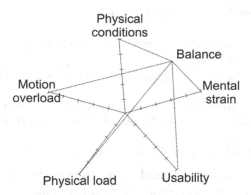

Fig. 2. Functions of changes in meeting the requirements of specific groups of criteria (own preparation).

4 Method Description – Presentation of Innovation Assessment Method with Examples

The author proposes a method of ergonomic evaluation of innovative solutions in terms of the criteria (Fig. 2) along with the application of systematic search methods for the assessment of the possibility of introducing simultaneous pro-ergonomic changes [12]:

1. Identify the components of the problem in question:

(a) variables which the designer can influence (decisional variables or design parameters). Example – for the change from CRT to LCD technology, physical conditions had to change – the electromagnetic field and usability related to legibility of the provided information, and the decisions which took into account the possibility of setting a different plane of the screen in relation to the plane of work – improving the working position.

(b) variables which the designer can not influence (contextual variables or independent variables). Example –to change a keyboard in the Dvorak layout content of deep rooted habits of users and content introduced independent of the software,

(c) variables which are affected by the design (objectives or dependent variables). Example –how will the load on the musculoskeletal system be affected by the use of touch screens.

2. Identify relationships between variables. Example – how will the usefulness of data entry solutions change if the load is transferred from the musculoskeletal system (hand and fingers), to speech organs (voice control).

3. Predict the probable goal values and their threshold values. Example – the threshold values of unloading during the use of intelligent reasoning.

4. Identify constraints or boundary conditions, i.e. the threshold values for each variable. Example – a threshold value for diagonal screen size above which the utility drops significantly during controlling movements.

5. Determine the value of each decisional variable (i.e. try out a range of design decisions), and calculate the values of dependent variables (i.e. calculate the resulting performance). Example – calculating the degree of an increase in efficiency due to the introduction of another type of information display.

The evaluation of innovative solutions regarding workstations must also take into account macroergonomic consequences such as the social effects of physical alienation [19], which, paradoxically, may be due to improvements in the field of communication.

5 Conclusion

The perception of each innovation in a positive light is a significant error. The changing working environment has led to a number of individual and social deviations. Hence the need for the use of a multicriterial evaluation of implemented innovative solutions in the field of computer workstations. The opportunity to evaluate solutions for far removed effects may in the future allow for adequate prevention of demographic phenomena, which currently seems to be unrealistic. Such far-reaching reasoning brings social engineering closer, still, the proliferation of virtual realities may help to adequately predict the effects of currently observed processes and to appropriately counteract them.

References

1. Allen, J.A.: Scientific innovation and industrial prosperity, p. 7. Longman, London (1966)
2. Bajda, A., Wrażeń, M., Laskowski, D.: Diagnostics the quality of data transfer in the management of crisis situation. Electr. Rev. **87**(9A), 72–78 (2011)
3. Butlewski, M., Jasiulewicz-Kaczmarek, M., Misztal, A., Sławińska, M.: Design methods of reducing human error in practice. In: Nowakowski, T., Młyńczak, M., Jodejko-Pietruczuk, A., Werbińska-Wojciechowska, S. (eds.) Safety and Reliability: Methodology and Applications - Proceedings of the European Safety and Reliability Conference ESREL 2014 Wrocław, pp. 1101–1106. CRC Press, London (2015). ISBN: 978-113802681-0
4. Butlewski, M.: The issue of product safety in contemporary design. In: Safety of the System, Technical, Organizational and Human Work Safety Determinants. Red. Szymon Salamon. Wyd. PCzęst. Częstochowa (2012). ISBN: 978-83-63500-13-9, ISSN: 1428-1600
5. Butlewski, M., Tytyk, E.: The assessment criteria of the ergonomic quality of anthropotechnical mega-systems. In: Vink, P. (ed.) Advances in Social and Organizational Factors, p. 298–306. CRC Press, Taylor and Francis Group, Boca Raton, London, New York, (2012). ISBN: 978-1-4398-8
6. Drożyner, P., Mikołajczak, P., Szuszkiewicz, J., Jasiulewicz-Kaczmarek, M.: Management standardization versus quality of working life. In: Robertson, M.M. (ed.) EHAWC 2011 and HCII 2011. LNCS, vol. 6779, pp. 30–39. Springer, Heidelberg (2011)
7. Freeman, Ch.: The Economics of Industrial Innovation, p. 7. F. Printer, London (1982)
8. Adam, G.: Assessment of compliance with minimum safety requirements in machine operation: a case of assessing the control devices of a press. In: Arezes, P.M. (ed.) Occupational Safety and Hygiene (i in.), pp. 497–501. Taylor and Francis Group, London (2013). ISBN: 978-1-138-00047-6
9. Hankiewicz, K.: Ergonomic characteristic of software for enterprise management systems. In: Peter, V. (ed.) Advances in Social and Organizational Factors, pp. 279–287. CRC Press, Boca Raton (2012)
10. Jasiulewicz-Kaczmarek, M.: The role of ergonomics in implementation of the social aspect of sustainability, illustrated with the example of maintenance. In: Arezes, P., Baptista, J.S., Barroso, M., Carneiro, P., Lamb, P., Costa, N., Melo, R., Miguel, A.S., Perestrelo, G. (eds.) Occupational Safety and Hygiene, pp. 47–52. CRC Press, Taylor & Francis, London, (2013). ISBN: 978-1-138-00047-6
11. Jasiulewicz-Kaczmarek, M., Drożyner, P.: Social dimension of sustainable development – safety and ergonomics in maintenance activities. In: Stephanidis, C., Antona, M. (eds.) UAHCI 2013, Part I. LNCS, vol. 8009, pp. 175–184. Springer, Heidelberg (2013)
12. Jones, J.Ch.: Design Methods. WNT, Warszawa (1977) (in Polish)
13. Kotler, Ph.: Marketing, Wydawnictwo Gebethner i S-ka, Warszawa, p. 322 (1994)
14. Mansfield, E.: Industrial Research and Technological Innovation, p. 83. W.W. Horton, New York (1968)

15. Mazur, A.: Application of fuzzy index to qualitative and quantitative evaluation of the quality level of working conditions. In: Stephanidis, C. (ed.) HCII 2013, Part II. CCIS, vol. 374, pp. 514–518. Springer, Heidelberg (2013)
16. Misztal, A., Butlewski, M.: Life improvement at work, Wyd. PP, Poznań (2012). ISBN: 978-83-7775-177-0
17. Mrugalska, B., Kawecka-Endler, A.: Practical application of product design method robust to disturbances. Hum. Factors Ergon. Manuf. Serv. Ind. **22**(2), 121–129 (2012)
18. Rogers, E.M.: Diffusion of Innovations, p. 12. Free Press, New York (2003)
19. Sadłowska-Wrzesińska, J.: Analysis of psychosocial risk in the context of the objectives of macroergonomics. In: Vink, P. (ed.) Advances in Social and Organizational Factors, AHFE Conference 2014, pp. 277–285 (2014). ISBN: 978-1-4951-2102-9
20. Schumpeter, J.A.: The theory of economic development, PWN, Warszawa, p. 104 (1960)
21. Truskolaski, S.: (2014)
22. The importance of knowledge transfer in the innovative activities of enterprises, Difin, Warszawa, p. 22
23. Whitfield, P.R.: Innovation in industry, PWE, Warszawa, p. 26 (1979)

A Freehand System for the Management of Orders Picking and Loading of Vehicles

Pedro J.S. Cardoso[1,2]($\boxtimes$), João M. F. Rodrigues[1,2], Luís Carlos Sousa[1,2], Andriy Mazayev[3], Emanuel Ey[1], Tiago Corrêa[3], and Mário Saleiro[2]

[1] Instituto Superior de Engenharia, University of the Algarve, Faro, Portugal
{pcardoso,jrodrig,lcsousa,amazayev,
eevieira,tiagodcorrea,masaleiro}@ualg.pt
[2] LARSys (ISR-Lisbon), University of the Algarve, Faro, Portugal
[3] Faculdade de Ciências e Tecnologia, University of the Algarve, Faro, Portugal

Abstract. The process of picking goods from a warehouse and loading distribution vehicles is done in a systematic manner which in general corresponds to a certain order. For instance in the delivery of goods, it may be important to load the transportation vehicles in the reverse order of the customers visit, in furtherance of better accessing the products when unloading/delivering. This management can be troublesome if the human-computer interface requires the use of devices, like mouses or keyboards, which are difficult to be used under certain condition (e.g., human with dirty hands or wearing thick gloves/clothes). In this paper it is presented a proof-of-concept in the area of picking goods from a warehouse and the corresponding vehicle loading when using equipments which do not allow easy use of common human-computer interfaces. In this sense, an application using a 3D sensor was programmed to implement the human-computer interaction based on simple swipe gestures to navigate through the options, menu and their (de)selection.

Keywords: 3D sensor · Leap Motion · Orders picking and loading · Vehicle Routing Problem

1 Introduction

It is quite easy to find definitions of Human-Computer Interaction (HCI). The most probable to be find on the web is "Human–computer interaction involves the study, planning, design and uses of the interaction between people (users) and computers. It is often regarded as the intersection of computer science, behavioral sciences, design, media studies, and several other fields of study" [12]. It is quite therefore easy to recognize that the boundaries of what is HCI are quite fuzzy. Historically, in a non-exhaustive overview, HCI evolved from a set of switches, to punched cards, monitors, keyboards, mouse pointers, etc. Things are changing fast. Dialogs like the ones in the "2001: A Space Odyssey" movie between the computer HAL 9000 and humans [14] or the library host hologram in "Time Machine" movie where the hologram communicates and interacts naturally with

© Springer International Publishing Switzerland 2015
M. Antona and C. Stephanidis (Eds.): UAHCI 2015, Part IV, LNCS 9178, pp. 422–431, 2015.
DOI: 10.1007/978-3-319-20687-5_41

a time traveler [25] were once science fiction. The truth is that, as J. Grudin says, HCI is a moving target [10]. We expect the future of HCI to be supported on ubiquitous communication where computers communicate to give universal access to data and computational services, high functional systems where accessing those functionalities is natural, mass availability of computer graphics, high-bandwidth interaction, wide variety of displays (e.g., on common surfaces, with flexibility, large and thin), and embedded computation.

Currently most computers and mobile devices have the computational capacity and are equipped to mimic human's capacities like sight and hearing, and even, with the appropriate sensors, temperature, taste, smell, touch, balance and measure acceleration [11,24]. Some of these capabilities (e.g., touch and gesture) can be used to control machines in a natural and intuitive way. A huge amount of sensors can be used to that purpose, such as embedded cameras, touch screens or mobile 3D sensors (e.g., Structure Sensor [22], the Leap Motion [16], or the Kinetic sensor [13]). Some examples are the interaction with art installations [2], in robotics [6], for head pose classification [26], in assistive technologies [5], in the operation of wheelchairs [1] or in the interaction with holograms for teaching technical drawing [7].

Bearing the previous context in mind, this article aims to present a proof-of-concept of a system designed to be used in the picking and loading area of a warehouse, where employees use clothes (e.g., gloves or thick clothes) or have dirty hands which make troublesome the use of common interfaces, like keyboards or mouses. In particular, we propose an application which makes possible navigate through a set of menus presenting routes, products and loading order. The HCI is supported on 3D sensor and uses simple swipe gestures to navigate through the options, menu and their (de)selection.

The remaining document is structured as follows. Section 2 presents a more deep contextualization and problem formulation. Section 3 explains the 3D sensor API and its configuration, while the interface implementation is shown in Sect. 4. The final section presents some conclusions and future work.

2   Contextualization and Problem Formulation

The present work was a study thought as part of the Intelligent Fresh Food Fleet Router (*i3FR*) project, developed by the University of the Algarve and X4Dev, Business Solutions. The project has the objective of building a system to manage and optimize the distribution of fresh and frozen goods by a distribution fleet [4]. In short, the system integrates an Enterprise Resource Planning (ERP) software with an optimization system (called *i3FR*) to minimize the costs of the distribution routes [3]. The routing optimization computes routes from the depots to the delivery points using cartographic information and takes into consideration multiple objectives to be minimized, namely: the number of vehicles and the total traveled distance.

In a sequence line the distribution process can be described as follows (see Fig. 1 for a sequence diagram of the procedure described next). First a client or a seller sends an order with a list of products and quantities to a seller that

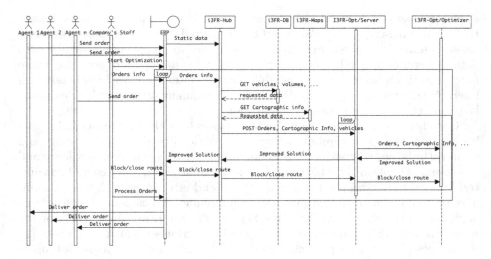

Fig. 1. Sequence diagram of the flow from the customers to the optimizer and reverse.

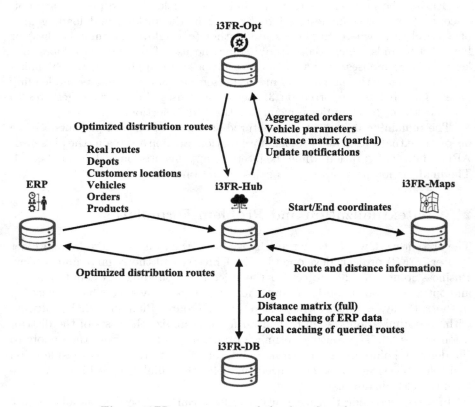

Fig. 2. *i3FR* components and the data flow them.

introduces the data into an ERP. This order is for one of the next days. Then, at a convenient moment, the system manager starts the optimization procedure by sending a signal to the *i3FR* system which, for modularity convenience, is divided in four main modules: *i3FR-Hub*, *i3FR-Opt*, *i3FR-DB* and *i3FR-Maps*(see Fig. 2). The signal triggered by the administrator goes to the *i3FR-Hub* which begins by requesting the necessary data from the ERP (e.g., orders, new customers data, available vehicles and new products data) and store it on the *i3FR-DB*. In this sense, updated data, i.e., data already fetched that was not changed since previous optimization sessions (e.g., older customers delivery locations, vehicle data), was stored in the *i3FR-DB*. The *i3FR-DB* acts as local database avoiding the overload of the ERP with repetitive requests of data.

The insertion of new customers trigger the *i3FR-Maps* module to update its distance matrix which stores the routes between all possible delivery locations. On other words, *i3FR-Maps* maintains a $n \times n$ matrix (n being the number of delivery locations) of routes including distances, travel time and corresponding routing directions details. The routes data is obtained from a Open Street Maps Routing Machine (OSRM) server [18] and Google Maps [9]. The use of the OSRM overcomes the limit of accesses to Google's API. The routes data is also stored in the *i3FR-DB*, which is supported on a MongoDB database [17].

Finally, in presence of the necessary data, the *i3FR-Hub* send a start signal (and the necessary data) to the actual optimization module, *i3FR-Opt*. The *i3FR-Opt* implements an hybrid algorithm based on the Push Forward Insertion Heuristic (PFIH) [20] which computes solutions for a Capacitated Vehicle Routing Problem with Time Windows (CVRPTW) [3,8], optimizing the number of routes and the total distance necessary to make all deliveries. Whenever good solution for the active CVRPTW are achieved, they are send to the *i3FR-Hub* which in turn sends them to the ERP. In the presence of the solutions, the ERP administrator can send signals to stop totally (or partially) the optimization process and start the loading of the vehicles.

A solutions is a set of routes. Each route starts at the depot and passes through a set of customers, returning to the depot. In order to better access the products when making the deliveries to the customers, it is important to load the vehicles in the reverse order of the customers visit, keeping the first products to be delivered near the doors and so forth. Given the routes, the loading order information is sent to the warehouse where the picking and loading of the vehicles is to be made by workers. Problems my arise if for instance the workers can't easily interact with the computers having the orders information. This problems can arise for instance if the worker are using thick clothes, gloves or, simply have dirty hand for directly operating products (e.g., fresh meat/fish).

The next sections present an HCI alternative to manage the picking and loading of the products. The solution is based on a 3D sensor which allows, with simple gestures, to interact with a loading and picking interface.

3   3D Gesture Recognition with Leap Motion

Leap Motion [16] has an Application Programming Interface (API) capable of detect multiple hand gestures, such as a circular movement by a finger, a straight line movement by the hand with fingers extended, a forward tapping movement by a finger/hand or a downward tapping movement by a finger/hand. The configurations and proper combinations of gestures detection, allow the recognition of a large set of actions, such as, open or close hand done with one or both hands, generally used to implement zoom in or out. Other examples are the movement from side to side with the hand to indicate a swipe gesture or a finger poking forward can indicate a screen tap gesture [15,19,21,23].

The Leap Motion senses the space as 3D space with standard Cartesian coordinate system, also known as right-handed orientation (see Fig. 3(a)). The origin of the coordinate system is centered at the top of the device. The x-axis is placed horizontally along the device, with positive values increasing from left to right, the z-axis is placed also on horizontal plane, perpendicular with x-axis with values increasing towards the user (the front side of the device) and the y-axis are placed is the vertical, with positive values increasing upwards.

A minimum set of intuitive movements where considered for the implementation of the problem in question, namely: the horizontal and vertical swipe gestures. The horizontal swipe gesture were used to navigate between options and menus, while the vertical swipe gestures were used to select and deselect options and menus (see Sect. 4). In this sense, the Leap Motion API has a direction vector for the swipe gesture that associates a 3D direction vector ranging from -1.0 to $+1.0$ in each direction, after a gesture is completely recognized, given the minimum length and velocity configurations properties. As this gesture was the only one used, it was necessary to detect various types of swipe. The interface was designed to react to two of the six different independent types of swipe gestures

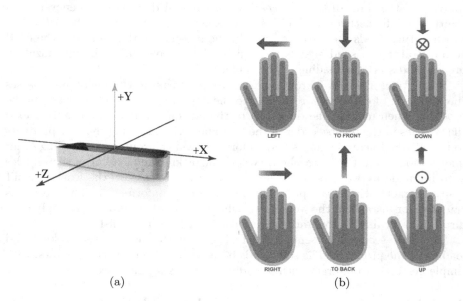

(a)   (b)

Fig. 3. (a) Leap Motion coordinate system; (b) Six types of swipes possibles with LeapMotion gesture recognition.

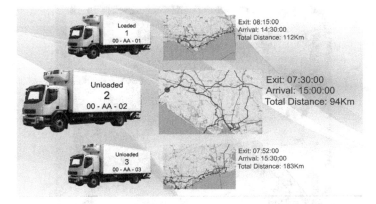

Fig. 4. Screen-shots from the user's interface: route/vehicle listing.

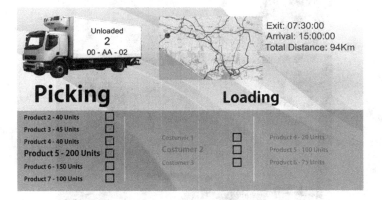

Fig. 5. Screen-shots from the user's interface: list of products to be picked.

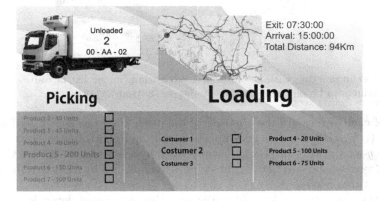

Fig. 6. Screen-shots from the user's interface: list of customers and products to be loaded in the corresponding order.

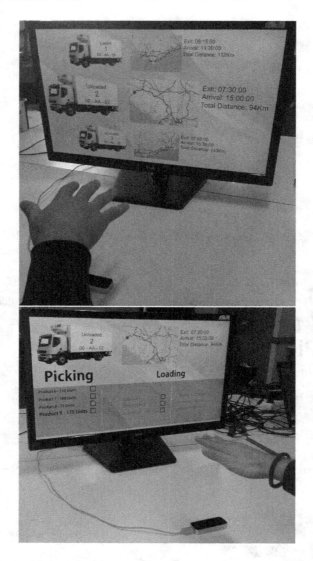

Fig. 7. User interacting with the interface, navigating: in the list of routes (top) and list of products to be picked from the warehouse (bottom).

(three of each swipes are the opposite of the other three) as shown by Fig. 3(b), namely: (i) Up/Down swipe, accomplished by a top to bottom or a bottom to top gesture (y-axis); (ii) Front/Back, accomplished by a front to back or back to front gesture (z-axis); and (iii) Left/Right swipe, accomplished by a left to right or right to left gesture (x-axis).

For the first case, of a up/down swipe, the movement depends mainly on the y-axis. The direction vector has an upward direction if $y \approx +1$ (used as a "deselect" action) and a downward direction if $y \approx -1$ (used as a "select" action). Since it is almost impossible to do a swipe gesture with a vector direction component of exactly $x = 0$, $y = \pm1$ and $z = 0$, it was considered a range of values to detect and differentiate between swipes types. Therefore, any swipe direction that agrees with the condition $y \in [-1, -0.5[$ and $x, z \in [-0.5, 0.5]$, is considered as a downward swipe. Oppositely, a swipe direction that agrees with the condition $y \in]0.5, 1]$ and $x, z \in [-0.5, 0.5]$, is considered as an upward swipe.

The remaining cases, (ii) and (iii), are defined by similar equation taking into consideration that the front/back and the left/right movements are defined along the z-axis and x-axis, respectively. These swipes are mutually independent that is, for every type of swipe there is only one possible choice.

4   Interface Implementation and Test

To provide a proof-of-concept we devised a simple interface composed by three main interface pages. These pages are associated with the routes, picking and loading actions.

The application starts by opening a page listing the routes (see Fig. 4). For each route is presented a set of informations namely: the vehicle license plate and number ID, the state of the vehicle (loaded/unloaded), the corresponding route represented in a map, the hour that the vehicle should leave the depot (such that the customer's time windows are satisfied), the estimated arrival time and the total distance. Some of these values, like the exit from the depot hour, is used to sort the loading of the vehicles (the ones exiting earlier are usually loaded first). For this interface, horizontal front/back or back/front (z-axis) swipes are used to navigate through the routes/vehicles. A vertical swipe selects the vehicle and moves to another interface showing the a list of products to be picked from the warehouse (see Fig. 5). Again, horizontal front/back or back/front (z-axis) swipes are used to navigate through the picking list. The active product has a larger font and a vertical down/up swipe activates/deactivates a check box, used to register the products already picked. When the products are to be loaded, a horizontal swipe from right to left (x-axis) is used to activate the loading page. The loading page presents a list of costumers in the vehicle's loading order. Horizontal back/front (z-axis) swipes allow to navigate between the customers and the corresponding list of products to be loaded (see Fig. 6). Again, a vertical down/up swipe activates/deactivates a check box, used to register the products/customers already loaded.

Figure 7 shows two examples of users navigating in the list of routes (top) and list of products to be picked from the warehouse (bottom). The tests where made with the sensor regulated a minimum length swipe of 130 mm and 200 mm/s of velocity.

5   Conclusions and Future Work

This paper presents a proof-of-concept study conducted to implement a HCI capable of overcome the difficulties of working with common devices (e.g., mouses or keyboards) when wearing thick clothes/gloves or having dirty hands. The study considers also the problem of picking products from a warehouse and their load into vehicles to be delivered to customers.

Test showed that the interface can be useful but some problems may arise at the beginning since it is necessary some adaptation to the use of the 3D sensor. Nevertheless, the used sensor has a finger tracking fast and accurate, is small (with dimensions of 13 mm × 13 mm × 76 mm and weighting 45 g) and inexpensive, which allows it to be placed almost with every display. Possible drawbacks are the supported conditions of operating like the temperature (0° to 45° C), the relative humidity (5 % to 85 %) or light conditions (bright sunlight, bright light sources or reflective surfaces are not recommended).

As future work, we intend to further explore the proposed prototype in other conditions and compare it with other 3D sensors.

Acknowledgements. This work was partly supported by project *i3FR*: Intelligent Fresh Food Fleet Router – QREN I&DT, n. 34130, PRHOLO: The realistic holographic public relations – QREN I&DT, n. 33845, POPH, FEDER, the Portuguese Foundation for Science and Technology (FCT), project LARSyS FCT [UID/EEA/5009/2013]. We also thanks to project leader X4DEV, Business Solutions.

References

1. Abedan Kondori, F., Yousefi, S., Liu, L., Li, H.: Head operated electric wheelchair. In: Southwest Symposium on Image Analysis and Interpretation, pp. 53–56. IEEE (2014)
2. Alves, R., Madeira, M., Ferrer, J., Costa, S., Lopes, D., da Silva, B.M., Sousa, L., Martins, J., Rodrigues, J.: Fátima revisites: an interactive installation. In: Proceedings of the International Multidisciplinary Scientific Conference on Social Sciences and Arts, pp. 141–148. SGEM (2014)
3. Cardoso, P.J.S., Schütz, G., Mazayev, A., Ey, E.: Solutions in under 10 seconds for vehicle routing problems with time windows using commodity computers. In: Proceedings of the 8th International Conference on Evolutionary Multi-Criterion Optimization, EMO 15. p. (accepted for publication)
4. Cardoso, P.J.S., Schütz, G., Semião, J., Monteiro, J., Rodrigues, J., Mazayev, A., Ey, E., Viegas, M., Neves, C., Anastácio, S.: Integration of a food distribution routing optimization software with an enterprise resource planner. In: Proceedings of International Conference on Geographical Information Systems Theory, Applications and Management, GISTAM-15. p. (accepted for publication)
5. Chiang, I.T., Tsai, J.C., Chen, S.T.: Using Xbox 360 Kinect games on enhancing visual performance skills on institutionalized older adults with wheelchairs. In: IEEE International Conference on Digital Game and Intelligent Toy Enhanced Learning, pp. 263–267. IEEE (2012)
6. El-laithy, R.A., Huang, J., Yeh, M.: Study on the use of Microsoft Kinect for robotics applications. In: IEEE/ION Position Location and Navigation Symposium, pp. 1280–1288. IEEE (2012)

7. Figueiredo, M., Sousa, L., Cardoso, P., Rodrigues, J.A., Goncalves, C., Alves, R.: Learning technical drawing with augmented reality and holograms. In: Proceedings of the 13th International Conference on Education and Educational Technology, pp. 11–20. WSEAS (2014)
8. Gambardella, L.M., Taillard, É., Agazzi, G.: MACS-VRPTW: a multiple colony system for vehicle routing problems with time windows. In: New Ideas in Optimization. Citeseer (1999)
9. Google: Google Maps (2015). http://maps.google.com. Accessed 20 January 2015
10. Grudin, J.: A Moving Target: The Evolution of HCI, 3rd edn. Taylor & Francis, New York (2012)
11. Halder, A., Mahato, M., Sinha, T., Adhikari, B., Mukherjee, S., Bhattacharyya, N.: Polymer membrane electrode based potentiometric taste sensor: a new sensor to distinguish five basic tastes. In: 2012 Sixth International Conference on Sensing Technology (ICST), pp. 785–789, December 2012
12. HCI: Human–computer interaction – Wikipedia, the free encyclopedia (2015). http://en.wikipedia.org/wiki/Human-computer_interaction. Accessed 20January 2015
13. Kinect: Kinect for windows (2015). http://www.microsoft.com/en-us/kinectfor windows/. Accessed 20 January 2015
14. Kubrick, S.: 2001: A space odyssey (1968)
15. Leap Developer Portal: Leap developer portal (2015). https://developer. leapmotion.com/documentation/skeletal/csharp/devguide/Leap_Overview.html. Accessed 20 January 2015
16. Leap Motion: Leap motion (2015). https://www.leapmotion.com. Accessed 20 January 2015
17. MongoDB Inc: MongoDB (2015). http://www.mongodb.com/. Accessed 20 January 2015
18. OSRM: OSRM - Open Source Routing Machine (2015). http://project-osrm.org/. Accessed 20 January 2015
19. Potter, L.E., Araullo, J., Carter, L.: The leap motion controller: a view on sign language. In: Proceedings of the 25th Australian Computer-Human Interaction Conference: Augmentation, Application, Innovation, Collaboration, pp. 175–178. ACM (2013)
20. Solomon, M.M.: Algorithms for the vehicle routing and scheduling problems with time window constraints. Oper. Res. **35**(2), 254–265 (1987)
21. Spiegelmock, M.: Leap Motion Development Essentials. Packt Publishing Ltd., Birmingham (2013)
22. Struture: Struture sensor (2015). http://structure.io/ Accessed 20 January 2015
23. Sutton, J.: Air painting with corel painter freestyle and the leap motion controller: a revolutionary new way to paint! In: ACM SIGGRAPH 2013 Studio Talks, p. 21. ACM (2013)
24. Villarreal, B.L., Gordillo, J.L.: Perception aptitude improvement of an odor sensor: model for a biologically inspired nose. In: Carrasco-Ochoa, J.A., Martínez-Trinidad, J.F., Rodríguez, J.S., di Baja, G.S. (eds.) MCPR 2012. LNCS, vol. 7914, pp. 126–135. Springer, Heidelberg (2013)
25. Wells, S.: Time machine (2002)
26. Yun, Y., Changrampadi, M.H., Gu, I.Y.: Head pose classification by multi-class AdaBoost with fusion of RGB and depth images. In: International Conference on Signal Processing and Integrated Networks, pp. 174–177. IEEE (2014)

Application of Infrared Technology
in Household Water Tap Design
and Evaluation

Ming-Shih Chen[1], Ming-Lun Li[1(✉)], and Yu-Chia Chen[2]

[1] Department of Industrial Design, Tunghai University, Taichung, Taiwan
msc@thu.edu.tw, e7228466@gmail.com
[2] Department of Visual Communication Design,
National Taiwan University of Art, New Taipei, Taiwan
t0329@mail.ntua.edu.tw

Abstract. Based on previous research results, this study examined the use of water taps and observes the experiences of different age groups when using new product designs. The results indicated that, although new designs can meet the demands of different generations, first-time users have a relatively low understanding of a product from its appearance; hence, if a new design deviates from common user cognition, even it could solve user problems, it still has low user acceptance.

Keywords: Infrared technology · Universal design · Washing behavior · Water tap · Use evaluation

1 Introduction

In Taiwan, it is common to see three generations living under the same roof, thus sharing the same toilet and bathing space. All family members, whether old or young, or those with limited physical mobility, use the same facilities every day. The toilet and bathroom space in Taiwan has area of about 4.95 m^2 on average, and the design does not separate the bathing and toilet areas. Based on previous research results [1], this study aims to investigate the user habits and problems of different generations, improve the washing equipment-water tap design, and construct an experimental model. It further re-investigates users to learn how different generations or people with different physical abilities use washstands and conduct washing behavior.

2 Literature Review

2.1 Main Equipment of Bathroom Space in Taiwan

The Construction and Planning Agency, Ministry of the Interior, issued a "Manual for the Residential Bathroom Experience", from which Taiwanese may gain some knowledge about bathroom equipment. The Manual specifies the dimensions of common bathroom equipment: washstands are categorized into desk type, rack mounting type, and wall mounting type (Fig. 1).

© Springer International Publishing Switzerland 2015
M. Antona and C. Stephanidis (Eds.): UAHCI 2015, Part IV, LNCS 9178, pp. 432–443, 2015.
DOI: 10.1007/978-3-319-20687-5_42

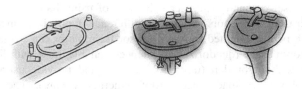

Fig. 1. Basic washstand types (Construction and Planning Agency, Ministry of the Interior, "Manual for the Residential Bathroom Experience")

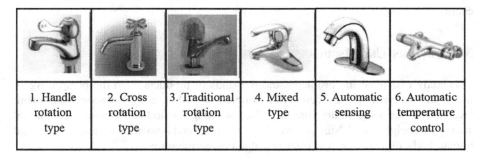

1. Handle rotation type	2. Cross rotation type	3. Traditional rotation type	4. Mixed type	5. Automatic sensing	6. Automatic temperature control

Fig. 2. Water tap types (Formosa bathroom website)

There are currently six types of household water taps for bathrooms in the market. The left three types are connected to pipelines through one hole, while the other three are connected through three holes (Fig. 2).

2.2 Introduction and Application of Infrared Sensors

New technology can change space opportunities. For example, bathroom equipment manufacturers have examined the elderly market and developed products for elderly people with limited physical mobility, which helps them solve various problems, such as difficulty in stand for a long period, cleaning the toilet in winter, and increased useful space in a bathroom. An induction power control device can automatically switch on or off power through infrared detection. Thus, even if the elderly forget to switch off the power, it can automatically control the switch, making it convenient for elderly people, as equipment and space design interact. Spaces change with advancement in science and technology; just as science and technology will change with space use.

2.3 Summary

Mostly areas of activity of the elderly are at home due to degeneration of physical functions, and the bathroom is the place with the highest accident rate in the home space. Currently most bathrooms do not have dry and wet separation design, which can no longer meet user demand. The user behaviors of using bathrooms are very complicated, as their usage behaviors vary due to difference in physical functions. To make bathrooms more people-oriented, infrared sensor technology can avoid awkward situations in bathroom usage (deodorization, silencer); enable those with limited physical mobility usage without burden (universal design); and provide users with a more comfortable and private space (peep-proof, emergency care). The application of infrared sensors can make bathrooms more comfortable, cleaner, and safer. Based on the current household bathroom equipment and the different use conditions and demands of users in Taiwan, this study proposed a water tap design for bathroom equipment for Taiwanese users, and validated the indicators of subsequent design and evaluation.

3 Previous User Issues

This study examined the problems and demands of products from the perspective of users, and summed up four factors that trouble users when using bathroom equipment: "water flow and temperature control", "face washing method and cleaning", "handrail setting and height", and "storage space" (Table 1), added human factor engineering and human body dimensions, and offer possible countermeasures.

Table 1. Improvement measures

Direction		Indicator	Problem	Countermeasure
Water flow and temperature control	Water flow control	Reduce repetitive operation	It will cause water to splash in all directions if water flow is directly adjusted to maximum amount	With infrared sensing, users do not need to switch it on and can use it directly
		It is easy to accurately control water flow		
		Tolerance for error operation		
	Water temperature control	Water temperature control is easy to understand	Hot water is normally not used	Put aside rarely used water temperature
		Operation instruction and feedback.		
		Tolerance for error operation		

(*Continued*)

Table 1. (*Continued*)

Direction		Indicator	Problem	Countermeasure
Face washing method and cleaning	Face washing method	Suitable for all kinds of methods	Different people have different face washing habits, but it is a complicated operation	Design a water flowing method for face washing that enables water to directly contact with the face
	Cleaning and drying	Easy to clean Durable without maintenance Keep the washstand table dry	The table can easily get damp after used, but few people clean or wipe it	Design an arc-shaped washstand, and adopt ultra repellent nano treatment to direct water drops to the wash port
	Wash basin	Easy to wash articles	Hair can easily become stuck in the wash port; small articles, such as earrings, can easily fall into the wash basin	Set the wash basin in the left-rear corner. Even when hair or earrings fall on the washstand, it will not be immediately washed into the wash basin
Handrail setting and height	Washstand height	Users will not get tired after a long time of use Suitable for all kinds of methods	The washstand is generally too low for users, and it is inconvenient for people with limited physical mobility	Select rack mounting washstands and raise the height to 77 cm; meanwhile, consider whether height is convenient for wheelchair users

(*Continued*)

Table 1. (*Continued*)

Direction	Indicator	Problem	Countermeasure
	Handrail setting	Secure and safe support structure	Metal external mounting handrails give people a cold, rigid feeling and are not aesthetically pleasing	Design a round handrail, and integrate it with the washstand to enhance its internal structure
Storage space	Articles storage	Provide proper storage space	It is not large enough due to too many family members	Though it can make it more convenient for users by increasing the storage space, it can also make it messier. A proper storage space shall be designed after evaluation

Supplementary: Human Factors Engineering and Human Body Dimensions — According to literature, in order to meet the demands of different users, the washstand height from the floor to the top of the washstand is 77 cm; however, with the change of times, washstands are now not only places where users wash their faces and brush their teeth, but more importantly have other functions, like cleaning. The useful area of washstands is larger. According to the behavior pattern of participants, the wash-stand is expanded: the sink is 33 cm long, 55 cm wide, and 11 cm deep. Water taps are used as the basis for subsequent design according to the best splash point (water out-let is 30–36 cm from users and 16–23 cm from the washstand).

4 Design Proposal

There are two behavior patterns in using water taps–water holding and splash cleaning; however, most water taps only provide the water holding function. When users want splash cleaning, they must splash by holding water in their hands, which can more easily wet the washstand top and wastes water. If a water flow method that allows splash cleaning is adopted, it would be more convenient for users and reduce the waste of water. Regarding water flow and temperature control, most users do not control water flow or temperature. They often switch on/off water taps and even let the water flow without switching it off. If infrared sensing replaces common switches, it is not only convenient to use, but can save water resources. Users only need to ignore the rarely used water flow and temperature, and adopt infrared sensing as the main function and control of the auxiliary function, thus, household water taps will be more human-oriented in operation.

5   Validation and Conclusion

This study made design improvements based on previous research and design coun-termeasures, while validation is mainly based on usage procedures of bathroom users. This study learned the demands of different groups of users through evaluation, questionnaires, and interviews, and offers improvement measures. This research involved 42 participants, and can be used as the judgment standard for comparison between product testing and importance, as well as among different groups of users (Fig. 3).

5.1   Questionnaire Analysis

To validate the improvements and evaluation of water taps, this research engaged common users, seniors (above 60 years old), children (above 8 years old), and disabled people, for evaluation and importance testing of the indicators of water taps, in order to learn the opinions and comments of different age groups on the use of water taps. The basic data of the participants are shown in Table 2.

5.2   Product Use Satisfaction Survey

This study measured on a 5-order evaluation Likert scale, as completed by participants. After the evaluation survey, this study sorted the survey data of participants, adopted SPSS software for data processing and statistical analysis, and obtained the average scores and evaluation of each indicator of use of water taps through independent t test. In the participant evaluation table, when t is negative, it means the measured value is lower than the expected value, in other words, it exceeds expectation; when t is

Fig. 3. Entity detection model

Table 2. Statistical table of basic data

Basic data		Number of people	Percentage
Gender	Male	22	52.4 %
	Female	20	47.6 %
Age group	Young adults	15	35.7 %
	Senior people	12	28.6 %
	Children	10	23.8 %
	Disabled people	5	11.9 %
Face washing habit	Splash by holding water in hands	15	35.7 %
	Cleaning with a towel	14	33.3 %
	Storing up water for cleaning	13	31.0 %
Type of household	Mixed type	28	66.7 %
Water taps	Rotation type	14	33.3 %

Table 3. Evaluation on use of water taps by participants

Indicators	Measured value	Expectation	t	Significance (single-tailed)
Easy to understand how to operate it from appearance design	3.60	4.19	−4.08	0.00*
Control water flow according to splash amount	4.05	3.86	1.26	0.10
Has specific operation instruction and feedback	3.81	4.26	−3.29	0.00*
Water temperature control is easy to understand	4.21	4.05	1.38	0.09
Columnar water flow from below can be easily and accumulatively controlled	3.98	3.95	0.21	0.42
Effectively reduce repetitive operation	4.36	3.88	3.39	0.00*
It can return to the original state if wrong use methods are used	3.79	4.21	−2.62	0.01*
Use method corresponds to different demands	4.29	3.86	2.82	0.00*
It can be easily cleaned	3.69	3.81	−0.83	0.20
Not easy to damage and durable	3.17	4.33	−7.05	0.00*

*P < .05

positive, it means the measured value is higher than the expected value, in other words, there is room for improvement. The presentation and explanation of the statistical analysis results are as follows:

Evaluation on Use of Water Taps by Participants. Table 3 shows that there is significant difference between "effectively reduce repetitive operation" and "usage method corresponds to different demands", meaning that all participants feel that the

Table 4. Evaluation on use of water taps by young adults

Indicators	Measured value	Expectation	t	Significance (single-tailed)
Easy to understand how to operate it from appearance design	3.87	4.67	−3.21	0.00[*]
Control water flow according to splash amount	4.40	4.20	0.62	0.27
Has specific operation instruction and feedback	4.00	4.40	−1.47	0.08
Water temperature control is easy to understand	4.53	4.47	0.31	0.38
Columnar water flow from below can be easily and accumulatively controlled	4.07	4.13	−0.27	0.39
Effectively reduce repetitive operation	4.27	3.93	1.14	0.13
It can return to the original state if wrong use methods are used	3.80	4.13	−1.08	0.15
Use method corresponds to different demands	4.53	4.00	2.26	0.02[*]
It can be easily cleaned	4.00	4.27	−1.00	0.16
Not easy to damage and durable	3.27	4.53	−4.50	0.00[*]

[*]$P < .05$

product can effectively reduce repetitive operation and meet different demands; however, as the product appearance is relatively novel, it cannot be immediately understood, and specific instructions and tolerance of errors are required. As water tap usage habits can differ, the new function of (splash face washing) is added; however, participants feel the new water taps are not durable. The temperature control handle in the design is not different from those currently on the market, thus, there is no cognitive difference among participants. As dual-purpose water taps are not common on the market, it is necessary to enhance operational instructions.

Evaluation on Use of Water Taps by Young Adults. Table 4 shows that young adults feel that it is difficult to understand how to use it from the appearance design, thus, it is necessary to provide operation instructions to enhance the operational interface and make it easier for users to understand how to use it; additionally, because operation is relatively more complicated than common water taps, young adults feel it is not durable. However, unlike common water taps, the design has a splash face washing device, which young adults feel can meet different demands and exceed their expectations.

Evaluation on Use of Water Taps by Seniors. Table 5 shows that it is relatively difficult for seniors to understand how to operate the water tap from the appearance design, they feel that it is difficult to return to its original state if they use it wrong, and that it is not durable. However, they feel the splash water amount and columnar water flow can be accurately and intuitively controlled. As the designs are consistent with

Table 5. Evaluation on use of water taps by seniors

Indicators	Measured value	Expectation	t	Significance (single-tailed)
Easy to understand how to operate it from appearance design	3.33	4.00	−2.60	0.01
Control water flow according to splash amount	4.00	3.50	2.57	0.01
Has specific operation instruction and feedback	3.75	3.92	−0.84	0.20
Water temperature control is easy to understand	4.08	3.92	0.98	0.17
Columnar water flow from below can be easily and accumulatively controlled	4.00	3.67	2.35	0.01
Effectively reduce repetitive operation	4.67	3.92	3.65	0.00[*]
It can return to the original state if wrong use methods are used	4.00	4.67	−2.97	0.00[*]
Use method corresponds to different demands	4.50	4.00	3.32	0.00[*]
It can be easily cleaned	3.75	3.92	−1.08	0.15
Not easy to damage and durable	3.08	4.75	−7.15	0.00[*]

[*]$P < .05$

their use habits, seniors find them easy to understand and operate. However, as the appearance is novel, it makes it relatively more difficult for seniors to judge how to use it from the appearance. Moreover, as operation is more complicated than before, it is easier to operate incorrectly; thus, operation instructions are required to prevent operational errors. In addition, as the operation is relatively complicated, seniors feel the water tap is easily damaged. Moreover, regarding "effectively reduce repetitive operation" and "use method corresponds to different demands", as an infrared sensor and splash device are installed, seniors feel the water tap can effectively reduce repetitive operation, meet different demands, and is more convenient to use.

Evaluation on Use of Water Taps by Children. Table 6 shows that children feel the water tap should have more specific operation instruction and feedback for users to read. Due to the height of children, it is necessary to reconsider the position of the water handle.

5.3 Interview Results and Analysis

In this research, participants first observed and operated the newly designed toilet and bathroom equipment, and then completed the questionnaire and accepted interviews, through which this study obtained the evaluations regarding the usage of the design by different age groups. This study recorded the problems arising from the use and

Table 6. Evaluation on use of water taps by children

Indicators	Measured value	Expectation	t	Significance (single-tailed)
Easy to understand how to operate it from appearance design	3.60	3.80	−0.77	0.22
Control water flow according to splash amount	3.70	3.70	0.00	0.50
Has specific operation instruction and feedback	3.60	4.50	−3.86	0.00*
Water temperature control is easy to understand	4.00	3.80	1.00	0.17
Columnar water flow from below can be easily and accumulatively controlled	3.80	4.20	−2.12	0.02*
Effectively reduce repetitive operation	4.00	3.70	1.15	0.13
It can return to the original state if wrong use methods are used	3.70	3.90	−0.85	0.20
Use method corresponds to different demands	3.70	3.70	0.00	0.50
It can be easily cleaned	3.30	3.30	0.00	0.50
Not easy to damage and durable	3.30	3.20	0.49	0.31

*$P < .05$

interaction of participants, and effectively obtained the data required for the experimental objectives, as based on the behavior and cognition process of the equipment described by the participants, which can provide a more complete new direction for solving problems of household bathroom equipment.

Interview Results of Young Adults. Young adults have the most suggestions regarding operation instructions and feedback, and feel that there is still room for improvement of the operational interface of the product, and it is necessary to make it easier for all users to understand how to use it. Some participants feel the splash water outlet position is not as good as expected, and can easily splash on clothes, thus, they feel it is better to allow users to actively contact it. As the water tap has more functions, they all think it can be easily damaged after long time use. However, it is impossible to test its durability during the testing period; thus, it is difficult to prove whether it is durable.

Interview Results of Seniors. It is relatively difficult for seniors to understand how to use it from its appearance, and relatively easier for them to use the product wrong, thus, they have many suggestions regarding the operational interface and instructions, and hope there are larger graphic signs, sounds, and other feedback. Regarding the infrared sensor on the columnar water mode, seniors feel that can reduce the body burden caused by repetitive operation and is more convenient for use. As the water tap has more functions, they all think it can be easily damaged after long time use.

However, it is impossible to test its durability during the test period; thus, it is difficult to prove whether it is durable.

Interview Results of Children. It is relatively difficult for children to understand the operational instructions, and required several times of wrong operation before learning correct usage. While some children could not use the splash face washing mode, and thus, have the most feedback regarding this mode. Regarding the handle near the water tap, it is relatively difficult for some children to control and switch on due to their height, thus, it is necessary to reconsider the position of the handle.

Interview Results of Disabled Participants. The disabled participants feel the water tap can effectively reduce repetitive operation and body burden. However, they all stated that durability is the primary factor they consider when choosing a water tap. The design appearance of the water tap makes it difficult for disabled participants to understand how to use it, and they initially used it wrong. Therefore, regarding disabled people, specific operational instructions are extremely important. As some disabled people are looked after by nurses, the water tap is switched on and off for them, which can save water and lessen the burden.

6 Research Conclusion

From the perspective of universal design, the household toilet and bathroom spaces are designed for seniors, disabled people, and all family members. Therefore, this research refers to domestic and foreign relevant information and research results in order to investigate the different use conditions and demands of existing household toilets, bathroom equipment, and users in Taiwan, proposes design planning and suggestions for toilet and bathroom equipment, and verifies lacking conditions that require improvement of washing equipment, according to the degree of satisfaction with the proposed design. It can be known through the questionnaire and interview analysis that, for all participants, there is still some room improvement in the under-standing of easy operation, difficult to damage, and good duration in the design appearance of water taps, especially because many appearances are different from the appearances used in the past, the participants must become accustomed to the new mode of use. Regarding the aspect of difficult to damage and duration, many participants raise questions; however, as water tap is not used for long duration testing, it is unable to judge its duration degree. The usage demands of elderly and disabled people are quite similar, and fault tolerance and reduction of repeated use are specially required, as repeated operation generates more burden than for young people, and they will experience more significant issues. For children, clear operation tips should be considered first, as children are relatively short, it is difficult for them to use the handle beside the water tap; however, duration and cleanness are not considered for children.

Overall, the design and operation tips of water taps are unclear, and while some users do not initially know how to operate the taps, through several wrong uses, they can learn. In the process of operation, there are some small details that require modification, such as the approximate range and sensitivity of the infrared sensor, and the feedback degree of the button for water pressure, have room for improvement. After overall analysis, it is found that, although more diversified operations, as compared with previous water taps, can meet the different usage demands, there should be more operation tips and feedback in order that users can accept such a new product. The duration degree can be accurately judged only when participants use the water tap for the long-term at home. For a new type of water tap, the users will first judge whether its appearance can be easily understood. If it is complicated, it is possible to make users understand how to operate more easily through clear operation tips and feedback; and provided that there remain operation errors, there should be a mechanism to recover the original mechanism. Correspondence to different demands and reduction of repeated operation are to reduce the physical burden of the user, while easy cleaning and duration are necessary conditions for everyone.

References

1. Chen, M.S.: Behavior and consciousness of bathroom space utilization of the elderly in Taiwan. Jpn. Soc. Sci. Des. **55**(5), 37–46 (2012)
2. Tzeng, S.Y.: From barrier-free design to universal design-comparisons the concept transition and development process of barrier-free design between America and Japan. J. Des. **8**(2), 57–74 (2003)
3. Chen, M.S., Lai, I.R.: An investigation of washing and dressing behaviors in bathrooms in Taiwan. In: The International Conference on Kansei Engineering and Emotion Research 2014 in LINKÖPING University, Sweden, KEER 2014, CD-ROM (2014)
4. Cheng, K.H.: A study of bathing space design form the perspective of universal design. Unpublished master's thesis, TungHai University, Taichung (2007)
5. Construction and Planning Agency Ministry of Interior: Manual for the Residential Bathroom Experience. Construction and Planning Agency Ministry of Interior, Taipei (2003)
6. Lin, C.Y.: A study of bathroom space utilization — a case study of "Dah-Penn Village" in Taipei County. Unpublished master's thesis, Chinese Culture University, Taipei (2002)
7. Narazaki, K., Tsuei, J.G.: Illustration of the Barrier-free Space for Elderly and Disabled. Jan's Books, Chan's Arch-Publishing Co., Taipei (2002)
8. Taiwan Design Center: Research Proposal on Universal Design. Taiwan Design Center, Taipei (2006)
9. Toto Corp.: Facilities for Elderly Users. Toto Co., Tokyo (2006)
10. Wu, M.L.: Statistical Application and Analysis. BookCity, Taipei (2003)
11. Universal Design Principle. www.ncsu.edu/ncsu/design/cud/about_ud/udprinciples.htm

Human Factor in Sustainable Manufacturing

Malgorzata Jasiulewicz-Kaczmarek[1] and Anna Saniuk[2(✉)]

[1] Chair of Ergonomics and Quality Management, Faculty of Engineering
Management, Poznan University of Technology, Poznan, Poland
Malgorzata.jasiulewicz-kaczmarek@put.poznan.pl
[2] Faculty of Mechanical Engineering, Institute of Computer Science
and Production Management, University of Zielona Gora, Zielona Gora, Poland
A.Saniuk@iizp.uz.zgora.pl

Abstract. This article describes sustainable manufacturing (a part of a sustainable development concept) and the role of human factor/ergonomics (HFE) in achieving it. This includes consideration of relevant human factor issues in advancing manufacturing operations and processes from the point of view of product life cycle phases.

Keywords: Human factor/ergonomics · Sustainable manufacturing · Product life-cycle

1 Introduction

One of first and most cited definitions of sustainability was coined in 1987 by the Brundtland Commission, which defined sustainable development as development that 'meets the needs of the present without compromising the ability of future generations to meet their own needs' [3]. Transferring this general definition on a corporate level leads to the concepts of —corporate sustainability. Wayne Visser [50] defined corporate sustainability as a values - laden umbrella concept, which refers to the way in which the interface between business, society and the environment is managed. It implies that the manufacturing organizations have to be seen as social partners not just as profit centres promoting the economic interests of their shareholders, but also as business entities having obligation towards various stakeholders including the employees in providing decent, safe and healthy working conditions [35]. The objective of sustainable development confronts business enterprises with three sustainability challenges:

- Ecological challenge: increasing ecological effectiveness
- Social challenge: increasing social effectiveness
- Economic challenge to environmental and social management: improving eco-efficiency and/or social efficiency.

In the article [17] the analysis reveals that six enablers 'Commitment from top management', 'Eco-literacy amongst supply chain partners', 'Corporate social responsibility', 'High level of supply chain integration', 'Waste management' and 'Logistics organization ensuring goods safety and consumer health' are ranked as Independent

M. Antona and C. Stephanidis (Eds.): UAHCI 2015, Part IV, LNCS 9178, pp. 444–455, 2015.
DOI: 10.1007/978-3-319-20687-5_43

enablers as they possess the maximum driver power. This implies that these variables are key barriers in the successful implementation of sustainability in the Supply Chain. The most important among them are 'Eco-literacy amongst supply chain partners', 'Commitment from top management' and 'Corporate social responsibility'. In the article [18] authors presented the model of the identification of enablers of sustainability collaboration between logistics partners. The results of this research can help in strategic and tactical decisions for a company wanting to create sustainability collaboration between logistics partners. The main strategic decision relies on 'Common business goals' and 'Training'. These enablers are the most important enablers that initiate strategic activities.

Enterprises must manage all these conflicting aspects of sustainability in an integrated manner, focusing not only on environmental or social performances, but also on sustainability of business.

On corporate level social sustainability is realized in concepts such as preventive occupational health and safety, human-cantered design of work, individual and collective learning, employee participation, workplace well-being and work-life balance [44]. The promotion of workplace well-being in the framework of sustainable development can be seen as a challenge and opportunity for organizations to achieve goal such as 'the ability of future generations to meet their needs'. Workplace well-being is considered by the International Labor Organization [22] as what is related to the aspects of working life, including safety and quality of the physical environment, workers feeling about their work and workplace, and their satisfaction level of work organization. According to this definition, workplace well-being aims at ensuring the workers are safe, healthy, satisfied, and engaged at work. Potential solutions or options to promote well-being at work may rise from the learning of ergonomics [36]. Human Factor/Ergonomics (HF/E) contributes to socially sustainable development and often also fosters productivity and effectiveness [43]. Steimle and Zink [43] encouraged ergonomists to make contributions through: understanding employment practices, complementing the design process of sustainability-oriented products, designing more efficient work systems, ensuring the safe operation of complex systems that may result in ecological and economic disasters, and through community ergonomics.

Sustainability is a topic that continues to gain the attention of safety, health, and environmental professionals. Legislative regulations provide an impetus to change from non-sustainable to more environmentally friendly operations, but their influence should be not overestimated. Sustainable manufacturing helps to overcome the problems resulting from increasing cost of energy, raw materials and waste disposal [12, 13]. Typically a board-level issue, sustainable growth strives to balance social, economic, and ecological issues. At their most basic level, sustainability and safety are really about the same thing: conserving resources. In the case of sustainability, those resources are typically thought of as environmental. In the case of safety, the resources are human. Despite this common ground, discussions of sustainability are only beginning to give attention to safety.

This article describes sustainable manufacturing (a part of a sustainable development concept) and the role of human factor/ergonomics (HFE) in achieving it. This includes consideration of relevant human factor issues in advancing manufacturing operations and processes from the point of view of product life cycle phases.

2 Human Factor

Human factors is not as directly about "humans" as the name might suggest. But it is about understanding human limitations and designing the workplace and the equipment we use to allow for variability in humans and human performance more efficient, safe, comfortable and satisfying [1]. Matching skills to the tasks performed is a priceless value in the long-term perspective of business management and strategy implementation [14]. As a discipline, human factors is concerned with understanding interactions between people and other elements of complex systems. All these complex systems need support, maintenance, monitoring, redesign and utilization, and this to be efficient requires a depth knowledge of ergonomics [5]. Human factors applies scientific knowledge and principles as well as lessons learned from previous incidents and operational experience to optimise human wellbeing, overall system performance and reliability [31]. The discipline contributes to the design and evaluation of organisations, tasks, jobs and equipment, environments, products and systems [6]. It focuses on the inherent characteristics, needs, abilities and limitations of people and the development of sustainable and safe working cultures. Human factors, can simultaneously affect a company's safety culture, and at the same time being a factor influencing job satisfaction [4, 15]. As suggest [30] 'The central focus of human factors relates to the consideration of human beings carrying out such functions as:

1. the design and creation of man-made objects, products, equipment, facilities, and environments that people us;
2. the development of procedures for performing work and other human activities;
3. the provision of services to people; and
4. the evaluation of the things people use in terms of their suitability for people.'

The term human factor has been used synonymously with ergonomics (Human Factor and Ergonomics – HFE), and evolves a unique and interdependent discipline that focuses on the nature of human – artefact interaction, viewed the unified perspective of the science, engineering, design, technology, and management of human-compatible systems, including a variety of natural and artificial products, processes, and living environment [41]. HFE focuses on systems in which humans interact with their environment. The environment is complex and consists of the physical environment ('things'), the organizational environment (how activities are organized and controlled), and the social environment (other people, culture) [53]. Today's ergonomics is an established discipline where professionals with interdisciplinary backgrounds work together in the designing socio-technical systems with the common goal of fitting them to human needs and well-being. From manufacturing companies context it recognizes that any complex technological system that involves people is critically dependent on the organizational and social context in which it operates. The objective is to ensure systems are designed in a way that optimises the human contribution to production and minimises potential for design-induced risks to health, personal or process safety or environmental performance.

For several years, there are discussions ongoing on the role and opportunities for active support of the pre-takings by HFE to meet the challenges of sustainable

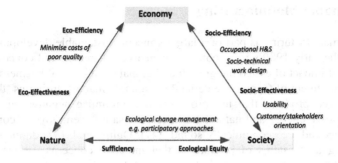

Fig. 1. Triadic model of sustainable development and ergonomics interventions [52]

development [7, 10, 11, 23, 32, 40]. Stanton and Stammers [42] argue that there is a natural link between ergonomics and sustainable development. Steimle and Zink [43] drew specifically on the WCED definition and the 'triple bottom line' approach. Steimle and Zink [43] encouraged ergonomists to make contributions through: understanding employment practices, complementing the design process of sustainability-oriented products, designing more efficient work systems, ensuring the safe operation of complex systems that may result in ecological and economic disasters, and through community ergonomics. Zink, Steimle and Fischer [52] extend on the triadic model to demonstrate the ways that existing human factors interventions have contributed to sustainable development (Fig. 1).

In the literature such terms as ergoecology, eco-ergonomics, green ergonomics [9, 20, 45] can also be found. According to [46] 'green ergonomics is focused on the bi-directional connections between human systems and nature. This involves looking at (1) how ergonomics design and evaluation might be used to conserve, preserve, and restore nature and (2) how ecosystem services might be harnessed to facilitate the improved wellbeing and effectiveness of human systems'. But regardless of how we define the scope of the relationship between human factor and sustainable development, human characteristics, behaviour and performance, and human interactions with technology are vital elements of sustainable development practices. There exists, it would seem, a natural synergy between these areas and ergonomics, with its goal of understanding and optimising the outcomes of human-system interactions. Ergonomic approach to the design of new and modification of existing products and processes is an approach aimed at meeting the requirements of both those who are users of the products or actors which resulted in the formation of these products as well as future users and participants of the manufacturing processes. The use of ergonomic requirements, described in conjunction with the human factor allows users to achieve the desired level of prohumanistic adjustment [16]. Than it should be noted that each product and the process of its implementation affects not only the direct users but also the local community and the environment, and company stakeholders.

Thus, ergonomics should also be seen as a stakeholder oriented approach.

3 Sustainable Manufacturing

Sustainable manufacturing is part of a larger concept, sustainable development, which emerged in the early 1980's in response to increased awareness and concern over the environmental impact of economic growth and global expansion of business and trade. The U.S. Department of Commerce defined sustainable manufacturing as 'the creation of manufactured products that use processes that minimize negative environmental impacts, conserve energy and natural resources, are safe for employees, communities, and consumers and are economically sound' [47]. Quinn et al. [37] define sustainable manufacturing as 'systems of production that integrate concerns for the long-term viability of the environment, workers health and safety, the community, and the economic life of a particular firm'. A more technical definition is given by Rachuri et al. [38] which define sustainable manufacturing as a 'system approach for the creation and distribution (supply chain) of innovative products and services that: minimizes resources (inputs such as materials, energy, water, and land); eliminates toxic substances; and produces zero waste that in effect reduces greenhouse gases, e.g., carbon intensity, across the entire life cycle of products and services'. Here Sustainable Manufacturing is defined as the essence of business, whose main purpose should be the creation of wealth throughout its whole system. Since there is no universally accepted definition for sustainable manufacturing, Javahir [24] describes it as a process that leads to: (i) improved environmental friendliness, (ii) reduced cost, (iii) reduced power consumption, (iv) reduced wastes, (v) enhanced operational safety, and (vi) improved personnel health.

Sustainable manufacturing implies that the processes and practices used for producing products meet the requirements for all three pillars of sustainability (....). From environmental perspective, sustainable manufacturing targets the consumption of less resources and generation of less hazardous materials in order to less jeopardize the environment by reducing global warming, climate changes and toxicity. From economic perspective, the economic advantages of sustainable manufacturing can be acquired by minimizing the cost through less material, energy, resource, and time consumption, and from social perspective, for better employment, well-being of the employees and livable communities; sustainable manufacturing considers workers' health and security with improved working conditions.

Taking into account such a wide spectrum of issues, sustainable manufacturing requires a holistic approach to the manufacturing process that monitors inputs and outputs in order to reduce the amounts of materials and energy being consumed, improve health and safety, and reduce the life-cycle impact of products. To achieve this, a successful approach to sustainable manufacturing must address all phases of product life-cycle e.g. design, production, exploitation and disposal (Fig. 2) and all stakeholders.

From Fig. 2, one can conclude that, sustainable manufacturing is extremely important to sustainability, and all phases of product life–cycle should be analysed and improved to meet the requirements of sustainability completely. Sustainable manufacturing is all about minimising the diverse business risks inherent in any

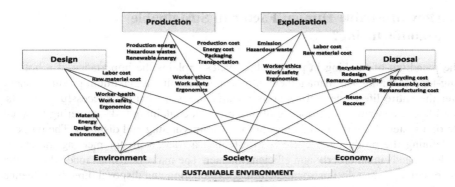

Fig. 2. Manufacturing contribution to sustainable environment [2]

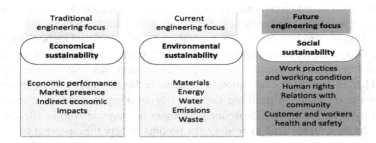

Fig. 3. Future engineering focus

manufacturing operation while maximising the new opportunities that arise from improving processes and products. Learning and practicing the new concepts, processes, methods and tools of sustainable manufacturing can be an exceptional opportunity for practitioners (engineers, ergonomists, etc.) that apply their knowledge and experience in developing new and improving existing products and systems of work friendly and safe for current and future users (Fig. 3).

One of example can be simulation of the transport tasks realization with taking into account different disturbances on process. By analyzing this process including different disturbances and impact of them to the whole process, the efficiency and an sustainability of the supply chain can be presented. Moreover, this approach includes human, ecology and other factors as disruptions (for example driving work time, congestion, suddenly weather changes) [21]. Traditionally, the scope of manufacturing is referred to product and production processes. However, the shift from management paradigm to sustainable development resulted in a change of the manufacturing paradigm towards of product life cycle management; as well as taking into account economic, environmental and social aspects.

4 How to Enable Human Factor in Sustainable Manufacturing?

The paradigm of thinking in product life cycles explains the importance of a holistic long-term planning and management approach to reaching a maximum product benefit over the entire life cycle and supports manufacturers in shaping successful products. The life cycle system is a sequence of phases, each containing tasks, covering the total life of a system from the initial concept to decommissioning and disposal. The purpose in defining the product life cycle is to establish a framework for meeting the stakeholders' needs in an orderly and efficient manner. The many decisions made during the process of a product design, manufacturing, exploitation and disposal directly influence the effect and outcome on the human well-being.

The first phase of the product's life cycle is its design. The conventional role of a product design in manufacturing firms has been to ensure that the product meets its desired objectives based on customer preferences taking into consideration performance, efficiency, ergonomics and aesthetics. However, with increased focus on sustainable manufacturing, the product designer is encumbered with additional responsibility of his decisions. This is due to, among others, the fact that the present definition of the customer goes beyond the classic 'customer as an organization or person that receives a product' [ISO 9001]. Starting from the definition of sustainable development and the challenges to be met by the company to meet the definition of an adequate customer seems to be suggested by J. Juran. Juran [25] defined customer as 'anyone who is affected by the product or by the process used to produce the product' where the customer can also be a local community, the environment, and even future generations. This broad definition of 'client' is close to the notion of 'stakeholder'. According to [8]: 'a stakeholder is any person or group that can affect or is affected by the achievement of the organization's objectives'. Product stakeholders are the people who are affect or are affected by the product during its life cycle. Thus, it becomes imperative for the designer to first acclimatize himself with the various issues concerning sustainability. From the point of view of sustainable manufacturing it is important to establish environmental and social (e.g. ergonomics) requirements and to apply a holistic view at product level as early as possible because, in early design phases of new products changes are less costly and easier to make than are late changes to the product, the work, or the workplace design. In addition, changes are increasingly difficult to make the closer it is to production start, and they become much more costly. When designing a product, not only the requirements for functionality and security should be taken into consideration, but also ergonomics. These requirements can be taken into account even at the stage of development of the concept of the product [33]. Thanks to such ahead in relation to the next stages of implementation of the project (construction of a prototype, serial production) so called thick errors can be avoided and significant savings of resources and time can be provided. Subsequent application of these requirements is burdened with too many risks, both financial (cost of improving the structure of already produced batch or serial), social (risk of hazards, accidents at work and occupational diseases users) and legal (legal consequences arising from marketing or putting into service of the product not in accordance with legal requirements) [34].

At this stage, aspects of the further phase, which is a production process should also be considered. Product design and engineering can benefit from the applications of ergonomics in both the design of the product for the end user and in design of a product that is easy to produce. Design for Assembly (DfA), or Design for Manufacturability (DfM), is an approach by which the ergonomics of assembly is considered in the product design stage. By considering production ergonomics in the product design phase it is possible to avoid all costs associated with corrective ergonomics processes, with little extra investment in the design phase. The aim in the production phase is to realise the design as physical components. Workers often pay the price for economic pressures on manufacturers to cut corners in order to meet demand for low cost products. Even if toxic inputs are eliminated from a product design, workers may be subjected to unhealthy working conditions, such as poor air quality, poor ergonomic design of work stations, involuntary overtime, and excessive pace. A product that is safe for consumers but presents significant hazards for those involved in its production is not a fully sustainable product. Similarly, a product that is polluting in its production and therefore harms the local community is not a fully sustainable product, even if this impact occurs far from where the product is consumed/used. How to ensure that working conditions are as safe as possible and humane? We spend eight hours a day at the workplace. Properties and workplace conditions have a significant impact on mental and physical health, not to mention the motivation of the employees [39]. The working environment may also play a significant role in both preventing the formation of non-conformity as well as the challenge of non-compliance of the product (economic aspect). Among the factors that may cause non-compliance of the product and human errors in the workplace the following are often cited: procedures, equipment, supervision, knowledge, time pressure, organization, fatigue [29].

In the literature of the subject, including ergonomics in this phase of the product life cycle is a shown to in the context of improvement activities most often carried out in system of continuous improvement. Lillrank et al. [26] defined CI as 'a purposeful and explicit set of principles, mechanisms, and activities within an organisation adopted to generate ongoing, systematic and cumulative improvement in deliverables, operating procedures and systems'. Realizing the program of joining employees in workstation improvement companies usually benefit from "Kaizen events" system for initiatives introduction. Initiatives of employees are mostly focused on various aspects of work processes and production. Participation of employees on all levels in the development of work and work environments is an important concept in modern ergonomics. The most common methods used in enterprises are 5S practices, machinery maps, process mapping, etc. [7, 27, 28, 49].

Including ergonomics in the design of work and workplaces may support productivity and quality, promote the health of the employees and also attract new employees. But most ergonomic interventions are designed to reduce relevant risk factors impacting the individual worker, ignores the potential health consequences of measures to improve competitiveness and productivity [51]. A shift for a more macro-approach should be expected from ergonomics interventions because they 'may have a better chance of success by focusing on insights that help balancing production performance and worker wellbeing, thereby moving towards more sustainable production systems' [51].

The next phase in the life cycle of the product is exploitation. In this phase, except of the obvious comfort of the device user it is necessary to draw attention to the comfort and safety of those who carry out maintenance and repair work. Generally the fact that maintenance operations involve some specific risks and that their operators are exposed to potential chemical, biological, physical (etc.) hazards that may influence their safety and health more than other workers is not taken into consideration. Repair work requires sustained awkward postures of the back, neck, and shoulders as well as repetitive manipulations and awkward postures associated with hand tool use. Sustained awkward postures restrict blood flow and can cause muscle fatigue as well as place the employee at risk of developing Work-Related Musculoskeletal Disorders. Repeatedly performing tasks in such positions imposes increased stress on the muscles and joints. Employees are exposed to contact stress to the hands from using small tools, while a lack of task lighting can increase eye strain and induce awkward postures as employees try to adequately view a part. The issues of ergonomics and safety at work of employees of the technical services is rarely subject raised in the literature. However, due to the automation of manufacturing processes on the shop floor more often we see the maintenance technician than the machine operator. A role of maintenance staff in the sustainable production is special.

The last phase of the product life cycle is liquidation. Waste from consumer products can be drastically reduced by adopting a design approach that facilitates: re-use of components in subsequent designs; the benign return of components to the environment through use of completely natural, no- or low-processed materials; and/or ease of recycling by ensuring the components are made from minimally processed, single type materials. In this way, we will cause that man is not only the participant in these processes, but mostly the involuntary recipient of their impact on the environment in which he lives will be better protected and his well-being will be assured.

5   Conclusion

Just as ergonomics benefits are often difficult to quantify, so too is 'selling' the benefits of sustainability. The goal is for both ergonomics, and sustainability, to become a central part of all phases of product life cycle. To do this it is necessary to show that by incorporating these practices both quality and productivity can be enhanced. A product designed to be usable and useful to the customer can contribute to companies' profit (economic perspective of sustainable manufacturing). Good ergonomics can be defined as appropriately applied ergonomics technology that also is cost-effective. According to [19, 48], most economics analysis of ergonomics and health interventions made clear that, from the company perspective, they are worth undertaking because they result in positive net values, benefit-to-cost ratios greater than 1, and relatively short pay-back periods.

References

1. Attaianese, E., Duca, G.: Human factors and ergonomic principles in building design for life and work activities: an applied methodology. Theor. Issues Ergon. Sci. **13**(2), 187–202 (2012)
2. Bi, Z.M.: Revisiting system paradigms from the viewpoint of manufacturing sustainability. Sustainability **3**, 1323–1340 (2011)
3. Brundlandt, G.H.: Our Common Future. Report of the World Commission on Environment and Development. Oxford University Press, Oxford (1987)
4. Butlewski, M., Misztal, A., Ciulu, R.: Non-financial factors of job satisfaction in the development of a safety culture based on examples from Poland and Romania. In: Duffy, V. G. (ed.) DHM 2014. LNCS, vol. 8529, pp. 577–587. Springer, Heidelberg (2014)
5. Butlewski, M., Tytyk, E.: The assessment criteria of the ergonomic quality of anthropotechnical mega-systems. In: Vink, P. (ed.) Advances in Social and Organizational Factors, pp. 298–306 CRC Press, Taylor and Francis Group, Boca Raton, London (2012)
6. Chapanis, A.R.: Human-factors engineering. In: The New Encyclopaedia Britannica, 15th edn., vol. 21, pp. 227–229. Encyclopaedia Britannica, Chicago (1986)
7. Dul, J., Neumann, W.P.: Ergonomics contributions to company strategies. Appl. Ergon. **40**, 745–752 (2009)
8. Freeman, R.E.: Strategic Management: A Stakeholder Approach. Pitman, Boston (1984)
9. Garcia-Acosta, G., Saravia Pinilla, M.H., Riba i Romeva, C.: Ergoecology: evolution and challenges. Work: J. Prev. Assess. Rehabil. **41**(1), 2133–2140 (2012)
10. Genaidy, A.M., Sequeira, R., Rinder, M.M., A-Rehim, A.D.: Determinents of business sustainability: an ergonomics perspective. Ergonomics **52**, 273–301 (2009)
11. Genaidy, A.M., Rinder, M.M., Sequeira, R., A-Rehim, A.D.: The role of human-at-work systems in business sustainability: perspectives based on expert and qualified production workers in a manufacturing enterprise. Ergonomics **53**, 559–585 (2010)
12. Golinska, P.: From traditional non-sustainable production to closed loop manufacturing: challenges for materials management. Corporate Environmental Management Information Systems: Advancements and Trends: Advancements and Trends, pp. 106–127 (2010)
13. Golinska, P., Kawa, A.: Remanufacturing in automotive industry: challenges and limitations. J. Ind. Eng. Manag. **4**(3), 453–466 (2011)
14. Gołaś, H.: Personal risk management. In: Stephanidis, C. (ed.) HCII 2013, Part II. CCIS, vol. 374, pp. 489–493. Springer, Heidelberg (2013)
15. Górny, A.: Application of quality shaping methods in the work environment improvement. A case of theoretical frames. Manage. Syst. Prod. Eng. **3**(15), 106–111 (2014)
16. Górny, A.: Human factor and ergonomics in essential requirements for the operation of technical equipment. In: Stephanidis, C. (ed.) HCI 2014, Part II. CCIS, vol. 435, pp. 449–454. Springer, Heidelberg (2014)
17. Grzybowska, K.: Supply chain sustainability – analysing the enablers. In: Golinska, P., Romano, C.A. (eds.) Environmental Issues in Supply Chain Management - New Trends and Applications, pp. 25–40. Springer, Heidelberg (2010)
18. Grzybowska, K., Awasthi, A., Hussain, M.: Modeling enablers for sustainable logistics collaboration integrating Canadian and Polish perspectives. In: Ganzha, M., Maciaszek, L., Paprzycki, M. (eds.) Proceedings of the 2014 Federated Conference on Computer Science and Information Systems, ACSIS, vol. 2, pp. 1311–1319 (2014)
19. de M. Guimarães, L.B., Ribeiro, J.L.D., Renner, J.S.: Cost-benefit analysis of a socio-technical intervention in a Brazilian footwear company. Appl. Ergon. **43**, 948–957 (2012)

20. Hanson, M.: Green ergonomics: embracing the challenges of climate change. Ergonomist **480**, 12–13 (2010)
21. Hoffa, P., Pawlewski, P.: Models of organizing transport tasks including possible disturbances and impact of them on the sustainability of the supply chain. In: Pawlewski, P., Greenwood, A. (eds.) Process Simulation and Optimization in Sustainable Logistics and Manufacturing, Eco Production. Environmental Issues in Logistics and Manufacturing, pp. 141–151. Springer, Heidelberg (2014)
22. ILO 2009. http://www.ilo.org/safework/areasofwork/workplace-health-promotion-and-well-being/WCMS_118396/lang–en/index.htm
23. Imada, A.S.: Achieving sustainability through macro ergonomic change management and participation. In: Zink, K.J. (ed.) Corporate Sustainability as a Challenge for Pomrehensive Management, pp. 129–138 (2008)
24. Jawahir, I.S., Dillon Jr., O.W.: Sustainable manufacturing processes: new challenges for developing predictive models and optimization techniques. In: Proceedings of the 1st International Conference on Sustainable Manufacturing, pp. 1–19 (2007)
25. Juran, J.: Quality Control Handbook, 4th edn., p. 23. McGraw-Hill, New York (1988)
26. Lillrank, P., Shani, A.B., Lindberg, P.: Continuous improvement: exploring alternative organizational designs. Total Qual. Manag. **12**, 41–55 (2001)
27. Lim, A.J., Village, J., Salustri, F.A., Neumann, W.P.: Process mapping as a tool for participative integration of human factors into work system design. Eur. J. Ind. Eng. **8**(2), 273–290 (2014)
28. Mazur, A., Stachowiak, A.: The framework of methodology for identification of organizational maturity with assessment of excellence level of logistics systems. In: Abrudan, I. (ed.) The Management Between Profit and Social Responsibility, Proceedings of the 4th Review of Management and Economic Engineering International Management Conference, 18–20 September 2014, Todesco Publishing House, Cluj-Napoca, Romania, pp. 415–423 (2014)
29. Mazur, A.: Application of fuzzy index to qualitative and quantitative evaluation of the quality level of working conditions. In: Stephanidis, C. (ed.) HCII 2013, Part II. CCIS, vol. 374, pp. 514–518. Springer, Heidelberg (2013)
30. McCormick, E.J., Sanders, M.S.: Human Factors in Engineering and Design. McGraw-Hill, New York (1982)
31. Misztal, A., Butlewski, M., Jasiak, A., Janik, S.: The human role in a progressive trend of foundry automation. Metalurgija **54**(2), 429–432 (2015)
32. Mitsch, W.J., Jorgensen, S.E.: Ecological Engineering and Ecosystem Restoration. Willey, New York (2004)
33. Mrugalska, B., Arezes, P.M.: Safety requirements for machinery in practice. In: Arezes, P.M., Baptista, J.S., Barroso, M.P. et al. (eds.) 9th International Symposium on Occupational Safety and Hygiene (SHO), Guimaraes, 14–15 February 2013, pp. 97–101. Taylor and Francis Group, London (2013)
34. Mrugalska, B.: Induction machine faults leading to occupational accidents. In: Stephanidis, C., Antona, M. (eds.) UAHCI 2014, Part IV. LNCS, vol. 8516, pp. 237–245. Springer, Heidelberg (2014)
35. Nicolăescu, E., Alpopi, C., Zaharia, C.: Measuring corporate sustainability performance. Sustainability **7**, 851–865 (2015)
36. Pitkänen, M., Naumanen, P., Ojanen, K., Louhevaara, V.: The Ergonetti-web-based ergonomics studies: a qualitative case study. Open Edu. J. **1**, 29–36 (2008)
37. Quinn, M.M., Kriebel, D., Geiser, K., Moure-Eraso, R.: Sustainable production: a proposed strategy for the work environment. Am. J. Ind. Med. **34**, 297–304 (1998)

38. Rachuri, S., Sriram, R.D., Narayanan, A., Sarkar, P., Lee, J., Lyons, K.W., Kemmerer, S.J.: Sustainable manufacturing: metrics, standards, and infrastructure - Workshop Report, NISTIR 7683 (2010)

39. Sadłowska-Wrzesińska, J.: Analysis of psychosocial risk in the context of the objectives of macroergonomics. In: Vink, P. (ed.) Advances in Social and Organizational Factors, AHFE Conference, pp. 277–285 (2014)

40. Scott, P.A.: Global inequality, and the challenge for ergonomics to take a more dynamic role to redress the situation. Appl. Ergon. **39**, 495–499 (2008)

41. Karwowski, W.: Handbook of Standards and Guidelines in Ergonomics and Human Factors (Human Factors/Ergonomics). L. Erlbaum Associates Inc., Hillsdale (2005)

42. Stanton, N.A., Stammers, R.B.: The future of ergonomics revisited. Ergonomics: Special Issue Future Ergon. **51**(1), 1–13 (2008)

43. Steimle, U., Zink, K.J.: Sustainable development and human factors. In: Karwowski, W. (ed.) International Encyclopedia of Ergonomics and Human Factors, 2nd edn, pp. 2258–2263. Taylor & Francis, London (2006)

44. Summers, J.K., Smith, L.M., Harwell, L.C., Case, J.L., Wade, C.M., Straub, K.R., Smith, H. M.: An index of human well-being for the U.S.: a TRIO approach. Sustainability **6**, 3915–3935 (2014)

45. Thatcher, A., Groves, A.: Ecological ergonomics: designing products to encourage pro-environmental behaviour. In: CybErg 2008: The Fifth International Cyberspace Conference on Ergonomics, Kuching, Sarawak, Malaysia, 15 September–15 October, 2008

46. Thatcher, A.: Green ergonomics: definition and scope. Ergonomics **56**(3), 389–398 (2013)

47. The US Department of Commerce, 2010, The International Trade Administration and The U.S. Department of Commerce's definition for Sustainable Manufacturing. http://www. trade.gov/competitiveness/sustainablemanufacturing/how_doc_defines_SM.asp. Accessed 28 June 2012

48. Tompa, E., Dolinschi, R., Laing, A.: An economic evaluation of a participatory ergonomics process in an auto parts manufacturer. J. Saf. Res. **40**, 41–47 (2009)

49. Törnström, L., Amprazis, J., Christmansson, M., Eklund, J.: A corporate workplace model for ergonomic assessments and improvements. Appl. Ergon. **39**, 219–228 (2008)

50. Visser, W.: Corporate sustainability and the individual a literature review, Cambridge programme for sustainability leadership paper series, no. 1, pp. 1–15 (2007). http://www. waynevisser.com/wp-ontent/uploads/2007/05/paper_sustainability_individual_lit_wvisser. pdf. Accessed 28 January 2015

51. Westgaard, R.H., Winkel, J.: Occupational musculoskeletal and mental health: significance of rationalization and opportunities to create sustainable production systems: a systematic review. Appl. Ergon. **42**, 261–296 (2011)

52. Zink, K.J., Steimle, U., Fischer, K.: Human factors, business excellence and corporate sustainability: differing perspectives, joint objectives. In: Zink, K.J. (ed.) Corporate Sustainability as a Challenge for Comprehensive Management, pp. 3–18. Physica-verlag, Heidelberg (2008)

53. Carayon, P., Schoofs Hundt, A., Karsh, B.T., Gurses, A.P., Alvarado, C.J., Smith, M., Brennan, P.F.: Work system design for patient safety: the SEIPS model. Qual. Saf. Health Care **15**(1), 50–58 (2006)

Model of OHS Management Systems in an Excellent Company

Anna Mazur[⊠]

Chair of Ergonomics and Quality Management, Faculty of Engineering
Management, Poznan University of Technology, Poznan, Poland
anna.mazur@put.poznan.pl

Abstract. In the paper the model of the Occupational Health and Safety management system (OHS management system model.) implementable in organizations striving for continuous improvement and excellence is presented. The concepts of excellent organizations and organizational maturity are explained. The model presented by the author is the result of the case study based research conducted in five manufacturing companies in the Wielkopolska region. All the analyzed companies in a very clear way focus their attention on the issue of improving OHS management system and are interested in are assessment of organizational maturity in this area and meet the requirements of any health and safety excellence model. The basic assumption of the model is application of the continuous improvement principle at three management levels: strategic, tactical and operational. As an extension of the model presented, the option of the implementation of Deming's fourteen principles to the area of health and safety management is introduced. Approach to the management of health and safety presented points to the ever increasing interest of enterprises in these issues, in addition it proves the fact that achieving and improving organizational maturity is only possible with regard to issues of health and safety.

Keywords: OHS management model · Excellence model · Organizational maturity

1 Introduction

The contemporary market and its tendency to continuous change and growing demands of the relevant stakeholders of organizations, force the search for solutions that ensure achievement of success in the long-term. Short-term thinking about the results of the organization does not guarantee success, and moreover is not sufficient to provide competitive advantage over the world-class companies. The desire to increase the value of companies and their ability to compete not only in domestic market but also in foreign one forces organizations to perform in a way, which in addition to making profit will enable development of a number of additional benefits for both the company and its stakeholders. This is directly linked with the idea of excellence and continuous improvement. The benefit is undoubtedly improvement of safety in organizations, as well as care for the health and safety of internal stakeholders. Safety should be considered here both in broad terms, understood as the absence of risk or protection against general risk, as well as in

© Springer International Publishing Switzerland 2015
M. Antona and C. Stephanidis (Eds.): UAHCI 2015, Part IV, LNCS 9178, pp. 456–467, 2015.
DOI: 10.1007/978-3-319-20687-5_44

narrower terms related strictly to production systems, implemented processes, people functioning in these systems and processes, as well as broad technical safety. Safety correlates with multiple dimensions of an organization, including reliability, but also other aspects of safety, such as financial or social, should be taken into account [1].

In the area of health and safety management in Poland the most popular models of management include Polish standard PN-N 18001:2004 and international standard OHSAS 18001:2007. The first of these standards defines the occupational safety and health as a state of conditions and the organization of work and behavior of employees to ensure the required level of protection of health and life against hazards in the work environment [20]. This definition clearly indicates that the object of interest in the management of occupational health and safety is a worker, that is the most important internal stakeholder, who is exposed to a nuisance, and harmful and dangerous factors. Thus, the objective of management of health and safety should be to reduce this exposure, inter alia by ensuring safe working environment. Requirements for safety and health at work may also include protection of persons exposed to work-related activities outside the immediate workplace, which is indicated in the OHSAS 18001: 2007 [18].

The objective of this article is to present a model of OHS management systems in an excellent company, which is the one for which the achievement of results at the highest level is the basic premise. The presented model takes into account the results of a case study conducted in five large companies in the Wielkopolska region. During the development of health and safety management model numerous aspects determining the level of organizational maturity in the area of health and safety management were taken into account, among which are:

- understanding the needs of employees,
- involvement of people,
- the level of motivation,
- safety culture awareness,
- improvement of the hygiene factors,
- ergonomic quality,
- quality of working conditions,
- industrial fatigue,
- ergonomic design criteria,
- occupational health and safety,
- optimization of the functions of equipment,
- safety of technical equipment,
- understanding the risks,
- benchmarking.

2   Improvement and Organizational Maturity in the Area of OHS Management

Improvement is a term often used in practical operation of enterprises. This is certainly related to the growing importance of management concepts such as TQM or Kaizen. Focusing on the implementation of tasks aimed towards continuous improvement is a natural action of companies managers of which understand the relationship between the economic results achieved and the continuous improvement of the functioning of the internal processes. The term improvement refers to projects undertaken to obtain additional benefits for the organization and its customers [10]. Analysis of the operation of enterprises in the management of occupational safety and health leads to the conclusion that improvement role is extremely important. System approach in this area, and operating in the traditional terms of the well-known Deming cycle: Plan-Do-Check-Act [3] is necessary to achieve long-term effects in striving for improvement of the area of health and safety in organizations. Undertaking one-time corrective actions aimed at the minimization of the negative influence of environment at human labor will not lead to the desired effects.

Focus on the issues of improvement in the area of health and safety has led to definition of the term of quality of working life, understood as the degree of satisfaction of employees with work, working conditions and, in particular, with such features as the quality of working conditions [4]:

- fair salary,
- occupational satisfaction (I like what I do),
- supervisors' respect,
- good organization of work and workstations,
- safety, hygiene, ergonomics,
- opportunity to prove one's independence (strict definition of responsibilities and rights).

Achieving this level of quality of working conditions that would guarantee benefits to the organization and its stakeholders requires the use of appropriate measures not only at the strategic level, but especially at tactic and operational levels (Fig. 1), with special emphasis on the human factor. The human factor can be considered as a determinant of obtaining the desired results [8].

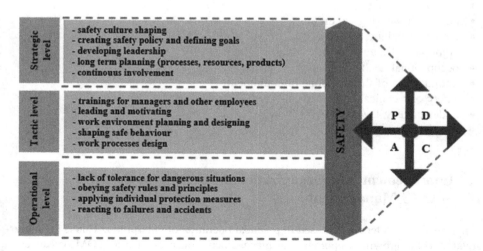

Fig. 1. Strategic, tactic and operational level in health and safety management

The implementation of the activities presented at all levels of health and safety management has an impact on the level of organizational maturity in this field. The idea is that the more "mature" organization, the greater is its ability to carry out processes in a way to achieve better product quality, vast improvements in the safety and thus better business results [2, 14].

Unfortunately, health and safety are rarely viewed as a main area of interest in business. However workers' health in a great manner influences the financial state of a company and next the company's development. While the managerial staff is interested mainly in the influence of workers' state of being on the company's business efficiency the workers are interested in the managerial and working processes that influence their health. Both aspects must be considered paralelly [21].

3 Excellent Organizations and Excellence Models in Health and Safety Management

The term excellent organization is an agreed idea referring to organizations heavily focused on continuous improvement, which enabled them to achieve the best possible position in their class. Improvement understood as a project undertaken to obtain additional benefits for the organization and its clients should focus on incremental improvements in every aspect of business, so that organizations could become the best in their class. Mature organization is the striving for achieving sustained success which is the result of the ability to achieve and maintain objectives in the long term [9]. Analyzing opportunities for improvement it is necessary to use the standards and guidelines to guide the organization's processes for continuous improvement, but also look for opportunities to recognize the effects of actions taken. This is why the models of excellence (e.g. MNBQA, EFQM) were developed, and meeting the criteria presented in them enables companies obtaining formal confirmation of improvement of their performance. Models of excellence, however, are still strongly associated with the area of quality management well developed in organizations. This is wrong thinking, because the success of an organization depends on the consideration of, and the strategy of sustainable development, which has become not only an idea, a political program, and the concept of loss prevention, but the paradigm of efficient management [23], taking into account the issues of health and safety management. Accordingly, excellence models were developed targeting the organization in such a way that they are aimed at improving the working conditions. A selection of these is presented in Table 1.

The evidence of interest in improving corporate issues is also developing by the most recognized manufacturers their own models of excellence defining world-class production standards (World Class Manufacturing - WCM). Among Polish organizations the excellent example is SABMiller's WCM model called "Manufacturing Way" [10] as well as the WCM model by Fiat Auto Poland [15]. Analyzing these models of excellence leads to the conclusion that in each of them one of the pillars is safety, which essence in the simplest terms, is the continuous minimization of accidents and incidents potentially dangerous, as well as improving the working environment and conditions.

Table 1. Selected health and safety excellence models

Models	Basic assumptions of the model
OHSAS 18001	Model primarily promotes safe and healthy working environment, offering a structure in which an organization can consistently set and control risks to health and safety, and reduce the likelihood of accidents, which favors the adjustment of applicable regulations and improves overall performance. The model can be used in any organization that wants to implement a formal procedure to reduce the risk to the safety and hygiene of work for employees, customers and members of the public [22]
PN-N 18001	It is the Polish standard that allows to carry out safety and occupational health management system certification. The standard indicates what should be done to effectively predict occurrence of circumstances which expose workers to injury or loss of life and prevent them. In addition, the PN-N standard requires the commitment, expressed in the safety policy, that the organization will act in accordance with applicable law and is committed to continuous improvement of safety management system [19]
International Safety Rating System (ISRS)	Model developed basing on the ISO 9000 series of standards and adapted to the needs of safety and risk management. Focuses on issues that relate to the management system and a loss as a result of accidents, incidents, industrial accidents, fires, explosions, occupational diseases and absenteeism of employees. ISRS takes into account requirements that are included in other international and national norms and standards, such as BS 8800, OHSAS 18001 and BS 18001 [19]
BS 8800	British and the first global standard that specifies guidelines for safety management systems and occupational health. It is worth noting that the standard BS 8800 became the basis for the development of the OHSAS 18001 [19]
Guide of International Labor Organization ILO-OSH 2001	Creates a guide on safety and health management systems. Includes guidelines (mainly organizational and institutional) that are not obligatory because they do not have the force of law, are not a substitute for national law regulations, or any standards. They are designed for the people responsible for the management of occupational health and safety in organizations and are used as practical advice in this area [19]

(Continued)

Table 1. (*Continued*)

Models	Basic assumptions of the model
SHE Model	Integrated management model of safety, health and the environment. It should be noted that this is one of the fundamental pillars of TPM. In this area focus is on to create a safe workplace and a surrounding area that is not damaged by their process or procedures. The general aim is to achieve zero accidents. Two factors help people acquire a zero accident – daily practice as part of workplace and strong, visible companywide support [10]

The issue of safety included in the models of excellence in world-class enterprises requires the adoption of a suitable methodology for the management of this area.

4 Health and Safety Management Model

The presented excellence model of OHS Management was developed basing on the results of a case study conducted in five large manufacturing companies in the Wielkopolska region. All of the analyzed companies in a very clear way focus their attention on the issue of improving health and safety management system, are interested in the evaluation of organizational maturity in this area and meet the requirements of any health and safety excellence model applicable.

As a result of the observation, it can be stated unequivocally that quality of work environment as a category itself has gained special importance. Ensuring adequate working environment is one of the primary responsibilities of company's management. Maintaining a working environment able to comply with legal requirements and expectations of stakeholders determines the possibility of obtaining the desired effects, while non-compliance should be treated as an important factor of disturbances [6]. Moreover modern enterprises are forced to constantly improve ways of management and to introduce changes. One of the changes is an alteration of organizational culture and acceptance of participation of employees in designing and implementing new solutions. Striving for general improvement of system efficiency involves joint design of technical and social systems to achieve the best fitness to goals and requirements of system and its parts possible. Not only technical objects, but also workers and workplaces (work environment) require keeping in good condition [11]. The human in technical system can exist in four roles: controller, operator, service technician, and performer. Different configurations of the human-technical object system are closely linked to the issue of the level and type of training of employees, the nature of their tasks and the type of workload [16]. Industrial production is an integrated process where a human plays the most crucial and vital role. The employees' ability to perform tasks at shift contributes to a significant loading of health. Thus, providing them good working conditions is necessary. In order to achieve it, safe and environmental friendly

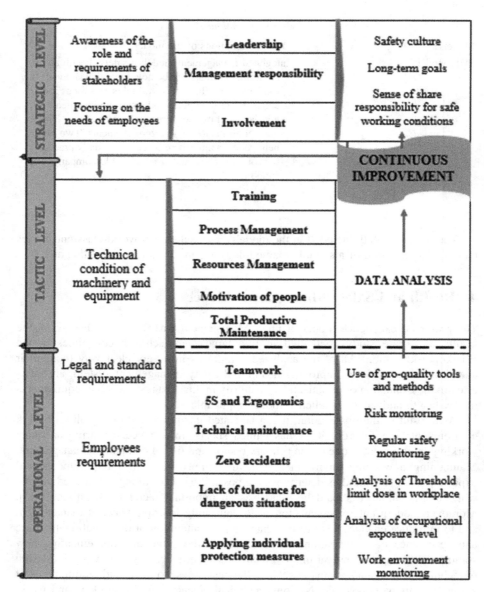

Fig. 2. Framework of the excellent model of OHS Management

systems of work should be assured. It should also be noticed, that in most cases poor working conditions are due to the lack of safety supervision and control [12]. An approach to the problem of analysis of the causes of accidents at work is also an important issue is also. Organizations that devote special attention to this issue gain better experience in eliminating the real causes of dangerous situations. It was noted that in the case of the use of appropriate methods to analyze the causes of accidents,

Table 2. Application of the 14 Deming's principles to health and safety

Deming's principle	Application to health and safety management
1. Responsibility of managers	Define a vision in terms of health and safety consistent with the general policy of the company. Make the leaders aware of the role of the occupational health and safety. Teach them the responsibility for the occupational health and safety, select the rules for implementing the vision and policies adopted with regard to the principle of continuous improvement.
2. New way of thinking	Accept new safety and hygiene of work management philosophies. Determine direction of efforts to realize adopted vision of security. Specify the basic rules applicable in practice in efforts to improve safety and improve the quality of working conditions
3. Lack of belief in efficiency of mass final control	Introduce the issues of quality of working conditions for all the areas of functioning of companies. Evaluation of the quality of working conditions is not only reflected in accidents at work and occupational diseases. Define the factors affecting the quality of working conditions during the performance of manufacturing processes
4. Change in decision making on purchasing concerning the price criteria	Implement method of assessing the cost of safe operation, analyze them, and use the results in deciding whether to allocate resources to different areas of health and safety management. Consider the costs of decentralization. Middle managers should be involved in decision on the necessary purchases (e.g. Personal protection means, training) that contribute to the improvement of the security situation
5. Continuous improvement of processes	Audit, assess, and improve all of the actions taken and affecting the quality of working conditions in order to achieve the highest effectiveness. Focus attention on improving the safety of your process
6. Courses and training	Ensure that all employees are educated, trained and made aware of health and safety. Use modern methods in this area. Improve their competences because once conquered and not embedded they do not

(Continued)

Table 2. (*Continued*)

Deming's principle	Application to health and safety management
	guarantee sufficient level of awareness of employees on safe working conditions
7. Leadership	Become a "superleader". Learn to listen to people and their opinions. Teach them to identify problems and solve them. Inform them on the actions taken to improve the level of quality of working conditions. Encourage such actions, constantly help. Encourage your middle managers to inform their superiors on the matters requiring adjustments in terms of quality of working conditions
8. Elimination of fear from management area	Try to make your employees not afraid to talk together about the risks and problems within the quality of working conditions. Teach employees that they should inform about the poor state of the safety, threats, loads not only physical and mechanical but also mental. Ask questions and listen
9. Break barriers in communication	Remove obstacles to cooperation between different levels of health and safety management in the company. Build teams to solve specific problems related to the safety of involving employees at all levels. Top management should play their roles according to the structure of the team and not the company
10. Eliminate slogans and inciting workers to overcome shortages and to a higher level of performance	Eliminate slogans on the safety of work for a real appreciation for the people working to improve safety. Instead of empty words create opportunities for the creation of programs and measures to warn about the dangers in the workplace
11. Limit standards on quantity	Do not impose quantitative targets to improve safety, such as the maximum number of accidents at work. Analysis of statistical data on accidents and occupational diseases is not sufficient for the development of safe behavior in the workplace
12. Remove barriers that rob workers of pride from their job	Ensure appreciation to employees and managers who obtain positive results in terms of safety, both in their workplaces and jobs of their colleagues. Build loyalty systems for those who follow the rules of

(*Continued*)

Table 2. (*Continued*)

Deming's principle	Application to health and safety management
	safety, give a good example and motivate others to follow them
13. Introduce training and self-learning schemes	Introduce the specific forms of professional skills improvement and learning on work safety. Provide a full understanding of employees on roles they play their actions in ensuring an adequate level of quality of working conditions as their decisions and actions affect the overall security posture
14. Commitment of all the employees	Apply the cycle of continuous improvement of all processes to improve the management of quality of working conditions. For this purpose, teach employees and executives using the appropriate methods and tools to identify and analyze problems concerning the quality of working conditions. Develop shared sense of responsibility for the safety and health status of the company

such as 5 Why analysis, FMEA (Failure mode and effects analysis), Pareto-Lorenzo analysis [5] or, for example, Ishikawa Diagram, the results are analyzed in greater depth and the actual causes are traced. The latter tool mentioned, in particular, allows to define the causes of accidents, which in many cases depend on the human factor [7]. Projects undertaken to ensure safety through strict control of the processes in which the main subject is a human and his/her appropriate response to alarms of the system also deserve special attention [17].

All observations made, analyzes conducted in the surveyed enterprises, as well as the conceptual framework resulting from the application of the principles of continuous improvement led to development of the excellent model of OHS management system (Fig. 2) (Table 2).

5 Conclusion

Excellent company is not just the one that effectively eliminates waste, depletes cost-absorption of resources, has a passion for standards, boasts the best leaders and dedicated employees. Excellent company is also the one for which primary value is the sensitivity to the safety of the workers. The managers of excellent companies have the expertise and are fully aware of the risks which are inherent to the implementation of processes, manufacturing of products or providing services. Striving to achieve the safety at the highest level brings many financial and social benefits, and above all helps to reduce the number of accidents, to develop a broad culture of prevention, improve the ergonomic quality of work environment and develop human sensibility and lack of tolerance to safety and hygiene deficiencies.

The model of health and safety management developed indicates what actions should be taken at different levels of organization management to achieve the benefits listed above. In addition, implementation of an attitude focused on continuous improvement of the organization, and of the fourteen Deming's principles as natural determinants of decision-making can bring nothing but benefits to organizations.

The issue of safety and health management is very important for enterprises striving for improving their maturity. Organizations focused on continuous improvement of their performance are not just interested in fulfilling the legal requirements relating to safety. Protecting the health of workers in the workplace and beyond, continuous improvement of competence in the area of safety excellence and taking actions to improve the design of technological processes and work space with respect to safety principles become unconditional requirements. Polish companies seeking to improve standards in the area of occupational health and safety, reaching to the PN-N 18001: 2004 are provided solely with the set of hints on the general direction of actions taken to plan and formulate a declaration aimed towards continuous improvement of safety. The presented model is currently being verified in the industrial environment, and the development of its components with specific guidance on implementation can bring tangible benefits to businesses. The further research of the author seeks to validate the model presented in the realities of the functioning of Polish manufacturing enterprises.

References

1. Butlewski, M.: The issue of product safety in contemporary design. In: Salamon, S. (ed.) Safety of the System, Technical, Organizational and Human Work Safety Determinants, pp. 112–120. Wydawnictwo Politechnika Częstochowska, Częstochowa (2012)
2. Butlewski, M., Misztal, A., Jasiulewicz-Kaczmarek, M., Janik, S.: Ergonomic and work safety evaluation criteria of process excellence in the foundry industry. Metalurgija 53(4), 701–704 (2014). ISSN: 1334-2576
3. Deming, W.E.: Out of the Crisis. MIT Press Canter for Advanced Engineering Study, Cambridge (1986)
4. Drożyner, P., Mikołajczak, P., Szuszkiewicz, J., Jasiulewicz-Kaczmarek, M.: Management standardization versus quality of working life. In: Robertson, M.M. (ed.) EHAWC 2011 and HCII 2011. LNCS, vol. 6779, pp. 30–39. Springer, Heidelberg (2011)
5. Górny, A.: Identification on accidents causes by the Pareto principle. In: Arezes, P., Baptista, J.S., Barroso, M.P., Carneiro, P., Cordeiro, P., Costa, N., Melo, R., Miguel, A.S., Perestrelo, G. (eds.) Occupational Safety and Hygiene, SHO 2015, pp. 143–145. Portuguese Society of Occupational Safety and Hygiene (SPOSHO), Guimarães (2015)
6. Górny, A.: The work environment in the structure of management system. In: Car, Z., Kudláček, J., Szalay, T. (eds.) Proceedings of International Conference on Innovative Technologies, IN-TECH 2013, pp. 217–220. Faculty of Engineering University of Rijeka, Rijeka (2013)
7. Górny, A.: The use of Ishikawa diagram in occupational accidents analysis. In: Azares, P., Baptista, J.S., Barroso, M.P., Corneiro, P., Cordeiro, P., Costa, N., Melo, R., Miguel, A.S.,

Perestrelo, G. (eds.) Occupational Safety and Hygiene, SHO 2013, pp. 162–163. Portuguese Society of Occupational Safety and Hygiene (SPOSHO), Guimarães (2013)

8. Górny, A.: The elements of work environment in the improvement process of quality management system structure. In: Karwowski, W., Salvendy, G. (eds.) Advances in Human Factors, Ergonomics and Safety in Manufacturing and Sevice Industries. CRC Press, Taylor & Francis Group, Boca Raton (2011)

9. ISO 9000:2005 Quality management system. Fundamentals and vocabulary (2005)

10. Jasiulewicz-Kaczmarek, M., Drożyner, P.: Preventive and pro-active ergonomics influence on maintenance excellence level. In: Robertson, M.M. (ed.) EHAWC 2011 and HCII 2011. LNCS, vol. 6779, pp. 49–58. Springer, Heidelberg (2011)

11. Jasiulewicz-Kaczmarek, M.: Participatory ergonomics as a method of quality improvement in maintenance. In: Karsh, B.-T. (ed.) EHAWC 2009. LNCS, vol. 5624, pp. 153–161. Springer, Heidelberg (2009)

12. Kawecka-Endler, A., Mrugalska, B.: Humanization of work and environmental protection in activity of enterprise. In: Kurosu, M. (ed.) HCI 2014, Part III. LNCS, vol. 8512, pp. 700–709. Springer, Heidelberg (2014)

13. Latzko, W.J., Saunders, D.M.: Four Days with Dr. Deming – A Strategy for Modern Methods off Management. Addison-Wesley Publishing Company, New York (1996)

14. Mazur, A.: Self-assessment of maturity of organization in terms of occupational health and safety with the recommendations of ISO 9004:2010. In: Stephanidis, C. (ed.) HCI 2014, Part II. CCIS, vol. 435, pp. 479–484. Springer, Heidelberg (2014)

15. Mazur, A.: Bezpieczeństwo jako filar modeli doskonałości przedsiębiorstw klasy światowej. Logistyka nr 5/2014, pp. 1067–1076, ILIM, Poznań (2014)

16. Misztal, A., Butlewski, M., Jasiak, A., Janik, S.: The human role in a progressive trend of foundry automation. Metalurgija 54(2), 429–432 (2015). ISSN: 1334-2576

17. Mrugalska, B., Nazir, S., Tytyk, E., Øvergård, K.I.: Process safety control for occupational accident prevention. In: Arezes, P.M., Baptista, J.S., Barroso, M.P. et al. (eds.) Occupational Safety and Hygiene III. International Symposium on Occupational Safety and Hygiene (SHO), Guimaraes, 12–13 February 2015, pp. 365–369, Taylor and Francis Group, London (2015)

18. OHSAS 18001:2007, Systemy zarządzania bezpieczeństwem i higieną pracy. Polski Komitet Normalizacyjny, Warszawa (2007)

19. Pacana, A.: Systemy zarządzania bezpieczeństwem i higieną pracy zgodne z PN-N 18001, Wdrażanie i audytowanie, Oficyna Wydawnicza Politechniki Rzeszowskiej, Rzeszów (2011)

20. PN-N-18001:2004, System zarządzania bezpieczeństwem i higieną pracy. Wymagania., Polski Komitet Normalizacyjny, Warszawa (2004)

21. Sadłowska-Wrzesińska, J.: Analysis of psychosocial risk in the context of the objectives of macroergonomics. In: Vink, P. (ed.) Advances in Social and Organizational Factors, AHFE Conference 2014, pp. 277–285 (2014). ISBN: 978-1-4951-2102-9

22. Sławińska, M., Mrugalska, B.: Information quality for health and safety management systems: a case study. In: Arezes, P.M., Baptista, J.S., Barroso, M.P. et al. (eds.) Occupational Safety and Hygiene III. International Symposium on Occupational Safety and Hygiene (SHO), Guimaraes, 12–13 February 2015, pp. 29–32, Taylor and Francis Group, London (2015)

23. Stachowiak, A., Hadaś, Ł., Cyplik, P., Fertsch, M.: Decision model for sustainable and agile resources management. In: IFAC Conference on Manufacturing, Modeling, Management and Control, MIM 2013, Sankt Petersburg (2013)

Ergonomic Aspects of the Architectural Designing of the Stairs in the Spaces for the Great Public Gathering

Zdzislaw Pelczarski[✉]

Faculty of Architecture, Bialystok University of Technology, Białystok, Poland
wa.dziekan@pb.edu.pl

Abstract. Spaces designed for large public gatherings, arranged both inside buildings and outside them, need to take into account a number of specific conditions. Among them the most important are design issues related to stairs. In this case, the main problems arise from the need to ensure a smooth and safe movement of the human masses, while fulfilling the relevant conditions of mental and physical comfort for each of the individuals, which are part of the moving crowd. In this context, the most critical design issues relate to the evacuation, taking into account the specific behaviours during the panic, especially when the crowd moves down the stairs from the upper to the lower floors. The article presents considerations, research results and conclusions of the author, based on his own experience of many years of architectural practice in the design of stadiums.

Keywords: Ergonomic · Stairs · Architecture · Designing · Crowd movement

1 Introduction

Contemporary realities of urban development, responsible for organizing the functioning of huge human clusters, require the use of solutions enabling for spatial displacement of their inhabitants. The most difficult are the displacement resulting from the need to change the utility levels - so called vertical communication. Used since time immemorial stairs and ramps, serving this purpose, have been supplemented in our times by a new inventions, such as escalators, moving ramps and elevators. To the issues that require special attention in this regard are the problems associated with the movement of crowd - movement of the large, dense masses of people. A special consideration requires the behavior of the crowd during the evacuation in a state of panic. In this case, provided mechanically vertical transport means are useless. Their performance reliability and safety are much inadequate. The only solution to these problems can be properly designed escape routes, taking into account the specificity of the crowd movement and behavior (Fig. 1). The phenomena of this kind are encountered in modern cities, and are connected, inter alia, to the functioning of large stadiums. In the design of modern stadiums, there are two trends in solving the problem of

© Springer International Publishing Switzerland 2015
M. Antona and C. Stephanidis (Eds.): UAHCI 2015, Part IV, LNCS 9178, pp. 468–479, 2015.
DOI: 10.1007/978-3-319-20687-5_45

Fig. 1. Slaski Stadium in Chorzow, Poland. Dangerous situation when leaving the arena by thousands of fans after the rock concert. Excessive density of the crowd caused complete blockade of the movement inside 60 m long and 12 m wide output tunnel. As seen in the photo, the stands are empty at this time, thanks to an efficient circulation. (Photo: author).

collective escape routes from the interior of the stadium to the grounds surrounding it. One of them uses the stairs, the other relies on a ramps with a gentle slopes. Based on own practical experience in the design of the stadiums and own research methods author has conducted an analysis of the advantages and disadvantages of both solutions. In the presented paper particular attention is focused on the study of the legitimacy of the stairs application for the purpose of organizing the main channels of escape, especially in terms of ergonomics and safety issues.

2 Definition of the Research Problem

The subject of detailed research undertaken by the author are the main escape routes leading from the interior of the stadium to the external safety zones. Analyses of the large stadiums, implemented in recent years, show that the mentioned above escape routes are solved in two ways. One of them involves the use of different arrangements of stairs, the second based on the use of several varieties of ramps (Fig. 2). In both cases, the design task is to bring down thousands of spectators from the zones situated at high floors on the level of external terrain. It follows that research mainly should concern the movements of the crowd down the stairs or down the ramp. In order to clearly highlight the rank of problem to analyze have been selected the extreme cases. To such include, in author's opinion, the solutions adopted, inter alia at Allianz Arena stadium in Munich (Fig. 2A), and also at the Stade de France in Paris (Fig. 2B). Their length results from the fact that they run continuously down to the ground level from the stadium concourses situated at altitudes exceeding 30 m. In fact, they form a kind of

Fig. 2. The examples of two different solutions of the major evacuation routes present in modern stadiums: - (A). *Allianz Arena* in Munich, (B). *Stade de France* in Paris (C). *The Stadio Giuseppe Meazza*, commonly known as *San Siro* in Milan (Sources: A.- http://www.silesiabl.pl/contents/ 02/img/027.jpg; B.- http://media.livenationinternational.com/lincsmedia/Media/x/g/s/0994544b-baa1-4c51-a3e8-8e7120d2314b.jpg; C.- http://www.came.com/fr/sites/default/files/1-san-siro.jpg ; admittance 2015-02-15).

linear staircase tunnels with a one-way up to down movement, inclined at an angle of approx. 30°. In extreme situations, during the hurried evacuation and panic, described inclined stair tunnel can be completely filled by moving down compact crowd. The possibility of occurrence of such a dangerous phenomenon has been the main motivation to undertake the research presented in the following parts of this paper.

3 Characteristics of Normal Movement Down the Stairs

The ability to move on the stairs is the result of biomechanical characteristic of human locomotive apparatus. The stairs have accompanied mankind since the dawn of history. However pioneering research on the geometry of comfortable stairs took place in the mid-17th century, and are attributed to Francois Blondel, the director of the Royal Academy of Architecture in Paris. Around the year 1672 Blondel had defined the algorithm, used to this day, enabling to set proper ergonomic relationship between height of rise and depth of tread, as depending on length of the human step. He discovered namely, that a comfortable stairway require to fulfil the condition according to

Fig. 3. Sensory role of the foot while walking up and down the stairs - overhanging heel or nose of the foot over the below tread of stairs enables to locate position edge of the step. (Photo: M. Pelczarski).

which: two risers + tread = step length. This principle results from the kinetic characteristic of the human body and as such is correct. The problem is, however, that for practical reasons the design of stairs is based on the average step length. Such stairs serve well only to part of the population.

Human gait, from the viewpoint of biomechanics is a spatial and cyclic mobility act, consisting in instantaneous change in center of gravity of the torso beyond the plane of the support leg, and then recovering the balance of the simultaneous implementation of the sliding movements on the ground. The above definition is correct also for a gait up the stairs. From the point of view of this research, the very essential fact is that while walking down the stairs each step has a long sequence of movement when the human body carries its weight on one leg only. This is the moment in which even a small impact of external horizontal force can lead to loss of body balance, and consequently to fall.

Long-term observations, conducted by the author and documented photographically shows, that the majority of people moving up the stairs behaves as shown on Fig. 3. It turns out that almost all people use just part of the foot while walking up or down the stairs. The sole of the shoe contacts the tread through some 75 % of its surface. Usually, while walking up the stairs the heels protrude outside the nose of tread, partially or completely. While moving down, the nose of the shoe extends beyond the edge of the stair tread.

On Figs. 4 and 5 have been presented comparative analysis of the human steps on a horizontal plane and on the stairs. The purpose of these studies is the definition of the differences in the two types of movement. It should be noted, when considering normal human step, the movement of the free of load leg in space, detached from the ground, from the rear to the front position is as long as about 4 treads of the stairs. The same kind of movement of the unloaded leg, while descending down the stairs reaches horizontal displacement distance equal to 3 treads of stairs. In the same time this leg lowers its location in space by 2 risers. On the stairs the muscles of both legs perform much more work than while walking on a flat surface. Especially the leg carrying the weight of whole body is very loaded. In sum it should be noted, that comparing to normal walking, descent down the stairs is for human much more complicated task

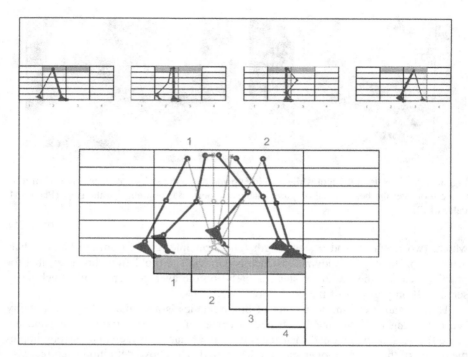

Fig. 4. The repeatable sequence of movement of both legs while walking on a horizontal surface (Source: author).

physically - very aggravating musculoskeletal system and carrying a significant risk of falling and getting hurt. Main safety limits of movement down the stairs arise due to the inability for support by the second leg on the middle level, when this leg is just above the third tread, in the last phase of its movement. This phenomenon is due to the fact that walking on the stairs is an automatic process that uses human psychomotor skills. The appropriate, subconscious placing the foot activate the sense of touch, allowing to locate the edge of the tread. It is well known that the easiest way to determine if the stairs were designed properly is to walk on them with closed eyes. Described above issues play an important role in the movement of large masses of people on the stairs. Moving in the crowd completely eliminates the possibility to control shape of the ground by the help of the sense of sight.

4   Issues of the Crowd Movement Down the Stairs

Crowd behaviors are not yet fully recognized and as such are still the subject of research undertaken by specialists in many fields. The greatest achievements in this area have been reached by psychologists, particularly with regard to an extensive knowledge on the psychology of the crowd. Rapidly develop new fields of science related to the management of the crowd. Among them there is also urban planning and

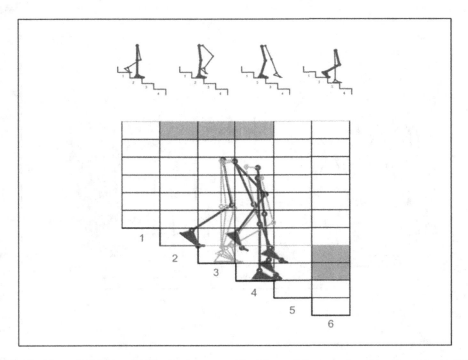

Fig. 5. The repeatable sequence of movement of both legs while normal walking down the stairs (Source: author).

the architecture Author's professional experience, related to the stadiums designing, indicates, that architects, undertaking such a tasks, ought to have deep knowledge concerning the mobility of crowd - particularly its spatial, dynamic, kinetic and bio-mechanic characteristics.

The scope of the analysis is limited to one exemplary case which is the most characteristic for defined earlier research problem. The object of the analysis is theoretical system of the main evacuation channels, modeled on the solution applied to the Allianz Arena in Munich. The system consist of the set of linear, long staircases with an one-way up to down movement, running continuously down to the ground level from the highest concourses, inclined at an angle of approx. 30°. It was assumed, for the purposes of analysis, the extreme situations, during the evacuation and panic. In such conditions, described above inclined stair tunnel could be completely filled by moving down compact crowd.

The configuration of the folded, falling down surface which is created by the treads arrangement determines dramatically location of individual persons creating the dense crowd (Fig. 6). Depth of stair tread is similar to a foot of the person standing on it. So, at every one tread can only stand as many people as number of lanes at the stair run. Some extreme cases, can lead to even greater density. This can occur when individual

Fig. 6. The crowd of extremal density on the stairs - the downward movement (Source: author)

person adopt a lateral position relative to the axis of the run of stairs. In this case crowd density will double. Considering the general conditions of the human mass movement down the stairs it should be noted, firstly, that this movement will only be possible when individual pedestrians will have guaranteed free space in front of them (Fig. 7).

Smooth movement of many people down the stairs in one lane requires that the distance between them, measured by number of free treads between the treads carrying the body weight was equal to at least 2 (Fig. 8). When the interval described above is only one step of the stairs smooth descend of many people on one lane is possible provided however that all of these people will be traversed synchronously. Disruption of this synchronization will cause a lack of free space on the tread in front of a person coming down the stairs and, consequently, a collision in the form of stepping on the heel of predecessor. It can also leads to disruption of the body balance of one or both person, threatening collapse. The described collision will stop one of the links of the chain. The consequence of this stopping will be the occurrence of a domino effect in the upper part of this lane. It will cover all the above part of the lane, where will occur the disappearance of free treads what is equivalent to the stop of chain movement.

The deficit of free space for normal movement will initiate the next phase of this very dangerous process. The compacted mass of human bodies will act like volcanic lava or other fluid matter on the hillside. Acting down, parallel to the slope of stairs

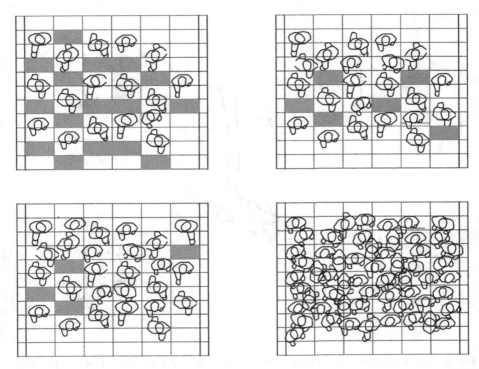

Fig. 7. The impact of the degree of compaction of the crowd on ease of the movement while descending the stairs (Source: author).

vector of force, derived from gravity will result in the flow of the crowd mass, leading to its further compaction with increasing internal destructive pressure. The history of disasters involving crowd proves that the described above situations often cause casualties, including death and serious injuries.

Figure 9 shows the analysis of the movement sequences while walking down the stairs in the conditions arising in the crowd. As has been previously demonstrated the lack of free tread in front of a person moving down the stairs causes stopping. Such an individual, standing on two legs, waits for a moment when the tread below will be released. Only then will be possible any movement in space, by lowering and horizontal shifting the position, equal to one rise and one tread of the stairs. The diagram shows that this locomotion activity requires the free space of motion greater than provided by the two treads. Lack of space hinders the proper body movements. It is rather a kind of sliding down the stairs than walking.

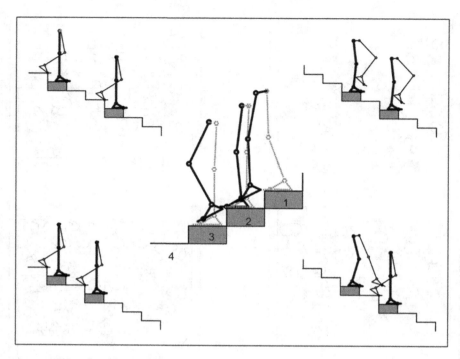

Fig. 8. The determinants of walking down the stairs many people in one lane of movement (Source: author).

5 The Use of Ramps for Escape Routes

As previously been found, an alternative way of providing to the masses of viewers an evacuation routs from the interior of the stadium leading to the external safe space could be based on the use of several varieties of ramps. One of the examples illustrating this is the system of escape routes serving the eastern stands at the *Silesian Stadium* in Chorzow (Fig. 10). Two pairs of wide ramps, North and South, in a much shorter time than 5 min, are able to lead all viewers from this part of stadium directly to the main exit gates [1]. Extremely interesting example, with regard of a sophisticated idea and the date of construction (1925) is the stadium designed as only of the for football, in the district of Milan, named San Siro (Figs. 2C, 11). Equally interesting are the effects of further renovations (1990) in the form of an extra tier being added to three sides of the

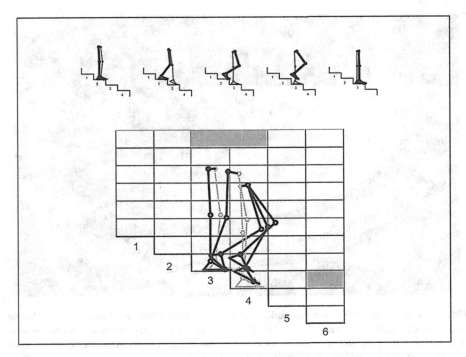

Fig. 9. The sequence of movement of both legs when moving by only one step of stairs down (Source: author).

pitch. This required the building of 11 concrete towers around the outside of the stadium, Four of them support a new roof. Around each of these columns wrap the spiral ramps, ensuring the evacuation of spectators from the highest parts of the stadium. In the United States and Australia have been built number of stadiums using the systems of ramps for the purpose of organizing the main roads of evacuation.

The most representative of these include among others: Melbourne Cricket Ground, Australia Stadium 2000 in Sydney, The Arrowhead and Royals Stadium at Kansas City, as well as Joe Robbie Stadium in Miami [2].

Fig. 10. Located in a 600 ha urban park, Silesian Stadium in Chorzow, Upper Silesia, Poland (the state after redevelopment 1994–2007). Two pairs of wide ramps, North and South, in time shorter than 5 min, are able to evacuate all viewers from this part of stadium directly to the main exit gates. (Source: Archives of WOSiR, photo - P. Oles).

6 Conclusions

Both the author's practical experience and research on architectural models of the main evacuation channels or, in other words, the main escape routes, leading from the interior of the stadium to the external safety zones show that solutions based on the use of stairs have a number of disadvantages.[1] These drawbacks do not occur in case of application for these purposes the solutions in the form of ramps, arranged in many ways. This general conclusion follows, in particular, the factors related to the efficiency and safety of spectators during extreme conditions of evacuation which accompany the movement of the crowd under the influence of panic. The most important of these are kinetic - motoric difficulties of a compact human masses in a movement down the stepped surface. Equally important problems are due to the relatively big steepness of the stair run. Declination of approximately 30° causes a formation of a downward force, acting in parallel to the run, being result of the gravity. This force depending on the mass of the crowd can reach very large, indeed destructive, values. It can lead to very dangerous situations that threaten the health and the lives of people. In this context, reported in the literature on the subject the advantages of the solutions of applying stairs, such as the construction economy, saving of the space and greater

---

[1] In the years 1994–2007 the author was the chief architect of the reconstruction of the *Silesian Stadium* in Chorzow, Poland.

Fig. 11. Efficient and spectacular spiral and peripheral ramps serving the circulation and evacuation movement at the *San Siro* stadium in Milan. (Photo: Timothee Nalet, http://www.timotheenalet.com/urban/milan-san-siro, admit. 2015-02-15).

speed of evacuation, should be taken with great care and restrain [3–6]. The safety and comfort of the users must be the primary criterion for choosing the solution. Both of these conditions are met completely only by the use of ramp systems of evacuation. Furthermore, an additional advantage of these structures is the attractiveness of their spatial forms, enriching the architectural values of the whole stadium.

References

1. Pelczarski, Z.: Widownie współczesnych stadionów. Determinanty i problemy projektowe (Grandstands of the Contemporary Stadiums. Determinants and Design Problems). pp. 57– 66, Oficyna Wydawnicza Politechniki Bialostockiej, Bialystok (2009)
2. John, G., Sheard, R.: Stadia. A Design and Development Guide, pp. 20, 35, 168, 238 (1997)
3. Nixdorf, S.: Stadium ATLAS. Technical Recommendations for Grandstands in Modern Stadiums, pp. 110 –111. Ernst & Sohn, Berlin (2008)
4. EN 13200-1: Spectator facilities - Part 1: Layout criteria for spectator viewing area – Specification (2003)
5. FIFA/UEFA, Technical Recommendations for the Construction or Modernisation of Football Stadia, FIFA, Zurich (1994–2003)
6. The Green Guide,Guide to Safety at Sports Grounds, HMSO, London (1990, 1997)

Typology and Ergonomics of Rooms in Contemporary Hotel

Elzbieta Trocka-Leszczynska and Joanna Jablonska(✉)

Faculty of Architecture, Wroclaw University of Technology, Wrocław, Poland
{elzbieta.trocka-leszczynska,
joanna.jablonska}@pwr.wroc.pl

Abstract. Depending on the hotel's standard, a variety of room types can be distinguished: Single, Twin, Double, Apartments (Polish "Apartament"), suites: junior, business, senator, etc. What is more, these are often found in a variety of standards, i.e. Standard, Superior, Luxury, Deluxe, Queen, King, Royal or Executive, just to name a few. With such a range of possibilities, and even more diversification based on cultural and architectural customs in a particular country, it seems that a proper typology of hotel services should be based rather on the grounds of ergonomics and room comfort than marketing labels. This article presents a study aiming at properly formulating tools for standardization of contemporary hotel accommodation. Scope of the study includes a range of European examples.

Keywords: Hotel design · Hotel room typology · Hotel room ergonomics · Contemporary hotels

1   Introduction

Contemporary hotel industry is extremely competitive. Namely, hotel chains and private hotel owners compete in making their offers increasingly more attractive. Their aim is to continuously expand the number of customers, who, in the process, become a more diverse group than ever before. As a result, new types of hotel services and hotel rooms, including various types of suites (e.g. junior, VIP, studio, business, classic and budget suite), as well as budget accommodation rooms (standard, economy, classic, budget), are on the rise. However, it is not only the abundance of accommodation types that may confuse visitors, as the latter often need also to become acquainted with room furnishing options and available accessories. This is due to the fact that different options provide different standards. It seems that even the traditional typology based on the amount and size of beds (Single, Twin, Double, etc.) is no longer a valid reference point.

Accordingly, a need to examine hotel facilities based on room types arises, in order to establish an accurate typology corresponding with the modern reality. This is crucial not only for travelers, for their physical and psychophysical sense of comfort, but also for creators and implementers of building and administrative law, architects, ergonomists, and even interior designers.

© Springer International Publishing Switzerland 2015
M. Antona and C. Stephanidis (Eds.): UAHCI 2015, Part IV, LNCS 9178, pp. 480–491, 2015.
DOI: 10.1007/978-3-319-20687-5_46

1.1   Methodology and Research Aim

The starting point for the research discussed in this article was an analysis of existing typologies, both in Poland and abroad, available in literature (according to the reference list). In order to modernize the source data, results were updated based on information acquired from Internet websites for travelers. A very important document in gathering the data was a regulation included in the Polish construction law, namely, the Minister of Economy and Labor Regulation of August 19 2004 regarding hotels and other facilities providing hotel services (uniformed text, Journal of Law 2006, No. 22, Item 169) with subsequent amendments, legislation in force as of January 1 2015 [Regulation]; later in the text referred to as the *Regulation.*

Another step included an examination of hotel facilities, so as to determine the currently circulating hotel room terminology. This data is presented in Tables 2, 3, 4, and 5. The research scope comprised of chosen facilities in Poland and other European countries, while the study was based on information available from the booking.com website, selected due to its: precision, trustworthiness and an international character. Hotel facilities taken into account were located in the downtown area of the city and ranged from 3 to 5 star accommodation types. All chosen buildings were adapted to modern architectural standards and customer's comfort.

The research was restricted to European hotels, due to different traditions in managing space in the American, Arab and Asian cultures. For example, furniture sizes together with their descriptive terminology are not standardized worldwide (see: [Rutes W. A., Penner R. H., Adams L. 2001]). It needs to be noted that Polish hotel facilities as well as legislature were at the center of this study, while references to European and, in selected cases, American literature was used for comparative reasons. However, presented results may be of use in scientific studies related to tourism in the whole Europe.

The gathered and described material served to initiate a discussion and a case study analysis. Both were based on a graphic, comparative and critical analysis, and were focused on determining basic room types, verifying random terminology, and also defining minimal architectural parameters as well as adequate furnishing for each type of rooms. In the concluding part of the text, a synthesis of findings together with a suggested collective terminology is presented.

2   Discussion

2.1   Existing Typologies

The basic definition of a hotel room, i.e. a residential unit, taken from literature [Programowanie, 2010 – Błądek, p. 53], runs as follows: "a separate residential unit [...], usually consisting of a bedroom, hall, toilet and a bathing facility, as well as other adjoining facilities (e.g. bar, kitchenette, balcony, loggia, etc.)". As the cited functional and spatial system is valid for the researched hotel standards of between 3 and 5 stars, the main factors taken into account in this study are the number of rooms and type of furnishing together with accessories.

Understandably, the most common typology divides hotel rooms based on the type of bed they are equipped with [Rutes W. A., Penner R. H., Adams L. 2001]. This type of classification one can find, for example, on the "eSKY.pl" website [http://www.esky.pl/porady-dla-podroznych/Hotele/Pobyt-w-hotelu/Typy-oferowanych-pokoi, Accessed: 26.01.2015], as well as in literature [Programowanie, 2010 – Błądek]. It involves the following categories: single, double for one person, double, triple, and quad, also called quarter (in the Ticekts.pl typology [http://tickets.pl/hotels/pub/hotels/faq-hotels/classification-of-hotels/types-of-hotel-rooms.html, Accessed: 26.01.2015]), and, finally, a dormitory (multiple) room. The first room mentioned is considered to be of around 8–14 m^2 with a single bed, while the double for one person is equipped with 2 beds. According to the website, the double is defined as the so called "twin", i.e. with two single beds, or "double", i.e. with one double bed.

Moreover, the sources state that the term "twin" is also used for rooms with a multiple even number of beds. Triple and quarter rooms are intended for the according number of people. The last category, a "dormitory" room intended for a multiple number of people, is characteristic for hostels and therefore has not been included in the research. However, the mentioned typology must be supplemented by information from the source literature [Programowanie, 2010 – Błądek] with the following: "studio" – a room with a single bed and an extra bed in the standard of a double room, usually with an adjoining kitchenette or a bar; junior suite studio – with at least two rooms, and residential studio – with multiple rooms or adapted for guests with disabilities [http://www.esky.pl/porady-dla-podroznych/Hotele/Pobyt-w-hotelu/Typy-oferowanych-pokoi, Accessed: 26.01.2015] [Programowanie, 2010– Błądek].

A slightly different classification is suggested by the Tickets.pl website [http://tickets.pl/hotels/pub/hotels/faq-hotels/classification-of-hotels/types-of-hotel-rooms.html, Accessed: 26.01.2015], enlisting additional categories: Extra Bed, basic room with an extra bed (also mentioned in [Programowanie, 2010 – Błądek]), and run the house, an undefined room area adjusted according to the customer's needs. Furthermore, the website presents an additional typology which includes: a Suite (Polish "Apartament"; equipped with a kitchenette), Balcony Room, Bedroom (with a separate bedroom), Business (furnished to provide working space), Connected Rooms, Corner room, Duplex (a bi-level suite), Family Room (for families with children, with one or multiple rooms), Honeymoon Room (for the newlyweds), Junior Suite (with adjoining day and night zones), President (luxurious, multiple rooms, with adequate zones for receiving guests and holding conferences), Standard Room (basic, with parameters adjusted to the functional-spatial structure of the building and available services), Suite (luxurious hotel accommodation type with at least 2 adjoining zones for night and day). Interestingly, the source also mentions a classification based on the available view, listing the following four types: Sea, Pool, Garden, Mountain [http://tickets.pl/hotels/pub/hotels/faq-hotels/classification-of-hotels/types-of-hotel-rooms.html, Accessed: 26.01.2015].

In order to present the discussed issue fully, it seems necessary to present one more typology, namely the classification of "suites" in American literature [Rutes W. A., Penner R. H., Adams L. 2001]. Accordingly, the mini suite (sitting room with an adjoining bedroom, classified as 1,5-unit area, situated in less attractive acoustically areas, close to the staircase or lifts), junior suite (2-unit with a sitting room and one bedroom), VIP suite (3-unit, a sitting room and 2 bedrooms), Conference suite (4-unit, sitting room, 2 bedrooms, conference table and a visiting room), Hospitality suite (4-unit, 2 large sitting rooms, 2 bedrooms and a pantry), Executive suite (5-unit, dining room, sitting room, large bedrooms), and, finally, Presidential suite (6-unit, one large bedroom, 3-piece sitting room area).

As we can see, already in the cited sources there is a significant disparity in terminology. Among others, the suite is at times defined as a single – or, at least, 2-unit area. In Poland, the requirement of 2 separate units in a suite is stated in the Regulation (see point 3.2) and cited in other sources [Programowanie, 2010 – Błądek]. However, in the course of research the authors have found that reality is usually not adherent with regulations in this aspect. Moreover, in foreign hotels, including those in the US, the Polish term "apartament" is substituted by "suite" which stands for a hotel room with a sitting room and one or more bedrooms [Rutes et al. 2001]. Similarly, while in certain facilities the Business standard stands for a hotel room with a specially dedicated working space area, in others it is a room simply equipped with office furniture [http:// tickets.pl/hotels/pub/hotels/faq-hotels/classification-of-hotels/types-of-hotel-rooms. html, Accessed: 26.01.2015], [http://www.esky.pl/porady-dla-podroznych/Hotele/ Pobyt-w-hotelu/Typy-oferowanych-pokoi, Accessed: 26.01.2015], [Programowanie, 2010 – Błądek], [Regulation].

2.2 Basic Features

In the majority of analyzed cases the basis for defining a standard for a residential unit was the floor surface. According to the Regulation [Regulation, Annex I Chapter IV], the standard room sizes for 3 to 5 star hotels are the following: (Table 1).

The floor surface is not determined for rooms for over 4 people and hotels above the 3 star standard. However, for 4 and 5-star hotels a "suite" is defined as follows: "encompassing at least a sitting room of 25 m^2 in the slightest, a bedroom with a bathroom and a hallway with an adjoining lavatory".

According to research results, as well as regulations, [Regulation, Anex I] the standard furniture includes a bed, a place to work, lavatory, bathtub or shower, closet and equipment, i.e. TV, hairdryer, phone, towels, bed linen, minibar, heating. Nowadays also Wi-Fi becomes a standard. It is worth noting that the Regulation mentions Internet accessibility in dedicated areas [Regulation I, Annex I, Chap. 2]. Also, the possibility to prepare coffee or tea in the room is becoming more and more popular, yet it is still optional. In regard to air conditioning the Regulation [Regulation, Annex I Chap. 2] requires maintaining room temperature at around 24°C in Summer and over 20°C in Winter, while keeping the humidity level between 45-60 % for the 4 and 5 star hotels. At the same time, heating is required for all standards.

The last feature is natural, mechanical or mechanical exhaust ventilation for bathroom facilities (3 star hotels). Additionally, as research has shown, sound insulation is considered to be an additional standard, similarly to a bar and kitchen facilities usually restricted to suites or studios [Programowanie, 2010 – Błądek], [Rozporządzenie], [booking.com]. As all the above mentioned features were present in the studied facilities they will not be discussed in the later part of the article.

Table 1. Floor surface according to the hotel room type (as established by the author based on [Programowanie, 2010 – Błądek]).

Category	5 star	4 star	3 star
Floor surface (without adjoining areas, i.e. bathroom, hall, alcove, loggia, etc.) in [m2]			
1-person	14	12	10
2-person	18	16	14
3-person	undetermined	undetermined	16

3 Case Studies

3.1 Types

In order to formulate the current typology it was necessary to determine actual type of accommodation in modern day hotels. Selected findings are presented in Tables 2, 3, and 4. Information in each table consists of data from 2 facilities of the 3, 4 and 5 star standard. An emphasis was put on selecting hotel chains as well as boutique hotels.

3.2 Floor Surface and Additional Equipment

Double rooms. For Double Standard (without additional names) rooms, with double or twin beds, present in all of the researched hotels, significant differences in floor surfaces have been established. For 5 star hotels floor surface ranges from 13 m^2 in the 5 star boutique Gródek hotel in Cracow, 20 m^2 in the majority of cases, and 34 m^2 in the 5 star Intercontinental hotel in Warsaw. Interestingly, the previously mentioned boutique hotel has not met the minimum floor surface regulation. However, as in Poland facilities are often located in the existing building stock they may fall under certain exemptions according to Sect. 3.1. of the Regulation [Regulation]. The referenced paragraph indicates that in the aspect of facilities on the national monument list certain exceptions from the building regulations are acceptable. For the 4 star Standard the floor surface ranges between 20 and 22 m^2, while for the 3 star one 16 to 17 m^2, thus exceeding the legal requirements. Usual width for single beds is set between 90 and 130 cm and 131–150 cm for double beds with furnishing equipment rarely deriving from the standard. Only in 4 and 5 star facilities other features were present, i.e. ergonomic chairs, beds over 2 m long, air conditioning, safe, ironing set, or, indicating a high standard, wooden furniture [booking.com].

Hoteliers refer to double rooms in many terms which are not mentioned in the cited typologies. For example, the 3 star Hotel Royal in Cracow offers the Twin Economy Room with standard equipment and a floor surface of 17 m^2. Based on interior solutions and floor surface, it is difficult to differentiate the mentioned room category from the standard one. One may assume that, perhaps, the equipment is slightly more modest than in the other Hotel Royal rooms [booking.com].

Superior stands for a higher standard, very popular among double rooms. The floor surface of this unit is similar to the standard one and ranges from 14 m^2 (PURO**** in

Table 2. Accommodation types – hotels in Wroclaw (comparative data retrieved from the Booking.com website, Accessed: 29.11.2014).

No.	Hotel name/location	Room type					
1	Europeum Hotel ***	Double Deluxe	Twin Deluxe (1 or 2 beds)	Triple Deluxe	Suite	Family Deluxe	Single Deluxe
2	Centrum Dikul***	Twin	Double	–	Suite	Single	Single Deluxe
3	Best Western Hotel Prima Wroclaw ****	Double	–				Single
4	PURO Hotel Wroclaw	Deluxe with king size bed	Double Superior	Twin Superior	–		Single Superior
5	Sofitel Wroclaw Old Town*****	Double Classic	Double Superior	Luxurious Double with panoramic city view	Apartament typu Junior Suite	–	
6	The Granary - La Suite Hotel ***** (boutique hotel)	Executive	Garden view	–	Premium Suite	Deluxe Suite	–

Table 3. Accommodation types – hotels in Warsaw (comparative data retrieved from the Booking.com website, Accessed: 02.12.2014).

No.	Hotel name/location	Room type					
1	Hotel Metropol***	Standard Double	Standard Twin	Double/Twin Executive	Family Room (2 2 or 1 +2)	Single Standard	Single Executive
2	Hotel „MDM City Centre***	Double/Twin Standard	Twin Deluxe	–			
3	Novotel Warszawa Centrum****	Standard Double	Twin Standard	Standard with one double bed and a sofa	Double Superior	Double Executive	
4	Polonia Palace Hotel****	Double/Twin Standard	Double/Twin Superior	Double Deluxe	Single Standard	Single Superior	Family Room (2 + 2)
5	Radison Blu Centrum Hotel"*****	Standard single or twin bed	Business Class		Executive Suite	–	
6	Hotel Intercontinental*****	with king size ort win bed	Deluxe with king size bed	Double Twin Club	Junior Suite	–	

Table 4. Accommodation types – hotels in Cracow (comparative data retrieved from the Booking.com website, Accessed: 02.12.2014)

No.	Hotel name/location	Room type								
1	Askot Hotel***	Double/Twin	Triple	Family	Single	–	Suite	Single Deluxe	Single Economy	Single Standard
2	Hotel Royal***	Twin Economy	Twin Standard	Double/Twin Deluxe	Triple Deluxe	Suite	Single Superior	–		
3	Hotel PURO****	Twin Superior	Double Superior	Corner Double Room	Suite	Single Superior	–			
4	Holiday Inn Krakow City Centre*****	Double/Twin Standard	Deluxe with king size bed for nonsmokers	–						
5	Hotel Gródek *****	Double Standard	Double Deluxe	–	Suite	–		Standard		
6	Sheraton Kraków Hotel*****	Double/Twin Classic	Double/Twin Deluxe	Double/Twin Club	Junior Suite	–				

Wroclaw), 18–20 m^2 (most common solution), to 26 m^2 in Aquila Atlantis Hotel, 5 star facility in Heraklion's city center in Crete (Greece). This type of room is characterized by interesting views on the city, harbor, or garden. Due to a relatively small cubature, comfort manifests itself mainly through interesting interior design and additional technical equipment, not furnishing. This includes: air conditioning, sound insulation, two safes (one for a laptop), tablet (PURO hotel in Cracow), touch panels for hotel staff ("PURO" in Cracow and Wroclaw), comfortable and ergonomic chairs, coffee makers, fast wireless Internet, as well as additional services. Interestingly, in one of the facilities (Aquila Atlantis Hotel) the Comfort standard is almost identical to the Superior [booking.com].

Often, for double rooms in standards higher than basic the "Deluxe" term is used. It is characterized by an increased floor surface unit in respect to other double rooms on the premises ranging from 18 m^2 and an adjacent closet in Europeum*** in Wroclaw, 30 m^2 in the Polonia Palace Hotel**** in Warsaw, to 34 m^2 in the InterContinental in Warsaw. Moreover, an increased bed standard is provided, with single beds ranging from 90 to 130 cm and double beds between 181 and 210 cm (the so called king-size) or length of over 2 m. Also in the aspect of equipment, Deluxe is enriched with an interesting view from the window, a balcony, safe, ironing unit, flat screen TV, air conditioning and other technological enhancements, e.g. controlling light temperature with a touch panel (PURO hotel in Wroclaw), or services not covered by the architectural design. For example, hotel guests may have access to a fitness or business center, clubs, coffee maker, or may be provided with newspapers or luxurious toiletry brands [booking.com].

The room type termed "Classic" also belongs to the higher standard class and was present in all of the researched hotels. Characteristic for a "Classic" is a larger floor surface of 24 m^2 (Sofitel Wrocław Old Town*****) and 28 m^2 (Sheraton Kraków Hotel*****), as well as a sitting room area and equipment of a higher than in the "Deluxe" type standard, e.g. additional furniture, sound systems or iPod charging spots. The "Club" type rooms are more or less similar (in two of the researched hotels), however the guests are additionally offered an entrance card to the hotel club. A similar class of comfort is provided in the Double Executive room type, which floor surface ranges from 20 to 35 m^2. For example in The Granary – La Suite Hotel interiors are divided into a bedroom and sitting room zone (in one room) with an interesting décor (exposed brick walls, glass ceiling) and a panoramic view of the city. Additional (other than the already mentioned) equipment consists of a closet-wardrobe and a laptop safe. Double beds are of a 181-210 cm width and there is a sofa bed in the sitting room. Having said that, in other facilities it is difficult to clearly define what is the difference between an Executive and a Deluxe room type. The case is similar with the Exclusive room type, provided, e.g., in the Warsaw Metropol*** hotel. The room has an area of 20 m^2, a separate sitting room area, with additional features: a great panoramic view of the city and air conditioning. Depending on individual requirements, the room may hold two single or double beds, with width dimensions of 131–150 cm and 90–130 cm respectively [booking.com].

One of the last categories is the Business Class hotel room, available, among others, in the 5 star Radison Blu Centrum Hotel. The room is 28 m^2 large and the nonstandard equipment includes an office desk with an ergonomic chair, fast and wireless Internet, air conditioning, coffee maker and services, i.e. press delivery and room preparation for a comfortable sleep in the evening. Depending on the selected option the hotel has units equipped with: 1 large double bed (151–18 0 cm wide), or 2 single beds (90–130 cm wide). A Business room with a panoramic view of the city is available also in the Aquila Atlantis Hotel in Heraklion in Crete. The room is 24 m² large and includes a large desk, 42-inch flat screen TV, air conditioning, safe, bed (1 double bed 151–180 cm wide or 2 single beds 90–130 cm wide) with a spring mattress, rainshower system in the shower and a separate lavatory [booking.com], [http://www.radissonblu.com/hotel-warsaw/rooms], [http://www.theatlantishotel.gr/?accommodation=business&lang=en].

Among the researched hotels the Double Corner Room was available in only one hotel, namely the 4 star PURO hotel in Cracow. Here, the floor surfaces equaled 27 m², the room had a modern design including windows of the interior's light height. The guests could dispose of a 40-inch TV, tablet, air conditioning, safe and one double bed.

Suites. Junior Suite is the most modest unit in the suite category. In researched facilities its size ranges from 37 m² (Sofitel Wrocław Old Town*****) up to 68 m² (InterContinental***** in Warsaw). A junior suite is characterized by a large sitting room connected with a bedroom (one room) with additional high standard equipment (similar to the one mentioned above), as well as interesting décor.

An example of a Classic Suite can be found in the 3 star Hotel Royal in Cracow. It is 80 m² large, has a balcony, wardrobe, flat screen TV, one single and one large double bed, as well as a bath tub. Despite a higher standard, air conditioning is not available. In the 5 star Hotel Gródek also in Cracow, the suite is 27 m² large and has a luxurious character. As other rooms in this facility, it is safe for people with allergies. Among the equipment one will find the following: bath tub, underfloor heating, ironing unit, air conditioning, very large double bed. Additionally, a press delivery service is offered. Also, in this room layout the bedroom and sitting room were not separate, while possibly the most surprising feature is the discrepancy in the floor surface among various described units.

A Suite is the first hotel unit discussed in the article, which consists of a division between a sitting room and a bedroom. The smallest suite among the researched hotels was located in the 4 star PURO hotel in Cracow (29 m²) and the largest in the Centrum Gikuł*** hotel in Wroclaw (45 m²). Alongside the additional equipment, these units usually include larger beds and, sometimes, kitchenettes.

In the boutique The Granary – La Suite Hotel **** in Wroclaw two suite types, with different names than in any other facility, can be found. The first one, the Premium Suite with a separate bedroom and sitting room is 40 m² large. The room is equipped with specially dedicated furniture, while the guests additionally have access to a fitness center. The second unit, the Deluxe Suite, is a bi-level unit with a bathroom and bedroom on the lower level and a dining room, kitchenette and an additional bathroom upstairs. Again, the suite is equipped with dedicated furniture and a bed 181-210 cm wide. The total suite size is 70 m². Finally, the Radison Blu Centrum Hotel in Warsaw offers an Executive Suite with the floor surface of 53 m². A bedroom is divided from a sitting room and working space area with sliding doors. The Suite features also a wardrobe.

Other. Single, triple and family hotel rooms are not very common. If so, they are usually available in the following categories: Standard, Deluxe, and Superior, and their level of comfort corresponds to the described above. However, it is worth to examine the functional-spatial layout of such interiors.

Deluxe family room in the Europeum hotel, 39 m^2 large, is created from two adjoining Twin rooms with one bathroom adapted to the needs of people with disabilities. In comparison, the Family room in the Metropol hotel in Warsaw is dedicated for 2 adults and 2 kids. It is 30 m^2 large and room features include two single beds or one double with a sofa bed. The room is also available in the one adult and two kids option and joined with a sitting room. At the same, a family unit in the Askot Hotel*** in Cracow, has standard parameters and equipment, is 30 m^2 large and is equipped with 4 single beds. Lastly, the Family Superior in the Aquila Atlantis Hotel in Heraklion in Crete in Greece is 36 m^2 large and includes a sitting room, a balcony, a rainshower system shower, 42-inch flat screen TV, coffee maker, safe, air conditioning and two double beds.

A Triple room (3 single beds) can be found in the Askot Hotel*** in Cracow. It is available in the standard option, larger than the double room by 2 m^2 (18 m^2 in total) and including 3 single beds. Hotel Royal*** in Cracow offers a Triple Deluxe room which is 28 m^2 large (a double room is 24 m^2 large). It has two single beds and a sofa bed or one single bed and one large double bed. Interestingly, as research has shown, single rooms were mostly doubles for one person with equipment and name matching the standards available in a given facility. Hotels rarely have actual single rooms characterized by a corresponding floor surface. One example is a Single Economy room in Hotel Royal*** in Cracow which is 11 m^2 large and is equipped with one single bed.

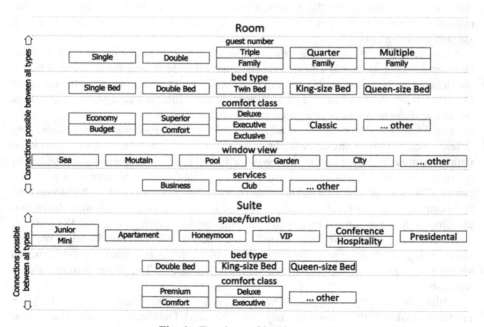

Fig. 1. Typology of hotel rooms

4   Conclusion

In the course of research an original typology dividing rooms based on the number of guests, type of beds, comfort level, view out of the window and additional services was formulated. Moreover, "suites", due to their specific character, were grouped according to separate classification standards. Additionally, the authors have adopted the European and not local definition of a suite, as a one chamber interior. (Figure 1).

The presented typology is intended for European facilities. There is no doubt that together with the development of the hotel industry, room types will be evolving, hence the given terminology may expand. Furthermore, in some cases, hotels may add up on or simply change the terminology, for example, due to the nonexistence of legislative regulations. For that reason, the "other" category has been included.

The authors hope that the presented typology together with the undertaken systematization of terms regarding hotel terminology, will inspire other research in the area, as well as prove useful to those involved in the travel industry.

References

http://www.esky.pl/porady-dla-podroznych/Hotele/Pobyt-w-hotelu/Typy-oferowanych-pokoi. Accessed 26 January 2015

Jaremen, D.E.: Ofensywa jakości dla hoteli i pensjonatów. Kierunki doskonalenia jakości. Metodologia badań, Jelenia Góra, 2006. www.vip.karr.pl/pliki/METODOLOGIA.pdf. Accessed 21 January 2015

Minister of Economy and Labor Regulation of August 19 2004 regarding hotels and other facilities providing hotel services (uniformed text, Journal of Law 2006, No. 22, Item 169) with subsequent amendments, legislation in force as of January 26 2015

Rutes, W.A., Penner, R.H., Adams, L.: Hotel Design. Planning and Development. Norton and Company Inc, Norton (2001)

Nowoczesne hotelarstwo: od projektowania do wyposażenia, ed. Błądek Z., Palladium Architekci - Błądek, Manikowski, Poznań (2010)

Author Index

Printed in the United States
By Bookmasters